THE ORIENTING RESPONSE IN INFORMATION PROCESSING

THE ORIENTING RESPONSE IN INFORMATION PROCESSING

Evgeny N. Sokolov
Moscow State University

John A. Spinks
The University of Hong Kong

Risto Näätänen
University of Helsinki

Heikki Lyytinen
University of Jyväskylä

Psychology Press
Taylor & Francis Group
NEW YORK AND HOVE

First published by Lawrence Erlbaum Associates, Inc., Publishers
10 Industrial Avenue
Mahwah, New Jersey 07430

This edition published 2013 by Psychology Press

Psychology Press	Psychology Press
Taylor & Francis Group	Taylor & Francis Group
711 Third Avenue	27 Church Road
New York	Hove
NY 10017	East Sussex, BN3 2FA

Psychology Press is an imprint of the Taylor & Francis Group, an informa business

First issued in paperback 2013

Cover design by Kathryn Houghtaling Lacey

Library of Congress Cataloging-in-Publication Data

The orienting response in information processing / edited by Evgeny N. Sokolov ... [et al.].
p. cm.
Includes bibliographic references (p.) and indexes.
ISBN 0-8058-3081-2 (cloth : alk. paper)
1. Orienting reflex. 2. Perception. 3. Cognitive neuroscience. I. Sokolov, E. N. (Evgenii Nikolaevich), 1920-

QP372 . 0754 2001
612.8'2—dc21

2001042312

ISBN 978-0-8058-3081-1 hardcover
ISBN 978-0-415-65253-7 paperback

10 9 8 7 6 5 4 3 2 1

Contents

Preface

Evgeny Nikolaevich Sokolov (ENS) was born in 1920 in Gorky (then called Nishney Novgorod). He was educated there and at the Pedagogical Institute in Moscow and at the Academy of Science, where he was later awarded the Pavlov Gold Medal from the Academy for his work in psychophysiology. Subsequently, he joined the faculty of Moscow State University, and became Chair of the Department of Psychophysiology when the department was reorganized into a Faculty of Psychology in 1966. One of his most famous colleagues along this road, Professor A. R. Luria, described him as an outstanding member of the young, postwar generation of Soviet psychologists. A more complete description of his life may be found in Graham (1989), this citation given at the 1988 Annual Meeting of the Society for Psychophysiological Research, when ENS was presented with an award for distinguished contributions to psychophysiology.

He is best known globally for his work on the "orienting response," his book *Perception and the Conditioned Response* having stimulated a large corpus of research worldwide. Frances Graham (1989), in her analysis of the citations of this book alone, noted that (up to 1989) it was referenced in some 267 different journals, including those in the fields of psychology, biology, developmental areas, the neurosciences, neuropsychiatry, clinical psychology, aerospace medicine, obstetrics, anesthesiology, political sciences, education, and industrial journals.

The current book, however, is testimony to his work over the years in developing our knowledge in the areas of perception, information processing, and attention, and to the research that it has spawned by ourselves, coauthors with Evgeny, of this book. It presents, on the surface, an historical account of a research program, written in a lecture style, complemented with numerous figures, diagrams, and photographs. It leads the reader toward a cognitive science approach to the study of perception and attention, where multilevel forms of inquiry and explanation converge on the same domain of interest, and where a neuroscience basis and mathematical modeling are requirements for an acceptable degree of explanation and description. More importantly, however, through the development of his ideas, of his theoretical and conceptual notions, and of his current views on methodology, it offers firsthand insights into the mind of a brilliant and avid scientist, philosopher, and theoretician.

He has been described in publications elsewhere as a "passionately dedicated scientist," and "one of the most perceptive and exciting brain–behavior theorists of the day." He has extensive mathematical and language skills, and was a translator during World War II. He displays, to all who work with him, an academic and cognitive vitality, and an energy that even now leaves many of the rest of us breathless. He has an overwhelming enthusiasm for research, for discussing his ideas, for debating issues, and for bringing research issues into sharp focus. He revels in hearing about others' work, and he shuns discussion that does not bear on the issues of his heart. He has received awards at home and abroad, but it is timely that the publication of this volume coincides with perhaps his greatest honor—in August 2001, ENS was presented with the President's Award by Russian President Vladimir Putin, for his achievements as one of the most distinguished researchers of Russian science.

The coauthors of this book all, of course, share a common research interest and commitment. We have collected data on orienting, attention, and information processing in the brain, using single-cell recordings, central, autonomic, cognitive, behavioral, and verbal measures. This communality brought us together for a series of research meetings, mainly at the University of Jyväskylä, Finland, which resulted in the production of this book. Earlier, in 1982, two of us (RN and HL) were in Moscow for one of the then-biennial meetings in the area of psychophysiology, these being part of an officially agreed program of scientific exchange between Finland and the former Soviet Union. This marked the beginning of our collaboration with ENS. There were many attempts within this program to try to arrange reciprocal visits by ENS to Finland, but constant visa difficulties meant that it was much later before he was able to visit Helsinki. The second coauthor (JAS) had completed a series of research papers based on Sokolov's work and theories, and had developed a link with HL through the common interests of anticipation and orienting.

However, it was ENS' lectures given in the Department of Psychology at the University of Helsinki somewhat later that set the groundwork for this book. The text of these lectures, together with his overhead sketches, formed the basis for the early chapters. In the course of several meetings between all the coauthors, in Finland, Russia, and Hong Kong, in particular, at the meetings at the Department of Psychology at the University of Jyväskylä over a number of weeks in the 1990s, the lectures were developed into a series of chapters that tell a story of developing ideas, maturing theories, and emerging concepts, as well as an intriguing journey through methodology and knowledge acquisition converging from different levels of explanation. The book finishes appropriately with a review of some of the studies by the coauthors that have developed from, or in parallel with, ENS' research. They investigate, in particular, the concepts of attention and anticipation, using a psychophysiological methodology. It is not intended that this book reviews in detail all subsequent studies that were stimulated by ENS' research. Rather, in keeping with his wishes, it focuses on the coauthors' research, giving details of those studies relevant to a furthering of our understanding of the concept of orienting.

It was also ENS' wish that his influence on the field of psychophysiology be downplayed in these introductions. His modesty is well known to those of us who have had the privilege to work with him. We were ourselves not convinced by his arguments in this respect, but we have attempted to comply to at least some extent. We would agree, however, that it should be left to the readers to make their own judgments and conclusions about the value of his work.

John A. Spinks
Risto Näätänen
Heikki Lyytinen

Introduction

This book deals with the mechanisms of information processing, mainly by reference to neuronal processes involved in the orienting reflex or response (OR) or to specific activity directed toward the coding of information from the external world. It is based primarily on the work of Sokolov and his colleagues in the development of theories of information processing and coding using the concept of the OR. The first 10 chapters are based on lectures that he gave on a visit to the Department of Psychology, University of Helsinki, Finland, and they describe, in chapters organized conceptually, much of his empirical work, typically presented in summary form. Generally, each chapter is organized historically, so that it is possible to see how research ideas about the OR arise and are tested. These research ideas and theories are tested and developed further in later chapters, thus providing a commentary on the life and work of Sokolov described earlier.

The book may be conceptually divided into several parts:

The first two chapters are devoted to a macrolevel analysis of the OR concept. The OR is a system of responses including automatic and motor components, electroencephalographic (EEG) components, driving responses, and event-related potentials (ERPs). The book is initially concerned with nonsignal stimuli, this term referring to stimuli that are not endowed with what has been termed *significance* by special instructions (usually human studies) or conditioning (usually animal studies). Chapter 2 concerns the operation of the OR in the context of conditioned responses.

The second approach of the book refers to a microlevel analysis of the OR. Chapters 3-6 cover two different methods for the evaluation of neuronal effectiveness—extracellular recording for identification of spikes and intracellular recording for understanding processing at a synaptic level.

In the third approach of the book, an attempt is made to elucidate as far as is possible the value of ERPs in the context of the OR and their relationship to the neuronal mechanisms of the OR.

Chapters 8-10 employ measures to develop information-processing explanations of the OR as indicated by perceptual, memory, and semantic spaces, particularly with reference to color vision. Mathematical modeling of psychophysiological data is then used to further our understanding of the mechanisms and properties of our perceptual systems.

Chapters 11-12 present some of the Western research in the area of the OR. There are many good reviews of the autonomic literature in this respect (e.g., Siddle, 1983), and there has been, therefore, no attempt to repeat this approach. Research using central measures, however, has made considerable strides in very recent years, and the review, therefore, covers this material comprehensively. These chapters complement the earlier research of Sokolov, offering insights into the influence that Sokolov brought to bear on the area, and the developments that have taken place in our understanding of the OR in information processing in more recent years.

One characteristic feature of the volume is an elucidation of the OR within the framework of the psychophysiology of information processing. A new approach to psychophysiology is suggested. Traditionally, psychophysiology has employed autonomic and motor responses, EEG and ERPs, in its inquiry into information processing, as well as other areas of psychology, but, at each and every point of inquiry within the area of psychophysiology, single unit recording can be made to elucidate the underlying mechanism. Many of the chapters of this book attempt to show the value of this research strategy. This process parallels the contribution to research progress of the development of conceptual structures and mathematical models. In this volume, then, it can be seen that psychophysiology can also be regarded as the science concerned with neuronal mechanisms of sensory phenomena, emotions, behavioral acts, learning, memory, and individual differences. The interest in the neuronal basis of subjective phenomena and individual characteristics can help shape a new research strategy in psychophysiology. Psychophysiology, within this framework, can find itself at the center of cognitive science.

This research strategy may be described by the term *man–neuron–model.* Such psychophysiological study starts with a psychophysical evaluation of input–output characteristics at the higher (macro) level of verbal, motor, autonomic, and global electrophysiological responses as dependent on sensory and symbolic stimuli. The present stage involves a paradigm that addresses itself to the neuronal basis of these input–output characteristics found at the macrolevel. This framework for experiments, now at the microlevel, is devoted to concentrating on a search for neurons specifically involved in sensory coding and response elicitation.

The integration of data concerning information processing at the macro- and microlevels may be achieved by construction of mathematical models composed of neuron-like elements, having the basic features of real neurons. The model is required to simulate overall the input-output characteristics found at the macrolevel. At the same time, each neuron-like element of the model should correspond to the characteristics of a real neuron involved in information processing, also taking into account function at the macrolevel. The model has to perform two basic functions. Initially, it serves to collect in a unified form divergent data from psychophysics and neurobiology. The next step is an application of the model as a working hypothesis.

The new perspective for this application of the model may be realized through computerized versions of the model. In such cases of computer modeling, a prediction of the working model can be obtained in a quantitative form for specified sets of input signals. The predicted characteristics can be obtained from the model for responses at the macro- and microlevels. The prediction from the model can then be tested at both the macro- and microlevels. If the predicted characteristics coincide with the experimental test data, the model is preserved. New predictive characteristics are generated as soon as the predicted results fail to correspond with experimental testing, in which case the model has to be modified. The depth of such modifications might be different—beginning from rearrangement of units or modification of the transformation functions between units without reconsideration of their properties, up to modification of the neuronal basis of the model. The generation of predictions from the model, their experimental testing, and the consequential readjustment of the model constitute a cognitive spiral of psychophysiological research.

A specific role in the integration of macro- and microlevel analyses within the unitary model belongs to event-related potentials. The most significant role of event-related potentials is in bridging the gap between psychophysical data and single unit activity. This bridge is based on the contribution of neurons to the generation of ERPs in man when direct single unit recording cannot be made. The identification of ERP components uniquely related to specific subjective phenomena or individual properties can help in identifying specific sets of neurons directly involved in the realization of functions at the macrolevel.

In information processing, a very important role belongs to the orienting response or reflex (OR)—a system specifically adjusted to emphasize novel events in the subject's surroundings. ORs are the building blocks of investigatory or exploratory behavior. The OR is not only evoked by suddenly occurring events but is characterized by an active search for new information based on comparison and re-evaluation of working hypotheses present in the brain. Such a voluntary form of OR is vividly expressed in the selection of fixation points during eye movements scanning a screen or monitor. The verbal control of the OR via external instructions and internal speech constitutes the basis of goal-directed attention.

A major problem that arises concerns the neuronal mechanisms that participate in the OR generation and the influence that it has on perceptual acts and complex forms of behavior. A quite new perspective on ORs may be realized from the hypothesis that novelty detectors in the brain may be sensitive, not just to new or unexpected events perceived in the environment, but also to new combinations in memory. The inference from this speculation is that the OR would play a role in the creative process that is based on the establishment of new combinations of memory traces, through the same novelty-dependent mechanisms that have been shown to underlie processing of novel environmental stimuli. The relationship between this idea and the more traditional concept of voluntary (cf. involuntary) ORs is one that demands more attention from researchers.

The volume also covers some of the other traditional concepts associated with the OR in the framework of information processing, such as temporal conditioning, anticipation, and exploration. This gives the book a very broad basis, and, as such, it has not been possible to include many details of the studies described, or, indeed, to go into detail on other authors' studies. It has been restricted, as much as possible, to a commentary on the present authors' research on the OR, and, more specifically, to research stemming from the first author's own development of ideas in this area.

In summary, it is hoped that this volume shows how different levels of analysis in psychophysiology can complement each other to produce a picture of information processing in the brain that is firmly based on underlying neuronal mechanisms, and that can explain aspects of information transformation and behavior. It shows how the OR lies at the heart of information processing, within a very broad framework of analyses in the brain, and how it can elucidate different levels of organization there, from neuronal levels, through perceptual levels and memory to semantic levels, and ultimately, behavior.

CHAPTER

1

A Macrolevel Analysis of the Nonsignal Orienting Response

This chapter covers the following issues:

1. The orienting response (OR) in the form of external inhibition in Pavlov's laboratory; the "Tower of Silence."
2. Exploratory behavior as a specific form of behavior directed to extract information from the environment.
3. The OR, adaptive response (AR), and defense response (DR) identified using vascular recording.
4. Sensory components of the OR.
5. The use of EEG recording to reveal phasic and tonic, localized and generalized ORs.
6. Driving responses and the OR.
7. Selective habituation of the OR.
8. Multidimensional self-adjustable filters.
9. The neuronal model of the stimulus.
10. Mismatch signal and its indirect expression.
11. Dishabituation.

THE OR IN THE FORM OF EXTERNAL INHIBITION IN PAVLOV'S LABORATORY; THE "TOWER OF SILENCE"

This chapter begins with a short historical summary of the discovery of the OR in Pavlov's laboratory. During his research on salivation and conditioned responses, Pavlov (1927) emphasized that this conditioning is very sensitive to any external stimulus presented at the same time to the animal. The external stimulus had the effect of depressing or facilitating the conditioned responses. In order to defend his ideas about the extremely important contribution of this unpredictable signal in the animal's environment, Pavlov decided at that time to build the first soundproofed room. It was constructed in the form of a tower, and therefore called the *silence tower.* This silence tower was used then for investigating the role of the OR in the development of conditioned responses. However, later on, Pavlov and his pupils emphasized a specific role for the OR of the animal during presentation of nonsignal stimuli. The emphasis at that time was on describing particular observable components–namely, eye movements directed toward the target, adjustment of the ears, and turning of the body and the head of the animal in the direction of the stimulus. As far as response components of the OR were concerned, this was just the tip of the iceberg.

The basic responses related to the OR were below the level of external observation. Therefore, the development of the study of the OR was related to new methods of recording such types of responses that cannot be directly observed, but that may be recorded through technical means. In particular, research progress in the area of this specific reflex was greatly enhanced by electroencephalograph (EEG) measurement, and later on, by single cell recording.

EXPLORATORY BEHAVIOR AS A SPECIFIC FORM OF BEHAVIOR DIRECTED TO EXTRACT INFORMATION FROM THE ENVIRONMENT

The importance of the research into the OR revolves around the biological significance of the OR. A view of the orienting response as a mere reflex-like adjustment to the stimulus would be an inadequate description, because the biological conditions in the process of evolution that might be considered additional to those reflexes necessary for sustaining life have led to the development of a specific system for collecting information. Therefore, it could be said that ORs should be regarded as a component of exploratory behavior. Exploration itself is a specific type of behavior, but it is not emphasized in the literature. Not only is there specific expression of such behavior through eye movements and other motor components, but there are very important emotional components of exploratory behavior. For example, experiments of Voittonis (1949), a Soviet psychologist, examined the behavior of rats in an open field that was divided into two parts by an electric fence. Although no specific food was present on the other half of the field, the rats nevertheless overcame the electric fence to explore the empty field.

The studies of Butter and Harlow (1954) provided another example with some experiments with monkeys; the reinforcement used was not food or water, but merely the opportunity to see the room. One such experiment was organized in the following way. A monkey in a completely shielded room received an auditory signal and if the animal responded correctly, a window was opened to enable the monkey to look into the laboratory where the experimenter was present. This reinforcement was effective across thousands of reinforcement trials, something that cannot occur with food or water because of satiation. Thus, it can be said that exploration is a specific form of behavior that is directed for the collection of information independent of its future use.

It is useful to emphasize a connection between the OR and exploratory behavior on one hand and some studies of learning on the other. Consider the studies by Tolman (1955) who discovered the so-called latent learning in animals, usually rats. Latent learning occurs whenever an animal is exploring a maze. After such exploration, any reflexes based on food or water reinforcement developed more rapidly because of the animal's knowledge of the map of the maze formed in its brain. So, exploratory behavior plays a specific role in behavior, and the OR is a component part of that exploration.

THE OR, ADAPTIVE RESPONSE (AR), AND DEFENSE RESPONSE (DR) IDENTIFIED USING VASCULAR RECORDING

The next point of this chapter is to show how ORs may be distinguished from other types of responses. This is very important, as it is easy to confuse the expression of different specific reflexes and specific exploratory behavior. To study this, the vascular components of the OR have been investigated. Before explaining why this problem was regarded as so important, it is necessary to turn to the results of some more recent brain research. It has been shown that the attentional level of different brain areas produces a local redistribution of blood according to the level of activation of neurons in this area. It is now possible to use thermographic techniques from the scalp or brain to observe a map of changes of temperature as an expression of the results of redistribution of bloodflow above the brain. Another method, using radioactive isotopes, has been used to identify the amount of blood in particular brain structures. All this data can now specifically localize these processes.

When this research began, plethysmographic recordings were made from one side of the head, and from the finger. One of the most important findings was that even a stimulus that has no specific relation to pain, to warmth, or to cold (such as light or sound) would nevertheless produce remarkable responses in the vascular system, even on the first presentation (Vinogradova & Sokolov, 1957). Light or sound stimuli would produce a vasoconstriction in the finger and a vasodilation in the head. So, the first presentation of the stimulus can evoke divergent changes in the two plethysmographic recordings. Figure 1.1a shows the first presentation of such a stimulus, in this case an auditory stimulus. If, however, these stimuli are presented 10 to 15 times, then no responses at all would be eventually observed in the vascular system. Thus, the sound was noneffective after 15 presentations, and this indicated that this response had habituated. If, how-

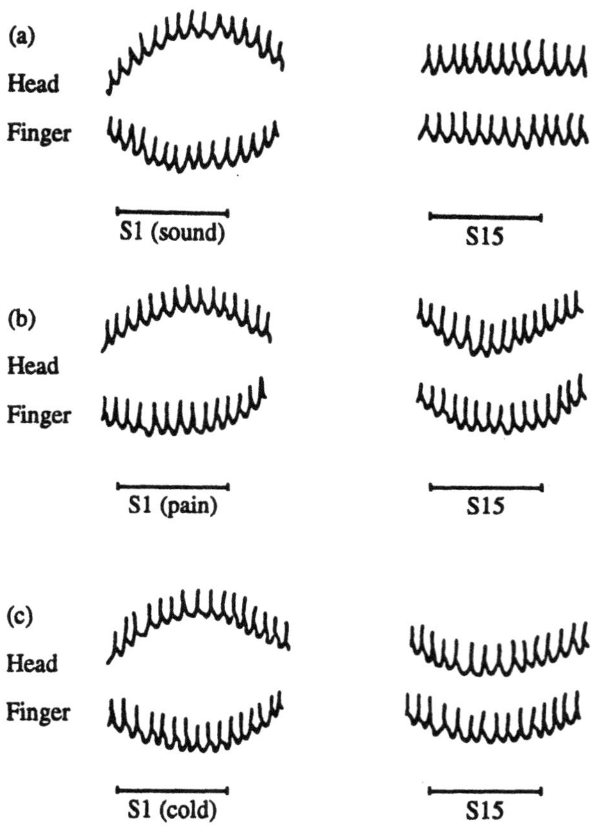

FIG. 1.1. The OR as related to the DR and AR. The OR is characterized here by a reciprocal response—vasodilation in the head and vasoconstriction in the finger to novel sound, rapidly habituating over repeated presentation of the same stimulus. A weak painful stimulus on the first presentation evokes an OR that habituates, and is replaced by defensive constrictions in the head and the finger. The first presentation of a long-lasting cold stimulus initially evokes an OR, which, following prolonged cold stimulation, is replaced by specific synergetic vasoconstriction at the head and finger. After OR habituation, the 15th cold stimulus produces specific responses to cold without OR involvement. S1 and S15 = 1st and 15th presentations of an auditory stimulus. Upward = vasodilation. Downward = vasoconstriction.

ever, an electric shock was presented to the finger of the hand not involved in the recording, sometimes the first presentation of this stimulus produced the same divergent effect in the plethysmographic recordings (that is, vasodilation in the head and vasoconstriction in the finger). Yet, if this painful stimulus was presented several times, a very remarkable change was observed. Instead of vasodilation in the head, vasoconstriction occurred in both the head and the finger recordings. Rather than a complete disappearance of these responses over repeated presentations, these types of stimuli resulted in some different responses that did not habituate (Fig. 1.1b).

These observations have shown that these two types of responses relate to two different reflexes. The one that habituates is a reflex to novelty and the nonhabituating one is a defense reflex to pain. However, at certain levels of intensity, the pain stimulus may be interpreted as a novel stimulus. Thus, if the pain is not very strong, there is a competition between the OR and DR. The OR dominates initially, but soon habituates, much like the responses to sound. Following this habituation of the OR, the re-establishment of the DR can be seen, which is stable and does not habituate. In order to make a comparison between these two reflexes and classical reflexes to cold and warmth, control experiments have been conducted. Very often, it is possible to observe OR-type responses to the initial presentation of cold stimuli, instead of the typical response to cold (Fig. 1.1c). However, if the stimulus is prolonged, instead of the vasodilation in the head, a classical vasoconstriction response to cold may be observed. Over repeated presentations, the classical vasoconstriction to cold stimuli is obtained, which again does not habituate, and is characterized by vasoconstrictions in the head and the hand. This (and the parallel classical vasodilation to warm stimuli) is a manifestation of the adaptive reflex.

How might the DR be distinguished from the cold-specific AR? Figure 1.2 shows the responses to warmth. The structure of these responses is very interesting because infrared illumination has been used as a method to produce pain. In an experiment where a standard intensity infrared stimulus was presented repeatedly (Fig. 1.2a), the first presentation of warmth was characterized by vasodilation in the head and vasoconstriction in the finger. The vasoconstriction in the finger was produced because of the involvement of the OR. Later on, after the habituation of the OR, there was vasodilation in the head and the finger, characterizing the AR. Prolonged illumination by infrared rays (Fig. 1.2b), on the other hand, produced DRs when the pain threshold was reached. From the beginning of the radiation, ORs are evoked, characterized by the usual reciprocal response. Later on in this prolonged stimulus presentation, vasodilation is observed in both the head and finger. This is the specific thermoregulatory response to warmth. Suddenly, when the subject perceives pain through radiation, a DR vasoconstriction may be seen in both head and finger recordings.

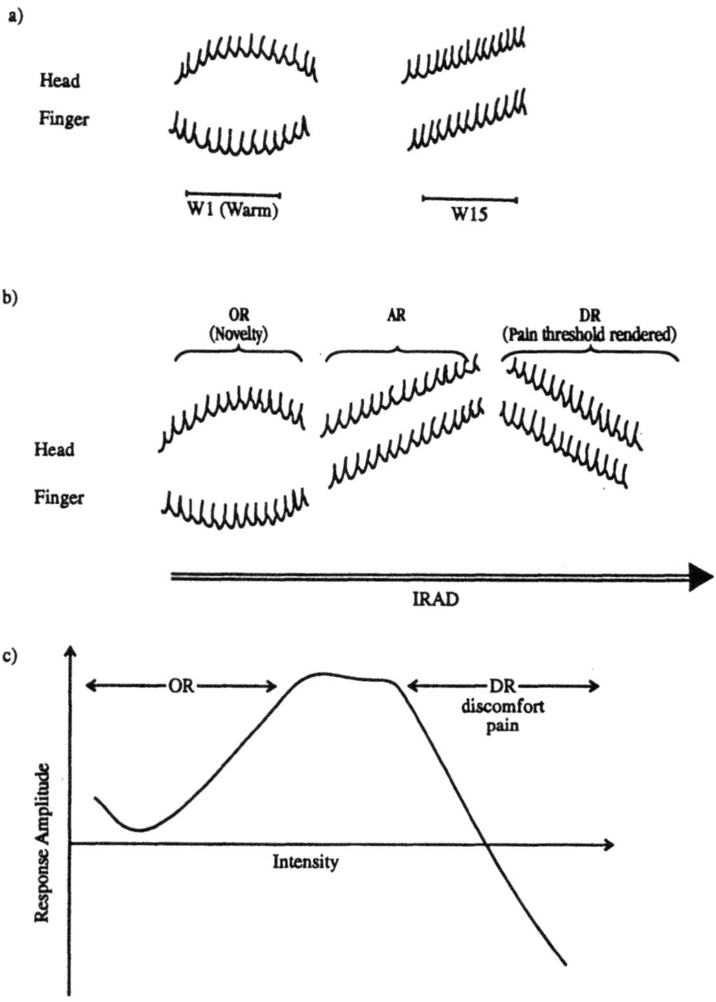

FIG. 1.2. The OR, AR, and DR sequence. (a) The first warm stimulus evoked an OR. After OR habituation, the AR to warmth is evident by parallel vasodilation in the head and the finger. (b) The beginning of perception of warmth is evident by OR reciprocal vascular responses. Prolonging the stimulus results in parallel vasodilation in the head and finger, indicating specific AR to warmth. When the radiation reaches the pain threshold, the DR is generated. This is evident from the abrupt vasoconstriction at the head and hand. (c) Presentations of repeated stimuli, gradually increasing in intensity, revealed a change from an OR to a DR as the subject experienced the discomfort of pain with intense stimulation. IRAD = infrared radiation. W1, W15 = 1st warm and 15th warm stimulus presentation.

Similarly, in the case where an infrared radiation stimulus was repeatedly presented, but increased in intensity over trials (Fig. 1.2c), two phases in the response were observed. At the beginning, there was an increase in the temperature below the pain threshold, until, suddenly, the intensity reached the pain threshold level. At this point, the response characteristics changed, indicating the evocation of a different reflex. What conclusion can be drawn from these facts, and what classification of reflexes can be made from this data? It has been shown that there exists a reciprocal response in the head and finger in the case of the OR, vasoconstriction in both recordings in the case of the DR. The ARs were characterized by a specific type of response to stimuli—classical vasodilation by warmth and vasoconstriction for cold in both recordings.

Therefore from this observation, it is possible to conclude that these three types of reflex exist—the OR, DR, and AR. What has happened to this classification in subsequent research? Graham (1979) used changes in heart rate for distinguishing between the orienting and defense responses. She has shown that the OR is characterized by a prolongation of the R–R (interbeat) interval in the electrocardiograph. Heart rate is lowered during an OR, and increased by the DR. She further developed the classification of reflexes by introducing a new reflex, specifically the *startle reflex*. This, as shown by Graham, is a short-lasting muscle tension and short-lasting increase in heart rate. This startle reflex has also been observed in the laboratories in Moscow. It was originally regarded as an artifact due to muscle tension, which may be observed in the plethysmographic recordings. However, because it is a motor artifact, it was not included in our conceptual scheme, as we prefer to keep to the three reflexes identified previously. Turpin (1983) also used this categorization of ORs, DRs, and ARs, although he had not (at the time of writing), analyzed the ARs in as much detail as the ORs and DRs. Graham elaborated evidence for distinguishing a fourth type of response—a transient-detecting response evoked by low intensity changes in stimulation—for a review, see Graham (1992).

Thus, to differentiate these different types of reflexes—OR, DR, and AR—one can use vascular responses, bearing in mind that there is a very flexible relationship between ORs and DRs (for example, if a painful stimulus is given on a new part of the skin, an OR may be initially obtained). It is also important in the context of the DR to consider response latency. Usually, the responses are measured from the beginning of the stimulus presentation. The DR that has been recorded is much longer lasting. Now Turpin (e.g., Turpin & Siddle, 1978) has, in accordance with this data, reported this longer-duration DR, showing gradual vasoconstriction in the head. At the Nenci Institute in Poland, measurement of the blood supply to the brain in dogs, using radioactive xenon, has revealed that low-intensity auditory stimulation is usually characterized by an increase in the radioactivity count, that is, an increase in blood supply. If very loud noises were used, an opposite effect was observed, indicating a reduction in the blood supply.

The DR evocation is of very great importance in its practical application, for example in different acoustic deficiencies in children as described in a study by Sokolov and Vinogradova (1957). One of the programs was devoted to the study of the phenomenon of recruitment, an effect that is characterized by an increase in the absolute threshold of hearing, and at the same time by a decrease of the pain threshold. This means that the range of sounds that can be perceived without discomfort by such children is very narrow. The measurement of this deficiency has been through the use of the amplitude and duration of the vascular response, and identified vasodilation or vasoconstriction in the head. The response magnitude obtained by multiplication of the duration with the amplitude was presented on a dB scale (Fig. 1.3). What is happening as the intensity of the auditory stimulus is increased? Below the threshold, no vascular response can be seen. If the sound is near threshold, the response is very strong, as indicated by the long duration of this OR. The response is smaller when the sounds are perceived more easily, as the intensity is increased. Then, the response increases up to a level of about 85 to 90 dB, where it turns in a reverse direction, that is, showing the presence of vasoconstriction in the head, indicating a DR.

For a child with a recruitment phenomenon (Fig. 1.3c), it may be seen that the absolute threshold is shifted upwards. The effect of the threshold stimulus is very small. With an increase in the intensity of the sound stimulus, after a short vasodilation, only vasoconstriction is observed in the head of such a person as the intensity of the eliciting stimulus is increased. This means that even moderate intensities produce discomfort. Similar results have been obtained in a subpopulation of children with deficiencies in sight. The experiments have been repeated with adults using an electrical current; by using electric pulses, the same type of curve can be produced. The difficulty in vascular recording is instability; although newer methods to measure the redistribution of blood supply are now available.

SENSORY COMPONENTS OF THE OR

Next, the sensory components of the OR are considered. If the vascular responses are regarded as specific mechanisms to improve the conditions for single unit activity in the brain, there has been an emphasis on the local redistribution of the blood supply. The role of such a blood supply as related to sensory function should be considered carefully. Experimentally, the problem in studying this phenomenon is to combine the OR recording with measurement of thresholds using classical psychophysical methods. In early research, the so-called self-writing adaptometer was used, in which the light intensity on a screen that the subjects watched could be regulated by the

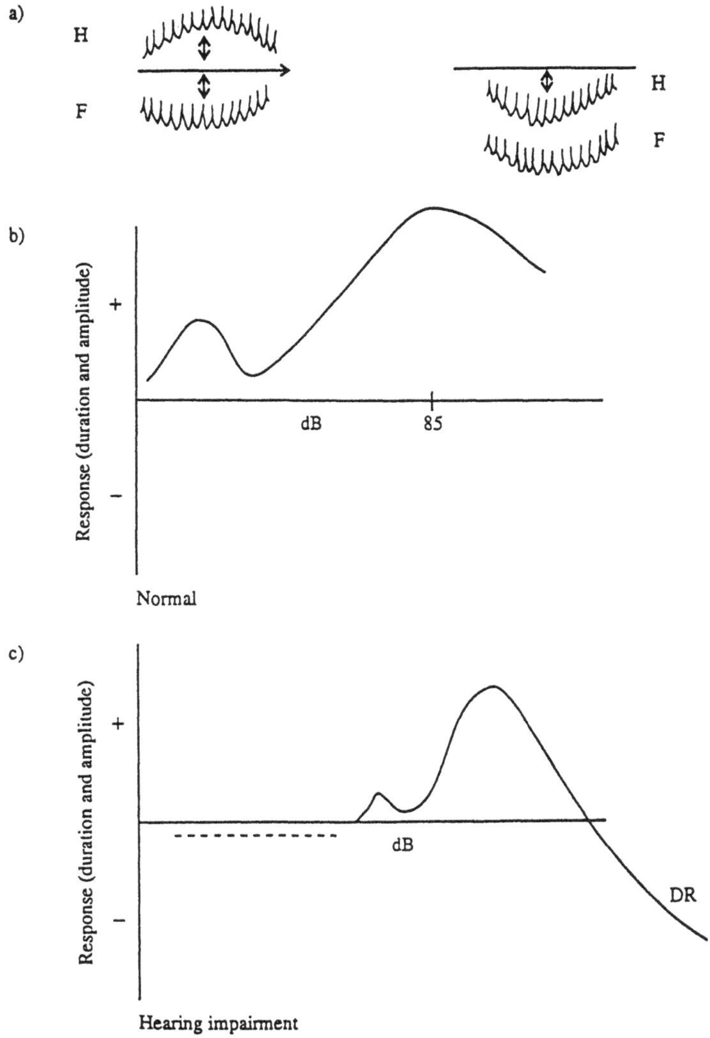

FIG. 1.3. Auditory recruitment. The OR and the DR are represented as examples. In normal subjects, the OR to threshold sounds is intensified. Reaching levels of discomfort, the sound evokes a DR interacting with the OR, resulting in a decrease of vasodilation and increase in vasoconstriction at the head. In persons with auditory recruitment, the sensory threshold is elevated. The threshold at which responses are intensified is small. The DRs to painful sounds are characterized by low thresholds in such subjects. The dynamic range between the intensities at which sounds are perceived and intensities at which DRs are evoked is rather narrow. H = head. F = finger. Upward = vasodilation. Downward = vasoconstriction.

subjects themselves by changing the filter to increase or decrease light intensity. This apparatus is thus very similar to the so-called Bekesy audiometer, which measures auditory thresholds (Von Bekesy, 1967). These devices have now been superseded by computer-based software—any such device can be programmed by using the computer to measure sensory functions.

The most important finding in these experiments was an increase in sensory visual sensitivity following the slightest sounds. This supports the work of Kravkov (1948), who used psychophysical methods to systematically study sensory interaction (that is, the influence of one sensory modality on another). The emphasis in the current studies has been the process of habituation of these effects. Thus, it has been found that only novel stimuli produce this increase in sensitivity. If the sound is repeated several times, then no increase in sensitivity accompanies later sound presentations.

For the purpose of combining the sensory recordings with an objective evaluation of thresholds, EEG recordings were employed, not in the classical way, but rather used to objectively measure the threshold of the visual system. The experiment was organized in the following way. A light was presented slightly below threshold and produced no alpha rhythm depression. Then, a sound was presented and later, the same test light. The sound produced a short depression of the alpha rhythm, which then recovered. At this time, the further presentation of the test light caused an alpha rhythm depression to be observed. Thus, in this case, a stimulus that was originally below threshold now produces a depression of the alpha rhythm, sometimes with, and sometimes without, a motor response from the subject. The sound increased the visual sensitivity and provided a time marker that helps the subject to invest his efforts at the appropriate time.

If, at the same time, electromyogram (EMG) recordings are made, it is possible to sometimes see the appearance of a long-latency EMG response (Fig. 1.4), indicating that, at first, an increase in the sensitivity is expressed in terms of alpha rhythm depression only. Later on, this increased level of sensitivity resulted in the subject voluntarily responding to the stimulus. It can thus be seen that combining EEG recordings with sensory measurement can be very useful in the study of the OR. Vascular components (as sensitive indicators of sensory components) may also be combined with measurement of EEG changes.

THE USE OF EEG RECORDING TO REVEAL PHASIC AND TONIC, LOCALIZED AND GENERALIZED ORS

The fifth point of this chapter relates to the EEG component of the OR. Berger (1929), who discovered the alpha rhythm, emphasized as its primary feature the rhythm's sensitivity to attention. In many of his publications, it is possi-

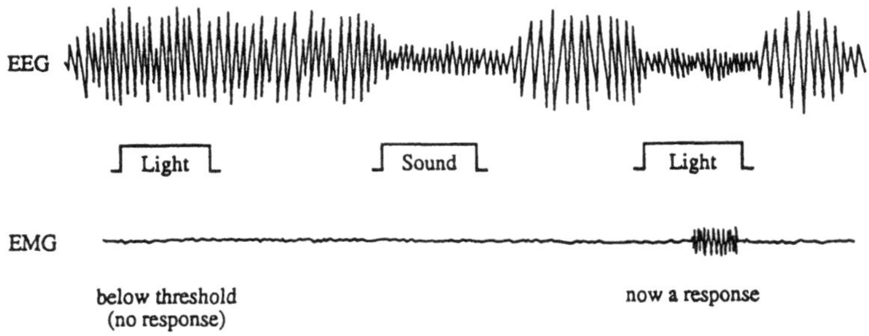

FIG. 1.4. Sensory components of the OR. EEG from the visual area. EMG from the constrictors. The subthreshold light stimulus close to threshold evoked no EEG depression and no EMG. The sound resulting in a short EEG desynchronization increases visual sensitivity. The same light now evokes EEG depression accompanied later on by EMG, showing that the light intensity after auditory stimulation exceeded the now-lowered threshold and triggered voluntary muscle activity.

ble to find different types of experiments where the alpha rhythm was depressed not by real stimuli, but just by changing the direction of visual attention in conditions of complete darkness. In our laboratories, the EEG has been studied under similar conditions to those used for discrimination of reflexes. The procedure for these studies is very simple. A stimulus is presented repeatedly, and the responses to this stimulus are decomposed into components due to novelty and other more specific components of the specific reflex under study. It has been shown many times that the repetition of a sound stimulus of low intensity results in a disappearance of the EEG responses to that stimulus. EEG responses are characterized by the same features as sensory and vascular components of the OR. Additionally, the galvanic skin response (EDR) has also been used to study the OR and this component is primarily sensitive to novelty.

The repeated stimulus presentations result in a complete habituation of the EEG and EDR responses (Fig. 1.5a). At the same time, some very specific features may be found in the analysis of EEG habituation. In this study, a light was presented while EEG responses were recorded from both the visual and motor cortex (Figs. 1.5b and 1.5c). Using the presentation of visual stimuli, about 20 to 30 presentations were needed in order to produce extinction of the response in the visual cortex. In the motor area, however, the responses disappeared after 7 to 10 presentations, in parallel with the EDRs. What has been shown here? Initially, a generalized alpha depression was observed. After about 15 presentations, this response was replaced by stable responses of shorter duration in the visual cortex and practically no responses in the motor area.

To stimulate the motor area, different procedures have been used, namely, actively making a fist, or passively changing the position of the

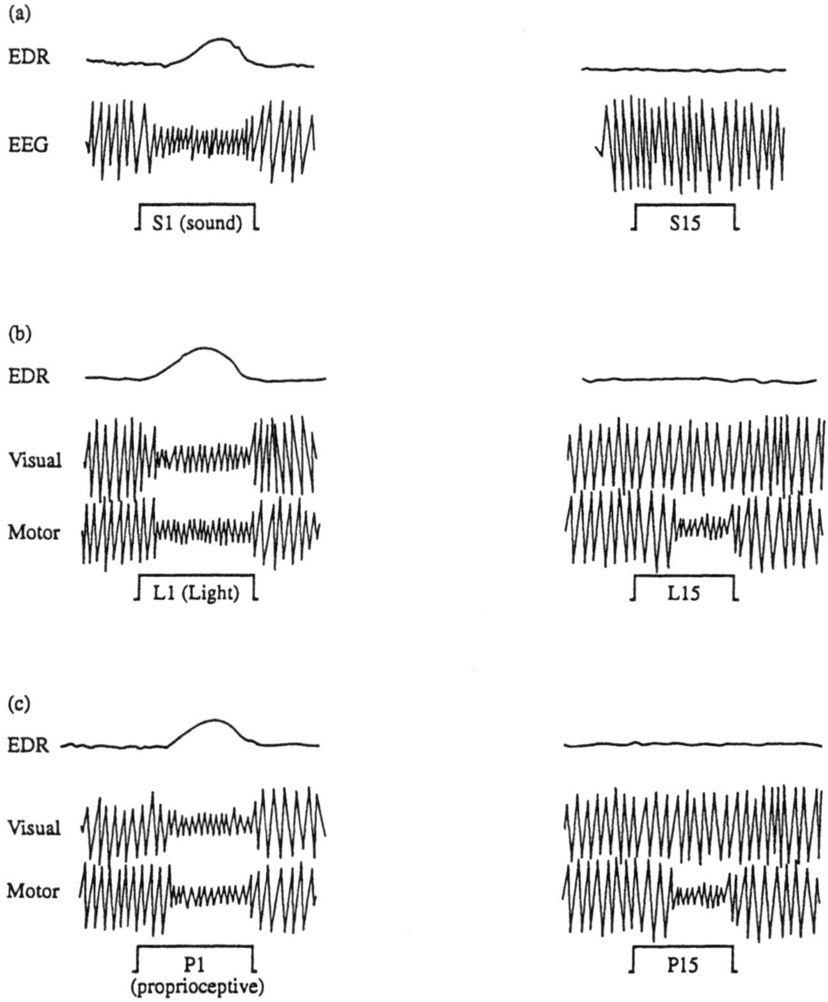

FIG. 1.5. The repeated presentations of sound results in habituation of EEG and EDR components of the OR. EDR—electrodermal (skin galvanic) response. The comparison of the light and proprioceptive stimuli show that after generalized arousal is over, the selective local arousal is preserved for light in the visual area, and for proprioceptive input in the motor area. These local responses that persist after many trials can be identified as indications of a local OR, as opposed to the initial generalized OR involving different brain areas and different behavioral manifestations. EEG = alpha rhythm of the visual cortex, S1, S15 = 1st and 15th presentation of sound stimuli, Visual = visual cortex, Motor = motor area, L1, L15 = 1st and 15th presentation of light stimuli, P1, P15 = 1st and 15th presentation of proprioceptive stimuli.

hand by elevating it with a system of blocks. Again, at first there is generalized depression in both the motor and visual cortex. However, after 15 presentations of proprioceptive signals, the EDR together with the EEG response in the visual cortex, is extinguished, but depression still continues in the motor area. These observations indicate two types of ORs—generalized and localized. The local OR is typically related to certain areas of the brain and can be seen only after habituation of generalized depression. It is very important to show concurrently the EDR, as this indicates the generalized nature of the OR. The EDR can be seen in all cases on the first presentation of a stimulus, but disappears when the stimulus is presented repeatedly (Fig. 1.5).

Thus, these experiments revealed specific generalized and localized responses, characterized as such because they refer to the whole of the brain or to just a specific focus within the brain. Another classification qualifies the duration of the response so that all EEG responses expressing the OR can be classified into tonic or phasic. It is reasonable to question whether this differentiation is necessary, and it has the support of this laboratory because sometimes the data shows a very long-lasting change in the background activity, which emphasizes a shift in the level of a tonic state of arousal. Underlying this arousal is a tonic activation of the OR and under such conditions, the phasic OR can be easily triggered. Local activation can also be tonic, that is, lasting for a long time in one brain area. At the same time, generalized arousal lasting a short period can be characterized as phasic. In summary, four types of OR are being suggested here—distinguished by a phasic-tonic dimension and a localized-generalized dimension. These descriptive explanations of the OR arise from the observations of a very simple procedure—the repeated presentation of a stimulus with some variations of stimulus parameters. Although simple, it is a very powerful method that can be modified for some other purposes.

DRIVING RESPONSES AND THE OR

Currently, the use of averaging techniques in event-related potential (ERP) research is very common. When the OR was first studied in the Sokolov laboratories, a Walter analyzer, which allowed adjustable frequency filtering of EEG, was employed. During recording of EEG, it was possible to get a summary of EEG activity in single frequency bands of alpha rhythms. Instead of single stimuli at that time, rhythmical visual or auditory signals were used. This is because, based on these rhythms, some resonance (and harmonic) effects in EEG responses were expected, which could be measured by the output of the Walter analyzer set to specific frequencies of EEG responses. The so-called driving response is an EEG pattern composed of brainwaves at the same frequency as a stroboscopic light that might be presented. This response is really more complex than the response to nonrhythmic stimuli, and it is very useful in understanding the mechanism of the OR.

This following or driving response is stable and is only modified to a degree, depending on the functional state of the subject. What is important about it is that the frequencies are switched on in the brain by the presentation of light. If the subject is stimulated at 9 cycles per second (Hz), different responses are produced, depending on the arousal state of the subject. If the subject is relaxed–not very sleepy, but not very aroused–then the same 9 Hz frequency, which is close to the background alpha rhythm, dominates the driving response. If, however, the subject is more strongly aroused, a modification of the frequency of the driving response is obtained, and, instead of the 9 Hz, the analyzer output reveals higher harmonics. An EEG might contain 18 Hz rhythms, or even 27 Hz, instead of 9. If the state of the brain is lower, then the reverse effect is observed. The subject may be stimulated by the same 9 Hz, but this frequency only partially characterizes the driving response, which may contain 6 and 4.5 Hz activity in the EEG spectrum. The driving response is thus very sensitive as a metric of the functional state of the brain, even more so than the EEG. This feature of the driving response has been used in our laboratories for studying the influence of the OR on brain activity. In this way, a new component of the OR has been identified, consisting of an activation mechanism responsible for amplification of brainwaves.

The experiment to be described is again a very simple one. The epoch of analysis in the Walter analyzer is usually 10 s but to adjust the epoch of analysis to the nature of the stimulation, an automatic device was connected to the analyzer that switched on the stroboscopic light at the beginning of the epoch and switched it off at the end of the analysis period. In this way, it was possible to obtain a correspondence between the driving response and the period of analysis of brain waves under the influence of this rhythmic stimulation. The experiment was as follows (Fig. 1.6).

The subject was presented with the stroboscopic light, so that the EEG response identifiable on the analyzer spectrum had the same frequency. If 9 Hz was used, then a 9 Hz activity was evident in the brain waves. In the next phase, an auditory stimulus was presented to the subject, followed by the same 9 Hz light again. This time, the EEG rhythm was no longer close to the 9 Hz used for stimulation. Instead, 18 or 27 Hz can be observed (Fig. 1.6a).

Now, it is possible to use the same procedure of habituation, using the stroboscopic light stimulus to evoke the driving responses and continue with the auditory stimulus to evoke an OR. After several presentations of this auditory stimulus, the response to the stroboscopic stimulus is close to the stimulus frequency again (Fig. 1.6b). It would appear that sound no longer affects the driving response of the brain. Thus, at the beginning of the ex-

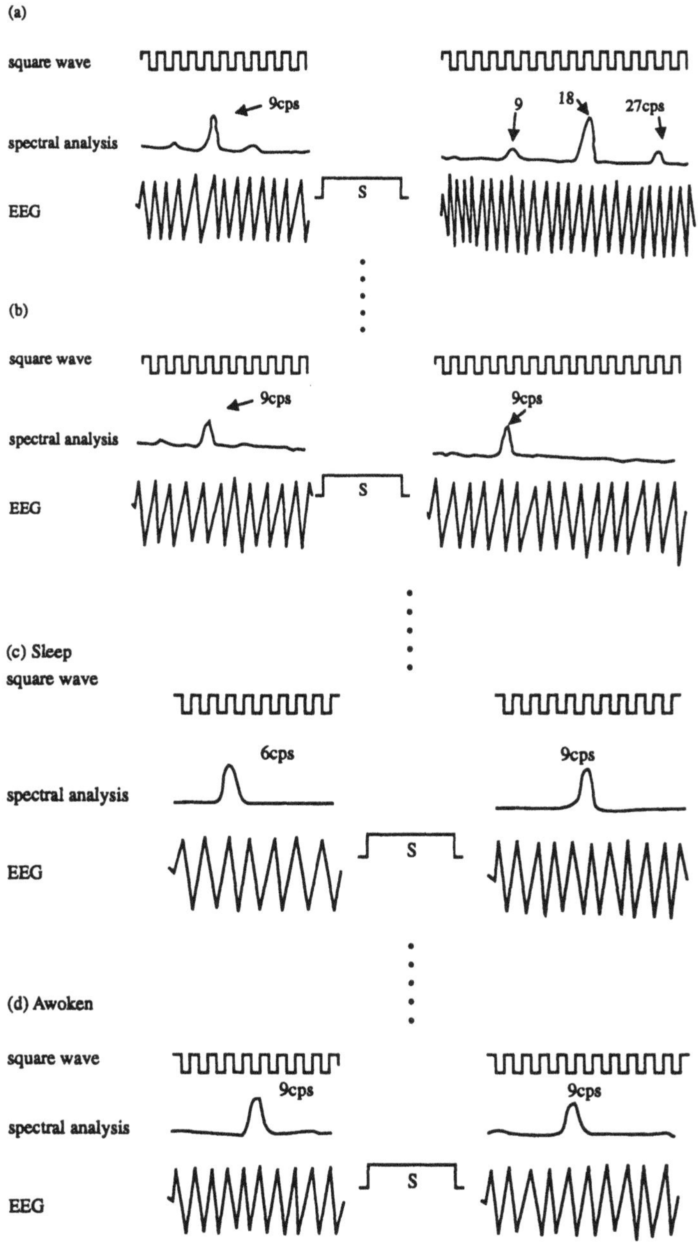

FIG. 1.6. Driving response and the OR. (a) The initial driving response is characterized by 9 Hz in the EEG spectrum. A novel sound modifies the driving response to 9 Hz light. The spectrum of the response reveals 18 Hz and 27 Hz components, instead of the stroboscopic light frequency of 9 Hz. (b) With the habituation of the responses to the sound, there is less modification of the driving response. (c) Repeated presentations of the sound induce drowsiness or sleep, and a transformation of the 9 Hz rhythm into one dominated by 6 Hz. (d) The termination of sleep is again characterized by the 9 Hz response, which is not modified by sound, because the OR to this sound has already habituated. S = sound stimulus.

periment, this sound produced arousal, and the frequency of the driving response was changed. After habituation, the frequency was the same as the original stimulation. This implies that the effect of the sound as an arousing stimulus is reduced due to repeated presentations. This very simple procedure of repeated presentations of the stimulus results in very remarkable changes in the brain.

A further experiment was conducted in which a subject was dark-adapted in a shielded room, and the stroboscopic stimuli were given through closed eyelids. The subject can be sleeping, but if the same procedures of the prior experiment are followed, then the result of the auditory stimulus was, remarkably, to induce deeper sleep instead of arousal. In sleep, the same 9 Hz light produced, for example, a 6 Hz driving response (Figs. 1.6c and 1.6d). If a novel stimulus is then given, it has the effect of arousing the subject, and, again, a 9 Hz rhythm was evident. More deep sleep again results in a 6 Hz response.

In drowsy subjects, repeated presentations of the auditory stimulus not only influenced the disappearance of a response, but also changed the functional state of the subject (arousal) and induced a state of sleep. Having observed this, it begs the question of whether the disappearance of the OR is related to this change in functional state. The series of experiments described were carried out to show that the initial phase of the habituation of the OR occurs without any evidence of change in functional state. Thus, OR habituation and the reduction of functional state or arousal levels (leading to the induction of sleep) are two different mechanisms.

SELECTIVE HABITUATION OF THE OR

It is suggested that the problem of habituation should be analyzed from another angle. What exactly is *habituation*? Is it a change of the overall functional state of the organism, or is it a very stimulus-specific process? To test these alternatives, the habituation paradigm can be used, together with the concurrent presentation of test stimuli. Such an experiment takes time, but it is an effective way of resolving this dilemma. One stimulus is repeated so that habituation results. This stimulus is then changed, thus inserting a new stimulus in the sequence of stimuli, evoking a response. Then, the same standard stimulus is repeated, followed by a new, changed test stimulus. For example, consider an experiment using auditory stimuli. A 1000 Hz tone could be used as the standard stimulus, and 700 Hz, 1200 Hz, and 1400 Hz could be used as test stimuli. Measuring the duration of the alpha-blocking responses to these test stimuli, it is possible to identify a very selective process. The frequency of 1000 Hz, on a subjective scale calculated as the logarithm of the frequency, comes eventually to evoke no alpha rhythm depression. Looking at the relationship between duration of responses to the test stimuli and the subjective frequency of these stimuli, it can be seen that the habituation process is not a total change in the level of arousal, but a very selective process concentrated around the standard 1000 Hz stimulus (Fig. 1.7a).

MULTIDIMENSIONAL SELF-ADJUSTABLE FILTERS

Thus, it is possible to show selective habituation that can be defined as a very specific process. How far does this selectivity extend? Does this selective habituation occur simultaneously to several parameters? To test this, another habituation paradigm was used, combined with the presentation of test stimuli with many modified parameters. After habituation is shown, the stimulus is changed, evoking a new response. Then, the original stimulus is again repeated, followed by another change stimulus, this time, however, changing along another dimension of the standard stimulus. By measuring the duration of alpha blocking to these test stimuli, it can be seen that the process of habituation is not a total change of the level of arousal, but a very selective one, selectively tuned to the stimulus under investigation. When these curves were first observed, it was very interesting to see how the research attitudes towards this field of investigation changed—instead of studying the OR per se, there was initiation of a new series of experiments, where the OR was used to study selective processing in the brain.

How has this multidimensional habituation been studied? Complex stimuli, varying along a number of dimensions, like color and the position of visual stimuli in space, have been employed. The most important results are obtained through the use of self-adjustable multidimensional filters. What does this mean? Using auditory stimuli, it can be seen that a single parameter, for example, frequency, is selectively blocked only within a certain window of frequencies. If several parameters are taken into account, then all these parameters can be considered as being recorded in the brain, constituting a multidimensional filter.

The results showed that, if frequency, intensity, and duration of the auditory stimulus are considered, this particular combination of features within a repeated stimulus results in a selective depression of the OR. Whether duration, frequency, or intensity are increased or decreased makes no difference to the result—a response to the changed stimulus is again elicited, confirming the conclusion that the original stimulus is encoded in multidimensional space, or, in this case, three-dimensional space. For a particular combination of these parameters, there is, in three-dimensional space, a certain area representing the particular combination of duration, frequency, and intensity of the sound. This area may be represented by a vector with the components of I, F, and D (Fig. 1.7b). This area will block the signals of these particular combinations. This leads to the conclusion that,

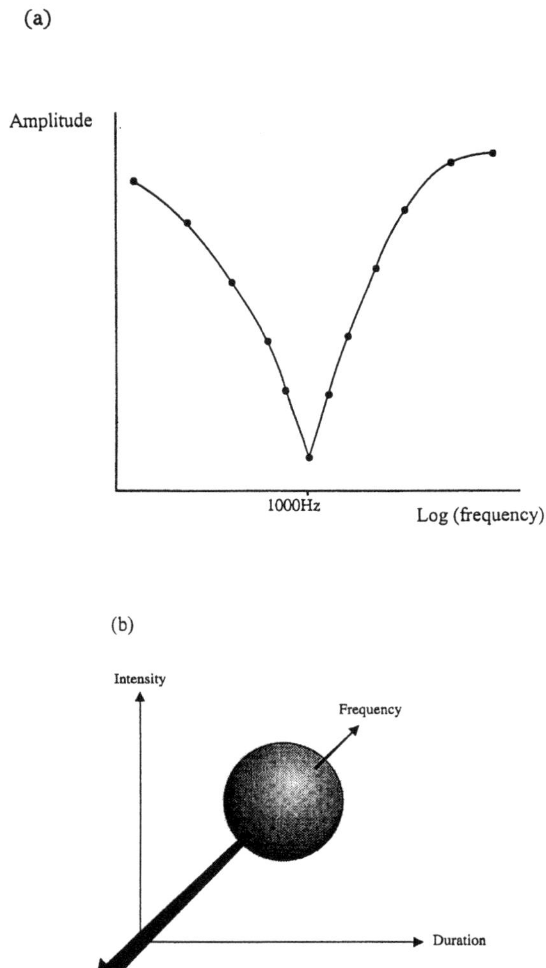

FIG. 1.7. Selective multidimensional habituation. (a) In this study of EDR responses to stimulus change, the amplitude of the response is shown as a measure of stimulus efficiency. After habituation of the EDR response to the standard 1000 Hz sound, the test stimuli evoked responses that increased in magnitude as a function of deviance from the standard. (b) If not only frequency, but also intensity and duration were used for test stimuli modification, the selective habituation appeared as an area in three-dimensional space. Stimuli with this exact combination of parameters produce no OR. Any deviation from this combination results in a mismatch signal and OR initiation. Similar results have been obtained using EEG alpha rhythm depression.

if a stimulus with different features is repeated, there is a selective filtering only for this combination of features. Thus, the brain appears to have established a self-adjustable filter due to the repeated presentations and it is this filter that selectively blocks particular familiar stimuli. Any nonfamiliar stimulus will be free to re-evoke the OR.

After these experiments that alter different parameters and their combinations, there has been a move one step forward through the employment of complex stimuli containing a combination of light and sound. A selective habituation to this combination can be achieved in the normal way. Then, however, either light or sound can be subtracted from the complex. The problem here was to investigate whether there existed in the brain a specific mechanism that integrates light and sound in one unit. If such a mechanism exists, elimination of one of the components should also produce an OR. It was found that such complexes do exist, indicating that there is in the brain a specific mechanism able to extract a combination of features.

THE NEURONAL MODEL OF THE STIMULUS

What is meant by filtering in this context, and how is the concept of filtering best handled? The results indicate that in the brain something has happened, and these modifications relating to current stimulation are retained. On the other hand, it is not a usual subjective phenomenon, because individuals do not subjectively realize the existence of such a filtering device. Common terms like *sensation* and *perception*, indicating subjective phenomena, are not appropriate for this type of data. Therefore, a new term has been suggested–the neuronal model of the stimulus. This means that, in some specific neuronal units, some changes occur that selectively modify the units in such a way that these modified units can be regarded as representations of a stimulus, because the modifications are always matched to the stimulus. In this respect, the OR has been observed from an alternative perspective, that which asks what is actually meant by the concept of the OR. The suggested answer is that the OR does not occur to the stimulus as such but is triggered by a mismatch signal when the stimulus and its trace or neuronal model do not coincide.

MISMATCH SIGNAL AND ITS INDIRECT EXPRESSION

Several very simple experiments were carried out to demonstrate such mismatch (Fig. 1.8). If a stimulus of a certain duration is presented, an alpha rhythm depression results. After several presentations, no response is seen (Fig. 1.8a). But this stimulus can be made shorter, and what is observed is an EEG depression beginning at the time when the duration of the stimulus

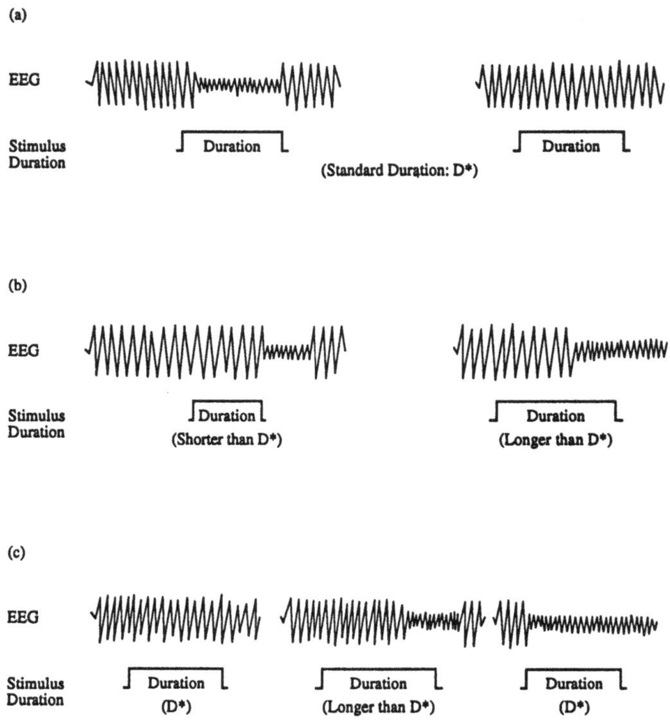

FIG. 1.8. EEG recording of mismatch signals. (a) The sound stimulus of a constant duration that evokes an OR on the first presentation results in no OR after habituation. (b) If the duration of the stimulus is shortened, the OR appears just after the unexpected termination. The prolongation of the stimulus results in a response when the test sound lasts more than the standard. (c) The sound presented with standard intervals evoked no EEG responses after habituation. If, however, the interval is modified, the stimulus results in EEG alpha depression and the dishabituation of the response to the next stimulus presented with a standard interval.

became shorter than the standard. Thus, it is not the stimulus that is triggering the EEG depression, but the mismatch between the previous model and the presented stimulus. The stimulus may also be lengthened in duration and in this case, there is also a response, and this response is triggered when the duration of the stimulus becomes longer than the standard (Fig. 1.8b). In all cases, the most important finding is that the response is triggered not by the stimulus per se, but by some mismatch signal. It is postulated that the existence of signals indicates a mismatch between the elaborated neuronal model and each stimulus. Before it is handled at the next level in the information processing sequence, each stimulus is compared with this trace. How this comparison is done is not yet clear, although an attempt to explain it will be made at the single unit level later in this book. Indirect evidence of mismatch is seen in dishabituation.

DISHABITUATION

Dishabituation is an effect that consists of the recovery of the habituated OR after presentation of a novel stimulus. This means that, once a repeated standard stimulus is no longer effective in evoking an OR, a novel stimulus presented will re-evoke a response, but, presenting the standard stimulus again results in a response once more (Fig. 1.8c). Thus, the novel stimulus not only produces a response, but also influences some other channels. This dishabituation effect may be regarded as indirect evidence of a mismatch signal that influences some other channels, not just this particular set of neurons constituting an informational channel used for the analysis of the standard stimulus. This has been the subject of some very heated discussion and debate about habituation. A very important theory in this debate was that of Thompson (1980), who postulated that habituation and dishabituation are controlled by two different mechanisms. Other authors believe that dishabituation is the result of the direct passage of a new stimulus through the same channel. Thompson argued that this effect occurs not only in the channel being stimulated, but in some other channels very widely distributed in the brain.

The data may be briefly summarized here. Nonsignal stimuli have been employed, where subjects are required to sit in a chair, with no instructions about how to process the stimuli. Yet, even under these circumstances, there is a learning effect, because the process of habituation may be regarded as a learning process, albeit negative learning. The term *negative learning* with respect to habituation was introduced by Thorpe (1956) in Cambridge University. In his observations on birds, he showed that during repetition of stimuli, the response of the animal disappeared, and this disappearance of responses was termed negative learning. OR habituation may also be seen as a form of negative learning. This learning is stimulus selective, and, at the same time, very complex in the sense that a total set of stimulus parameters is fixed and preserved in the brain systems in the form of a neuronal model. The mismatch signal is widely distributed, evoking a number of responses that can be a common property of selective habituation.

CONCLUDING COMMENTS

The identification of the OR as a particular reflex has opened up a new area of experiments devoted to the selectivity of its habituation. Such experiments have suggested that the OR is evoked by a mismatch signal arising from coincidence of a new stimulus with the trace established during presentation of the standard. Using different stimuli, one can evaluate the shape of the trace as being an exact replica of the standard. This indicates that the nervous system can create a neuronal model of the standard stimulus during the process of OR habituation.

CHAPTER

2

A Macrolevel Analysis of the Signal Orienting Response

This chapter covers the following issues:

1. The role of the orienting response (OR) in the establishment of CRs.
2. Facilitation of the OR due to reinforcement.
3. OR conditioning.
4. Habituation of the OR during CR stabilization.
5. Re-establishment of the OR during difficult tasks.
6. The role of verbal instructions in OR activation.
7. The role of the frontal lobe in the control of the OR.
8. The OR and threshold experiments.
9. The standard stimulus memory trace and the OR.
10. The OR as an information regulator.
11. Informational load: Geometric space for EEG and ERP and functional connections.
12. The psychophysiology of computerized teaching.

This chapter is devoted to a macrolevel analysis of the orienting response (OR), and is related specifically to the response to signal stimuli. The term *signal* is taken to describe such stimuli that, having been under the influence of previous instructions, or influenced by a process of prior conditioning, may be regarded as significant stimuli. In this sense, signal stimuli may be identified with significance. This chapter covers how the OR behaves under the influence of such significance, or, as may be preferably understood, under the influence of different kinds of conditioning, including verbal conditioning. Verbal instructions are a specific type of this procedure.

Before the role of the OR in the establishment of conditioned responses (CRs) is explained, it is necessary to summarize the basic standpoint concerning the OR. First it should be emphasized, as has been noted earlier, that the OR is a multicomponent system. For the identification of ORs, it is usually necessary to look to polygraph recordings to identify a specific pattern of components constituting the OR. It has also been emphasized earlier that the OR is different from at least three other reflexes: startle, defense, and adaptation reflexes. The OR is characterized by selective habituation. This process can be represented in the form of a multidimensional selective filter blocking a particular stimulus and preventing ORs to this particular stimulus. The deviation of a stimulus from the standard one results in the evocation of a new OR. Using this terminology, it could be said that the OR is not a response to the stimulus per se, but that it reflects the results of a comparison between the elaborated trace and the new stimulus. It is possible to analyze the content of this trace by using OR measurements. From this, it can be seen that stimulus parameters are exactly represented in the trace, thus giving rise to the concept of a neuronal model as a trace reproducing in the neuronal structure different aspects, or different properties of the stimulus.

It has been noted in the previous chapter that the first observations of the OR were carried out in Pavlov's laboratory, in relation to its inhibitory effect on the conditioned response. From this statement, it may be deduced that the OR is a specific component of the conditioned response, but such a conclusion would be premature. It is correct only insofar as the OR and current activity are affiliated with different behaviors associated with conditioning and orienting respectively. However, to establish the CR more efficiently, it is necessary that orienting occurs in the first phase of conditioning to the conditioned stimulus (CS). This was evident from the work in different laboratories, including observations in the Sokolov laboratory (Sokolov, 1963). In order to condition a CR in man to a particular stimulus, it is usual to go through a procedure of habituating the OR. When the conditioning procedure starts, then, the OR has already been habituated. This habituation of the OR results in prolongation of the period of the establishment of the conditioned response.

This observation was made earlier at the Nenci Institute by Konorski (1948) and colleagues, who studied the establishment of CRs in dogs both with the previous presentation of a signal and without such a session of habituation. They found strong support for the proposal that the preliminary presentation of a stimulus before this stimulus became a conditioned stimulus (CS) had the effect of inhibiting the establishment of CRs. It seems likely, therefore, that this stimulus became an inhibitory one; the reinforcement should then initially eliminate this inhibition somehow, re-establish the OR, and then start the elaboration of the CR. Thus, there is a seeming contradiction in the effects of the OR in conditioning. On the one hand, the OR, as seen in Pavlov's laboratory, has an inhibitory effect within the conditioning process, temporarily halting ongoing behavior. On the other hand, the OR has an activating influence on acquiring information about the conditioning arrangements, in order to facilitate learning of such associations. In both cases, the common feature is that the OR is a response to novelty and information, helping to acquire and analyze information from new, unknown situations.

What happens initially when a stimulus is first reinforced? The relevant experiments were done in man, using previously habituated auditory stimuli as conditioned stimuli and pain by electrical stimulation of the skin as an unconditioned stimulus (UCS). These experiments were carried out in order to discriminate two types of reflex: the OR, seen in the vascular reactions as a divergent change of vascular responses in the head and the finger, and the DR, characterized by constriction of vessels in the head and the finger. The process that is characteristic of the establishment of the conditioned response using a painful stimulus as a reinforcement is as follows. As has been made clear in the previous chapter, novel stimuli evoke an OR, characterized by specific vascular responses. On the head, there is vasodilation; on the finger, vasoconstriction. After several presentations, the same stimulus, being a nonsignal stimulus, evokes no further responses in the vascular system. The reinforcement may be started at this point; whenever a sound is presented at a particular time, it is followed by pain stimulation (Fig. 2.1). What happens during this period?

As has been explained, the sound was no longer effective in evoking an OR because of the prior habituation. If the pain stimulus is given, a marked vasoconstriction in both records may be seen. This indicates that the reinforcement, pain, produces a DR. The nervous system of course, could not predict what would happen on this particular trial. What would be the response on the next trial when the first reinforcement trial was presented—that is, the sound was combined with the painful stimulus? Perhaps one might expect that the first results would be a response to sound typical of pain. This is not so at all and the outcome was very striking. The sound given after the first combination of sound and pain produces a remarkably strong OR. Additionally, when the pain stimulus was presented as reinforcement in the second trial, the effect of the pain was reduced. In different experiments, it has been noted either the absence of the DR, or sometimes the pain, instead of a DR, produced a marked OR. Instead of getting a directly conditioned DR by such a procedure, it may be systematically observed that the OR is intensified both to the sound and to the electric shock. Thus the first stage of defensive conditioning is profound activation of OR as OR habituation.

What is happening here? During conditioning the process can be described thus. The OR evoked by the pain gradually habituated and the pain initiates a normal DR. What is particularly important is that, under conditions of reinforcement by pain, the sound remains effective as a OR trigger for much longer than simply indifferent stimuli. This suggests that, under the influence of biologically significant reinforcement, the first effect is an orientation towards the stimulus. Of course, during subsequent sessions of the experiment, the response to the sound is continuously modified, until finally the classical effect is observed, where the sound produces a DR that is accompanied by a second DR to pain. These DRs may then be called *conditioned DR* (to sound) and *unconditioned DR* (to the pain itself). Thus, the stages of development of the conditioned response are as follows. The initial phase is the activation of the OR, which is sometimes intensified to the extent that it prevents the expression of the DR to pain. Subsequently, the OR is eliminated in the face of defensive reinforcement, while, finally, there is a full expression of the classically conditioned DR.

Extinction of the CR is a remarkable process. It should be noted that, in Pavlovian physiology, the term *extinction* is used in its classical sense, that is, gradual elimination of the conditioned response due to nonreinforcement of a conditioned stimulus. This nonreinforcement period begins with the presentation of the sound stimulus alone. If sound alone is used to stimulate in this way, a conditioned DR is evoked, because the nervous system is not aware of the nature of the reinforcement. Yet, when the pain is omitted, there is a remarkable OR of great magnitude and duration at the time of omission. This means that the nervous system has identified the elimination of the reinforcement from the sound and pain complex, because the specific pattern of sound and pain combined is stored. Thus, elimination of pain initially has the effect of intensifying the OR during pain omission (Fig. 2.1).

The response to the next presentation of the sound, again without any pain stimulus, is also modified due to an activation of the OR. Thus, the first stage of extinction of the conditioned reflex consists of an intensification of the OR to sound. The sound, which previously resulted in a conditioned DR, now evokes an OR. The final outcome of this paradigm is the complete habituation of the OR, and, at the same time, the disappearance of the conditioned DR. When the sound produces no responses at all, then complete habituation has occurred.

Under the influence of pain reinforcement, the first effect of conditioning consists of the activation of the OR to the conditioned stimulus. Similar results can be obtained not just by the use of biologically relevant stimuli, but also by procedures that are more appropriate for human subjects. This conditioned reinforcement has been used in the Sokolov laboratories. This requires the use of an additional light if the conditioned stimulus was

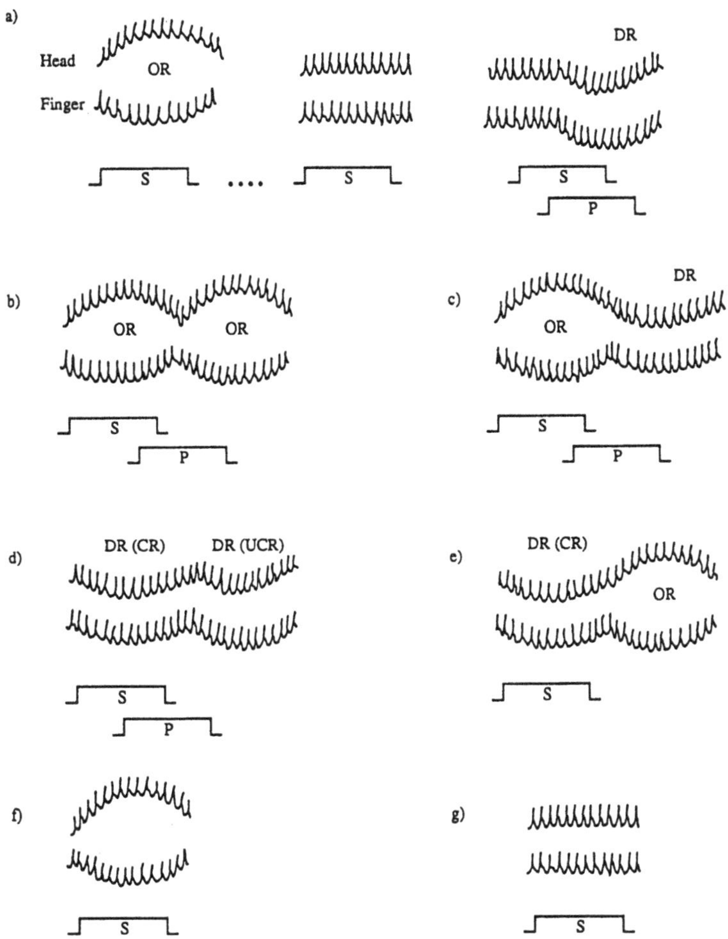

FIG. 2.1. The OR in the conditioned DR. OR = orienting reflex. UCR = unconditioned reflex, CR = conditioned reflex. UCS = unconditioned stimulus, CS = conditioned stimulus, DR = defense reflex, S = sound, P = pain. If the OR is initially habituated to sound, subsequent addition of a pain stimulus results in a pain-dependent DR (a). If there is no initial habituation to the sound stimulus, then the reinforcement of sound by the addition of a pain stimulus results not only in an OR to the sound, but also an OR to the pain stimulus (b). The initial stage of the establishment of the CR is characterized by a DR to the pain, with an OR to the conditioned sound stimulus (c). The stabilization of the CR is characterized by a conditioned DR to sound followed by an unconditioned DR to pain (d). The omission of the UCS results in an OR at the time of omission (e). The elimination of pain (extinction) results eventually in the recovery of the OR to the sound stimulus (f). Finally, the repeated sound stimulus eventually produces no responses at all, as these responses habituate (g).

sound, or sound if the conditioned stimulus was light, which is declared by instruction as a reinforcement of a correct response. The absence of this signal is negative reinforcement. Using such a procedure, it has been possible to eliminate verbal reinforcement, which can evoke different responses depending upon, for example, the tone or duration of the verbal reinforcement. The subject is instructed to respond to the light stimulus by moving his fist. He is told that wrong responses will be followed by sound but that correct responses will not.

It is necessary to measure a number of systems in such a study: EEG, EDR, eye movements, respiration, muscle tension, heart rate, and plethysmographic magnitude responses. The verbal instructions of the subjects result in a tonic OR activation that gradually returns to the initial level. The light as a conditioned stimulus evokes a set of OR components and EMG of finger muscles as conditioned responses to light. The absence of the sound as a negative conditioned reinforcement indicates that the response was correct. In the process of repeated associations, the latency of EMG decreases and OR evoked by light stimulation reduces. The stabilization of the CR parallels the habituation of OR to the conditioned stimulus. If unexpectedly, sound as a negative conditioned reinforcement is given, the OR activation is produced. The next presentation of the conditioned stimulus (light) evokes OR accompanied by inhibition of the conditioned motor response.

Under the influence of reinforcement, or in this case, a negative conditioned reinforcement, the activation of eye movements, EEG, alpha depression, and other OR components are evident. It is not only biologically strong stimuli that result in an activation of ORs, but also verbal stimuli, or stimuli that became significant through verbal instructions, and that remain effective stimuli through memory mechanisms evoked by specific experimental procedures or instructions (Fig. 2.2).

The facilitation of ORs is evident during or after presentation of verbal reinforcement. Their effect may also be seen in driving responses. Exactly how are driving responses changed after the influence of verbal instructions, or under the influence of reinforcement introduced by verbal instructions? The spectra of EEG recording and driving responses in a resting state of the subject are dominated by the slow frequency range. EEG potentials during driving, as has been shown, follow the frequency of the stimulating light. If the light is terminated, then an alpha rhythm at the initial frequency is re-established. If a rhythmic stimulus is followed by conditioned reinforcement, this reinforcement, as has already been noted, results in OR activation, and the ensuing presentation of the stroboscopic light results in a doubling of the dominant EEG frequency. The effect of the verbal reinforcement making rhythmic light a conditioned stimulus is characterized by this appearance in EEG of the second harmonic. This suggests that the introduc-

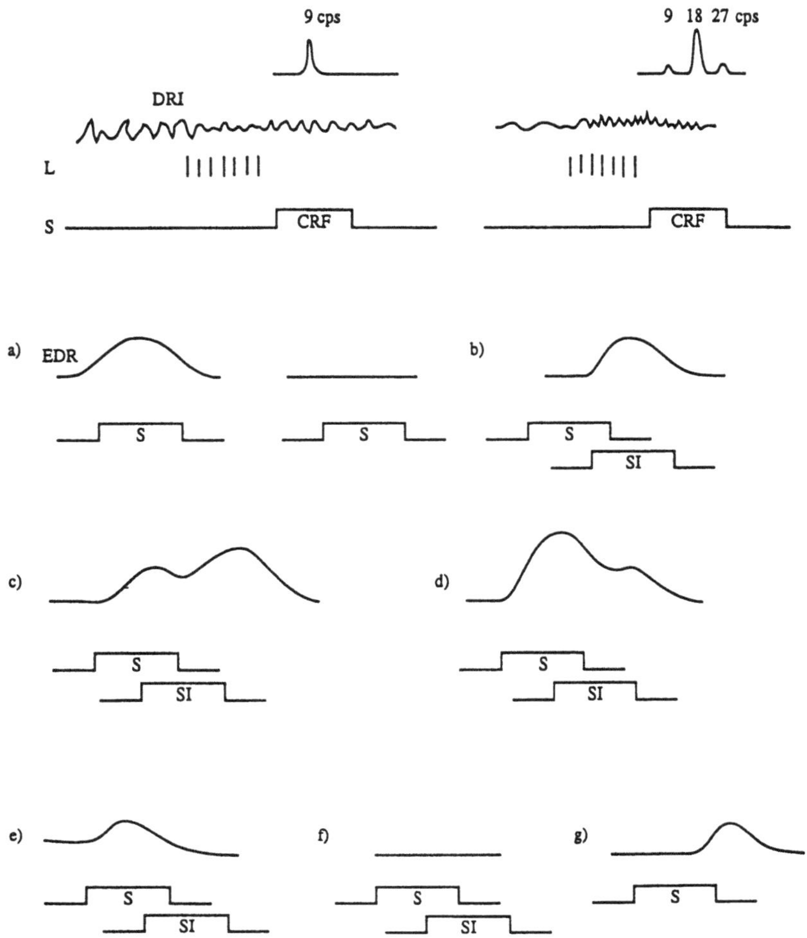

FIG. 2.2. Driving response as an indication of arousal and OR conditioning. The rhythmic light as a nonsignal stimulus produces under a low level of arousal no high harmonics. After a verbal instruction, that elevated arousal level, the same stimulus generates high harmonics. The presentation of sound results in a habituation of the EDR (a). After habituation, the combination of sound with high intensity sound initially produces an OR to the SI only (b). Continual repetition of this stimulus combination results in first, a reactivation of the OR to the sound, an increase in the OR to this stimulus (d), a reduction of the OR to this stimulus combination, (e) and, finally, total habituation (f). There is recovery of the OR to omission of the intense sound (g). DRI = driving response. EDR = electrodermal response. CRF = conditional reinforcement. S = sound. SI = high intensity sound.

tion of the reinforcement results not only in a change of the vascular system, but also changes in the pathway for transmission of visual signals to cortical levels. Facilitation of the driving response is marked by the appearance of second harmonics instead of the basic frequency or lower harmonics that are present in under a state of OR inactivation. Under the influence of such conditioned reinforcement, the driving response change parallels the galvanic and vascular responses increase.

This issue of facilitation of the OR is closely connected with OR conditioning. OR conditioning is a very complex problem, not so much because of theoretical difficulties, but mainly because of habituation of the ORs to the OR reinforcement itself. If one indifferent stimulus is used as a conditioned stimulus, and another indifferent stimulus is employed as reinforcement for the first, then at the end of the experiment, there will be a complete habituation of OR to both signals. Under specific conditions, when the OR used as a reinforcement for the establishment of the conditioned OR is very powerful, it is possible to see a phase when the initially conditioned OR is enhanced and then gradually habituated, insofar that the OR to the reinforcement itself is habituated. The information on OR conditioning can be obtained from the conditioned galvanic skin response. It consists of a change in the slow potential or modification of the skin resistance under the influence of an indifferent stimulus. An auditory stimulus evokes an EDR as a component of general arousal produced by the novelty, which may then be identified as an OR. After several trials, the sound is no longer effective.

Considering now, what happens when a combination of two indifferent signals is used, that is, one sound as a conditioned stimulus and the second following as a sound of greater intensity as a reinforcement? What may be observed is the OR, reflected in the EDR and vascular components, triggered not by the first sound, but by the second strong sound. When the two stimuli are combined, it is possible to observe the activation of the OR to the first sound, accompanied by a second OR to the more intensive sound. Such a combination of stimuli makes it possible to observe a very striking phenomenon—the total OR response is gradually shifted over trials towards the beginning of the stimulus complex. In other words, the first (weaker) stimulus evokes an OR that is now greater than it was originally. This is not a local facilitation effect due to arousal, but some kind of conditioned reflex.

During subsequent presentations, the OR gradually diminishes again. The first sound produces a response of smaller magnitude and finally, the two sounds produce no EDR at all. Thus, elaboration of a conditioned OR is followed by its extinction due to a habituation of OR to the reinforcement. What may be seen here is the process of integration of two signals into a complex. Furthermore, the neuronal model mechanisms should be taken into account in this analysis. One of the signals can be eliminated. If the second signal is eliminated, an OR may be seen at exactly the place where the signal has been omitted. This means that these two signals, the first and second, have been integrated in time in such a way that these two parts depend on each other. This is evident from the elimination experiment, when a decrease of the total energy of the stimulus nevertheless results in a response. This response is time-dependent, occurring only after the neuronal mechanisms can identify that the second stimulus is not present at its expected time (Fig. 2.2).

Reference has already been made to the problem of general activation under the influence of reinforcement and the specific effect of OR in the process of conditioning. An account should also be taken of some other important features of this conditioned OR, because of its importance in learning procedures. Using children as subjects, Ivanov-Smolensky (1927) suggested the presentation of an interesting picture as a reinforcement. From the perspective of biological significance, this picture should not be too effective, yet it produces a strong OR and makes other signals given in association with it more effective for the subject. The problem of the interaction between the CR and the OR is very important, but has not yet been studied in enough detail and needs to be illuminated more precisely. The problem to be considered refers to the motivational aspect of the OR as response to novelty. In addition to different vegetative, motor, and EEG responses, the novelty evokes some powerful hormones, including beta-endorphines that influence positive emotional attitude and reduce sensitivity to pain. This reciprocal relationship between OR and DR might be based on reciprocal emotional mechanisms.

The next point concerns the habituation of the OR during stabilization of the CR. It has been pointed out earlier that, using vascular responses, a final stage of CR extinction, where the OR to a signal stimulus has habituated, may be observed. At the same time, a very important phenomenon should be taken into consideration, namely, the habituation of the OR during the stabilization of CR. During the first stages of the development of the CR, there is an enhancement of the OR. If the stimulus is very stable, that is, presented in the same order and without any involvement of any additional signals, it is possible to see a very striking effect of habituation of the OR during CR stabilization. This is shown using alpha rhythm depression during a conditioned motor response. A conditioned stimulus, sound, is reinforced by conditional reinforcement; that is, a light substituting the verbal command to respond by moving a fist. The CS itself evokes an electromyographic (EMG) response as a CR. If the CR is developed, the EMG activation starts with short latency. This is a stage when the CR to sound is already elaborated at the beginning of the experiment. Two effects may be observed—arousal in the form of an OR, and the motor response. The experiment should involve repeating the same stimulus, sound, over long periods of time, to see what happens. With repetition, no changes in EEG are evident. The motor response, with a short latency, is very stable. It can be said that the conditioned response has stabilized. The short latency is indicating that the EMG response however, has been adjusted to the beginning of the stimulation with no signs of an OR. This suggests that, if the signals are not difficult to analyze, then the CR can be effected without any involvement of the specific activity of the OR. Thus, OR habituation takes place not only for nonsignal stimuli, but also during the procedure of stabilization of the CR (Fig. 2.3).

A new set of considerations applies when so-called differentiation procedures are employed in the experimental studies. This means that several (at least two) stimuli are employed. One is positively reinforced by conditioned reinforcement, while the other is negatively reinforced. What will happen? Regarding the first effect when a novel sound is introduced into the schedule. The first presentation of the new sound evokes an OR to this stimulus. At this stage, nothing new actually happens. If EMG activity is analyzed however, it is possible to observe a parameter of EMG latency response that is weaker than that evoked by normal sound. This is as a result of the mechanism of generalization, because the nature of the signals that are specifically associated with particular reinforcement is not yet defined. It is possible to observe an abortive type of EMG and OR. If the old conditioned stimulus is presented, this old stimulus, to which habituation had already occurred, now produces a marked OR. The EMG reveals that the CR to this sound is inhibited—the latency of the motor response is increased and the EMG magnitude reduced. The conditioned reinforcement is an additional intensifier of the EEG alpha depression, indicating that the OR is present. The first effect, where the OR is intensified, can be explained as just a novelty effect. It does not seem to be very important at this stage. However, as the procedure is continued and the sound is repeated several times, the OR during the discrimination of the signals is not habituated, but remains more evident.

Reinforced and nonreinforced signals produce striking ORs, with the CRs less stabilized. The phase of this intensification of ORs depends also on the discriminability of the signals. If the sounds are very different, this process of OR intensification is neither strong nor long. If these signals are close to each other, the intensification of the OR is marked, and long training is necessary in order to get differentiation of closely related signals. After a long period of training, the stimulus to be differentiated comes to evoke no OR and no motor response. The reinforced signal stimulus also evokes no OR, but results in a stable motor response. There is now stabilization of the conditioned reflex and differentiation of stimuli. Thus, the discussion has returned to the habituation of the OR and stabilization of the CR, but through a long-lasting activation of the OR, which is remarkably enhanced and prolonged in the process of differentiation of stimuli (Fig. 2.3).

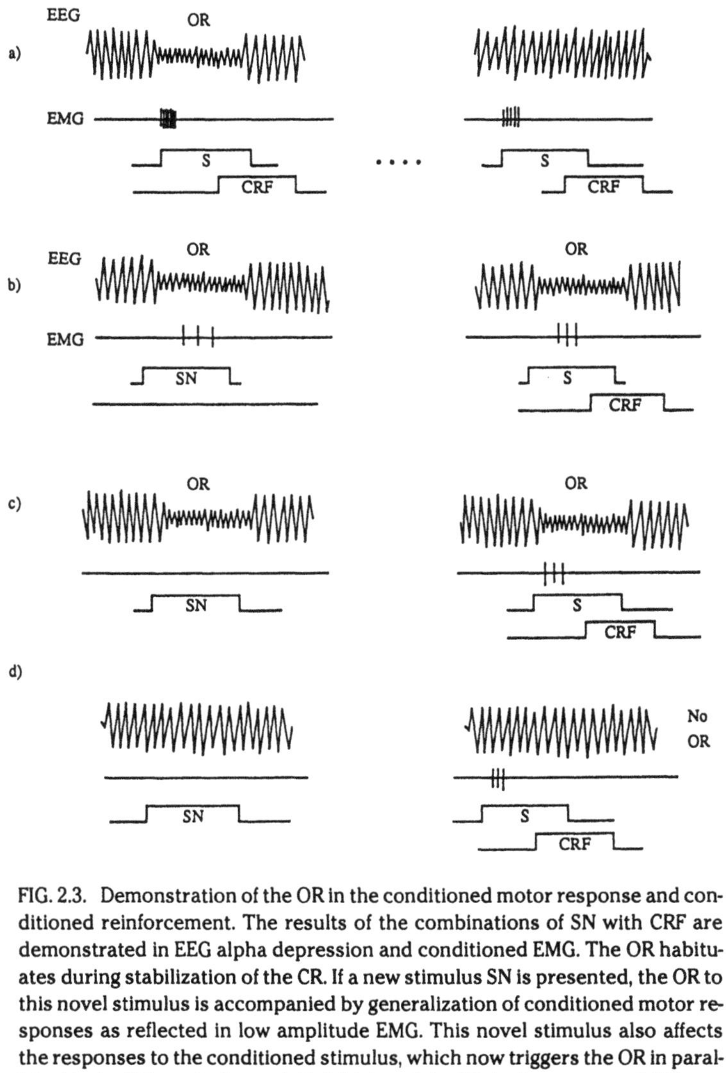

FIG. 2.3. Demonstration of the OR in the conditioned motor response and conditioned reinforcement. The results of the combinations of SN with CRF are demonstrated in EEG alpha depression and conditioned EMG. The OR habituates during stabilization of the CR. If a new stimulus SN is presented, the OR to this novel stimulus is accompanied by generalization of conditioned motor responses as reflected in low amplitude EMG. This novel stimulus also affects the responses to the conditioned stimulus, which now triggers the OR in parallel with the OR results in partial inhibition of the CR. In the process of differentiating signals S and SN, they evoke an OR. At the final stage, the SN evoked no OR or CR. The S stimulus evoked a stable CR without any OR manifestations. SN = novel stimulus. CRF = conditioned reinforcement. OR = orienting reflex.

The effect of differential training may be illustrated by a schematic presentation of ORs and DRs (Fig. 2.4). Note that these two reflexes can be distinguished, the OR eliciting vasodilation in the head, whereas DRs are indicated by vasoconstriction here. The conditioned stimulus in this example is an auditory stimulus of 500 Hz. At the final stage of conditioning, these 500 Hz stimuli evoke DRs. Frequencies close to 500 Hz generate reflexes of an

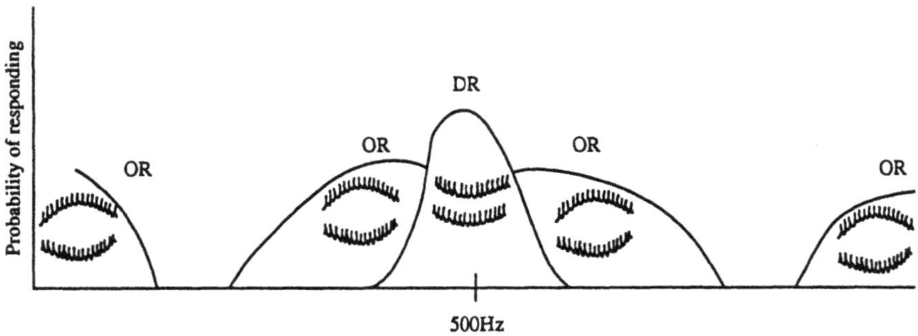

FIG. 2.4. A scheme of OR–DR relationship. The signal stimulus, 500 Hz, at the end of conditioning evokes a DR. The frequencies around this frequency of 500 Hz evoke ORs. More distant neighboring sounds were not effective. Sounds located on the frequency scale far away from that used in the experiment again produce ORs. The memory trace of the standard stimulus can activate the OR to signals close to the standard stimulus, even after a number of weeks when traces of the standard is kept in long-term memory.

orienting type. Thus, on both sides of the conditioned DR response area, there is an intensification of ORs. They are intensified for more precise analysis of these signals, in order to make decisions about whether they are conditioned stimuli or not. Finally, at frequencies distant from that used in this experiment, whether much higher or much lower, there are no ORs evoked. These frequencies are not actually involved in the conditioning procedure. If signals of extremely high or low frequency are used, ORs are again evoked. The structure of the OR and DR relationship is where an area of specific DR evocation is surrounded by an area of OR evocation. Outside these areas, frequencies evoke no responses, but more extreme frequencies evoke ORs. This particular paradigm of CR learning demonstrates the complex relations between OR and DR.

It is important to consider the role of verbal instructions in evocation of ORs. Verbal instructions have effects that are the results of previously elaborated verbal conditioned reflexes. When verbal instructions are used, it is possible through such means to change the contacts between neurons of different systems. Particular attention should be drawn to the experiments using driving responses. Evoked potentials (EPs), in the form of driving responses, were recorded to light flashes. These EPs were integrated and presented in the form of a spectrum, so that the total effect of light flashes could be evaluated. When instructions were given to attend—either to count signals or by asking subjects to evaluate a particular property of the stimulus—the same signals now come into the focus of attention as a result of the instructions. The result of this is that there is an enhancement of the responses to the stroboscopic light. This effect is a long-lasting increase in the driving responses; under verbal instructions, the effect of driving is greatly intensified. The mechanisms involved in the effects of instruction such as this are quite difficult to understand.

Luria and Homskaya (1970) in Moscow University conducted some relevant clinical experimentation in this area. Patients with damaged frontal lobes were instructed to pay attention to a particular set of signals, and the OR to such an instruction was investigated. The most important result of these experiments was that verbal instructions did not activate ORs in such patients. This suggests that there is some descending pathway from the frontal lobes that control the level of excitement of the OR system. At the same time, however, the OR to indifferent stimuli was intact.

Similar results were obtained in the study of eye movements in the same patients. For this purpose, Luria (1973) used a technique developed by Yarbus (1965) in Moscow. This technique involves a small mirror attached to the sclera, so that all changes in the position of the eye are recorded on a screen. Complex figures were used for the task, which consisted of an identification of figures in these pictures. The most important result of this research was that eye movement control by verbal instruction has no effect on systematic selection of different informational points in these pictures. The regulation of eye movements as one of the most important components of the OR was damaged in accordance with the damage to the frontal lobe control, and this coincided with the deficit in the control of the vegetative components of the OR. This means that the total set of OR response components was reduced or eliminated in relation to verbal instructions. This provides good evidence for the unitary OR concept. Basic verbal mechanisms regulating the OR should be considered. The incoming signal is not just compared with the active trace obtained by repeated presentation of this stimulus, but also with memory traces left earlier in the nervous system, but activated under particular tasks by verbal instructions.

It was explained earlier that after repeated presentations of the stimulus in the nervous system, a trace is formed that is used for formal comparison of incoming signals. The result of a mismatch between this trace and incoming signals results in the generation of a specific reflex called the OR. A lot of discussion has been devoted to the problem of significance as a specific parameter that regulates the OR. This problem has been studied from the standpoint of elaboration of CRs and has then moved toward the problem of the relationship between the OR as a response to novelty and elaboration of stabilized CRs. Earlier, it was shown that following the influence of reinforcement, a paradoxical result was obtained whereby before the conditioned response is established, the first result of the reinforcement is the enhancement of the OR. If the CR is stabilized, there is a reduction of the OR, even its complete elimination. If a differential conditioning procedure is used, where, rather than using a signal conditioned stimulus, a conditioned stimulus plus a stimulus for differentiation are introduced, the first result of this procedure is the enhancement of the OR with parallel inhibition of the elaborated conditioned response. In order to extinguish the OR under such circumstances, a longer period is needed. The closer the two signals that should be differentiated are, the greater the intensity of the OR. This main conclusion is not emphasized in learning theories when the OR is often neglected and not analyzed. The question arises as to how relevant conditioned responses and experiments on conditioned responses are for human studies.

Some experiments are now described that are very important for understanding the OR and are, at the same time, closely related to objective psychophysics. The OR can be used for measurements of thresholds. The easiest way to do this is by the presentation of a light signal. This light stimulus can be given without demanding a specific motor response. The subject can be asked to look at a particular fixation point. The light stimulus is presented somewhere near to this fixation point, while EEG is continuously measured. Sometimes, additional control of muscle tension can be used under instruction to perform conditional motor responses. A very weak light stimulus produces a very interesting effect in the EEG, namely a response with a long latency period. The first part of this latency period is when the EEG is not influenced by light, while the light accumulates. Alpha depression then indicates a response to this light. Using a logarithmic scale of intensities, it is possible to measure the probability of responses to light of different intensities. By so doing, a curve can be constructed that can be used for objective evaluation of the visual threshold. In some cases, this curve can only be obtained from EEG studies.

A problem originally formulated by Tanner and Swets (1954) was how sensitivity and response criteria might be differentiated. This differentiation was achieved by signal detection theory methods. It is, however, possible to use the OR for this purpose. Instead of differentiating sensitivity and criterion from analytical data, it was decided to do this directly from the experiment. To understand this procedure, it is necessary to make a comment about the concept of a standard stimulus. A particular light intensity, near threshold was presented on a screen to a subject. The subject was given verbal instructions that this was a stimulus, to which a motor response should be given and EMG was concurrently recorded alongside EEG. The subjects were instructed to make a fist continuously during the time that the light was seen. This response was of course reflected in the EMG. The most remarkable occurrence was that by decreasing the light intensity, there was an increase in the latency of EEG to the light. The second important feature was a shift of the EMG activity backwards from the beginning of the EEG alpha depression.

The next very important result was that, in parallel with the increase in EMG latency, was an increased period when the subject was seeing the light, even after termination of the light stimulus. The conclusion drawn from these experiments is that the OR, while being evoked by the weak light, is prolonged along with the motor response above a termination of light because of a low signal-to-noise ratio. A decision that the signal is off requires an equal amount of time as the decision that the light is switched on. This was the case when no response criterion was introduced into the experiment. Examination of the EEG and EMG data when the criterion for a motor response was shifted toward a higher intensity revealed that although no motor responses were present, there were EEG responses. Measuring the probability of EEG responses produced the same function relating response probability to stimulus intensity as without instruction. By shifting the criterion along the intensity scale using verbal instructions, such as asking the subject to only respond if the stimulus is above a criterion, the motor responses were shifted in accordance with these instructions.

Under conditions of no such instructions, the motor response curves were very similar to those for EEG reactions. When a higher level of response criterion was introduced, the EEG curve remained the same. This curve was as that for nonsignal stimuli, because these responses are merely reflections of OR evocation. The change in the motor response curve during the high criterion condition, however, was very striking. The latency of the EMG became longer, but the motor response stopped as soon as the light was switched off. This indicates that the OR was triggered by the light, but the EMG indicating decision that the light was above criterion needed some additional time, because the criterion was set higher than the threshold. At the offset of the stimulus, there is a change from a high level of intensity to just noise, and this is a very simple change to perceive, so that the latency of the off response is reduced (Fig. 2.5).

This experiment may be extended by modifying the instructions. For studying memory traces, a direct experiment was carried out to investigate the difference between the memory trace and OR curves within a similar paradigm (Sokolov, 1969a). A stimulus was presented, with instructions to remember it, and the subject is then invited back to the laboratory a week or a month later, when he has to distinguish this stimulus from distracters in a recognition test. As before, the subject's task here is to make a motor response in the form of a fist when the standard stimulus is perceived. At the same time, EEG and EMG are recorded. The probability of EEG and motor responses are given in Fig. 2.6. A week after the presentation of the standard stimulus, identification of the standard stimulus was very high. There is no overt reinforcement in this experiment. The motor responses were distributed normally around this standard stimulus. ORs were more widely distributed around this stimulus, so that the signals that would be discriminated from the standard by the subject still produce EEG responses. So, the curve of motor responses is surrounded by an intensification of the OR. In

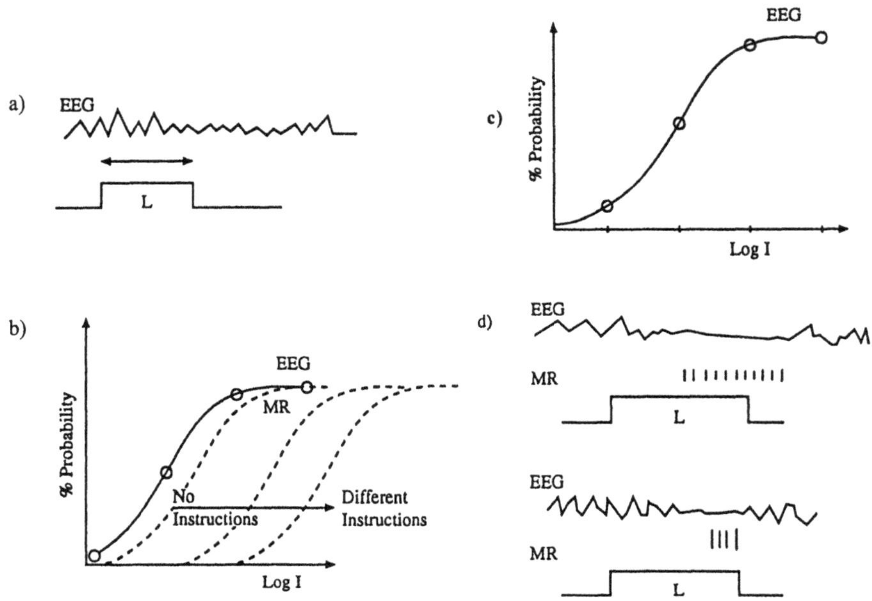

FIG. 2.5. The OR in threshold measurement. The light at threshold level produces an EEG response with a long latency and long after-effect in the form of EEG desynchronization (a). The probability of EEG responses to nonsignal stimuli plotted against log stimulus intensity shows that the curve is close to absolute threshold (b). A shift in the criterion along the intensity scale results in a parallel shift in EMG curves toward higher intensities, with the EEG response moving to the place indicative of absolute threshold (c and d). L = light. MR = motor response.

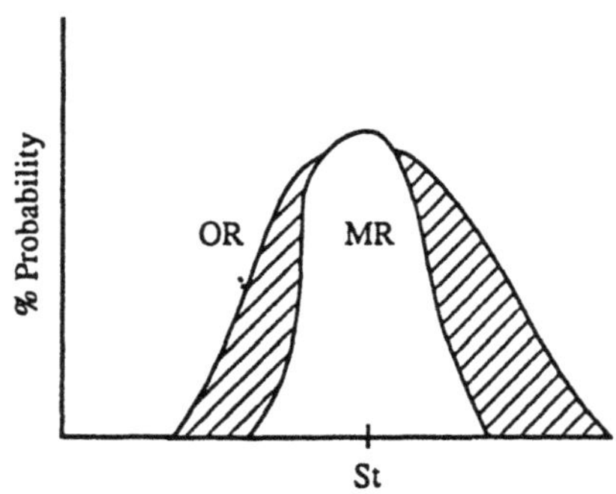

FIG. 2.6. When a standard stimulus is kept in memory, the probabilities of EMG responses indicate the precision of its participation in EMG response evocation. The ORs are triggered by a wide area of stimuli, demonstrating OR contribution in uncertainty. St = standard stimulus.

our laboratory, verbal instructions have been used to develop a relationship between the signal defined by traces in long-term memory and ORs. It has to be said, however, that the regulation of the OR in this particular procedure is not as simple as in the case of the development of neuronal models by repeated stimulus presentation. The regulation of the OR in this case is defined by a second mechanism—the long-term memory traces. It has been possible to prolong this experiment up to a month, and the subject is able to keep the standard stimulus in mind. A very precise ability to retain memory for a particular frequency or even intensity of sound had the effect of stimulating the OR on subsequent presentation of stimuli close to the memorized standard.

These experiments imply that the memory trace can be activated by verbal instruction and now participates in activation of the OR. This means that through frontal lobe channels, verbal instructions can steadily activate a particular trace and make it operational with respect to a set of signals according to the given instructions. Of particular importance is that these responses, as indicated in Fig. 2.6 are surrounded by activation, indicated by recorded OR components. In situations of complex information processing, the simple concept of the OR presented until now is inadequate, because the processes that are set in action when the OR is triggered are complicated by participation of long-term memory. In the previous cases, there is only one memory trace, which regulates the OR. Yet, under conditions when the identification of a certain figure is required, for example a letter, in the selection of informational points within this figure, that is, those points that are efficient in the discrimination of symbols, the OR is regulated step-by-step by a set of memory traces. This means that the OR does not operate via a random search of points in the visual field, but rather is controlled to search for such points that have maximum informational value to the subject in efficiently discriminating the complete stimulus array. This search strategy is based on sets of previously experienced signals given as long-term memory traces. So, actually, the OR is a very complicated structure, which includes not only the mechanism of matching non-signal stimuli, but it also participates in conditioning, and memory search, constituting a very important mechanism in information processing. This regulation of information acquisition by the OR leads to the assumption

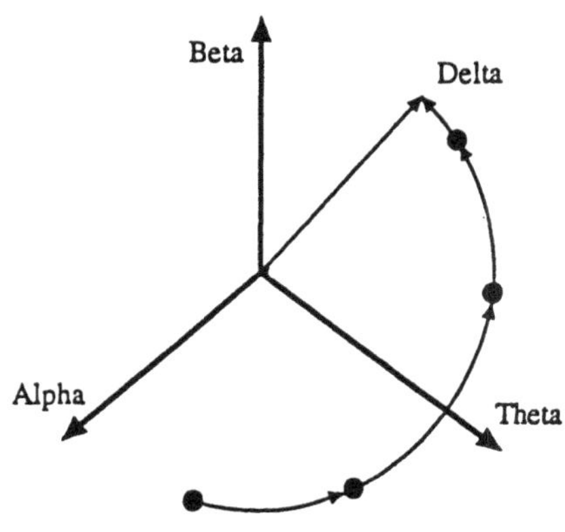

FIG. 2.7. The representation of the process of functional state modification in multidimensional space of EEG spectrum. Alpha, beta, theta, delta = EEG frequency bands. The vector is moving from alpha to delta waves as the subject goes to sleep.

that the OR may be regarded as an information regulator or as a control system in information processing (Sokolov, 1969b).

This domain of information processing is very important now, because many problems of ergonomics and training operators to search through visual displays are very much related to the intake and transformation of information with minimal motor tension connected with informational stress. The problems arise as to whether this handling of information can affect the brain, and, if so, how. The observation of very important vascular redistributions in the brain during the OR indicates that the handling of information is a very hard job, because the maximum energy that is spent in the brain is used by neurons for the sodium/potassium pump. This is continuously activated, and if the energy is not enough, this pump stops reestablishing the normal potential, and the neuron cannot maintain normal operation. Information processing has an energy-consuming effect, able to produce a remarkable fatigue and most remarkable changes in the brain.

When considering the information currently described in books on symbolic processing, rather than information processing, it is important to examine these from the point of view of energy resources. This approach leads to the aspect of informational load, which means the degree of information which can be handled within a particular time interval. Khananashvili (1978) from Georgia in the former Soviet Union has developed a theory of informational neurosis, whereby he postulates long-term changes in the modification of responses under three conditions of excess informational load within a limited time under emotional stress. He has called this the *triad of informational neuroses*. The problem of how to construct a test for informational load was addressed in order to measure this informational load (Sokolov, 1966). For physical exercise, this has usually been done using bicycle ergometers, which can measure energy expenditure. The introduction of an informational load was made and the subsequent response was observed. The stimulus sequence was a number of sets of closely related auditory signals. Nine psychophysiological components were measured, including EEG, muscle tension, eye movements, electrocardiogram, heart rate, and respiration, all analyzed on a heartbeat by heartbeat basis to keep them time-locked. These parameters were cross-correlated, revealing a number of basic factors, the most important of which were heart rate, respiration, and vascular tone. These three can be represented graphically and it is possible then to describe each person, at each state, by a modification of this graph. In this graph, values of the cross-correlation functions have been drawn, showing some shifts between the studied responses. The question is how changes in informational load can influence this graph.

Another problem area at that time was the psychophysiology of computerized teaching. As an example, take a book prepared in the computer department of the University of Moscow (Brusentsov, 1982). Fortran programs were used to teach computerized classes of 20 to 30 students, each at a "dumb" terminal linked to a computer in such a way that each step in the student's study was controlled by the computer. The computer displayed information, and set exercises for the student, the results of which determined the direction that the program subsequently took. This was a very economical system. Such a teaching method was used with dumb terminals in attempts to teach ninth grade students Basic and Fortran using this computerized system.

What psychophysiological problems arose here? Usually, the sequence of the programmed instruction depended on the earlier results of the teaching, but insufficient attention was paid to the price of this method of teaching, that is, the price from the standpoint of the well-being of the student. Two organized loops in the computerized system were suggested. One controls the level of knowledge, whereas the other is based on our results of informational load control. At minimum, each student's electrocardiogram was relayed to the computer, and the total process of teaching could be represented as conducted in the corridor of optimal arousal states. This means that, if the exercises were too simple, and the students switched off from studying, then the course of the program was altered. It was changed so that the students were always active enough, the computer giving tests to shift the students' level of activation to optimal. In this system, the intention was to put together the process of control of knowledge acquisition and the objective evaluation of the results of this informational load. Psychophysiological indicators helped to obtain the optimal computer assisted teaching.

A very convenient method for the evaluation of the arousal state of the subject is the spectral analysis of R–R intervals extracted from the EKG of the student under informational load. Three main peaks can be identified in the power spectrum of the heart rate. Respiratory arrhythmia indicates the contribution of the parasympathetic control of the heart rate. The peak corresponding with blood pressure shows sympathetic input. The thermoregulation and metabolic channels are evident in the slowest peak of the heart rate variations. The OR contribution is seen in a decelerating shift and respiratory arrhythmia. The stressful situation is shown by an increase of blood-pressure dependent oscillations.

There is always a problem in these studies of how to represent the functional state of the person, and to evaluate how this changes. One convenient method is to represent the subject's arousal in vector space. For example, in Fig. 2.7, there are coordinates representing alpha, beta, gamma, and delta waves from the EEG spectrum. A particular point indicates an initial state of the subject. According to the functional state and the redistribution of these components, the trajectory that leads either to sleep or to a more aroused state can be seen (this being in the direction of increased beta waves). The same multidimensional presentation can also be used for the evoked potential.

CONCLUDING COMMENTS

There are many components of the OR. The EEG is the most reliable measure for OR because it can identify local arousal in specific brain areas. The OR components can be divided into generalized and localized. As soon as an EEG component becomes localized and specifically adjusted to a particular stimulus, the generalized components are not visible. The OR depends not only on the significance of the stimulus, but also on the difficulty of the behavioral task. The more complex and demanding the behavioral pattern, the greater the contribution of the OR.

When a tone stimulus is repeated, it is still possible to see the EMG response while the EEG response could not be seen. The latter is a sign of the disappearance of the OR when CR is stabilized during a simple behavioral task. This means that conditioned muscle responses are stable, accurate, of very short duration and with short latency, but all the visible components of the OR are lacking in such situations. As soon as you introduce a new task to differentiate signals or delay responses depending on the time schedule, the OR is activated towards the conditioned stimulus. The differentiation of light signals is a rather difficult task especially when signals are given in a random order. It was practically impossible to get extinction of local OR components under such situations. This means that, if the task is very difficult, the OR is present as a specific phase in the build-up of conditioned reflex structures.

CHAPTER

3

A Microlevel Analysis of the Orienting Response Using Extracellular Recording

This chapter covers the following issues:

1. Randomization and synchronization of spikes in the nonspecific thalamus as related to the orienting response (OR).
2. Phase-specific neurons of the nonspecific thalamus.
3. Driving response of neurons in the lateral geniculate body, nonspecific thalamus, and visual cortex.
4. Neuronal contribution of the nonspecific thalamus and lateral geniculate body to the EEG.
5. Septal neurons and theta rhythm.
6. Rhythmic modulation of behavior.
7. Comparison of filters at the detector level with novelty and sameness neuron filters, macrolevel habituation, and memory traces in conditioning.
8. Neuronal analyzer as a set of detectors.
9. Modulating neurons.
10. Command neurons.
11. Principles of the information coding in the brain pattern of spikes, neuronal ensembles, and channel-dependent code.
12. Conceptual reflex arc.

In the search for habituatable neurons, two types of habituation have been found. One type was a partial habituation, when the response was divided into two spike groups. One discharge was stable and did not habituate. The other one, mainly a late component, habituated by repeated stimulation and recovered during dishabituation. If a novel stimulus was presented, the standard stimulus to which the organism had earlier habituated then produced a complete response, including the habituatable part as well as the stable part. The second type of habituation—total habituation of the spike response—could be found in neurons in the hippocampus. Two kinds of neurons were found: novelty neurons that responded with activation of spike discharge to a novel stimulus and response elimination during repeated stimulus presentations, and sameness neurons. The term *sameness* was used because the firing of spikes in this type of neuron was present if the stimulus was familiar. Presentation of a novel stimulus always results in a depression or elimination of spikes in such neurons.

In addition, two subpopulations of neurons were found in the hippocampus, located in CA3 and CA1, respectively. The two populations of neurons differ in their influence on the reticular activating system. CA1 neurons mainly influence the thalamic area of the reticular formation, yet CA3, represented by novelty and sameness neurons, affect the brain stem reticular activating system and reticular synchronizing system, respectively. The problem now arises as to how these responses of novelty or sameness neurons can influence behavior. Before the behavioral level can be examined, through the control of motor responses, attention should be paid to the relationship between novelty responses and the neuronal structure of the nonspecific thalamus.

In the resting condition, the responses of neurons in the nonspecific thalamus are characterized by bursts of spikes. These spike bursts are interrupted by periods of silence. The burst sequence coincides with the EEG frequency that is usual in the rabbit, that is, 3 to 4 Hz. The most remarkable characteristics of these neurons is their close relationship to the orienting response (OR). If a novel sound stimulus was presented, then these bursts were changed from this shaped pattern of bursts to a random generation of spikes. This response has been labeled a *randomization response* (Fig. 3.1a). The frequency of spikes during such a randomization response may remain the same as the averaged frequency in spike sequences under the bursts condition. The most pronounced randomization response was seen following novel stimulation. If, however, the stimulus reappears, then this response disappears (Fig. 3.1b). After several trials, the same sound produces no randomization effect. The habituation effect in these neurons was therefore characterized by a decrease in the randomization effect produced by the stimulus. If the animal was from the beginning of the experiment in an excited state, the thalamic reticular neurons were initially characterized by random spikes (Fig. 3.1c). If a period of rest is introduced, sending the animal into a state of relaxation, then instead of random spikes, the regular bursts of spikes may be observed (Fig. 3.1d).

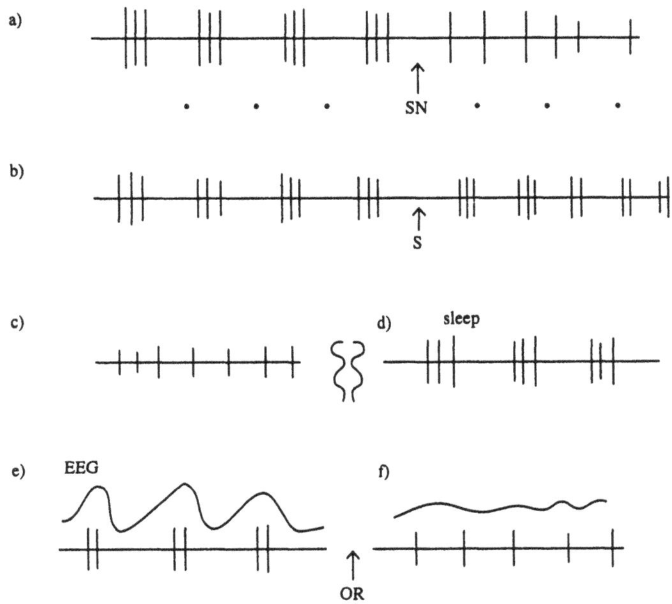

FIG. 3.1. Randomization response and EEG desynchronization. (a) The nonspecific thalamic units under conditions of relaxation in the rabbit generate bursts of spikes. The novel sound, S, results in a randomization of spikes. (b) Repeated presentation of sound results in habituation of the randomization response. The bursts of spikes now remain unchanged following the presentation of the sound. (c & d) The shift from arousal, characterized by random spikes, to sleep is expressed in the formation of burst patterns. (e) Parallel recording of the nonspecific thalamic neurons and surface EEG reveals a state of relaxation as indicated by a synchronized EEG record and, at the same time, bursts of spikes from the nonspecific thalamus. (f) A stimulus evoking an OR results in two parallel effects: EEG desynchronization and spike randomization. SN = novel stimulus. S = stimulus.

The relationship between bursts and randomized patterns of neural firing can be correlated with the OR. By looking at both the EEG recording and the thalamic spike recording either directly from microelectrodes in the thalamic area or from superficial electrodes on the surface of the cortex, a correlation may be seen between bursts of spikes and slow waves in the cortex (Fig. 3.1e). Under the influence of novel stimulation that evokes orienting, randomization of spikes accompanied by EEG desynchronization occurs (Fig. 3.1f). The close correlation in the rabbit between spike bursts in the nonspecific reticular nucleus of the thalamus and slow brain waves indicates that the novelty signals of the hippocampus can trigger a mass effect of firing level in the nonspecific thalamus that results in an EEG arousal.

The most exceptional feature of the reticular thalamic spikes is their specific temporal location with respect to the phase of the slow wave recorded in the cortex. If 3-Hz slow waves are observed in the rabbit's brain, it can be seen that a single unit recorded as a spike sequence does not occur at any temporal location with respect to the slow wave, but is related to a particular phase of this slow wave. Because of this property of reticular thalamic neurons, they have been called *phase specific cells.* This effect is seen when several neurons are recorded in parallel, and it may be observed that the responses of different cells are specifically adjusted to a particular phase of the slow waves. This means that a generation of slow waves is a sequential process and that the high amplitude of the slow wave is dependent on a neuronal loop in which impulses may circulate. Generation in such a loop of a slow wave depends not on the total amount of spikes generated, nor on the summation of units, but on their sequential participation in the wave. The desynchronization effect is the result of synaptic interruption of connections within the loop. This indicates that these cells constitute a sequence with constant time intervals (Fig. 3.2a).

This particular shape of spike organization in the thalamic neurons can be tested using a stroboscopic light. The idea tested here states that if a loop exists and in this loop the neurons are sequentially influenced, a frequency selective resonance effect could be expected. For this purpose, a wide range of frequencies of stroboscopic lights was used, while measuring

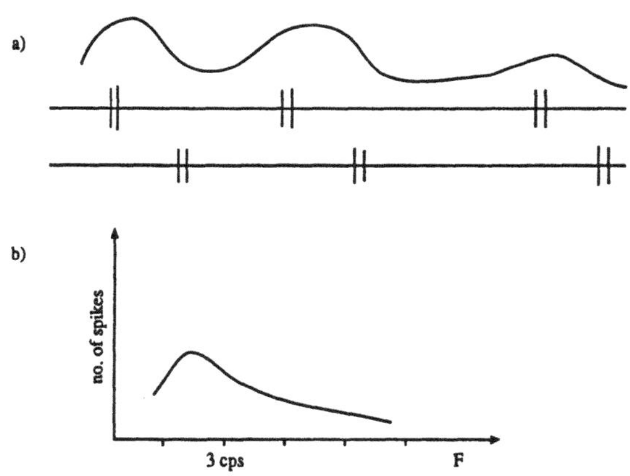

FIG. 3.2. Phase specific neurons. (a) The observation of many neurons in the nonspecific thalamus reveals their phase specificity with respect to alpha waves (3 Hz) in the rabbit visual cortex. This phase specificity suggests a neuronal loop circulating with EEG frequency. The EEG is formed by the sequential contribution of phase-specific neurons. The EEG desynchronization of the loop may be associated with the prevention of OR impulses in the loop resulting in diminution of burst formation. (b) The presence of a loop suggests a resonance effect that is revealed by stroboscopic light stimulation at 3 Hz coinciding with the frequency of spike bursts and EEG oscillation. The number of spikes generated at different light frequencies demonstrates a resonance peak in the responses of nonspecific thalamic neurons.

single unit responses to each particular frequency. The response can be represented in the form of a graph, with the frequency of light stimulation on the abscissa and the number of spikes on the ordinate (Fig. 3.2b). The curve, as expected, demonstrated a resonance effect that was particularly evident at the basic frequency of the brain waves. This means that the light frequency of about 3 Hz produced a maximal response. The response dropped in both directions from the resonance frequency as measured by the number of spikes generated by each stimulus.

It is very important to understand whether this particular property of the nonspecific thalamus is a unique one or whether this is only one form of a general property, referred to as a *resonance effect* in the brain. The specific visual nuclei at the thalamic level, lateral geniculate body were selected to compare with the reticular nuclei. Using the same sequence of stroboscopic light by recording neurons in the lateral geniculate body, it is possible to observe that the responses of the lateral geniculate body closely follow the stroboscopic light frequency. Each flash of light produces a compact spike discharge up to 40 Hz when fusion occurs. The curve plotting number of spikes against stimulus frequency shows a gradual diminution of responding with an increase in frequency, but, importantly, without any specific resonance effect such as that seen in the nonspecific thalamus (Fig. 3.3a).

The driving responses in the nonspecific thalamus and the specific visual thalamus, therefore, were completely different, but they interact at the cortical level. From psychophysical studies, there is known to be an effect of an apparent increase in the subjective intensity of light if that light is presented with a frequency close to the alpha rhythm frequency, about 10 cycles per second. At this frequency, the subjective brightness is enhanced. This point is raised because there are now data indicating that there is a nonspecific pathway, independent of the lateral geniculate body, taking information from the nonspecific thalamus. At the cortical level, these two channels–from the nonspecific reticular thalamus and from the specific thalamic pathway–are superimposed. This superimposed effect observed in psychophysics as a subjective enhancement of intensity can represent the interaction of two channels when the nonspecific input can increase its contribution in addition to the specific input.

The driving response is also expressed in the visual cortex. The frequency effects in the visual cortex depend on the state of the nonspecific system and the frequency that has been used. If a randomization effect is present, as shown by EEG arousal, the nonspecific input via the synchronizing system is depressed, and the higher frequencies through the specific pathway are generated. On the other hand, if low frequencies are used and the state of the animal is shifted toward a drowsy state, then there is domination by the nonspecific contribution characterized by low frequency re-

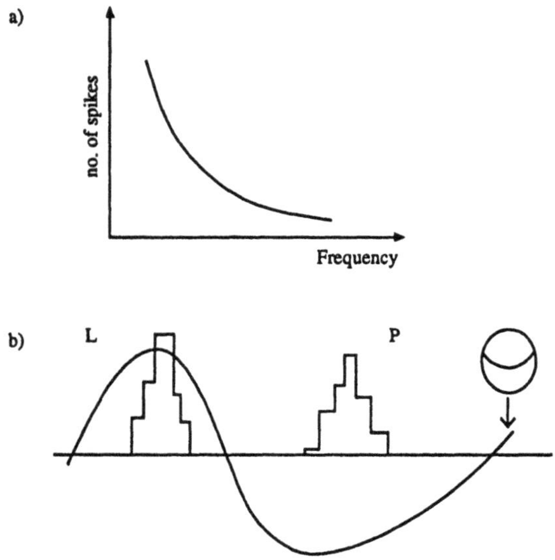

FIG. 3.3. Response characteristics of the specific visual pathway (lateral geniculate body–LGB) and the functional role of theta waves. (a) The frequency of groups of spikes generated in the LGB by the stroboscopic light closely corresponds to the light frequency in a broad range of frequency change. The number of spikes per flash falls as the frequency of stimulation rises. (b) The theta waves take part in the frequency modulation of behavioral acts. The pressing and lifting motor responses are produced in different phases of the theta waves. This effect suggests that the theta rhythm may affect the output information transfer. It is assumed that phase-specific septal neurons rhythmically modulate different command neurons, organizing a time schedule for different reflexes. L = lifting, P = pressing, θ = theta.

sponse. The two different channels, with their two different properties and different contributions to the OR, are associated at the level of the visual cortex.

What happens alongside the thalamic spike randomization effect and EEG desynchronization in the cortex? The main feature of the initial cortical desynchronization in the rabbit is the appearance or increase of a specific new rhythm, the so-called *theta rhythm*. It is difficult to try to explain the role of this theta rhythm because, in man, the theta rhythm is a slower rhythm than alpha rhythm. In the rabbit, alpha-like oscillations are of 3 Hz. The shift from 3 Hz up to 6 Hz that is observed during theta rhythm activation is obviously an increase in frequency. This shift in frequency of a rhythmical generator from slow waves to fast waves is equivalent in man to the depression of alpha rhythm and a shift to beta rhythm. In the rabbit, the appearance of theta rhythm was closely correlated with the OR—novel stimuli produce an increase of both the amplitude and frequency of the theta rhythm. Thus, theta rhythm in the rabbit is an analog of beta rhythm in man.

Theta rhythm is shown in the septal area by spikes in specific neurons that are not synaptically connected with each other for rhythm generation. The use of cadmium instead of calcium in physiological solutions interrupts all synaptic contacts between neurons, but still the septal neurons generate groups of spikes at theta frequencies. These septal spikes traveling to the hippocampus produce hippocampal rhythm which, in the rabbit, extends all over the cortex and is one of the most noticeable frequencies seen during arousal. Thus, there are two generators in the rabbit. One generator in the slow frequency range is related to the thalamic area, and the other generator of higher frequency is connected with theta rhythm in the hippocampus.

What is the functional role of these generators? There were several attempts to understand the role of the alpha rhythm, but, unfortunately, no definite results were shown. Only recently, Sheveler (Moscow) has shown that alpha waves may scan the visual field influencing latencies of responses. For theta rhythm, it was shown that the particular phase of the theta wave influences the choice of the type of behavior. If a rat was required to lift and press a lever, then these responses each only occurred in one particular phase of the theta rhythm. Integrating theta waves and measuring the probability of these pressing and lifting responses, it may be found that the probabilities of these two types of responses are different during different phases of the theta wave. If the rat missed pressing the lever, it had to wait one cycle, and only during the next cycle did it perform this behavior. The frequency of the theta wave then seems to be a regulator of transfer of information of the organism. It can be said that for each phase of the theta wave, there are different reflexes generated. Each specific septal neuron can produce a modulating effect for a particular time interval for a particular response mechanism. In this way, the probabilities of responses are different for different reflexes in different time intervals (Fig. 3.3b).

It is very important to relate this rhythmical modulation of behavior to the specific time regulation that is present in behavior. It might be thought that the modulating effect does not influence motor output directly, but affects some premotor neurons. This time selectivity is not directed toward a single muscle, but is referred to behavioral patterns. This can be explained as a modulating effect in sequencing behavior into single acts.

The interaction between novelty neurons and ORs affects behavior according to the following scheme. At the input of the signal, there is a set of selectively tuned detectors. The signal produces a selective excitation of a particular line in a set of detectors. These channels converge on plastic hippocampal neurons, where these inputs are selectively switched off when the stimulus is repeated. This produces a selective diminution of the re-

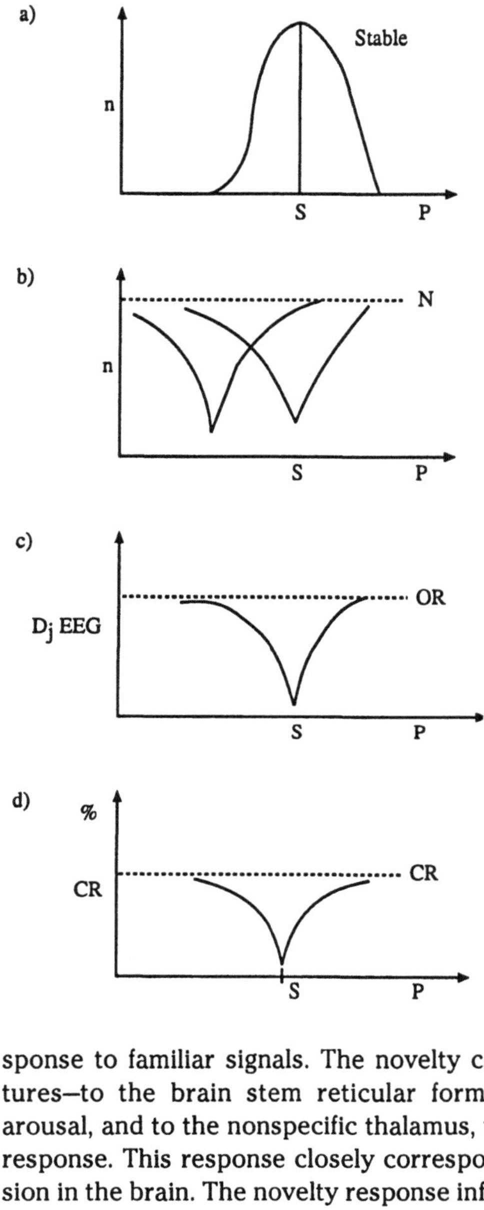

FIG. 3.4. Characteristics of the filter at the micro- and macrolevel. (a) The stable pass filter of a detector is selectively tuned to stimulus S. (b) The adaptive novelty reject filter to the same stimulus S in novelty neurons. Correspondence of filter characteristics suggests that the detectors build up the inputs to the novelty neuron. Using a stimulus exciting another detector, a parallel filter to this signal can be elaborated in the same novelty neurons. This proves the parallel input of detectors onto novelty neurons. (c) The stimulus S, by repeated presentations, results in the development of a filter, and, at the same time, results in selective habituation of the OR. (d) The generalized conditioned reflex to a set of stimuli can be selectively extinguished with respect to stimulus S, demonstrating a selective reject filter based on switching off of the detector from the command neuron. CR = conditioned reflex, D_j EEG = EEG desynchronization under the influence of novelty detector D tuned to stimulus j, n = number of spikes, N = novelty detector filter, P = a parameter of the stimulus.

sponse to familiar signals. The novelty can be fed to two different structures—to the brain stem reticular formation for generation of overall arousal, and to the nonspecific thalamus, which produces a more localized response. This response closely corresponds to the alpha rhythm depression in the brain. The novelty response influences neurons of the activating reticular formation that produces cortical arousal.

The interest is in what system is involved in the handling of information in the brain by selective filters. The filters of different detectors are given in Fig. 3.4. The abscissa represents certain parameters of a stimulus, in abstract form. The ordinate represents the number of spikes generated by the detector. A detector is characterized as a selective filter to a particular parameter of the stimulus. This filter is not modified. Other detectors extract some other properties by stimulus repetition. What happens in the novelty detectors? By novel stimulation, all novelty detectors are switched on in parallel. If the same stimulus is repeated, it may be observed that the responses in all novelty detectors have habituated. In each novelty detector, a selective filter is built up. This filter has similar characteristics to the detector described previously, except that its response characteristics are reversed. The detectors show responses matched to the signal features. Novelty detectors generate responses of minimum value to the repeated signal. What is the difference? The filter of the detector is stable, having been built up in early stages of ontogenetic development (Fig. 3.4a). Novelty neurons can produce a formation of different filters depending on the nature of the presented stimulus, that is, depending on which detector was stimulated under the particular experimental procedure (Fig. 3.4b). A comparison between filters of single detectors and elaborated filters of a novelty detector suggests that the general scheme of these mechanisms to develop filters is plastic convergence of many detectors into one integrating novelty neuron of the hippocampus.

Returning to an examination of habituation at the macrolevel recording EDR or EEG, all signals, being novel, produce EEG desynchronization and if the stimulus is repeated, a selective habituation of the EEG develops (Fig. 3.4c). This can be explained in line with previous neuronal explanations. The signals that are blocked by novelty detectors cannot now reach the mechanism for EEG alpha depression. The EDR also disappears. The parallel, but not coinciding, habituation of different OR components indicates that there exist many parallel output cells in the hippocampus. It could be said that many different reflexes are regulated by different neurons. Each novelty neuron can be selectively tuned to the repeated stimuli contributing to evoke one of the OR components.

The final problem of filtering refers to the development and formation of the conditioned response (CR). To make the logic of filtering more understandable, it is necessary to first examine the generalized CR. At the beginning of an experiment, an animal may be given different signals and all these signals are reinforced. This produces a generalized CR—all signals can evoke CRs. In extinction, one stimulus is selected, which will not be reinforced. The others remain reinforced. In this way, selective extinction of the CR to a particular stimulus can be developed. This selective extinction can be represented in the form of a signal-rejecting filter (Fig. 3.4d). From the characteristics of this filter, it is possible to deduce that the detectors that regulate habituation at the micro- and macro-level are not only used in the control of the OR, but also can explain selective extinction of a generalized CR. The scheme of organization is the same for OR habituation and CR extinction. As the CR is developed, so the detectors converging on the command neurons increase the responses. The detectors are stable whereas the novelty neurons are plastic. The plasticity is also present in command neurons. The main problem of plasticity is related to finding how such a concept operates at the synaptic level.

In order to find single synaptic contacts and single patches of the membrane of the command neuron to demonstrate selective plasticity at the level of the single synapse it is useful to summarize the main principles of coding of information. There are at least three principles of coding of information in the nervous system. The first principle can be called *spike pattern coding*. It assumes that for each specific stimulus, a different spike pattern is generated in the neuron. In Fig. 3.5a, Stimulus 1 produces a pattern consisting of three early and two late spikes in a sequence. Stimulus 2 in the same neuron triggers a different spike pattern—one early spike followed by a burst of spikes. The information in this case is contained in the pattern of spike discharges in the single neuron. A single neuron generates a different

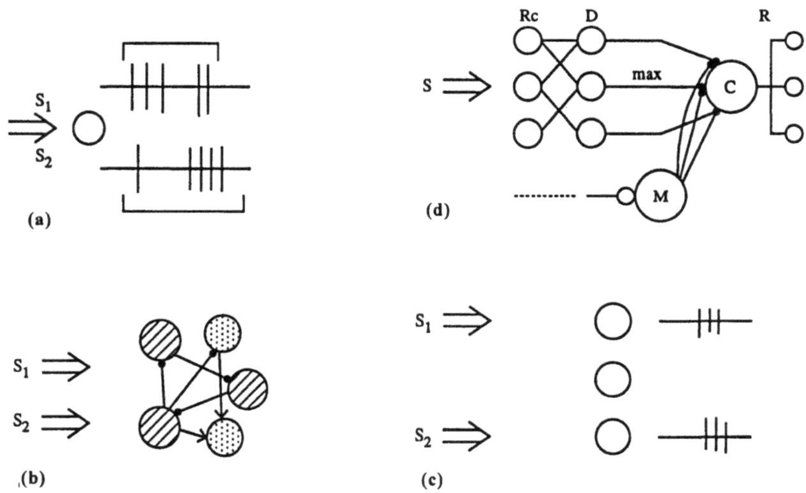

FIG. 3.5. Principles of coding. (a) The spike pattern code—S1 and S2 always evoke two different patterns of spikes in the same neuron. Each spike pattern is a code symbol for the input stimulus. (b) The neuronal ensemble code. Each stimulus excites a unique combination of cells—a cell ensemble. Stimuli S1 and S2 are represented by different ensembles of excited cells. (c) The channel-dependent code (labeled line code) detectors. Each stimulus selectively excites only one neuron, which represents this stimulus in the nervous system. The detectors represent a single labeled line by transmission of information. Command neurons are used in labeled lines for generation of output. (d) The conceptual reflex arc—receptors, detectors, command neuron, reflex dependent on this command neuron, modulating neuron modifying synapses of the detector on the command neuron. C = command neuron, D = detectors, M = modulating neuron, R = response, Rc = receptors, S = stimulus.

spike pattern and each pattern can be related to the symbolic coding of this signal.

The second principle was suggested by Hebb (1949). One of his contributions to neuroscience was the principle of ensemble coding. Stimulus 1 may excite only three out of five neurons in a population of cells. These three neurons are combined into an ensemble (Fig. 3.5b). Stimulus 2 excites other neurons in this same population of cells, resulting in a second ensemble. In a set of cells, each combination of neurons can correspond to a particular stimulus. This stimulus is therefore coded by this ensemble in terms of the selective activation of a particular pattern of cells.

The final principle, which is called the channel-dependent code or labeled line code, assumes that there is a selective excitation of a particular neuron for each stimulus. If the neuronal net is stimulated, there is a maximal excitation in one line, and this line then represents the stimulus. This means that the coding of the stimulus is performed according to the labeled line principle. It is of interest to look at the history of the labeled line concept. The first person to develop this concept was Wirsma, who found giant axons in the crayfish, and observed that electrical stimulation of these giant fibres always evoked a specific defensive response. The term channel-dependent code suggests that the channel is a neuron. The code depends upon the excitation of this representative labeled-line. If the stimulus is changed, then the line that is excited is also changed. If a stimulus is moved against the skin, then different receptors and different lines are activated. In the internal structure of the brain, the collection of such detectors can be regarded as a quasireceptive surface. It is a map of detectors in the brain. If the stimulus is changed, the maximum excitation moves across this map, thus coding the signal. The code depends upon the point on the map which is excited by a particular stimulus (Fig. 3.5c).

The channel-dependent code can be used for construction of schemes for transfer of information within the nervous system. The transfer of information might be viewed in the following way. The input is represented by a layer of receptors. The receptors are connected to a receptor layer (Fig. 3.5d). This connection can be very complex, but the most important aspect is that each stimulation produces the maximum excitation in one of the detectors. If the stimulus is changed, the position of the maximal response from the detector layer is changed. The detectors, as labeled lines, converge on a command neuron. The term *command neurons* was first introduced as a logical concept, but later on the real command neurons were found. For example, such command neurons are present in the superior colliculus, involved in the eye movement mechanism. In fish, Mautner cell activity may result in an excitation of motor neurons in the spinal cord, with the behavioral result that the fish swims away. The command neurons are connected to many motor neurons, which result in some final response.

Additionally, a stimulus can influence a modulating neuron. The modulating neuron can in turn change the efficiency of synaptic contacts on the command neurons from detectors. Thus, three types of interneurons with different functions were identified–detectors which extract aspects of information from the environment, command neurons that generate the response, and modulating neurons that can change the efficiency of different synapses of the command neurons.

In higher vertebrates, several layers of detectors, several layers of command neurons, and a variety of types of modulating neurons, including phasic modulating, tonic modulating, local modulating, and generalized modulating neurons constitute a system. The basic mechanism of the reticular formation can be regarded as based on different types of modulating neurons, which can change the synaptic contact between neurons within the brain. The modification of synaptic efficiency by internal modulating effects, rather than by external stimulation, is a very important function. This main scheme can be called a conceptual reflex arc useful for the single unit study of the nervous system. The term conceptual reflex arc is based on Hebb's idea of a conceptual nervous system (Hebb, 1949).

The test of the conceptual reflex arc organization has provided incentives to study single units using intracellular recording in a simple nervous system such as that of the snail. This concept could be visualized directly by injecting dyes into particular neurons, and observing not only how the signals travel, but also what the structures are via which the signals arrive. In the snail, the scheme is very close to the real structure. If this main concept can be shown in the snail, the next step would be to move to more complex systems. The task of such a study would then be to understand how the signals are transmitted and how detectors perform their function of extraction of information from the environment, and how the OR operates in more complex tasks.

The basic problem of the CR formation is the reinforcement at the single unit level. The experiments done by Feher and Barany on cats were conducted as follows. A cell in the motor cortex was penetrated by an intracellular electrode, the pyramidal tract being used to stimulate the cell antidromically. In the specific thalamus, the wire was used to produce a synaptic effect in this intracellularly recorded cell of the motor cortex. The stimulation of the thalamus as a conditioned stimulus produced a postsynaptic potential in the cell of the motor cortex. Stimulation of the pyramidal tract that contains the axon of this particular cortical neuron produces antidromic spikes in the cell bodies. So, the postsynaptic potential is followed by a train of spikes evoked by the antidromic stimulus. In the process of combining the thalamic and pyramidal tract stimulations, an increase in postsynaptic potential was observed in the cell of the motor cortex. When the reinforcement was not given for approximately 30 trials, the amplitude of the postsynaptic potential returned to normal level.

In the control experiment, two types of stimulation were used for the thalamus. One population of synapses was related to the conditioned stimulus and another one represented the stimulus to be differentiated. It was shown that only the population of synapses that was reinforced by antidromic spikes became greater according to conditioning laws. The other population of synapses that was related to differentiated stimulus and was never reinforced, remained unchanged. This means that only synapses that were excited before the spike generation in the neuron were reinforced and modified. This corresponds well with the Hebbian principle. The synapses that were excited just before spiking of the postsynaptic neuron increased their efficiency. From the standpoint of Hebb, reinforcement at a single unit level is excitation of the neuron (Fig. 3.6).

The problem is not so easy, however. Singer, of the Max Planck Institute, studied the formation of detectors in the visual cortex of kittens, and showed the following effect. If the kitten is completely immobilized, but stimulated by light, the detectors sensitive to light orientation are not formed. If, however, in such an immobilized kitten, the reticular formation of the brain stem or nonspecific thalamus are electrically stimulated, then the selective detectors under light stimulation are formed. Singer suggested

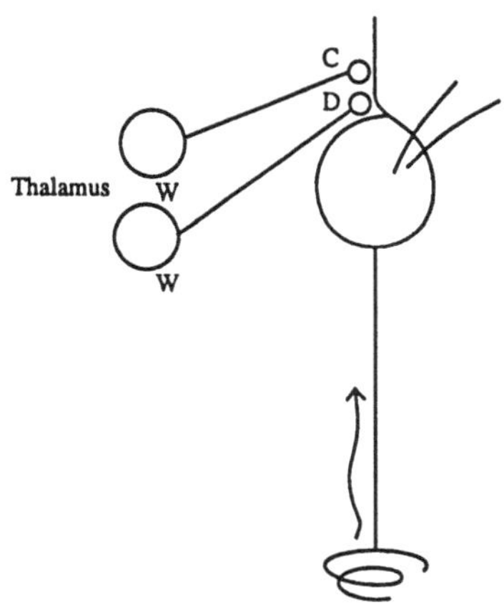

FIG. 3.6. Scheme of intracellular conditioning. The cell of the motor cortex penetrated by a microelectrode for recording synaptic potentials and spikes. Two local wires in the specific thalamus generate analogies of conditioned and differential stimuli. Stimulation of the pyramidal tract for reinforcement of the cell via antidromic spikes. The combination of excitatory postsynaptic potential with antidromically evoked spikes results in a gradual enhancement of this postsynaptic potential. The nonreinforcement of conditioned input results in its gradual diminution. The differential input remains unchanged. The experiment shows that according to the Hebbian principle only the synapse active before neuronal firing became more efficient resulting in a selective conditioned reflex. C = conditioned, D = differential, W = wire.

that the Hebbian principle should be extended, by adding in the influence of the nonspecific system, which takes part in learning, in addition to the spike discharge of the conditioned neuron (Singer, 1990). The area is still controversial. Following the Hebbian principle, attempts are being made, in the Sokolov laboratory, to study associative learning in completely isolated neuronal soma where no specific emotional reinforcement is present. An analog of conditioning was obtained. The methodology of the experiments on isolated soma is very promising, because only intracellular recording in isolated soma can directly reveal the postsynaptic modifications. This cannot be achieved using extracellular recordings, where only the amplification of the number of spikes, but not the mechanism of this amplification, can be seen, that is, it is not possible to see what happens in the neuron. Thus there are different types of reinforcement.

CONCLUDING COMMENTS

The question of whether detectors are plastic or nonplastic is often raised. It is correct to say that detectors are nonplastic in adult animals or in man. There exist, however, in ontogenesis, sensitive periods for the formation of detectors. This is very well known for visual detectors, but now it has also been demonstrated in the auditory system. Most importantly, for different detectors there exist several sensitive periods. Thus, for the parietal cortex, the sensitive period is shifted forward in time compared with the formation of visual detectors. A monkey kept in complete darkness became practically blind because the detectors formed in the visual cortex did not reach the integrating neurons in the parietal cortex. The neurons in the parietal cortex in such a study lose visual input completely. The auditory and somatic inputs develop normally. One can imagine several sensitive periods in which the formation of detectors occurs. In more primitive organisms, detectors are mainly formed by genetic mechanisms without any specific role of the environment. From this perspective, the formation of detectors in a sensitive period is a kind of learning.

The refractory period for detectors that have been stimulated, is rather short. Thus, the fusion frequency for flickering light at the critical level is about 40 cycles per second. In the bat there are detectors which have very short refractory periods and they extract information about distance by measuring the interval between sound and its echo. Some other detectors are more slowly responsive. The oscillatory neurons are specifically related to the process of time quanta that transfer the information relatively independently of the preceding and the following informational content. The other aspect of the oscillatory neurons is to separate different behavioral acts using time windows. The domination of a particular behavioral pattern strongly depends on the modulating neurons emphasizing the signals and selecting the behavioral pattern.

CHAPTER

4

A Microlevel Analysis of the Orienting Response Using Intracellular Recording

This chapter covers the following issues:

1. Snail preparation.
2. Command neurons.
3. Habituation to skin stimulation.
4. Receptive field of the command neuron: Focus and periphery, habituatable and nonhabituatable synapses.
5. Selective habituation at a nonsynaptic level.
6. Pacemaker potential habituation and dishabituation.
7. Correlation of pacemaker spikes of command neurons with motor responses.
8. Modulating neurons, modulation of synaptic contacts, motor responses, and receptors.
9. The giant neuron as the nerve center.
10. Intracellular reverberation of impulses.
11. Plastic calcium channels.
12. Nonplastic sodium channels.

The macrolevel and microlevel analysis of the orienting response (OR) in man and vertebrates has already been discussed and this chapter now describes studies using single unit recording in the snail. In the central nervous system of the snail, neurons have been found that demonstrate three basic properties of the OR–habituation (extinction), dishabituation, and a selective trace that can be compared with the neuronal model postulated in vertebrates. What additional information can be found in such experiments? The most important information concerns the synaptic organization of all these processes, assuming that in this there is similarity between vertebrates and invertebrates.

The chapter begins with a discussion of the habituation process, and moves on to synapses as the mechanism for habituation. A new type of intracellular habituation connected with pacemaker potentials will be discussed, and then attempts are made to analyze the plastic changes of the neuron using the concept of a single ionic channel.

Figure 4.1a refers to what can be called the split body preparation. The snail with an intact nervous system can be stimulated selectively by using von Frey's hair method where hairs are used to stimulate different parts of the body (von Frey & Golgman, 1914). The skin is divided into two parts, one part is used for stimulation, the other for recording the motor re-

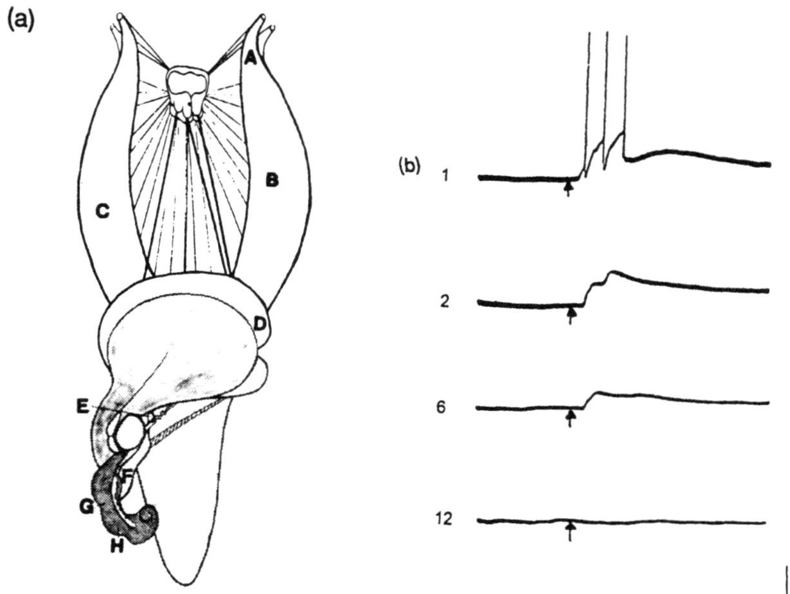

FIG. 4.1. Methods of intracellular recording. (a) Semi-intact preparation split-body of Helix enables separate stimulation of different body areas in combination with intracellular recording and stimulation through two independent electrodes. (b) The habituation of the intracellular response consisting of spike discharge overlapping excitatory postsynaptic potentials (EPSPs). The habituation of spike discharge is followed on later trials by complete reduction of the EPSP. The giant command neuron has a very broad receptive field demonstrating selective habituation for each point except the nonhabituatable focus around the pneumostome.

sponses. In such a way, direct motor responses at the locus of stimulation are prevented. The skin area can be stimulated and a central motor effect on the other side of the body may be observed, and vice versa.

Figure 4.1b moves to more common features known from the observation of habituation by intracellular recording. Tectal stimulation is given by an electromechanical device that stimulates a local piece of skin of the animal. In the first response, the excitatory postsynaptic potentials (EPSPs) may be seen. All these potentials are pure synaptic potentials. Spikes are generated when the threshold of spike firing is reached (Trial 1). Later in this chapter, it is seen that in the synaptic response of the cell, there are not only the usual postsynaptic potentials but also endogenous oscillations related to so-called pacemaker potentials, which are of great importance in the amplification of the responses of the animal. During repeated stimulus presentation, the following processes can be seen. At the first stage of habituation (Trial 2), the spikes disappear and pure excitatory postsynaptic potentials consisting of two independent peaks can be observed. These represent the inputs from the two channels from the stimulated parts of the skin converging on the command neuron that may be seen in Figs. 4.3 and 4.5.

Palikhova in the Sokolov laboratory (Palikhova & Arakelov, 1990) identified several detectors that have local, point-like receptive fields representing different parts of the internal organs. All these detectors are characterized by stable nonhabituatable responses. The intracellular stimulation of such detector cells generates spikes that result in the cell body of the command neuron for defensive behavior through single EPSPs. By repeated intracellular stimulation of a detector, the EPSPs in the command neuron are selectively habituated with respect to a particular detector and its local receptive field on the internal organs.

With stimulus repetition, there is also elimination of just a single input into the cell. This secondary peak is more rapidly habituated, as shown in the parallel recordings of pacemaker spike discharge (upper trace) and the motor response of the mantle (lower trace) in Fig. 4.2a. A gradual decrease of the other postsynaptic potential demonstrates a habituation of longer duration. Finally, all responses are habituated. The stimulus is presented, but no response is evident (Trial 15). If the stimulus is moved over the skin just 1 mm or 2 mm, it becomes stronger, then the total response may be again observed (Fig. 4.2a and 4.2b, Trial 17).

This indicates that the receptive field resulting from many sensory inputs converging onto giant neurons is organized in parallel channels. The neurons converging from all parts of the body, including the total skin area plus all internal organs, onto this particular neuron, constitute the receptive field of one giant neuron. This neuron regulates the defensive response of the animal. It means that every point of the body is represented on the

(a)

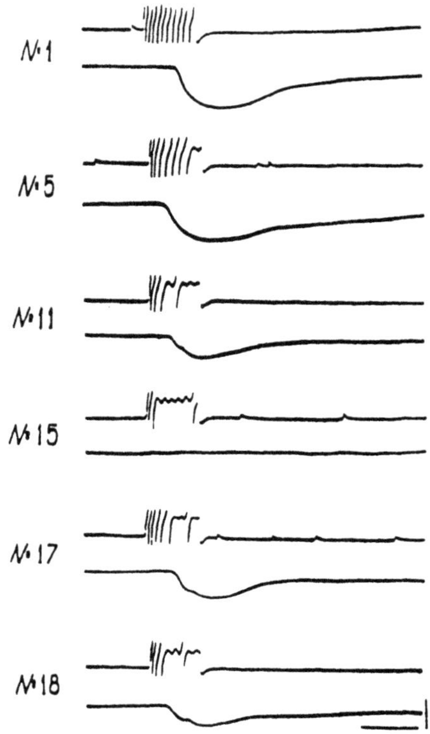

FIG. 4.2. *(Continued)*

dendrites of this particular neuron. In this receptive field, however, two areas can be distinguished. A very wide area of the skin and internal organs is plastic. Around the *pneumostome* (an area responsible for respiration in these animals, by opening a local part of the mantle) is an area from where no habituation can take place. Thus, two types of synapses may be distinguished which have different inputs to the same neuron—habituatable synapses coming from all parts of the body, and nonhabituatable synapses representing the most important part of the body for defensive reflexes. This area of respiratory function is most important for the animal and is thus appropriately protected.

In the experiments by Palikhova, modulating functions of a neuron that produced no motor response were expressed in activation of muscles at the synaptic level and in augmentation of sensory input to the defensive command neuron. Balaban, Zakharov, and Chistyakova (1988) found and identified a group of modulatory neurons directly related to defensive behavior. The electrical stimulation of the modulatory neurons intensifies the synaptic links between detectors and defensive command neurons. This modulating effect on the defensive behavior is effected by the release of se-

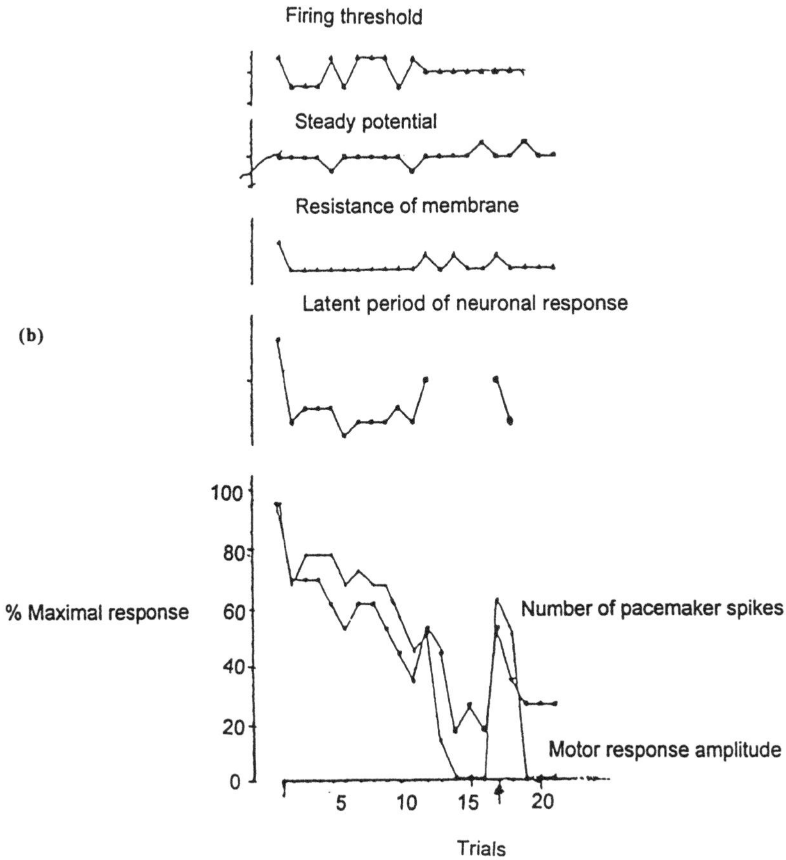

FIG. 4.2. Correlation between pacemaker spikes and motor responses. (a) Parallel recording of pacemaker spike discharge and motor response of the mantle demonstrates their parallel habituation. A change in stimulation (Trial #17) results in a dishabituation effect. (b) The magnitude of the motor response and number of generated spikes on the ordinate demonstrate parallel modifications against trials presented on the abscissa. The pacemaker modifications during habituation do not depend on firing thresholds and membrane resistance.

rotonin from the modulatory neurons on the presynaptic terminals of the detectors converging on the defensive command neuron.

Figure 4.3 shows real command neurons that are located in the left and right parietal ganglia. These two neurons were injected with cobalt after the experiment, and a symmetrical system of giant neurons that produce far-reaching axons can be observed, arranged in such a way that the most important area of the pneumostome is directly innervated by command neurons. The total area of the body is covered by two axonal trees from the left and from the right giant command neurons. If just one neuron is stimulated,

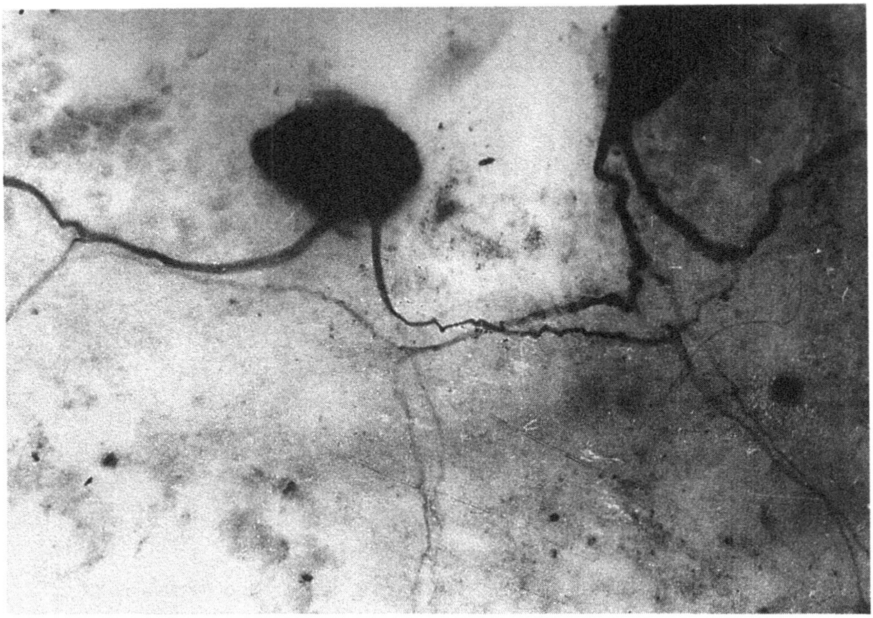

FIG. 4.3. Two symmetrical command neurons associated with the defense response injected with cobalt are characterized by a wide net of axonal terminals responsible for generation of a complex defense pattern. The structure of fibers of command neurons represents part of the hardware of the defense program. The software is incorporated into the system through plastic patches of the membrane, modified by environment and by learning.

then a complete defensive behavior results. This indicates that the neuron as such is responsible for a very complex behavioral act.

The role of the command neuron in behavior may be demonstrated using concurrent recordings from the neurons and from the body of the animal. The intracellular recordings and intracellular stimulation are usually made from two microelectrodes penetrating the cell body. A photorecorder measures the diameter of the pneumostome. The neuron is then directly stimulated, while the other microelectrode penetrating the cell produces the current for depolarization of the cell. The current is enough to trigger so-called *pacemaker spikes*. Why are these action potentials called pacemaker spikes? In Fig. 4.4, the sine-wave-like slow potentials—pacemaker potentials—may be seen, which, once they reach the firing threshold, trigger spikes without any EPSPs. The spikes triggered by pacemaker waves are called pacemaker spikes. The selective electrical stimulation of the command neuron produces a very remarkable motor response in the area of the pneumostome. This experiment is very important for demonstrating so-called intracellular habituation.

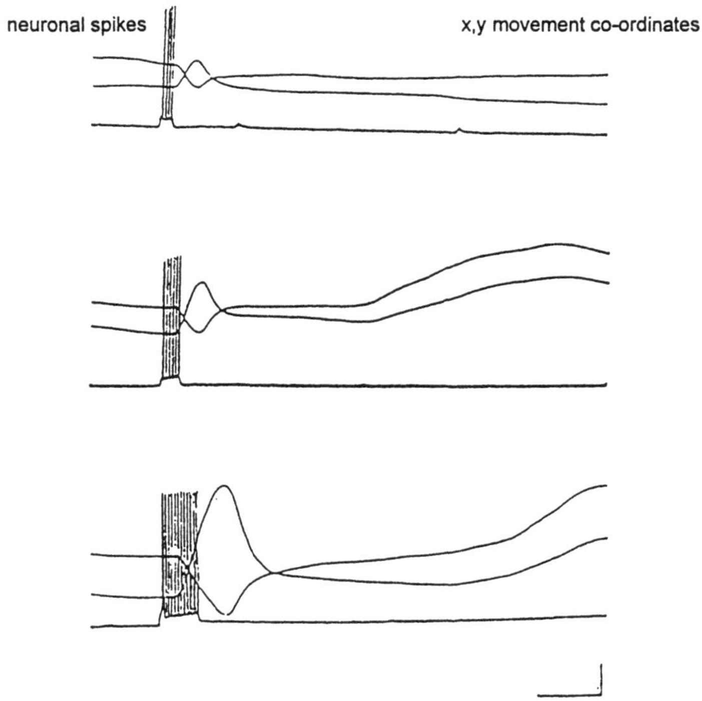

FIG. 4.4. The mantle motor responses triggered by the command neuron through intracellular stimulation. The amplitude of the motor response, the slope of motor reaction and the after-effect depend on the spike frequency generated by the neuron.

Usually, the role of the presynaptic mechanism has been emphasized in the study of habituation. The other phenomenon—intracellular habituation of pacemaker potential—has been discovered and very systematically studied. This refers to repeated presentation of electrical current into the cell producing a decrease in the number of spikes. During habituation, instead of spikes, there are only pacemaker oscillations of the membrane potential, these being called *pacemaker potentials*. Their reduction in amplitude is the reason for the disappearance of spikes, because the pacemaker spikes are not directly triggered through the mechanism of pacemaker depolarization. This depolarization results in the triggering of spikes. When such internal oscillation becomes smaller in amplitude, the spikes are no longer triggered, and intracellular habituation therefore takes place. If the number of generated spikes at the end is reduced to a minimum (only one or two), then no motor response is seen (Fig. 4.2b). It is therefore possible to talk about correspondence between the number of pacemaker spikes and the magnitude of the motor response. Behavioral responses are completely determined by the pacemaker activity of the command neuron.

The effect of disinhibition has now been tested, not at the level of synaptic processes, but in the mechanism of the internal pacemaker. After the development of habituation, a stronger electric stimulus has been given, producing a more powerful neuronal response and recovery of the motor response. After that, the standard stimulus that had been used in habituation was tried and it also evoked the motor responses. This noneffective stimulus, under the influence of a stronger stimulus, produces the disinhibition effect. This effect is a real disinhibition because the increase of intensity can only increase the adaptation, and can only increase the threshold of spike generation. Instead, it results in a recovery of the pacemaker mechanism similar to that seen by synaptic dishabituation. Attention should particularly be drawn to the new mechanism of habituation and dishabituation that is not related to synaptic potentials nor to the electroexcitable membrane of the neuron as such. The specific contribution of the pacemaker potential is evident from the additional measurements.

The firing threshold, the steady potential, the membrane depolarization potential, the resistance of the membrane, and the latent period of the neuronal response remain unchanged during the experiment (Fig. 4.2b). If the biophysical parameters of the cell are constant, what has happened? Two parallel lines may be seen on the graph that indicate the amplitude of the motor response and the number of pacemaker spikes in percentage terms, from the beginning of the experiment. The parallel decrease in these two responses may be seen in Fig. 4.2b, up to a period of the experiment when there are only two spikes. These two spikes cannot trigger a motor response. The motor neurons that control this command neuron are not effective, resulting in a complete motor habituation. But several spikes in the command neuron are still present, showing that this command neuron is a premotor neuron operating at the behavioural level by means of motor neurons. The response is again recovered for spikes and for the motor response, under the influence of the pacemaker potential triggered by application of a strong stimulus. There is thus a complete correspondence between the habituation of spikes in the command neuron and the habituation of a defensive reflex controlled by this particular command neuron. A single command neuron and not a neuronal system is responsible for a particular behavioral act.

In the same command neuron, the influence of the number of generated spikes on the magnitude of the motor response was also studied (Fig. 4.4). Recording was done not by a photorecorder, but by a sensitive two-coordinate induction sensor. Thus, two coordinates from one part of the body were measured. This means that this sensor represents information concerning two dimensions of change in the position of a specific part of the body. Most important is the correlation between the number of spikes per unit time and the magnitude of the response, with the appearance of some secondary responses. This suggests the existence of some long-lasting feedback loop related to the control of the pneumostome.

For more detailed analysis, look again at the preparation of the command neuron (Fig. 4.5). The cell actually has several axons going to the periphery. A very powerful control system could then be imagined, influencing the periphery not by one axon only, but by many axons running through many of the nerves of the animal. Most important for this experiment was the investigation of the responses around the pneumostome. It has already been pointed out that the receptive field of the pneumostome is stable with respect to repeated stimulation. The problem is whether this particular area around the pneumostome is controlled by this command neuron directly or in some specific way, or whether there is a common mechanism for its regulation via motor neurons. It has been found that the pneumostome area is controlled by direct axons reaching the motor cells. Some other more complex responses evoked by the stimulation of these neurons are involved through additional links via motor neurons. Yet, the most important area for a very rapid response is under the direct influence of the command neuron.

These command neurons combine the properties of the premotor neurons and motor neurons. The motor neurons are used for a selective rapid regulation and premotor neurons function to integrate complex behavior. Different spike frequencies influence the response differently. At low spike frequencies, very small motor deflections are seen to be associated with each spike (Fig. 4.4). This demonstrates the direct effect of spikes on muscle cells. After a certain period of stimulation, a more complex response is generated, which cannot be divided into single deflections. One might assume that now motor neurons are involved. At other frequencies, there is again a period of single deflections of the muscle, but later triggering of the whole response. With an increase in the frequency of spikes, the resultant slope of the response is increased and there is a doubled response. The structure of the response is determined by a direct input (direct influence on muscles) and an indirect one through the motor cells involved in the system of defensive behavior.

The plastic properties of the detectors on the command neuron can also be demonstrated during conditioning. The microelectrodes are inserted into the command neuron of a defensive behavior. Feeding behavior was used as a conditioned stimulus for defensive behavior, with food as the unconditioned stimulus for the feeding behavior. Isolated presentation of food resulted in a spiking within the command neuron of feeding behavior. No spikes were generated in the defensive command neuron. The presentation of food was associated with a painful current on the lip of the animal. After several trials, the food decreased the spiking in the command neuron of the feeding behavior. Instead, food started to generate spikes in the defensive command neuron triggering behavioral manifestations of the defensive behavior.

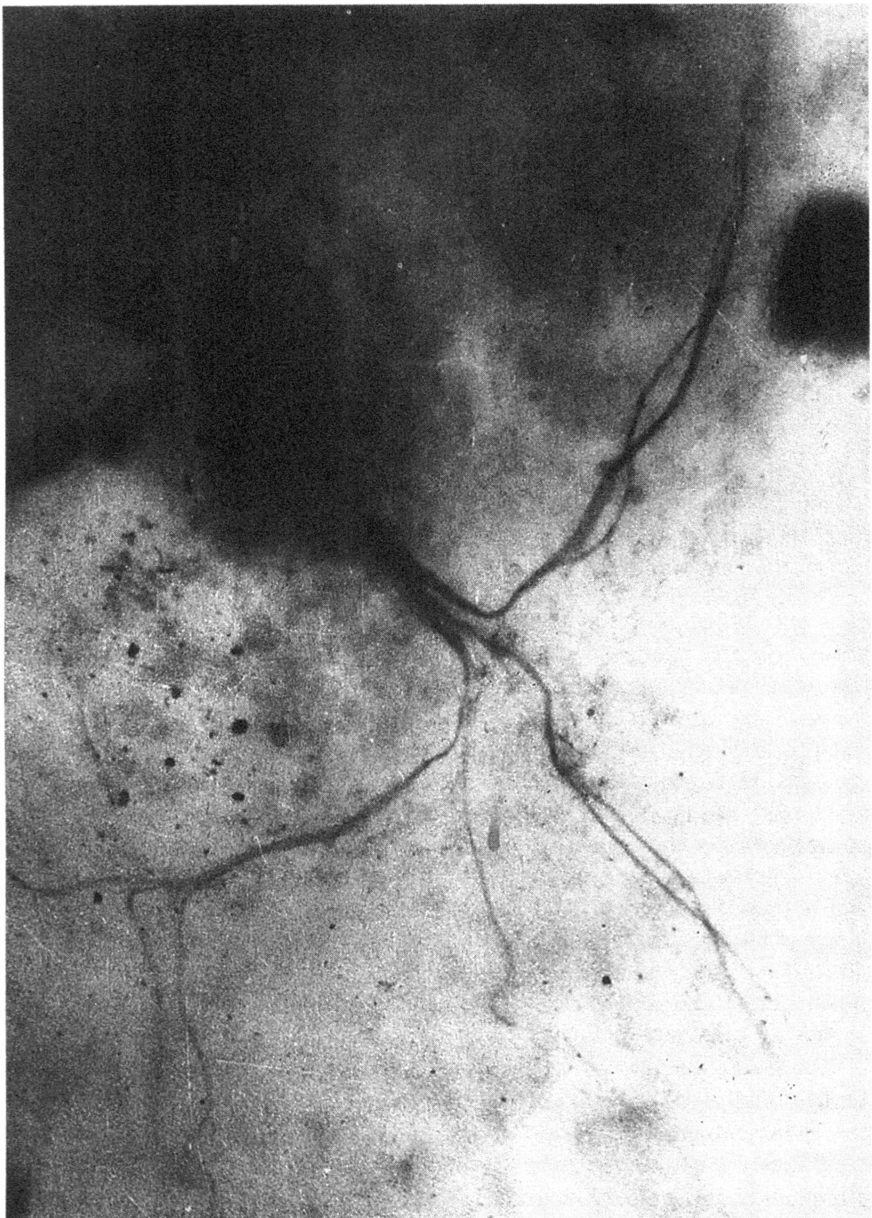

FIG. 4.5. Right parietal neuron (RPa3) with command functions, located in the right and left parts of the body, has a wide extension of axonal trees.

When cobalt is injected into the cell, it demonstrates the presence of powerful processes that reach the opposite ganglion and run within different nerves. At the same time, in some of these axonic areas, very fine dendrites can be seen which belong to a system of selection of information from the entire body. The giant neuron, with its multiaxonal network, resembles a nervous center. Its study is a more complex problem. The idea of these experiments was to combine intracellular recording and stimulation with recording and stimulation of single axons by stimulation of different nerves. Each axon can be selectively stimulated because in these nerves single axons run from the command neuron. This neuron can be directly stimulated through the intracellular electrodes.

It is also possible to make recordings from different nerves. This is the simplest example. The stimulation of the cell produced by injection of the depolarizing current initiates the pacemaker mechanism that generates spikes, and a spike can be recorded later on in one of the axons. This means that the spike is leaving the cell body and is travelling down to the periphery. This is the normal sequence of events. It is also possible to observe spikes moving from the periphery to the cell body, which in some cases, failed to reach the threshold for generation of somatic spikes, and are recorded as electrotonic potentials—so-called *A-spikes*. The electrotonic potentials indicate that between the axon and the soma of the cell, there is a certain portion of the membrane that has no active properties. A spike coming from the periphery can therefore be recorded in the soma as an electrotonic axonic input. In some other cases, the picture is even more complex. The spike reaching the soma from an axon may be big enough to reach the threshold of somatic spike generation. Now, this electrotonic potential reaching the threshold generates a spike in the soma. From the soma, spikes move back to the periphery and a double spike can be seen in the axon. The first one occurs in the periphery and is moving towards the cell body, which, in turn, generates another one that leaves the cell body going back to the periphery. Similar effects can be seen in different nerves. Thus spikes can travel from periphery to the soma in this way generating a trail of spikes.

The existence of command neurons in general terms was explained earlier. In the mollusc, they have been seen directly, but command neurons have not actually been seen in vertebrates. Returning to the modulating neurons, these neurons, although they evoke no behavioral response, can affect the other neurons and in this way modify behavior. In experiments conducted in Moscow University, Palikhova (1991) discovered a neuron that has the same distribution of axons as a command neuron. However, whatever the stimulation of these neurons, it has not proved possible to find any motor, vegetative or other responses. The neuron was active and responsive, but it did not prove possible to find any function for these neurons. It was concluded that this type of neuron can perform a modulating function, not controlling the synapses in the central nervous system, but controlling peripheral parts, because the axons of this modulating neuron correspond exactly with the axons of the command neurons. Two hypotheses were suggested. One of these was that the modulating neuron results in a potentiation of muscles. The other hypothesis was that this neuron can potentiate the receptors.

The following experiment was carried out to see what would be the results of artificially stimulating the modulating neuron. While stimulating the modulating neuron, a single stimulation was given to the command neuron. What happened to the magnitude of the motor response? The results were not clear. However, the main idea behind the experiment was to increase the function of the modulating neuron and to look at the complexity of the responses evoked by command neuron stimulation. As a preliminary result, one can say that the modulating neuron can modulate the activation of muscles at the pre- or postsynaptic level or at the level of the membrane.

Another experiment was designed to test for potentiation of receptor function by the modulating neuron. In this experiment, the modulating neuron was continuously electrically stimulated, and responses in the command neuron to skin stimulation were recorded. The responses were superimposed because they did not correlate in time. In a very mixed picture of command neuron responses, it was seen that if the modulating neuron is silent, only a small activation of the command neuron is seen. An increase in stimulation of the modulating neuron augments the sensory input to the command neuron that is somehow amplified. These experiments are being continued. It is not yet possible to present detailed observations and explanations of the mechanism of these modulating functions. The results were very unusual in that no direct effects whatsoever of the identified neuron were found and only indirect influences could initially be discovered. The neuron hypothesized to perform a modulating function was characterized by spontaneous background activity. Its intracellular stimulation produced an additional burst of spikes. At that time, some increase in motor response was seen following each single intracellular stimulation of the defensive command neuron. Parallel recording of the spikes within different axons and the cell body demonstrates the following cases (Fig. 4.6):

- Somatic spikes (S-spikes)—trigger following spikes in an axon.
- Axonic spikes—trigger following A-spikes in the cell body.
- Axonic spikes in another axon trigger A-spikes in the cell body that, in turn, generate following spikes in the axon under recording. Depending on the axonic branch, somatic spikes can precede or follow the axonic spikes.

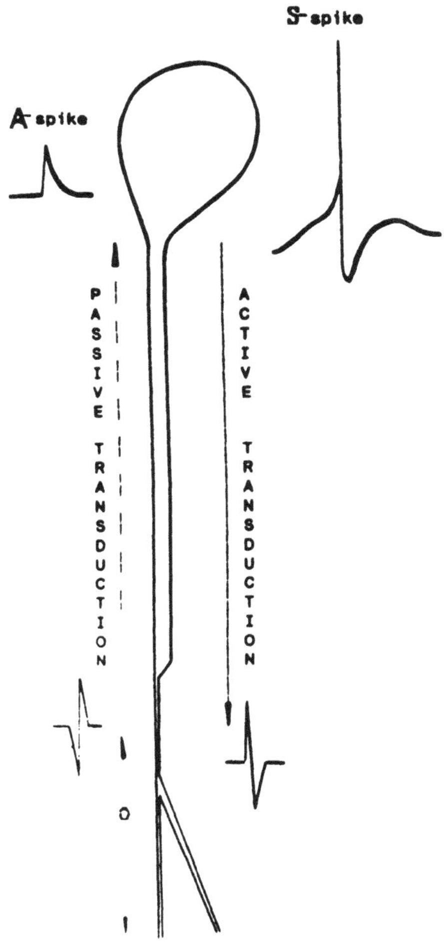

FIG. 4.6. The neuron as a nervous center (intracellular reverberation). RPa6 neuron demonstrates somatic and local axonal triggering areas where spikes can be initiated. Somatic pacemaker spikes result in the retardation of spikes in several axons. The spikes generated in the active axon areas are recorded in the soma as A-spikes, which may, in turn, reach firing threshold and generate a somatic spike (S-spike). Such an effect results in the appearance in the axon of two spikes—one generated locally in the axon and descending to the periphery, and the second spike of somatic origin following the first one.

The complex functions of a neuron as a nervous center were studied in detail. A combination of processes in the neuron is expressed in the distribution of axons and in the very complex activity, including EPSPs and A-spikes of this neuron. What is the nature of this complex activity? The circulation of impulses is due to a very powerful interaction between the soma and single axons. Together, they produce many different types of reverberation of nervous impulses within the neuron.

Figure 4.7 shows a schematic representation of a neuron with three different axons. Each axon has its own triggering zone and it is possible that from the soma, the spike arrives at the active zone in the axon. The next spike, which can be secondarily produced in this triggering zone, moves back to the soma and is recorded there in the form of an electrotonic potential, or so-called *A-spike*. Sometimes, the impulses can migrate from one

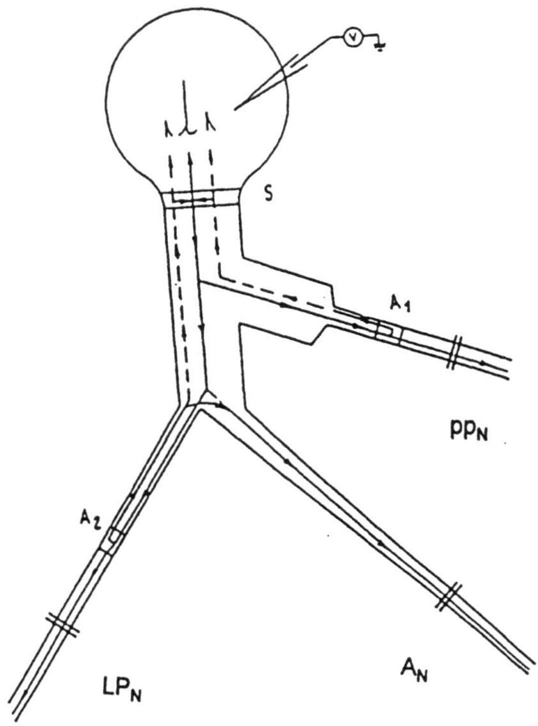

FIG. 4.7. Scheme of intracellular reverberation. The single axonal branches may operate independently or cooperatively under the influence of cell body spikes. The spikes may travel from an axonal branch to another without the involvement of the cell body. The interaction of axonal and somatic spike generation mechanisms produces a long-lasting train of spikes ("intracellular reverberation").

axon to another without passing through the soma, but they are still seen in the soma as small electrotonic potentials. In this way, many internal reverberations of action potentials may be seen. How is it possible to prove that this is really an internal process? A complete blockade of all chemical synaptic contacts occurs in the preparation using cobalt. Cobalt closes the calcium channels in presynaptic terminals, of course, preventing calcium entering the presynaptic part of the terminal. Calcium is the essential second messenger that triggers a cascade of processes that produce the release of a quantum of transmitter on the next neuron. If the calcium channels in presynaptic contacts are blocked, then all chemical synapses are eliminated, but not electrical synapses. It has already been demonstrated that, under cobalt, all reverberating processes are preserved, and it was concluded that this cycling of excitation in the neuron between different branches of axons, between soma and single branches is an intracellular reverberation.

Say, for example, one spike is generated in the axon. The somatic spike will, of course, be delayed with respect to this axonic spike, but the somatic spike triggers in the axon a new spike, and this spike moves both to the periphery and to the soma. Travelling back to the soma, such a spike produces an A-spike here. This A-spike is above threshold and triggers another somatic spike. The somatic spike then goes back to the axon. So, instead of two spikes, there are now three spikes in the axon. Sometimes, a long train of spikes is produced by such reverberation. Thus, a train of spikes moves to the periphery due to this soma-axon reverberation. In a simpler example with double spikes, the first spike from the soma generates in the axon a new spike that returns to the soma and produces there an A-spike, which on reaching the threshold generates a somatic spike. This is a very characteristic pattern that depends on the distances between these active zones in the soma and axon.

In the next experiment, the problem was to explore the mechanism of the habituation of pacemaker potential or, in more general terms, the mechanism of intracellular habituation. The hypotheses were that mainly calcium (Ca) spikes are located in the soma, and sodium (Na) spikes are located on the axon, except for the presynaptic terminals where again calcium channels are available. In this experiment, the number of spikes and the magnitude of depolarization have been recorded in the same command neuron. The experiment consisted of an increased stepwise depolarization of the cell. When the maximum depolarization was reached, the current intensity was reduced. Of particular interest was the appearance of hysteresis that can be interpreted as a trace that is a kind of memory in channels. To separate Ca-channels and Na-channels, four experiments were carried out where each neuron was studied in four different solutions:

- Normal physiological solution, where Ca^{++} was available.
- Sodium-free solution.
- Normal solution plus cobalt to close the Ca-channels.
- Sodium-free solution plus cobalt.

After each experiment, the neuron was washed out in a normal solution. The intensity of depolarization was systematically changed. The number of spikes and the change in membrane potential generated by the neuron are shown in Fig. 4.8a. Low-level depolarization produces no spikes, being below threshold. The arrows show the increasing stimulation, and, with this increase in current, an increase in the number of spikes generated by each depolarization can be seen. As the high stimulus intensities are then gradually lowered, there is a return in the graph along different pathways. The strong current has now shifted the firing thresholds. This results in a hysteresis effect, which indicates that "something" has happened, and this

Normal solution

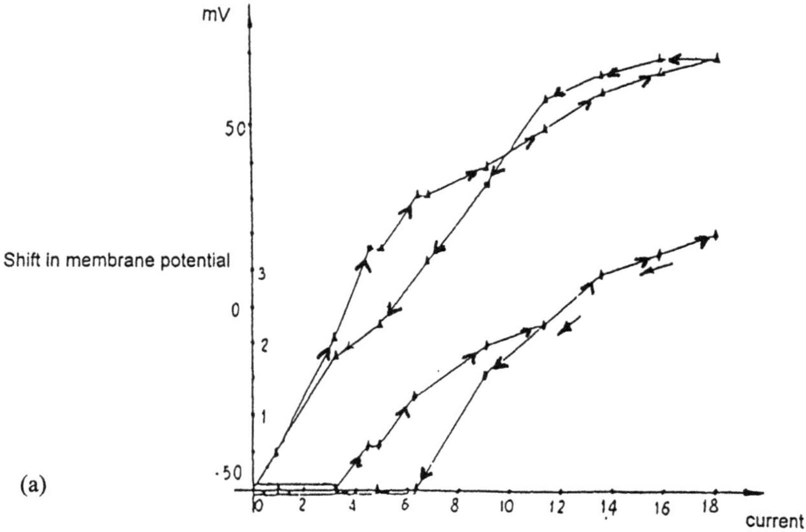

(a)

Sodium-free solution

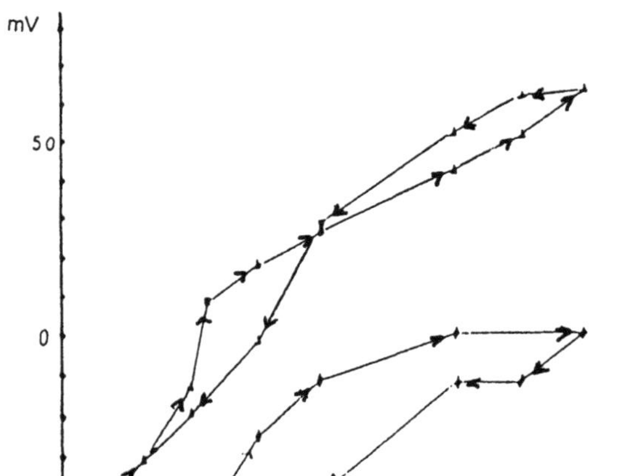

(b)

FIG. 4.8. *(Continued)*

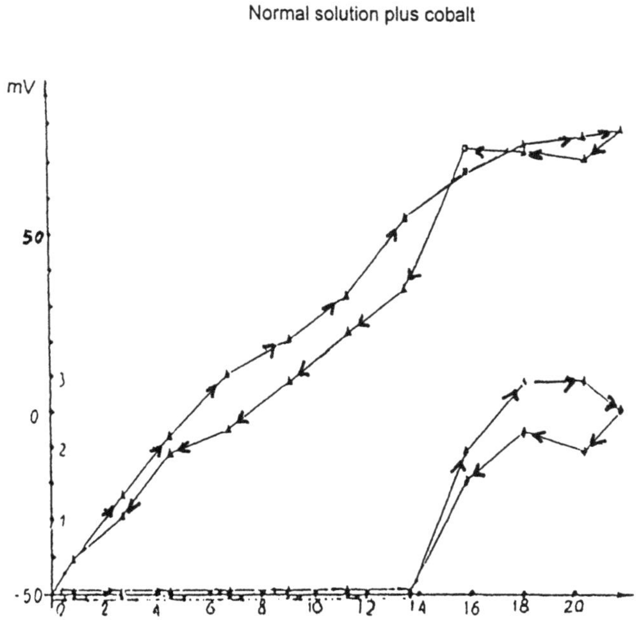

(c)

FIG. 4.8. Plasticity of calcium ionic channels. The abscissa is the current used, while the ordinate indicates the shift of the membrane potential, as well as the number of spikes. The arrows indicate the sequence of changes in the current applied over trials. (a) In the normal solution, a hysteresis effect is seen. The threshold of spike generation after many strong currents is elevated (plastic effect). (b) In a sodium-free physiological solution, the neuron with intact Ca-channels demonstrates plastic properties of spike generation. (c) Cobalt in normal physiological solution results in an elimination of plastic Ca-channels elevating the threshold of spike generation.

"something" influences the increase of the threshold of spike generation of during decreasing current presentations.

In the experiment using the sodium-free solution, nothing changed (Fig. 4.8b). The lack of Na-current does not eliminate any hysteresis effect, implying that they are not involved in plastic changes. The cobalt, which has the effect of blocking Ca-channels, results in an increase of the firing threshold and disappearance of the hysteresis effect. This means that the Ca-channels are plastic and their closure causes a blockade of the hysteresis (Fig. 4.8c). Using cobalt in a sodium-free solution as a control condition, it was found that the membrane potential was the same, having no modification. However, no spike was generated to any current intensity. Finally, a return to a normal physiological solution produced data similar to those of Fig. 4.8a.

This indicates that, in this neuron, two types of ionic channels participate in generating action potentials: Ca-channels and Na-channels. Na-channels are stable and nonhabituatable, while Ca-channels create spikes in the soma and are plastic. It can now be suggested that the intracellular habituation that is observed by intracellular stimulation of the cell and expressed in the reduction of pacemaker potentials is dependent on the plastic properties of ionic Ca-channels. Several hypotheses concerning the mechanisms of such plasticity can be suggested. One is that the calcium entering the membrane closes the channel from the inside, preventing the next portion of Ca^{++} ions entering the cell. The other hypothesis explains this plasticty because of the activation of Ca-dependent dephosphorylation of proteins constituting Ca-channels.

The study of the same processes in the completely isolated cell has supported the conclusion that plastic changes in the cell are due to calcium channels. The OR has been explained in terms of extracellular observation earlier on. In this case, only modification of spikes has been observed. The final picture of OR habituation may be drawn following intracellular data obtained from completely isolated neurons.

The intracellular mechanisms of habituation can be linked to the plasticity of Ca-channels participating in the generation of pacemaker waves. Intracellular habituation results from a calcium-dependent cascade of reactions resulting in the dephosphorylation following the inactivation of proteins constituting the Ca-channels.

CONCLUDING COMMENTS

The somatic membrane contains Ca-channels and Na-channels. Complete elimination of spikes has been achieved under conditions where Na is eliminated from the solution at the same time as Ca-channels are blockaded. In this case, only RC-potentials dependent on membrane resistance and capacitance are generated. Under normal conditions, Na- and Ca-spikes are generated resulting in a complex interaction between axons and the cell body.

The command neuron might be regarded as a closed neuronal net within which the intracellular reverberation can be observed. This is sometimes possible in successful preparations of isolated soma. If four microelectrodes are inserted into the cell, two in the soma and one in each of two axons, then it is possible to notice how the spike travelling from the soma to the axon is modified by participation of the Na-spike. Due to Ca^{++}, the spike at the soma is very broad. As it moves to the axon, it becomes very sharp because of the rapidity of acting Na-channels.

It may be argued that there is a large conceptual leap between this chapter and the previous one. If one looks at the main scheme of information processing, the gap between vertebrates and invertebrates is not so wide.

The detector-like sensory elements identified in the nervous system of the mollusc are similar to the detectors of vertebrates. A sensory element can be small, but it acts on five command neurons. If a sensory neuron is stimulated, a monosynaptic response in every identified command neuron occurs. By observing both sensory and command neurons, the distribution of one detector among several command neurons can be determined. For a particular defensive command neuron, the process occurs in a single synapse. It is possible to look at the total reflex arc, putting the microelectrode in the sensory neuron, in the command neuron, in the motor neuron, and additionally in the modulating neuron that can influence behavior acting on a command neuron. All the important elements transfer information accordingly. This is the channel-dependent code. If the detector cell is stimulated electrically, a single spike is generated and is distributed in labeled lines towards the command and modulating neurons. The most important elements are the sensory neuron, command neuron, and modulating neuron. These three different neurons are repeated in all the explanations of the OR given here. So far, there has been a discussion about detectors and the labeled line principle, and about modulating neurons as neurons of the reticular formation related to novelty detectors. The OR, with many components including different types of modulating neurons and input detectors, regulates the relationship between extraction of information and performance of behavioral acts. The basic neuronal structure of the OR is based on the same principles of the channel-dependent code.

The detector of the system can be tested for receptive field. In the snail, these neurons collect signals from the skin or from internal organs. The problem is to what extent the loop can modify the input information. This input information cannot be changed too much, otherwise adjustments to the environment would be made impossible. There should be objective information even if different loops are operating. The loops mainly operate not with respect to modification of information as such, but mainly by changing the sensitivity of the detectors. For example, Rasmussen tracked the hearing system and has shown that the role of this efferent pathway for hearing is a change of the signal-to-noise ratio.

The problem of sensory feedback is very important. In the snail experiments, where there is a very simple system, it is possible to identify exactly the premotor command neurons that trigger specific patterns of defensive behavior or food reflexes, depending on the stimulated cell. However, the contribution of detectors to excitation of a particular command neuron depends on the excitation of relevent modulating neurons.

It was shown that a modulating neuron alters the efficiency of synapses of detectors on command neurons by serotonin that changes the density of activated Ca-channels on presynaptic terminals. The modulating neuron has been regarded as a mechanism of presynaptic control. However, the modulating neurons that can control the somata of command neurons by operating with peptides introduce a completely new mechanism into the play of modulating neurons. In this case, it is not a synaptic change, but a change of the pacemaker activity. Under the influence of peptides produced by modulating neurons, the command neurons switch on the pacemaker mechanism.

How specific is this kind of modulation? The command neurons and detectors are modulated specifically by relevant modulating neurons and nonspecifically by global modulation. Two kinds of modulating neurons exist—local and general modulating neurons. The local modulating neurons produce and emphasize the responses of one behavioral system. The generalized modulators increase the total activity in detectors and command neurons, and produce general activation. The type of modulation depends on the state of the organism and the characteristics of stimulation.

The behavior is triggered by a key stimulus represented by detectors leaving strengthened synapses on the relevant command neuron. These enhanced synaptic contacts can be regarded as a memory trace. This trace is in an operational mode when a given command neuron is amplified by a specific modulating neuron. Thus, the hunger (deficit of glucose) would stimulate the modularity neuron of the feeding behavior and elevate the pain threshold for the evocation of the defensive reflex. In vertebrates the memory trace has a more complex organization. Näätänen (1982, 1990) has suggested that the goal can be operationalized by an attentional trace as a kind of representation of the target. It is a temporarily activated representation of the stimulus.

The experiments on delayed response by Batuev (1981) can somehow explain the problem of the target in neurophysiological terms. Delayed response is a conditioned response that should be performed by making a learned movement of the monkey. There is a warning conditioned stimulus that triggers the process of delay. The interval between the warning stimulus and the signal for performance of the response is variable. The interesting aspect is what happened in the frontal lobe neurons during this delay period. It was found that neurons are not silent. The time interval of the delay was occupied by activity of the neurons in such a way that the bursts of spikes in each neuron are time-locked. The bursts of spikes were seen stepwise from one neuron to another, finally reaching neurons that trigger the delayed motor response. Thus, the target stimulus represented in the brain by a trace controls a sequence of time-selective neurons through a period of delay.

CHAPTER

5

A Microlevel Analysis of the Orienting Response Using Intracellular Recording From the Isolated Soma

This chapter covers the following issues:

1. The isolated soma of an identifiable command neuron.
2. Comparison of pacemaker waves and spikes in isolated soma and different preparations.
3. Postsynaptic and transmitter potentials.
4. Habituatable and nonhabituatable loci on the membrane of the isolated soma.
5. Associative conditioning in the isolated soma, due to the pairing of transmitter potentials (as CS) and electrically triggered firing (UCS).
6. Differential learning in the isolated soma.
7. Inhibitory learning in the isolated soma.
8. Conditioning as an intracellular process.
9. The role of plastic calcium channels.
10. Extinction of associations in the soma.
11. Protein synthesis and habituation.
12. Membrane projection on the genome: Suggestions.

In earlier chapters, the command neuron has been discussed and the cobalt preparations of command neurons displayed a highly developed system of axon branches and dendrites. The same neuron which has already been identified as a command neuron, and which is functionally related to the defense response, can be extracted from the isolated ganglion. Under

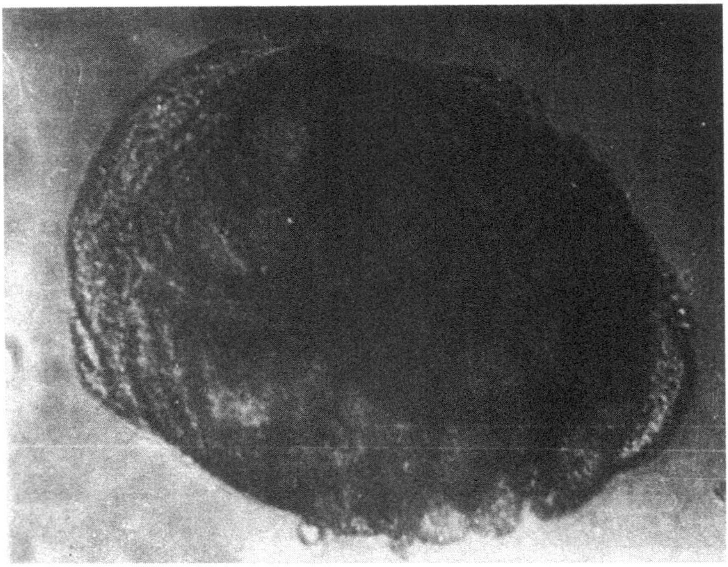

FIG. 5.1. Isolated soma of a command neuron. The cell body is characterized by stripes on the membrane. The hillock is seen as a short extension of the soma.

the microscope, the shape of this neuron can be seen (Fig. 5.1). When the axon of this isolated neuron is cut, the membrane is closed so that the cytoplasm of the neuron is preserved. Such a neuron can live in physiological solution for several days without the special contribution of any additional substances. This neuron can then be penetrated by microelectrodes, usually using two electrodes. Sometimes, two microelectrodes are put on the soma and two are put within the soma. In some cases, two axonic branches were present (Fig. 5.2).

It may be noted that each neuron is characterized by the specific structure of the membrane. Stripes may be seen on the membrane of the cell body (Fig. 5.1), suggesting the existence of different compartments of the cell. Perhaps this is the reason why it is possible to record several independent spikes from the one cell, for example, one spike of 20 mV, one of 80 mV, and a third of 5 mV. It is believed that this is the result of independent involvement of portions of the membrane in spike generation, such that, in between the parts of the membrane participating in spike generation, there are nonexcitable areas.

These neuron preparations have been used by Grechenko (Grechenko & Sokolov, 1987) to conduct some very specific experiments in which she has been able to preserve the isolated neuron with four microelectrodes for 3 to 4 days for observation. It is possible to put microelectrodes into the ax-

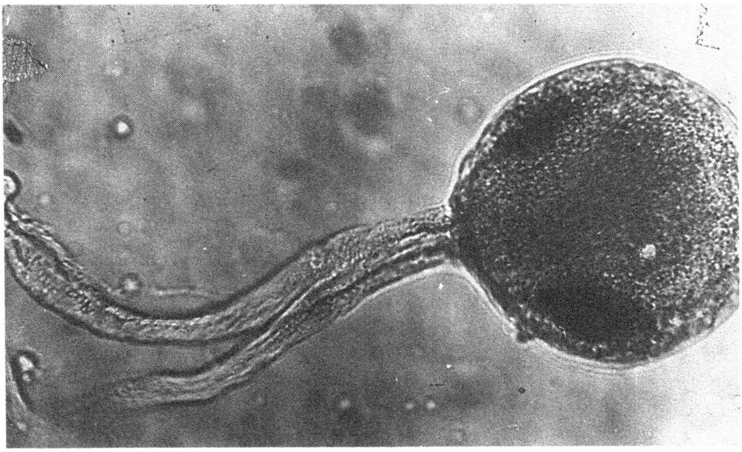

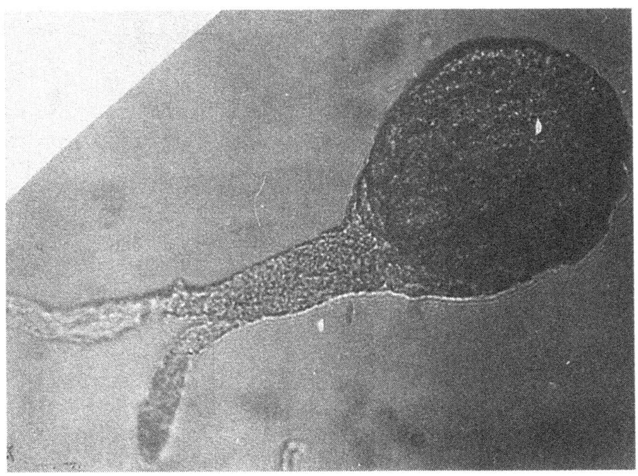

FIG. 5.2. Isolated command neuron with two axonal segments preserved after tripsinization and washing.

ons and in the soma to study neuronal responses that have been shown in the complete preparation. In the isolated nervous system, the neurons are connected with each other via synaptic contacts. This property is lost in a completely isolated neuron.

In an attempt to find out what is lost when the command neuron is completely isolated in this way, comparisons were made between the identified command neuron in the isolated nervous system and the completely isolated neuron. Figure 5.3a shows that the activity of completely isolated neu-

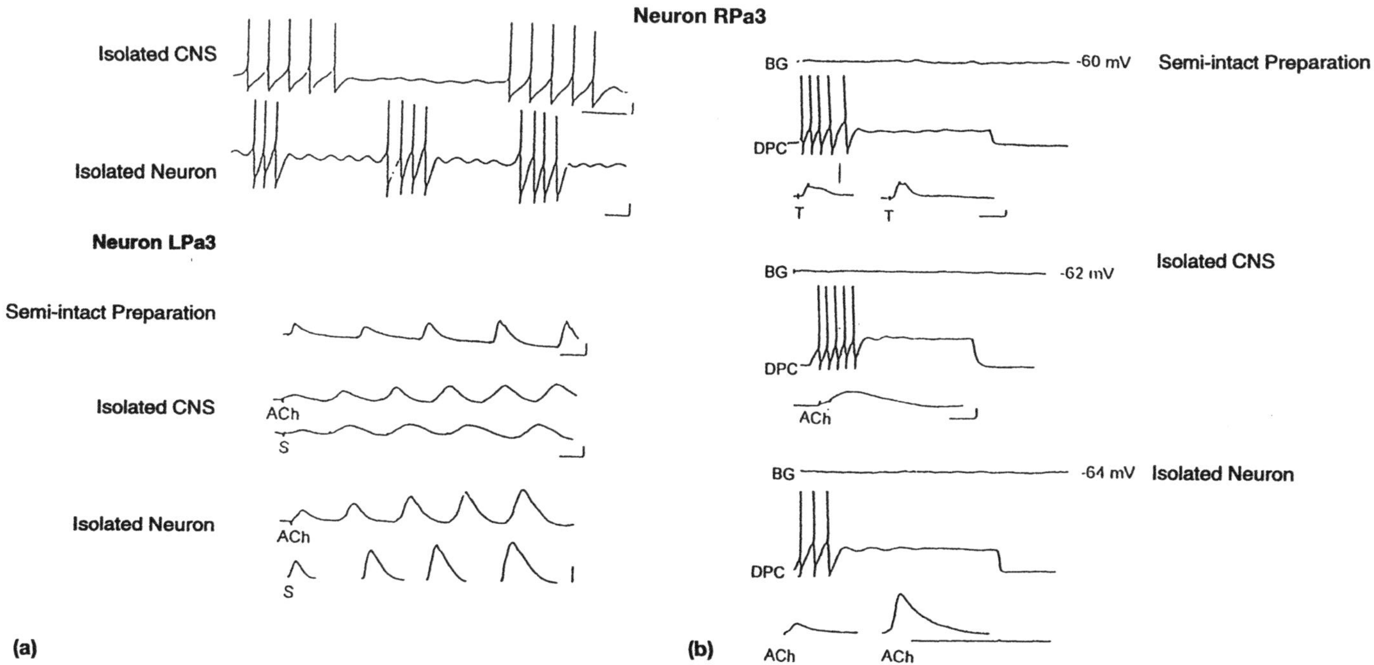

FIG. 5.3. Comparisons of pacemaker waves and spikes in the semi-intact preparation, isolated nervous system and isolated soma. Demonstration of identity of these processes for an identified command neuron. The postsynaptic potentials in the semi-intact preparation can be stimulated by iontophoretic application of transmitters participating in the transfer of information (acetylcholine and serotonin). Ach = Acetylcholine, BG = Background, DPC = Depolarizing current, S = Serotonin, T = Tactile stimulation.

ron preserved the main features of the responses observed in the isolated nervous system. This figure also shows the pacemaker potentials that trigger spikes. It could be inferred from the isolated nervous system preparation that the pacemaker potentials could have been due to synaptic interaction, since the neurons in the isolated nervous system possess synapses. The control, the isolated neuron, has no synapses, no interaction with other neurons, but still beautiful oscillations of the pacemaker potential can be seen. If the pacemaker potential reaches the threshold, then the pattern of spikes appears. The isolated neuron can not only respond to stimuli, but can also generate an endogenous pattern of spikes depending on its internal generator, seen as a pattern of pacemaker waves.

In the third type of preparation, the semi-intact preparation, the nervous system and a part of the body are preserved. The same identifiable neuron is studied in a split body preparation. One can see the same kind of activity (Fig. 5.3b). When a depolarizing current is applied, low pacemaker potentials and spikes are again seen. If mechanical stimulation is given to the skin, then postsynaptic potentials are seen in the command neuron. The neuron in the isolated nervous system and the completely isolated neuron functionally operate as in the semi-intact preparation except that the direct connections from the receptors to the neuron are eliminated.

In order to study the effects of acetylcholine (ACh) on an isolated neuron, a comparison between tactile stimulation and direct application of acetylcholine was made. A similar comparison was done for intracellular stimulation. Figure 5.3b shows the responses of the neuron in the isolated nervous system to electrical stimulation. Background activity shows no spikes and no pacemaker activity. A depolarization by intracellular current produces oscillations of the pacemaker potential and spiking. Acetylcholine is applied iontophoretically on the soma and produces a potential similar to EPSP. To identify this potential, a specific term was employed—*transmitter potential.* Excitatory transmitter potentials and inhibitory transmitter potentials are analogs of excitatory and inhibitory synaptic potentials. Such transmitter potentials were demonstrated in the completely isolated neuron. Thus, ACh stimulation in the semi-intact preparation, the isolated nervous system, and the isolated neuron produced the same effects.

Stimulation was also applied to demonstrate the effect of tactile stimulation of the skin in the semi-intact preparation, and the responses produced by a direct application of acetylcholine. Serotonin to which the neuron is also sensitive was then used as stimulator and the same effect was seen in the semi-intact preparation and in the isolated neuron (Fig. 5.3a).

Figure 5.4a shows the results from an isolated command neuron, having different local properties. In different loci of the membrane, the effects of habituatable loci and nonhabituatable loci are demonstrated. If acetylcholine was presented many times, the response gradually diminished, demonstrating good habituation. The serotonin produced a facilitation effect. This means that the receptors for acetylcholine and serotonin are different. A train of acetylcholine pulses produces habituation. Serotonin pulses, instead of producing habituation, produce a facilitation effect. This suggests that processes in the serotonin receptor do not influence the other locus where the acetylcholine is presented. So, to study the possibility of interaction or independence between the two loci, the acetylcholine locus and the serotonin locus, these substances were presented in a random order (Fig. 5.4a, bottom trace). It can be seen from the diagram that acetylcholine responses gradually diminished and eventually completely disappeared, but serotonin, despite the fact that it was presented in parallel with the acetylcholine, still produced the same potentiation or sensitization effect. The most important conclusion from this experiment is that the neuron operates by single loci, independent from each other, and the problem of their interaction is a specific one. One cannot speak about the excitation of the total neuron except in cases where the spike involves the whole membrane. Usually, each neuron can operate according to activity at single patches of the electrical and chemical membranes.

Thus, in addition to habituation, a facilitation effect of other loci on the same neuron can be demonstrated. An effect of potentiation can be seen if the stimuli were presented for a certain period of time. For example, Fig. 5.4b shows a potentiation of the spike as a result of acetylcholine stimulus presentations. Only after 60 minutes does the response return to its initial level. The other locus operates independently from the first, demonstrating, over 40 min, the same effect of potentiation evoked by serotonin.

The first part of this chapter has been devoted mainly to the subject of habituation and facilitation evoked by direct application of transmitters. However, conditioning has not yet been discussed. The same procedure has been used in the isolated neuron for the habituation of the orienting response (OR)—of extracellular spikes recording and of the postsynaptic po-

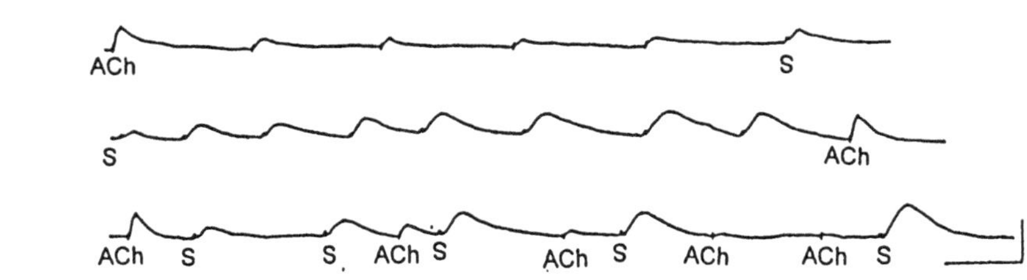

FIG. 5.4. *(Continued)*

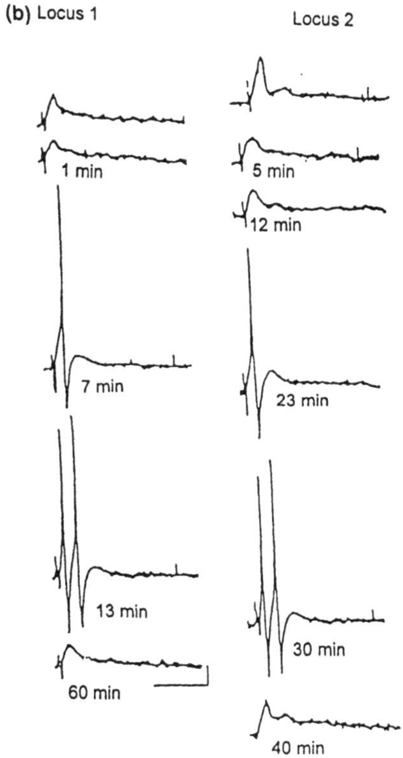

FIG. 5.4. Habituatable, nonhabituatable, and facilitable membrane receptors. (a) The application of acetylcholine results in a gradual habituation, whereas serotonin does not produce habituation. Random presentation of both transmitters shows the independence of the operation of single loci. (b) Local differences in the membrane receptors. The repeated presentation of acetylcholine in one locus results not in habituation, but in facilitation in two independent loci. The facilitation is evident in the spike generation and with time, the facilitation effect disappears. Both loci demonstrate independent, but similar, dynamics. The facilitation is a process opposite habituation. Habituation disappears over time and results in a re-established response. The elimination of facilitation reduces the response to the initial level. The process of facilitation can be represented by two mechanisms–the sensitization of membrane receptors and mobilization of plastic ionic channels (possibly calcium). This recruitment of calcium channels in a close surrounding of chemically sensitive loci determines spike generation. The disappearance of the spike response over time shows that these processes are local and short-lived. They require local stimulation of receptors of the chemosensitive membrane to be kept in an operational state.

tentials in the simple nervous system. New knowledge about conditioning is always connected with a question about where these plastic changes occur—at the presynaptic or the postsynaptic level. In the isolated neuron, there are only postsynaptic structures, and every plastic change that occurs in this isolated neuron must therefore be dependent on processes in the postsynaptic membrane.

The investigation then moved on to studying conditioning. The first formally published hypotheses concerning conditioning as an intracellular process were made by Anokhin (1974) in his book on the biology of the conditioned reflex. It was decided to investigate this problem directly using the isolated neuron. The conditioned stimulus (CS) was the application of acetylcholine, since it produces the same effect as stimulation of the skin. In the absence of synaptic contact in the isolated neuron, the microelectrode was inserted inside the cell to simulate reinforcement, and acetylcholine as the CS was applied directly on the membrane. The unconditioned stimulus (US), however, was more of a problem. Several types of experiments were conducted. The most effective was the use of a depolarizing current as the US. The acetylcholine was given in combination with spike activity evoked by intracellular electrical stimulation. These data are in good agreement with the results of Feher, who demonstrated neuronal learning using intracellular reinforcement stimulating the axons of the cortical cells. In the present experiment, then, the conditioned stimulus was acetylcholine which when applied produced a depolarization transmitter potential. The US given separately was intracellular stimulation evoking spikes. The pairing of acetylcholine and electrical stimulation of the cell was given with a time interval of 30 ms between the beginning of the CS and US.

The first session of the experiment consisted of 20 pairings of CS and US. By the pairing of acetylcholine and evoked depolarization, it is possible to see the beginning of the transmitter potential, and, overlapping this transmitter potential, there are spikes evoked by electrical stimulation (Fig. 5.5). This pairing was repeated several times, and after 15 min there was a test, giving the CS alone. There was no change in response to acetylcholine from the initial response level. Then, the association was continued, and during these trials, an increase in spikes to ACh was observed. The potential evoked by acetylcholine now reached the threshold necessary for spike generation. After the third association experiment (Fig. 5.5; bottom), test stimuli were given 1 min, 90 min, and 120 min following the end of the experiment to see how long the associative trace is kept in a single neuron. It can be seen that the cell gradually recovers to its initial level, but not until 120 min after the last training trial.

An important characteristic of the conditioned reflex is its selectivity, because it is always possible to say that the observation at one point is not the selective association at that point but a total excitation of the neuron.

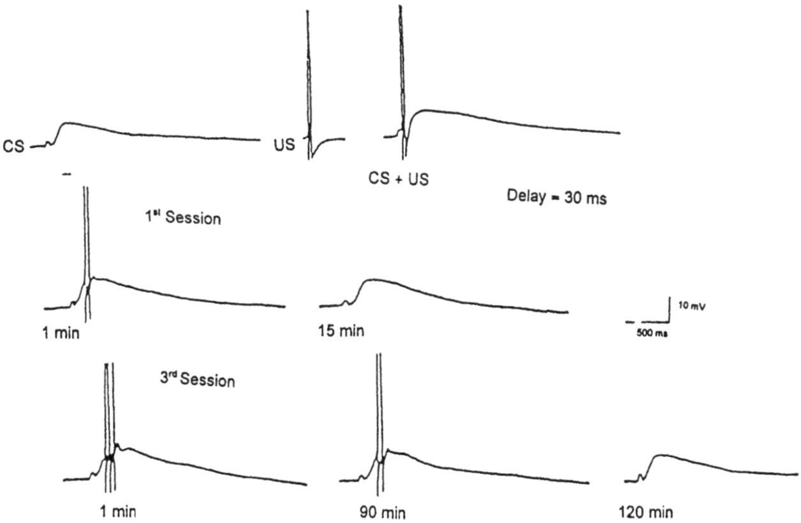

FIG. 5.5. Associative learning in the isolated soma. CS—application of acetylcholine evoking transmitter potentials. US—intracellular stimulation resulting in spike generation. The repeated pairings of acetylcholine and intracellular electric depolarization leads to augmentation of transmitter potentials as training progresses. The effect of conditioning is evident from the fact that the CS alone generates spikes. The effect lasts for about 2 hr.

To ensure that the conditioned process is a very local one, it was necessary to use a differential conditioning procedure that could be used for intracellular recording in the isolated neuron. A differential stimulus (CS^-) was presented by having a second pipette, with acetylcholine put on the other place on the membrane. So, one micropipette with acetylcholine was the CS, and, whenever acetylcholine was applied through this pipette, it was combined with shock. The other pipette was never combined with electrical stimulation. It was only used to test whether the changes were local to one place on the membrane or whether the effects occupied the total membrane, including where the CS^- was located.

Designating a number for each of the two pipettes—acetylcholine (or Ach_1) is a conditioned stimulus CS^+, and acetylcholine (ACh_2) is the CS^-. After 10 pairings of ACh_1 with shock, with a 50 ms interval between the two associated stimuli, an important kind of learning was demonstrated. This was the so-called *postponed learning* that has also been shown on the intact snail. It was shown under the following conditions (Fig. 5.6). During learning, no results were seen. The termination of the learning schedule and of the CS test gradually revealed the enhancement of the conditioned response (CR). This effect increased with repetition. It can be seen that after about 15 min, spikes gradually arose. After 20 min, the response to ACh_2

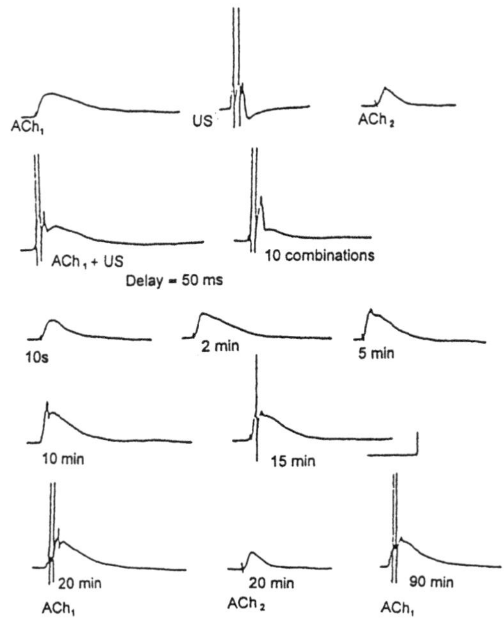

FIG. 5.6. Differential conditioning in the isolated soma. Two acetylcholine micropipettes were used as the CS^+ and CS^-. The spike train evoked intracellularly was used as the US, being paired with conditional acetylcholine (CS^+) only. The augmentation of the transmitter response occurred only at the locus associated with spike discharge. The differential acetylcholine (CS^-) did not change the amplitude of the transmitter potential. The experiments show the participation of single patches of the neuronal membrane in the learning process.

was unchanged, although spikes could be seen to ACh_1. Even after 90 min, ACh_1 was still effective. This type of learning could be very important because of such stable effects observed over long periods (Fig. 5.6).

Again using two loci, one conditional (for the CS^+) and one differential (for CS^-), it is possible to show another effect of gradual learning, and how the effect of acetylcholine is modified because of the pairing with depolarizing current. During an initial conditioning session, a very slow and gradual increase in the response to acetylcholine may be observed (Fig. 5.7). This local facilitation of the response increases in size or the CS finally generates spikes. The learning in this case is a modification of the membrane in such a way that the chemical membrane produces a kind of mobilization of plastic ionic channels around the area of stimulation. This mobilization of channels becomes greater and the transmitter potential reaches the firing level, up to a point where the endogenous opening of voltage-dependent channels is initiated, resulting in the generation of spikes. After rest, at the end of the conditioning phase, a return to the initial stage is seen. The second session of conditioning is a repetition of the first one. It was used to demonstrate the results of secondary conditioning because after one session of an experiment, the CR is more easily elaborated. It can be seen that, during the second session, a local potential is produced and a spike formed much earlier in the stimulus series. Furthermore, the spike is preserved not for just 15 min as in the first session, but for 25 min, and even after 45 min the local

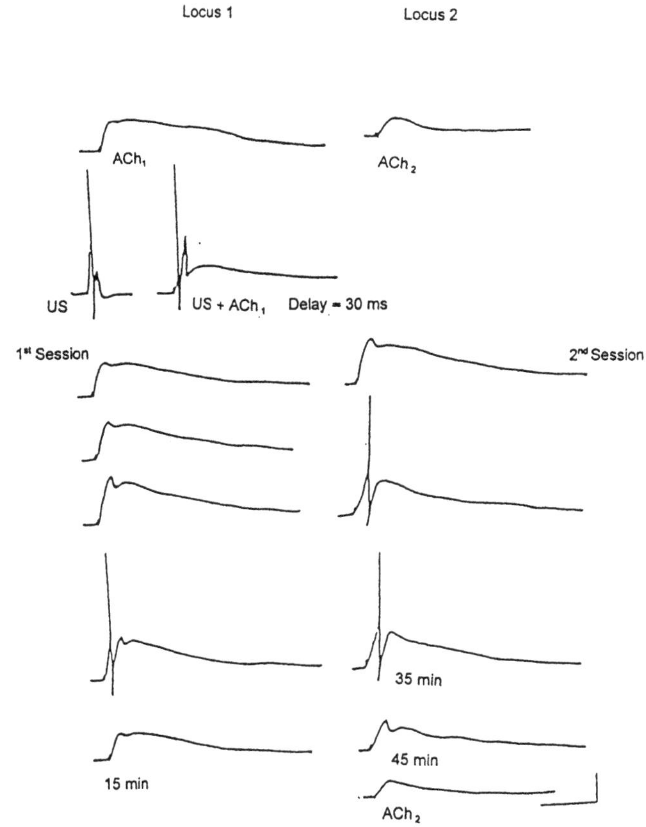

FIG. 5.7. Differential conditioning in the isolated soma. The reinforcement of one membrane activated by acetylcholine results in its long-lasting potentiation, as shown by the faster conditioning in the second session. The other locus, being nonreinforced, remains unchanged.

potential is still present. The response to ACh_2, the CS^-, is practically unchanged (Fig. 5.7).

Several type of CSs and USs were used, acetylcholine as the CS and electric shock as the US. Electric shock has also been used as a CS, plus electric shock through other electrodes as USs. This shock as CS was combined, at some delay interval, with another shock as US given to other places on the membrane. The result of this type of study was a considerable increase in the number of spikes to CS. Later, however, the CS produced only local, aborted responses, but no spikes, that is, spikes were depressed because of this pairing. Only later was there recovery of the response to the CS, but, if this conditioning procedure was again employed, then some diminution of spike generation was again evident. This depression effect is not always the same for different electrodes. In one experiment, four electrodes were used for different stimulation, and it is possible to use each one as the CS or as the US.

A question may arise as to whether the response to the CS can be modified during habituation. It can be demonstrated that the electric pulse produces stable responses to the CS and US. The intracellular electrical stimulation of the cell as CS combined with the stronger electrical stimulation as US may result in not only an inhibitory effect, but also conditioned augmentation of the response to the electrical stimulation used as a CS. Thus, if initially a CS evokes only a local potential without spike generation, so under the influence of reinforcement by electric shook, the local potential increases and becomes a full-sized action potential. The duration of such augmentation may be sometimes as short as 25 min.

Several questions may be asked concerning conditioning in the isolated soma. The first one is the duration of the results obtained by the conditioning procedure. The longest effect is up to several hours. Of course, this is not a very long-lasting memory. The main difficulty for such a long period of observation is to try to keep the neuron with the microelectrode(s) through the night and the next day to attempt the conditioning procedure again. Long-lasting processes are associated with specific ionic channels. The local potential evoked by an electrical depolarizing current given into the cell consists not only of a classical potential dependent on the resistance and capacitance of the membrane, but there is an additional local potential which can gradually increase. There is evidence to suggest that these increases in local potentials and spikes in the soma are due to some plastic Ca-channels that are involved in the process of formation of Ca-spikes.

The mechanism of long-lasting memory is connected with the synthesis of proteins responsible for habituation and learning. Insofar as learning is concerned, more research is needed. But for habituation using the isolated nervous system and long-lasting stimulation of nerves, for producing postsynaptic potentials in the neuron, the distinction between short-term and long-term memory has been tested. The result was very surprising and very interesting. When the synthesis of proteins was blocked, habituation was intact. After 2 days, when all these synaptic contacts were completely habituated, a remarkable result was discovered. The synapses were transformed from habituatable to nonhabituatable. This result was completely unexpected because the expectation of the protein synthesis blockade was elimination of long-lasting memory. Suddenly, the nonhabituatable synapses appeared.

It was fortunate that the receptive fields of command neurons had been studied previously, where two types of synapses could be identified: habituatable and nonhabituatable. The synapses around the pneumostome produced postsynaptic potentials without any change (a sign of habituation). Up to 300 stimulations were given and no habituation took place from this defensive area of the receptive field. The other parts of the receptive field have habituatable synapses. Thus, the idea of two types of synapse, one being habituatable and the other being nonhabituatable, was not a new phenomenon to the Sokolov laboratory. A conclusion was reached concerning the existence of a specific enzyme that regulates the functions of synapses, making these synapses plastic. The plastic property of the synapse is thus a secondary one. After protein synthesis blockade, synapses can still operate, but in a nonmodifiable manner, meaning that they now become nonhabituatable.

The results of this experiment suggested that in the nucleus of the cell, the RNA is transcribed and used for protein synthesis, the proteins of which are brought to the synapse in the form of enzymes to make the synapse plastic. Different proteins have different lifetimes, and the enzymes that make the synapses plastic may have a short life. The specific plasticity enzyme, being relatively short-lived, would disappear during the period of blockade of the protein synthesis. Thus, the time of blockade excluding the synthesis of that protein, would be enough to eliminate the link regulating the plasticity of the synapse, but not its function. Such a conclusion concerning the mechanism of short-term memory and habituation have influenced attempts to understand the role of the nucleus of the nervous cell in memory functioning.

The problem can be set out as follows. How can single neurons make different patches of the membrane operate independently? The main idea here is that the membrane is projected on the genome. To preserve the specificity of the cell, there should be a continuous restoration of proteins that are selective with respect to the locus of the membrane. This means that the proteins of the ionic channels, the proteins of the receptors, and some other proteins should be replaced in accordance with their location on the membrane. How can these different loci on the membrane be controlled by long-lasting memory traces? For selective control of different loci of the membrane, it has been suggested that each locus of the membrane has its representation on the DNA, so that each part of the membrane is controlled in two ways. If stimulation changes a locus of the membrane, the signal in the form of a particular protein reaches the specific locus of the DNA, the code for the plasticity enzyme. The signal protein releases this operon from depression or enhances its function. Now the information, encoded in DNA, is transcribed by RNA from this part of the genome. On the basis of the RNA the plasticity protein is synthesized. The problem is how this protein is transported to a particular locus of the membrane to make its receptor plastic. Now, translocating proteins, which are attached to the basic protein, have been discovered. The translocating proteins specific to different loci of the membrane enable transport of the protein to a particular locus of the membrane. A local activation of the locus of the membrane results in expression of gene coding for specific translocating proteins which produces an informational RNA. Synthesized proteins are selectively transported to particular places on the membrane.

The main hypothesis here is that long-lasting memory is encoded by the participation of the steady expression of a particular portion of DNA in neurons. At the same time, this hypothesis establishes a connection between the differentiation of the cells in ontogenesis and the process of learning in adults. The ontogenetic differentiation of cells is followed by their differentiation through environmental influences, known as an *effect of selective deprivation*. Differentiation of tissues is mainly the result of internal contacts between the cells. The next stage of their differentiation is when the environment, through the receptors and nerve cells, influences the formation of a specific type of neuron. The following stage, a very long one, is the stage of learning. Differentiation of cells, formation of detectors, and learning are all processes characterized by specific features, but they are of the same nature. Thus, the genome not only preserves the stable cell structure, but always changes it dynamically with respect to expression and depression of particular parts of DNA in accordance with demands. The goal of the study of learning, then, is to understand these intracellular control processes evoked in the cell by external events through intracellular informational channels.

CONCLUDING COMMENTS

The main task of the study was to isolate postsynaptic events in the process of habituation and learning. According to these ideas, Ca-channels were studied using the same procedure of conditioning in the completely isolated cell. The other approach is to study identifiable synapses. This approach was concerned with finding an identified sensory neuron and a command neuron. To identify the synapse between these two cells, two different dyes were injected into these two neuron types. The study of the properties of the synapse at different stages of the process of habituation and learning is a key problem. Using isolated neurons and identifiable synapses as the main objects of study means a shift towards the genetic machinery of learning. Using this knowledge, one can move to a reasonable explanation of behavior at a molecular level.

The main logic of the research was as follows. After a selective habituation at the level of macroresponses, when searching for habituation of the cells in the hippocampus, it was found that some cells can reproduce a selective habituation and dishabituation which simulates the responsiveness of the macrocomponents of the OR. How is this possible? It was concluded that external events are coded by detectors, and the detectors are finally represented in the cell as synapses. The array of detectors constitutes a matrix of synapses. It implies a membrane with many synapses, some of which were blocked–if signals were sent through these channels, there was no response; if signals were sent through other channels, a response is evoked. How can this be tested? It was necessary to investigate the membrane for such a study. Snail neurons were used because they have giant receptive fields and it is possible to use intracellular recording. The same basic rules of habituation as for hippocampal cells were found. This means the following sequence: external event, detector, synaptic contact. The difficulty was in knowing how to differentiate the processes at presynaptic and postsynaptic membrane. The best way found was the removal of the neuron from the nervous system and its study in isolation. This has been done in the current research, but instead of synapses there were only postsynaptic receptors. Applying a transmitter substance to the membrane of an isolated neuron, a selective effect of habituation was achieved.

If all these neurons are depressed, does it mean that is not possible to produce dishabituation? In the exploration of the interaction of habituation and dishabituation, it is possible to find support for the dual-process theory of Thompson (1980). In the process of habituation, a signal is sent repeatedly and the response to it is diminished. In order to examine how dishabituation operates here, the entire scheme should be considered. In order that dishabituation can occur, a stimulus should be given, not in the area that was habituated, and this becomes represented by a particular detector. The detectors involved in response to a novel stimulus send different contacts to novelty neurons and some of these are directed to modulating neurons. The modulating neuron ends with its serotonin synapses on the synapses of the command neuron. Habituation occurs due to the closure of Ca-channels because if there is repeated stimulation, the number of Ca-channels operating decreases, Ca^{++} is not entering the presynaptic terminal and so the transmitter is not released, and does not influence the postsynaptic membrane. The modulating neuron produces serotonin, which influences, through several steps, the responsive state of the Ca-channels. The number of responding Ca-channels is increased under the influence of the modulating neuron. This increase of Ca-channels increases the output of the transmitter. In this respect, the dual-process theory of Thompson is supported because for dishabituation there is a specific loop. By stimulating the skin, the sensory neurons also send signals to the modulating neuron. In the process of habituation, the stimulus produces no responses of command neurons and eliminates the mechanism of dishabituation by habituation of the modulating neuron. To produce dishabituation, the stimulus intensity should be increased or the detectors in the other sensory area that stimulate modulating neurons producing a wide effect of synaptic enhancement should be stimulated. In general, enhanced synapses are where the Ca-channels are closed. This is a very reasonable assumption because the total number of channels is limited. If a neuron has a very great number of operating Ca-channels, the modulating neuron will not add anything. However, if the level of operating channels is low, then the modulating neuron will substantially increase the number of Ca-channels, and enhance the sensitivity of synapses that were previously inactivated in the process of habituation.

The other explanation of the dishabituation is applicable for the isolated neuron. The habituation of the pacemaker activity to intracellular electrical stimulation can also demonstrate dishabituation after a change in stimulation to a stronger or even to a weaker stimulus. Putting this into the context of the inactivation of plastic Ca^{++} channels, the dishabituation means that new plastic channels are recruited by a modified stimulation. The increase in the amplitude of the transmitter potential due to combination with intracellular stimulation again suggests the transformation of some of the sleepy receptors into a responsive form.

CHAPTER

6

A Microlevel Analysis of the Orienting Response: Extracellular Recording From Detectors and Novelty-Dependent Neurons

This chapter covers the following issues:

1. In search of habituatable neurons.
2. Intensity detectors.
3. Time detectors.
4. Color detectors.
5. Complex detectors (gnostic units).
6. Neurons with stable responses.
7. Partial response habituation.
8. Novelty detectors: habituation and mismatch.
9. Sameness detectors: habituation and match.
10. Selective self-adjustable filtering with a single neuron.
11. Multidimensional filters in a single neuron.
12. Neuronal model of the stimulus as a matrix of modified synapses.

This chapter examines the orienting response (OR) from the standpoint of extracellular recording using the same procedures that were used in human subjects. The first part of this chapter is entitled "In search of habituatable neurons." Why was this study initiated? This research was started when it was decided to research what was meant by habituation, the processing of the OR, and precisely the factors that trigger the OR. The simplest stimulation was selected–a light flash and an auditory click, as the main purpose of this study was to discover neurons that show a regular decrement in their response. The first hypothesis concerning the organization of the OR was based on our assumption that the plastic neurons are located mainly at the neocortical level. Moving among structures in the rabbit brain, the visual cortex, auditory cortex, and motor cortex have been examined. The lateral and medial geniculate bodies have also been studied and in these areas, hours have been spent stimulating single neurons, keeping these neurons on the tip of a tungsten microelectrode, but neurons with stable responses were mainly found.

Using these simple stimuli, the variables that can initially be examined in stable neurons were intensity and time parameters. Very excitingly, feature detectors have been found among the stable neurons. These neurons may be called *intensity-selective*; each neuron was adjusted to respond to a particular range of intensities. Figure 6.1a shows the number of spikes triggered by the light flash plotted against the log of the light intensity: The characteristic look of a selective filter can be seen. The result of this experiment was that the number of spikes generated by the neuron initially increased as stimulus intensity was increased, but following further increases in intensity, the number of these spikes gradually fell to zero. Other neurons were selective at different intensity intervals. So, it is possible to construct from all the data a set of stable filters each of which is selectively tuned to a particular stimulus intensity. If the intensity of the stimulus is changed, the maximum of excitation will move along this array of intensity detectors. This was the first indication that the code of signals in the central nervous system is a channel-dependent code or labeled line principle. This means that, for each level of intensity, there exists in the cortex a specific line with maximum response to a particular intensity.

At the same time, no such intensity-selective neurons were found at the level of the lateral geniculate body. Instead, neurons were found there that have the same characteristics as those which were described very well by Jung, the neurophysiologist and psychophysicist, who identified so-called B- and D-neurons (brightness and darkness neurons). With the increase in stimulus intensity, the B-neurons gradually increase the number of spikes per unit time, being saturated by the most intense lights (see Fig. 6.1b). The D-neurons have the opposite characteristics with respect to the B-neurons. If the light intensity is absent or its intensity is very small, the neuron is most active, while as the stimulus intensity is increased, so the number of spikes gradually diminishes until they are completely abolished (Fig. 6.1c). These two populations of neurons interact in the selective coding of intensity information (Fig. 6.1d).

Although at the time it was found, it was thought that the next type of cortical neuron with stable responses was perhaps the most unusual, it was discovered later that such neurons are not rare in the nervous system. These stable neurons are selective to time, meaning that the magnitude of

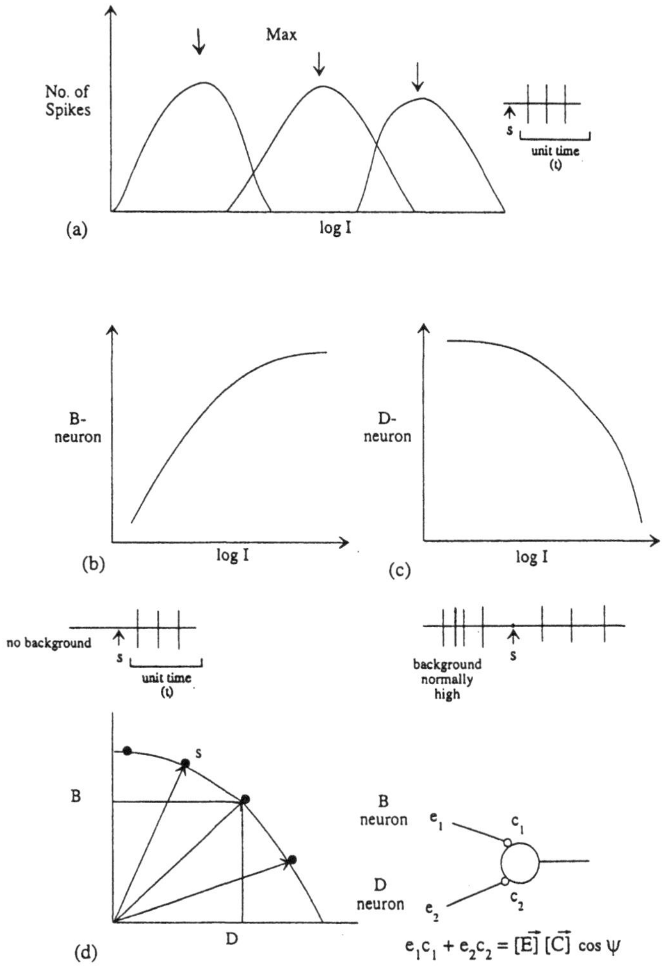

FIG. 6.1. Detectors for light intensity. (a) The spike characteristics of neurons selective with respect to intensity level. The particular intensity on log(I) scale (arrowed) results in a maximal response in a neuron labeled *max*. (b) Measuring the number of spikes during unit time, the characteristics of the intensity detectors may be plotted. One type of intensity coding neuron is characterized by a gradual increase in firing with an increase in light intensity (B-neuron). (c) The other type (D-neuron) show a gradually diminishing firing rate as intensity increases. (d) The formal presentation of this intensity coding analyzer may be represented by a set of detectors each realizing the scalar product of the vector of excitation consisting of excitations of B- and D-neurons, and the vector of synaptic coefficients. The response of the detector D_j is given.

$$D_j = e_1c_1 + e_2c_2,$$

where e_1 and e_2 are components of the excitation vector, and c_1 and c_2 are coefficients of synaptic efficiency. The signal producing an excitation vector results in a selective maximal response in a detector having collinear synaptic contacts directly proportional to the coming excitations. The excitation vector rotates with the increase of light intensity.

the interval between two signals is transformed into an activation of a specific neuron. This is suggestive of a channel-dependent code or labelled-line code. In other words, for a specific interval between light flashes, there is a specific neuron representing it. The characteristics of such neurons can be represented in the following scheme (Fig. 6.2a). On the horizontal axis is time, and on the vertical axis is the number of spikes generated in experiments, when the time intervals between stimuli are fixed from 1 s up to 30 s. Of course, the best statistics were collected in the area of 3 to 5 s. One neuron responded well to stimulus intervals of 2 sec, but if the interval between light flashes increases, the response diminishes. The other neurons are selectively tuned to longer intervals. Thus, it is possible to represent time intervals as a set of selectively tuned neurons. If the time interval between signals is changed, then the maximum excitation is shifted along the array of detectors. Again, in the lateral geniculate body, gradual time-dependent neurons have been found. One type of neuron gradually decreases firing when the interval between stimuli is increased (Fig. 6.2b). The other type of

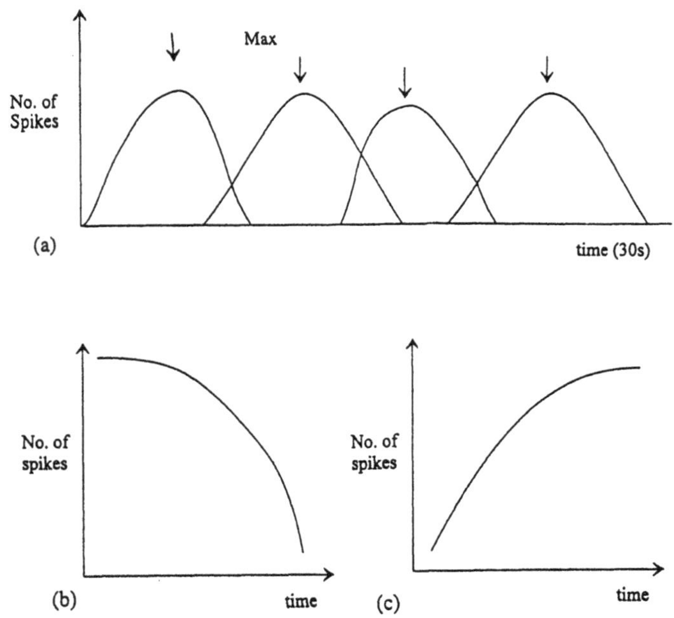

FIG. 6.2. Detectors for time. The selective characteristics of time detectors generating in unit time a specific number of spikes. Time intervals between stimuli range between 1 s and 30 s. Two types of time-coding neurons are characterized by rising (6.2b) and falling (6.2c) curves, respectively. The mechanism of time coding is similar to that of intensity. Each time interval is transformed into maximal excitation of one time-detector according to the labeled line or channel-dependent code principle.

time-dependent neuron increases firing as the interval between stimuli in increased (Fig. 6.2c).

It might be queried whether this is an exceptional case, or whether there are other specific time-coding neurons. The best example was presented in Suga's experiments (Suga, 1965) which were part of a study of time perception of bats in their use of the ultrasonic range. In a specific acoustic area of the cortex of the bats there are neurons which measure the time intervals between the emission of the ultrasonic burst and the reception of the echo of this sound burst from the target. A set of neurons exists which are selectively tuned to different time intervals. These intervals are not within the time range that were found in the studies in the Sokolov laboratory (Sokolov, 1975). They are adjusted to the very small time scale that is related to the distances between the bat and the insects that are the usual targets for this animal.

During these experiments, it was found that light flashes and clicks are very limited means for extracting information about a neuron's specificity. The introduction of colour as an additional parameter for use in light stimulation tests allows an expansion of ideas. In the rabbit, colour selective units and gradual color-coding neurons have been found. Gradual neurons are very well known in the visual system, associated with so-called opponent cells. But selective color detectors were discovered as a specific set because the search was specifically in the visual cortex. Later, the study of color detectors was carried out with very great precision by Zeki (1990). He showed the existence of a collection of color-coding neurons, tuned selectively to particular wavelengths in V4 of the monkey neocortex. This work has been supported by Kumatsu, Ideura, Kaji, and Yamanc (1992). Each color detector is selectively tuned to a particular band of wavelengths in the visible spectrum. Using a limited set of signals composed of light flashes and clicks, a very important type of neuron, that is, neurons selectively tuned to complexes have been discovered. The experiment used animals, but simulates the effect in human subjects, and was carried out in the following way. Light and sound were presented at the same time, with this combination being repeated several times. This combination produces responses in some neurons of the animal, but if a single stimulus was presented, then no response could be recorded. Such neurons are of great value for extracting information about complexes composed of different modalities.

Konorski (1948) in Poland introduced the concept of a gnostic unit. The reality of this concept was treated initially with extreme scepticism. But in the 1980s, Grusser from the Max Planck Institute and Rolls (1989) at Oxford University found a collection of neurons in the inferotemporal cortex that were selectively tuned to a particular combination of features of the face. Only a particular set of features of the face were effective in generating a response from this gnostic neuron; if the same signals were presented on the screen in random order, then there was no response from the neuron. However, these gnostic neurons also belonged to the category of stable neurons, and did not therefore display any habituation.

Summarizing the data, it can be seen that there is a certain population of stable neurons having responses that are not modified at all by repeated presentations of stimuli. At the same time, these neurons extract information from different aspects of the stimulus. There is a very wide range of applicability of these mechanisms for extraction of information, starting from simple features up to a combination of features. The appropriate term for neurons extracting elementary features is *detectors*, or *feature extractors* and for neurons that extract complex combinations of features, the term *gnostic unit* is adequate. All the observations so far, however, have been in the range of stable units and there is not yet any evidence of real plastic modifications.

During these experiments, however, some observations on so-called partial habituation were made. If light or sound is presented, a specific response may be observed which can consist of several phases of nerve impulses. These responses can be divided into two parts—the early one and the latter one (see Fig. 6.3a). What can be seen in such a response pattern? During repeated stimulus presentation, some components, mainly early components of the response, are stable, but some late spikes habituated. This is the partial habituation effect (Fig. 6.3b). If any novelty is introduced into the situation, then there is recovery of the initially habituated part of the response (Fig. 6.3c). The conclusion may be drawn that there is a widespread nonspecific activation, which can interact with specific responses of detectors, activating and increasing their responses. If a standard habituation curve is constructed, plotting the number of spikes against the trial number of a repeated stimulus, then there is a certain asymptotic level of response below which the curve does not extend (Fig. 6.3d). This is because of the presence in the pattern of the response of the stable component that does not habituate over repeated stimulus presentations.

The search for habituatable neurons was moved to the hippocampus. The main contribution to this research came from Vinogradova (1975, 1976) who worked in the Sokolov laboratory and carried out a number of experiments in this area. The shift to the hippocampus was crucial because it was possible to see for the first time neurons there that really simulated the basic properties of the OR seen at the macrolevel.

In terms of the research into habituatable neurons, it should first be noted that hippocampal neurons generate a series of spikes to any novel stimulus (Fig. 6.3e). If these neurons are stimulated several times, the response greatly diminishes (Fig. 6.3f), leaving only a background frequency of spike generation on the recording. In practice, this means a complete ha-

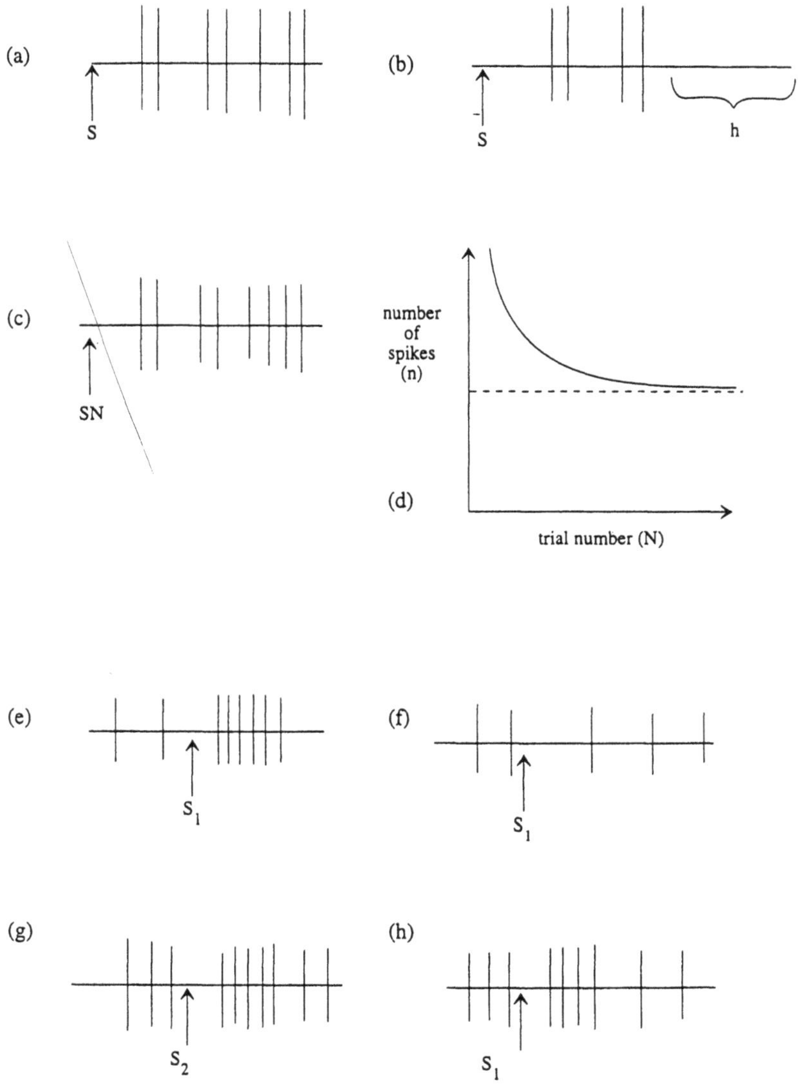

FIG. 6.3. Partial habituation of spike discharge and novelty neurons. (a & b) The partial habituation results in elimination of the plastic (later) part of spike discharge. The stable component remains unchanged. (c) The dishabituation results in a recovery of total discharge. (d) On the graph, the number of spikes n diminishes with trial number N, reaching a constant asymptotic level. (e, f, g, h) Novelty neurons (activating type of plastic neuron) habituate with repeated presentation of stimulus S1. The novel stimulus S2 results in an activation during its presentation and dishabituation of the response to stimulus S1. h = habituation, SN = novel stimulus.

bituation of the response. This was the characteristic feature of the first type of neuron, having an excitatory pattern of spikes generated by stimulus presentation. This type of neuron has been termed *A-neuron*, because they were activated by the stimulus. Because only novelty was a triggering factor for these neurons, they have been called *novelty neurons*. However, another type of neuron was also found. This type of hippocampal neuron was characterized by the opposite response—where stimulus presentation led to the inhibition or elimination of spikes. If the stimulus was repeated several times, this inhibition response disappeared, due to habituation of the inhibitory response that led to the reappearance of the spikes from the cell during stimulation.

After several presentations, therefore, the same stimulus resulted in less and less inhibition. If the stimulus is changed, the inhibitory response may again be seen. Novel stimuli not only result in the recovery of the inhibitory response, but also produce dishabituation, the restoration of the inhibitory response to a habituated stimulus. This means that a novel stimulus not only evokes inhibition of spikes to that new stimulus, but also results in a dishabituation of inhibition so that the old stimulus again generates spikes (Figs. 6.3g and 6.3h for A-neurons).

So, this type of neuron was characterized by responses in the form of inhibition of spikes. This inhibition disappeared in a parallel way as did the excitation in A-neurons. These neurons have been labeled *T-neurons* from the Russian word for inhibition, but are termed *sameness neurons* due to their function. The spiking of the novelty neurons reflect the fact that the stimulus is novel with respect to the surroundings of the organism, but the T-neuron produces spikes only if the stimulus is familiar. Later in this research, Vinogradova (1976) found that axons of these two systems extend to two different structures in the midbrain. Novelty neurons stimulate the reticular activating system, whereas sameness neurons are fed to the synchronizing system. If the stimulus is repeatedly presented, not only does habituation of the OR take place, but also a gradual initiation of activity in the synchronization system, which, according to Moruzzi, induces sleep. Thus, different types of hippocampal neurons are differentially related to activating and inactivating systems.

The most important feature of hippocampal neurons is that they form self-adjusting filters, which have already been discussed at the macrolevel based on recordings of the total response of the organism. Now, it is possible to see that the same filters are present in these single neurons. Such filters can be built in parallel in an array of neurons of the CA3 field of the hippocampus. The question is, how exactly may these filters be identified and represented? The relevant experiments on hippocampal neurons simulated the OR studies. Using rabbits, a particular frequency of standard stimulus was presented. After the response to this standard stimulus had habituated, a test stimulus of a different frequency was presented. The magnitude of responses increased as the difference between the repeated standard and test stimuli increased. A filter selective to a particular standard stimulus frequency may be observed in one neuron. After a rest, it was possible to test other standard stimulus frequencies; it was demonstrated that the same neuron can retune to a new frequency and can organize a filter to another frequency. This means that an enormous number of different frequency-selective channels are converging on a single neuron. This is in accordance with the data showing very extensive dendrites of hippocampal neurons receiving signals from the neocortex. Such a mechanism of adjustable selective filtering exists in all hippocampal neurons. These novelty neurons, then, can generate, depending on the destination of their output fibres, different types of responses, constituting OR components.

The sameness neurons have completely the opposite function (Fig. 6.4a–6.4d). If their inhibitory responses are extinguished, a maximal spiking would be reached. Spikes generated by sameness neurons during habituation produce inhibition distributed via a synchronizing system to different brain areas. Figure 6.4e illustrates the filter characteristics of the novelty and sameness neurons.

A comparison made between the characteristics of detectors, selective filters of the OR and self-adjustable filters in hippocampal neurons suggest that there is a common principle for information processing in the brain. The incoming signals pass through arrays of detectors and each detector extracts some particular information from the stimulus. The information contained within the stimulus is transformed into excitations along a number of parallel labeled lines. Each labeled line represents a particular feature or a particular magnitude of this feature. This enormous number of detectors converges in a parallel manner onto many hippocampal neurons. Each hippocampal neuron in the CA3 area collects inputs from all the detectors, and each detector carrying external input is represented on the hippocampal neuron by a single synapse. Each detector is transformed at the level of the hippocampal neuron into the activity of a single synapse. If the animal is presented with a particular stimulus, it is represented by an array of detectors. These detectors are activated and change their synaptic contacts with the hippocampal neurons.

This modification of synapses is the mechanism behind the selective habituation of the OR. The filters observed using behavioral criteria or EEG recording coincide with the filters obtained from hippocampal neuron studies. At the same time, each self-adjustable filter at the macrolevel or at the hippocampal neuron level match one of the detector filters. The detector filters are stable however, and can continuously extract information. The filters in hippocampal neurons are plastic and their purpose is to adjust the organism appropriately to its environment by emphasizing new events and neglecting familiar stimuli.

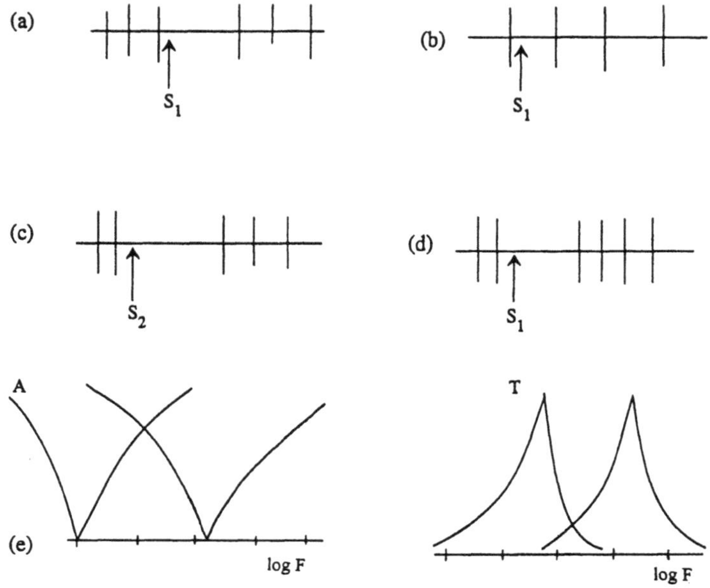

FIG. 6.4. The filter characteristics of novelty and sameness neurons. The initial presentation of stimulus S_1 results in an increase of spikes in the novelty neurons and (a) inhibition of spikes in the sameness neuron. After several trials, the increase of spikes in the novelty neurons and the (b) inhibition in the sameness neurons disappear. The firing in the sameness neuron indicates that the stimulus is a familiar one. A novel stimulus S_2 evokes (c) inhibition in the sameness neuron and excitation in the novelty neuron and additionally (d) a dishabituation effect with respect to the previous stimulus S_1 is evident. (e) The responses of A-neurons selectively habituated are represented as selective adaptive band-rejection filters. The sameness or T-neurons represent adaptive band-pass filters. In one of the neurons, several different filters can be set up at different times.

The conclusion that external events are represented at the level of hippocampal neurons by a matrix of potentiated synapses is very important. Transformed synapses representing the external event constitute a neuronal model of the stimulus. This term can be used because they exactly match the external stimulation. After studying different neuronal aspects of the OR in the rabbit, there has been further research to study this problem at the level of a single neuron. Molluscs have been studied to show that different channels represented by detectors can really be identified as synaptic processes in the single neuron. This was the logic which forced the movement from behavioral experiments and to extracellular and intracellular recording, in order to find such simple events that can explain the process of selective habituation and formation of the representation of external events in the nervous system in the form of a neuronal model.

The literature supports this scheme very well. At the time when these experiments were done, there was no real evidence concerning time detectors, intensity detectors, or the relationships between detectors and novelty neurons. After discussion of the event-related potential studies, this book returns to the issue of integrating the results within the context of information processing in the complete system. It will examine, as an example, color vision, which, because of the initial experiments in our laboratory on the OR, was transformed into a field of research in its own right.

One of the main questions is where exactly does habituation occur—at the receptor sites or in presynaptic structures? Some evidence suggests that cells become habituated by a mechanism that involves a very selective inhibition of receptor sites. In the parietal ganglion of the snail, defensive command neurons trigger the closure of the pneumostome. The receptive field of this neuron occupies the total surface of the skin of the organism, even its internal organs. By touching a point of the skin and measuring synaptic responses in this neuron, one can see habituation. Habituation has shown that each point on the skin is represented by a specific line; if the skin is stimulated at a particular location, then habituation occurs in the neuron. If, however, if a point of stimulation is moved 1 mm to the side of this point is stimulated, then a response is evoked again. This suggests a parallel input from all the skin points where selective habituation takes place. Yet, there is still a question about the role of the presynaptic and postsynaptic mechanism that concerns the amount of transmitter released from the presynaptic terminal—is it really reduced?

There is now data concerning the role of postsynaptic events, including not only the modification of receptors, but in a cascade of secondary messengers. The secondary messenger in the postsynaptic cell can amplify or decrease the response in a very specific way by phosphorylation and dephosphorylation of proteins constituting the receptors and ionic channels. Not only do receptors participate in these events, but also a number of ionic channels can be responsible for postsynaptic modifications. That is the reason why the study of the local plasticity of the neuronal membrane is so important to our research. It seemed that some ionic channels are plastic and participate in habituation. There is modification of single patches on the membrane that has a good correspondence with the selective processes of the neuron. The neuron does not habituate as a whole, but single patches on the membrane are modified.

Thus, by the means of selective detectors a synaptic contact on the hippocampal neuron represents an external event. The cells that are tuned to certain interstimulus intervals are time-selective detectors. Such time-tuned neurons can explain the learning function and mismatch negativity (MMN). MMN can be triggered by cells selective to time intervals. They can trigger the MMN with the same mechanism used by other detectors. If presented with signals of the same interval and then suddenly the interval is made short, then in addition to the obligatory response a mismatch of signals arising from the change of time detectors would be expected.

The question could be raised as to how these cells detect the change in time? To explain how time is transformed into the excitation of a labeled line, one should touch on the scheme of information processing in general. It is possible to demonstrate it by reference to color vision, and the main idea is very simple. The main assumption is that in the nervous system signals are coded not by the scalar magnitude of this excitation, but by excitation vectors. Thus, intensity coding is connected to the B- and D-neurons. If the stimulus is presented, the combination of excitation of the B- and D-neurons arises. Looking at their characteristics, the B- and D-neurons are very close to sine and cosine functions, so that the stimulus of particular intensity produces an excitation vector.

Depending on the contribution of B- and D-neurons, the vector will change the orientation. The detectors have a number of synapses that correspond with the number of excitations; in this case, each detector receives two excitations. The detectors have a different coefficient of synaptic contacts. These produce a summation of the product of excitation and synaptic contact. This summation is a scalar product of two vectors, a vector of excitation and a vector of synaptic contacts of this particular detector neuron. If the stimulus is changed, the combination of excitations is altered. The vector has changed its orientation. When the excitation vector is collinear with the vector of synaptic contacts in a particular detector, the response reaches maximum. For each stimulus, there is an excitation vector. In this way, the intensity results in a selective excitation of a single detector. This scheme can be applied to different features. A similar structure is suggested for time detectors. The gradual time-dependent neurons generate a time-dependent excitation vector that results in an excitation of time-selective detectors.

Modifications of activity in the hippocampus may last days and weeks. Anderson has studied selective long-lasting potentiation in the hippocampus. This effect is very selective to particular synapses and is due to the presence of the postsynaptic mechanism. But the hippocampus is not a specific place for long-term memory record. Long term memory neurons were found by Miyashita (1988) in the antero-temporal area. The role of the hippocampus is related to a memory mechanism for the OR.

CHAPTER

7

Event-Related Potentials and the Orienting Response

This chapter covers the following issues:

1. The glia-neuronal hypothesis of event-related potentials.
2. Detector participation in evoked potentials.
3. Reconstruction of perceptual space using predetector–glia interaction.
4. Reconstruction of color space using the electroretinogram of the frog.
5. Detector map and selective depression of evoked potentials.
6. Selective adaptation and modulating neuron participation in mismatch negativity.
7. Processing negativity in selective detector activation.
8. Expectancy wave and orienting response anticipation.
9. Readiness and motor potentials in the orienting response as a targeting reaction.
10. The orienting response neuronal structure and event-related potentials.

The main task of this chapter is to find a correlation between the transfer of information at the neuronal level and event-related potentials (ERPs) which are recorded during this process of information transfer. The specific task to be accomplished here is to suggest some approach to ERPs that can be useful in explaining the correlation between these electrical events and neuronal responses as related to the orienting response (OR). There are two main hypotheses about ERPs. One refers mainly to the problem of postsynaptic potentials. The ERP is regarded as a result of summation of excitatory postsynaptic potentials and inhibitory postsynaptic potentials. However, there is another theory of generation of ERPs, which is related to neuronal-glial interaction. This hypothesis was used mainly with respect to steady potentials in the brain, and to expectancy waves. An analysis of short-lasting evoked potentials (EPs) is less evident in this approach, and this is the main obstacle in the way of analyzing the correlations between the neuronal and ERP activity. How can the relationship between glial cells, neurons, and ERPs be conceptualized? Schematically, this can be represented in the following way (Figs. 7.1a and 7.1b).

Figures 7.1a and 7.1b show the results of experiments which were done by Somjen (see Somjen, 1972) in fibers and Schwann cells. The same results were obtained for the central nervous system pathways for oligodendroglia. It is possible to show for these cases a difference between nerve fibers with fast action potentials and glia cells with gradual responses. During the generation of action potentials, there is often a hypopolarization that is due to outflow of potassium ions into the surrounding tissue. The glial cells are

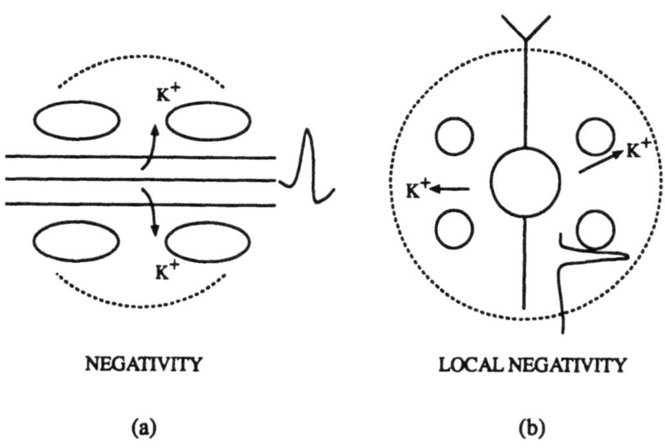

FIG. 7.1. Glial-neuronal interaction in ERP generation. (a) The spikes transmitted through nerve fibers represent a sequence of inward (sodium) and outward (potassium) currents. The Schwann cells or oligodendroglia around fibers respond to an increase of potassium with local depolarization fulfilling the role of amplification and integration of spike signals. The potassium outflow by traveling spikes via axons (a) and excitation of central neurons. (b) The potassium depolarizes the glial calls, Schwann or oligodendrocytes, and astrocytes in the nerves and brain, respectively. The glial summated slow potential overlaps with the spike discharge and can be recorded from the surface of the nerve. The glial potential moves along the nerve with retardation dependent on the time constant of the glial response to potassium. K^+ = potassium ion.

very sensitive to the concentration of potassium such that an increase in the potassium level results in depolarization of the cells. This results in a local source of depolarization that moves along as the transmission of nerve impulses due to the outflow of potassium ions. How can this approach be applied to the central nervous system?

The neuron generates spikes during which the surrounding neuroglial cells are depolarized by the outflow of potassium ions from the neuron. This neuron can be a detector or another cell. In any case, a stationary local negativity is set up around the neuron being stimulated (Fig. 7.1b). How can the very well-known N100 vertex potential be interpreted in this light? The negativity of N100 can be regarded as a depolarizing neuroglial response to the generation of spikes in phasic detectors (specific nonhabituatable part of N100) followed by spikes evoked by nonspecific activation that constitutes the habituatable part of N100. To understand the N100 following positivity, it is necessary to study lateral inhibition that was discovered by Hartline (1949) in the eye of Limulus. It was shown that excentric cells are combined together through inhibitory synapses using gamma-aminobutyric acid as the transmitter. Lateral inhibition is greater with stronger excitation and closer distance between excentric cells (Fig. 7.2a).

The theory of lateral inhibition can be applied to different sets of detectors, because the detectors of many species have shown much more selective responses than can be predicted from their direct stimulation. It is not difficult to imagine that detectors of a detector map are linked via inhibitory connections. The detector map can be understood topologically only with respect to connection between detectors. If this detector map is presented with stimulation in such a way that one of the detectors is maximally excited, then the process can be described in the following way (Fig. 7.2b). Initially, the detectors respond according to their tuning to the stimulus. This detector mobilization produces the ascending limb of the response. The greater the excitation of several detectors, the greater is the lateral inhibition, which then produces a descending limb of evoked potentials followed by positivity. There is some overshoot, due to overregulation produced by lateral inhibition. Thus, spiking results in an increase of K^+ producing negativity. The inhibition of spikes decreases K^+ and leads to positivity. From this standpoint, the smooth modifications of EPs can be explained according to the participation of glial cells in such a way that each negative amplitude at a particular point on the time scale reflects the response activity of a number of spiking neurons. The number of excited detectors and spike density determines the output of potassium and, thus, the amplitude of local depolarization.

If this scheme is carefully considered, it is possible to find a new application of this approach. In the concept of a system of detectors, there are so-called predetectors that are stimulated by receptors. The excitation vector

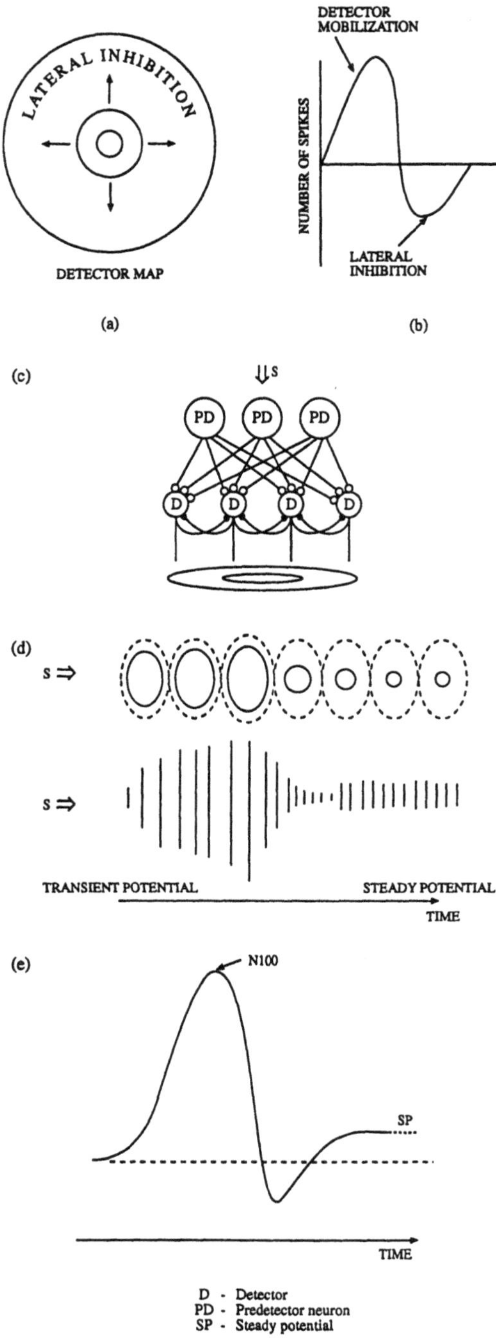

FIG. 7.2. The participation of detectors in ERP generation. (a) Lateral inhibition on a detector map. The lateral inhibition between detectors results in a negative feedback decreasing spiking around the excitation maximum. (b) The time-dependent rise of lateral inhibition results in a time-selective peak of detector activity. (c) This behavior of the response pattern of the detector map depends on inhibitory links between detectors decreasing with the increase of respective distances. (d & e) The excitation area of spiking detectors on the detector map is gradually diminished up to a particular magnitude. This corresponds with transient and steady potentials related to N100 and steady potential shift, respectively.

from these predetectors influences, in a parallel way, the detectors (Fig. 7.2c). The detectors are connected with each other by inhibitory synapses. When the stimulus begins, the detector map produces a rather widespread excitation of the detectors. Of course, they are excited to a different degree, but there is still widespread excitation. Due to lateral inhibition, this area of excitation is reduced and finally only specifically tuned detectors remain excited, all other detectors are switched off. This can be shown in the following way. From the stimulus onset, the excited detectors respond during the full duration of the stimulus and define the so-called steady potentials, which follow the N100 negative component and depend upon specific features of the stimulus (Fig. 7.2d). The N100, on the other hand, is due to the process of transient responses to stimulation where lateral inhibition is involved. The steady potential is a long-lasting steady activation of specific detectors during all periods of stimulation.

This can also be shown as a modification of the detector map (also Fig. 7.2d). From the onset of the stimulus, the detectors are involved in the response and the area of the excited detectors increases. Then, due to lateral inhibition, this area decreases, and is stabilized. This is shown by the descending limb of the N100, and the subsequent steady potentials along the time axis. The same can be also shown as a modification of EP amplitude (also Fig. 7.2d). The stimulus produces an ascending effect of N100 because of the involvement of detectors, and then a descending effect until a steady potential is stabilized (Fig. 7.2e). In this approach, a close correlation between the detectors involved in the response and the shape of the ERP (in this case, an EP) can be found. Many new areas of study could follow from this line of reasoning.

When several independent fibers or neurons are stimulated, it is possible to see a certain distribution of spike activity and, accordingly, a specific pattern of depolarization of glial cells (Fig. 7.3). If the stimulus is changed, the distribution of spikes changes and, accordingly, the shape of the glial potential changes. This can produce the following result. A stimulus that is presented produces a response—however, if this stimulus is changed later, there is an additional response because some new channels are involved that were previously not activated. Now, if the stimulus is switched off, there are responses of off-cells, which generate spikes dependent on termination of the stimulus. Consider the change in spike distribution when a switch from one stimulus to another results in a component that is the neuronal equivalent of stimulus change. If the nervous system detects the difference between physical stimuli, it generates this spike response and the neuronal difference between the two stimuli can be regarded as an analog of subjective difference. This neuronal difference is, of course, an objective difference, but it can be treated in such a way. If there are now two different stimuli that are not differentiated by the nervous system, then there

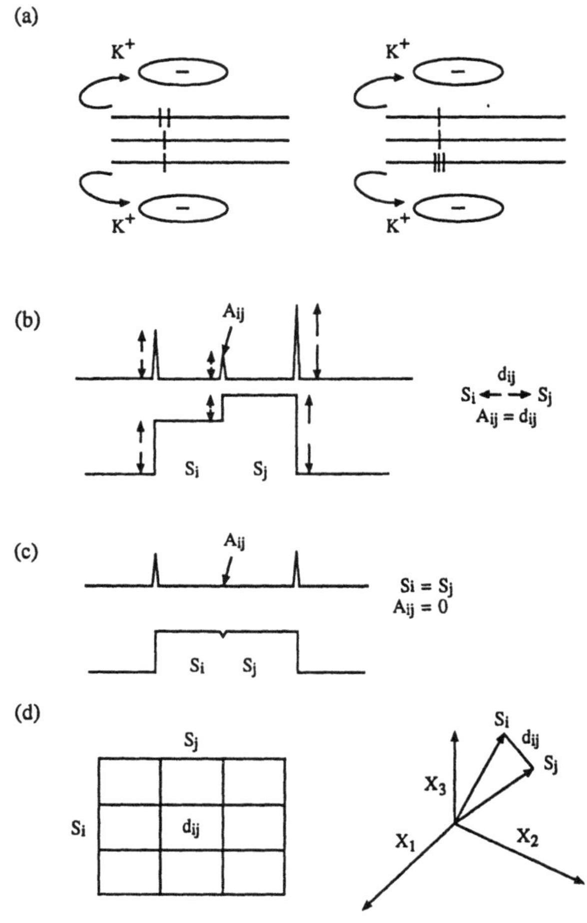

FIG. 7.3. The generation of evoked potentials in response to stimulus change. (a) Due to lateral inhibition, the train of spikes disappears by stimulus prolongation. Through stimulus change, the spikes originate within a different channel producing an evoked potential to change. (b) Two step functions of different amplitude, stimuli S_i and S_j, following each other, produce on-response, response to change and off-response. The amplitude of the response to change is a neuronal measure of the difference between S_i and S_j. (c) The identical step functions evoking on-and-off responses generate no EP to change. (d) Systematic change of S_i and S_j stimuli results in a matrix of neuronal differences (d_{ij}) that can be used to extract information concerning the excitation vectors constituting a geometrical space for representation of signals. A = amplitude, d_{ij} = neuronal differences between S_i and S_j, K^+ = potassium ions, S = stimulus, S_i and S_j = different stimuli, X_n = vectors.

will be no response to the change. Different stimuli can generate responses of equal amplitude, but the response to a transition from one to the other will be generated only if these physically different signals are differentiated by the nervous system's response amplitude to change, which is regarded as the *neuronal difference* between signals.

If such a neuronal difference is an analog of the subjective difference obtained in psychophysical experiments, then these data can be put into a matrix for the construction of an analog of subjective space. The matrix consists of responses to all combinations of signals given in the experiments. Each element of this matrix is the neuronal difference between two signals. This matrix can be treated by the methods of multidimensional scaling described earlier for psychophysical data. It is possible to find the eigenvectors and eigenvalues for this matrix. For example, the matrix can be approximated by three orthogonal axes, in such a way that Euclidean distances closely match the initial neuronal differences. In this way, it is possible to obtain an analog of perceptual space from these neuronal responses. The analysis of responses of detectors to a stimulus change can be substituted by the respective amplitudes of negative peaks of ERPs. If that population of neurons takes place in the evaluation of subjective phenomena one can assume that the subjective space obtained in psychophysical procedures would correspond with the objective analog of perceptual space based on ERPs generated by change of stimulus used in the psychophysical experiments. Thus, in finding a biological object whose neurons are not to generate K^+-dependent depolarization of glial cells one can test this suggested procedure.

Such a study was done in Moscow University in collaboration with Näätänen (Zimachev, Shekhter, Sokolov, Izmailov, Näätänen, & Nyman, 1991; see also Näätänen, 1992). This was a study of color vision in the frog. The frog ERG consists of at least two important waves—the b-wave at the beginning and the d-wave at the end of the light stimulus (Fig. 7.4). These waves result from the potassium outflow from bipolar cells in the retina and the action of the potassium of glial Müller cells. The latter are located in the retina, dividing the retina into small columns. If the retinal cells are stimulated, Müller cells are depolarized by outflow of potassium. This has been shown in several experiments, and this has been used for color vision testing in the frog.

The method of triads was used, the three-stimuli paradigm where at the beginning and end of the stimulus series, the standard stimuli are the same, and the test stimuli in the middle can be changed, either made stronger or weaker. In the case of a red–blue–red triad, a b-wave is generated at the beginning, and the d-wave at the offset of the triad. Increasing the test stimulus intensity generates a b-wave, and a decrease in intensity results in a d-wave. The intensity of the blue test color can be increased or decreased

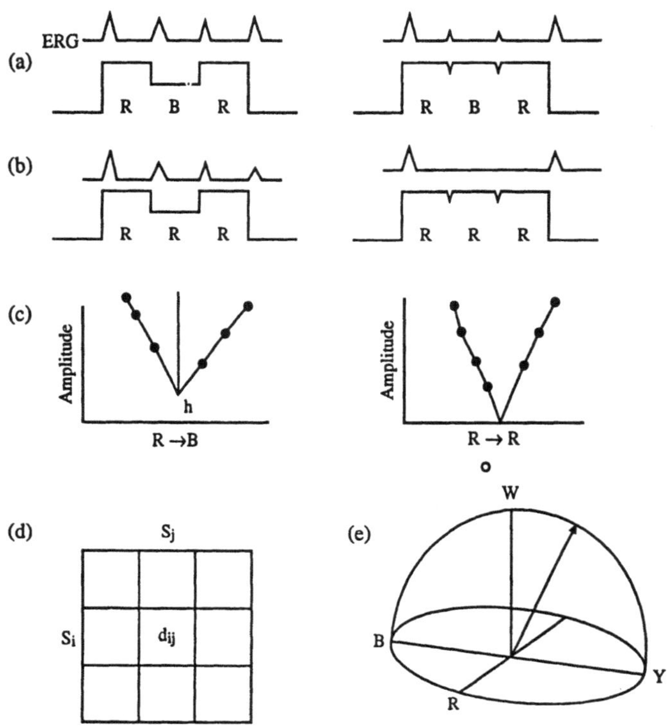

FIG. 7.4. The responses of ERG of the frog as a basis for the construction of the frog's color space. (a) The triad of colors red→blue→red of different intensities for red and blue generate a sequence of b- and d-waves. Changing the intensity of blue color attempts to eliminate responses to the transitions from red to blue and from blue to red. It cannot be obtained. Minimal responses are there, showing color-dependent ERG wave. (b) In the control experiment with the sequence red→red→red→, an appropriate selection of the middle stimulus abolishes the waves. (c) The graphs constructed from transitional responses show that the graph for different colors is above the horizontal axis. For equal colors, the graph reaches the horizontal axis. (d) The magnitudes of minimal ERG responses represent measures of neuronal color differences. Systematic substitutions of colors result in a matrix of neuronal differences $||\hat{d}_{ij}||$ between stimuli S_i and S_j. From that matrix using multidimensional scaling (MDS), the color-coding predetector neurons constituting the color space can be found. (e) It was shown that it is a three-dimensional sphere for equiluminant color. The projection of colors on the red–green and blue–yellow plane demonstrate the common aspect of color coding in frog and man. B = blue, ERG = electroretinogram, G = green, h = color dependent component of ERG, R = red, W = white, Y = yellow.

(Fig. 7.4a). However, even if the intensity of all these signals is equal, then the ERG response to switching from red to blue or blue to red is not abolished. These waves are specifically related to colors. These waves have been called *hue waves*, indicating their use in color discrimination. For the control condition, a decreasing or increasing test stimulus (in the middle of the triad) of red color was employed (Fig. 7.4b).

Of course, at one level of intensity of this red test stimulus, all the red stimuli will be identical, and there will be no response in the ERG except at the beginning and the end of the triad. If the amplitude of the response is presented against the difference between the standard and test stimuli, then a very important difference can be seen. With an increase and decrease in the intensity of the test stimulus in a red–red–red triad, there is an increase in amplitude of the response with both an increase and a decrease in the intensity of the test stimulus, as this is dependent upon b- or d-intensity channels. The curve is always positioned on the horizontal axis (zero amplitude) when all red signals are equal in intensity (Fig. 7.4c, right). For different colors that can be distinguished by the frog, there is always the same shape, but shifted above the horizontal axis by a particular magnitude *h*, which is a specifically color-dependent component of the ERG (Fig. 7.4c, left). If the h-wave is regarded as an analog of subjective differences, it can be used as an input variable to the matrix for subsequent multidimensional scaling (Fig. 7.4d).

The result of this treatment is a three-dimensional color space of the frog for equiluminant colors, with a reduction of the red–green axis and a more powerful contribution of the yellow–blue axis. The white color is on the pole, and the vector of the hemisphere characterizes different equiluminant colors that can be discriminated by the frog. The colors of different brightness reveal a hypersphere of four-dimensional space (Fig. 7.4e). It should be added that a behavioral discrimination depends on more central structures, but the retinal level discriminative ability is a necessary precondition of the behavioral discrimination.

At the level of the retina, where the predetectors generate only limited numbers of components, this approach is very promising for computation of color-coding space. Yet, in the case of ERPs, recordings were done from cortical detectors and the interpretations are more complex. Starting with the concept of local depolarization of the glial cells by neuron spiking, if the detectors are selectively tuned to different signals, their responses will be very localized. If one stimulus is given and it stimulates one detector only, and if the other stimulus activates a different detector, there will be no increase in responding with a difference between stimuli. Any deviation from the standard stimulus will produce the same response. However, for EP generators it is not a single detector, but the detector map that is responsible, via the activity of glial cells. If the stimulus is changed, substituting the standard stimulus by a test stimulus, no response will be obtained if the test stimulus does not differ from the standard stimulus. As the difference between these stimuli increases, the EP increases, reaching a constant asymptote when the difference reaches maximum (Fig. 7.5).

When stimulus S_i is active, it generates detector excitation vector D_i. The stimulus S_k presented independently generates detection excitation vector D_k. If, however, S_k closely follows S_i, then the response to S_k depends only on the excitation of detectors that can be additionally stimulated. Thus, if S_i and S_k are identical, no response to S_k after S_i will be generated. The total response to S_k will equal the sum of all additional excitations. Evoked poten-

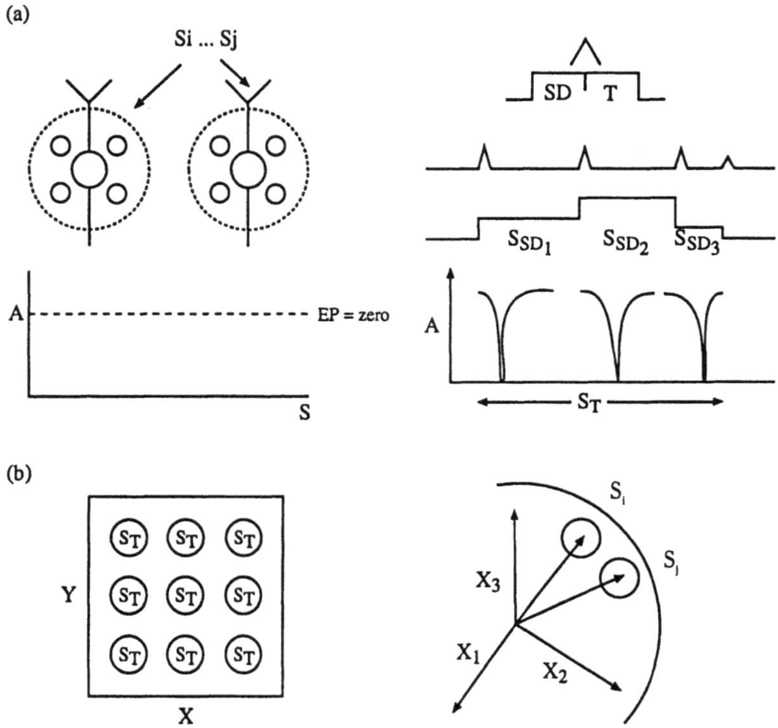

FIG. 7.5. The application of stimulus substitution technique for measuring the neuronal differences between stimuli. (a) The stimuli S_i and S_j address different detectors. Each stimulus evokes responses of equal amplitude. If, however, the standard stimulus continuously acting is replaced by a test stimulus, the EP equals zero when the standard and the test stimuli are identical. Selecting standards sequentially means that a set of selective filters can be obtained. (b) At the detector map, different standard stimuli are selected. Using a set of test stimuli, a matrix of responses is obtained with coordinates of stimuli in a four-dimensional space. A = amplitude, S = stimulus, $S_i + S_j$ = stimulus addressing different detectors, S_{SD} = standard stimulus, S_T = test stimulus, X_n = vectors.

tials to change of a transition from stimulus S_i to stimulus S_k are measured by the sum of absolute values of excitation differences generated by these stimuli.

$$d^*_{ik} = \sum_{j=1}^{n} | d_{ji} - d_{jk} | = | D_i - D_k |$$

where d* is an ERP measure of difference excitation due to change in stimulus from S_i to S_k.

It means that EP to a stimulus change equals the absolute value of vector difference of two vectors D_i and D_k. Thus, from a matrix of EPs to stimuli changes, it is possible to get information about the structure of detector space. To do this, one should use a set of stimuli and use transitions from one stimulus to another to collect a matrix of evoked potentials from such transitions.

Thus, if the test stimulus coincides with the standard stimulus, there is no evoked response, but by changing the test stimulus, responses are seen again. In such an experiment, it is possible to get information about the characteristics of selective filters for each standard stimulus. These filter characteristics are obtained by evoked potentials that are generated by a population of neurons. If two stimuli by substitution produce a response, this means that at the detector level they are also discriminated. Using different standard stimuli, one by one, and then changing the test stimulus for each standard stimulus, a detector map can be constructed. For each detector, there is a certain excitation area measured on the map for which this detector is selectively tuned. In other words, these elements of the map are different loci in the perceptual space if the detector map coincides with subjective space. Thus, a neuronal space can be studied on the basis of EPs to a set of substituted stimuli.

With these ideas in mind, the problem of N100 can be considered. Therefore if two signals are presented, the test stimulus following the standard separated by a short interval, they produce a N100, which because of the short interval between the stimuli is rather small. These test and standard signals are presented with the same probability (Fig. 7.6a). If the standard stimulus is fixed, the same standard can be used as the test stimulus, in which case the standard and test stimuli are equal. In this case, there is a maximal adaptation of detectors and a selective depression of the N100 potential. If the test stimulus deviates from the standard, then an N100 of higher amplitude can be recorded (Fig. 7.6b). The amplitude of the N100 can be represented as a function of the parameter of any stimulus (Fig. 7.6c). The amplitude of the N100 can characterize the degree to which the receptive fields of stimuli overlap. There are receptive fields of the detector that are involved in the generation of the response to the standard and the receptive field involved in the response to the test stimulus. If these two sets of receptive fields are the same, then this produces maximal depression. If these areas do not exactly overlap, then there will be an increase of amplitude up to the point where these two areas are completely separated. In this case, a plateau is reached, which is not modified by the following change of stimulus (Fig. 7.6d). By repeated presentation of the stimulus, there is a stimulus selective adaptation of detectors that is reflected by the selective depression of the N100. Also, from the matrix of such responses, information can be obtained about the detector space structure.

It was shown by Verbaten et al. (Verbaten, Poclofs, Sjouw, & Slangen, 1986) that N100 has two parts: nonspecific (habituatable) and specific (nonhabituatable). The habituatable N100 is habituated in parallel with SCR demonstrating its direct link with OR. Specific N100, evident even by short interstimulus intervals, results from the contribution of phasic detectors. The more similar the test and standard stimuli, the smaller the specific N100 under constant interstimulus interval. The response reaches minimum for identical stimuli. A set of standard and test stimuli can generate a matrix of responses to different combinations of test and standard stimuli. This matrix can be used for reconstruction of the detector space as described previously.

The nonspecific N100 repeatedly habituated in parallel with OR is difficult to study using averaging techniques. In order to do this, Verbaten suggested the computerized reduction of background activity, thus achieving recordings of isolated N100 evoked by stimuli separated by 20 s to 30 s. In such a case, specific N100 has a constant value and the habituation refers to nonspecific N100. It was shown that such a habituation was stimulus selective that corresponds with SCR selective habituation. Using a standard for

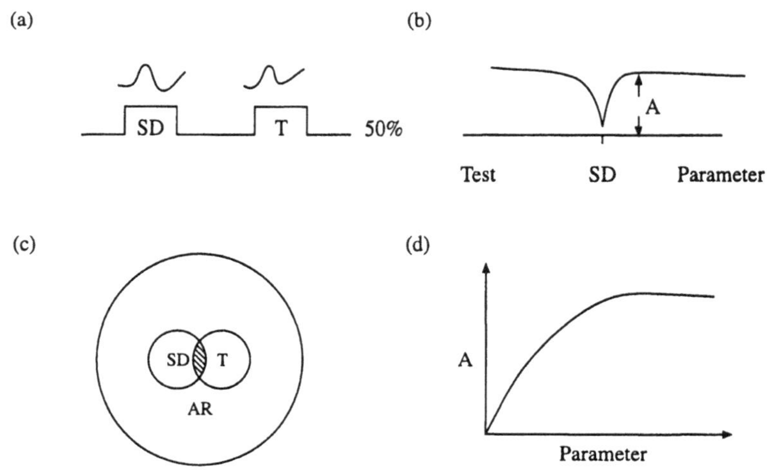

FIG. 7.6. *(Continued)*

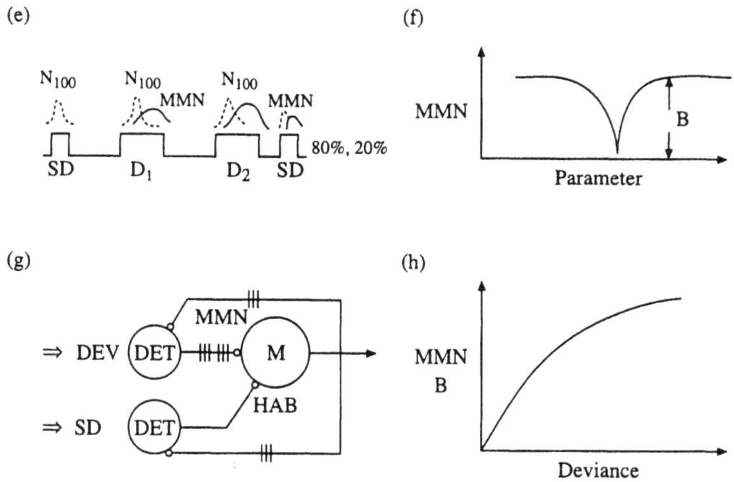

FIG. 7.6. The application of specific N100 and mismatch negativity (MMN) for getting information on stimulus neuronal coding. (a) The standard (SD) and test (T) stimuli are close to one another with 50% probabilities. Setting a specific parameter of the standard, it is possible to change that of the test stimulus. When the standard and test stimuli are identical, the response reaches minimum. The amplitude (A) of responses (AR) to different test stimuli correspond to representation of the parameter in a given neuronal population. (b) The degree of overlapping of responding detectors to standard and test inversely corresponds to the amplitude of the response that measures the stimulus parameter. (c) In the case of different probabilities for standard (80%) and test (20%), a new wave (MMN) to deviant stimuli is evoked. The amplitude of MMN is larger when the deviance is greater. (d) The evocation of MMN is related to specific plastic neurons obtaining information from detectors via habituating synapses with short-term plasticity. In the amplitude of MMN is coded the parameter of the deviant (DEV). (e) If the probability of standard and test stimuli differ (80% and 20%, respectively), mismatch negativity results from the modulating neuron obtaining strong stimulation from difference detectors (DET) that have not habituated. The modulating neuron acting with delay is more efficient to the second deviant (D_2) than to the first (D_1). (f) The receptive field of the modulating neuron can be obtained from the signals generating MMN. There is selective habituation (HAB) to the standard stimulus, with the response reaching asymptotic levels as the change in the parameter of the stimulus increases. (g) Short-term memory unit (M) is habituated to a standard stimulus in response to a deviant one. (h) The amplitude of MMN increases with deviance from the standard stimulus. B = Negativity.

selective habituation of N100, a test stimulus can be used to get a response under such selective habituation. The decrease of the response that simulates the selective habituation of the hippocampal neurons is due to the formation on the hippocampal neurons of a synaptic link vector orthogonal to the detector excitation vector. If the stimulus evokes excitation vectors that are orthogonal to the link vector, no response is generated. The closer the excitation and link vectors are to collinearity, the greater the response. From the matrix of the responses to test stimuli, one can get information about memory space involved in OR control. However in Näätänen's studies, it was shown that, by different probabilities of standard and test stimuli, some other modifications occur. A new phenomenon is generated. This phenomenon is a negative wave, which is called mismatch negativity (MMN) because it is only triggered when the stimuli deviate from the preceding ones. The following sequence of events is shown in Fig. 7.6e.

The standard stimulus produces only an N100. The deviant stimulus produces an N100 and MMN, which is decreased by the second presentation of the deviant. If the standard stimulus is presented again after the deviant(s), it can be seen that, in addition to the N100, some MMN also occurs. The probability level of the standard and deviant stimuli is 90% and 10%, respectively; however, it is better to have a lower probability for deviant signals. The amplitude of the MMN is dependent on the difference between the standard and the deviant. Again, the MMN can be represented as a function of the parameter of the stimulus (Fig. 7.6f). It can also be seen that, as for N100, there is an asymptotic level, above which there is no more increase in the response despite the fact that the standard and the deviant become increasingly different.

The MMN representing the short-term memory can be used for construction of the short-term memory space. In order to do this, different standard and deviant stimuli are combined to get a matrix of MMNs. This matrix contains information about vector space. The short-term memory space is possibly represented by specific neurons having short-lived habituation traces similar to novelty detectors of the hippocampus but located in specific areas. The repeated stimulus results in their selective habituation to stimuli of specific modality. Such a modality specific short-term memory can enhance deviant stimuli in the stream of sequential events. The plastic changes result in a formation of an orthogonal link vector with respect to the standard stimulus excitation vector.

How can the appearance of MMN be explained? The standard stimulus acts on detectors that send signals to habituatable neurons with habituatable synapses. This means that, if a standard stimulus is repeatedly presented with short ISIs, the synaptic contact in use, being depressed, does not operate and therefore the short-term plastic neuron is no longer efficient in detector activation. If the stimulus is changed, and it activates another detector, then this other detector is switched on. Habituation does not take place in this pathway, since the deviant stimulus is rare and the synapse recovers. Therefore, these new detectors have a strong effect on the plastic neuron. The latter's response, having a certain delay, is now added to the response evoked by the deviant. This means that the detector channel response is prolonged due to the participation of the plastic channel. Due to rapid selective habituation, the following deviant is less efficient. At the same time the standard following as a deviant producing MMN (Fig. 7.6g). The greater is the deviance, the greater the MMN (Fig. 7.6h).

Next is the more complex structure, which is described in studies of EPs as well as those of the OR (Fig. 7.7). This is the study of *processing negativity*, a negative wave evoked by the stimulus under active attention. What are the prerequisites of this response? The first is verbal instruction. The frontal lobe neurons are stimulated through speech perception. From the long-term memory storage (memory map), a particular memory trace is set to operational memory where it can be matched against the test signals. Such a stable function of the unit in operational memory is supported by the frontal lobe neurons. The incoming signals are compared with the operational memory trace (template) in the same way as in the command neuron. The response maximum is reached when the input excitation vector results in a scalar product with the link vector of the memory unit. The closer the

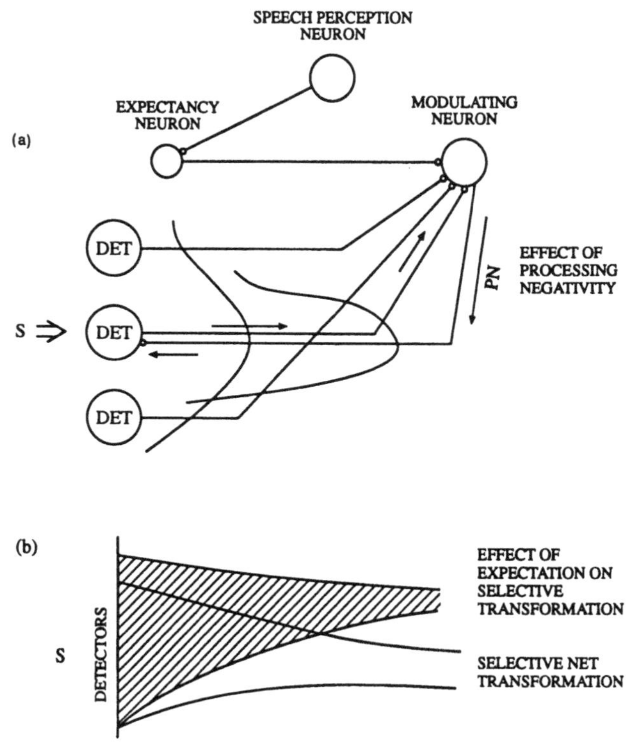

FIG. 7.7. The model of generation of processing negativity (PN). The verbal instruction activates the expectancy neuron. (a) If the stimulus corresponds with the expected one, the PN is generated, possibly activating relevant input detectors (DET). (b) In the process of learning, the corridor of effective signals becomes more narrow.

relationship of the two vectors is to collinearity, the greater the response of the memory unit.

The frontal lobe neurons thus keep active a specific memory trace, a long-lasting effect that switches on modulating neurons in the reticular system. Such modulating neurons are connected to a particular subset of detectors. The modulating neurons do not operate if no signals are presented; they only potentially influence particular detectors. What happens when the stimulus is presented and it matches the template? The signals arrive from the modulating neuron, which fires impulses to the detector selectively tuned to a particular stimulus. This means that, through speech perception in the act of voluntary attention, initial information is passed through memory traces forward to a particular modulating neuron that activates a particular subset of detectors.

Due to lateral inhibition, there is a redistribution of excitation of detectors. This process is more rapid and more efficient if additional excitation is sent to the detector that already has a very high level of excitation. So, the shape of the distribution of excitations among the detectors in the detector map will be sharper due to the firing of modulating neurons of the tonic type at the detector level.

The problem of expectation refers not only to the category of the stimulus but to the time interval as well. To understand expectancy in time (the extrapolation used in predictive control systems), the representation of time in the nervous system must be considered. For short interstimulus intervals, time is represented by a channel-dependent code by time-selective detectors. Each detector is tuned to a particular time interval. The time detectors converge on an expectancy neuron. Thus, expectancy neurons can, in principle, respond to different intervals. Yet, some synaptic contacts from time detectors on expectancy neurons are modified by learning according to the Hebb principle (Fig. 7.8).

If a certain time interval is reinforced by a biologically significant stimulus, its synaptic contact is increased. In this way, a particular channel, meaning a particular time interval detector, will more efficiently act on an expectancy neuron. The expectancy neuron can be connected with different types of neurons. Take, for example, novelty neurons. These are expectancy neurons that can be taught a particular time interval by reinforcing particular time signals by biologically significant inputs. Repeated stimulation with constant interstimulus intervals produces habituation of novelty neurons and facilitation of expectancy neurons, so that omission of the stimulus makes it fire, even with no reinforcement. The correlation between expectancy neuron firing and the expectancy wave has been suggested by the experiments of Batuev (1981) in St. Petersburg. It was shown that there exists a system of neurons that discharge in sequence, one neuron following the response of another. The responses are phase shifted against each

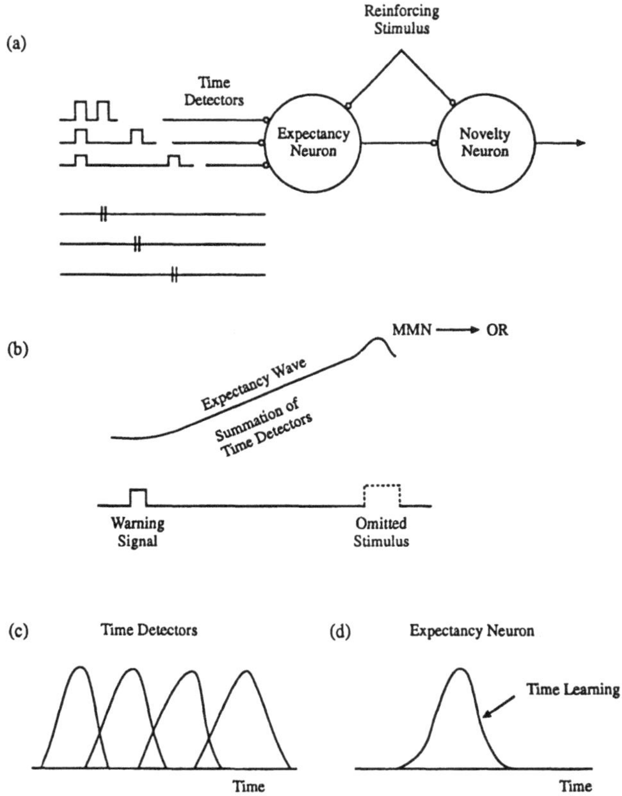

FIG. 7.8. The model of operation of expectation mechanism. (a) The time is coded by time-selective detectors that converge on the expectancy neuron. The time-selective learning of the expectancy neuron is reinforced by significant stimuli. The expectancy neuron is linked with the novelty neuron. (b) The warning stimulus activates the time detectors' sequential spiking. The only specific learned time detector generates a response. The summation of time-detector spiking results in an expectancy wave. If the stimulus at a specific time is omitted, the MMN and OR are generated. (c) The time detectors are selectively tuned to different time dimensions. (d) The expectancy neuron is selectively tuned to specific time intervals.

other in time and the summation of these responses produces an expectancy wave. The most efficient contact produces a behavioral reaction. A warning stimulus initiates an expectancy wave with expectancy neuron activation. An omitted stimulus that is expected at a specific times, produces MMN. Via expectancy neurons, the time detectors can be combined with the command neurons; that is, taught by means of a reinforcement of a particular time schedule. Through the omission of the stimulus at a specific time, the time detector excites the expectancy neurons to a sufficiently high level to produce a response. The property of expectancy neurons thus depends on time detectors.

Each time detector is tuned to a particular time interval, but the expectancy neuron learns to extract a particular one. This means that a particular channel is switched on to an expectancy neuron, so that one of the time detectors can switch on the expectancy neurons, and in this way, the expectancy wave is selectively adjusted to such time intervals that are used in the particular conditioning procedure. The expectancy neuron can be taught to respond to any time interval.

The roles of activation and different types of arousal are usually emphasized in discussion of the OR, but their basic role in OR deals with motor responses. The OR can be regarded as a targeting response, a response that makes a certain object the target of attention. The term *targeting response* was introduced by Konorski in Poland. How does this particular targeting reflex operate? This reflex selectively habituates to a particular stimulus. At the same time, the saccade generated by the eye movement mechanism is selectively directed to a particular point of space. How can this habituation at the same time as very selective adjustments of the eye movements be explained? To understand this, it is necessary to analyze the output system of eye movements and novelty neurons in the OR. At the level of the superficial layers of superior colliculus, there is a representation in the form of a retinotopic map. If a visual stimulus is presented, it is projected onto the retina, and, according to retinotopic projection, is localized in a particular area of the superior colliculus. This is a visual local detector. Each neuron is selectively tuned to a particular place on the retina. If a microelectrode is introduced into the depths of the superior colliculus, it is possible to find the other type of neurons. These neurons can be called *command neurons*, because, if such a neuron is stimulated through local microelectrodes, a saccade of a particular direction and amplitude is produced. This means that each of these neurons is selectively connected to a particular saccade, or each neuron corresponds to a particular saccade. At the level of the pons, there are two types of neurons—horizontal and vertical premotor neurons. These neurons are connected with motor neurons directly generating eye movements via their connections with the eye muscles. The stimulus occurring at a particular point in the visual field is projected onto the superior colliculus and a particular command neuron is activated. The command neuron generates a particular vector that is defined by synaptic contacts on horizontal and vertical neurons, the signals from which are distributed among the motor neurons. In such a way, a particular light stimulus can produce a particular saccade that brings the eye directly onto a target stimulus.

Figure 7.9 illustrates a stimulus in the external field, where particular command neurons automatically generate the saccade that brings the fovea in line with the stimulus. In this neuronal net, a very important point to note

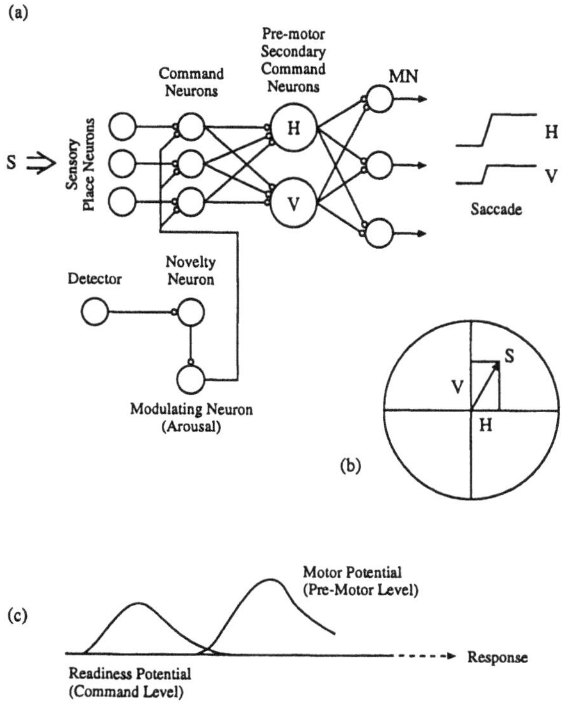

FIG. 7.9. The participation of arousal in saccadic eye-movement generation. (a) The stimulus is projected on the place selective detectors of the retinotopic map of the superior colliculus linked with a map of command neurons generating prewired saccades via second level command neurons (these are vertical and horizontal premotor neurons that converge on motor neurons [MN] that produce horizontal [H] and vertical [V] saccade components). The selective saccade command neurons are influenced by modulating neurons of the reticular formation switched on by the novelty neurons. The habituation of OR results in the inactivation of the command system. (b) The saccade (S) is represented by excitations of horizontal and vertical premotor neurons. (c) The preparatory mechanism of saccade generation is related to readiness potential at the command neuron level and motor potential at the premotor-neuron level.

is that direct, prolonged stimulation of these command neurons produces a sequence of saccades of equal amplitude and direction (a staircase of saccades). There is no habituation if the command neuron is stimulated directly. Why do saccades habituate through sensory stimulation? It should be noted that an additional input from a novelty neuron through modulating neurons of the reticular formation elevates arousal levels at the command neuron level. The stimulus, on the one hand, stimulates a particular locus of the superior colliculus, according to its place in the visual field. But, on the other hand, the stimulus can be of a particular color or a particular shape, and these features are analyzed via the geniculate body and at the cortical level by detectors. Novelty neurons, on which the detectors converge, selectively habituate to stimulus parameters. After several presentations, arousal is no longer generated, the command neuron receives no additional excitation, and the stimulus produces no specific targeting response.

How are these motor responses related to the generation of the ERPs? The readiness potential that can appear even when no response at all is evoked, can be connected with the expectancy neurons and command neuron, pre-excitation. The motor potentials that precede the real motion but do not result from motor feedback can be related to the premotor level in the motor areas of the brain. Thus, a sequence of ERPs can be suggested, each of which is specifically related to a particular part of the neuronal net. There are two groups of ERP, stimulus-dependent and response-dependent potentials.

Figure 7.10 shows the relationship between the basic processes in evoked potentials and a simplified OR neuronal structure. Starting with the ERP, the

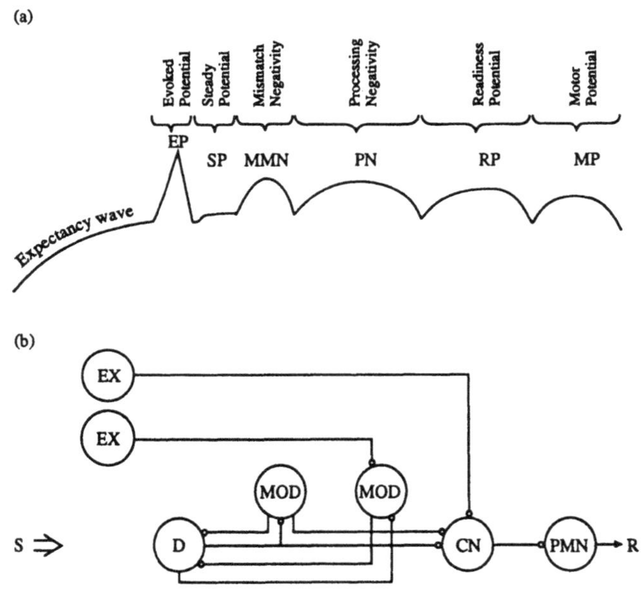

Simplified OR structure with corresponding ERPs.

FIG. 7.10. The neuronal basis of the ERP sequence. (a) The sequence of ERPs is divided into sensory dependent (specific N100, steady potential), memory related (MMN, PN, expectancy wave, nonspecific N100), response executive-related (readiness and motor potentials). (b) The neuronal net responsible for the sequence of ERPs contains expectancy neurons, activating modulatory neurons, and command neurons for the two forms of expectations, sensory and motor. CN = command neurons, D = detector, EX = expectancy neurons, MOD = activating modulatory neurons, PMN = premotor neurons, R = response.

following processes are evident: Expectancy wave, EP, steady potential, MMN, processing negativity, readiness potential, motor potential. In a simplified structure of the OR, expectancy neurons define the responses to all kinds of expectations, including the so-called learned attention and expectancy wave. The detectors generate specific N100 and steady potential signals and send these to modulating neurons via their links with the novelty neurons. The feedback from modulating neurons onto detectors produces nonspecific N100. Then, processing negativity is produced from the operation of memory units matching the signals. MMN results from modality-specific habituatable plastic neurons. If the signals reach command neurons, the motor response is initiated. Expectancy neurons can also participate in command neuron excitation. If the signal is not presented, but the neuron was previously taught to respond to a particular time delay, the command neuron generates a response. These responses correspond with the readiness potential and premotor neurons are connected with motor potentials.

CHAPTER

8

Neuronal Organization of Color Space

This chapter covers the following issues:

1. Characteristics of cones in fish.
2. Horizontal cell responses to different wavelengths.
3. Spectral characteristics of horizontal cells as an excitation vector.
4. The photopic seeing curve and vector length.
5. Spherical structure of colors of equal luminosity in fish.
6. Hue in fish color vision.
7. Saturation in fish color vision.
8. The prediction of detector characteristics.
9. Wavelength thresholds.
10. Saturation thresholds in fish color vision.
11. Prediction of behavioral characteristics of color vision from horizontal cells.
12. The neuronal color analyzer.

Tomita's results of intracellular recording from three types of cones in the carp (Tomita, 1965) demonstrate overlapping characteristics with peaks in the short, middle, and long wavelengths (Fig. 8.1). The same characteristics are found in the goldfish, so it is possible to make a comparison between different data. The most important finding is the overlapping functions of blue, green, and red cones. The main task of this study was to find the neural basis for color vision. Having formulated (chaps. 9, 10) the con-

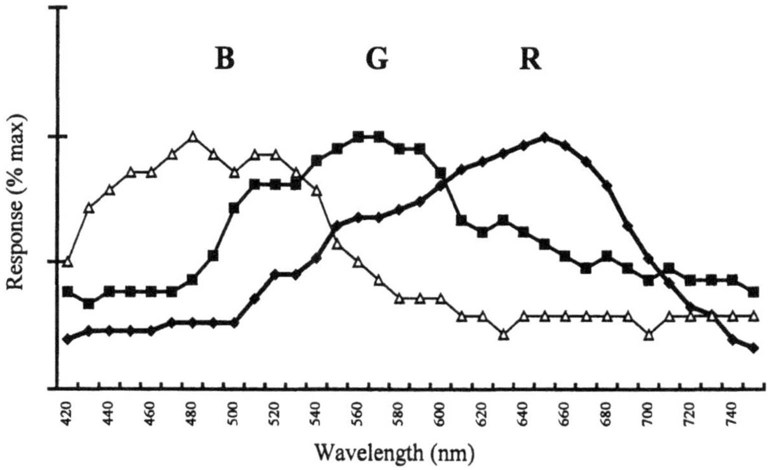

FIG. 8.1. The spectral characteristics of carp cones obtained by intracellular recording (data from Tomita, 1965). The abscissa shows wavelength. The peaks of the functions shown correspond with short-wave, medium-wave, and long-wave cones of trichromatic vision obtained by equal numbers of quanta at each wavelength.

cept of the spherical structure of color space and the concept of the excitation vector, and having identified, from multidimensional scaling, the characteristics of red–green, yellow–blue, and achromatic cells, the question now was whether it would prove possible to re-establish the spherical structure of color vision from the neural response characteristics of opponent cells of an animal having color vision. In order to check this, it was decided to study horizontal cells of fish because the cells participate very much in the integration of responses from the cones. The responses of horizontal cells approximate the linear combination of the responses generated by different cones. The nonlinear transformation in the color analyzer is connected with the cone itself. When an electrical recording is made from the cone, a logarithmic function is already apparent. Thus, the potential of cones is linearly related to the next stage of the responses at the horizontal cells level.

The experiments described in this chapter (see, for example, Ismailov, Sokolov, & Chernorizov, 1989) were done in the isolated retina of the carp, using superfine electrodes, less than 1 μm diameter. The stimulation consisted of visual projection of monochromatic lights. The recordings were carried out on a population of photopic horizontal cells. The purpose of this cell sampling was to be sure that the horizontal cells really are represented by a limited number of groups. It is known that horizontal cells can be divided into two populations. One group that is used for vision in the dark is connected with rods rather than cones. This is a separate channel and these cells have not been examined; scotopic vision was not studied in these experiments. The concern here was with the horizontal cells for photopic color vision. There are three types of photopic horizontal cells in the retina–red–green, yellow–blue, and luminosity horizontal cells. The task was to test whether any additional type of horizontal cells is present in the fish retina.

The study first revealed that there were different types of horizontal cells in terms of the nature of their responses to stimulation of different wavelengths. The responses of these cells to different wavelengths of light stimuli are shown in Fig. 8.2. The first type of cell demonstrated no change in the direction of the response with a change of wavelength. There was always a hyperpolarization of the cell, increasing in magnitude as the wavelength increased. The second was a biphasic component cell. When the wavelength was increased, there was a reversal of the sign of the response. Instead of hyperpolarization at short wavelengths, the cell produced a depolarization to stimuli of longer wavelengths. The third type of cell can be regarded as an analog of the blue–yellow system, which had three phases as the wavelength changed. In the first change of response direction, the hyperpolarization response to short wavelengths became a depolarization response. As the wavelength increased, so the depolarization decreased and was again followed by recovery of a hyperpolarization response. This type of cell may be referred to as a *triphasic cell.*

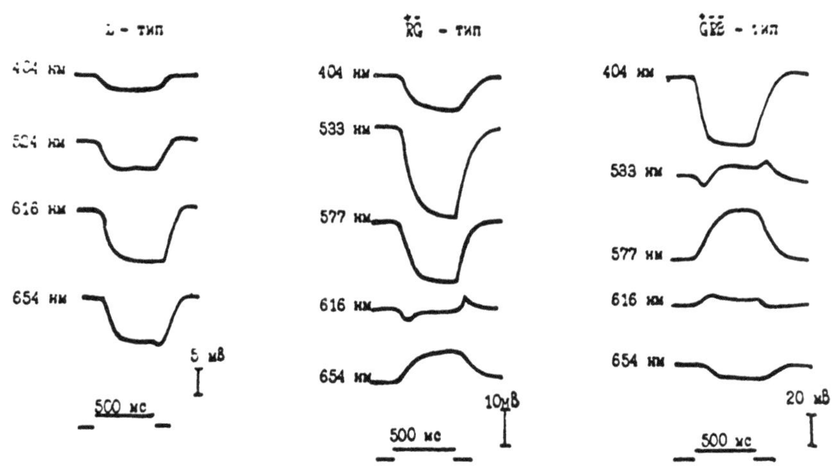

FIG. 8.2. The intracellular recording from three types of photopic horizontal cells. The intracellular recording from three types of photopic horizontal cells of the carp obtained in our laboratory using stimuli with equal numbers of quanta. The gradual responses to light with wavelength-dependent polarity in different cells are shown vertically. The monophasic, biphasic, and triphasic photopic horizontal cells taken together correspond with a local color analyzer at the retinal level.

One of the achievements of this set of experiments was the prediction of the responses of horizontal cells from the data obtained by measurements of potentials in cones. Only one assumption was made, that the responses of the horizontal cell were a linear combination of inputs from cones. Now, if the responses of cones are known, it is possible to obtain the responses of horizontal cells. For each type of horizontal cell, three equations are needed to calculate the synaptic coefficients that characterize the contributions of cones in different responses of the horizontal cell. These coefficients have been calculated; then, from the data of Tomita the curves of the responses of the horizontal cells have been recalculated. The problem is whether, knowing the synaptic coefficients, any response of the horizontal cell can be obtained by using only a linear combination of cone inputs. The predictions were made for all three types of horizontal cells. The response curves obtained in the actual experiment and the curves calculated from this linear combination of cone inputs are shown in Fig. 8.3.

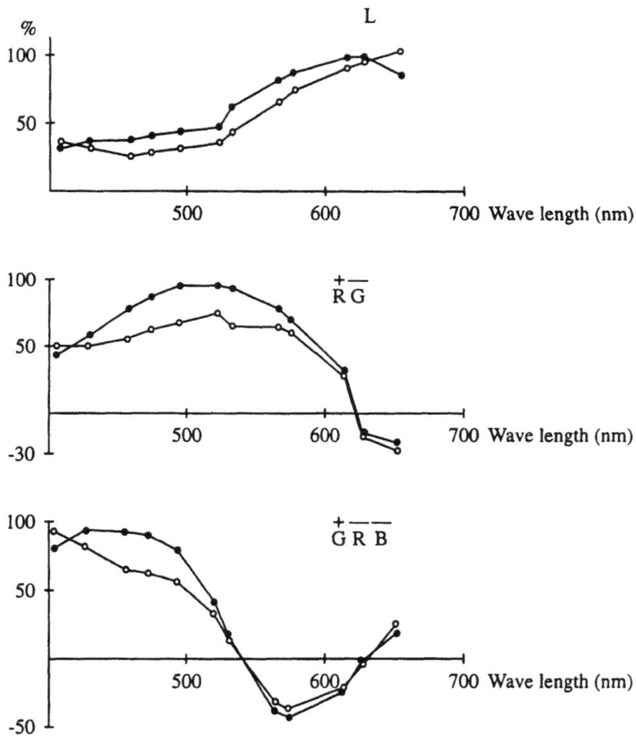

FIG. 8.3. The result of amplitude estimations for three horizontal cells as a function of wavelength. The excitation of each cell at a particular wavelength can be regarded as a component of the three-dimensional excitation vector. For each wavelength, there exists a particular combination of the vector component. This means that each color is coded by an excitation vector.

Response data was collected for horizontal cells using stimuli of equal numbers of quanta. In human subjects, it is possible to subjectively evaluate colors of equal brightness, but what does subjectively equal intensities of colors mean for fish? The conclusion was that the response of the b-wave of the electroretinogram (ERG) can be used. This characterizes the sensitivity of the total retinal system to different wavelengths. In parallel, the lengths of the excitation vectors obtained from measurements of responses in three types of horizontal cells were calculated. The amplitudes of the responses to particular wavelengths in the three cells may be regarded as components of one excitation vector. The excitation vector is a combination of the three excitations of horizontal cells. For each wavelength, it is possible to find three coordinates, and so each monochromatic color can be represented by a vector composed of excitations of horizontal cells.

The amplitude of the ERG obtained from the preparation exactly matched the length of the vector. Figure 8.4 shows that the calculated length of the vector for each wavelength coincides with the experimentally found amplitude of the ERG. This means that color is coded in the following way at the level of the horizontal cells. The length of the three-dimensional

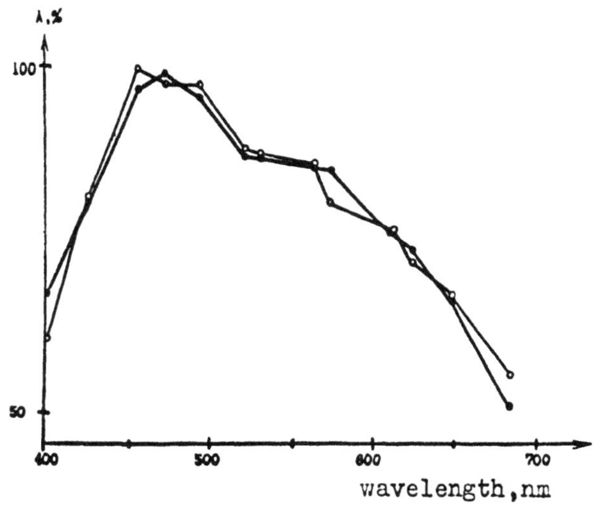

FIG. 8.4. The test for spherical structure of fish color vision. The excitation vector obtained directly in experiments from excitations of horizontal cells is characterized by a particular length. The values for the photopic sensitivity curve were obtained using the amplitude of the b-wave of the ERG. The amplitude of the b-wave at different wavelengths was compared with the length of the vector obtained from horizontal cell responses at the same wavelengths. It is evident that the b-wave and vector length completely coincide at all wavelengths under similar photopic conditions. This implies that the perception of colors of equal brightness is located in fish on the sphere in three-dimensional space.

vector characterizes the intensity of the light, and the orientation of the vector characterizes the color of the stimulus. If the lengths of the vectors are known, then it is possible to project all subjectively equally bright colors onto a sphere of unitary radius. Thus, dividing the responses by the vector length, it is possible to obtain a representation of the colors on the sphere. This is because the intensity of light is related to the length of the vector and the colors of equal brightness are related only to the orientation of the vector. The unitary sphere in three-dimensional space shows the color vision of the fish for colors of equal luminosity (Fig. 8.4).

Using a projection of all colors onto the red–green and yellow–blue plane in a similar way to that shown later for human subjects, the color vision in fish can be compared with color vision in human subjects. In man, the data from subjective differences were calculated by multidimensional scaling. In fish, the contribution of horizontal cells in the establishment of color space has been directly measured. In both cases, there are two opponent cells—yellow–blue (triphasic) and red–green (biphasic). The trajectory on the plane is the trajectory of monochromatic light projected onto the equatorial plane. In fish, monochromatic colors are represented in the three-dimensional space located on a hemisphere. On this projection, the characteristics of each color are given by the orientation of the vector. The closeness of each point to the center where white is projected characterizes the degree of color saturation. The more distant the point from the center at each wavelength, the more saturated the color. The position of the white color can be formally obtained from the assumption that white light should be located in the center of the plane when red–green and blue–yellow channels are not excited.

The comparison of results of the projection of colors in man and fish shows that in fish, the trajectory is shifted towards long wavelengths, but the sequence of wavelengths is based on the same principles. Each wavelength follows the previous one without changing their order (Figs. 8.5 & 8.6).

A schematic representation of information flow starts from cone responses. The coefficients for the synapses between cones and horizontal cells were calculated using data concerning the characteristics of cones and horizontal cells. Three different wavelengths taken for calculation result in three different equations. The composition of wavelengths can be changed and, using the same procedure, a new set of coefficients can be calculated, thus allowing a measure of the reliability of these coefficients. For each horizontal cell, there is a set of three synaptic contacts. An initial vector of the excitation is generated at the level of excitation of receptors. The vector for synaptic contacts is called a link vector—this means a vector of coefficients that combines excitation from all cones onto a particular horizontal cell. The response of the horizontal cell is a scalar product of the excitation vector and the link vector. The characteristics of color detectors

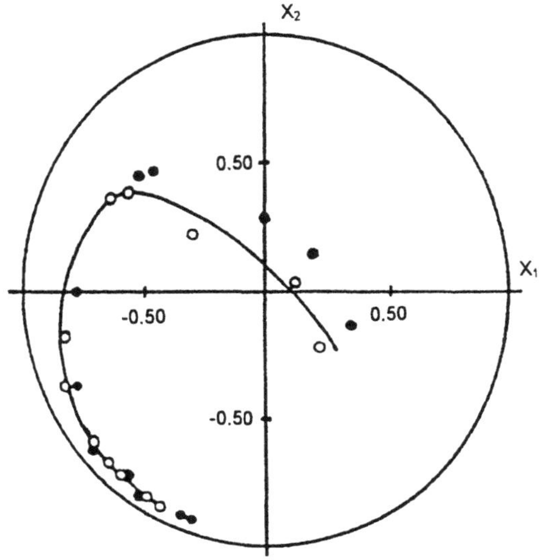

FIG. 8.5. The opponent horizontal cell used as coordinates for red–green and blue–yellow plane. The monochromatic colors of different wavelength form on the equatorial plane a sequentially ordered trajectory similar to that trajectory obtained by multidimensional scaling from subjective estimations.

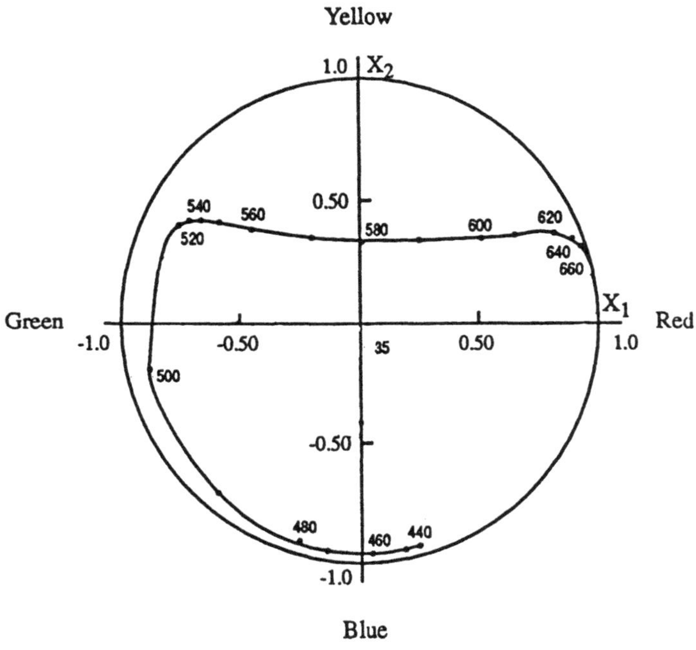

FIG. 8.6. The monochromatic equiluminant light on red–green–blue–yellow plane trajectories for color vision in man. The representation of color vision in fish occupies a more restricted area of the equatorial projection plane, in comparison with that for human subjects. Additionally, some monochromatic lights cross the white point, indicating a local deficiency in discrimination of white and monochromatic lights. The color system of human subjects occupies a larger area, and monochromatic lights do not cross the white point.

were calculated theoretically in the following way. For a detector sensitive to a particular wavelength, it is necessary to know the excitations that provide the input to this neuron. Then, these magnitudes can be regarded as components of the link vector. If the detector receives an excitation vector coinciding with the link vector, there will be a maximal excitation at the detector. The inner product of vectors that equals the lengths of vectors is multiplied by the cosine of the angle between these two vectors. If the excitations coming to the detector are proportional to the coefficients of synaptic contacts that have been selected for this detector, then the response of the detector reaches maximum. When the excitation vector and the link vector are collinear, by changing the input wavelength and the corresponding excitation vector at the horizontal cell level, the characteristics of selective detectors were obtained (Fig. 8.7).

How are color signals transformed in the neuronal net? The input signal is characterized by a certain spectrum. It produces a particular combination of responses in the cones. This results in the excitation of a combination of horizontal cells. At the level of these horizontal cells, there is an orthogonal system. Horizontal cell responses can be characterized by a very simple description of linear combinations of cone responses. The same description can be applied to detectors. Each point or locus on the color sphere is represented by a particular detector so that the total hemisphere consists of patches, each corresponding to a detector. The excitation of a detector corresponds with an equivalent subjective experience in human subjects. If a color stimulus is presented, its spectrum defines the combinations of horizontal cells that are excited. The excitation vector changes its orientation and produces in a particular detector an excitation maximum. Different colors projected on a sphere are characterized by angles. Hue corresponds to the angle on the red–green, blue–yellow plane. Saturation is characterized by the vertical angle (see Fig. 8.8).

If single detectors represent different colors, then it should be possible to measure a threshold that is constant for the total sphere. It can be measured by angles—the threshold angle has a constant value. To produce a constant value, different wavelengths should be differently modified at different points on the sphere. The magnitude of the wavelength shift to produce a fixed angle change characterizes the threshold in wavelength differences. The thresholds measured in wavelength differences ($\Delta\lambda$) against wavelength (λ) indirectly from our model corresponds to a threshold obtained in behavioral experiments (Fig. 8.9).

The behavioral measurements of the color threshold by Yaeger (1967) and the results of the model closely correspond (Fig. 8.10). The calculated threshold corresponds with saturation measured by behavioral methods. The saturation thresholds in fish closely resemble those in man. The main difficulties of this long-lasting project were related to the maintenance of

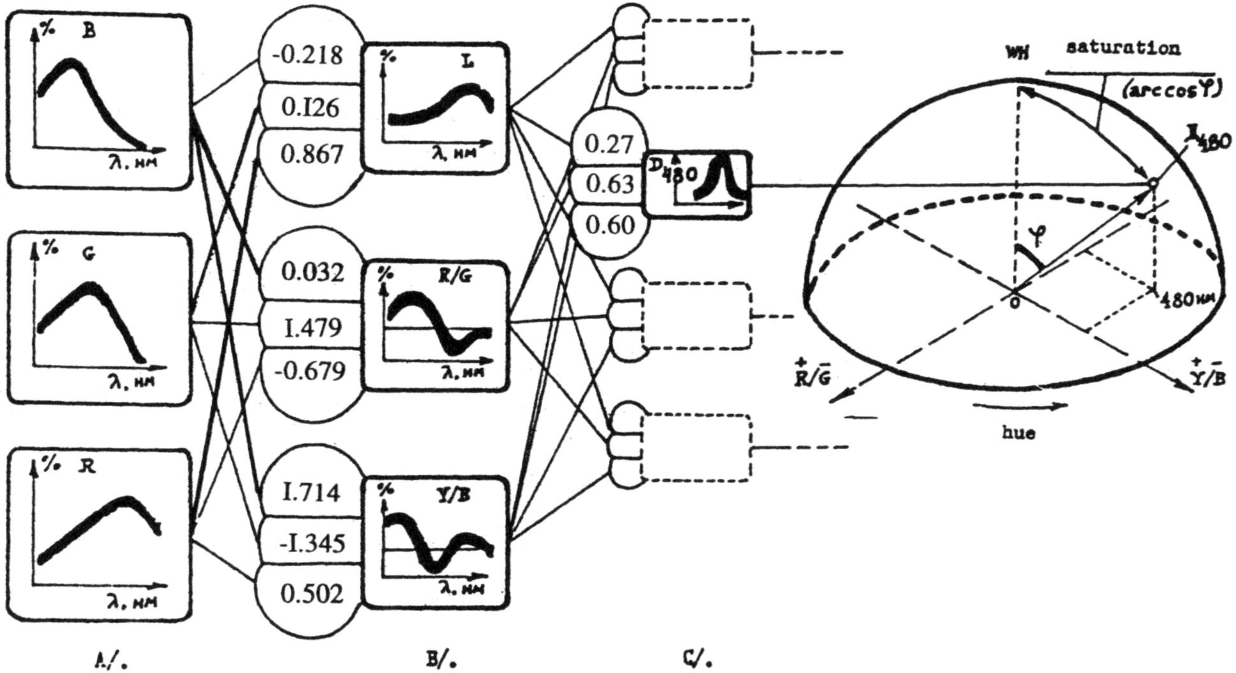

FIG. 8.7. The scheme illustrating the structure of the color analyzer supported by experiments on fish retina (for equiluminant colors). The signals are logarithmically transformed in the cones. After the cones, the signals are linearly summated at the horizontal cells. Omitting several stages of transformation because the scheme only accounts for processing of equiluminant colors, one can say that the signals converge in parallel on a set of color detectors selectively tuned to particular colors. The excitation vectors that converge on detectors and the link vectors of the synapses for each detector are all of a constant length. This results in a projection of all colors on the surface of the sphere in three-dimensional space determined by the excitation of three real predetector neurons—horizontal cells. Thus, the color analyzer is a neuronal net projecting an n-dimensional set of spectral signals on the spherical surface in three-dimensional space.

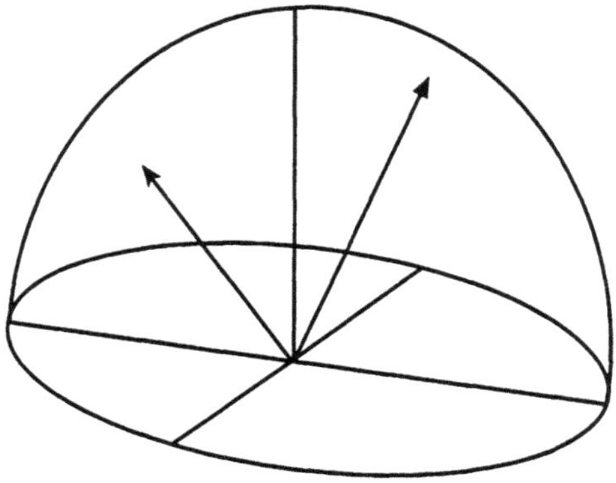

FIG. 8.8. Mathematical modeling of color analyzers. The structure of the color analyzer expressed in the form of linear combinations of signals after they pass a logarithmic input in cones. The model can predict the color responses to different spectral inputs in terms of vector algebra.

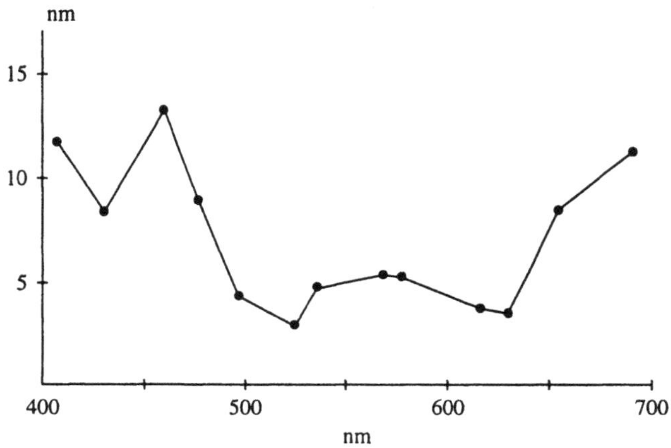

FIG. 8.9. The wavelength thresholds obtained from spherical model of fish color vision. The constant minimal angles found as thresholds on the sphere are recalculated in wavelength differences corresponding to these angles at different wavelengths.

the cells in the experiment. After calculating coefficients, it is possible to construct an artificial, simulated, color analyzer for fish that will produce the responses in close correspondence with the vision of this animal. This cannot only be done for fish; it is also possible to construct a model that simulates color vision under simple conditions in human subjects. The specificity of the model is in its structure that is based on very simple parallel processing. The evaluation of information in these artificial systems is a parallel channeling of signal with calculation of maximum in one of the parallel channels. This model is a realization of a channel-dependent code.

Using ERG recording from a frog eye under conditions when one color was substituted by the other color, b-wave measures of color differences were obtained. The matrix of b-wave amplitudes was studied by a multidimensional scaling procedure. It was found that frog's color space is a four-

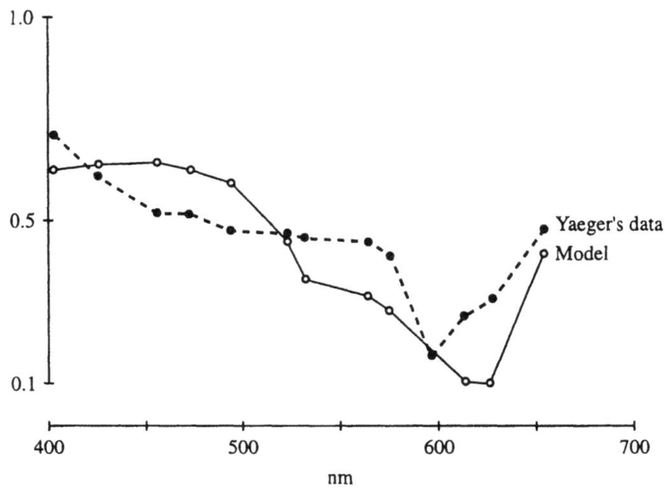

FIG. 8.10. The comparison of the wavelength thresholds calculated from the neurophysiological data of the carp and behavioral thresholds found in the carp by Yaeger (1967). The close correspondence shows that the known neuronal organization of color vision underlies the observed color-dependent behavior.

dimensional structure in which the colors are located on the hypersphere. Since the b-wave corresponds with the excitation of the bipolar cell, one may conclude that at the level of bipolar cells, a transformation from three-dimensional space of horizontal cells to a four-dimensional space occurs by adding D-neurons active in darkness.

CONCLUDING COMMENTS

Is the predetector system a universal for different modalities? Insofar as hearing is concerned, the orientation in space is performed by selective units that respond to a particular difference between intensity or sound phases coming to each ear. This occurs through two populations of cells closely resembling the predetectors. They have ascending and descending characteristics, respectively. There are other neurons selectively tuned to sound moving in space. There is a debate about what is the role of the broadly responsive neurons and how very selective detectors of location operate. One approach is based on the assumption that broadly responsive cells represent a level of predetectors.

The second layer of detectors results from a combination of predetector excitations. In the visual system, such predetectors have been identified. In the auditory system, the predetectors are not identified, but selective detectors for location and intensity have been found. Are there cells with good color detecting properties operating in the human brain? Selective detectors of light intensity have been found in the visual system. It is possible to see intensity detectors in the auditory cortex of the monkey and bat. A selectively tuned detector is a major principle of the coding of intensity. Zeki (1990) showed color coding neurons in V4 of the monkey neocortex.

The main difficulty is the transfer from the horizontal cell where there is a three-dimensional vector to the four-dimensional sphere that was found from multidimensional scaling. From three horizontal cells, excitations reach four types of bipolar cells–bright (B-neuron), dark (D-neuron), red–green, yellow–blue. The main assumption is that the signals of these four cells are normalized. Thus, instead of a three-component vector, which changed length with intensity, a four-dimensional vector of constant length was obtained. The next stage of the study of the neuronal mechanism in the frog has shown that bipolar cells constitute the structure of the excitations generating the sphere in four-dimensional space.

The essence of this approach is the integration of psychophysics with neurophysiology within a computerized model. One can study color vision using multidimensional scaling and then halt the investigation there, but it is possible to go further. The coordinates obtained through MDS are regarded as components of a real excitation of neurons and the search was to specifically look for these neurons. The fish experiments were therefore initiated in order to do this. To check whether the neuronal approach and the psychophysical approach are similar, one has to create a model. Now, there are many models of color vision, but in this case, there are two requirements that eliminate a great number of models. This is because on the one hand, a model should reproduce psychophysical functions, and on the other hand, each element of the model constructed from neuronal-like elements should reproduce a single neuron in the real nervous system. To create such a model under these two conditions is very difficult. Many models are completely unacceptable because at the same time they cannot reproduce functions of neurons as well as psychophysical findings. The process of creation of models cannot be stopped. If the model is created, the next step of research begins–there is extension of the conditions under which the model is tested, looking to see whether the model can explain something else. If it cannot do this, then it should be modified. There are three components in psychophysiological study–man, neuron, and model. Thus from this model, it is theoretically possible to predict behavioral data for discrimination of colors.

What about those detector maps? If someday a detector for color is found, this model may have suggestions for how they could be organized. It is most important that the map organized by detectors coincides with subjective space. The closeness of the detectors on the map is defined by the similarity of their synaptic contacts and the map is topological. You can press it into any form you like. At the same time, the pressed map is a screen of detectors. The concept of a map of detectors is very important. Some researchers believe that detector theory principally eliminates a complex projection of signals. This is wrong because when they use the term *detector*, they forget about the possibility of creating from these detectors a very complex structure. The detector map represents, by position on it, a variety of signals. If the detector responses are measured against the wavelength, the shape of the threshold areas along the wavelength will be different. If thresholds are measured in angles, they will be circles. The subjective threshold and the threshold calculated from the sphere are defined by the same detector mechanisms.

The next stage should be the objective evaluation of these maps using evoked potential techniques. Without penetrating the brain, according to detector theory it is hoped that one can extract information about detectors parallel to subjective characteristics. How this can be done is a specific problem because there should be a correspondence between detector levels and evoked potentials.

CHAPTER

9

The Orienting Response and Subjective Space I

This chapter covers the following issues:

1. Detector map.
2. Subjective differences as geometrical distances in perceptual space and multidimensional scaling.
3. Perceptual space for light intensity.
4. Coordinates of perceptual space as excitations of independent predetector neurons; excitation vectors.
5. Spherical structure of perceptual space for intensity; subjective distance, differential threshold.
6. Detector representation of perceptual space, the concept of link vectors, scalar products of excitation vectors and link vectors, detector characteristics and detector map.
7. Fechner's law and Stevens' law as interpreted by spherical structure of perceptual intensity space.
8. Perceptual space for colors of equal intensity as a sphere in three-dimensional space.
9. Neuronal opponent channels as components of vectors of excitation.
10. Color detectors as representations of color space.
11. Saturation and hue as polar coordinates of spherical model.
12. Threshold measurement using color space.

There are three different approaches to coding in the nervous system. The first is the code by pattern of spikes, the second the code by the ensemble of neurons, and the third the labeled line principle or channel-dependent code of detectors. According to the first principle, it is believed that each stimulus can produce in a neuron a particular train of spikes that represent this stimulus by specific combination of interspike intervals. In this sense, each neuron can generate different representations of different signals. The second principle is assumed on the basis that each stimulus produces a unique combination of neurons that are excited. According to the third principle, the detector channel code or the labeled line principle, each feature of the signal, each variation in the parameter of the signal is processed in parallel channels by means of specific lines that can be called labeled lines, detectors, or channel-dependent code. The term *index code of the neuron* can also be used.

The problem is how a single line can be used in the representation of signals of more complex structure than the variations in a certain parameter. Here, a new concept, which is very important in neurophysiology, should be introduced. This is the concept of a *detector map*—a collection of specific detectors that represent, by means of excitation, at a particular point on the map a particular feature of the external signal. In this sense, the principle of a labeled line that at first seems to be completely independent of the relationship between signals, is used as a method of projection of signals on maps composed of specific detectors. Cortical areas are collections of maps, even blocks of maps, where different aspects of the stimulus are selectively represented.

The methods by which such maps can be studied raises some problems. The most direct approach is by touching a microelectrode onto a single element of the map, and characterizing the responsive area or the receptive field of this detector with respect to the coordinates of the map, thereby constructing the map through a step-by-step recording of such detectors. This is a very time-consuming process and is not always sufficient to reveal the dimensionality this map possesses, because this method only looks at local properties of this structure. The other approach is a psychophysical one. It is possible to express subjective differences between signals as distance on these maps. Collective excitation in a block of maps can also be related to the subjective phenomenon known as *perceptions*. If this is correct, then it should be possible to find a specific approach for detector map reconstruction, which is derived not from the detectors themselves, but from the subjective phenomena associated with the excitation points of the detector maps. This approach can be described as follows.

The first assumption for this use of sensations in reconstructing such a map is based on understanding the properties of our subjective evaluations of the differences between signals. Experimental results reveal that, if a matrix is constructed from subjective evaluations of paired presented signals, when each pair is evaluated by numbers from zero (when the two stimuli are subjectively equal) to nine (when the difference is maximal), then the elements of this matrix possess a specific property. They obey the axioms of a matrix space. This means that, first, the differences between subjectively equal signals is zero, then the distance between signals does not depend on the direction of the comparison. Second, three independent differences taken together form a triangle, so that two differences are greater than the third one. These are the axioms of matrix space. If the matrix of subjective differences obeys the axioms of matrix space, then it would be possible to find an orthogonal system of vectors in which these signals can be represented as points in such a way that the geometrical distances between points exactly corresponds with subjective differences from which the data were derived. Using this approach, a number of independent coordinates can be obtained that are necessary to approximate the position of points in multidimensional space with a high degree of precision with respect to experimental subjective differences. From these data, it is also possible to obtain some indication about the dimensionality of the space. In the Euclidean metric space, the distances between points equal the square root of the sum of squared differences between coordinates of the two points.

The first step is to obtain the matrix of subjective differences. The second step is to prove that these matrices obey the axioms of metric space. The next step is to apply one of the available algorithms to obtain the orthogonal base of vectors in which these points can be represented. The best known algorithms are the Young–Torgerson procedures of multidimensional scaling (MDS) that measure the number of independent coordinates (Torgerson, 1958; Young & Housholder, 1938). The strategy of research is as follows. The hypothesis is suggested that detectors selectively tuned to particular features of stimuli collectively constitute a detector map. Each stimulus feature is represented by a point on the detector map in accordance with the excitation of the respective detector. The subjective differences between signals are measured by geometrical distance between the points on the detector that represents respective stimuli. Using a matrix of subjective differences and regarding these differences as geometrical distances, one can reconstruct the structure of a detector map.

Using such procedures, it is possible to obtain an understanding of color vision through detector maps of color detectors. A study was initiated in the Sokolov laboratory in an area that has not been fully researched—that of scaling the intensity of light. The problem here was whether the intensity is represented in the nervous system as a scalar or as a vector in such a way that intensity detectors constitute a detector map.

The experiment was very simple. Using procedures with a test field and an induction field, it is possible to extend the variations of darkness, because darkness on an illuminated screen can only be obtained using a strong induction field surrounding the test field. The experiment was carried out in the following way: the test field surrounded by the induction field constitutes a stimulus that was followed by a similar structure but with different intensity of the test field and the induction field. The subject's task was to compare the test fields under different intensities of the induction fields presented sequentially and to quantify in numbers from one (identical lightness) up to nine (maximal difference of lightness).

The subjective differences between intensities of lights of the test fields under different intensities of the induction field were estimated and put into a matrix that was then analyzed by the Young–Torgerson method.

The most important result of this analysis was that the perceptual space of lightness has two dimensions, that is, for describing subjective differences between light intensity, two variables are needed. More specifically, the points representing different lightness are located on a semicircle (Fig. 9.1). The points representing different stimuli do not occupy the total two-dimensional perceptual space, but are located in a thin layer that can be regarded as a result of small deviations from a circumference line with constant radius. In this sense, different light intensities are coded by two coordinates. The orientation of the two-dimensional vector characterizes the

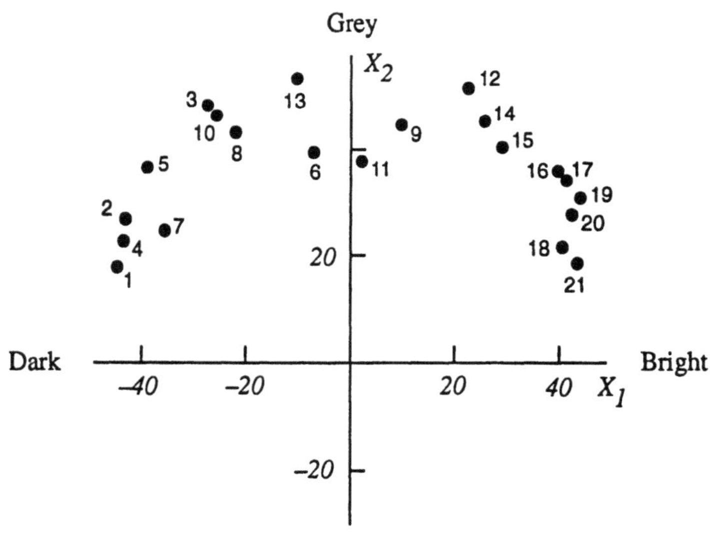

FIG. 9.1. Perceptual space for light intensity. The subjective differences between lights of different intensities presented under different induction fields were put in a matrix. Elements of each obey the metric space axioms. The multidimensional scaling procedure reveals a two-dimensional space in which all signals are located on a semicircle with the brightest and the darkest at the ends of the semicircle. The gray color was located in the middle. Every light was characterized by two coordinates. One coordinate for all light does not change the sign. The other axis changes sign for bright and dark light, respectively.

subjective intensity. Negative and positive coordinates define the brightest and the darkest signals, respectively. The gray is between the very bright and the very dark with an orthogonal axis. Using a normalization procedure with respect to a constant radius, a unitary sphere was obtained (Fig. 9.2). Most importantly, when the data were normalized in this way, the position of single stimuli did not change with respect to any other stimulus. The original sequence or ordering of stimuli was preserved. The intensity of light, therefore, appeared to be coded by a vector represented in normalized form, by the sine and cosine of the angle characterizing the position of the signals of the semicircle (Fig. 9.3). It should be emphasized that it is not possible to put all the signals of different intensities along one line, in one dimension without distortion of interstimulus differences. They were located on a plane, with two independent coordinates needed to specify the position of any signal on this plane. Each stimulus was characterized by a vector. The intensity in the nervous system was represented not by a scalar, but with a vector.

Among the bipolar cells in the retina, there are two types of neurons: B (brightness) and D (darkness), with elevating and descending response characteristics. The B-neuron is more effectively excited as the intensity of

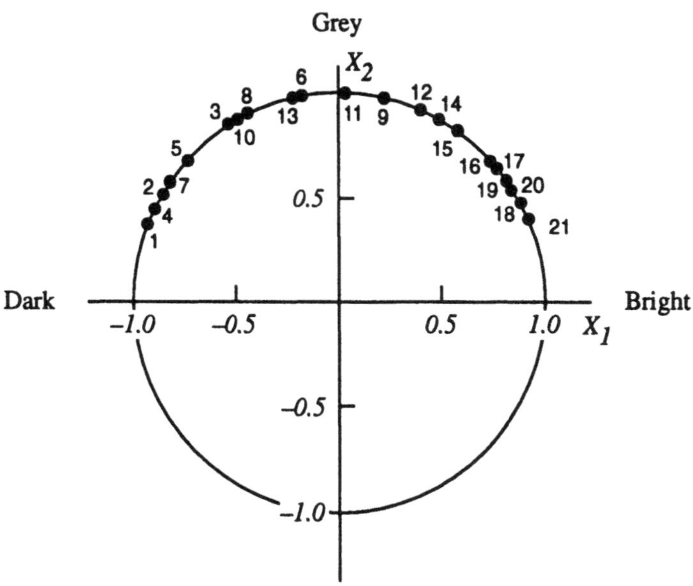

FIG. 9.2. Perceptual space for light after their location on a circle of constant radius. The position of any light with respect to each other does not change, indicating only random variation of the radius. The correlation between geometrical distances and initial subjective differences remains very high. Thus, the light intensities are represented in subjective space along the semicircle—a sphere in a two-dimensional geometric space.

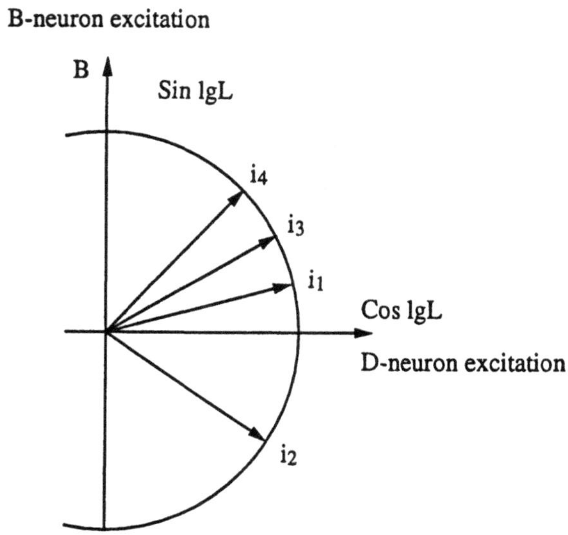

FIG. 9.3. Scheme of the subjective space for light intensity. Each point on the semicircle represents a particular intensity represented by intensity selective detectors. The light intensity detector excitation depends on input in the form of excitations from predetectors constituting an excitation vector. Each excitation vector corresponds with a specific detector. This is achieved by different combinations of synaptic contacts on each detector constituting its link vector. The selective response of a detector to a particular stimulus depends on its link vector. The response reaches maximum when the excitation vector is collinear with the link vector.

the stimulus increases. The D-neuron shows decreasing excitation if the stimulus is bright. The coordinates of this vector are the sine and cosine of the logarithm of intensity. (Figure 9.4a shows these coordinates plotted independently against the log of the stimulus intensity.) It might be asked why the B-axis extended below zero. That occurred because a test surrounded by an induction field was used. The hypothesis is that the B-neurons from the induction field send their signals as an additional neuron from the test field to the induction field when the impression of darkness on the test field is of higher intensity than the test field. If the test fields were compared under conditions when the induction field is not illuminated, then the lights of different intensities occupy only one quadrant of the circle in such a way that dark and bright lights were located on two orthogonal axes with lights of various intensities positioned on the circle between the brightest and darkest stimuli. Thus, each light intensity evoking an impression characterized by lightness was represented by two coordinates that parallel sine and cosine functions of the angle that correspond with the logarithm of light intensity.

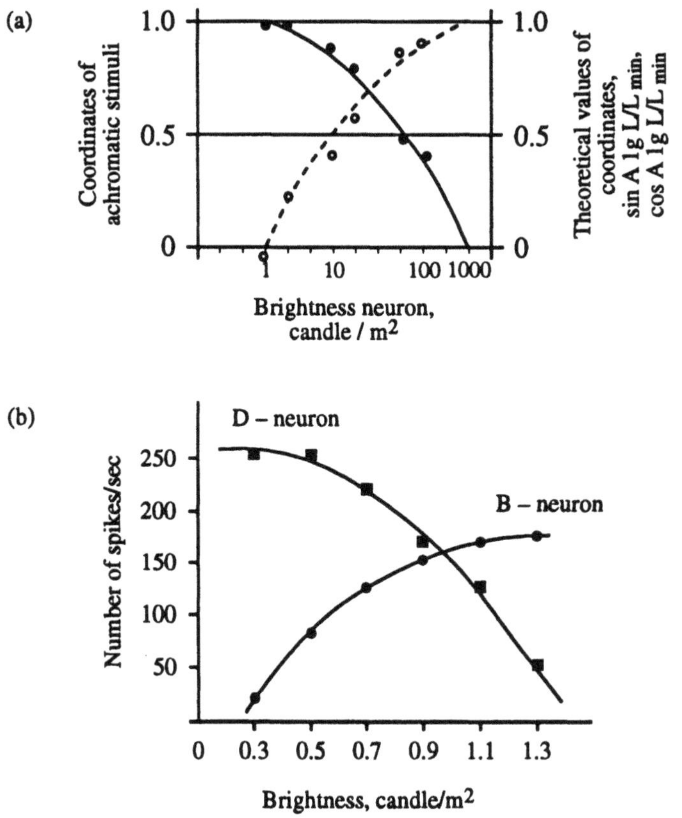

FIG. 9.4. Comparison of two coordinates of light intensity perceptual space with spike responses of B- and D-neurons. (a) Representation of coordinates (ordinate) obtained by multidimensional scaling from subjective estimations of differences between lights varying along a log(intensity) scale (abscissa), which closely match the cosine (left ordinate) and sine (right ordinate) functions. (b) The responses of B- and D-neurons in spike discharges (ordinate) are very similar to the sine and cosine functions if presented along a log(intensity) scale (abscissa). The comparison of coordinates of subjective perceptual space obtained from magnitude estimations of differences (top), with spike responses of B- and D-neurons (bottom) shows their close correspondence, suggesting that light signals of different intensities are organized into a sphere in such a way that each stimulus is represented by a two-dimensional vector of a constant length.

Figure 9.4b shows the electrophysiological characteristics of the D-neuron and B-neuron, with spikes discharges plotted against light intensity. The characteristics correspond with sine (B-neuron) and cosine (D-neuron), respectively. The coordinates obtained in the psychophysiological experiment plotted in Fig. 9.4a and the electrophysiological characteristics of these neurons plotted in Fig. 9.4b are very similar to each other. B- and D-neurons represent the real excitations found in subjective intensity space as coordinates. If the intensity of light changes, the composition of the components dependent on the excitation of B- and D-neurons also changes.

The vector of excitations given by excitations of B- and D-neurons is acting in a parallel manner on the array of intensity detectors. Each intensity detector is characterized by two synaptic contacts for B-neuron and D-neuron signaling. The response of the detector results from the summation of products obtained from the multiplication of incoming excitations and specific synaptic weight (strength). The response characteristics of intensity detectors are selective with respect to specific light intensity.

Figure 9.3 is a scheme that shows the principle coding of intensity by detectors. For each light intensity, there is a specific excitation vector. One of the problems of intensity coding is to understand the nature of the transform of the excitation vector into excitation of the detector. In the studies of the rabbit cortex in the Sokolov laboratory, (Izmailov & Sokolov, 1991), it has been found that neurons are selectively tuned to particular light intensities (Fig. 9.4). If the intensity of the signal is changed, the response of the neuron is decreased. As seen in Fig. 9.5, the intensity changes with respect to optimal value. The next neuron tuned to another intensity again decreases its firing as intensity is changed. The characteristic of each detector can be approximated to the cosine function. An array of detectors represents a sequence of cosine functions, selectively tuned to particular intensities.

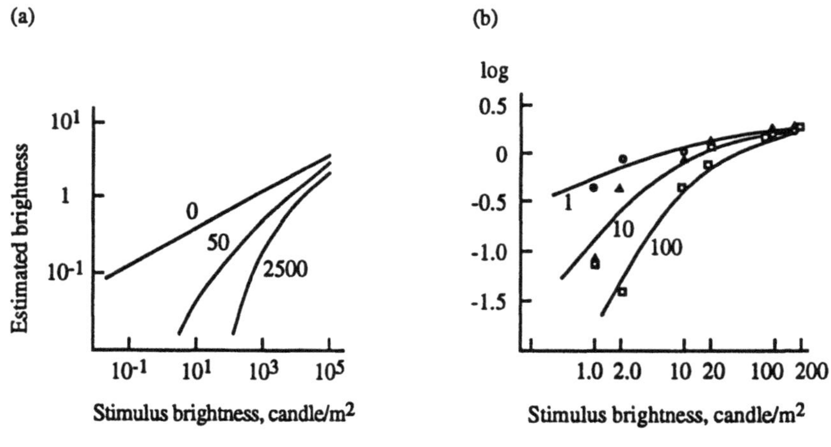

FIG. 9.5. The comparison of Stevens magnitudes of subjective light estimations with geometrical distances obtained from the spherical model and regarded as analogies of subjective differences between signals. Depending on the background illumination, the subjective estimations produced functions with different slopes. The close correspondence of Stevens' values of subjective differences with geometric distances from the multidimensional scaling suggests that the Stevens' law follows from the spherical organization of perceptual space.

How is the system for coding intensity organized? Take photopic vision as an example. At the input level are three cones that converge on the B- and D-neurons, which are called *predetectors*. Each predetector generates one component of the excitation vector and from each predetector, the excitation arrives at a set of detectors. A formalization of this process is presented in Fig. 9.6. Predetectors generate an excitation vector representing a combination of excitation of two predetectors. This excitation vector acts in a parallel manner to all detectors, achieved by having a fan of connections coming from each predetector to each detector. Each detector has a specific synaptic weight. All detectors receive the same excitation vector, but each detector possesses a specific combination of synaptic contacts. The detector performs the following procedure. The detector multiplies in each channel the arriving excitation by the magnitude of the synaptic weight and the same is done for the other channels. The results of this multiplication are summated in the detector.

Formally, the detector is characterized by synaptic weights that can also be regarded as a component of a link vector. The result of the summation is an inner product of two vectors, excitation vector X and link vector C. The inner product is equal to the multiplication of the lengths of these vectors and the cosine of the angle between these vectors. This angle is that between the vector of excitation and the link vector of synaptic contacts for a particular detector neuron. The lengths of the excitation vector and the link vector are of constant values. From this computation it can be seen that, if the excitation vector coincides with the direction of the link vector, the detector response reaches maximum. This takes place when the excitations are in direct proportion to the magnitudes of the synaptic contacts. In this

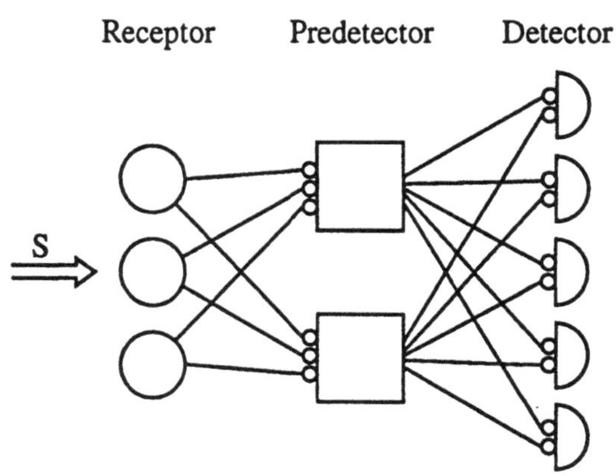

FIG. 9.6. Schematic representation of light intensity analyzer. The stimulus generates logarithmic responses in three types of cones that are connected with two predetectors–B- and D-neurons. The signals of the predetectors represent a "fan of excitation vectors" acting in parallel on a set of intensity-selective detectors differing in their link vectors. The "fan of excitation vectors" produces in each detector a scalar product of the excitation vector and the link vector. The maximum excitation would be reached in a selective detector whose link vector is collinear with the excitation vector generated by a given stimulus.

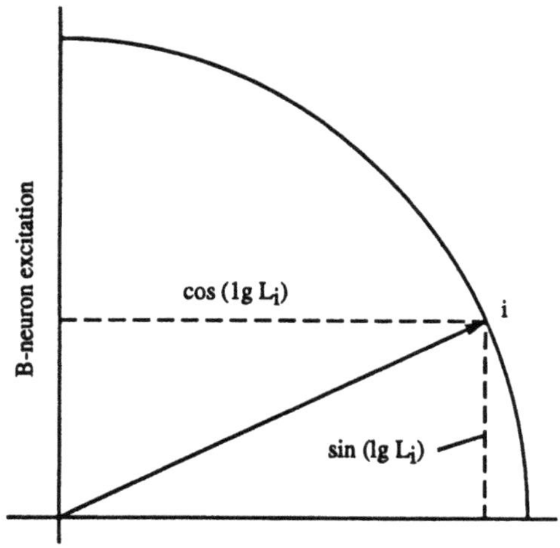

FIG. 9.7. Vector representation of light intensity. The components of the excitation vector are excitation of B- and D-neurons functioning as predetectors with characteristics sine(logI) and cosine(logI) determining the position of the detector on the circle according to the intensity, I, of the stimulus. The excitation of a selective detector is maximal when its synaptic contact constitutes a link vector collinear with an excitation vector generated by a signal.

case, the vectors are collinear and in this case the angle between them equals zero, the cosine equals one and the response then reaches maximum (Fig. 9.7). The stimulus intensity is first coded as a vector of excitation. This vector of excitation produces a selective excitation maximal at one of the detectors. If the stimulus is changed, the composition of the excitation vector components is also changed, and the maximum of excitation moves along the array of detectors. This mechanism of selective detector excitation determines the perception of light intensity. It is evident from the fact that B- and D-neurons characteristics correspond with coordinates of the vectors obtained from psychophysical experiments.

The next challenge was to study colors of equal intensity. It has just been shown that the intensity space is two-dimensional. Using color signals of equal intensity, the subjective differences between the colors has been studied. In different experiments, between 10 to 15 different colors were used. These monochromatic colors were presented to the subject, with a 1-s interval. The subject's task was to evaluate the subjective difference between the colors, using numbers from zero to nine. A matrix was then obtained for all these subjective differences, using data averaged over five presentations of each pair. The Young–Torgerson MDS procedure was used to find the coordinates of points representing colors. The results showed that the colors could not be localized on a plane as many previous studies have suggested. The colors of equal intensity were instead located on a sphere in three-dimensional space. The coordinates were obtained from the experiment without any special instructions concerning the evaluation of subjective differences.

At the start of the experiment, the subject saw all the colors that would be presented. No information was given about the minimum and maximum differences between colors, or details of the criteria that the subject had to use. Nevertheless, after just a short period of training, they had very stable responses about color differences. If, in several subjects, the coordinates were close to each other, the data was integrated into a group of normal subjects (Fig. 9.8). The three coordinates of color space closely resemble green–red, yellow–blue, and white color-coding neurons. A three-phasic and a two-phasic opponent process were found. When the third achromatic coordinate is examined (Fig. 9.9), it can be seen to have a very unusual shape that does not correspond to the photopic vision curve. A specific shape of the third coordinate has to be analyzed further. Using this method, it is also possible to obtain maps of abnormal color vision. An analysis of different variations has not yet been carried out, but normal and abnormal color vision has been precisely distinguished.

The results of color testing can be represented by the projection of the sphere on a plane defined by two coordinates: green–red and yellow–blue (Fig. 9.8). No purple colors were presented in this experiment, because only monochromatic colors were used; the dots in Fig. 9.8 show where the purple colors could be located. It can be seen that the colors with very low saturation (for example, yellow, 570–580 nm) are very far from the circumference of the circle. It is not possible to present this data in two-dimensional space, because of the very great deviations of the initial subjective differences from Euclidean distances calculated from the coordinates. If distances are calculated using only two coordinates, then there are very substantial deviations from the initial subjective differences (cf. Fig. 9.10; see also later). Individual curves are given in Fig. 9.11.

The results obtained for different levels of intensity show that the red and blue colors are very close to the limits of saturation for all intensities (Fig. 9.12). There is an intensity-dependent modification of trajectory of monochromatic colors corresponding with the Bezold–Brucke effect. The spherical surface for the equiluminant colors can be regarded as occupied by color-sensitive detectors for the colors of equal intensity. The change of monochromatic light resulting in modification of the three-dimensional excitation vector would selectively excite a particular color-detector that is based on the same principle explained for intensity coding. That principle is characterized for color-detector by the scalar product of the three-dimensional excitation vector and the three-dimensional link vector of the equiluminant color detector.

Thus, for representation of color signals there is a sphere. For achromatic colors of different intensity, a semicircle is required if the test field and induction field are used, or a quarter of a circle if a test field is given without an induction field. The distance between the ends of the excitation vectors equals the distance between the detectors excited by respective stimuli. What is the differential threshold in such a model? The detector code of light intensities and equiluminant colors suggest that the differen-

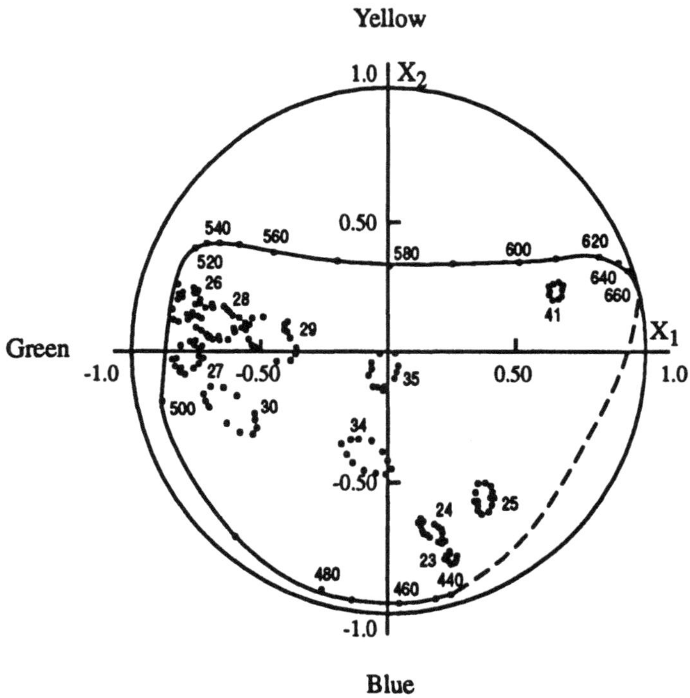

FIG. 9.8. The color perceptual space of equiluminant colors. The subjective differences between equiluminant color treated by multidimensional scaling revealed that all stimuli are located on the sphere in three-dimensional space. The basis of this space is represented by red–green and yellow–blue opponent orthogonal axes, and an achromatic unipolar axis orthogonal to the opponent axes. Monochromatic light occupies a curve located in a hemisphere only. Each monochromatic light is then represented on the sphere by a three-dimensional vector of constant length with components defined by the contribution of red–green, yellow–blue, and achromatic neurons functioning as predetectors. The projection of monochromatic light on the red–green and yellow–blue plane demonstrates a curve that is not closed, because of the absence of purple colors in the experiment. The circle is closed when the purple colors obtained by a mixture of violet and red lights were used in the experiment. The white color positioned on the pole of the sphere is projected on the centre of the plane. The coordinates of two opponent and one achromatic channels given as functions of wavelength closely correspond with the respective opponent and achromatic neurons in the geniculate body of the monkey. The model states that different loci of the sphere are represented by color detectors having three-dimensional link vectors and that are selectively tuned to different colors according to the appropriate three-dimensional excitation vector generated by the particular color.

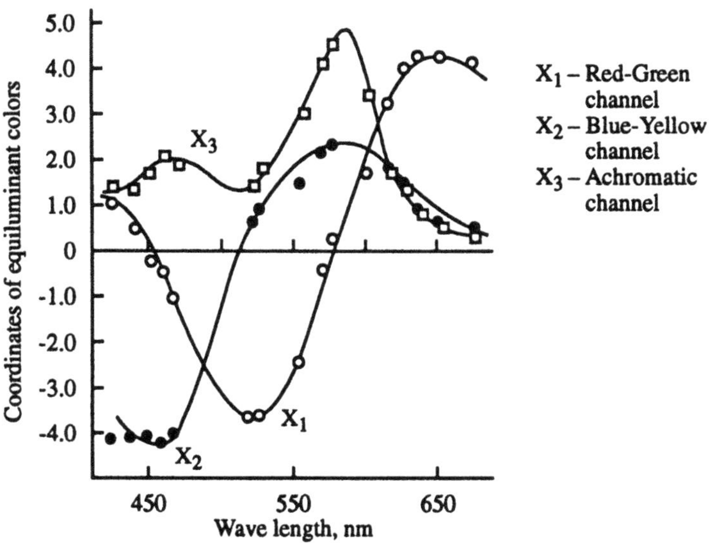

FIG. 9.9. The coordinates of monochromatic isoluminant light as a function of wavelength. The coordinates of monochromatic isoluminance lights constitute a vector of constant length projecting the light on a unitary sphere in three-dimensional Euclidean space. The Euclidean distances between the ends of the vectors representing color closely correspond to the initial subjective differences between the colors obtained from the experiment and treated by multidimensional scaling procedures. The shape of the wavelength coordinate functions corresponds with the opponent and achromatic color coding neurons in the trichromat monkey.

FIG. 9.10. Cross-correlations between the Euclidean distances between points representing colors in the spherical color space and the initial subjective estimates of differences between the corresponding colors. Abscissa—Euclidean distances between points representing colors on the surface of the sphere. Ordinate—Subjective estimation of color differences. There is clearly a very close relationship between the color-space model and the corresponding subjective color differences used in multidimensional scaling for the construction of color space.

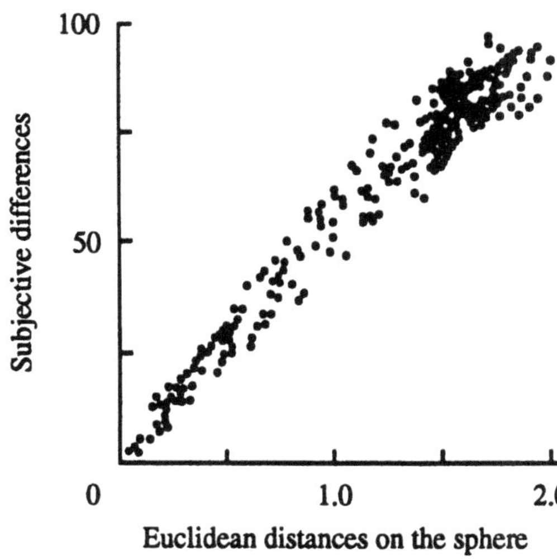

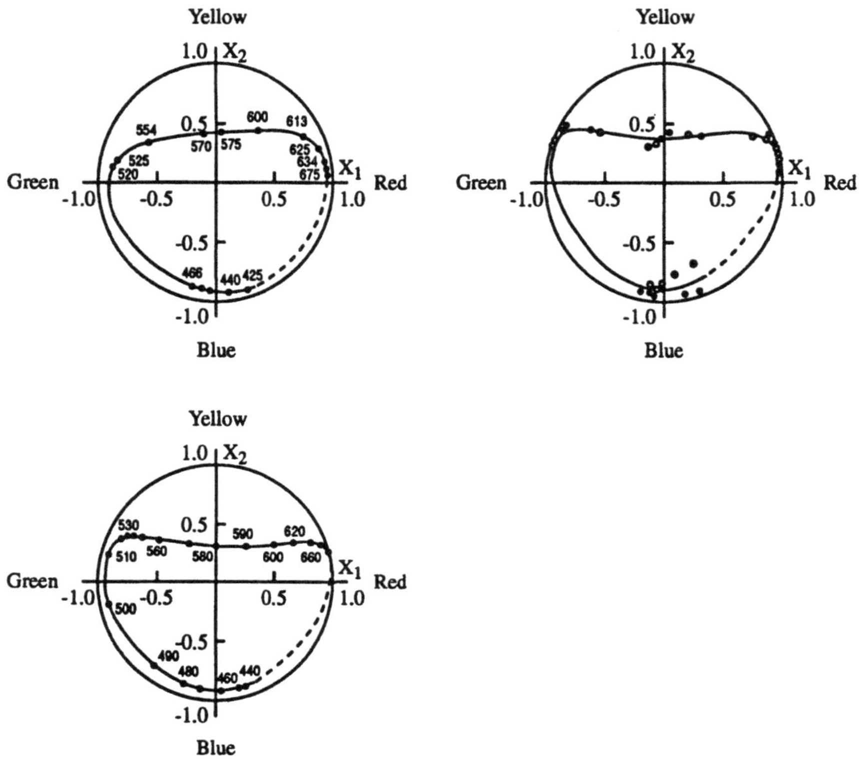

FIG. 9.11. Individual projections of the spherical color space on the red–green and yellow–blue plane. The spherical color space can be obtained not only directly from the matrix of subjective differences but indirectly from a procedure of verbal categorization of color stimuli. The weighted probabilities of verbal responses are regarded as components of the categorization vector. The analogs of direct subjective differences between colors are calculated as the Euclidean distances between the categorization vectors in the form of a matrix of analogs of subjective differences. The matrix is treated by multidimensional scaling procedures in the same way as was done for a matrix of subjective differences. The results of these two methods corresponds, indicating that a common perceptual color space is operating in both experimental procedures.

tial threshold equals the distance between the neighboring detectors. As the Euclidean distance and the angle for small angles are close to equality, the threshold can have angular measure. The difference between two sequentially presented colors would be perceived as if an excitation vector is "jumping" from a particular color detector on the neighboring one.

For colors of equal intensity, a sphere in three-dimensional space is needed. The subjective difference between signals is measured as the distance between the ends of excitation vectors representing these signals.

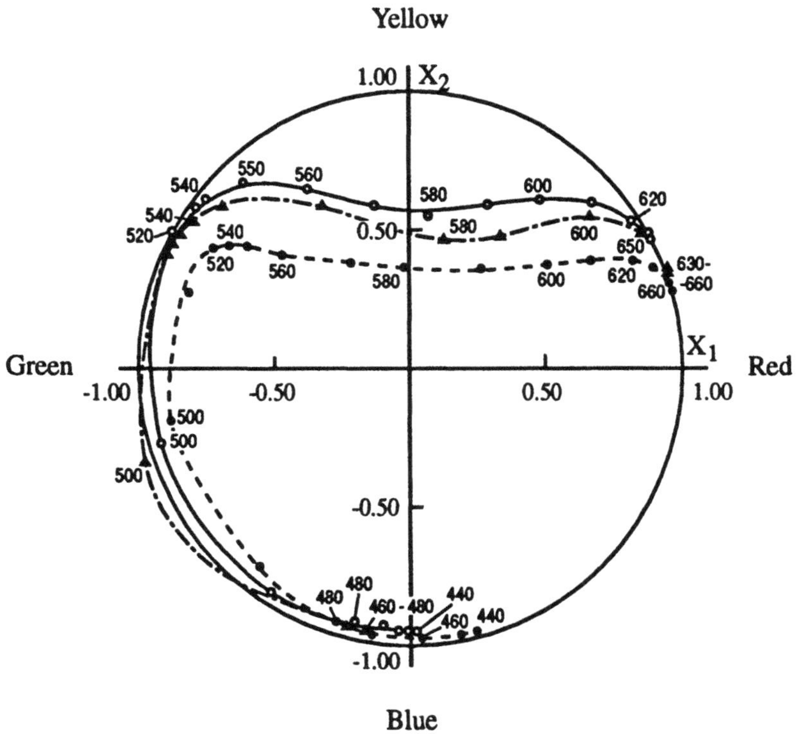

FIG. 9.12. The influence of intensity level on the structure of color space for equiluminance–luminance colors. The projection on the sphere of the plane of the opponent process mechanism shows the effect of an increase in intensity on the trajectory of monochromatic light, demonstrating the perfection of color perception with an increase in illumination of the equiluminant colors used in the experiment.

The threshold on the sphere is an abstract threshold. For each such unitary angle, it is possible to calculate for monochromatic light a particular difference between wavelengths. The excitation vector shift along the line of monochromatic lights on this unitary angle corresponds to the subjective threshold, expressed in $\Delta\lambda$. The points obtained from the sphere are plotted in Fig. 9.13, and they closely match those obtained by direct measurements of color threshold. From the color spherical model obtained, it should be remembered, by estimations of superthreshold differences between colors, it was therefore possible to obtain data concerning the color thresholds.

The comparison of saturation for experimental data extracted from the literature with saturation obtained from the color sphere shows their similarity (Fig. 9.14). Saturation was measured by the magnitude of the vertical angle (the angular difference between the color point and the pole), be-

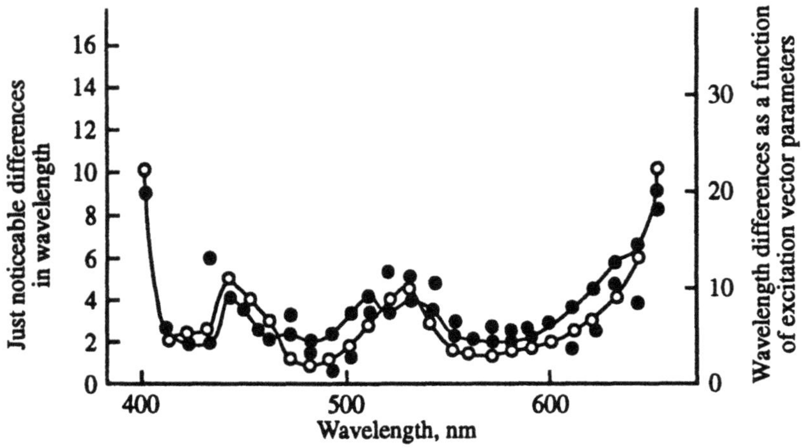

FIG. 9.13. Threshold measurements of hue extracted from the spherical model. The spherical color space obtained from superthreshold subjective distances allow an opportunity to obtain data about thresholds. The evaluation of color thresholds in the just noticeable differences of wavelength is obtained directly from the spherical model by calculation of the modification of wavelength $\Delta\lambda$ corresponding to the rotation of the excitation vector on minimal constant angle. At different wavelengths, this constant angle of the rotation of the excitation vector corresponds with different $\Delta\lambda$ values. The $\Delta\lambda$ values thus obtained from the model as a function of λ coincide with independently measured thresholds presented as a function of wavelength.

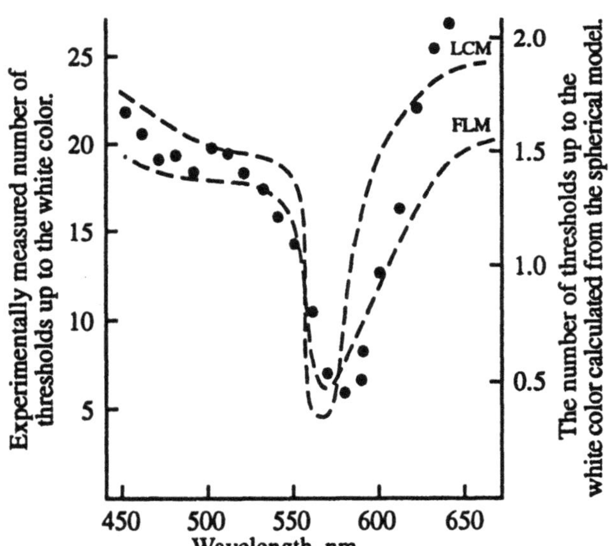

FIG. 9.14. The saturation function obtained from the model. In the model, saturation is given by the vertical angle (angular difference between color point and pole). The closer to the equator is located the color point, the greater is the saturation. The calculated vertical angles of the sphere corresponds with independently subjectively measured saturation.

cause white light is located on the pole of the sphere, saturation varies from the pole up to the equator where saturation reaches maximum. The color sphere represents an isotropic color space. This can be seen from an analysis of MacAdam ellipses shown in Figs. 9.15 and 9.16 (MacAdam, 1963). The question is why the MacAdam ellipses are of different magnitude and orientation. The solution is that two-dimensional space results in a distortion of the geometrical representations of subjective color thresholds. The projections of the MacAdam ellipses on the color sphere now shows that their magnitudes are more regular and the ellipses are closer to circles.

The significance of the color sphere for representation of initial subjective differences was studied using the following procedure. Initial color differences were obtained in the experimental matrix. Then, the coordinates of color points can be obtained by MDS, each color being defined by three coordinates. Using these coordinates, it is possible to calculate the geometric distance that, according to our hypotheses, should be exactly equal to the initial subjective differences. The two sets of data were then correlated and Fig. 9.10 shows this correlation, with subjective magnitudes along the vertical axis and Euclidean distances calculated from the unitary sphere on the horizontal axis. All coordinates were normalized

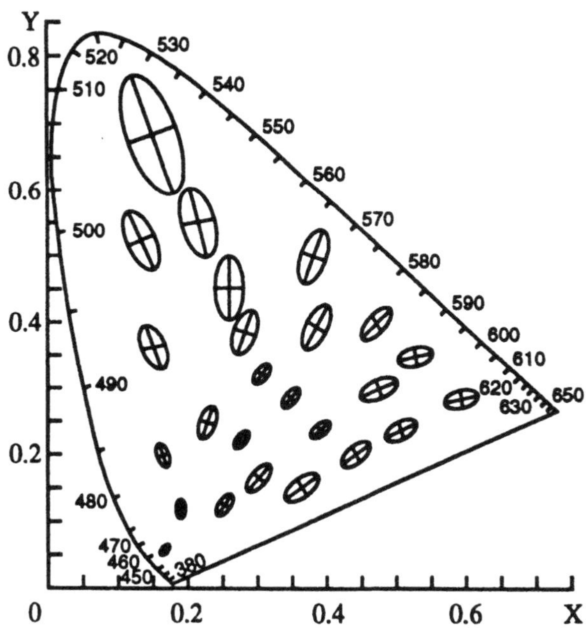

FIG. 9.15. The representation of two-dimensional thresholds on the X-Y plane (MacAdam ellipses). The ellipses are not equal in different parts of the diagram. This is evidence against isotropy of this representation.

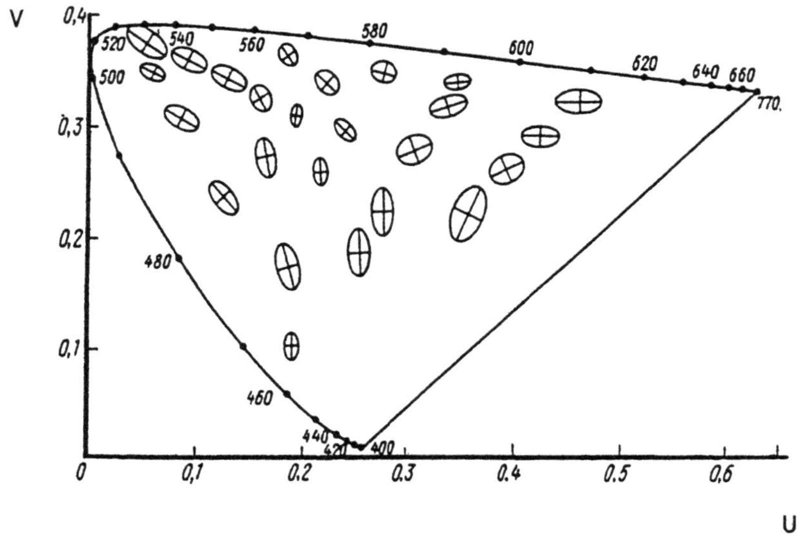

FIG. 9.16. The correction of the XY diagram with respect to two-dimensional thresholds. This has been attempted in UV systems as isotropic space approximation. It is evident that the degree of approximation is not sufficient; although the MacAdam ellipses are more regular, they are still of different magnitudes and orientations.

with respect to the radius. The magnitudes of correlation reached values of between 0.95 and 0.98. There were thus very high correlations between initial subjective differences and Euclidean distances. This gives very strong support to the view that the subjective color experience is determined by color vectors.

The same logic that was applied to intensity detectors can also be applied to color detectors. The vector of excitation for colors is, however, a three-dimensional vector. Theoretically, the color detector is a neuron that is selectively tuned with respect to specific combinations of the coordinate of the excitation vector. Color detectors have been studied in the rabbit, and several color-selective units were found in the visual cortex. In the lateral geniculate body, red–green and yellow–blue neurons have been seen. After several years, an excellent study of Zeki (1980) showed that there were, in the visual cortex of the monkey, neurons that were very selective with respect to wavelength. Stimulation of this color analyzing system produced a certain combination of excitation of cones. At this level, there is a nonlinear transformation of light intensity, the transformation being a logarithmic function of the input stimulus intensity. After that, there is a linear combination of excitations. Thus, the horizontal cells provide linear combinations of cone excitation. Scotopic vision is enabled by horizontal cells having input only from rods. There are three types of photopic horizontal cells connected with cones. These are the red–green, yellow–blue, and luminosity horizontal cells. At the level of horizontal cells, a vector of excitation is of different length, depending on intensity. If the intensity of the colors is constant, the equiluminant colors are located on the sphere in the three-dimensional space. Coding of color of equal luminosity is achieved by a three-dimensional vector. It is only by using stimuli of equal intensity that it is possible to encode colors on the sphere in three-dimensional space.

How do these color-selective units operate? From the standpoint here, there is a neuronal color net with colors being represented by single color detectors, single color selective neuronal elements. The scheme works in a similar way as for intensity, except that, for equiluminant colors, there are three coordinates. The color detectors generate excitations defined by the scalar products of a three-component excitation vector and a three-component link vector. Each color detector has three synaptic contacts of different value. The formula for color is the same as that for intensity because the vectorial representation does not depend on the number of vector components. Responses of color-selective detectors depend on the extent to which the excitation of color predetectors corresponds to the magnitudes of the synaptic contacts. If they are proportional and the vectors are collinear, then the detector response reaches maximum. If the input spectrum is changed, then the vector of excitation is changed. Through a fan of synaptic contacts, there is parallel processing of a great number of color selective cells detectors. In a cell where the link vector corresponds with the direction of the excitation vector, the excitation reaches maximum. Thus, the maximum excitation on the surface of the color sphere in this three-dimensional space, which reflects the color of the stimulus, moves around as the input spectrum is changed.

In the sphere, it is possible to obtain the three Cartesian coordinates and polar coordinates-angles. The Cartesian coordinates correspond with the physiological mechanism; they are closely related to real neuron characteristics. The polar coordinates characterize the subjective aspects of the color. Because the sphere in three-dimensional space has a constant radius, there are only two independent subjective variables and two angles, hue and saturation. The line of monochromatic light is located above the equatorial plane. Each color can be characterized in physiological terms by excitations of three independent neurons: green–red, yellow–blue, and white–black. Hue corresponds with the angle on the equatorial plane, and saturation corresponds with the vertical angle.

It has been found that intensity needs two dimensions but that colors of equal intensity need three dimensions. The problem is how many dimensions are required for a combination of different intensities and colours. One expectation, from simple summation, is that the number of dimensions should be five. However, it has been shown that only four dimensions are needed and the sphere in four-dimensional space explains all three subjective variables—hue, saturation, and brightness.

CONCLUDING COMMENTS

The correlations between subjective estimates and Euclidean distances are really high. Is it still a unique representation of colors? The search has been for a unique mathematical description, from the standpoint of physiological mechanisms. A spherical structure has also been found in fish, measured by intracellular recording of the magnitude of responses in three photopic horizontal cells. This psychophysical approach was chosen because of the correspondence with physiological systems. Psychophysiology is a science that integrates psychophysics with neurons through models built from neuron-like elements. This model should reproduce characteristics of each element and, at the same time, its output should represent the psychophysical functions. Insofar as the mathematical aspect is concerned, it is very remarkable that in Kohonen's studies (Kohonen, 1990), similar vector formulae were obtained using a completely different point of view of self-organization. Kohonen regards the external signal as a vector whereas here the concept of an excitation vector generated in the nervous system is used. The main principles are also present in a channel-dependent code by detectors organized in the map. This detector map is organized in two layers. Before a particular point on this map is reached, a vector representation of signals at the lower levels of the nervous system is obtained. The basic difference is in the multidimensional representation and spherical surface of the detector map.

This is a new approach among the theories of color vision. Such a spherical model had never been published before. It is very important that all color detectors are on the surface. The space is empty, signals are represented on the map. This study was initiated by finding a neuron that is selectively tuned to light intensities. When the shape of the responses of intensity detectors were examined, it appeared that they were well represented by the sine and cosine function. Some evidence on color detectors that has been collected in the rabbit and other data obtained by Zeki (1980) is, however, difficult to account for using this model. Zeki measured along wavelengths, and thus comparisons can only be made with the model for monochromatic light. Each detector has a circular configuration of receptive area, so that the sphere is divided by detectors into patches and each patch refers to a particular color sensation.

Light intensity detectors have been seen and the principle of coding of intensity by selective neurons is not unique. The question concerns detectors in the visual system. Flashes of light have been used and the characteristics of intensity detectors are very selective. Thus, with an increase of intensity, a decrease in the response is seen.

The strength of this response was measured by the number of spikes per unit time. It is very important to evaluate the selectivity of the neuron tuning because the detectors represent a basic mechanism. Some other spaces of detector-neurons have been found. In experiments with motion detectors in the cat visual cortex, area 18, responses were measured with respect to direction and speed of target motion. At first, it was found that some neurons are selective for speed, and some for direction. It was decided to organize an experiment to combine these two variables and to study the whole map of neurons responding to a combination of direction and velocity. It was found that this map was occupied by such units that were selective to a combination of speed and direction of motion. It was possible to explain the characteristics of these cells by reference to the spherical model, where two predetectors code the orientation and two predetectors code the speed. The spherical structure is thought to be a basis for the organization of detectors. The vector code of stimuli on the predetector level can explain the spherical representation of stimulus-selective neurons on the detector level.

CHAPTER

10

The Orienting Response and Subjective Space II

This chapter covers the following issues:

1. Perceptual space for colors of different intensities as a sphere in four-dimensional space.
2. Cartesian coordinates of the four-dimensional space as two opponent neurons and B- and D-neurons.
3. Polar coordinates of the color sphere: hue, saturation, and brightness.
4. Correlations between polar coordinates of a sphere and cylindrical coordinates of the Maunsell color body.
5. Detectors of color space.
6. Normal vision.
7. Protoanomalous vision.
9. Protoanopic vision.
10. Deutoranomalous vision.
11. Deutoronopic vision.
12. Deficiencies of color vision by local brain damage: Local color abnormalities, the color-naming deficiency.
13. The color names as symbolic representation of colors.
14. Subjective difference between color names.
15. Isomorphism of perceptual and semantic color spaces.
16. Combined space for colors and color names.
17. The isolation of memory color space.

18. Artificial color names and the modification of their semantic space in the process of learning.
19. The relationships between perceptual, memory, and semantic color spaces.
20. Generation of new gnostic units using link between memory units.
21. Spontaneous OR as response to internal novelty.

In the previous chapter, the work on intensity perception and color perception was discussed. The research on intensity perception has shown that all intensities can be represented on a semicircle on a two-dimensional plane. Each intensity is represented by a vector having two independent coordinates that are not just formal mathematical statements but indicate real excitations of two types of neurons—the B- and D-neurons. For color vision, when subjective intensities of all stimuli were equal, the colors were located on a sphere in three-dimensional space. Each color of constant brightness was characterized by a vector having three components. Two of these components characterized the hue. These components are due to the participation of opponent cells—red–green and yellow–blue. The third component defines the presence of whiteness in these equal illuminosity colors. This whiteness axis results from the contributions of B- and D-neurons. The problem is how many dimensions would be required if colors of different intensity are considered? A likely answer is that all coordinates are independent, and therefore that these stimuli would be represented in five-dimensional space. Another possibility is that some components are common for intensity and color. This would result in a reduction of the total space required.

To solve this problem, a special technique for studying color vision was used. The subject has several categories for the names of the colors—yellow, blue, green, red, bright, dark. Subjects can use any of them in a particular order. Each place in this order is weighted, and from these weighted values the vector of color names was constructed. Each color was characterized by a different contributions of color names. Thus, each color was characterized by a specific vector derived from these color names. From these vectors, the subjective differences between the colors were obtained indirectly. The Euclidean distances between the color name vectors were measured, and these distances between the color name vectors were regarded as equivalent to the subjective evaluation of color differences in order to construct a matrix of subjective differences between colors.

For the purpose of analysis, 126 different colors of different intensity, hue, and saturation were used. Using the technique of color naming, the experimental procedure of comparison of pairs of monochromatic lights of different intensities was reduced. Finally, a 126 by 126 matrix of subjective differences between colors of different intensities was constructed. This matrix was analyzed using multidimensional scaling procedures. The results show that for colors of different intensities, there are only four independent axes. The other specific findings were that the colors are not all randomly distributed in all parts of this four-dimensional space, they are positioned with equal distances from a central point which can be found—a center of gravity of color points. This means that the colors do not occupy all the four-dimensional space, but are located on the surface of the sphere in four-dimensional space.

Finally, these color points were projected onto two planes defined by basic axes (Fig. 10.1). One plane was defined by the red–green and yellow–blue axis, and on this plane many trajectories of monochromatic lights with differing intensities were located. On the other plane, defined by B- and D-neuron coordinates and the brightness of colors were characterized by the vector angle. The different wavelengths were characterized by the length of the vector. In this way, each radius on this B–D plane was a representation of a certain subjective intensity of monochromatic light. A very important point is that the wavelengths are located very regularly on the plane. The white and gray colors were characterized by the angle of the

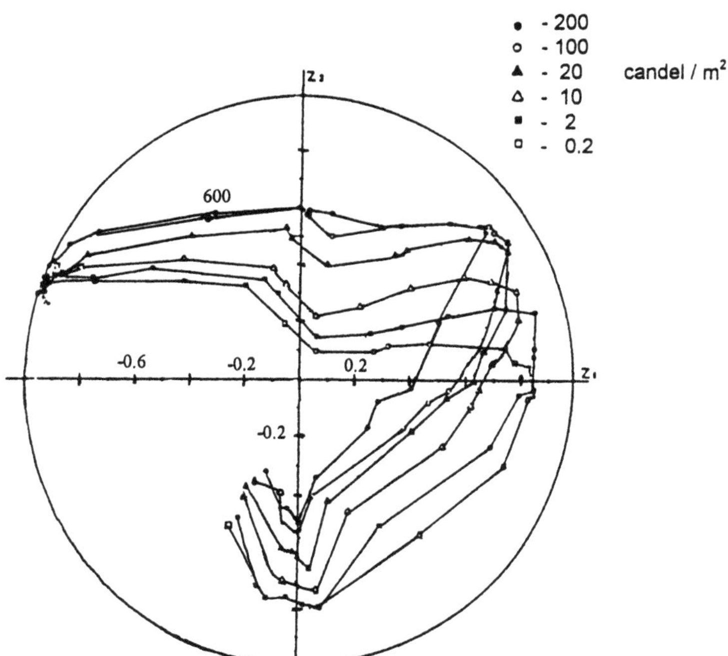

FIG. 10.1. The trajectory of monochromatic lights of different intensities on the red–green and yellow–blue color plane. The angle on the plane estimates the hue of colors. The white color is in the middle of the plane. The length of the vector indicates saturation on the red–green and blue–yellow plane.

vector but not by its length. The lengths of the vectors do not characterize the subjective brightness, which is defined by a combination of two coordinates represented by the B- and D-neurons, respectively. In turn, the length of the vector was related to the saturation; the shorter the vector, the more saturated the color (Fig. 10.2).

The total experimental material shown on the B–D plane again demonstrated that white and gray have the greatest vector length. The change of vector angle is characteristic for specifying brighter or darker stimuli. Here, all stimuli are located in just one octant of the four-dimensional sphere. The black color is absent in these experiments because combinations of test and induction fields were not used, only a test field without any induction field. This means that the range of subjective intensities is only from bright to gray. The black part of the stimulus array can only be generated by means of an induction field that was absent here (Fig. 10.3).

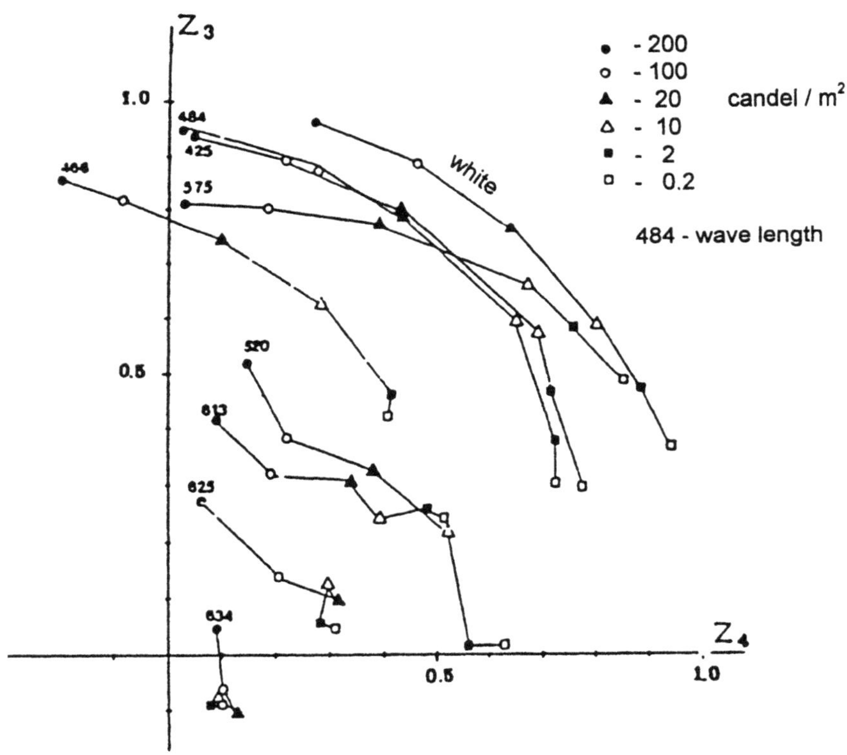

FIG. 10.2. The projection of monochromatic lights on the coordinate plane equivalent to B- and D-neurons. The angle characterizes the lightness of the color. The length of the vector measures the reciprocal value of saturation. Thus, the whiter colors of different lightness are located mostly far from the center, where the most saturated colors are situated close to the center.

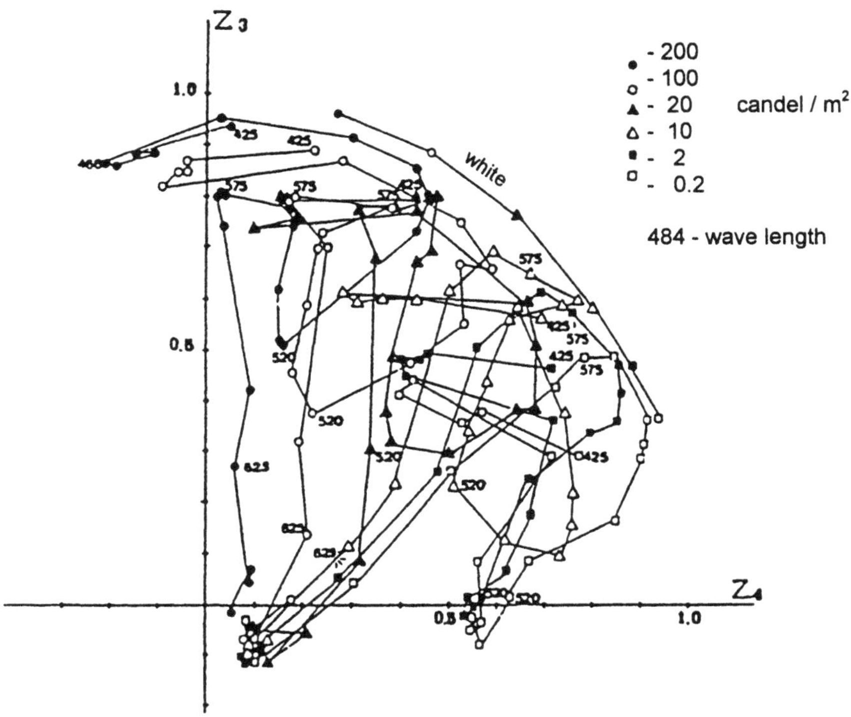

FIG. 10.3. The representation of all colors from the matrix on the B- and D-coordinate plane, plotted according to intensity of light stimuli. The angle corresponds to brightness. The vector length indicates the contribution of "whiteness," based on the excitations of the B- and D-neurons.

Several remarks should be made about the coordinates. In all, there are four coordinates generated by green–red, yellow–blue, B-, and D-neurons. The coordinates of the color space correspond with the real excitation of neurons. These neurons, the so-called predetectors are gradual and not selectively tuned to a particular color. Using monochromatic lights of different wavelengths for each color point, four independent numbers were obtained—excitations of red–green, blue–yellow, bright, and dark neurons. Each coordinate can be plotted out against wavelength, forming independently constructed curves for the different intensities.

These color curves for different intensities have closely corresponding coordinates constructed from the experiments using multidimensional scaling in man. The graph of coordinates of monochromatic lights for the blue–yellow system can be regarded as analogs of the blue–yellow cells in the geniculate body (Fig. 10.4). The graph of coordinates for monochromatic stimuli for red–green corresponds to the same characteristics of real red–green neurons in the geniculate body of the monkey (Fig. 10.5). The

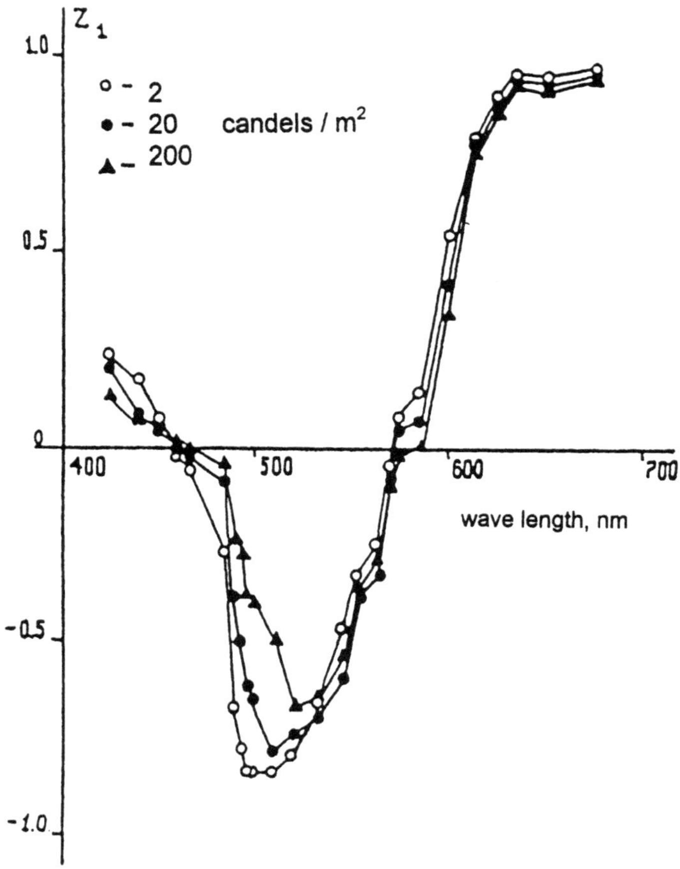

FIG. 10.4. The characteristics of the red–green system. Abscissa is wavelength, ordinate is coordinate amplitude. The shape of this opponent element is not strongly influenced by intensity.

next figures (Figs. 10.6 & 10.7) show white and gray coordinates obtained from the results of multidimensional scaling (MDS) and plotted against wavelength. The white coordinate corresponds to the B-neuron coordinate. Similar results were obtained for the gray system. The coordinates of a gray system also obtained by MDS correspond with the D-neuron. A number of comments should be made at this stage about terminology. The term *gray* rather than *dark* is used, because there were lights only on a test field–no induction field was present. So, there were excitations of B-neurons and D-neurons in the test field only.

If the stimulus is very bright, there is maximum excitation of the B-neuron. As the signal on the test field is gradually eliminated, maximum excitation of the D-neuron takes place. If an induction field is introduced

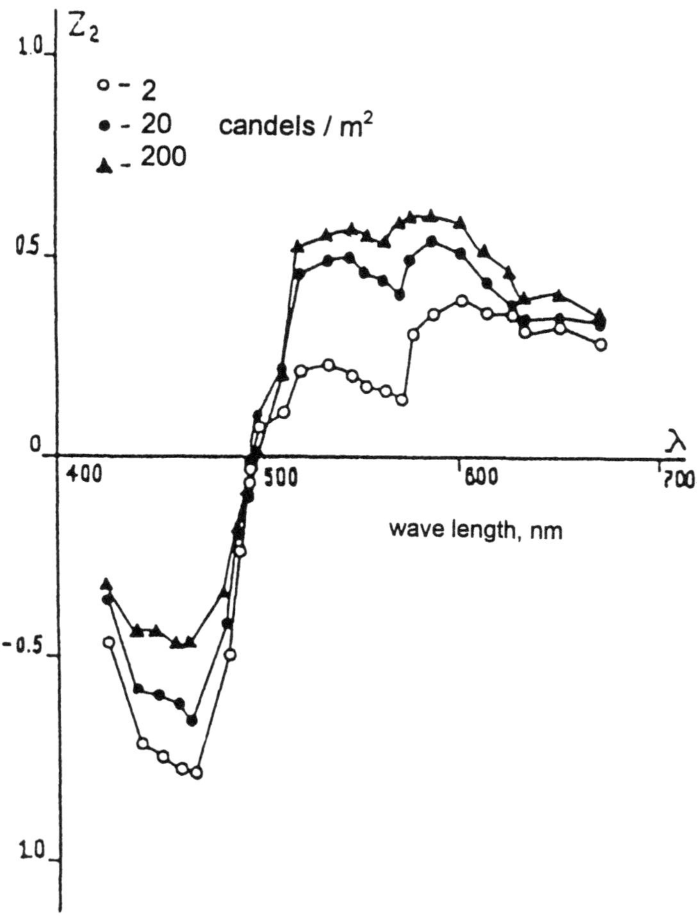

FIG. 10.5. The characteristics of the blue–yellow system. Abscissa is wavelength, ordinate is coordinate amplitude. The shape is more affected by light intensity.

around the test field, it is possible to obtain negative values for the B-neurons corresponding to the black color. This can be explained by the theory that B-neurons from the induction field act on the test field in the opposite direction and result in prolongation of the B-axis into the negative region. The following scheme has been postulated: B-neurons activated by the test field respond when a stimulus is presented in the test field. The B-neurons excited by the induction field contribute as a specific black predetector for the test field. This contribution of B-neurons from the induction field results in a black color on the test field. The D-neuron should be called a gray detector, because it participates in the processing of both bright and dark sig-

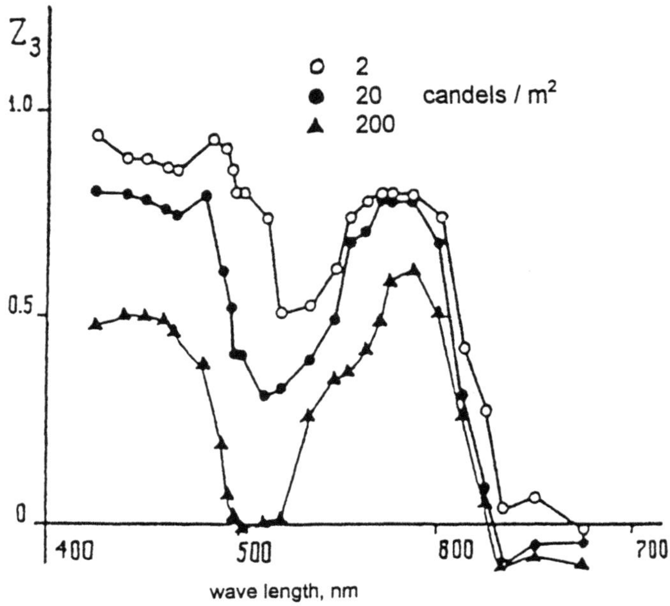

FIG. 10.6. Spectral functions of analogs of B cells along wavelength axis demonstrates strong intensity dependence.

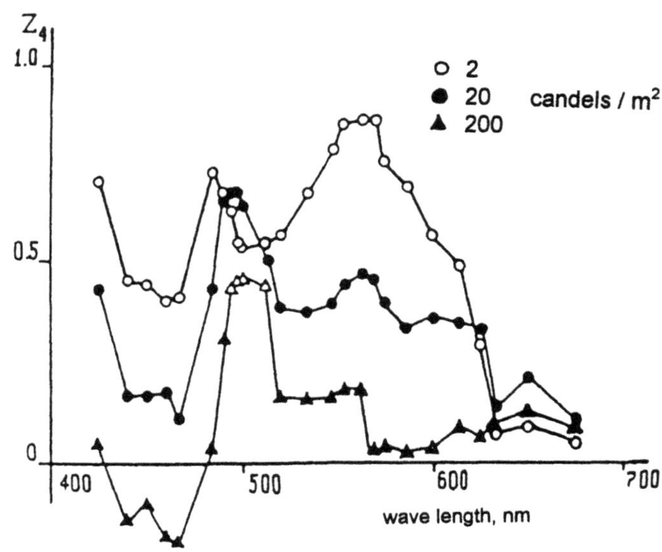

FIG. 10.7. Spectral functions of analogs of D-neurons along wavelength axis demonstrates strong intensity dependence.

nals. The conceptual reflex arc for name color response is given in Fig. 10.8. When two stimuli, S_i and S_j, are compared at once, two color analyzers are used to generate the value of S_i and S_j subjective differences (Fig. 10.9).

To summarize, the combinations of components of vectors are different for dark and bright signals. Accordingly, different light intensity detectors are excited by each of these excitation vectors composed from B–D neurons activated by the test field or B-neuron excited by the induction field and D-neuron from the test field.

The lights illuminating the test field only excite B-neurons and D-neurons, which participate in this case in the perception of intensity between bright and gray. The introduction of a high intensity induction field results in coordinates of B-neurons of negative value. This can be explained by the contribution of the B-neurons from the induction field in the perception of intensity of the test field. It is, in fact, a real excitation of B-neurons from the induction area coming to the test area, and producing in combination with the gray D-neuron a new vector for dark signals on the test field. The gray D-neuron participates in perception of light and dark signals. At the neutral point, when no signals from B-neurons are presented, this D-predetector

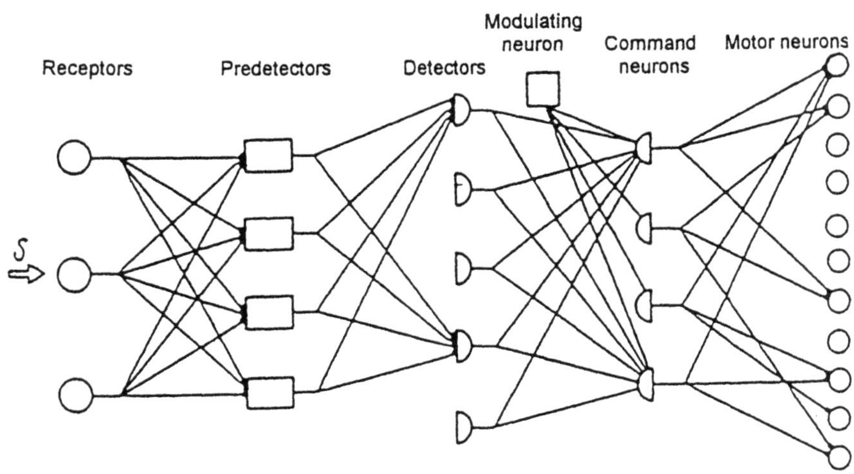

FIG. 10.8. The scheme of signal transfer in the reflex arc with color analyzer at the input. The signal acts on three types of cones, which linearly combine on four predetectors (bipolar cells). The horizontal cell level is omitted for clearer demonstration of the four-dimensional structure of the neuronal net. The four predetectors generate an excitation vector acting in parallel on the set of color-coding detectors, which constitute a four-dimensional Euclidean space. The detectors occupy in this four-dimensional space only a surface of a hypersphere constituting subjective color space. The color-selective detectors via modulating neurons are switched on or off from command neurons responsible for verbal responses and realizing color naming with the musculature of the articulation system.

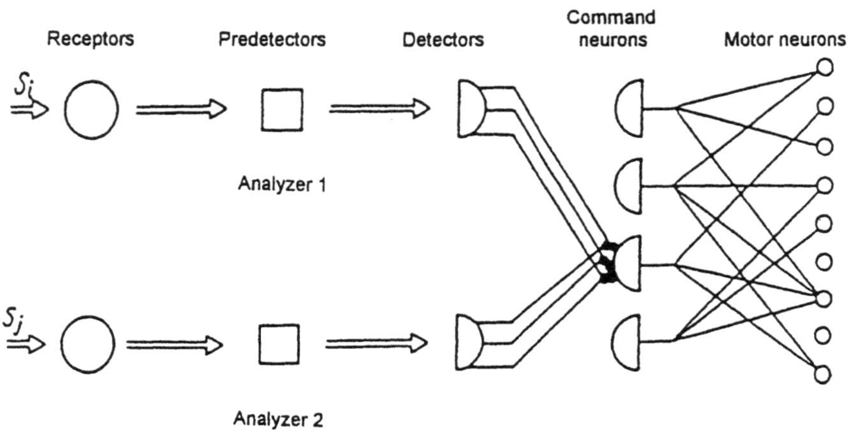

FIG. 10.9. The generation of numerical estimation of difference between two simultaneously presented colors requires two color analyzers for such an operation. The subtracted difference is after that analyzed in the structure similar with intensity detectors, which were discussed for brightness estimation. The command neuron of verbal responses selectively generates a particular number estimating the difference between colors.

has maximal value that corresponds to the perception of gray. Thus, the Cartesian coordinates refer to neuronal mechanisms.

The next problem refers to the polar coordinates. The sphere in four-dimensional space having four independent orthogonal Cartesian coordinates has three angles characterizing the color points on the sphere. The first angle on the plane, comprised of red–green and blue–yellow axes characterize hue, the specific aspect of color. The second angle on the plane represented by B- and D-axes corresponds to lightness, the value of the light stimulus. The third angle composed of combined axis taken from hue and lightness corresponds with saturation. Thus, the three angles of the hypersphere in the four-dimensional space are linked with subjective aspects of colors: hue, lightness (or value), and saturation. These constitute coordinates of the Maunsell color body. The problem arises as to how the polar coordinates of the color sphere correspond with coordinates of the Maunsell color body.

It was shown that the angle characterizing subjective brightness/lightness corresponds with the values in Maunsell color body (the term for lightness). The angle characterizing the position of the vector between the hue plane and the lightness plane characterizes the saturation. For each stimulus, three angles can be calculated. The angle for each stimulus was measured and compared with coordinates from the Maunsell body. In the Maunsell body, cylindrical coordinates are used to integrate the data concerning the colors of different intensities. The angle from this set of cylindrical coordinates in the Maunsell body characterizes hue. The length of the vector represents saturation whereas the height of the cylinder represents value. According to Maunsell, value means the position between very bright and very dark colors (Fig. 10.10). Calculating correlations between the three angles of the color sphere in four-dimensional space and the data from the Maunsell body, very high correlations between the angles obtained from the four-dimensional sphere and the Maunsell body characteristics were found. However, when subjective differences were calculated between the colors using cylindrical coordinates, it was found that these calculations did not match real subjective differences between these colors. This happens because the Maunsell body is obtained empirically by the subjective threshold method. The Maunsell body is a very convenient representation of colors in cylindrical shape, but this shape does not reproduce the real subjective space of colors.

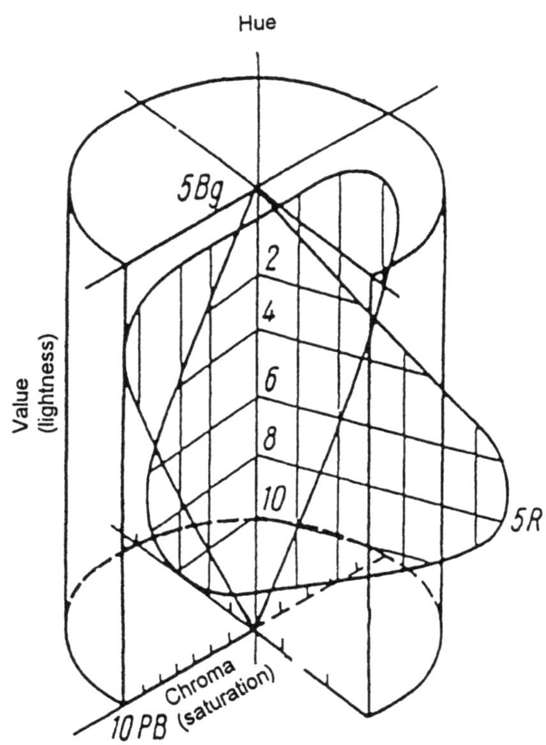

FIG. 10.10. The Maunsell body is characterized by hue (the angle), value or lightness (the height of the cylinder), and saturation (length of the vector). The polar coordinate of the sphere in four-dimensional space closely matched the cylindrical coordinates of the Maunsell body. The Maunsell body is, however, not isotropic. The calculations of subjective differences using the Maunsell body cannot be carried out. The four-dimensional spherical model enables a calculation of any subjective difference using Cartesian coordinates as four-dimensional vectors for Euclidean distances.

The data shows that it is possible to regard Maunsell coordinates as angles in the spherical model. Then, from these angles, four Cartesian coordinates can be calculated and from these the distances in four-dimensional space can be measured. This Euclidean distance in four-dimensional space exactly matches the subjective differences between corresponding colors. The conclusion is that the Maunsell body is an empirical representation of colors. The real structure of color space is four-dimensional Euclidean space based on the underlying verified neuronal mechanisms, which can be called a *coding by vector principle*. The stimulus activates a combination of excitations that build up an excitation vector that is useful at the next stage of information processing when the detectors are selectively excited. This is because this vector acts in parallel on a map of detectors having different synaptic contacts. This excitation vector produces a selective excitation of a detector as a locus on a sphere.

The structure that produces this four-dimensional sphere is a neuronal net. There are three cones with independent spectral characteristics, with maxima in the blue, green, and red regions. These receptors produce a logarithmic transformation. After that, through an intermediate stage, the signals from receptors converge with different weights on the four predetectors being normalized. These predetectors converge on selective detectors. Using particular light stimulation, a four-dimensional vector is obtained that results in a selective excitation of one of the detectors. The problem is how color detectors generate the verbal response of color naming. Here the concept of command neurons can be employed. It is believed that the generation of verbal responses is also organized by a specific command system triggering different speech articulation patterns. The responses, according to the verbal responses required, are modified by modulating neurons controlled by verbal instructions. This modulating neuron can change the synapses between detectors and speech command neurons. As a simple example, the colors can be named in Russian, English, or German. There are different systems of command neurons that the color detectors can switch on, resulting in different responses to the same colors. During the study of a particular language, these connections are established and can be controlled by such a modulation mechanism.

The next theoretical scheme demonstrates how subjective differences between two colors are generated. If the colors are presented simultaneously, two systems for analyzing the colors are operating simultaneously. Receptors, predetectors, and detectors are the same in both systems. Two colors are analyzed in parallel. There is convergence on a system of command neurons that generates the difference between two signals for the production of the verbal response. The main idea of this schematic representation is that two independent channels are operating and their signals are evaluated in each one in vector form. The subjective difference between colors is an absolute difference between two excitation vectors.

The spherical model can be tested using television colors. A computer-controlled color television can be used to obtain the color space of a subject. This subject looks at a color television and responds using a mini-terminal. The coordinates for the colors generated in this arrangement can be calculated using multidimensional scaling (Fig. 10.11). The television colors on the hue plane are within the area obtained for monochromatic stimuli. Using the computerized test of color vision, a group of normal subjects

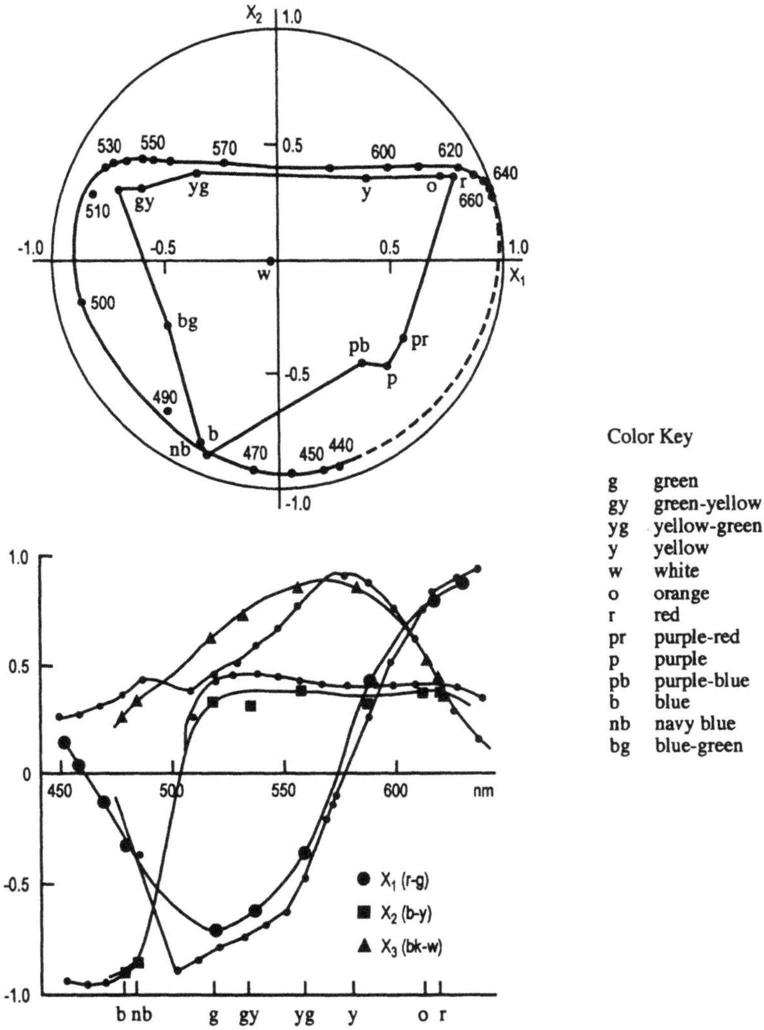

FIG. 10.11. The computerized TV system for automatic diagnosis of color vision deficiencies and representation of color vision malfunction in the form of a map. The figure represents a normal vision with normal coordinates for equiluminant colors on the red–green and yellow–blue coordinate plane.

was studied, that is, those with normal representation of the colors that have been generated on the television to see the degree of deviations in normal patterns of colors. The very similar results (Fig. 10.12) obtained from this group of normal subjects showed the efficiency of this computerized color system. Such a system has been used to generate maps of televi-

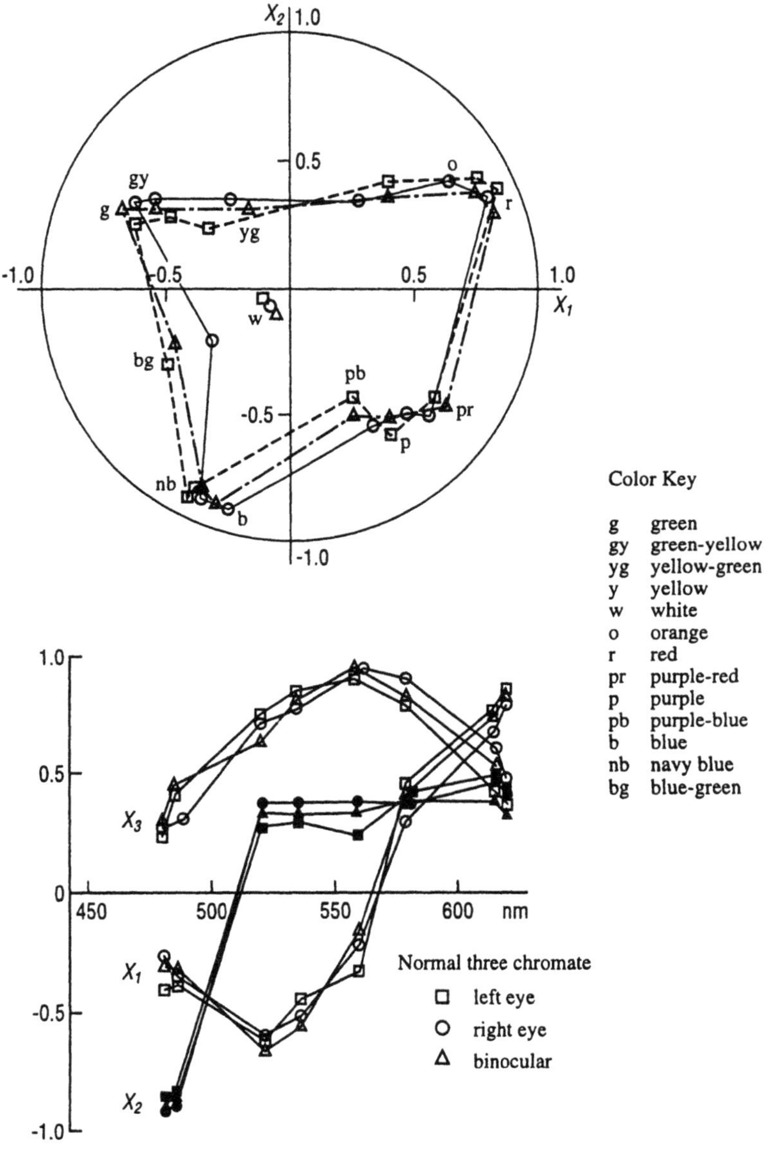

FIG. 10.12. The group of normal subjects demonstrate a very high level of correspondence of the results of color testing.

sion colors for people with normal color vision, as a standard for comparison of the shape of this color trajectory for subjects with different types of color deficiencies. Coordinates obtained from subjects with deficient color vision can be represented also on the color sphere, but all coordinates of colors are modified in comparison with those from subjects with normal color vision.

In the case of protanomaly, there is a reduction of the red–green system, with a preservation of (or intensification of) the blue–yellow system (Fig. 10.13). All colors are located along the blue–yellow meridian of the sphere.

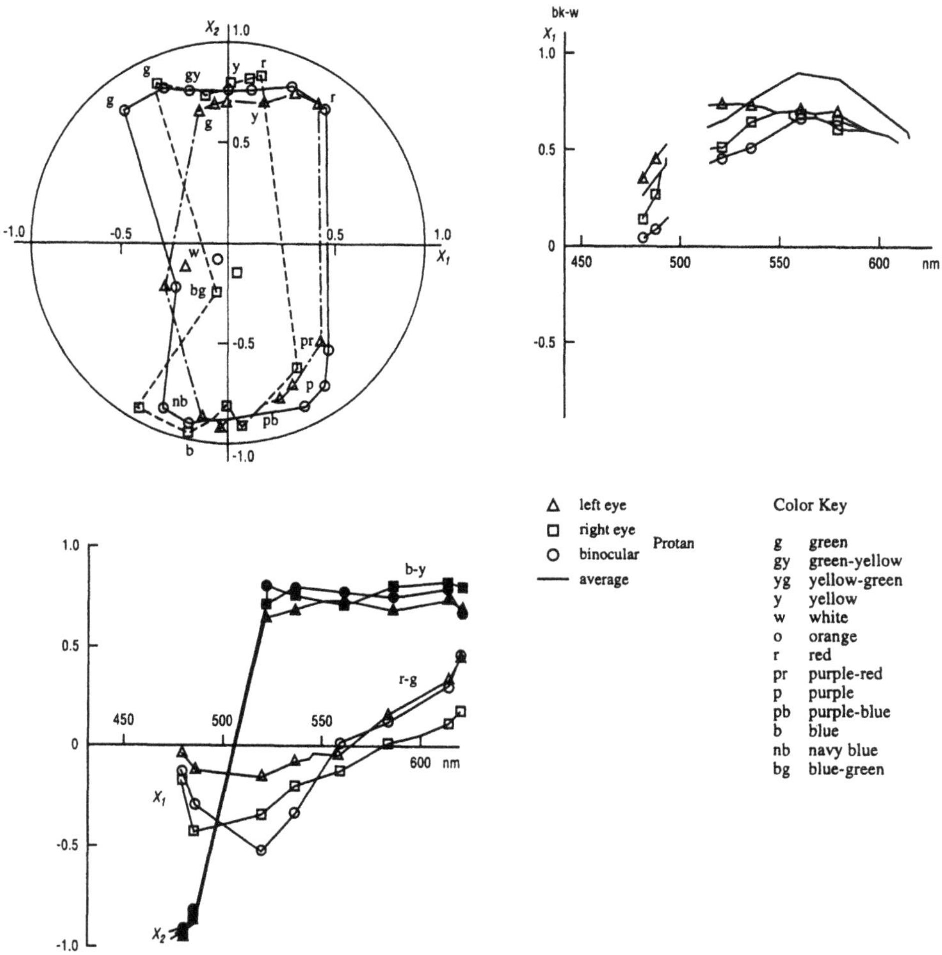

FIG. 10.13. The protanomalous vision is characterized by spherical structure, but the total amount of colors is distributed along the yellow–blue meridian as seen on the red–green and yellow–blue projection.

This test is done with colors of equal brightness so all colors should be represented on the sphere in three-dimensional space.

In a subject with protoanopic vision, the reduction of the red–green system is even more pronounced (Fig. 10.14). Practically all colors are situated along one line of the blue–yellow meridian. Many red–green colors cannot be distinguished from white. The next deficiency, deutoranomaly, is more complicated. A reduction of red–green may be seen in Fig. 10.15, but there is also some reduction of the yellow–blue axis. All colors are concentrated around the white area (also see Fig. 10.16).

Several hypotheses about the deficiencies of color vision exist and within these, color blindness is mainly regarded as the result of the absence of some receptors. The findings detailed in this chapter indicate that the process could be even more complicated. In subjects with protoanomalous and protoanopic vision, the predetectors are the same, but because of a change in the absorption spectrum of red cones, they become similar to green cones and the two types of cones converge on the same red–green predetector, but with a different polarity. If the red cones change the absorption spectrum to green, but send signals to the predetector, they are subtracted from the excitation signals sent off by the green cones, resulting in a total reduction of the red–green predetector response. There is a substitution of genetically changed pigment in red cones but for green cones, their links with predetectors is preserved. Therefore, reduction of the red–green component occurs. The reduction of the red–green predetector and an increase of the blue–yellow predetector results in a modification of the area of perceived colors on the sphere.

For subjects with deuteroanopic vision, the green pigment in green cones is substituted for red pigment resulting in the reduction of red–green axis. This substitution for blue–yellow predetectors results in a reduction of the blue–yellow axis. Thus, the area of perceived colors in such subjects is swollen around the white color (Fig. 10.15 and Fig. 10.16). In a study of color vision in patients with different types of brain damage, indirect evidence for the existence of predetector and detector level color vision has been found. The first results suggest that in some patients the equiluminant colors are on the sphere in three-dimensional space. Despite that there was partial elimination of color space, for example, the green colors were absent.

In the nervous system, the negative signals cannot be transmitted. In order to transmit negative signals, all channels should be duplicated. To transmit red and green signals, which at the horizontal cell levels have plus-and-minus characteristics, two channels are needed—red-plus–green-minus and green-plus–red-minus. Similarly, to transmit yellow–blue signals, yellow-plus–blue-minus and blue-plus–yellow-minus channels are required. In this patient, a lesion affects only one channel of two parts of a red–green

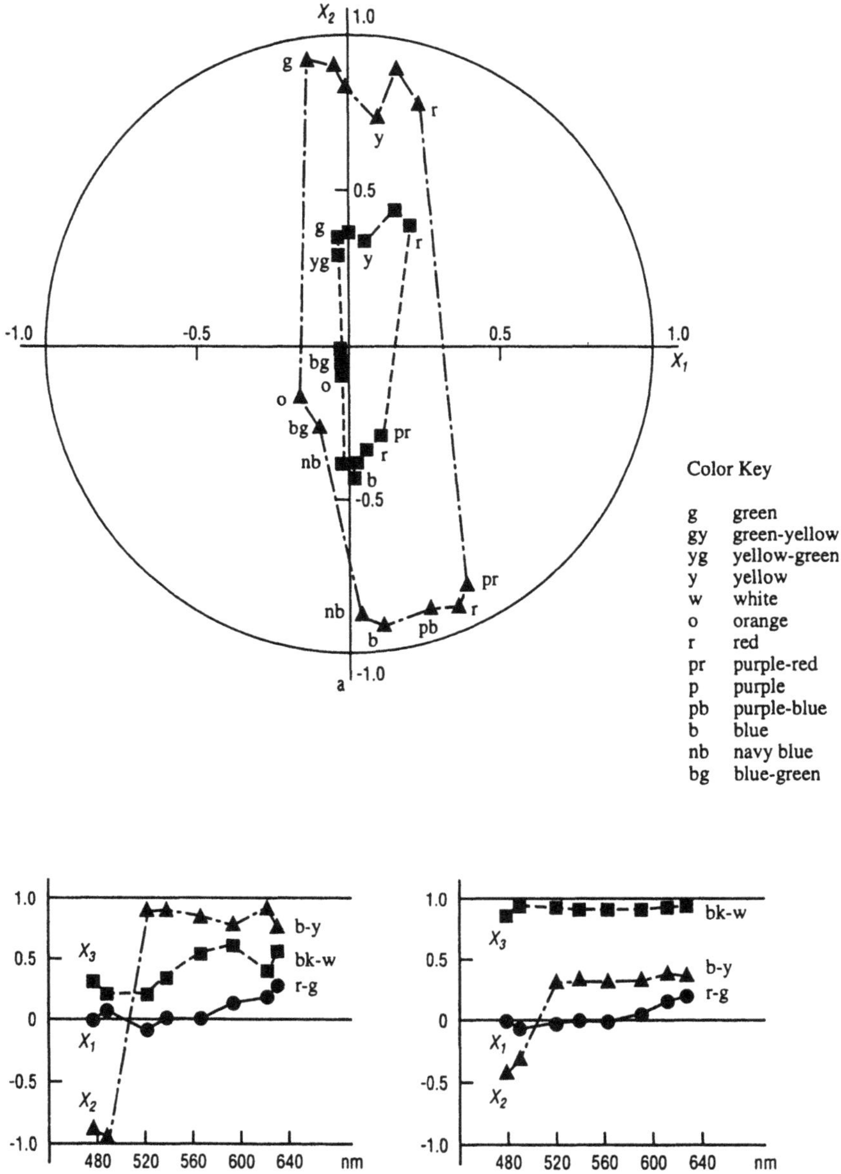

FIG. 10.14. The increase of red–green blindness results in even narrower location of all colors along the yellow–blue axis on the red–green, yellow–blue plane.

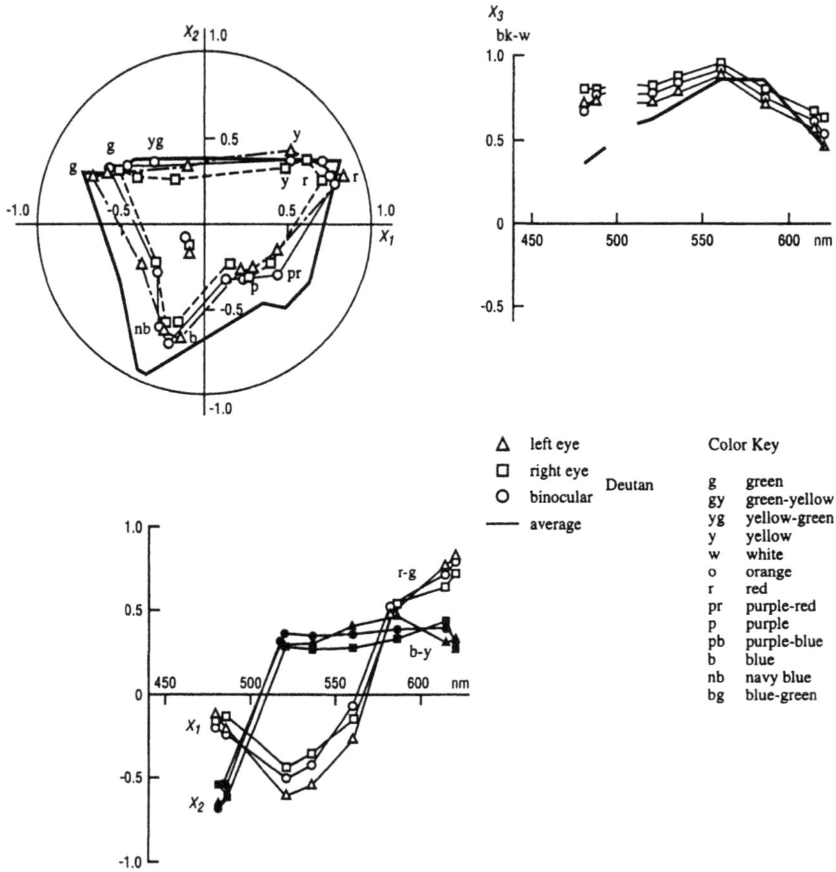

FIG. 10.15. The deuteranomalia is characterized by reduction of color area around the center on the equatorial plane.

predetector. In this case, the green-plus–red-minus could be damaged resulting in an elimination of a set of green colors.

The results of the experiment with another type of patient showed a very local disappearance of colors. This means that a certain color is not perceived. The color space is modified, within a very localized area. The suggestion is that this is a result of elimination of detectors at the detector level, because the total color system is preserved and only a small part of color space is eliminated. One subject showed a very remarkable change. This person cannot name any color; rather, the names of the colors are used randomly with respect to the real colors presented. The problem is whether this is due to an absence of color vision, or to the lack of links between the color detectors and the command verbal mechanism. To solve this problem, a subjective comparison between two colors was explored,

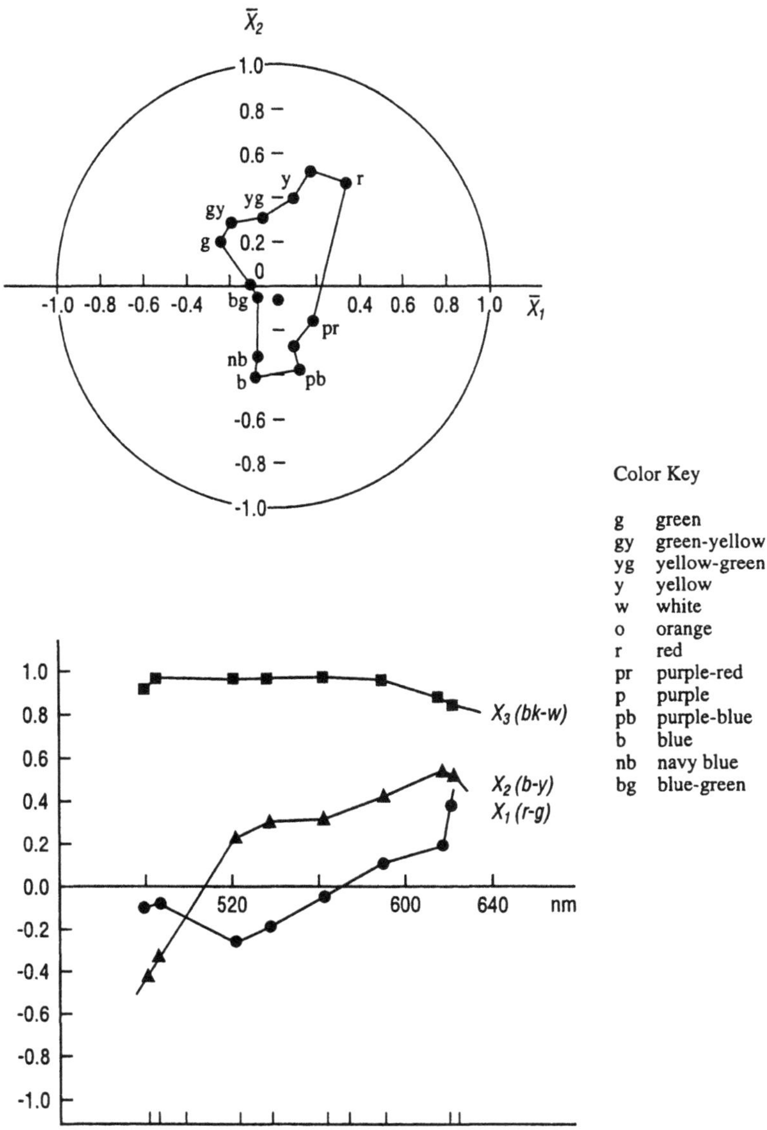

FIG. 10.16. The increase of deuteranomalia corresponds with a progressive reduction of differences between colors on the red–green, blue–yellow plane.

asking the subject for numerical estimations, but these numerical estimations of color differences were also very random. Then, a method of cross-modal comparisons suggested by Stevens was used. Direct nonverbal estimations of subjective differences consist of demonstrations of the subjective differences as a length of a line. When the patient received these instructions, she made color estimations correctly and demonstrated a normal color vision.

The conclusion is that the connection between color detectors and the verbal system of command neurons is either destroyed or functionally damaged. It is important to emphasize that it would be very difficult to explain these facts obtained in clinics if attention was not concentrated on the neuronal organization of the color system. The color space is constructed from selective color detectors. Excitation of these specific color detectors corresponds with the subjective experiences of color. The subjective differences between color is related to Euclidean distances in color space. In addition to a perceptual space, it would also be possible to study a mnemonic space and discover semantic space. Usually, these spaces are isomorphic with each other. In this experiment, 56 Russian names for colors were presented to a subject who was previously studied with regard to his normal color vision. A personal space for color names was constructed for him. It turned out that this was also four-dimensional and the color names correspond very well for this subject with real colors. This semantic color space was isomorphic to the perceptual color space. This comparison of color according to their names requires a memory representation of colors—a color memory space. The memory space was studied in the following way. A color was presented to the subject for memorizing it and later on some other colors were given and the subject was asked to make a subjective estimation between memorized and real color. Using different colors for memorization, a matrix of subjective differences between the memorized and real colors was constructed.

These spaces are integrated into a complex main structure. The perceptual space refers to real colors. If a certain color is presented, one can generate its name. When one is asked to make a comparison between two colors by presenting their names, this cannot be done without a memory screen, a memory map. When subjective differences between colors using their names are measured, these names are projected to the memory space, and the verbal response is obtained from this memory space, according to the respective differences between the colors. The precision of these measurements depends on the projection of these colors on the memory space. Verbal responses result from this memory space according to the respective differences between the colors. The precision of these measurements depends on the projection of colors on the memory space and preservation of memory traces of these colors. In formulating the role of the orienting response, reference should be made to the concept of memory spaces. It is believed that several memory spaces of different trace durations exist. The orienting response is an attempt to find out certain traces not by subjective methods, but by objective methods. The selectivity of orienting response habituation is a demonstration of a specific memory trace.

Thus, for perceptual, memory, and semantic color spaces, there is similar spherical structure in the four-dimensional space. The Cartesian coordinates of the perceptual color space correspond with red–green, blue–yellow opponent cells on one hand and with brightness (B) and darkness (D) neurons on the other hand. Three polar coordinates of the hypersphere represent subjective aspects of colors: hue, lightness (value) and saturation. The surface of the sphere is composed of color detectors selectively tuned to particular light spectra in accordance with the four-dimensional color excitation vector that selectively excites a particular color detector. The change of the light spectrum results in a modification of excitation vector and a shift of the excitation maximum with respect to the color detector map.

The color detector map is projected on memory units that register the color stimuli on the color memory map. The color memory units are associated with color names constituting semantic color space. The color names generate on the color memory map specific profiles of excitations of memory units. The degree of the overlapping of memory unit excitations is a measure of the semantic closeness of respective color names. The four-dimensional structure of the color space is evident when colors are changed in hue, saturation, and lightness. The equiluminant colors are projected on the sphere in the three-dimensional space with two polar coordinates matching hue and saturation.

Achromatic colors of different lightness are located on the semicircle because red–green and blue–yellow channels are not excited. In the perception of lightness of achromatic color, only B- and D-neurons are involved. The angle corresponds to the lightness as subjective aspect of achromatic colors. The three angles of the hypersphere in the four-dimensional space closely correspond to hue, lightness (value), and saturation measured by coordinates known from the Maunsell color body.

The experiments using color naming technique showed that treating different probabilities of color categories as vectors characterizing each specific color, one can obtain the perceptual color space corresponding to the color space obtained by evaluation of subjective differences between pairs of color. It means that color names as symbolic representatives of color contain a bulk of information concerning real colors. It is possible to construct a semantic color space using their symbolic representation instead of their real color. Such experiments were done by Vartanov. The presentation of two color names to the subject allowed him to create the numeric measure of difference between symbolized colors in the same way as is done for real colors. The matrix of subjective semantic differences between color names may be analyzed by a multidimensional scaling procedure. The color name space obtained was to be matched against perceptual color space. The color names were located on the hypershere in the four-dimensional space in such a way that basic color names are closely related with basic color.

More specifically, the color names projected on the plane with red–green and blue–yellow axis are positioned in accordance with a Newton circle with white and gray in the center. On the plane corresponding to brightness and darkness axis, color names are positioned in accordance with their designated lightness. Finally, the color names on the plane represented by combined chromatic and achromatic axes are regularly located in accordance with saturation symbolized by each color name (Fig. 10.17). Such results suggest an isomorphic relationship between perceptual and semantic color space. To test this suggestion, the combined matrix of subjective differences was obtained in experiments with Fedorovskaya (1992a, 1992b) where real colors and color names were matched against each other. When multidimensional scaling was applied to the matrix of the common space obtained by combination of semantic and perceptual color space, it revealed four coordinates as was shown for colors and color names in separate experiments. In the common color space, related colors and color names were located in a close neighborhood (Izmailov & Sokolov, 1992). Thus, the isomorphism of perceptual and semantic color spaces is supported (Fig. 10.18).

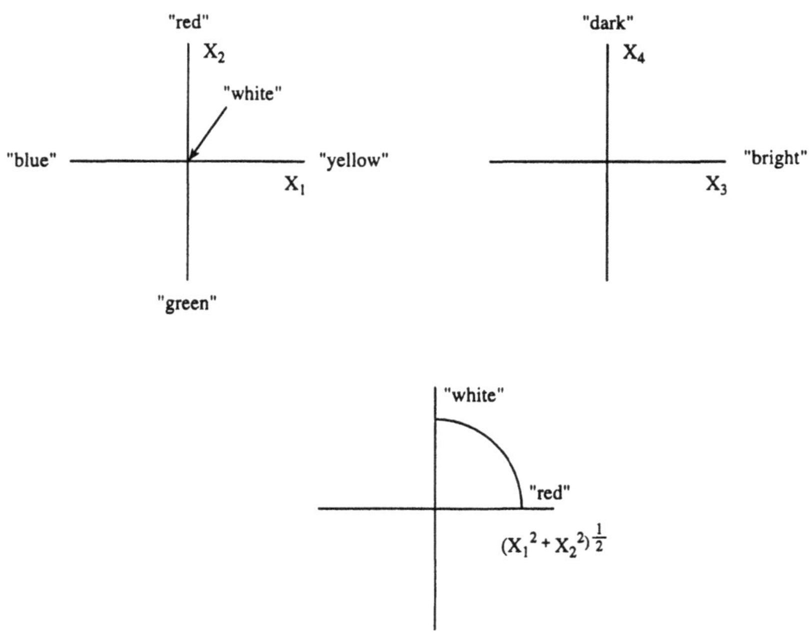

FIG. 10.17. The hypersphere in a four-dimensional space as representation of color names. The color semantic map corresponds closely with perceptual color space.

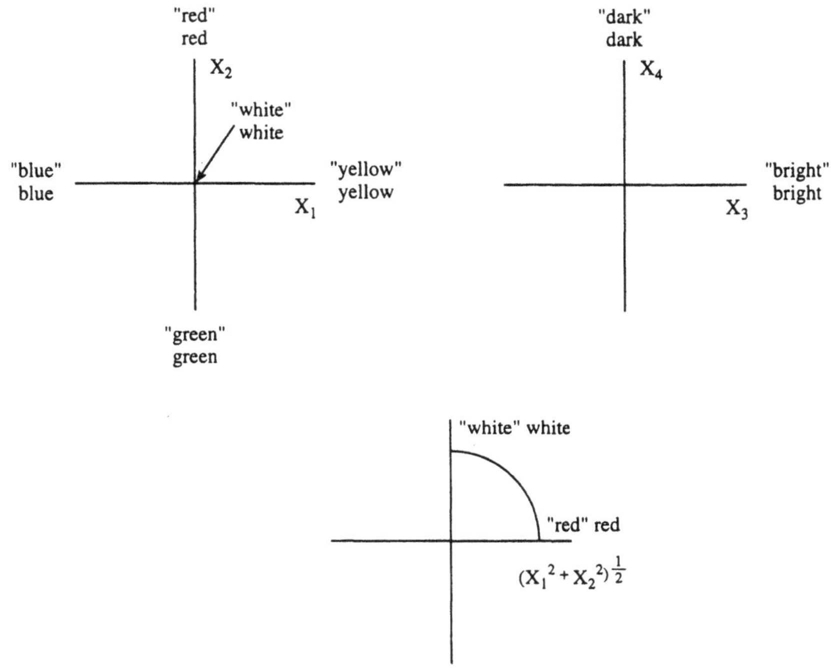

FIG. 10.18. The common space for real colors and color names. The common subjective space for real colors and color names is a *hypersphere* in the four-dimensional space. The isomorphic relations between perceptual color space and semantic color space are seen in that colors and their names are located in a near neighborhood from each other.

How is it possible that the subject can estimate differences between color names? The assumption is that between color detectors and semantic units an intermediate layer of memory units exists. The endeavor to isolate the memory color space from semantic and perceptual color spaces posed problems that the experiments of Fedorovskaya (1992a, 1992b) were designed to elucidate. The subject was presented a color that was to remembered and later on the subject was tested by test–colors. The instruction was to evaluate the subjective differences between the memorized color and the test–color. Using different colors for memorization and a constant set of test–color, one can construct a matrix of subjective differences that can be treated by multidimensional scaling. The results of such a procedure reveal red–green, blue–yellow, brightness, and darkness axes (Fig. 10.19). How can symbolic elements become color names? To study this in the experiments by Izmailov, artificial color names were used. The quasi-words composed from consonant–vowel–consonant were used as color symbols. Initial semantic space of such quasi-words having no associations with colors was very multidimensional with random order of the quasi-words.

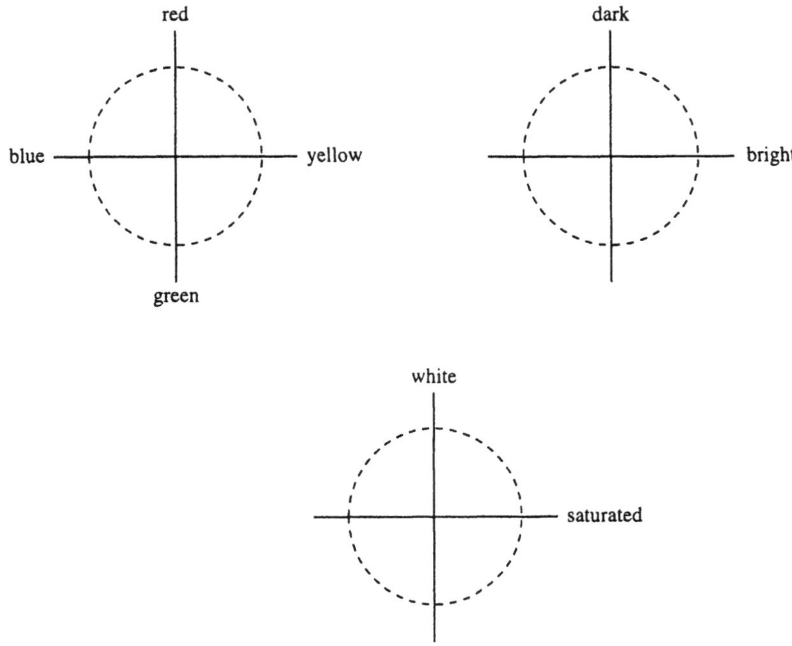

FIG. 10.19. The color memory space obtained by comparisons of memorized and real colors. The memory map is closely related to perceptual color space and semantic color space. The memorized colors are located in the same coordinate systems that colors and color names are located.

The quasi-words were associated with real colors presented by computer. After the confusion matrix indicated an exact correspondence between quasi-words and colors, the semantic space for these quasi-color names was constructed. Two stages in the process of learning were identified. At the first stage, the color names were concentrated in clusters around the basic axes. At the second stage, the quasi-color names were distributed in color semantic space in accordance with colors with which they were associated.

The fact that quasi-color names have generated semantic differences in accordance with associated colors indicates that in the process of learning not only feed-forward links from memory units toward semantic units are established, but also feed-back connections from semantic units toward memory units. The magnitude of the semantic similarity seems to be dependent on overlapping of memory unit populations evoked by each semantic unit. The total coincidence of overlapping populations of memory cells corresponds with synonymatic relation between respective symbols. The possibility of generating responses about subjective difference between a memorized color and a real color suggest that from the total volume of color traces available in the brain, only one identified by verbal instruction is continuously matched against test-colors. Such an operation requires a specific unit representing color trace for comparison with real colors. It is suggested that frontal lobe neurons can activate a copy of color memory trace transferred from long-term memory into operating memory. The neurons of operating memory are functioning insofar as they are enhanced by frontal lobe neurons. Otherwise, the operating memory can change its content, resulting in a new version of the behavioral goal.

The total system—perceptual, memory, and semantic color spaces can be presented as three maps composed of color detectors, memory units, and semantic units. The set of frontal *goal setting units* transfers the selective features of a particular long-term memory unit identified by verbal instruction to short-term operating memory unit. This unit as a template representing memory trace is used for matching the input test signals against it (Fig. 10.20).

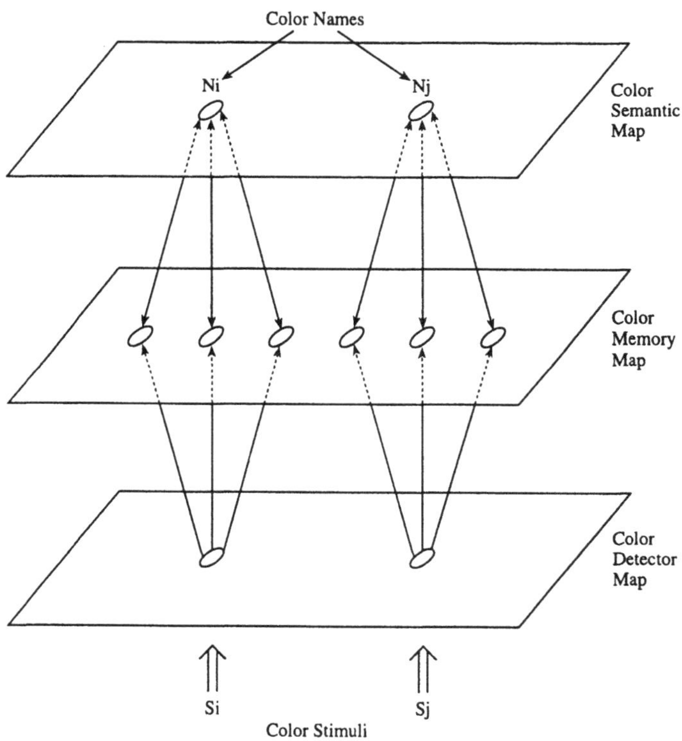

FIG. 10.20. The interaction of perceptual, memory, and semantic color spaces. The color stimulus is initially recorded on the detector map. Stimuli S_i and S_j in different times produce several versions of their records on the memory map through down–up links. These memory units become associated with respective semantic units and via the semantic units, two different color names, N_i and N_j evoke on the memory map via up–down link excitations of population of memory units.

A mostly remarkable characteristic of the long-term memory is the transformation of a time sequence of events in the surroundings into a multilayered field or map of events. This makes possible a new operation termed *internal looking*, as if the events given on the memory map are directly perceived surrounding events. In this line, a new problem arises as to whether the memory units can interact, thus generating new elements, which themselves can constitute elements of the memory map.

A similar suggestion can be made with reference to semantic units. Some time ago, Izmailov and Sokolov (1992) posed a hypothesis that novelty detectors enhancing new external events can participate in emphasizing the appearance of such super novel memory units. It is expected that spontaneous ORs appearing in a resting state might be related to such "internal novelty signals." Such ORs generated in the absence of external stimuli can characterize the creativity as a function related to generation of new elements of memory and semantic spaces using information already available in memory and semantic nets. The role of novelty detectors in the process of a creative solution implies an intensification of novel combination above the noise level. This function can be studied by observation of spontaneous ORs in combination with the following verbal report concerning subjective experience relevant to OR evocation.

CHAPTER

11

Orienting, Information, and Anticipation

This chapter covers the following issues:

1. Orienting, cognitive processing, and mismatch negativity (MMN).
2. The OR and information.
3. Information coding and representations.
4. Information-processing changes and the OR.
5. Behavioral changes and the OR.
6. Conditioning and anticipation.
7. Orienting and anticipation.
8. Workload effects on orienting.
9. Covariation of ANS and ERP measures.
10. The OR during sleep and early infancy.

The analyses of the OR so far in this book have employed a particular strategy—the so-called *man–neuron–model* approach. This includes studies at the microlevel and the macrolevel, attempting to integrate micro- and macrodata within a framework of a model uniting these phenomena. Later chapters examine orienting from the point of view of cognitive processes based on experiments with human subjects from a psychophysiological perspective. One of the main tools for studying brain functions are evoked and event-related potentials (ERPs), including brain-mapping and identification of dipoles that represent active neuronal populations under consideration. Some of the experiments to be reported, however, also use the more traditional autonomic somatic measures to assess orienting and anticipation.

The importance of different levels of explanations in the descriptions in this book of orienting behavior should be apparent. At the lowest level of explanation–novelty responses–the activity within individual neurons has been examined. Knowledge of the changes in ionic flow, EPSPs, and IPSPs is then used as a basis for an understanding of novelty based on formation of neuronal models, as prepotentiated matrices of synapses. Studies using autonomic responses and brain ERPs, in particular, mismatch negativity (MMN), may elucidate processes at perceptual, memory, or semantic space levels. Cognitive level explanations might be used in conjunction with ERP analysis, giving an opportunity to look at relevant brain mechanisms. Biosocial descriptions represent the highest level of description, although these still remain amenable to autonomic–somatic and ERP studies of the brain functions involved. Different levels of explanation require upward and downward links, or translations, so that a fuller understanding of the phenomena under study may be achieved.

This chapter therefore also aims to build new bridges between different levels, in an attempt to link cognitive functions to the OR. It will attempt to build bridges between some of the OR research previously described and current research on cognitive processes linked with the OR, thus providing a test of some of the theoretical concepts derived from Sokolovian theory, attempting to develop it further. The final goal of this chapter is to link the OR concept to those related to cognition, including such phenomena as anticipation, control of information, symbolic representation, attention, action, and action schemata. This requires a development of the OR construct, to also cover the results of earlier learning, and the memory and semantic spaces described previously.

ORIENTING, COGNITIVE PROCESSING, AND MISMATCH NEGATIVITY (MMN)

ERP research has provided new means for the study of OR phenomena at the human level, making it possible to illustrate functional aspects of the OR. Studies show that not only at any waking moments but also during sleep, an organism maintains a preparedness to orient to the external world. The current context, the content of cognition, and the flow of consciousness, may be disturbed by an external or internal stimulus, which may accordingly initiate a reorientation. Any stimulus is apparently analyzed preattentively up to a certain level to ascertain the need for calling up resources for response preparation. The current action program may not be affected very much by a change in the environment, but it may change various activities within the brain. This is very clearly shown in the ERP study of initial orientation to change in a homogenous stream of auditory stimulation. A model example of this is a condition when the subject is concentrating intensively, for instance, on reading and is concurrently exposed to repetitive auditory stimuli, but where occasionally tones are presented that deviate (for example, in pitch) from the repeated stimuli (standards). These deviant tones very consistently elicit an ERP deflection called mismatch negativity (MMN).

If the deviation is large enough, the subject is distracted from reading, when the stimulus elicits a call for attention to search for the possible consequences this change may have. This switch is based on brain processes, which may have multiple manifestations, depending on the results of the stimulus evaluation concerning its possible consequences. The responses can be seen as preparation for action for the anticipated following events. Even in these cases, the MMN may be observable, although for technical reasons there may be some confounding between ERP components associated with these latter stages. These typically include a negative ERP shift called *N2b*, occurring slightly later than MMN. N2b often continues to lead to *P3a*, the two together forming a well-known negative–positive complex associated with the OR process, as is shown in detail in chapter 12. This has been shown to accompany behavioral orientation to the change, which may be subjectively experienced as a disturbance. The change intrudes into consciousness and leads to the typical OR manifestations such as electrodermal responses and heart rate responses, whose pattern simulates those seen as responses to the anticipated events that the orienting stimulus is signalling, this reflecting the preparation for the consequences.

Whereas MMN can be observed in a situation where the subject is unaware whether any auditory change during reading has been heard, the N2b–P3a complex occurs when the subject is attending to the change and, for example, counts the number of deviant tones that have occurred during the tone sequence. In the traditional orienting response study, the stimulus presented to a waking human subject is seldom a purely nonsignal stimulus. This may only be the case where the current cognition concerning the environment includes knowledge clearly indicating that the stimuli are meaningless, as in the case of, for example, ordinary background noise. But even a small violation of the known tonal pattern in this noise may initiate—as suggested by the elicitation of an MMN—a search for the possible consequences that this new signal pattern may have for subsequent action. This has been shown to occur even during sleep (Sallinen, Kaartinen, & Lyytinen, 1994).

The violation of the existing model of a complex scene resulting in the evocation of an OR may occur when a stimulus event is novel, or when there is a large or significant deviation from the anticipated stimulation. In the case of the traditional OR, the violation stems from a comparison with the content of working memory, whereas MMN responds to a deviation from a model held in sensory memory and maintained for only a few seconds. Both may initiate further processing, leading to the need to access relevant association networks in long-term memory. This processing may lead to a conditioned (orienting) response if it results in finding a match in long-term memory. Often, if no such readily conditioned response is available, a longer process of coping may be needed. Any such process is intimately linked with the anticipation or preparation for the event signalled by the OR. In the case of mismatch or a failure to find an immediate automatic response to the violation of the expectations from the earlier experiences, a search for information from memory and from the immediate environment is initiated and this can be called *orienting*, following the traditional usage of this concept. The results of these processes lead to an update of the present schema concerning the situation. Where this occurs, several changes will inevitably be required—these may be behavioral in order to prepare for responding to the new situation, or perceptual as in the case where information would be expected from the new stimulus events, or cognitive where a new set of anticipated events will be constructed. Thus, the search for information is a self-supporting process—a chain of ORs.

It is possible to separate the initial orientation (including the biological preparedness of the brain reflected in MMN) directed toward identification of a change in the environment (but that may not necessarily lead to its conscious perception) from the traditional OR resulting from the perception of the change. Most of the changes one experiences in everyday life may be so meaningless that the initial analysis suffices and there is no need for further analysis or attentive involvement in the events. This initial analysis may, however, lead to a call for attention where the results of this perceptual process demand further processing, which would then require attentive effort (controlled processing). A decision about which changes are of sufficient importance for an organism to call up controlled processing depends on learning, on the existing store of coping programs. Mechanisms based on conditioning can handle basic coping, thus saving the limited resources needed for handling situations under conscious control.

It seems that an analogical separation of stages may also be differentiable among animals like the cat. Observations of a cat's orientation show at least two types of ORs, one having a brain manifestation similar to MMN without behavioral concomitants and another being an OR-like parallel of the behavioral anticipation of the event. In the human case, we may be able to separate more than two ORs that have observably distinct manifestations. In addition to the previously mentioned MMN–OR and the traditional OR, an anticipation/preparation OR can be seen. The last differs from the traditional OR elicited by a novel stimulus in that it includes features determined by the results of the processing of the eliciting stimulus event. A typical case is that of word recognition, which can be said to elicit a conditioned

OR that, in the case of a command, initiates a sequence of relevant behaviors. The bodily manifestations of this preparation for action may be observed immediately after the subject identifies the stimulus as requiring action. The stimulus may lead to anticipation of certain further information or request certain behaviors. The interesting point here is that this OR contains features—if measured to a sufficient extent—that demonstrate that it is a part of organism's preparation for an event that the eliciting stimulus has led the subject to expect, as experimental evidence to be presented next will show.

In experimental studies by both Lyytinen (for review, see Lyytinen, 1983, 1985) and Spinks (e.g., Spinks, 1989) carried out for documenting these effects, S1–S2 paradigms are typically used. The S1 updates the current expectations and the subject, in these paradigms, will thus be able to prepare for S2 on the basis of the cue(s) provided by S1. Therefore, the preparation can refer to controlled changes, either explicitly conscious or implicit, the latter being the case in conditioning studies. The more information S1 contains, the stronger are the needs for updating the current preparation and the more specific it can be. This will be shown with physiological observations of OR and anticipation below. The functional significance of the OR can be seen in the variation of both responding systems and their response amplitudes, according to the amount of expected information or the type of S2 event. Thus, the electrodermal response (EDR) system may be highly responsive in anticipation of an avoidable event such as a loud tone, although the cardiovascular system (but not the EDR) may respond in anticipation of a cognitive task like mental arithmetic; the somatic system may be active in anticipation of a motor task, with other response systems being relatively silent. These then are not generalized arousal responses, but specific task-oriented responses in anticipation of future requirements.

The initial screening OR—the filter mechanism, which saves the organism from unnecessary alarms potentially initiated by any change in its environment—is interesting for many reasons. It shows the extreme adaptability of the organism. It is highly effective and probably also automatic in that it is not affected by any current workload of the sensory mechanisms. On the other hand, there are clear limits or bottlenecks in the later stages of orientation at the conscious level. The adaptive variation of the initial orientation is manifested in the MMN amplitude that usually does not decrease in size, as the load demanded by the other (foreground) tasks increases. This mechanism assures the survival of the organism by checking out potentially significant changes in the environmental stimulation, even in the case of high concurrent workload. Under certain conditions, even a sleeping brain seems to be continuing to effectively monitor the environment, as will be shown later.

One highly interesting aspect of the work to be described is the interaction of the initial analysis seen in the MMN–OR, the novelty OR and the anticipatory OR, through recording autonomic activity. This chapter describes and discusses how these different ORs appear in concomitant recording of ANS, somatic nervous system, and brain ERPs when the stimulus conditions are varied in order to examine the effects of the requirements for further processing or anticipatory preparation.

THE OR AND INFORMATION

It is possible to go back to Pavlov in order to see the historical derivation of some of the ideas linking the OR with a conditioned reflex to time. This phenomenon was developed more fully by Sokolov, emphasizing the role of the OR in adapting to and anticipating the environment. The OR is seen as not only being a direct response to novelty or other environmental events, but also in helping the organism itself to be appropriately receptive to, and responsive to, such changes in the world around. Two major parts of this brain–behavior interaction of interest here are, first, the exact functional significance of the OR in tuning the organism to the environment, and, second, the anticipatory facility of organisms in predicting the future state of this environment, so that such tuning can occur in advance of the environmental changes.

The psychobiological foundations of the OR are that it forms part of the arousal, activational, and attentional systems of the brain. As such, it may be viewed as a system for determining under what conditions this tuning should take place. Early work on the OR showed that this adaptation could be both central and peripheral. Related research on the functional significance of the OR is reviewed briefly later. As can be seen in this book, the conditions that evoke an OR can be the presentation of both nonsignal stimuli (usually those that are novel or that lead to uncertainty) and signal stimuli (where such stimuli predict events in the environment that might be of significance to the organism). Both types of stimuli lead to situations in which the organism would be led to acquire further information from the environment. In the case of nonsignal stimuli, which are novel or improbable in terms of their likelihood of occurrence, the organism, because of their occurrence, has probably failed to predict environmental events accurately. The resulting failure to respond efficiently to such events can lead to difficulties of adaptation, and so information is gathered to try to improve the quality of its prediction of (and thus preparation for) such events. In the case of signal stimuli, these predict significant or information-carrying events. So, in both cases, the OR can be seen to be related to acquisition of more information from the environment.

One possible way to evaluate the efficiency of prediction is to plot the probability of hits in advance of an imperative stimulus. In the case of a reaction time measure, the probability density of responses is shifted, from a skewed distribution with a median around, say, 200 ms following the presentation of the imperative stimulus, to one with a median around the onset of the imperative stimulus when a warning stimulus with fixed foreperiod is presented, where the measure of variability will give an indication of the inaccuracy of prediction. (Usually, a bimodal distribution combining these two distributions may result). The same effect may be seen in eye movements when subjects follow a regularly moving target. Here, the gaze position may also have zero phase shift against the stimulus, demonstrating that eye movements are controlled by extrapolatory input.

One of the goals of an organism, therefore, is to continually attempt to predict future events in the environment, and the organism will respond through attentional, arousal, or activational changes if this prediction breaks down at any moment in time. The nature of, and the distinction between, some of these concepts has been discussed by a number of authors including the present ones (e.g., Kahneman, 1973; Pribram & McGuinness, 1975; Spinks & Siddle, 1983). This goal of the organism is what is meant in this chapter by *anticipation*. Prediction is made on a probabilistic basis, using, for example, past conditioning history, in which an organism might anticipate a significant event by virtue of the prior occurrence of an UCS. The concomitant alerting or attentional changes are then part of the OR, and such anticipation is clearly advantageous to the organism in terms of its ability to deal with the world around, as it is responding in advance of the event itself, in order to be optimally set once the stimulus does actually occur.

The concept of anticipation is rooted within classical physiological psychology. In I. P. Pavlov's works (1927), it was transformed into an experimental study of conditioned reflexes to time. These conditioned reflexes to time constitute a neurophysiological basis of predictive control as a powerful mechanism of adaptation. The existence of time-coding neurons has already been discussed previously. The mismatch between anticipation and an actual event triggers an OR and sustained exploratory behavior. This aspect of neuroprediction was emphasized in P. K. Anokhin's research related to the acceptor of action theory. The main mechanism of switching from a particular behavior to another one depends on the prospect of future results of a particular behavioral act. This idea of the future being imprinted into specific neuronal mechanisms—the so-called acceptor of action—allows for the control of the following behaviors. As soon as the results do not match the prediction, the OR is triggered to collect information for the organization of new behavioral strategy. Bernstein (1969) put forward a more general perspective, where he argued that there is more than one (match–mismatch) stage in OR elicitation, the OR being a more complex interaction of cognitive and motivational variables. In this sense, each outcome of an action is evaluated with respect to the goal of the behavior.

An important contribution to this issue of anticipation was made by L. V. Krushinski, who suggested that there is a specific group of exploratory reflexes that differ from unconditioned reflexes and classical conditioned reflexes. At the neuronal level, the anticipation can be specifically related to the OR in the framework of a neuronal model of the stimulus (Sokolov, 1969b). The time-selective detectors act in parallel with other feature detectors to establish a trace of a stimulus in hippocampal neurons. The predictive control in the hippocampus may be recorded as spikes in exploratory neurons against a background of regular stimulation.

INFORMATION CODING AND REPRESENTATIONS

Previous chapters have shown how the OR can reveal the extent to which information has been encoded in the brain. A nonsignal stimulus that is repeated produces habituation of the OR to this stimulus. This occurs as a neuronal model of the stimulus is built up by extraction of information from the stimulus until it is identified. When the neuronal model is exactly specified, then habituation takes place, as the incoming stimulus will no longer produce a mismatch with this model.

In order to test the principle of the buildup of the neuronal model and its influence on the habituation process, an experiment was performed that also enabled a further understanding of the nature of the information content of a stimulus array as one of the determinants of this habituation process (Spinks & Siddle, 1976). Briefly, subjects were presented with repeated visual stimuli featuring nonsense shapes (Fig. 11.1) for 20 trials, while their EDRs to the presentation of the stimuli were monitored. The subjects' task was to pay attention to the target stimulus, so that they could recognize it within a set of distractors at the end of the experiment. The stimuli varied between subjects in their complexity, this being measured in bits, according to the methods of formal information theory. The actual values of the

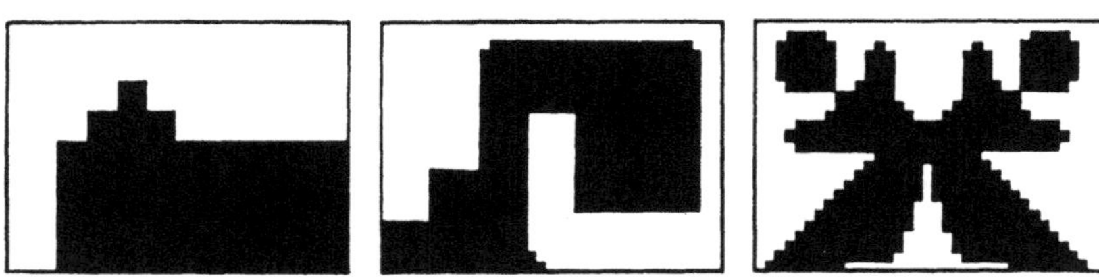

(a) (b) (c)

FIG. 11.1. The visual stimuli that subjects were required to attend to, for later recognition. Stimulus information was estimated at (a) 12 bits, (b) 26 bits, and (c) 60 bits. (From Spinks & Siddle, 1976. Copyright © 1976 by North-Holland Publishing Company. Reprinted with permission).

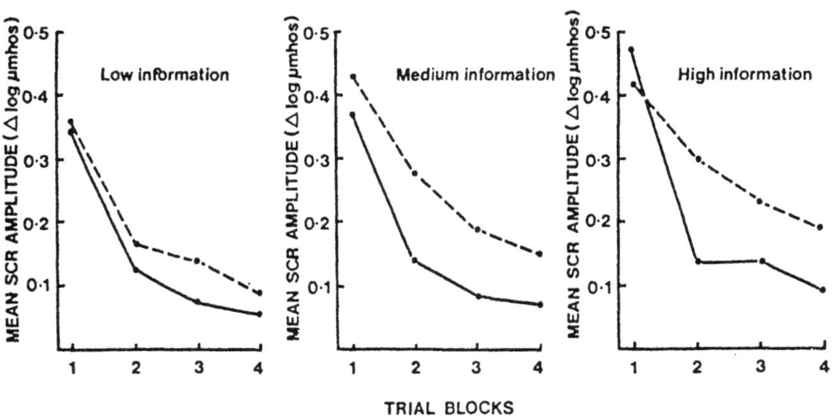

FIG. 11.2. Mean SCR amplitude plotted against blocks of trials for low-information, medium-information, and high-information (complexity) stimuli. (From Spinks & Siddle, 1976. Copyright © 1976 by North-Holland Publishing Company. Reprinted with permission).

stimuli were 12, 26, and 60 bits, respectively. The results showed that the number of trials to an EDR habituation criterion was related to stimulus complexity, habituation being retarded for the subjects who viewed the most complex stimuli (Fig. 11.2). This supports the notion that habituation occurs as the representation of the stimulus builds up, this taking longer when the stimulus is more complex.

The stimuli were also presented for either a short (0.5 s) or a long duration (4.5 s) on each trial. Long-duration stimuli resulted in faster habituation, also confirming that habituation is a function of the amount of information extracted on each trial (the stimulus being subjectively more familiar and objectively conveying less information, as it became more predictable across trials). When the stimulus is presented for a longer period of time, then it is possible for the subjects to extract more information per trial, and thus for habituation to occur with fewer stimulus repetitions. Autonomic ORs may thus reflect this process of familiarization or building representations of the stimuli, as the characteristics of the stimuli or environment are identified. At a neuronal level, more complex stimuli could be said to trigger more feature detectors, and more synapses are involved in the process of formation of a representation, as indicated elsewhere in this book. This may postpone the formation of a neuronal model and retard habituation.

Thus, stimuli that are repeated, and whose characteristics have been identified, produce habituation of the OR to these stimuli. The information from the stimuli is encoded in the form of a neuronal model, a CNS representation of the stimulus. As further stimuli impinge on the organism's receptors, these are compared with the neuronal model built up from previous presentations, and an OR is evoked if there is a mismatch between the incoming stimulus and this internal representation. In this way, there is a subsequent dishabituation whenever any change from the originally repeated stimulus is noted. The actual information encoded, then, can be determined by the nature of the dishabituation function.

This neuronal model may be thought of as a prepotentiated matrix of synapses that corresponds to the internal representation of that stimulus. The details of such a neural network may be found in the chapter by Sokolov in *Neuronal Mechanisms of the Orienting Reflex*, edited by Sokolov and Vinogradova (1975). Repeated stimuli whose central representations map onto each other build up this prepotentiated effect. As the number of repetitions increases, these stimuli will be more quickly (or perhaps automatically) processed through the operation of this matrix, and habituation will gradually result. Dishabituation will not occur until the representation of the incoming stimulus differs from the matrix.

As has been seen previously, representations can be organized on at least three levels, perceptual, memory, and semantic levels. The perceptual level may be further subdivided into two levels—detector and predetector neuron levels. Perceptual space corresponds to the representations of incoming stimuli, as indicated by detector cells, along dimensions revealed by multidimensional scaling (MDS) of responses to (e.g., differences between) perceptual stimuli, as shown earlier. Such MDS reveals an n-dimensional space, where the n dimensions correspond to n types of predetectors in the sensory system (such as red–green cones, blue–yellow cones, B(rightness)-neurons, and D(arkness)-neurons). The limited number of these predetector cells is the limiting factor determining the dimensions in space at all levels. A study is currently underway by other researchers to see whether perceptual space may be reflected in ERP components.

Semantic space can be similarly realized by reference to MDS of verbal output (e.g., color-naming). Again, it is hypothesized by Sokolov that there are cells (command neurons) that are the elements controlling verbal responses. However, semantic space may be better understood in terms of vector descriptions, where the vectors describe features of the multidimensional space model. Vector mathematics can then provide detailed and exact descriptions predicting semantic data. This cellular structure is the basis (the building blocks) for more holistic representations of complex stimuli, which may be similar to the prepotentiated synaptic matrices described in Sokolov's 1975 chapter.

The correspondence between perceptual and semantic space is determined by memory space. The variance of semantic space will inevitably be greater than that of perceptual space, because of the involvement of memory. Operating memory [see also Näätänen's (1982, 1990) *attentional trace*] can be viewed as a subset of long-term memory, pulled out by verbal instructions, expectations, or extrapolations. Short-term memory is a set of representations of perceptions of recent events in the outside world. Features of such a memory may be reflected, for example, by processing negativity. The OR can be triggered from any of these levels. Yet, sensory and verbal stimulation are, of course, more efficient because the exact times of events are known. The ORs triggered from memory are expressed in terms of spontaneous responses that are more difficult to interpret than stimulus-evoked ORs.

It has been noted that the OR is evoked whenever there is a mismatch between an incoming stimulus and the representation of the earlier repeated stimulus. The nature of these representations and the different levels at which they may be organized has been elucidated. However, OR evocation is not just related to representations of incoming stimuli. It has already been noted that, at a more general level, ORs may be evoked whenever there is uncertainty in the environment. This may come about not simply because the subject has encountered a novel stimulus where there is such a mismatch. It may occur where an unanticipated (that may or may not be novel) stimulus has been perceived. These situations may be reinterpreted as being where the prognosis of future stimuli, built up by the subject in anticipation of changes in the environment, has failed to correctly predict.

At a further level of generalizations, the OR is evoked whenever there suddenly is information in the environment to be analyzed. This may occur in many situations. One would be when the stimulus is novel, and therefore contains information that has to be extracted. Another would be when the stimulation is unexpected or unpredicted, where information must be absorbed in order for the organism to be in a better position to predict its future. A further situation would be when a stimulus occurs that signals a significant future event, as might be the case with a CS during conditioning. An example of this situation would be when the individual's name is called out, or when someone shouts "Fire!"

It is important here to stress the emotional aspect of the OR that is part of the mechanism of informational self-reinforcement. Thus, one piece of information has a positive value as a reinforcer, making possible a sequential analysis of the environment. Organisms may, in this regard, habituate to one particular stimulus, but there is still a tendency to acquire further information from other stimuli.

Thus, it is possible therefore to classify OR-eliciting events according to the information that is conveyed by these events. Some stimuli carry information within them, as in the case of a complex visual stimulus—such stimuli could be said to contain high *intrinsic information*. Other stimuli carry information by virtue of their unpredictability, as in the case of highly unexpected or improbable stimuli—these could be said to have high extrinsic information. These two sources of information are orthogonal to each other. Stimuli can have further information by virtue of the stimuli that they signal—there is anticipated information following the occurrence of such stimuli. Finally, whenever there is uncertainty in the environment, an OR is evoked because of the necessity of taking in information from the world around. In all these cases, the OR is evoked because the component responses aid analysis of the stimuli. This is the topic of the next section of this chapter.

In summary, this close relationship between the OR, information coding, and information extraction was earlier developed in some detail by Sokolov in his paper published in English in 1966. The OR is seen there as being a response to uncertainty or entropy, with the OR aiding in the extraction of information from environmental events. This information is then represented in various representational spaces (e.g., perceptual space, semantic space) in the CNS, and these representations are the basis on which the dishabituation function is built.

INFORMATION PROCESSING CHANGES AND THE OR

The previous section showed how the OR may not only reveal the nature of the representation, through the dishabituation function, but how central the extraction of information required to build up this representation is in the OR process. These two processes are complementary, in that an OR is evoked whenever there is a need for further or more rapid information extraction. This can occur at times when a mismatch occurs between the internal representation of the stimulus (or anticipated stimulus) and the current input from the perceptual system—or, in more general terms, when there is uncertainty in the environment. As has been noted, this information extraction is part of the organism's adaptation to the environment. The biological significance of prediction of future environmental events and the anticipation of such events by behavioral, autonomic, or CNS responses is clear.

This process has been shown in an experiment (Shek & Spinks, 1985) where subjects were presented with the same simple visual stimulus for 15 trials. On the 16th trial, the stimulus was either the same, changed to a novel, but similarly meaningless, nonsignal stimulus, or changed to a novel and significant stimulus (the subject's name). Almost immediately following (500 ms) this stimulus on the 16th trial, subjects were shown a visual stimulus containing four words, which they were then, unexpectedly, asked to recall. EDRs to the 16th-trial stimulus showed that the significant stimulus evoked a much larger response than the other conditions, a typical result from studies using signal stimuli. Heart rate responses discriminated all three conditions. The data revealed that more words were recalled or recognized when the presentation of these words followed a novel, nonsignificant change stimulus or a significant change stimulus than in the no-change condition.

The data from this study show that stimuli that produce orienting appear to enhance perceptual processes or memory consolidation (or both). The close link between orienting and memory consolidation may be seen in the following experiment (Spinks, 1984). Subjects had a series of nonsense syllables presented, some of which had to be remembered (these were distinguished from those that did not have to be remembered by being of upper or lower case letters). Either 0.5 s or 2.0 s after the presentation of this nonsense syllable, there was a visual search task (Fig. 11.3), following which subjects had to report the syllable memorized (where appropriate). The to-be-remembered stimuli produced larger ORs, as reflected by EDRs, than control stimuli or the no-stimulus condition. Further, performance on the subsequent visual search task deteriorated (longer search times, see Fig. 11.4) when it followed the to-be-remembered stimulus, compared with other conditions. This study thus shows that encoding or consolidation of the stimulus in memory produces orienting, in order to facilitate the task, this task producing a deterioration in performance of other tasks. In this way, the OR acts as a regulator of information processing, controlling processing priorities and producing CNS states to optimize performance in the high priority tasks. More specifically, in this study, the OR may reflect the cen-

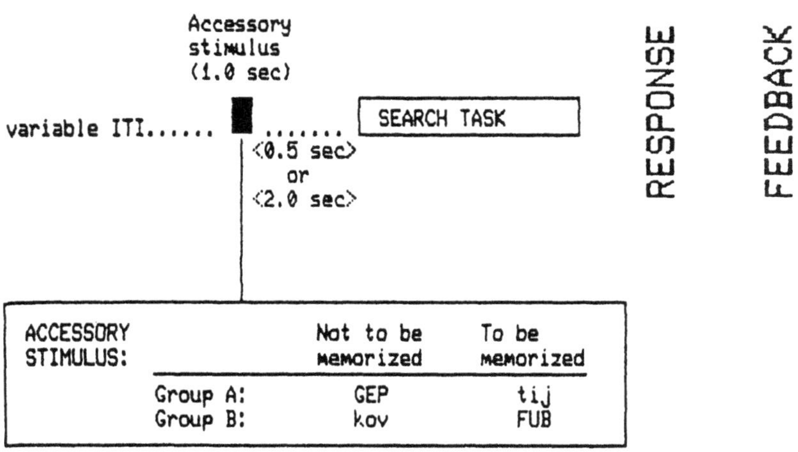

FIG. 11.3. Trial procedure and experimental design. Subjects were presented with a series of nonsense syllables, some of which had to be remembered. Either 0.5 s or 2.0 s after the presentation of this nonsense syllable, there was a visual search task, following which subjects had to report the syllable memorized (where appropriate).

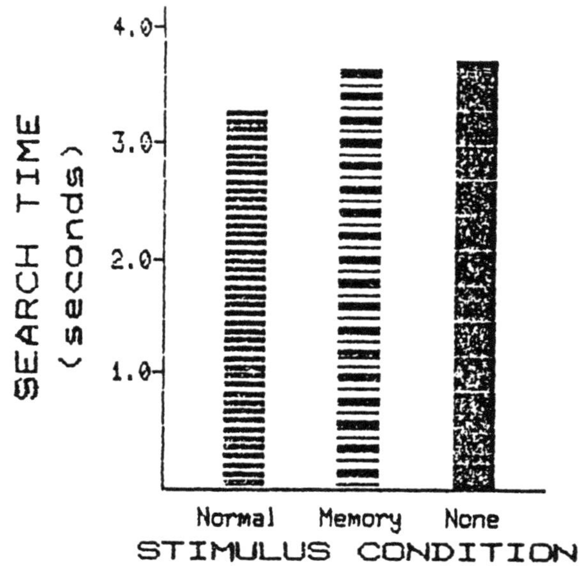

FIG. 11.4. Performance data for the three trial conditions. The to-be-remembered stimuli (*Memory*), which evoked the largest ORs, resulted in statistically significant performance deterioration on the subsequent visual search task (longer search times) compared with the not-to-be-remembered stimuli (*Normal*).

tral processing capacity allocated to the memory task. Search task performance deteriorates as a result, either because there is less central capacity to allocate to the search task while memory processes occur, or because it takes time to switch between tasks.

A third study (Siddle & Spinks, 1992) also illustrated the deterioration in background performance that occurs while a subject is orienting to a novel stimulus elsewhere in the environment. An accessory stimulus (visual or auditory) occurred while subjects were engaged in a visual search task (Fig. 11.5). This accessory stimulus, if present, was either novel or familiar. Novel accessory stimuli evoked larger SCRs and produced greater deterioration in performance on the visual search task than familiar stimuli or no stimuli (see Fig. 11.6).

These studies suggest that the OR is closely associated with perceptual and/or memory processes. Specifically, the OR may be linked to facilitation of these processes with respect to the OR eliciting stimulus, which then has a negative effect on performance of any other task competing for the same limited capacity pool of resources. This reallocation may be seen as a major part of the functional significance of the OR. More specifically, OR components can be seen as enhancing the discriminatory powers of both central and peripheral parts of the perceptual system, providing optimal

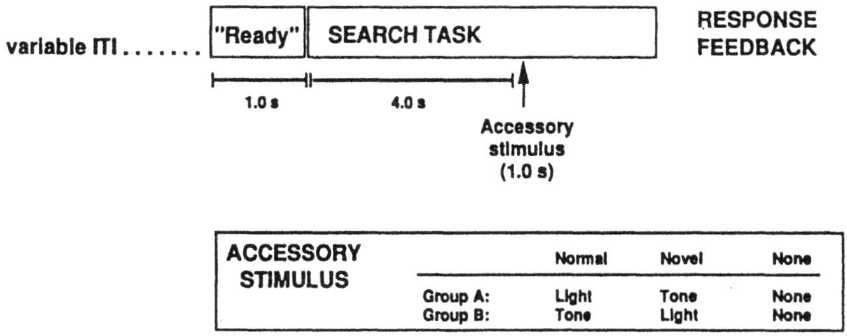

FIG. 11.5. Trial procedure and experimental design. A novel or familiar visual or auditory accessory stimulus might occur while subjects were attempting to detect target letters in an ongoing visual search task. (From Siddle & Spinks, 1992. Copyright © 1992 by Lawrence Erlbaum Associates. Reprinted with permission).

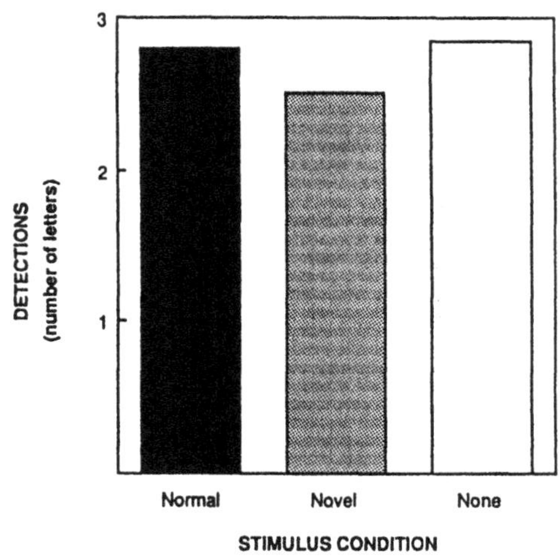

FIG. 11.6. Performance data showed a performance decrement when a concurrent novel accessory stimulus was presented, compared with a familiar stimulus, or no stimulus. (From Siddle & Spinks, 1992. Copyright © 1992 by Lawrence Erlbaum Associates. Reprinted with permission).

conditions for the subsequent perception of the eliciting stimuli (Sokolov, 1963). As is seen later, these changes will be more beneficial to the organism if brought about to coincide with the presentation of the stimulus, rather than by being effected as a result of, and therefore after, the presentation of the stimulus. The role of the OR in regulating informational flow and analysis through changes at the cortical, subcortical, and peripheral levels is discussed further in other parts of this book.

The role of the arousal system and ANS in the OR complex is particularly important in terms of the functional significance of the OR. Autonomic reactions serve the same purpose as somatic reactions, in that they facilitate analyzer sensitivity (Sokolov, 1963). The reticular activating system (RAS) maintains the activity of the cortex as a whole and, as P. K. Anokhin argued, contributes to the mechanism of the OR. The relationship between the activity of the RAS and the functional state of the analyzers had been shown by Granit (1955), who suggested that there are positive feedback mechanisms in the CNS that can heighten receptor sensitivity. A number of attempts have been made to formulate such a feed-forward principle and describe how it might work. For example, Livingston (1958), in reviewing the central control of receptors, hypothesized a mechanism which actively selects and organizes messages from the perceptual system at the earliest stages of their generation. The very same goal directiveness was linked by Alexandrov and Järvilehto (1993) to the theory of functional systems (Anokhin, 1974), based on the argument that forthcoming events, as the results of behavior, in a sense also guide behavior, perhaps more so than do current stimuli.

Accordingly, functional systems emerge during an individual's development (and learning) that organize behavior to be goal-directed in such a way that a heightening of receptor sensitivity can be defined by the anticipation of future events or the results of action based on actual behavioral goals. This idea is congruent with Sokolov's description of different types of neurons that subserve the specific categories of goal-directed behavior.

The facilitation of receptors corresponds to RAS activation, constituting a mechanism whereby the OR participates in an increase of sensory functioning. Activity in the RAS, realized as modulating neuron activity, may be triggered by novel stimuli, via novelty neurons. Also, however, hormonal reactions play a part in control of reflex activity in maintaining the activity of the cortex via the RAS and hypothalamus, and in analyzer sensitivity, to the extent that K. M. Bykov described analyzers as being tuned by the "neuro-humoral control system" (Sokolov, 1963).

Western authors, in particular, Kahneman (1973) and Pribram & McGuinness (1975) have also stressed the interrelationship between a state of generalized arousal and orienting. One of the central indices of orienting is alpha blocking, which some researchers have argued leads to an increased capacity to handle information (Lindsley, 1960). More specifically, Surwillo (e.g., 1975) argued that the frequency of the EEG determines (or is a reflection of) the frequency of a cortical timing or gating function, which, in turn, determines the rate at which the CNS processes information.

Sokolov (1966, 1969b) further speculated on the neuronal basis for an increased ability to analyze information during orienting. There are changes in the rate at which simple nervous processes operate in the analyzers and facilitation in the afferent pathways from the receptors, resulting in a similar increase in the speed of neural impulses. At the same time, there is a reduction in the signal-to-noise ratio for neurons that do not convey information at that time, and an opposite effect for information carrying neurons. Two mechanisms for extension of informational capacity under the OR can be identified. At the sensory level, the OR increases the fusion frequency of a flickering light. At the ERP level, the critical period when two ERPs are separable to sequential light stimuli shortens. At the single unit level of the visual cortex, the flickering light generates distinguishable bursts of spikes with greater frequency. In all cases, the amount of transmitted information per unit time increases.

The results of Caspers' (1961) experiments recording steady potentials from cortical structures of the cat have shown two interrelated effects. The shift of the steady potential towards positivity demonstrates a transition from high frequency EEG oscillations to a lower frequency. At the same time, the behavior of the animal changes dramatically, demonstrating a chain of acts related to preparation for sleep and sleep itself. The shift of the steady potentials toward negativity produces a higher EEG oscillation, arousal, and behavioral exploration. Recent studies using intracellular recording from cortical pyramidal cells reveal depolarization and high frequency endogenous oscillations of membrane potentials up to 80 to 100 Hz during the active state produced by direct application of acetylcholine to the surface of the cortex. Blockade of the muscarinic receptors by atropine results in deactivation, hyperpolarization, and a shift of the spectrum of intracellular oscillations toward the low frequency band. The intracellular study demonstrating a shift of the spectrum toward the high frequency band under arousal suggests that steady potentials and the EEG spectrum reveal that intracellular pacemaker potentials are critically important for neuronal spiking.

Although it has been suggested that various central changes during orienting result in facilitation of processing within the analyzers, sensory thresholds may also be lowered through centrifugal excitatory control of receptors during orienting. One example of these peripheral effects is pupil dilation changes and photochemical changes in the retina that may lower visual thresholds. Another is heart rate deceleration that may facilitate the intake of information through neurophysiological processes elaborated by Lacey (1967). Cephalic vasodilation and peripheral vasoconstriction together represent the diversion of blood to the brain in order to satisfy the additional energy requirements. PET and fMRI methodologies have demonstrated that brain information processing is highly energy demanding. First, this energy is used to run Na/K pump mechanisms to keep polarized neurons from being depolarized by spiking. Thus, the OR operates to intensify the supply to the brain of energy required for its activity. The vascular system is a very important mechanism within this positive feedback system when the demand for information is linked with an increased demand for energy supply to the brain. Automatization of behavior results in a lower demand on the brain's energy supply as shown by PET studies (e.g., Posner & Raichle, 1995)

The changes in the state of the sensory systems under the influence of the OR produce effects too numerous to discuss here. Even as early as 1954, London had reviewed over 500 Russian studies showing that all modalities undergo modifications of sensitivity on presentation of a usually contiguous accessory stimulus. Later, Razran (1971) made an extensive further analysis of Russian studies of these and many other aspects of OR theory. The heteromodal cueing literature also shows changes in sensitivity of the second stimulus, with a maximum increase in thresholds occurring some 500 ms after the presentation of the accessory stimulus. There is also supporting evidence from the foreperiod reaction time field (for a review, see Niemi & Näätänen, 1981).

One experiment (Spinks & Shek, 1982) showed how the nature of this perceptual facilitation process is further complicated by whether perception of stimuli at the center of the visual field or at the periphery of the visual field are examined. Subjects were presented with a picture or a set of words in which there was one central component and several peripheral components. Prior to the presentation of this imperative stimulus or S2, an accessory stimulus (S1) was presented. Trials varied in terms of the duration of S1 and S2, and the interval between these two. Exploratory data analysis techniques (Figs. 11.7 and 11.8) revealed that there was an inverted U-shaped relationship between the recognition of the S2 and the S1–S2 duration; recognition was poor when the interval was below 80 ms, improved between 80 to 360 ms, and gradually deteriorated as the interval increased up to the limit in this study of 15 s. This is an indication of the temporal course of the cognitive changes that form part of the OR. As the duration of S1 itself increased (at reasonably short S1–S2 durations), the recognition of central information deteriorated, but peripheral recognition improved. It could be argued that a short S1 produces a generalized enhancement of perceptual processing, but that this facilitatory effect becomes more focused on central target items as the duration increases.

BEHAVIORAL CHANGES AND THE OR

Pavlov (1927) had originally noted that one of the more obvious components of orienting was behavioral (What has to be done?), rather than perceptual (What is there?), the latter being emphasized more by Sokolov and others. In order to examine the effects of the OR on motor (behavioral) processes, the following experiment was performed (Shek & Spinks, 1986). Subjects were presented with a simple visual stimulus for 15 trials. On the 16th trial, the same stimulus was presented for some subjects, and others were shown different forms of change stimulus (an innocuous change stimulus, a significant change stimulus [the subject's name], or a change stimulus that

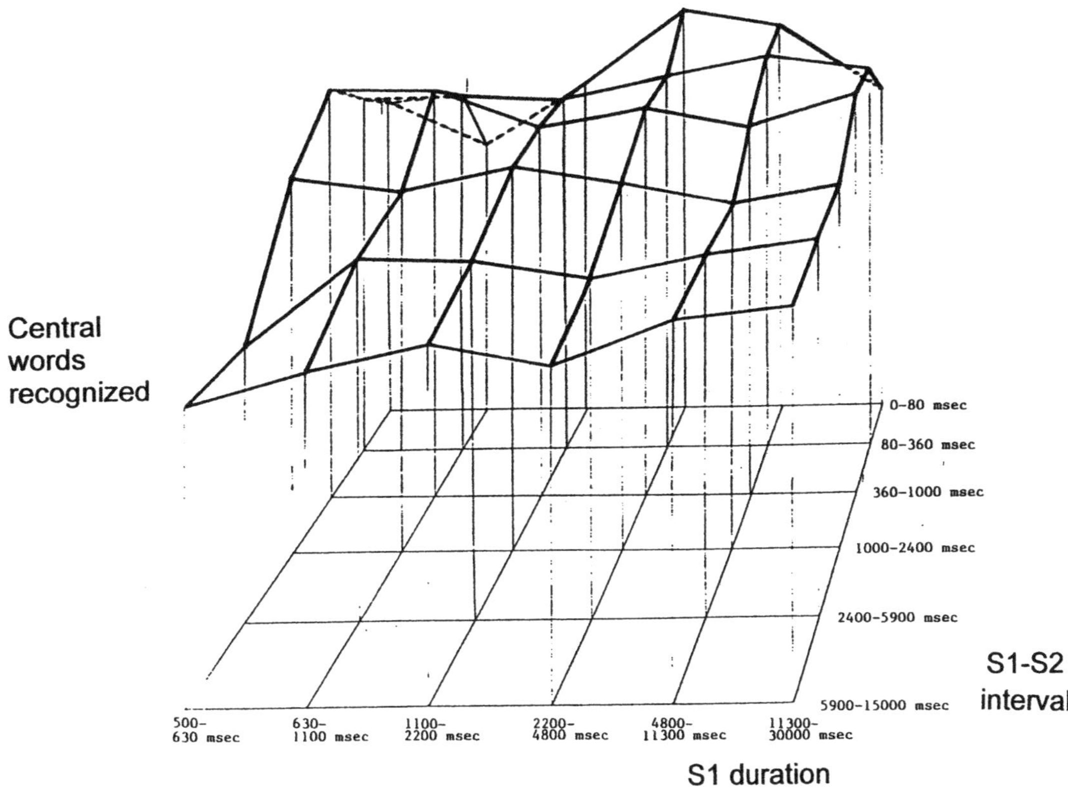

FIG. 11.7. The amount of information (number of words or characters) at the periphery of a visual stimulus S2 that was subsequently recognized as a function of the duration of the warning stimulus (S1) and the duration of the interval between S1 and S2.

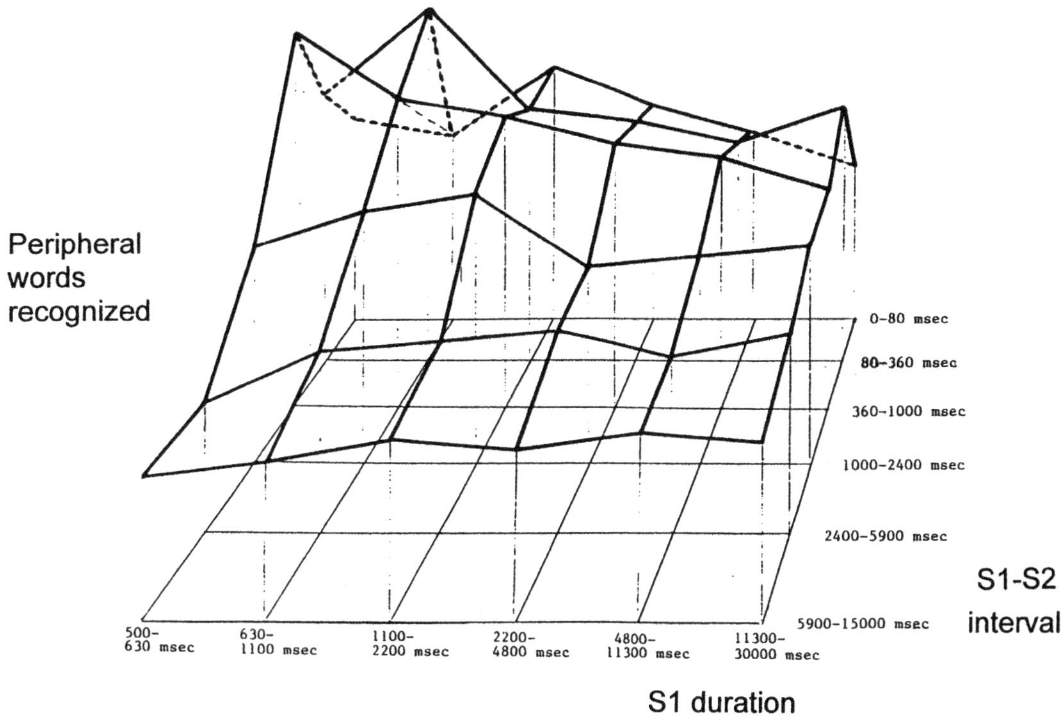

FIG. 11.8. The amount of information (number of words or characters) at the center of a visual stimulus S2 that was subsequently recognized as a function of the duration of the warning stimulus (S1) and the duration of the interval between S1 and S2.

warned them of stimuli to come and therefore directed their attention forward in time [the word "COMING," about which the subjects had been forewarned]). One second following the onset of this 16th stimulus, two words were presented, to which subjects had to press a reaction time key (to indicate whether they were the same or different, as instructed earlier in the study). The results showed that, in general, the significant and innocuous stimulus changes resulted in a deterioration of RT performance (Fig. 11.9).

These results can be contrasted with those from the previous study on perception, where recall of words was better, rather than worse, following a stimulus change. One interpretation of the two studies is that orienting produces a generalized enhancement of perceptual processes (or perhaps memory consolidation processes), but tunes the organism for specific motor activity, depending on the nature of the stimulus. In this study, it could be argued that motor activity is simply inhibited by orienting stimuli during the time that the organism processes the OR eliciting stimulus, perhaps because these particular orienting stimuli do not immediately prime any specific motor behavior. Data to be presented later suggest that generalized orienting is not linked to specific behavioral acts. Rather, particularly with nonsignal-orienting stimuli, general motor inhibition is more likely to occur as this should enhance the perceptual processing that might help to identify the nature of the change in the orienting stimulus. This interpretation is given support from the results of the final type of change stimulus in this

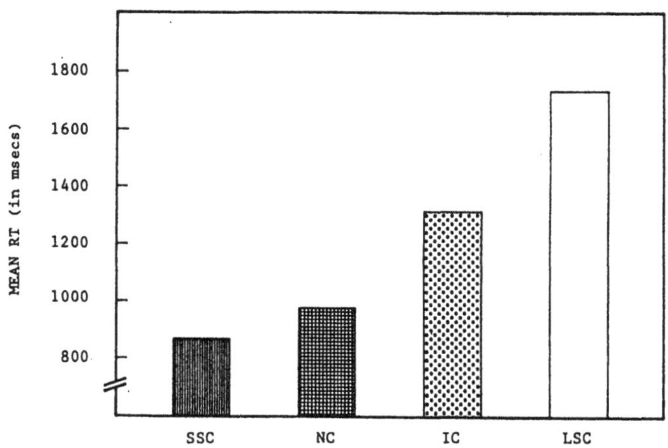

FIG. 11.9. Results showing the mean reaction time to the probe words, as a consequence of different types of orienting stimuli presented one second earlier. SSC: Short-term Significant Change (the word *COMING*); NC: No Change condition (same slide as previous 15 trials); IC: Innocuous Change (same slide as previous 15 trials, but rotated); LSC: Long-term Significant Change (subject's name). (From Shek & Spinks, 1986. Copyright © 1986 by Elsevier Science Publishers B.V. Reprinted with permission).

study, where the word "COMING" produced a facilitation of RT (Fig. 11.9). Subjects had been told earlier in the experiment that this word might occur, and that the encoding task would shortly follow the presentation of this stimulus. Thus, specific motor behavior was indeed primed in this condition, with facilitatory results. This effect illustrates one of the major issues of this chapter, that is, the linkage of the OR with anticipatory mechanisms.

The effects of the OR, then, are not confined to covert peripheral and central changes, but may be behavioral (see also Germana, 1969). Humans are clearly motivated, with obvious benefits in terms of their adaptation to the environment, to acquire information while they suffer various negative consequences from a lack of informational inflow. These negative effects can range from boredom and fatigue to the more complicated and serious results of sensory deprivation. Pavlov (1927) originally noted the relationship between the OR and a complex series of exploratory acts, aimed at investigating the environment in detail. Another part of the behavioral components of the OR was noted to be the temporary cessation of ongoing activity, in order to deal with extracting information concerning the novel situation, as was seen in the study described previously.

Sokolov (1969b) identified behavioral searching movements with the OR, the aim of these being to secure and transmit information about external objects. In studies with Arana on recognition of different objects by touch, it was shown that the tactile movements used by subjects were determined by the system of neural models (hypotheses) developed by the subject, these being the most complex, and generating the largest number of hypotheses, when the object was novel. The probabilities of each of these hypotheses are revised continually according to information obtained, until such time as the stimulus is identified. The total uncertainty in the system, or entropy, calculated from the probabilities of the various hypotheses, determines whether the OR will be evoked. When a novel stimulus is introduced, the entropy will be highest, because such uncertainty is characterized by large numbers of low probability hypotheses and the absence of any one hypothesis of reasonably high probability. This approach makes an additional distinction between the conditioned reflex and the OR. At the beginning of conditioning, the number of equiprobable a priori hypotheses is high. This uncertainty triggers the OR. The CR occurs to signal stimuli with only a low probability. After the formation of the CR, however, the probability of one (a posteriori) hypothesis increases, and the CR is triggered consistently. The entropy of the set of hypotheses is low, and the OR is therefore absent.

The idea of hypothesis generation is central to many views of information processing. For example, concept formation and problem solving in humans is usually seen as based on the generation and then a test of hypotheses about the concept or answer. Theories of perception usually accept that it is, in part at least, an active process, where hypotheses and expectations determine, through top–down processing, the analysis of the stimulation. This process of generating hypotheses may be fast and preattentive, as shown by Marcel's (e.g., 1983) semantic priming studies, where word primes produce spreading activation in the cortex to activate semantically related words that are, probabilistically, the most likely to follow. These words can be recognized more quickly and easily than improbable, semantically unrelated words. This process of expectation (or hypothesis generation) and testing has been related to the OR by Feigenberg (1969), who argued that the organism makes a probabilistic prognosis (prediction) of future environmental events. Any deviation from this prediction results in uncertainty, and then orienting, in order to take in information to reduce this uncertainty and allow the organism to generate more reliable prognoses.

One of the conclusions that Sokolov (1966, 1969b) drew about the OR is that it has the property of maximizing information uptake in both space and time. In terms of space, it has already been pointed out that behavioral activity, particularly eye movements and orientation of the head, but also including the finger movements investigated in the tactile exploration study of Sokolov and Arana, all have the effect of bringing relevant stimuli and the information they contain within the field of the receptors. More importantly for this chapter, however, the OR is also located in time in such a way as to maximize the information extracted from the environment (Sokolov, 1966). The nervous system is primed, at this moment (or moments) in time, to be optimally receptive, and this mechanism constitutes the major component of the anticipation and prediction mechanism. Later sections of this chapter describe studies on how the OR is related to anticipatory responses and analysis.

CONDITIONING AND ANTICIPATION

Anticipation may be defined in terms of neuronal models of expected stimuli or stimulus–response combinations, which the organism is continually making and updating, in order to best adapt to its present and future environment. One of the most studied forms of anticipation occurs in a selective attention situation, where Ss are trying to follow one channel in a dichotic listening paradigm (processing negativity studies), and identify target stimuli having certain features that differ from other attended stimuli. In this situation, an early ERP deflection can be found to the attended stimuli. It is so early (reported to commence at about 50 to 60 ms from stimulus onset) that the information can only have just reached the cortex (requiring some 10 ms) before the first manifestation of a differential response may be seen. This suggests that an anticipatory set must be present before the stimulus presentation. Näätänen (1982, 1990) argued that such a speed is possible because the stimuli are automatically analyzed via a process of a voluntarily maintained representation (attention trace) of the physical features of the stimulus that are relevant during such "selective maintenance." So, if the to-be-attended stimulus is clearly different from the other stimuli, the comparison process is terminated quickly, making an early ERP index of the distinction possible if the trace is actively maintained. The rehearsal required for this maintenance can be seen as a form of active anticipation. The rehearsal can be at different speeds. Short-lasting rehearsal is like reverberation of impulses in closed neural circuits. On the other hand, voluntary rehearsal as a tool for aiding memory can be long-lasting.

Sokolov's original data (1963) concerning the OR came from electrodermal and vascular recordings. Later, a number of other physiological measures were used to demonstrate basic OR-phenomena such as habituation and dishabituation. Conditioning studies demonstrated that if the CS and UCS are paired with a long (>6 s) interval to allow in practice the separation of two autonomic response components, an immediate response to the CS can be shown to behave like a habituating OR to this stimulus, and a later response represents the conditioned response. This typically occurs just in time before the UCS onset. In his book *Perception and the Conditioned Reflex*, Sokolov (1963) demonstrated that OR habituation and CR development may be concurrent but usually proceed so that the OR fades out at the same time that the CR becomes visible. This can be easily shown. One interpretation is that the latter response component is merely a conditioned orienting response.

In human subjects, the perception of the CS–UCS relationship occurs rapidly, with the result that the autonomic OR habituates quickly and an anticipatory CR or conditioned OR may be observed after a few pairings. Usually two to three paired presentations are sufficient for habituation to take place as well as for the full development of the anticipatory response. This latter response seems to represent preparation for the UCS-event in a conditioning situation. It usually starts to decrease soon after reaching its asymptote. The specificity of the pattern of the physiological changes preceding the UCS-event that is cued (informed) by the CS may reveal whether this response reflects the anticipation of information and/or behavioral preparation for a response (depending on the expected UCS). Whether this is the case or not was the goal of the following experiment (Lyytinen, 1984). The terms S1 and S2 are used instead of CS and UCS for the first (information) event and the second (critical) event, in order to provide consistency with other studies of this chapter.

Different types of S2 events were employed in the same experimental session of recording physiological manifestations of orientation and anticipation, in order to observe the event-related specificity of the responses preceding each. The S1–S2 trials with these different S2 events were presented in random order and the mean intertrial interval was 12 to 25 sec. Four groups of 20 subjects each were given different amounts of information concerning the S2 in a stimulus (S1) preceding S2 by 8.8 s. The first, Fully Informed group (FI) received a warning stimulus (S1-slide), which always informed the subjects in advance of the nature of the coming critical event S2. The second Partially Informed group (PI) had to decipher the cue given in the S1 slide so that subjects could, following an active search, slowly learn to correctly anticipate the coming S2 event. The third Noninformed group (NI) received only temporal information by always having an empty slide presented as S1, but with the same fixed interstimulus interval (8.8 s) before the S2. The last group, a Sensitization group, experienced all the S1 and S2 events in random order, so that responses to the single stimuli could be measured for comparison purposes.

The six S2 events contained cognitive tasks—mental arithmetic, memory, and sensory tasks (given in the S2 slide, and to be answered immediately), motor tasks (to be carried out according to an imperative stimulus included in S2), and sensory stimuli (loud tone and shock, occurring concurrently with S2 containing *tone* and *shock* words). Each such S1–S2 trial was repeated four times in the whole sequence of 4 × 6 = 24 trials. The sequence followed a pseudorandom order where none of the S2 events could occur on two successive trials.

The autonomic–somatic orientation processes were followed (Lyytinen, 1984) by measuring fourteen total autonomic or somatic (EMG) parameters continuously throughout the experiment and by computing three average scores from the different stages of the S1–S2 event sequence for all variable × group × condition units (see Fig. 11.10 for a summary of design and variables). The measured variables consisted of EDRs, heart rate acceleration and deceleration, finger pulse amplitude and blood volume, and pupillary dilation and constriction reactions. The EMG measures were taken from orbicularis oris and flexor muscles. The first category of scores represented the traditional OR (or first interval response, as defined in the conditioning literature) and was defined as the maximum response occurring within 1.0 to 5.0 s from the onset of S1. The second (interval response) category represented the anticipatory response, and was defined as the peak deflection occurring within −3.8 to +0.2 s in relation to S2 onset. The third UCR-type category was based on the peak responses within the period +0.2 to +4.2 s from the onset of S2.

As can be seen from Figures 11.11a–11.11c, the EDR results support the contention that the pre-S2 responses represent anticipation and/or preparation. In the Fully Informed group, this response was highly mapped onto the S2 event that it preceded; even in the Partially Informed group, it was more specifically mapped onto S2 than in the Noninformed group. The temporally informed Noninformed group, however, showed something like a

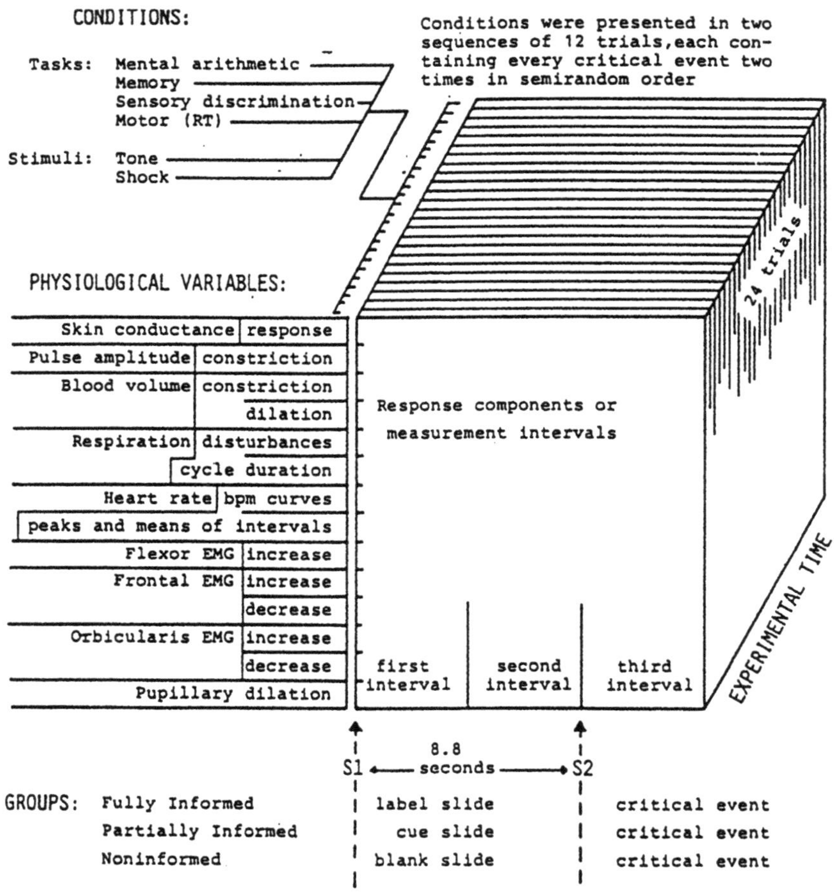

FIG. 11.10. The design, stimuli, event-timing, and measures of the ANS anticipation study by Lyytinen (1984).

flat, relatively high response profile of pre-S2 amplitudes, implying that these subjects were perhaps prepared for any of the possible events that the subject had learned to anticipate in the study. Thus, the autonomic and somatic variables used were able to very clearly show the subjects' use of the available anticipatory information, leading to event-specific preparation for each of the S2-events. The profiles of the pre-S2 responses simulated satisfactorily the post-S2 profiles in the Fully Informed group. It might be noted that although for the sake of simplicity only EDR results are shown, the mapping results were also clearly seen in HR, FPA, and EMG responses.

The second interesting result was that the OR to S1 was shown to habituate more quickly, the more the warning stimulus (S1) reduced uncertainty (FI > PI > NI). In fact, no habituation occurred in the Sensitization group that

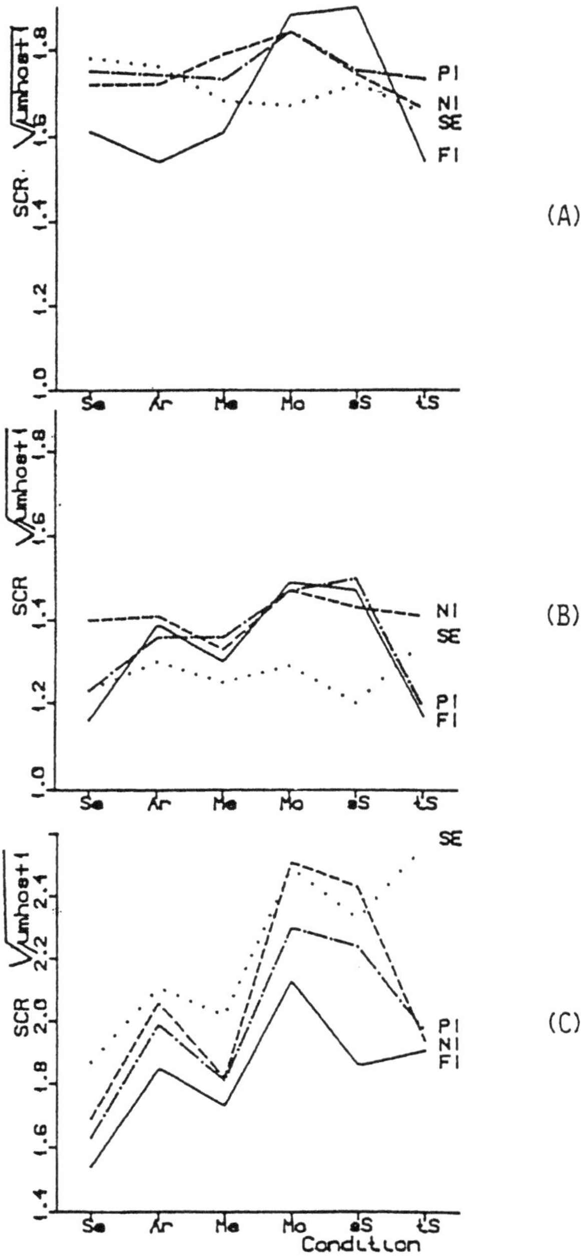

FIG. 11.11. The electrodermal responses during (a) the post-S1, (b) pre-S2, and (c) post-S2 intervals in the differentially informed groups during the different S2-event types (from Lyytinen, 1984).

received no advance information about the coming events (see Fig. 11.12). Figure 11.12 shows also that the habituation of the other groups follows the function of advance information they receive from S1. As shown by Fig. 11.11, the post-S1 responses cannot contain any specific mapping of, or specificity toward, S2 in this or the NI group.

Figure 11.11 shows also that the responses following S2 were affected by the preceding information so that the better the subjects' preparation opportunities were (on the basis of the preceding information), the lower were the relative amplitudes of the responses to the S2 events.

Thus, anticipation can refer to the OR with its arousal and facilitating properties and to different behavioral acts. The role of the OR as the immediate response to a signal stimulus is linked with informational or cognitive aspects of processing, but not necessarily to specific behavioral acts. The preparatory aspect moves during learning to the time when it is needed for making the brain and body optimally prepared for the act required. As recent animal model studies of nictate membrane response from Thompson's laboratory from the University of Southern California showed, this learning process and the movement of the pre-UCS preparatory trace of the CR can be recorded also from the brain and can be prevented by making nucleus interpositus neurons nonfunctional (e.g., by cooling) in the cerebellum (Krupa & Thompson, 1997).

These results reveal how orienting to anticipated events is reflected in the body in several different ways and stages. The first, immediate response represents a relatively nonspecific orienting response to the cue (S1), which is a physiological manifestation of a brain process involving an update of the current knowledge of the subject's scheme for the immediate

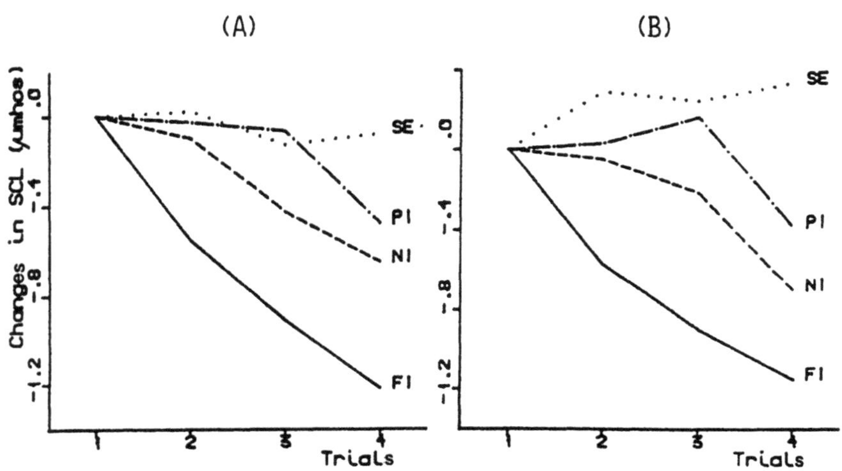

FIG. 11.12. Electrodermal habituation in the groups of differentially informed groups (from Lyytinen, 1984).

future or (as shown in the present experiment) the anticipated event. The more informative such a cue is, the more explicitly is this knowledge used by the subject for preparation—as manifested in the bodily responses—for the anticipated event. This information also affects the adaptive or defensive responses following the critical events, showing how the preparation facilitates coping with or responding to these future events. In this sense, less sensory regulation or metabolic mobilization is needed for coping with an event if the appropriate adjustment or mobilization can be initiated in advance. The processing of information is linked with brain metabolism—thus, the OR indicates vascular activation and glucose and oxygen uptake.

What is the relationship between the OR and these later response components? Insofar as these studies support the idea that these responses help coping with the present or future events in terms of the information collected, one could argue that these belong to orienting processes. This interpretation is supported also by the finding that all response components showed habituation. On the other hand, at least part of the autonomic and somatic pre-S2 changes can be seen as preparatory responses for task performance (as in those prior to the motor reaction) or for coping with aversive stimuli (as in those prior to the loud tone). This can be seen to minimize further learning in respect of responding to, or coping with, anticipated stimuli. The amount of learning needed for optimal coping decreases as the experiment progresses and as the subject automatizes the coping processes. Coping can be defined as a process whereby behavioral acts are performed with optimal levels of information. Excessive information is abolished. This occurs because of a reduction in the evoked OR. Thus, OR reduction and stabilization (coping) are two sides of the same coin.

A detailed analysis of the data from the previous experiment reveals that the immediate responses to the cue (S1) informing subjects about the coming event already showed some specificity to the anticipated event, although the later responses occurring just before the critical S2 event were clearly more specifically mapped onto the S2 event responses. The distinction between these two response components may be arbitrary and only show the time course of the perceptual analysis of the situation and behavioral preparation, which are simply two different aspects of the same adaptive process of orientation to the events. Of interest, however, is the fact that autonomic–somatic changes observed in such a situation show clearly how the information extraction from S1 is related to the immediate future and how it helps the organism prepare for this by initiating the same kind of changes which would have occurred on perception of S2. This has the effect of minimizing both stimulus and response uncertainty with regard to future events.

The preparations that specifically adapt the organism for the coming event include, not only the basic sensory analysis, but also the cue-deciphering-based decision making, as well as the efferent preparatory processes for the coming event. All these could be seen as components of the OR. In such a context, the feed-forward nature of the OR as a set of processes serving the needs of coping with the flow of events an individual faces in time and especially in the near future are clearly demonstrated. The experiment shows explicitly the future orientation of the autonomic–somatic adjustments when an individual is actively engaged with a goal. A real-life example of the role of active anticipatory orientation in autonomic–somatic adjustments may be seen in the passenger of a moving car. The passenger who follows the movements of the car along a winding road is much less liable to nausea than is one who is not engaged in attending to environmental cues ahead of the car. The sensory information helps the brain in this case to initiate anticipatory adjustments (centrally or behaviorally) needed to avoid the imbalances that result in nausea.

Thus, in summary, anticipatory arousal, as indexed by the OR, increases the inflow of information that is very important, at the stage when a behavioral strategy is not defined. When a selected behavior pattern has been shown to be effective and efficient, the reduction of the OR helps the organism to concentrate on only task-relevant information, without the distracting influence of extra environmental information. The anticipatory arousal also is more time-specific, shortly preceding the stimulus.

ORIENTING AND ANTICIPATION

Evidence has been presented thus far that the functional significance of the OR lies in its role in enhancing aspects of information processing, so that environmental stimuli can be more efficiently analyzed. As has also been noted, this facilitation occurs particularly at moments in time that are likely to convey information to the organism, that is, at times of uncertainty, where an unusual or a novel stimulus (i.e., an informational event) has occurred, or where a significant (signal) stimulus (i.e. one which results in anticipation of an informational event) has occurred. From the perspective of adaptation to the environment, the organism would be better able to interact with it surroundings if it could anticipate these information carrying events, and prepare in advance to process the information therein. Indeed, it makes little sense for the organism to orient in order to process a stimulus event that has already past. In order to assess the information value of a stimulus, it must be analyzed. Orienting as a response to this information is thus too late to have a useful effect on analysis, particularly perceptual analysis, unless the OR is evoked immediately following an initial, perhaps preattentive, analysis of the stimulus and is very fast in its facilitatory effects. Notwithstanding this latter comment (which will be examined later in this chapter), the organism would be psychologically (and therefore biologically) better prepared if orienting is related to predicted or anticipated information.

In order to examine, then, the relationship between the OR and future incoming information, the following studies were carried out. In the first of these (Spinks & Siddle, 1985), visual stimuli were presented in pairs, 6 to 8 s apart. S2 was a simple (low intrinsic information) or more complex (high intrinsic information) array of letters, which the subject had to recognize and subsequently report. For some experiments, the array presentation could be of short (60 ms) or long (75 ms) duration. Both these factors were varied within subjects, from trial to trial. S1 warned the subject of which stimulus would follow on that particular trial (for example, S1 = "ONE LETTER, LONG DURATION"). Thus, S1, although it conveyed information to the subject about the complexity and the timing of the forthcoming S2, actually conveyed itself the same amount of information, regardless of the condition of that trial.

In this experiment, the EDRs evoked in the interval between S1 and S2, just prior to S2, were of larger magnitude when a higher information, more complex S2 was to follow (Fig. 11.13). Thus, it would appear that the OR, at least as measured by the EDR at this time point, is affected by the anticipated information rather than the information actually conveyed by S1 itself, thus showing results which are in line with the earlier speculation concerning the goal-directed nature of behavior. In terms of the development of ideas earlier about the functional significance of the OR, this mechanism is clearly adaptive, in that it alerts the organism to be optimally receptive to analyzing information in advance of the presentation of this information. This increase of anticipatory OR activity is relevant to the optimal intake of information that has to precede the decision making process and response performance.

Further findings (Spinks, 1989; Spinks, Blowers, & Shek, 1985), however, showed that varying the information in S1 (giving no information except temporal information, giving the number of letters to appear in the imperative stimulus, or giving the actual letters that would also appear in S2) also influenced the magnitude of the SCR-ORs evoked immediately following S1. The design for this study (Spinks, et al., 1985) is shown in Fig. 11.14 and the relevant results in Fig. 11.15. In this sense, the data replicated the findings of the experiment described earlier (Spinks & Siddle, 1976) that varied stimulus complexity. Thus, it would appear from these two studies that the OR is sensitive to *both* anticipated information *and* the information actually conveyed by the stimulus. The OR does, therefore, in part at least, appear to be part of a forward-directed information processing mechanism. The Spinks et al. (1985) results have been replicated in a subsequent study examining both EDRs and P300 ERPs to S1 (Blowers, Spinks, & Shek, 1986). P300 amplitude in this study appeared to be most closely related to the amount of uncertainty regarding subsequent (or anticipated) stimulus processing.

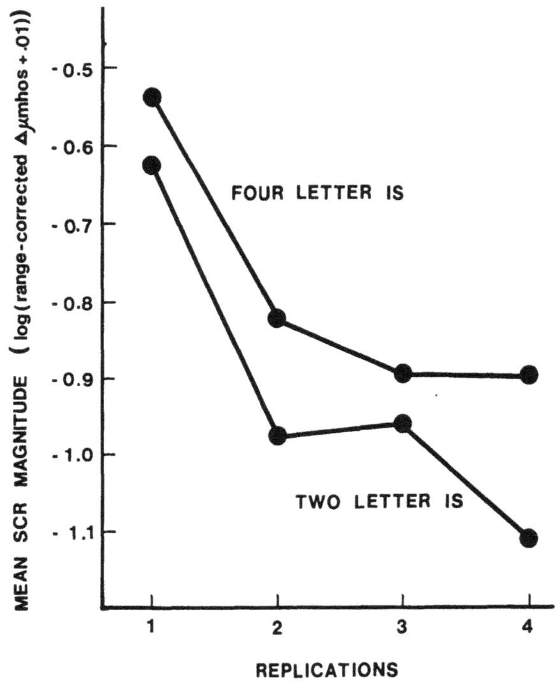

FIG. 11.13. Habituation of SCRs in the interval between S1 and S2 in a two-stimulus paradigm. When S1 warned of a simple (two-letter) S2, SCRs prior to the S2 were smaller in magnitude and habituated to a zero response criterion more quickly than when the S1 warned of a more complex (four-letter) S2. (Adapted from Spinks & Siddle, 1985. Copyright © 1985 by Elsevier Science Publishers B.V. Reprinted with permission).

The duration of the imperative stimulus had mixed effects in these studies. Earlier experiments had found no influence of this variable on OR magnitude, whereas later studies, which, it could be argued, were more sensitive to this factor, found larger ORs when a longer duration S1 has been perceived or a longer duration S2 was expected (Fig. 11.16). This would certainly fit well with the view that the OR is related to the actual or predicted amount of information extracted, this presumably being greater when the stimulus is available for a longer duration. These studies were followed up by one (Spinks, 1989) in which reaction times to a secondary task probe stimulus were measured. S1 and S2 were presented visually, in a design similar to that of Spinks et al. (1985) described before (Fig. 11.13). At several fixed times around these stimuli (randomly chosen from trial to trial), visual or auditory probes were presented that were subjectively matched for intensity. The instructions given to subjects were to make a speeded motor response to these probe stimuli. The results are presented in Fig. 11.17. If it can be assumed that such probe reaction times reflect the commitment of

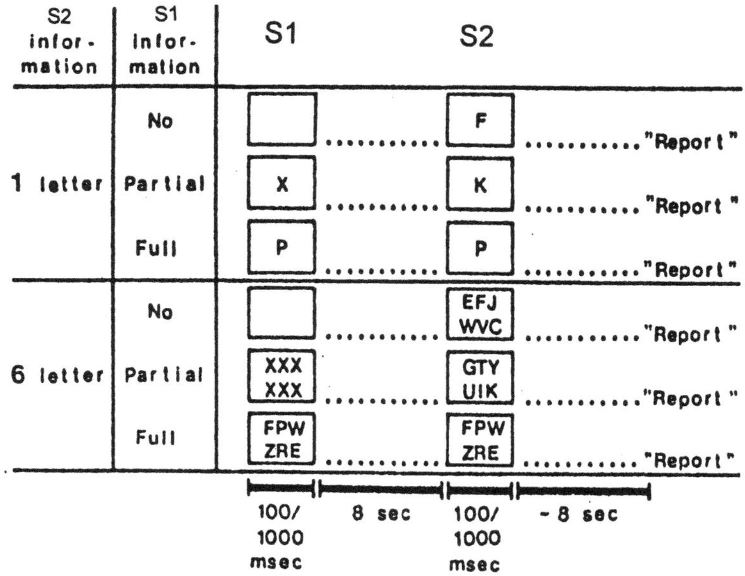

FIG. 11.14. Summary of experimental design. S2 could be a simple (one-letter) or complex (6 letters) stimulus, and S1 gave with no information, partial information (the number of letters to appear), or full information (the actual letters) about S2. (Adapted from Spinks, Blowers, & Shek, 1985. Copyright © 1985 by The Society for Psychophysiological Research, Inc. Reprinted with permission).

processing resources as a result of the S1–S2 combination, the data suggest that there is only a reallocation of such processing resources when S1 warns of a high complexity S2 (six-letter condition). Following S1 presentation in this condition, as well as just prior to S2, reaction times slow, suggesting that both the orienting to S1 and anticipatory orienting prior to S2 have engaged processing resources. When S2 is simple, on the other hand (one letter condition), reaction times change very little. This study thus shows the specificity of the central changes that take place during orienting and anticipation. Interestingly, in terms of the distinction between generalized and localized ORs, there was little difference between the curves for auditory and visual probes (although one could argue that the task had not become familiar enough for localized orienting to develop).

WORKLOAD EFFECTS ON ORIENTING

Well-established views of human information processing suggest that it can be conveniently divided into two general modes. The first of these is automatic, where the organism has genetically preprogrammed or learned programs of neuronal activity to accomplish some goal (e.g., recognition,

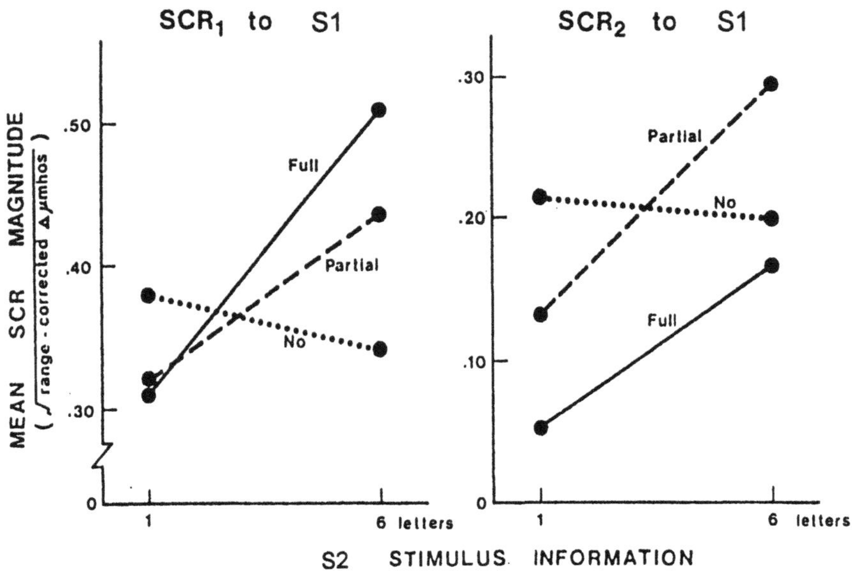

FIG. 11.15. Electrodermal results show that, even in the partial information condition, where S1 simply warned subjects of the number of letters to subsequently appear in S2, SCRs in the S1–S2 interval were greater in magnitude when a more complex S2 was anticipated as a result of this warning. SCR_1 was defined as the first SCR to occur whose onset was within the period 1 to 5 s after S1. SCR_2 was defined as the largest SCR to occur whose onset was within the period 5 to 9 s after S1. (Adapted from Spinks, Blowers, & Shek, 1985. Copyright © 1985 by The Society for Psychophysiological Research, Inc. Reprinted with permission).

appropriate responding). These programs are not affected by other concurrent activity and do not require effort on the part of the organism. Some of these automatic processes have well-known manifestations like mismatch negativity that can be recorded using EEG-, MEG-, or even PET-based (Näätänen, Medvedev, et al., submitted) techniques.

Mismatch negativity (MMN—see chapters 7 and 12 in this book for more details) can be seen as an example of an initial OR component. The elicitation of this ERP component to any change in the stream of auditory stimulation is not generally affected by attention. In some conditions, the MMN amplitude can in fact be even larger in a situation where more attentional resources are needed for processing other simultaneous events that the subject is actively processing. There are some studies, on the other hand, which show MMN amplitude to be attenuated with strongly focused attention elsewhere. No study has shown elimination of the MMN by attention to peripheral events. To examine whether MMN amplitude is dependent on attention to competing events, the following experiment was conducted. Sub-

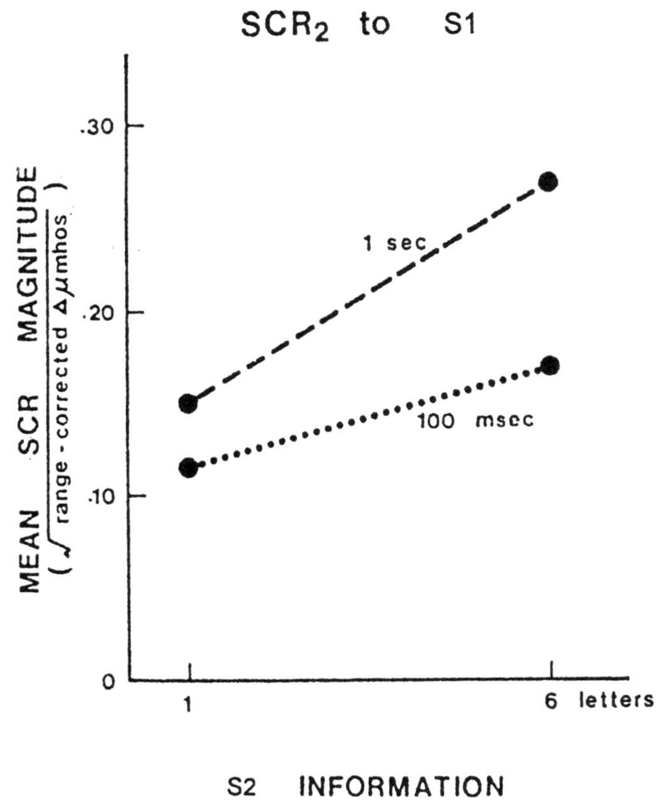

FIG. 11.16. Electrodermal results from the same study showed that short-duration stimuli produced no differential effect for anticipated S2 complexity or information. On the other hand, SCRs prior to a more complex S2 were larger in magnitude than those prior to a simple S2 when the duration of the stimuli was longer. SCR_2 was defined as in Fig. 11.15. (Adapted from Spinks, Blowers, & Shek, 1985. Copyright © 1985 by The Society for Psychophysiological Research, Inc. Reprinted with permission).

jects performed tasks with sensory requirements and received feedback about their performance.

Each trial consisted of two stimuli. S1 was a four-letter set like NSDP, which then had to be remembered. An example of S2 would be XSXP containing the same/different letters in non-X positions. The interval between S1 and S2 was 6 s. The subject's answer, 2 s after S2, was immediately followed by feedback on whether the answer was correct or not, by means of a change in the color of the display. Three seconds later, subjects received a loud tone (UCS) if the answer was incorrect. MMN was recorded to infrequent (10%) tone pips (50ms, 1030 Hz) in a stream of standard (90%) tone pips (50ms, 1000 Hz) occurring at 1-s intervals during presentation of the

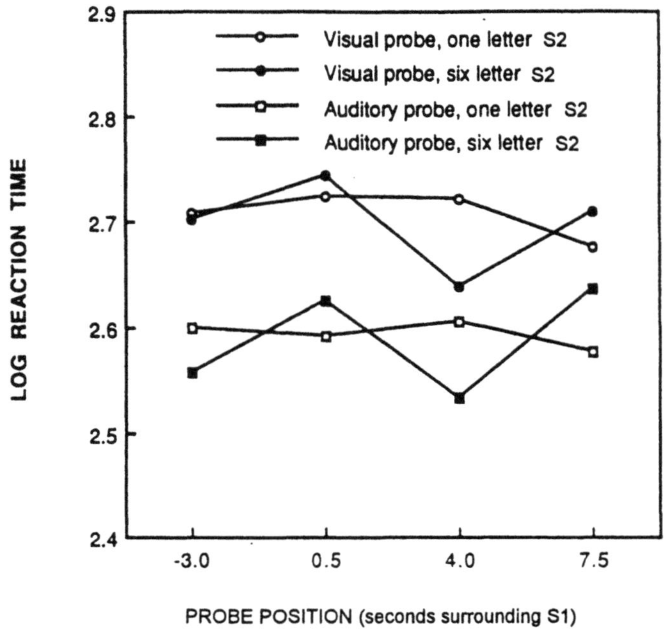

FIG. 11.17. Performance data, showing reaction times to probes presented at various times around S1 and S2. (Adapted from Spinks, 1989. Copyright © 1989 by Elsevier Science Publishers B.V. Reprinted with permission).

earlier described S1–S2 task. The intertrial intervals were defined as low attention (to task events) epochs, the first 3 s of the interval between S1 and S2 and the first 3 s between S2 and UCS as intermediate attention situations, and the last 3 s of both these intervals as high attention situations. As shown in Fig. 11.18, the MMN amplitude was a function of the attention to the active tasks, being smaller when attention to the other main tasks was greater. MMN appears to be evoked regardless of the workload or by how much attention, or perhaps even conscious effort, is directed to the competing events. It is, in this sense, a metric of some automatic processing routine within perception.

These automatic processes usually involve information handling routines that are very common. The other mode of processing is controlled processing, where the organism has to invest effort. It usually involves processing that is new to the organism, unusual, unexpected, or especially difficult. This may be reflected by an increase in arousal, longer processing times, and interference from other ongoing controlled processing routines. In practical circumstances, however, there is a dynamic interaction between automatic responding and activity that is primarily controlled, where the relationship between the two can be shifted in a particular direction. Thus, the task is to evaluate at each particular stage of

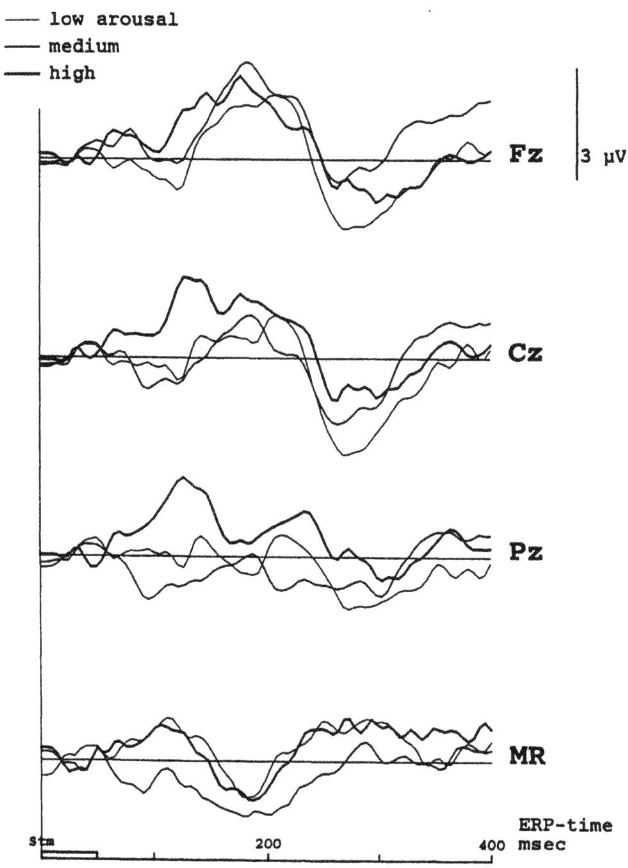

FIG. 11.18. MMN responses to deviant stimuli occurring during different levels of work load in a continuous performance task (from Lyytinen, Aro, & Leppäsaari, 1992).

information processing the relative contributions of automatization and informatization. The word *informatization* is preferred to *controlled*, because all responses and actions are in a sense controlled. In fact, automatized processes are far better controlled than others, in that they are usually more highly practised or conditioned, leading to more skilled performance. Thus, the preference is to use the term *informatization*, indicating that extra information has to be acquired and utilized before an appropriate outcome occurs, and this takes time, thus delaying the response. When processing becomes more automatic, as seen earlier, it is beneficial for the organism to decrease informational inflow, because such information may disrupt the automatic process. Thus, the OR should be inhibited under these conditions, for optimal processing.

It could be argued, however, following the earlier discussions about orienting enhancing information processing in novel or unusual situations where a large amount of information is being processed, that the OR would be required during informatized (controlled) processing. The extent to which orienting is a reflection of a call for, or a change to, informatized processing was examined in the following experiment (Spinks, 1989).

The design was similar to the two-stimulus paradigm described previously. The second stimulus of the pair, a visual imperative stimulus, S2, contained either one letter of the alphabet or six such letters. The subjects' task was, again, to identify as many of these letters as possible. At 8 s prior to this stimulus was a visual warning stimulus, S1, this being a number simply indicating how many letters would subsequently appear in S2. Thus far, this experiment was identical to one described earlier (Spinks, et al., 1985). In the present experiment, however, there was an additional task for the subjects (Figs. 11.19 & 11.20). About 8 s either side of the presentation of S1, a visual search task also appeared on the screen in front of the subjects, where subjects were asked to search for particular targets, and press a foot pedal every time they recognized one. This search task varied in difficulty. On some trials, there was simply no target to search for, although the letters still appeared. On some trials, the target letter was easily distinguished from the distractors. On the remaining trials, the target was visually similar to the distractors, and the distractors on one trial might become the targets on another, a situation that could be said to require informatized processing.

The results confirmed those found in the two studies described previously, in that they showed larger EDRs to S1 when an S2 with more information was anticipated. Of more interest here, however, was the finding that these EDRs decreased in magnitude as the search task became more difficult. Figure 11.21 shows the relevant data from this (left) and a subsequent study (right). One explanation of these findings is that the facilitation of information processing mechanisms discussed previously and by Sokolov (1966) could not be effected under the difficult search task condition, as there was less information processing capacity available for the anticipatory preparation shown in the earlier experiments and in the no-search task condition. The differential EDR magnitude prior to the two S2 conditions was not seen under the difficult search task condition. This result has important implications. It suggests that the autonomic OR is not evoked by an initial (perhaps preattentive) analysis of the stimulus as the background search task difficulty should not influence EDR magnitude, this only being determined by the anticipated information in S2.

Two further points can be made about the results of this experiment. First, one has to refer to two different types of OR—tonic and phasic. It is important to differentiate the arousal level and the phasic OR that can be quite independent. It would appear that the previous data are not the result

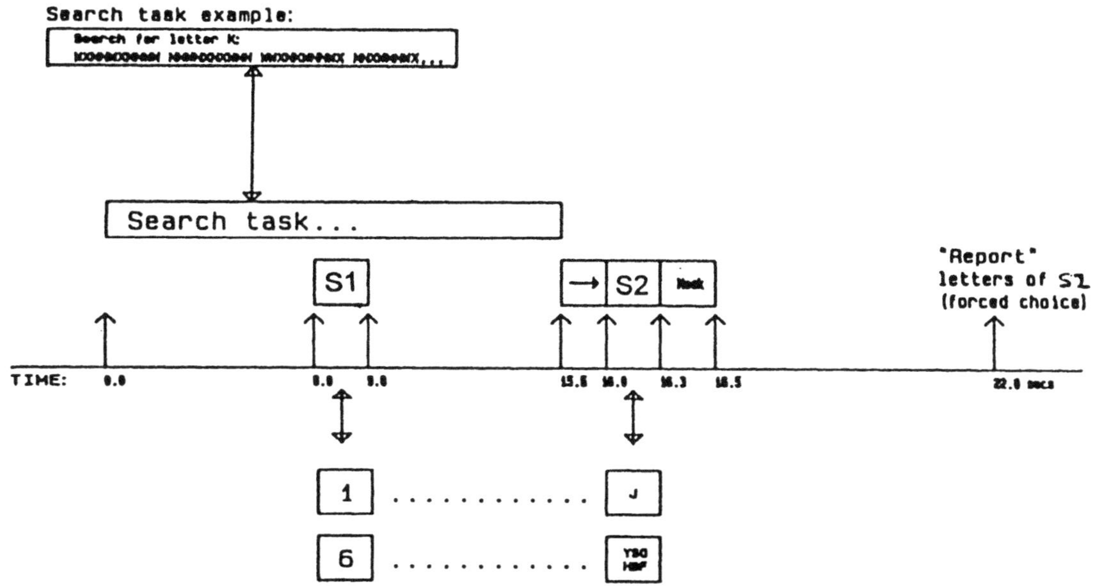

FIG. 11.19. Trial procedure. This study was similar to the S1–S2 studies described previously, but with an additional search task, which was ongoing at the time of the presentation of S1. (Adapted from Spinks, 1989. Copyright © 1989 by Elsevier Science Publishers B.V. Reprinted with permission).

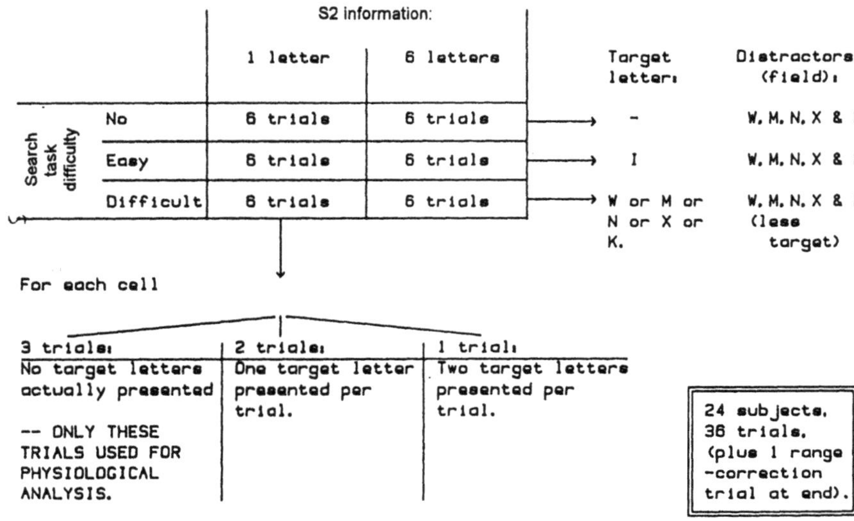

FIG. 11.20. Overall design. There were three levels of search task difficulty (no search task, easy search task, and difficult search task), employing differing levels of processing resources. Manipulations were on a within-subjects basis. (Adapted from Spinks, 1989. Copyright © 1989 by Elsevier Science Publishers B.V. Reprinted with permission).

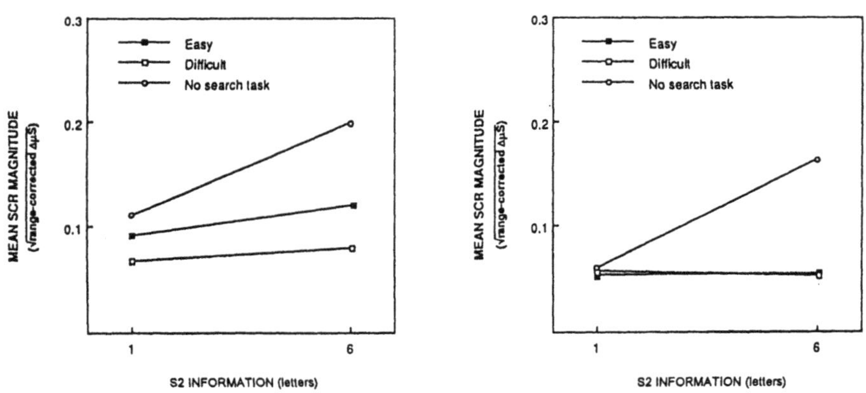

FIG. 11.21. Results from two studies employing the design illustrated in Figs. 11.19 and 11.20, where the factors of interest were the level of difficulty of the background search task, and the anticipated complexity (information) of S2. Data show the mean magnitude of SCRs to the warning stimulus, S1. (Adapted from Siddle & Spinks, 1992. Copyright © 1992 by Lawrence Erlbaum Associates. Reprinted with permission).

of varying arousal levels, although there is some evidence to suggest that these also change. Figure 11.22 shows the averaged skin conductance levels during this experiment, where phasic responses to S1 and S2 can be seen. In the six-letter condition, it is possible to also see responses just prior to the S2. In the one-letter condition, the effect of the background search task is much less pronounced than in the six-letter condition, as the information processing requirements in this one-letter condition are minimal and therefore unaffected by the availability of processing resources. Second, the ANS–OR is unlike MMN in terms of elicitation under automatized and in-

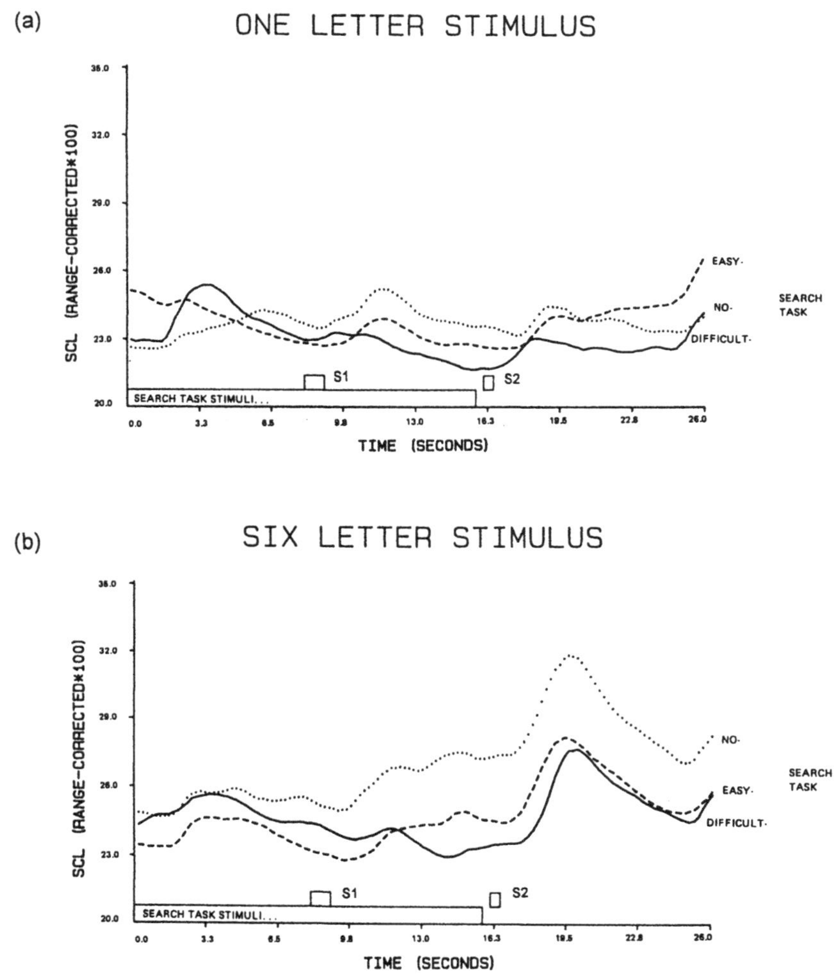

FIG. 11.22. Averaged skin conductance levels (resolution of 100 ms) for (a) an anticipated simple (one-letter) stimulus, and (b) an anticipated complex (six-letter) stimulus.

formatized processing conditions. A more detailed examination of this issue may be found in Spinks and Kramer (1991a, 1991b). The relationship between MMN and the ANS–OR is discussed further later in the next section.

The OR appears to be sensitive to other current goal-directed activities because it is goal-directed itself. *Goal-directed* implies forward-directed behavior, where the changes that take place within the ANS and CNS are directed at some future, anticipated events in the environment. As is well known from the literature, priorities within the environment determine goal-directed activity—instructions, conditioning, novelty, and uncertainty all call for high priority—and these are instrumental in eliciting orienting and alerting/arousal. The results from these studies can also be seen from this perspective. Goal-directed behavior may differ with respect to specific goals. The OR can be directed not to a particular goal, but to the source of information needed to reach a particular goal.

COVARIATION OF ANS AND ERP MEASURES

Of the basic mechanisms of the organism's adaptation to the environment in a Darwinian sense, the OR has come to assume a central theoretical importance. Evgeny Sokolov's theoretical developments not only describe behavioral orientation but propose brain systems that optimize the detection of environmental changes that have survival value for the organism. These changes are, most importantly, associated with novelty and signal value. For the first of these, Sokolov proposed a mechanism of novelty detectors based on specialized neurons in the hippocampus. At the time that Sokolov developed his theory, the measures available to studying orienting were limited to ANS and EEG alpha-blocking recordings. Later, Näätänen proposed the use of brain ERPs, and was able to develop, through this measurement, a specific index of change detection occurring below consciousness.

As described earlier, this response to change could even be seen when a subject's information processing capacity or work load is maximally employed on another task. The brain continually monitors changes in the auditory world and responds to any change of any quality in it, where the incoming stimulation differs from the temporary models of the preceding stimulation held in sensory memory. Where Sokolovian orienting follows the perception of novel or signal (or significant) stimuli, the specific ERP, the MMN response that Näätänen identified, may be a reflection of the processes related to the preconscious initiator of a further change detection—an initial selector of the information—that may require a further analysis. It may initiate (or may index the initiation of) a call for informatized processing where conscious attention will be focused on the stimulus. Näätänen labelled the ERP as *mismatch negativity*, as it occurs to a stimulus that fails to match the subject's memory that has built up following repeated presentations of the same stimulus, and because it is a negative polarity EEG deflection.

Although the main sources of the MMN are cortical and located in auditory areas, some indications of responses like MMN–OR can be recorded from the hippocampal areas (CA1, CA2, and dentate fascia), as shown by Ruusuvirta, Korhonen, Penttonen, Arikoski, and Kivirikko (1995a, 1995b). If the deviant stimuli are followed by an UCS, an OR response having both behavioral and ERP manifestations develops as a hippocampal OR at a latency of about 80 ms. In animals like the rabbit, MMN and the OR seem to merge together because, in an oddball paradigm, the hippocampal responses to deviant tones present within and outside a stream of standards are similar, and have manifestations in the cerebellar cortex as well, although not in the visual cortex. The data from these studies show a phasic negative wave in the hippocampus, overlapping a stable negativity. The phasic part of the wave then corresponds to behavioral orienting in the form of head movements. It can be suggested that the tonic part of the wave corresponds to axonic spikes travelling along pathways perforating the hippocampus. This tonic response then can be seen as a replica of the MMN, whereas the phasic response is more similar to responses of novelty detectors.

The process continues from the initial detection to perception, and, if needed, automatic responding—according to prior conditioning history and situational demands. Following Darwinian principles, one could say that the brain has evolved to initially detect change, novelty, or significance in such a way that the information or warnings given by these stimuli that elicit MMN or an OR are then taken into account by the organism and acted on in some way, in order to ensure the organism's survival. It is the potential consequences of stimuli and actions that have led to the development of this detection mechanism in the brain, and to the development of ways of handling these warnings so that these consequences are taken into account.

The best known characteristics of the OR are habituation and dishabituation, which show how an environmental event that is repeated without apparent consequences to the organism will automatically demand progressively fewer resources. The most direct measure of habituation has been the decrease in amplitude of ANS responses, typically considered as markers of energy mobilization. Similarly, if the eliciting stimuli for the OR have any consequences, rapid conditioning is possible. However, in the case of a stimulus change that evokes MMN, this does not in itself have marked somatic or psychological consequences, and does not lead, automatically, to awareness or a demand for resources. Thus, MMN need not, and should not, habituate. MMN is a stable response to deviant stimuli. If it is responsible for triggering of an OR, one has to explain why the OR habituates. The only relevant explanation is that this processing of deviant stimuli represents an earlier stage of OR initiation.

The differences in habituation are shown in an experiment where ANS–ORs were recorded in an oddball paradigm where MMN could be demonstrated. As shown by Fig. 11.23, the MMN does not differ on those trials on which a deviant stimulus (here a stimulus with a slightly faster rise-time than that of the repeated standard stimulus) elicited an autonomic OR, in comparison with those trials on which no autonomic OR was seen. This is the case, regardless of whether the trial selection is made on the basis of EDR or heart rate indications of the OR. On the other hand, the later ERP components usually associated with P3 are related to the ANS–ORs as can be seen from Fig. 11.24, although the correlations were not particularly strong. Blowers, Spinks, & Shek (1986) had also reported similar findings for

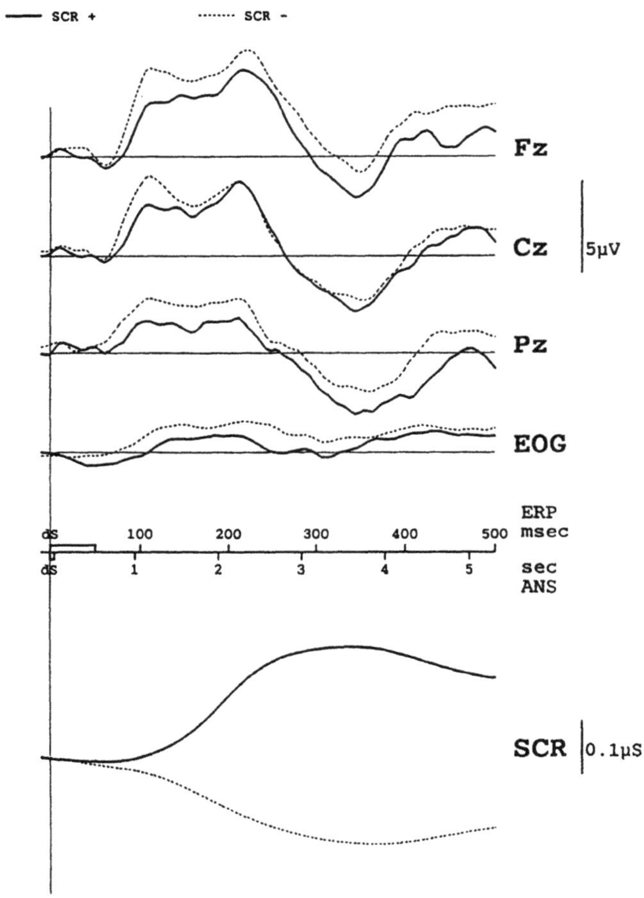

FIG. 11.23. MMN occurring to a deviant stimulus that is or is not eliciting autonomic (EDR) OR. As seen MMN is not affected by the OR. See text for description of the stimuli and explanation of the responses (from Lyytinen, 1989).

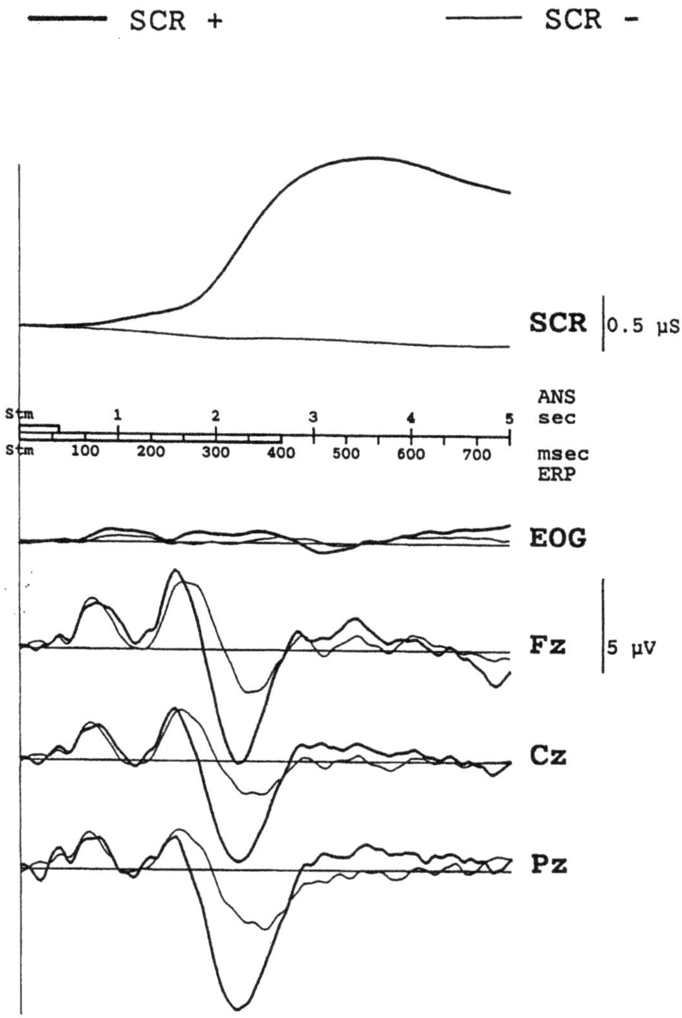

FIG. 11.24. The ERP associated with the ANS OR is a N2b–P3a complex to a deviant stimulus. Responses are categorized according to EDR occurrence to nontarget (slow rise-time) stimuli when subject is counting fast rise-time stimuli and the rise-time of the repeated standard is between those two (from Lyytinen, 1989)

P3 amplitude as were shown for ANS–ORs in the anticipation study of Spinks et al., 1985, described previously.

Slightly deviant stimuli in a stream of auditory tones occasionally result in a call for attention or attention being allocated, which may then be reflected in an autonomic OR and in a positive (P3a) ERP deflection shown by Fig. 11.24. These EDR–P3a association data are from a situation where the deviant stimulus is of slower rise-time than that of the standard stimulus and subjects are instructed to count the faster rise stimulus stimuli occurring as frequently (10%) as those of slow rise-time stimuli. Postexperimental interviews suggest that stimuli that elicit these latter responses have switched the focus of attention, yet the MMN may occur without the subject remembering hearing or remembering paying attention to the deviant tones. Further, there is, as expected, a dramatic change in the ERPs and ANS–ORs under conditions where the same stimuli are presented with an instruction to count the deviant tones.

Figure 11.25 shows the different type of ERP and ANS responses occurring to different types of changes in the auditory stimulus stream. Practically no response occurs to a repeated stimulus but any change, even when presented to a subject who is ignoring (not attending to) the stimuli in question, elicits a response (MMN). If the same stimulation is given in a

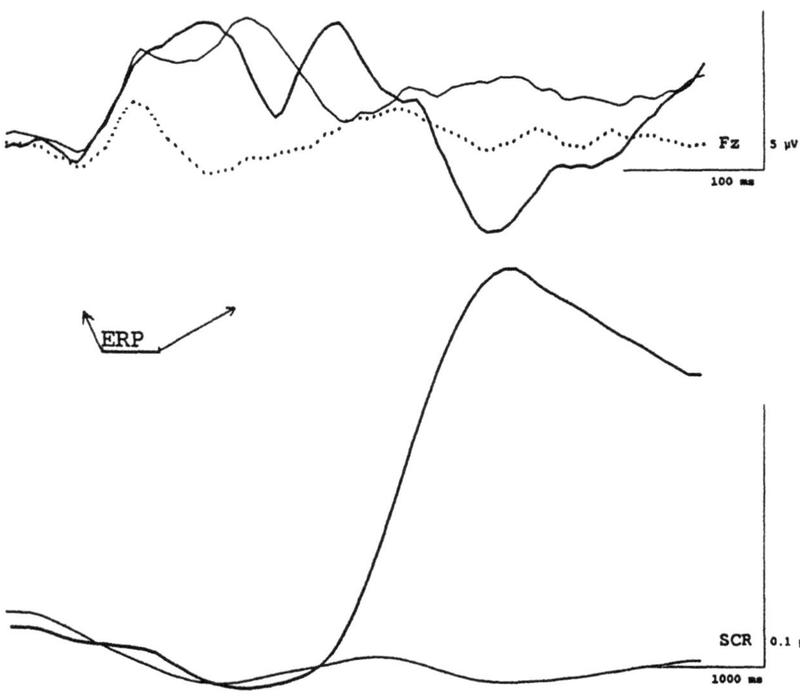

FIG. 11.25. Effects of stimulus deviance and attention to stimulus in a stream of tones. EDRs and ERPs to auditory stream of stimuli of which 10% are deviants (higher pitch) in comparison with the repeated tones from two *ignore* and *attend* situations. EDRs only to deviant stimuli. The dotted line shows the average ERP to the standard stimuli; thin line shows ERPs to the deviant stimulus in an *ignore* situation; and thick line shows ERPs in an *attend* situation (from Lyytinen, 1989).

situation where the subjects are instructed to count the deviant stimuli, a pronounced response is elicited to such to-be-counted (and thus attended) stimuli. In an *attend* situation, other stimuli deviating from the frequently repeated stimulus elicit both cortical and autonomic responses. It seems that conscious perception of the stimuli is an important determinant of an autonomic orienting response. If a deviant stimulus in an *ignore* situation occasionally becomes attended, it elicits both ANS–OR and a N2b–P3a complex but may not affect the occurrence of MMN. However, MMN may be a necessary condition for an attention switch to the stimulus change leading to its conscious perception. As shown by the figure, the attended stimulus elicits a huge EDR (thick line in the lower portion of the figure), yet a deviant stimulus in an ignore condition elicits only a barely detectable EDR (thin line), if any.

In an oddball task where subjects ignore the stimuli, ANS–ORs show habituation but MMN does not, as expected (Lyytinen, Blomberg, & Näätänen, 1992). In fact, even if the whole experiment is divided into thirds according to the trial sequence, and MMNs are averaged from each third separately, these show no (or very little) difference, although ANS–ORs show a clear reduction in amplitude (see Fig. 11.26). Chapter 12 describes some of the results of these ERP–ANS experiments in more detail.

So, MMN is like a basic change detector, but autonomic orienting only occurs if the consequences of the stimulus occurrence require the mobilization of the resources of the organism. These are thus different levels of analysis. The lower levels are more reflexive, more automatic, often innate, or well learned. At higher levels, there will be increasingly informatized processing, requiring more and more effort and perhaps arousal, guided by higher level nervous activity, and the responses will depend more on the situation (taking into account previous learning and long-term memory). Mobilization can include perceptual enhancement, motor preparation, appropriate sensorimotor tuning, even avoidance of or defense against future adverse stimuli. The exact nature of these mobilization changes will depend on the organism's prediction of the future, and will be, at least to some extent, mapped onto this prognosis. Although this higher level orienting is usually associated with awareness, this need not necessarily be the case.

THE OR IN SLEEP AND EARLY INFANCY

The normal brain responds, of course, to auditory changes in the environment immediately after birth. This can be shown to be the case at a very early age and also, interestingly, during sleep. Figure 11.27 shows the development of ERP amplitude to deviant tones recorded during the first few days of postnatal life as a function of maturity (gestational/conceptual age; from Leppänen, Eklund, & Lyytinen, 1997). The ERPs illustrated here, possibly identified as MMN, are elicited by pitch changes, but differential re-

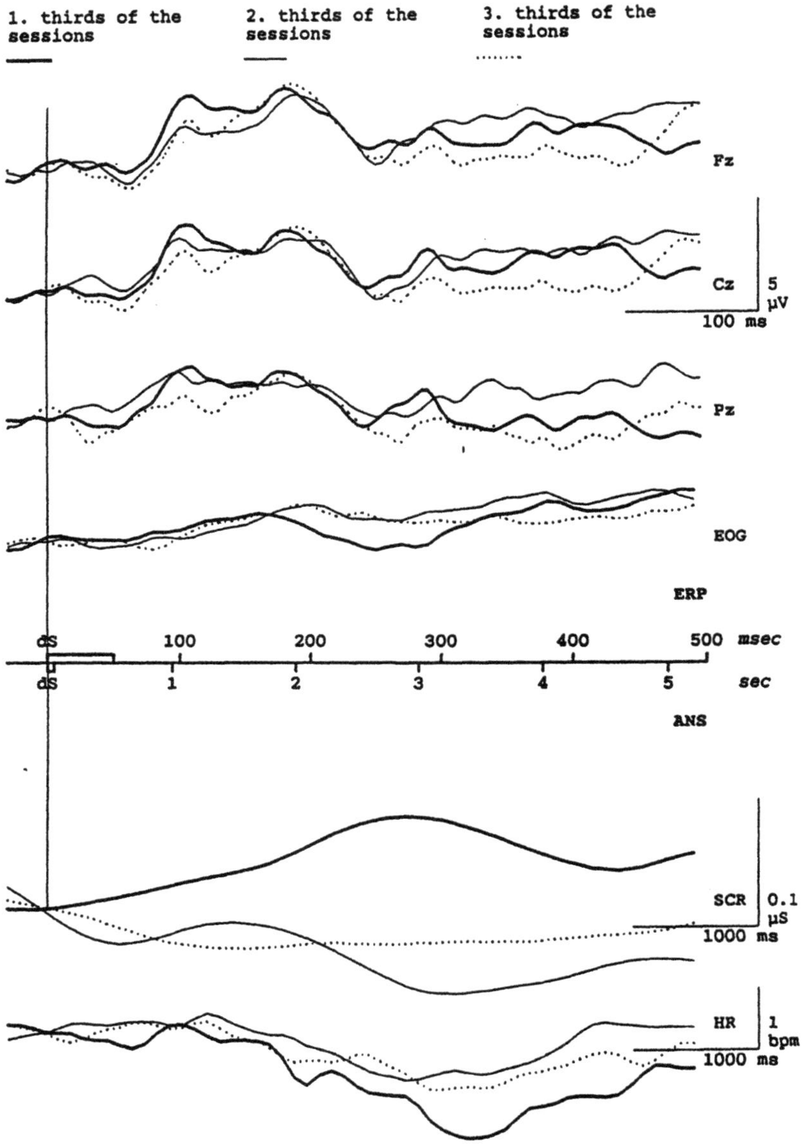

FIG. 11.26. The MMN, EDR, and HR to deviant stimuli during different stages (thirds) of the stimulus sequence during an *ignore* session when subjects are reading and the standard stimuli are of 1000 Hz and deviant ones are of 1030 Hz tones.

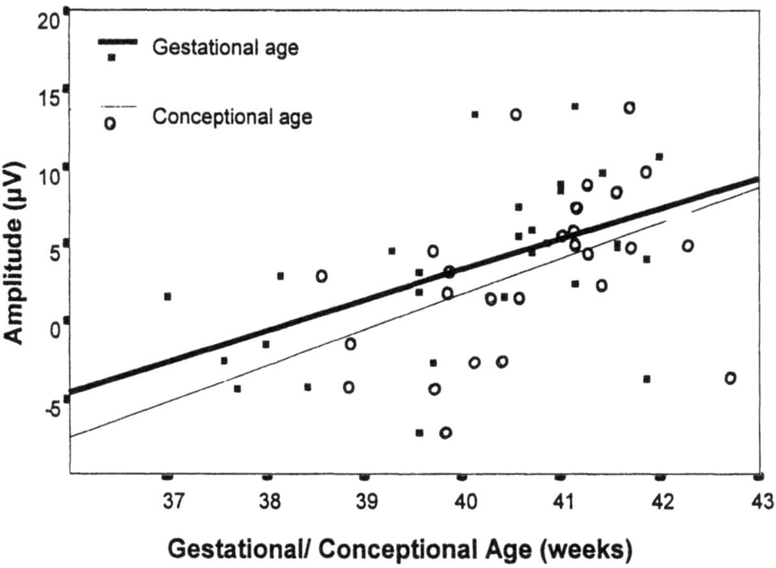

FIG. 11.27. Average ERP difference wave (response to deviant minus standard tone) of 2 to 10-day-old sleeping infants to occasional deviant (1100 Hz) and repeated standard (1000 Hz) tones as the function of the gestational–conceptual age (from the study of Leppänen, Eklund, & Lyytinen, 1997. Copyright © 1997 by Lawrence Erlbaum Associates. Reprinted with permission).

sponses to changes (amplitude to the deviant stimulus minus that of the standard one) have also been shown by other kinds of stimulus change, such as that of stimulus duration. What is seen in the figure is the change of not only the amplitude but also of polarity of the amplitude. Cheour-Luhtanen et al. (see Cheour-Luhtanen et al., 1995, 1996, 1997) have repeatedly demonstrated an MMN-like response in their recording of infant ERPs. It seems that the type of the response (even the polarity) and thus possibly the whole nature of the ERP responses to deviant tones may depend on the maturity of the brain, as shown by Leppänen et al. (1997).

The brain of the adult human seems to be sensitive to changes in the auditory environment also during sleep. Even relatively small pitch deviations among low-intensity tones elicit autonomic responses like HR acceleration. The so-called K-complex and heart rate acceleration responses can be, however, interpreted as responses that reflect a process to protect the sleeping state and the brain from external stimuli, rather than a readiness to orient to them (Sallinen & Lyytinen, 1997). There are also some indications of MMN to occasional deviant tones among sequences of repeated tones during Stage-2 sleep (Sallinen, Kaartinen, & Lyytinen, 1994). It seems, however, that an OR to stimuli presented at a longer interval (like 5 to 30 s) increases substantially the probability of an elicitation of the K-complex (which may

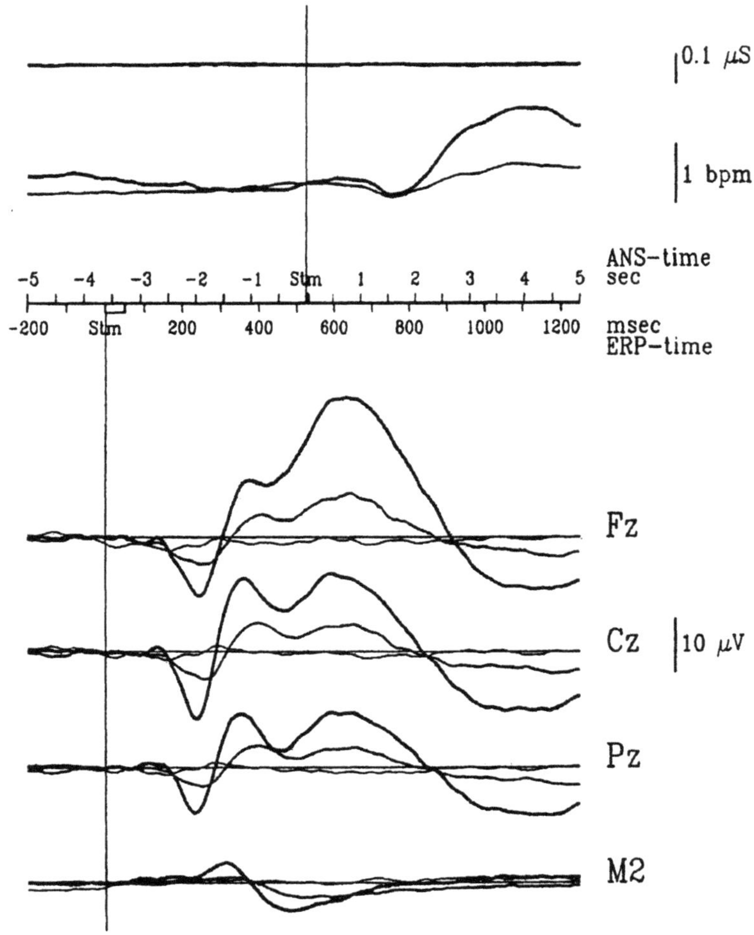

FIG. 11.28. Average EDR (top), HR (middle), and ERP (bottom) responses to tones presented with long ISIs (thick lines) and to the same tones presented as deviant tones among repeated standard tones (intermediate lines) during Stage-2 sleep. Both ERP types resemble K-complex. Note the substantial HR response occurring to both stimulus types and the failure to show any EDR to tones presented during sleep. Thin lines show the ERPs to standard tones (of slightly lower pitch) alone.

also occur without any external stimulus). Figure 11.28 shows the average ERPs to a low intensity tone when presented with long ISIs (thick line) or when the same tone is presented with same ISIs but among repeated standard (intermediate line) tones. It also shows the ERP to the standard tones of slightly lower pitch and EDR and HR responses to the two first tones. HR shows sensitivity to both stimulus types; EDR is unresponsive. The differential response (MMN) fails sometimes to occur during sleep without a subsequent elicitation of the K-complex to the same stimulus, as shown by Sallinen, Kaartinen, & Lyytinen (1997). This finding may support the sleep protection function. In fact, a closer look at the brain events preceding the elicitation of the K-complex shows that the standards that usually elicit very small or no responses during sleep tend to elicit a larger response at this time, showing that somehow the brain is in a more responsive state before an elicitation of the K-complex.

It seems that the brain response to external events is affected by its state. When moving from an awake state to drowsiness, the amplitude of the MMN decreases as a function that follows about the same course as the relationship between RT performance efficiency and, for example, the amplitude of the parietal P3 in an active task (Sallinen & Lyytinen, 1997). The sleeping brain is in a fluctuating state where it is occasionally more open to external stimulation. This openness seems to vary between both microstates within a sleeping stage and between sleeping stages. Thus, a P3-type response to a deviant tone can be elicited relatively consistently in REM sleep, increasing in amplitude as a function of the size of the deviancy from the repeated standard and the length of the REM period, as shown by Sallinen, Kaartinen, and Lyytinen (1996).

SUMMARY

This chapter reviewed a number of aspects of the OR within an information processing system, which complement or develop parts of the OR model described in the earlier chapters of this book. Evidence concerning the functional significance of the OR within such an information processing system has been presented, showing that the OR plays an important role in the perception of change or novelty, but perhaps more importantly, in the anticipation of events and information in the environment. Its psychological concomitants may include perceptual enhancement, motor preparation, and appropriate sensorimotor tuning, the nature of these changes being mapped onto a prognosis of future events, action, or information processing. The OR concept has been extended by incorporating MMN into a model of information processing. This, and other responses, may not fulfill the most restrictive criteria of the OR (e.g., habituation, dishabituation), but require that they are consistently elicited by novel, deviant, or significant stimuli. The organism must have the capacity to adapt to environmental events with minimal short-term costs (that is, it should not be maximally prepared at all times), but also with the goal of minimizing longer-term psychological costs or effort (such as dealing with the impact of a forthcoming event).

The nature of these anticipatory adjustments has been shown in a series of experiments. Thus, the organism responds to any perceptually separable differences in the sequence of stimuli occurring within the time span of working memory (about 10 s, from the MMN studies) or to any new stimulus where newness is defined by the fact that the same stimulus has not occurred within the present context of working memory (traditional OR studies). The signal OR occurs to any stimulus involved in any association (retrievable from long-term memory) with arousing (i.e., UCR-producing) events or behaviors that are effortful. In this sense, it is specific to the individual's learning experiences. The MMN is not specific to earlier learning. Finally, the chapter has presented some of the evidence that looks at the relationship between the OR and what has been termed *informatization*, and between the OR process and the automatized MMN process.

CHAPTER

12

Auditory Event-Related Potentials in the Study of the Orienting Response

This chapter covers the following issues:

1. Sounds presented at long intervals.
2. Short trains of auditory stimuli with long intertrain intervals.
3. Unattended sounds presented at short intervals.
   MMN: Evidence for the involvement of a memory trace.
   MMN: Is a constant standard stimulus necessary?
   MMN: Evidence for primitive sensory intelligence.
   Representations of stimulus events as neural models.
   Neural models as predictions of future stimulus events.
   MMN–its intracranial origins.
   MMN and attention switch.
4. Attended sounds presented with short ISIs.
5. The contribution of auditory ERPs to understanding the OR in the classical OR paradigm.
6. The contribution of auditory ERPs to understanding the OR in short-ISI paradigms.

Although Sokolov's orienting-response theory postulated brain events causing the orienting response, the overwhelming majority of the empirical OR research has used peripheral measures. These data, in general, have not provided more than a very indirect test for this theory on the cerebral OR initiation and control, leaving many of the most central issues without a satisfactory answer. For example, there has been a long-lasting debate, known as the significance controversy in the literature (see Bernstein, 1979, 1981; Maltzman, 1979; O'Gorman, 1979; Siddle, 1979), on whether stimulus change per se is sufficient for OR elicitation, or whether this stimulus change must also be perceived as significant or potentially significant in some way by the organism for OR elicitation. Bernstein (1979), one of the leading significance theorists, argued that although an orienting response may follow a stimulus change, it is the experienced significance, rather than the change per se, a physical event, that elicits the orienting response. Hence, on the significance hypothesis, the cortical interpretative and evaluative processes are crucial; if they do not occur, then no orienting response is elicited. This of course means rejecting Sokolov's neuronal-mismatch theory. An orienting response elicited by stimulus change per se was described as very disastrous to behavior and performance by significance theorists. "We would be continuously orienting to insignificant stimulus changes." (Bernstein, 1969).

One way toward settling this issue, and toward a better understanding of this vital response in general, would be to try to clarify whether any neuronal-mismatch kind of process to a mere physical stimulus change occurs in the human brain. In this chapter, recent electrophysiological and magnetoencephalographical (MEG) data suggesting the existence of such a mechanism are examined.

Second, the role of attention in OR elicitation has also been viewed very differently by different authors. Attention is, of course, a factor of central importance in trying to understand the essence of the OR. Sokolov (1963) observed that attention to stimuli, introduced for example by asking the subject to press a button to each stimulus, increased the strength of the OR and made it more resistant to habituation. Some later authors, however, wished to make a clear distinction between the two cases, introducing dichotomies such as nonsignal and signal cases (see Kimmel, van Olst, & Orlebeke, 1979) or involuntary and voluntary ORs (Maltzman, 1979). Even the assumption of the OR theory that the brain mechanisms of OR initiation are the same in both cases was questioned (Näätänen, 1979). Considerable light on this issue is furnished from ERP studies to be reviewed here later.

Third, some researchers (e.g., O'Gorman, 1979) questioned Sokolov's assumption that the OR elicited by the first stimulus in the sequence (initial OR; O'Gorman, 1979) and that to stimulus change in that sequence (change OR; Näätänen & Gaillard, 1983) are initiated by very similar brain processes. According to Sokolov, in both cases, a neuronal model corresponding to the eliciting stimulus would be lacking, and therefore could not prevent the sequence of processes initiated by feature-detection activation from reaching hippocampal novelty neurons and thus from initiating the OR. ERP data to be reviewed here later seem also to illuminate this issue.

The relevant ERP research is examined in two parts. Studies with long ISIs such as those used in the traditional OR research mainly employing

ANS measures are reviewed first. These ISIs were on the order of 20 to 30 s. This is followed by studies using short ISIs (1 s or so) typical to most ERP studies employing the repetition–change (oddball) paradigm.

SOUNDS PRESENTED AT LONG INTERVALS

When a homogeneous sound is repeatedly presented at long intervals, a large N1–P2 wave can be observed. This wave complex attenuates with stimulus repetition, and faster when the ISI is shorter. In one of these studies, Rust (1977) presented his subjects with loud tones of 1000 Hz lasting for 1 s, which were described to them in advance. The ISI was constant at 33 s. No task instructions other than to keep the eyes closed were given. ERPs were recorded between O_z and T_3, making them rather difficult to interpret. These ERPs were averaged into three classes: the first 10, the second 10, and the third 10, omitting, however, the most interesting response, that to the very first sound that appeared to have caused a startle reflex: "Some subjects tend to jump a little on hearing the first stimulus" (Rust, 1977, p. 124). The strong intensity (95 dB) of the sound used makes it possible that also the defensive response was elicited at times (see Graham, 1973).

Four ERP waves were, according to the author, clearly present with all subjects, a large negative deflection at about 100 ms (N100), a large positive deflection at about 200 ms (P200), a smaller positivity at about 50 ms (P50), and a late negative deflection (N400). In addition, some subjects showed a late positivity. These measures, in general, attenuated in amplitude from the first 10 trials to the second 10 trials, whereas no further amplitude decrement occurred between the second and third sets of 10 trials. The amplitude attenuation was strongest for the P50–N100 (P1–N1) and N100–P200 (N1–P2) measures.

The SCR and the HR response to sounds were also measured to determine whether the ERP-amplitude decrement correlated with the OR habituation as indexed by these ANS measures. It was found that the N1–P2 attenuation correlated significantly but rather weakly with the SCR amplitude attenuation and with the attenuation of both the HR-deceleration response and the subsequent HR-acceleration response. Thus, these data provided some evidence for a relationship between ERP-amplitude attenuation and OR habituation when a sound is repeated at long intervals. Unfortunately, the data were not averaged separately for each trial (as was done by Ritter, Vaughan, & Costa, 1968).

Becker and Shapiro (1980) presented 59 clicks rated by subjects as being of medium intensity or slightly above but were experienced as startling at first. Two conditions were used: *Ignore* (relax) and *Attend*, with the ISI being 15 s. In contrast to Rust (1977), these authors observed a P3 as a regular component in response to auditory stimuli. This P3, recorded from the vertex, occurred in both conditions although it was larger in amplitude in *Attend* than *Ignore* Condition. The P3 amplitude (averaged for each group of the consecutive 10 trials) attenuated with stimulus repetition, and this effect was somewhat stronger in *Attend* than in *Ignore* condition: After the last (59th) click, this attenuation was about 30% in *Attend* condition and about 50% in *Ignore* condition. Also, the N1 and P2 amplitudes attenuated significantly with stimulus repetition.

In contrast to the P3, the alpha-suppression response and the SCR were elicited at the same amplitude in the two conditions. Further, both responses strongly attenuated as the click was repeated, and after the 25th click they were practically absent. This is in a considerable contrast with the P3-amplitude attenuation that occurred at a much slower rate. This result indicates a clear difference between OR habituation, as indexed by traditional OR measures, and ERP attenuation as a function of stimulus repetition.

Also Simons, Rockstroh, Elbert, Fiorito, Lutzenberger, and Birbaumer (1987) presented their subjects with auditory stimuli (1000-Hz tones at a moderate intensity) at very long ISIs but used only an *Ignore* condition, the instruction being no more specific than just "stay alert." In their first experiment, the ISI was variable rather than constant (range 14–30 s, mean 22 s). An important addition to the paradigm was that at the 21st trial, the tone frequency was 500 Hz instead of the regular 1000 Hz. The first 20 trials were averaged in groups of 4 consecutive trials.

The SCR behaved as a classical OR measure should: Its amplitude attenuated with stimulus repetition, was increased considerably when a deviant stimulus was presented, and was larger to the standard stimulus immediately after the deviant stimulus than to the standard stimulus immediately before it. That is, the SCR showed dishabituation (Fig. 12.1). The same was true with regard to HR deceleration but the effects were not always statistically significant.

In examining the ERP components, special attention was paid to the O-wave, usually interpreted as an expression of the orienting function (Gaillard, 1976; Loveless, 1979, 1983; Loveless & Sanford, 1974a, 1974b; Rohrbaugh, 1984; Rohrbaugh & Gaillard, 1983; Rohrbaugh, Syndulko, & Lindsley, 1976, 1978, 1979). This is a slow negativity elicited by single auditory stimuli with long ISIs, and by S1 in the S1–S2 paradigms. This measure, however, behaved in quite an odd manner: Its amplitude increased with stimulus repetition, decreased when the deviant stimulus was presented, and increased again in response to the return of the original 1000-Hz stimulus (Fig. 12.1). Nor did the N1 and P3 amplitudes correlate well with the ANS measures. Both diminished in amplitude within the first set of 4 trials but not thereafter.

In their Experiment 2, 1000-Hz tones each lasting 10 s were presented at 60 dB with constant ISIs of 50 s (offset to onset). Tones 11 and 12, however,

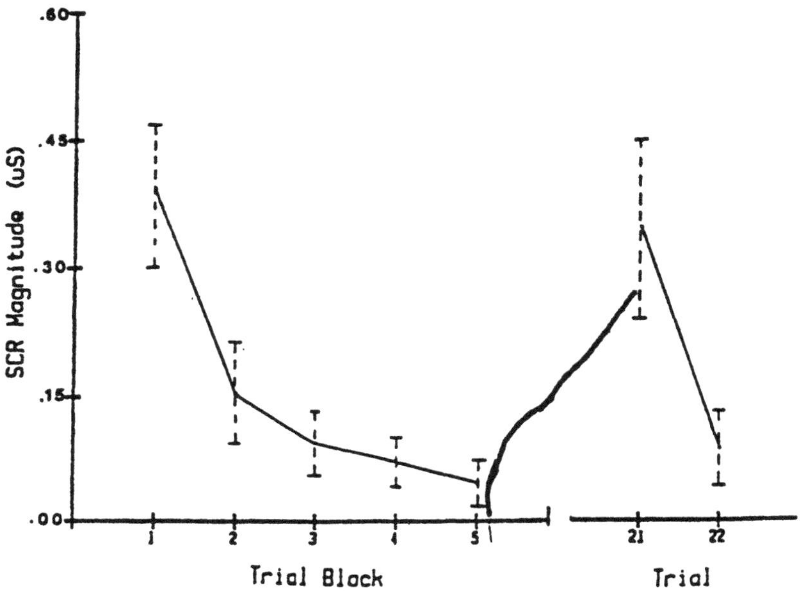

FIG. 12.1. The SCR magnitude (±1 standard error) as a function of trial block (left) and separately for trials 21 and 22 in Block 5 (right). (From Simons, Rockstroh, Elbert, Fiorito, Lutzenberger, & Birbaumer, 1987. Copyright © 1987 by Oxford University Press. Reprinted with permission).

were considerably louder, at 80 dB. Subjects were instructed to remain relaxed and to listen passively to the tones. Again, the SCR behaved according to the expectations derived from the OR theory, whereas now the HR-deceleration response failed to show the expected habituation. The alpha-desynchronization response occurred only to the first stimulus of the sequence and to stimulus change, thus showing no gradual habituation typical to the ANS measures.

Importantly, the ERPs were now averaged trial-by-trial, permitting one to observe the very rapid amplitude decrease of the vertex potential (negative peak at about 150 ms and positive peak varying between 240–350 ms, probably the N1–P3) when the tone was repeated (Fig. 12.2). It can be seen that the amplitude decrement occurs within the first 4 trials but not thereafter. Also the separately measured N1 and P3 amplitudes showed a significant attenuation with stimulus repetition. In addition, the stimulus-change trial enhanced the response amplitude (Fig. 12.2) but this might be simply due to the higher intensity of the deviant stimulus. The 0-wave behaved very similarly to that recorded in Experiment 1, that is, in a way contradicting its name.

Essentially similar result were obtained by Roth, Blowers, Doyle, and Kopell (1982), who delivered a sequence of very loud (115 dB SPL) white-

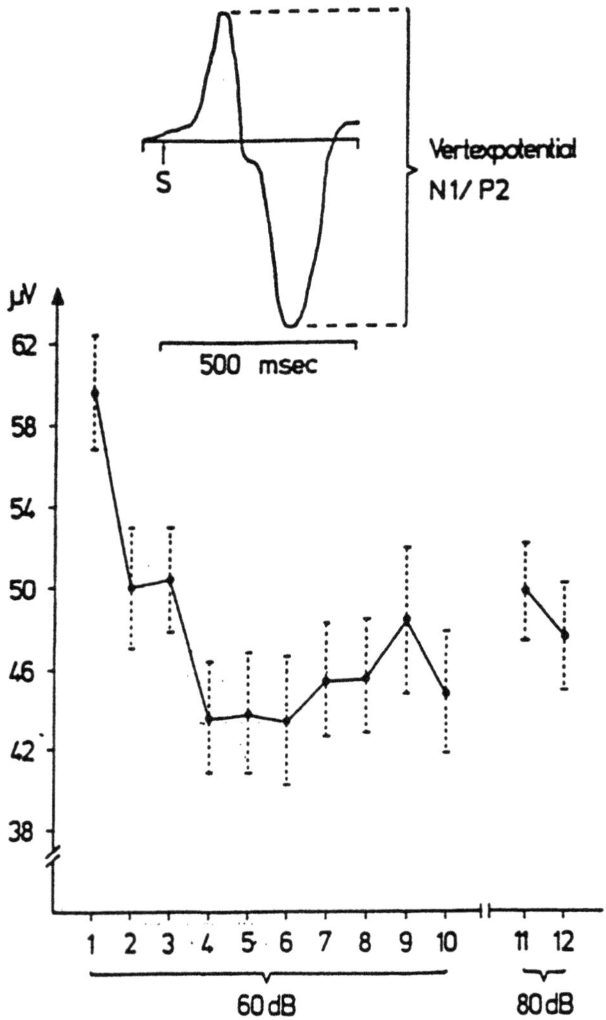

FIG. 12.2. *Top:* The ERP during 500 ms following stimulus onset, averaged across subjects and trials. *Bottom:* The amplitude of the "vertex potential" (in µV ± 1 standard error) averaged across subjects separately for each trial. (From Simons, Rockstroh, Elbert, Fiorito, Lutzenberger, & Birbaumer, 1987. Copyright © 1987 by Oxford University Press. Reprinted with permission).

noise pips at long ISIs irregularly varying between 10 and 90 s in a nonsignal (no-task) condition. About 10% of the stimuli were deviants, formed by adding a 1000-Hz tone pip to a noise pip. The N1 and P3 amplitudes significantly decreased, but to a quite modest extent, in the course of the session. The stimulus change affected the ERP neither to the deviant stimulus itself nor to the subsequent standard stimulus.

Dishabituation was attempted also by introducing a verbal message between two stimuli. This did not affect the ERP but dishabituated the SCR. Further dissociations between the ERP and the SCR were found by Roth, Dorato, and Kopell (1984), who observed that while the SCR amplitude for auditory stimuli varying in intensity (mean ISI 14.5 s) rapidly habituated, that of the P300 and other ERP waves did not.

Lyytinen (unpublished data) delivered blocks of 11 auditory stimuli of 800 ms in duration at irregular ISIs of 14 to 28 s. The 10th stimulus in each block lasted only 400 ms (deviant). The first two blocks were nonsignal blocks. These were followed by three signal blocks: counting the number of different stimuli in a block (Counting), pushing a button to the offset of each tone (Motor Response), and to the anticipated onset of each tone (Anticipation).

Figure 12.3 shows data from the first nonsignal block. The first stimulus elicited a SCR that fully habituated with stimulus repetition. The deviant stimulus re-elicited the SCR but at a low amplitude. No SCR dishabituation, that is, in this case, a SCR to the next stimulus after the deviant one, can be seen. The N1 wave to these long-ISI stimuli reached its amplitude maximum at the vertex, which suggests a major contribution of the nonspecific N1 component to this wave (Hari, Kaila, Katila, Tuomisto, & Varpula, 1982; Näätänen & Picton, 1987). Some amplitude decrement occurred with stimulus repetition but only to a modest extent in comparison with that shown by the SCR. The deviant-stimulus ERP showed still further amplitude attenuation, for a decrement in stimulus duration (from 800 to 400 ms) cannot, of course, be reflected in response to stimulus onset. Interestingly, the figure suggests that some N1 recovery in response to the subsequent standard stimulus occurred. In contrast, the long-latency part of the ERP showed only one clear difference between the trials: A large, widespread P3 (P3b) positivity, spanning the latency range 250 to 400 ms, was elicited by the first stimulus but not by any subsequent stimuli. In this condition, the 0-wave showed a small tendency to habituation.

The introduction of the very simple stimulus-classification task (Counting) greatly increased the SCR amplitude to the first stimulus and also to the deviant stimulus. A distinct SCR dishabituation can also be observed in response to the stimulus immediately following the deviant one. In contrast, the ERP effects again appeared to be quite modest. The N1 amplitude showed no clear effect, whereas the P2 amplitude suggested some habituation and dishabituation. The 0-wave showed a clear habituation.

In the Motor–Response Condition, SCR amplitude was further increased and its habituation was retarded (Fig. 12.4; notice the scale change for SCR). Yet, some dishabituation seems to have occurred. The N1 amplitude was larger, especially at the vertex, than in the previous, less demanding conditions. It attenuated at the vertex and parietal electrodes with stimulus repetition, but no dishabituation was seen. The P2 amplitude showed a very

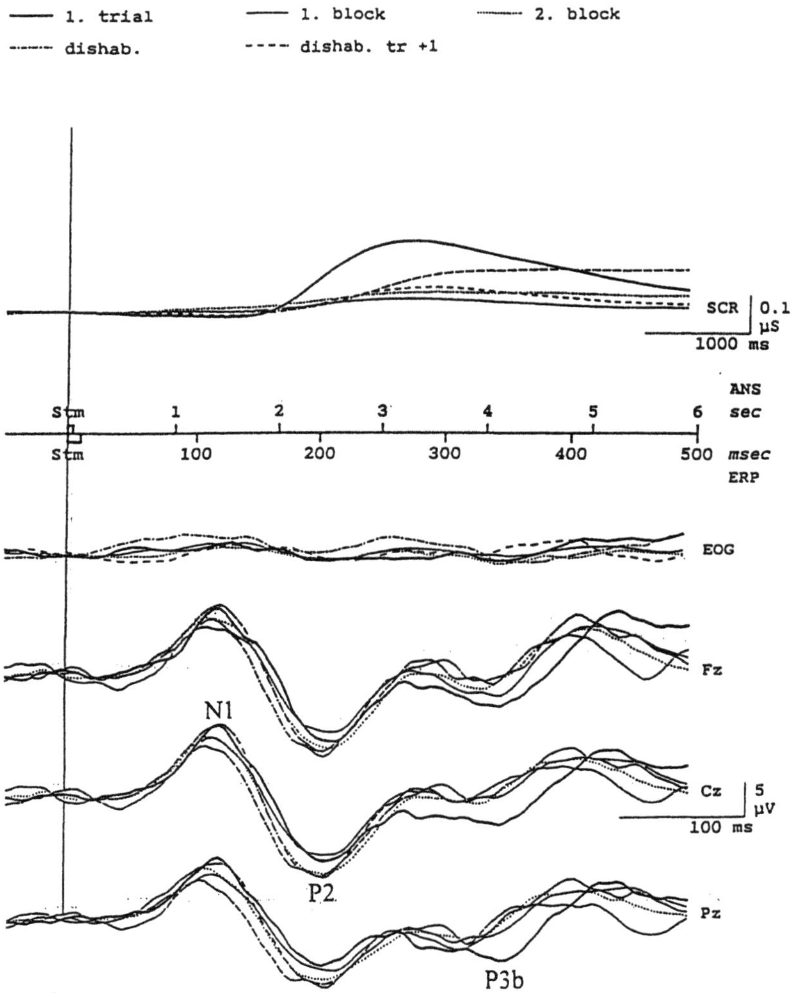

FIG. 12.3. Data from nonsignal conditions. SCR, EOG, and ERP (at Fz, Cz, and Pz) to the first stimulus (1. trial); to stimuli 2–9 in the 1st block ("1. block"), to stimuli 2–9 in the 2nd block ("2. block"), to the deviant ("dishab") stimulus, and to the next standard stimulus after the deviant stimulus ("dishab. tr + 1"). Notice the different amplitude and time scales. (Lyytinen, unpublished data).

clear amplitude decrement with stimulus repetition and possibly some recovery, too, after the deviant stimulus. There were no later systematic ERP effects related to stimulus repetition and change.

In the Anticipation Condition, no SCR attenuation with stimulus repetition occurred. This held true also with regard to the different ERP waves. In Fig. 12.5, the first-stimulus responses under the different conditions are

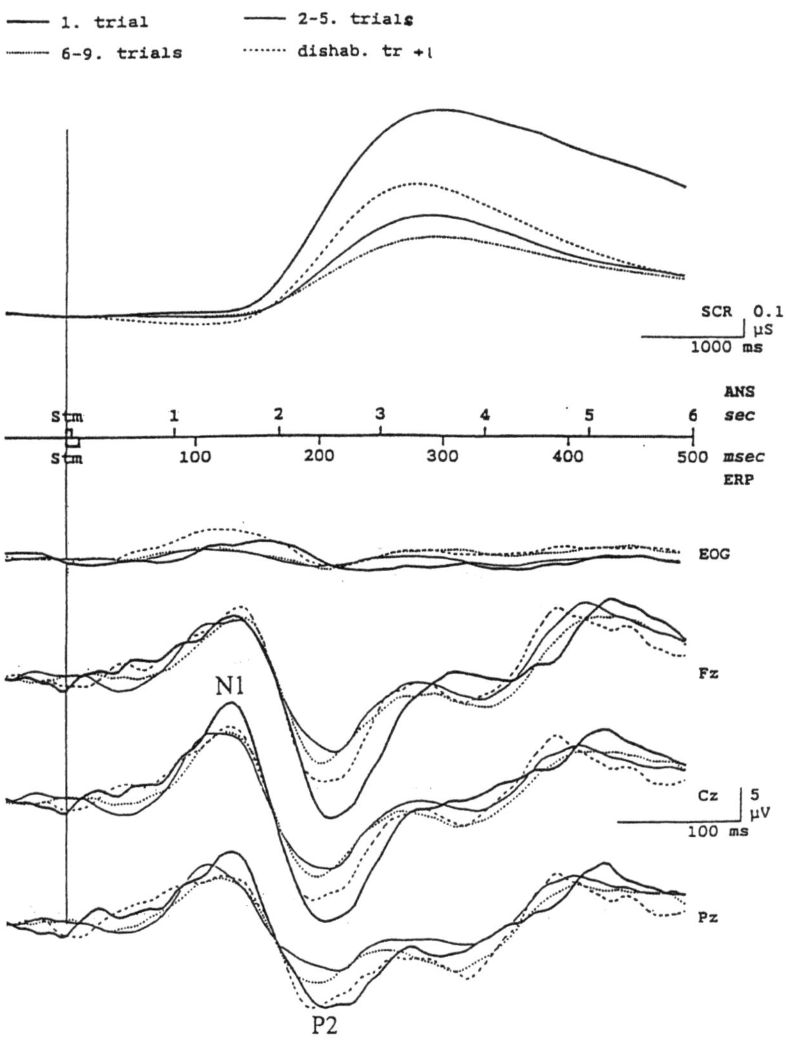

FIG. 12.4. Data from motor-response condition. SCR, EOG, and ERP (at Fz, Cz, and Pz) to the first stimulus (1. trial); to stimuli 2–5 (2–5 trial), to stimuli 6–9 (6–9. trials), and to the deviant stimulus ("dishab. tr"). Notice the different amplitude and time scales. (Lyytinen, unpublished data).

compared with each other. The signal conditions show enhanced SCRs, Motor-Press Condition in particular. The N1 amplitude at the vertex shows a similar rank order between the conditions, due presumably to condition effects primarily on the nonspecific component. The P2 amplitude behaves in a similar manner, and it differs between the different conditions considerably more than does the vertex N1. Unfortunately, however, such orderly

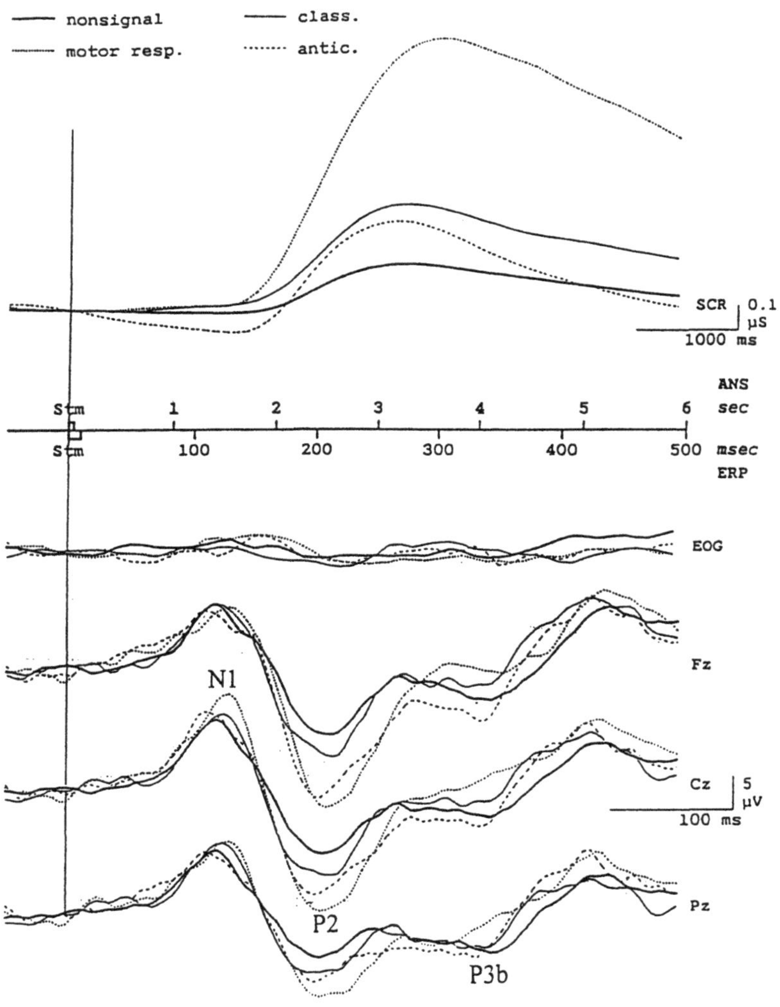

FIG. 12.5. Responses to the first stimulus of the block separately for the nonsignal, classification (class.), motor-response (motor resp.), and anticipation conditions (antic.). The measures from top to bottom are the same as in Figs. 12.3 & 12.4. (Lyytinen, unpublished data).

relationships could not to the same extent be seen in responses to the subsequent stimuli.

In conclusion, it is evident from these long-ISI studies that ERPs, at least the measures used, do not correlate well with the traditional OR indices. Let us first consider the habituation of the OR with stimulus repetition, which is reliably shown by ANS measures such as the SCR and the HR deceleration: With stimulus repetition, both responses are quite soon extinguished. However, although ERP measures such as the N1 (or N1–P2) and P3 do show amplitude attenuation with stimulus repetition even when long ISIs are used, this occurs at a much slower rate than with the ANS measures. Typically, at the moment of the total disappearance of the ANS responses, the ERP responses still reach at least a half of their initial amplitude. Clearly, these ERP responses reflect somewhat else, or more, than the orienting function.

Looking at the component structure of these ERP waves is illuminating here. Starting with the N1 (N1–P2), one of the components of the auditory N1 is the nonspecific N1 component (for a review, see Näätänen & Picton, 1987). This component, with an unknown generator structure (but see Alcaini, Giard, Thevenet, & Pernier, 1994; Lu, Williams, & Kaufman, 1992), is elicited in each modality, and it has very long refractory periods (Alcaini et al., 1994; Hari et al., 1982). In the Alcaini et al. study, the N1 amplitude was enhanced when the constant ISI was prolonged from 16 s to 2 min. It is probably this nonspecific N1 component that primarily caused the N1-amplitude reduction observed in the previous studies, for the auditory-specific components of the N1 have much shorter recovery periods (Hari et al., 1982; for a review, see Näätänen, 1992) and could therefore be expected to recover fully even during the 16-s ISI. For an illustration, see Fig. 12.6. With the MEG, one can separately determine the ISI dependence of the specific N1 components generated in the supratemporal plane as shown by Mäkelä, Hari, & Leinonen (1988) and Lu et al. (1992). That the specific N1 components are elicited even with short ISIs is probably related to the fact that their generator processes obligatorily belong to those underlying perception (Giard, Perrin, Echallier, Thevenet, Froment, & Pernier, 1994; Näätänen, 1990).

Given that the nonspecific component of the N1 attenuated in amplitude with stimulus repetition to a much larger extent than did the total N1 wave, could we then regard this nonspecific N1 as a correlate of the OR? Probably not because, apparently, no genuine habituation was involved: No dishabituation could be demonstrated in studies trying to dishabituate the N1 (or N1–P2) response (e.g., Simons et al., 1987). This is consistent with the assumption that in the neural circuitry generating the nonspecific N1, no memory mechanism plays a role (Näätänen & Picton, 1987). If no memory-comparison process participates in neural events leading to the nonspecific N1 generation, then no habituation and dishabituation could, by definition, occur anywhere in this neural circuitry.

Why, then, did the nonspecific N1 component attenuate in amplitude with stimulus repetition with these very long intervals? Näätänen and Picton (1987) proposed that the refractoriness in this generator mechanism lasts for at least 30 s, so that the generator would be fully recovered from the effects of the previous response only when the ISI between consecutive stimuli clearly exceeds 30 s. This might be better understandable in the

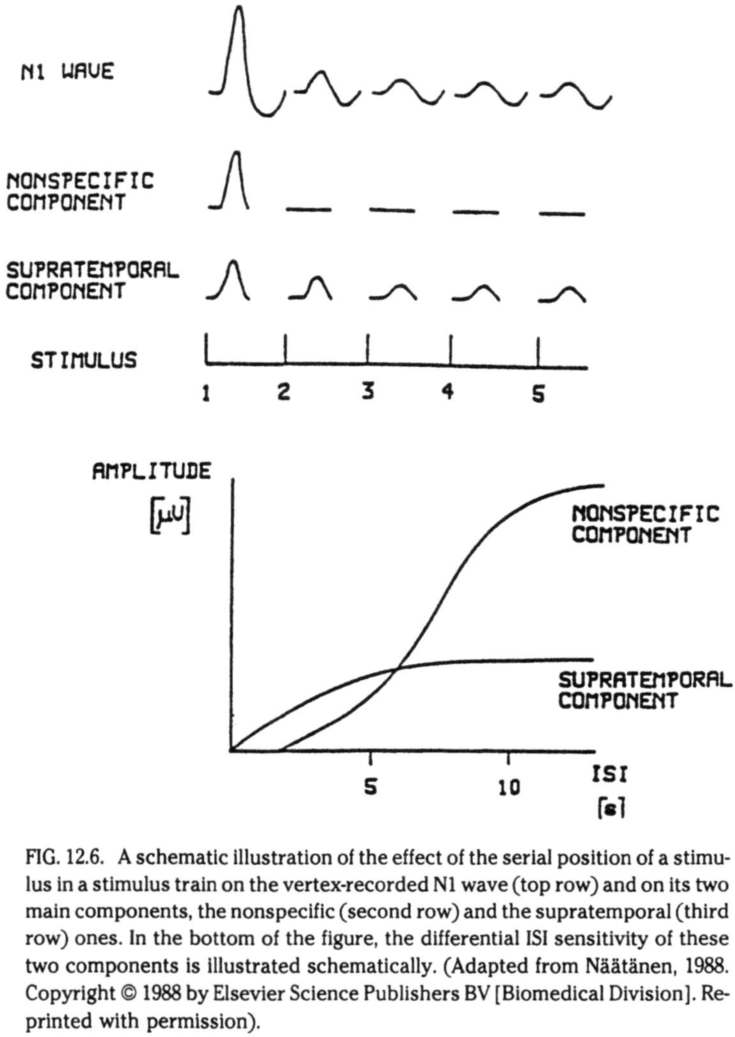

FIG. 12.6. A schematic illustration of the effect of the serial position of a stimulus in a stimulus train on the vertex-recorded N1 wave (top row) and on its two main components, the nonspecific (second row) and the supratemporal (third row) ones. In the bottom of the figure, the differential ISI sensitivity of these two components is illustrated schematically. (Adapted from Näätänen, 1988. Copyright © 1988 by Elsevier Science Publishers BV [Biomedical Division]. Reprinted with permission).

light of the functional significance that these authors assign to the brain mechanism(s) of the nonspecific N1 component. According to Näätänen and Picton (1987), the generators of this component (Component 3 in their classification) belong to an extensive cerebral mechanism that functions to produce a widespread transient arousal reaction of the organism, which facilitates sensory and motor responses to the eliciting stimulus as well as the associated central integrative processes, and thus shifts the organism to a more efficient functional state.

This is supported by the evidence relating the N1 wave (probably the nonspecific component) to a transient increase in spinal excitability (Fig.

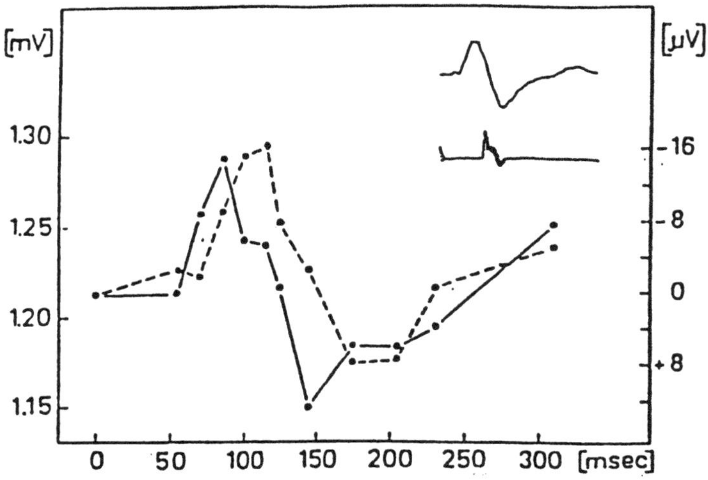

FIG. 12.7. Average amplitudes of the H-reflex (solid line) and the vertex (Cz) ERP (dashed line) of one subject as function of the interval between the click, presented at 0 ms, and the shock eliciting the H-reflex. The millivolt scale belongs to the H-reflex, the microvolt scale to the ERP. In the right upper corner, a typical averaged ERP (above, time scale 480 ms from stimulus onset) and a single H-reflex (below, time scale 120 ms) of this subject are shown. (From Fruhstorfer, Järvilehto, Soveri, Lumio, & Partanen, 1970. Unpublished manuscript).

12.7). "The long refractory period, the vigorous response when recovered, and the multimodal nature of this component support its interpretation as a transient arousal response with widespread facilitatory influences. Component 3 may also serve some aspects of detection and perception by alerting sensory association and motor cortex when a stimulus occurs after a period of quiescence." (Näätänen & Picton, 1987, p. 415).

In light of this interpretation of the nonspecific N1 component, the N1-amplitude attenuation with stimulus repetition at long ISIs could be explained in terms of decreased general cerebral excitability associated with decreased vigilance and lower functional state, as the subject gets used to the experimental situation, relaxes, and perhaps eventually gets a little drowsy in the boring situation.

This interpretation of course implicates that cortical excitability would recover if something alarming happens. This would alert the organism and bring it back to a high functional state. It is often forgotten that Sokolov incorporated a general-arousal type of factor in the elicitation of the OR to the first stimulus of a sequence. Thus, according to him, this OR is a joint consequence of (1) a neuronal-mismatch process due to the lack of a neuronal model corresponding to the stimulus; (2) memory-unrelated arousal reaction to stimulus-energy onset (see Lynn, 1966, pp. 14–17).

The P3 wave of the ERP was proposed by many previous authors as a possible correlate of the OR (see Donchin, 1981; Donchin et al., 1984; for a critical review, see, however, Roth, 1983). Again, it can be observed that stimulus repetition attenuates the P3 amplitude usually relatively much more slowly than it attenuates the ANS responses (Becker & Shapiro, 1980; Roth et al., 1982, 1984) and, further, no response recovery of the P3 in the "dishabituation trial" occurs (Lyytinen, unpublished data; Roth et al., 1982). Here it might be useful to take a look at the component structure, as the earlier, and usually sharper P3a with a central or fronto-central scalp distribution can be separated from the P3b which has a longer latency and a clearly posterior scalp distribution. It is the P3a that is the more promising correlate for the OR of these two P3 subcomponents (see later).

With regard to the 0-wave, from its behavior in this paradigm, orthogonal to that of the ANS measures (Simons et al., 1987), it is evident that the functional significance of its generator process is very different from what was initially believed when this component was termed the 0-wave. However, Simons and his colleagues collected their data in nonsignal conditions. Previous studies showed that in signal conditions, the 0-wave behaves much more like an 0-wave should (for reviews, see Loveless, 1979; Rohrbaugh, 1984).

SHORT TRAINS OF AUDITORY STIMULI WITH LONG INTERTRAIN INTERVALS

Ritter et al. (1968) were the first to average ERPs to auditory stimuli of a short stimulus train according to their serial position in the train. These authors presented short trains of tones separated by intertrain intervals of several minutes. In one of their conditions, the within-train ISI was 10 s. In this condition, apparently with no task instructions other than to maintain a steady ocular fixation, the N1–P2 amplitude did not attenuate statistically significantly as a function of stimulus position in the train. The lack of the first-stimulus effect in this condition is probably due to the fact that the subject "knew when a run was to begin." In contrast, in their 2-s condition, the vertex N1–P2 amplitude rapidly decreased over the first few stimuli and then stabilized at about half the amplitude of the first response by the second, third, or fourth tone, depending on the subject. When the tone frequency in a stimulus train was unpredictably changed from 1000 Hz to 2000 Hz, the first stimulus of the new frequency elicited a large positive wave peaking at about 350 ms, however, which also occurred in response to the first stimulus of the train when the subject did not know when the train was to begin. However, no dishabituation could be observed as the subsequent stimuli evoked responses that were not significantly different from those preceding the stimulus change. Ritter and his collegues (see also Roth & Kopell, 1969) therefore concluded that the ERP attenuation over time represented no genuine habituation but rather refactoriness within the auditory system.

The decrease in the N1–P2 amplitude during a brief train of auditory stimuli was soon confirmed by other investigators. Roth and Kopell (1969) found that this response to the first stimulus in a train of five was significantly larger than that to the subsequent stimuli, with the amplitude attenuation being greater for more rapid rates and for more intense stimuli. The subject was instructed to push a button on hearing an occasional, slightly longer tone.

Fruhstorfer, Soveri, and Järvilehto (1970) presented trains of eight clicks using ISIs of 1 or 3 s and intertrain intervals of 100 s. They recorded their auditory ERPs between an electrode near the vertex and one on the forehead while the subject was reading a book. The N1 amplitude for the first stimulus of a train was very large, about 10 times that for the second stimulus in the trains with the 1-s intervals, and more than two times that for the second stimulus in the trains with the 3-s intervals (Fig. 12.8). The amplitude decreased further until the third or fourth stimulus and then stabilized. The authors interpreted this reduction in terms of short-term habituation but did not try to demonstrate dishabituation.

Öhman and Lader (1972) found a significant decrement of the N1–P2 amplitude, and also of the P1–N1 amplitude, over a brief train of clicks presented with a mean ISI of 10 s (range 8–12 s). ERPs were measured bipolarly between Cz and T3. This decrement occurred both in their *Attend* and *Ignore* conditions, and was proportionally of about the same magnitude in the two conditions, the amplitudes being larger in the Attend condition. Also the skin-conductance level (SCL), measured before each of the 10 clicks forming a train, significantly decreased over the train of clicks.

In contrast to the results of Fruhstorfer, Soveri, and Järvilehto (1970), the ERP to the first stimulus was not considerably larger than that to the subsequent stimuli, although the intertrain interval was on average 30 s. This is probably due to the fact that the start of each train was heralded by switching on a red lamp preceding the first stimulus by an interval corresponding to that of the block. The lack of the "first-stimulus effect" (Loveless, 1983; Wastell, 1980) was also observed by MacLean, Öhman, and Lader (1975) who used similar stimulus arrangements. This is consistent with the results of several studies that have shown cross-modal refractory effects on the auditory N1 (Davis, Osterhammel, Wier, & Gjerdingen, 1972; Gjerdingen & Tomsic, 1970; Hay & Davis, 1971; Kevanishvili, Pantev, & Khachidze, 1979; Larsson, 1956, 1960a, 1960b; Rothman, Davis, & Hay, 1970).

The ERP amplitude in the above-mentioned Öhman and Lader's (1972) study decreased also when analyzed train-by-train. However, the skin-conductance level did not show a similar long-term effect. Also, the RT in both conditions (the subject performing a visual RT task in the ignore condition)

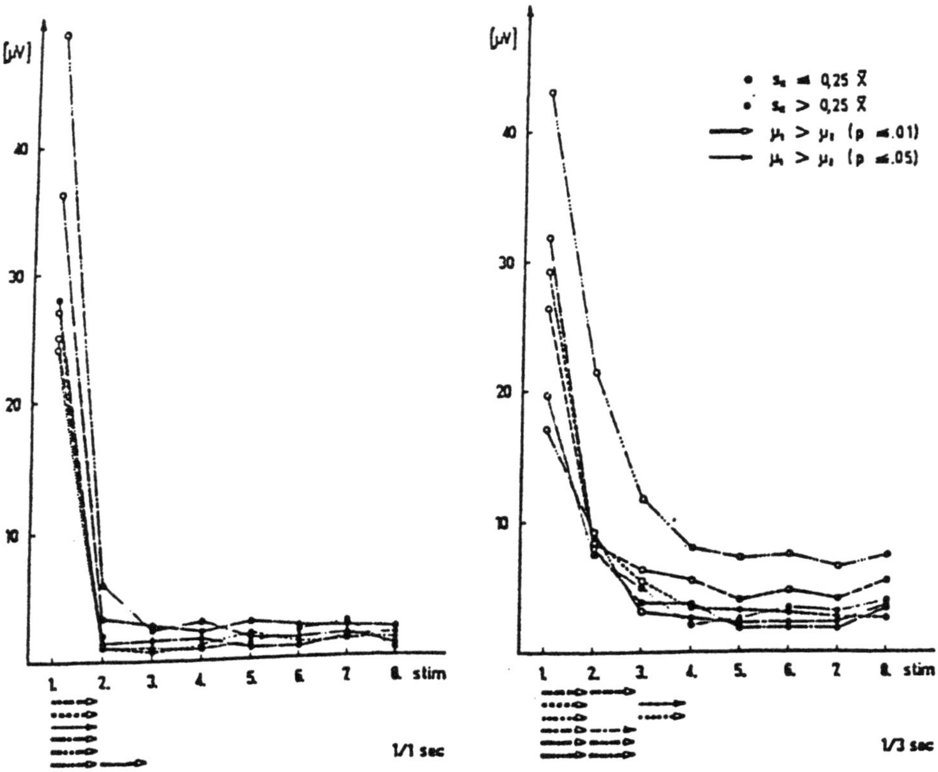

FIG. 12.8. The N1 amplitude as a function of the position of the stimulus in a block separately for each subject. The subject was in an inattentive state when the first stimulus was presented. (Open circles indicate that the value of the standard deviation is equal to or smaller than a quarter of the mean.) Arrows below the diagrams indicate the cases in which the amplitude reduction reaches a significant level (one-tailed, rank-sum test). (From Fruhstorfer, Soveri, & Järvilehto, 1970. Copyright © 1970 by Elsevier Sciences Publishers, Ireland. Reprinted with permission).

remained at a relatively stable level throughout the experimental session. The authors consequently concluded that the long-term ERP decrement observed is not "in general explicable solely in terms of a decrease in general, diffuse activation" (Öhman & Lader, 1972, p. 84).

In another related study, Roth (1973) presented a sequence of auditory stimuli at a constant ISI of 1 s. In some blocks, a 1000-Hz tone was the frequent stimulus and a burst of white noise the infrequent stimulus. In other blocks, the two stimuli exchanged their roles. The subject was instructed to ignore all auditory stimuli. Three different probabilities for the deviant stimulus were used. No evidence was found for dishabituation of the ERP to the standard stimulus following a deviant stimulus. Similar results were obtained by Sams, Alho, and Näätänen (1984).

Fruhstorfer (1971) found that a somatosensory stimulus inserted into a train of clicks evoked an N1 wave that was larger than that evoked by the clicks, and larger than what would have been evoked had it been preceded by a train of somatosensory stimuli. (During recordings the subject was reading a book.) These results are illustrated in Fig. 12.9. The next standard stimulus after the deviant somatosensory stimulus evoked an N1 that was not significantly different from the N1 prior to the deviant stimulus (that is, no dishabituation occurred). Analogous results were obtained when an auditory stimulus (a click) was inserted into a train of somatosensory stimuli.

The increase in the N1 amplitude for the deviant stimulus by virtue of being from another modality may be explained on the basis of release from specific refractoriness. The attenuation of the N1 with stimulus repetition is to some extent specific to the precise characteristics of the repeating stimulus and to some extent generalized to other stimuli (see Näätänen & Picton, 1987). This generalization was demonstrated by Fruhstorfer (1971) who found that the modality-deviant stimulus evoked an N1 that was not as large as the N1 it would have evoked if not preceded by the repeating stimuli in the other modality. As already mentioned, several studies have shown that the N1 response to a sound stimulus can be dampened by having it preceded by a stimulus in another sensory modality.

According to Butler (1968), within the auditory modality, there is both specificity and generalization of the refractory effects. He found that chang-

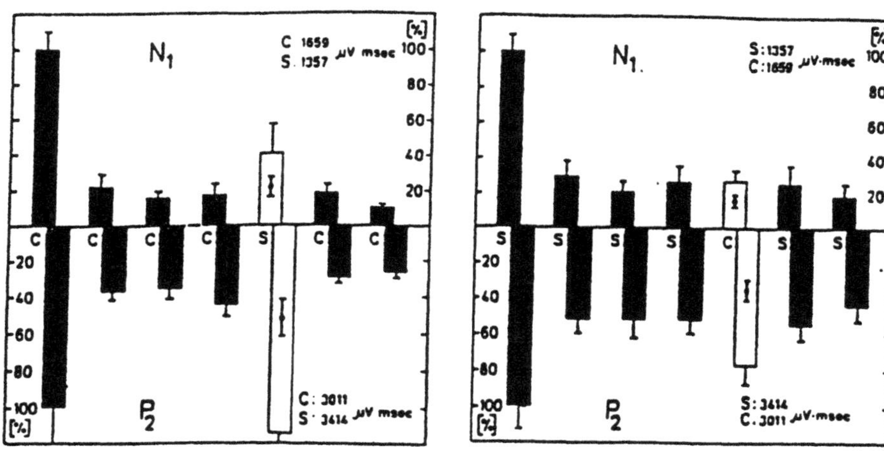

FIG. 12.9. LEFT: Mean changes in the voltage integral of N1 and P2 (in % of the size of the first-stimulus response) during a CCCCSCC train. C denotes a click stimulus; S, a somatosensory stimulus. The bars indicate the standard error to one side. RIGHT: Mean changes in the voltage integral of N1 and P2 during an SSSSCSS train. (From Fruhstorfer, 1971. Copyright © 1971 by Elsevier Science Publishers, Ireland. Reprinted with permission).

ing the stimulus could enhance an N1 that had been attenuated by stimulus repetition. Butler presented his subjects with a 1000-Hz tone of 600 ms in duration every 5 s. The intervals between these 1000-Hz test tones contained either no tones or three intervening tones. The amplitude of the response to the test tone was largest when there were no intervening tones. When these did occur, the amplitude of the response to the test tone varied with the frequency of the intervening tone, being smallest when this frequency was identical to that of the test tone. This selective-adaptation effect was replicated by Butler (1972) and by Picton, Woods, and Proulx (1978).

Butler (1968) proposed that the decrement in the N1–P2 response was specific to the frequency of the stimulus: "When the frequency of the intervening stimuli was progressively removed from that of the test stimuli, the population of neural units activated by the two categories of stimuli became more and more disparate. Hence, each time the test stimulus was presented, neural units not activated by the preceding three intervening stimuli were brought into play" (p. 949). In a subsequent paper, Butler (1972) suggested that the response was generated in the auditory cortex and, further, that, although this cortex was tonotopically organized, each frequency had a widespread neural representation. Näätänen, Sams, Alho, Paavilainen, Reinikainen, and Sokolov (1988), however, showed that under some conditions, the N1 can be highly stimulus specific. Their results are illustrated in Fig. 12.10.

In a further study along these lines, Megela and Teyler (1979) evaluated the change in the N1–P2 amplitude over brief trains of tones presented at ISIs of 1 s and intertrain intervals of 5 to 10 s. A test tone with a different intensity from that of the repeating tone was randomly given after five to nine

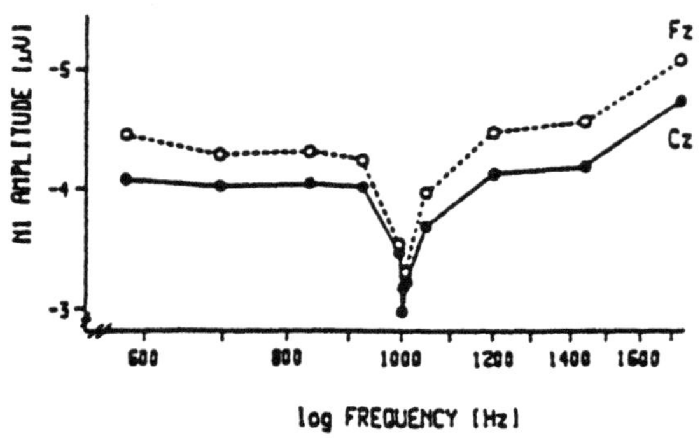

FIG. 12.10. The across-subject averaged N1 (P1–N1) amplitude at Fz and Cz for the test tone of 1000 Hz as a function of the frequency (log scale) of the intervening tone. The test and intervening tones were equiprobably delivered in random order. In different blocks, the test-tone frequency was varied from 578 Hz to 1728 Hz. (From Näätänen, Sams, Alho, Paavilainen, Reinikainen, & Sokolov, 1988. Copyright ©1988 by Elsevier Scientific Publishers, Ireland, Ltd. Reprinted with permission).

tones. The subject was instructed to attend to the incoming stimuli. It was found that the N1–P2 amplitude for a loud test tone was larger when it followed a series of soft tones than when it followed a series of loud tones. (This effect, however, was not significant for the baseline-N1 measurement.) The opposite effect was not true, however, the response to a soft tone being no larger when it followed a series of loud tones than when it followed a series of soft tones.

These results suggest, according to Näätänen and Picton (1987), that the process underlying the decrement in the N1–P2 amplitude with stimulus repetition involves decreased synaptic efficiency (cf. Thompson & Spencer, 1966) and not a comparison of incoming sensory information with a neuronal model (Sokolov, 1963, 1975). A soft stimulus would activate only a subset of the synapses activated by the loud stimulus, and thus the generalization of the decrement from soft to loud would be less than the generalization from loud to soft. In contrast, decreasing the intensity of the stimulus should be similar to increasing the intensity for a process comparing the sensory input with a neuronal model.

Woods and Elmasian (1986) obtained data that they interpreted as suggesting that the response decrement is a function of the acoustic resemblance between the successive stimuli. They presented sequences of 6 identical auditory stimuli but in half of these sequences, the fifth stimulus was replaced by a different stimulus. The stimuli used were different kinds of tones and speech sounds, administered in different combinations of standards and deviants. The N1, recorded with maximal amplitude at the vertex, rapidly decreased with stimulus repetition to 35% of the response to the first stimulus in the sequence with the ISI of 0.5 s, and to 60% in the sequence with the ISI of 1 s. The amplitude of the temporal negativity (corresponding to Component 2 in Näätänen and Picton's (1987) classification) peaking at some 50 ms later than the vertex N1 showed a similar decrement. The decrement in the vertex N1 amplitude with stimulus repetition was greater for speech than nonspeech sounds.

The N1 amplitude was larger to the deviant stimulus occurring in the 5th position than to the standard stimulus when it occurred in the same position. When the deviant stimulus differed from the standard stimulus in phonetic structure (but was more similar acoustically), the amplitude recovery to the deviant stimulus was smaller than when the two stimuli were different tones (less similar acoustically). The N1-amplitude to the standard stimulus immediately following the deviant stimulus showed no amplitude recovery (dishabituation) in comparison with the response to the standard stimulus immediately preceding the deviant stimulus.

In sum, it appears that the results from studies using short stimulus-trains (with long intertrain intervals) do not significantly alter the conclusions based on the long-ISI studies. Even when stimuli were repeated at short intervals, the N1 and P2 were elicited by each stimulus of a train (though the amplitude usually dramatically dropped from the first to the second stimulus). It is quite obvious that this initial N1-amplitude attenuation is for the most part due to the disappearance of the nonspecific component (cf. Hari et al., 1982) although also the specific components of the N1 are elicited at a lower amplitude when the stimulus is repeated soon after its first presentation. (With the MEG, one can separately determine the ISI relationship of the specific N1 component generated on the supratemporal plane; Mäkelä et al., 1988).

Consequently, it appears that the N1 wave as and of itself cannot be regarded as a correlate of the OR, one obvious reason being the involvement of some of its generator mechanisms in basic sensory and perceptual processes which cannot be inactivated, or very strongly suppressed, by stimulus repetition (see Näätänen, 1990, 1992; Näätänen & Picton, 1987). In contrast, if one examines the nonspecific N1 component separately, then some relationship might be proposed, however not with the OR based on the neuronal-mismatch process (change OR) but rather with one caused by a sudden energy increase (transient; see Graham, 1973; Loveless, 1983; MacMillan, 1973) after sensory quiescence (Näätänen, 1986a; Näätänen & Gaillard, 1983), that is, with the initial OR. Consistent with this interpretation, no N1-response recovery to the standard stimulus immediately succeeding the deviant stimulus could be found (e.g., Fruhstorfer, 1971; Woods & Elmasian, 1986).

The behavior of the P3 in a short-ISI stimulus train is somewhat different from that of the N1 wave in that the P3 is elicited only by the first stimulus of the train but not thereafter. This resembles the OR, of course, but a clear difference is revealed by the presentation of the dishabituation stimulus, with the subsequent standard stimulus eliciting a clear ANS response (see Lyytinen, Blomberg, & Näätänen, 1992) but no P3 (Ritter et al., 1968; Roth, 1973; Sams et al., 1984).

UNATTENDED SOUNDS PRESENTED AT SHORT INTERVALS

The use of long sequences of stimuli presented at short ISIs is a natural paradigm of ERP studies because of the necessity of response averaging. Therefore, this type of paradigm has been the predominant one even in studies addressing OR-related issues. A considerable drawback is the difficulty in trying to record also ANS responses in such a paradigm, for example to occasional deviant stimuli, because of the long latencies and durations of these ANS responses relative to the short ISI. However, the combination of ERP and ANS recordings in this paradigm, to be discussed later, is not impossible (Lyytinen & Näätänen, 1987; Lyytinen et al., 1992; for a review, see Halgren & Marinkovic, 1995; Näätänen & Lyytinen, 1989).

The response to the standard stimulus, including a small P1–N1–P2 but no distinct later ERP waves, and certainly no ANS responses, when short ISIs are used, is of no major interest from the point of view of the OR theory. Instead, when a deviant stimulus is delivered, the mismatch negativity (MMN) can be recorded in these short-ISI paradigms. The MMN occurs both in passive (nonsignal) conditions and active (signal) conditions. The MMN is accompanied by several other ERP components in active conditions, whereas in passive conditions, only the P3a is a more or less regular concomitant of the MMN.

When the OR theory with its central neuronal-model and neuronal-mismatch constructs was developed by Sokolov (1960, 1963), these were just assumptions of brain events causing and controlling the OR elicitation measured mainly from the periphery of the organism. The advent of the MMN signified a verification of the basic principles of cerebral initiation of the OR in humans as proposed by Sokolov (but of course only for the circumstances under which an MMN can be elicited).

The MMN is a negative, change-specific ERP component peaking at 150 to 200 ms from stimulus onset, which was isolated by Näätänen and his collaborators (Näätänen, 1979; Näätänen, Gaillard, & Mäntysalo, 1978, 1980; Näätänen & Michie, 1979, Näätänen, Simpson, & Loveless, 1982; Sams, Paavilainen, Alho, & Näätänen, 1985) from the N2 deflection and the N2–P3a complex elicited by deviant sounds occurring among standard sounds (Ford, Roth, Dirks, & Kopell, 1973; Ford, Roth, & Kopell, 1976a, 1976b; Klinke, Fruhstorfer, & Finkenzeller, 1968; Snyder & Hillyard, 1976; Ritter, Simson, & Vaughan, 1972; Ritter, Simson, Vaughan, & Friedman, 1979; Simson, Vaughan, & Ritter, 1976, 1977; Squires, Donchin, Herning, & McCarthy, 1977; Squires, Squires, & Hillyard, 1975). (The existence of a deviance-specific ERP component elicited even with no experienced stimulus significance was predicted by Näätänen, 1975).

Figure 12.11 presents the MMN from the Näätänen et al. (1978) study. These authors used dichotic stimulation instructing the subject to detect occasional deviant stimuli in a designated ear. When subtracting the standard-stimulus response from the deviant-stimulus response, a relatively slow negativity peaking at about 200 ms from stimulus onset was found which, interestingly enough, was very similar for deviants in the attended and unattended channels (inputs to the two ears).

This deviance-specific response was interpreted by the authors as a manifestation of a neuronal-mismatch process causing an attention switch to stimulus change and thus serving OR initiation. Näätänen et al. (1978) proposed that "it may well be that a physiological mismatch process caused by a sensory input deviating from the memory trace ('template') formed by a frequent 'background' stimulus is such an automatic basic process that it takes place irrespective of the intentions of the experimenter and the

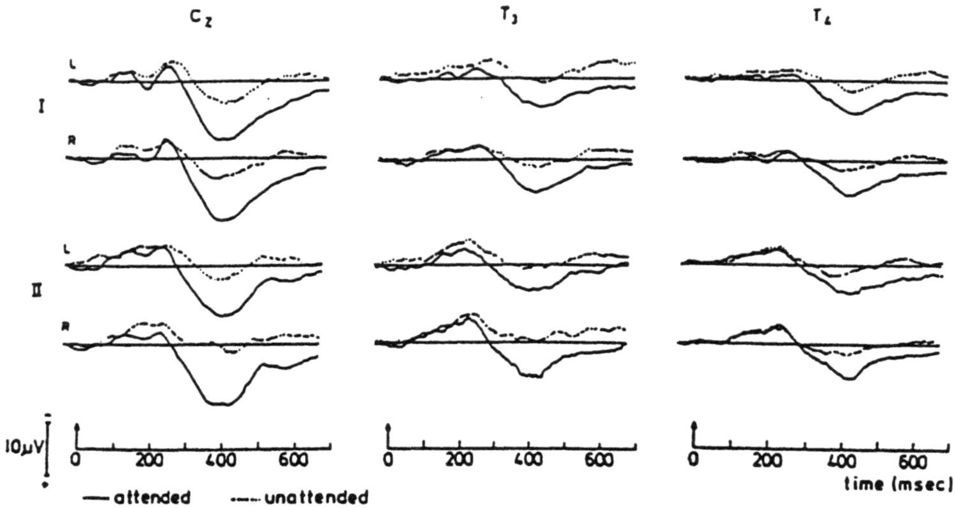

FIG. 12.11. The difference between ERPs to deviant and standard tone pips (averaged across nine subjects) for three electrode positions (C_z, T_3, T_4) separately for the left (L) and right (R) ear when attended and when unattended. These difference curves were obtained by subtracting ERPs to standards from those to deviants. *I* refers to Experiment *1* in which deviants were of higher frequency than standards, *II* to Experiment *2* where deviants were of higher intensity than standards. From Näätänen, Gaillard, & Mäntysalo, 1978. Reprinted with permission.

subject, perhaps even unmodified by the latter. This view is supported by the fact that the mismatch negativity was similarly observed both for the attended and the unattended sides. Hence, we may here be dealing with a *deviation* effect rather than *relevance* effect, whereas the much larger P300 in the EPs to the attended signals than to the unattended signals certainly represents a relevance effect" (pp. 324–325).

The sensitivity of the MMN to small stimulus changes is illustrated in Fig. 12.12. In this study (Sams, Paavilainen, Alho, & Näätänen, 1985), subjects reading a book were presented with blocks of auditory stimuli (short tone pips) consisting of standard stimuli of 1000 Hz (80%) and deviant stimuli (20%) of a slightly higher frequency. The deviant stimuli were, in different blocks, either 1004, 1008, 1016, or 1032 Hz. The order of the standard and deviant stimuli was randomized, and the ISI was constant at 1 s.

The N1 wave elicited by the various deviant stimuli was very similar to that evoked by the standard stimulus because the two stimuli were quite similar, activating strongly overlapping neuronal populations (Butler, 1968; Näätänen et al., 1988). As shown by the difference waveforms in the bottom of Fig. 12.12, a clear MMN was elicited by deviant stimuli with frequencies higher than 1008 Hz. The MMN appears as a negativity that commences at about 100 ms from stimulus onset, peaks at about 200 ms, and lasts until

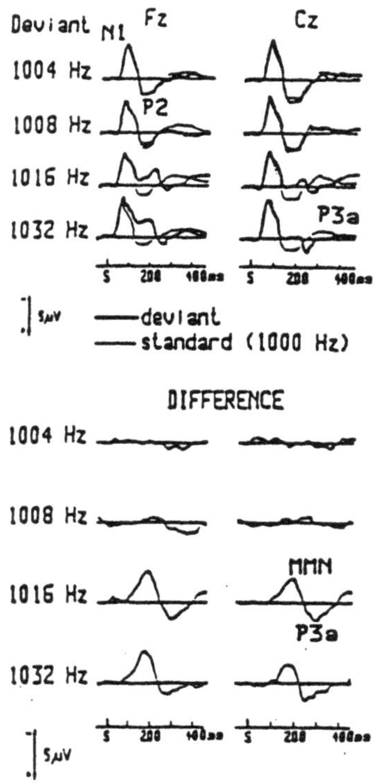

FIG. 12.12 *Top*: Grand-average ERPs to standard stimuli of 1000 Hz (thin line) and deviant stimuli (thick line) of 1004, 1008, 1016, and 1032 Hz. In each block, 80% of stimuli were standard stimuli and 20% were deviant stimuli in a random order (one type in a block). *Bottom*: The corresponding difference waveforms obtained by subtracting the standard-stimulus ERP from the deviant-stimulus ERP. (From Sams, Paavilainen, Alho, & Näätänen, 1985. Copyright © 1985 by Elsevier Science Publishers, Ireland. Reprinted with permission).

about 250 ms poststimulus. Even the 1008-Hz deviant stimuli, which in a separate discrimination task were found to be at the discrimination threshold, elicited an MMN, although a very small one. The more recent results of Tiitinen, May, Reinikainen, and Näätänen (1994) illustrated the orderly amplitude increase as well as latency and duration decrease of the MMN with the increased magnitude of frequency deviation (Fig. 12.13).

An MMN can also be elicited by occasional changes in stimulus intensity, both by intensity increments and decrements, which is consistent with the predictions from the OR theory. Such data (Näätänen, Paavilainen, Alho, Reinikainen, & Sams, 1989) are illustrated in Fig. 12.14. The standard stimulus was of 80 dB SPL and, in different blocks, the deviant stimulus was either of 77, 70, 57 (intensity decrements), 83, 90, or 95 dB (intensity increments). In the other attributes, the standard and deviant stimuli were identical.

In examining the vertex (Cz) responses to the 77-dB deviants, it can be seen that the N1 to these slightly softer stimuli was attenuated in amplitude in comparison with that to the standard stimulus. This amplitude decrement reflects the dependence of the N1 on stimulus intensity (Picton, Goodman, & Bryce, 1970). The N1 to deviants was followed by the MMN, not present in response to the standards. When the deviant-stimulus intensity was

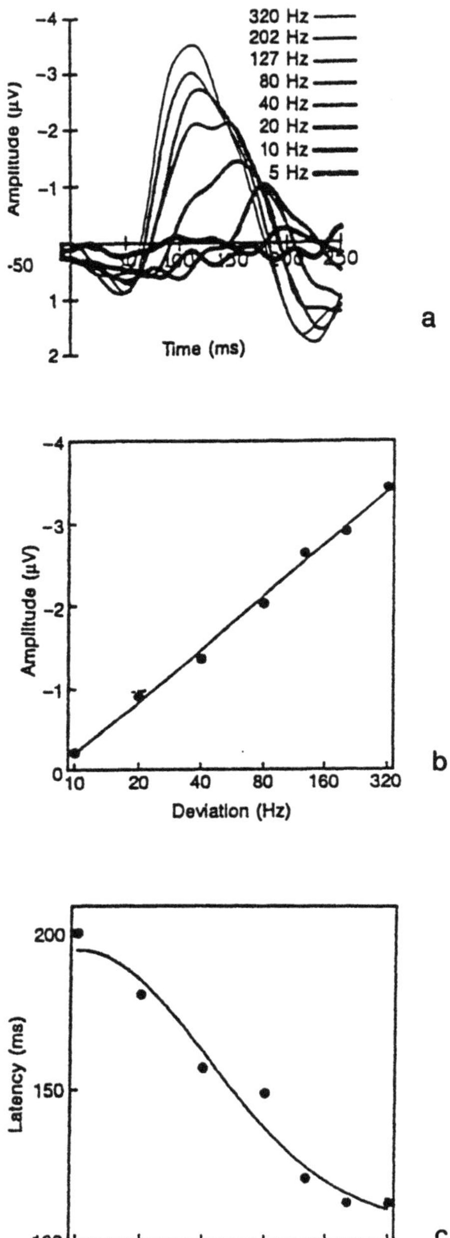

FIG. 12.13. (a) MMN to frequency deviation: Grand-average difference waves calculated by subtracting ERPs to 1000-Hz standard tones from those to deviant tones with higher frequencies as indicated, each occurring among standard tones in separate stimulus blocks at a probability of 0.05. Note that the MMN amplitude is increased and latency is shortened with increasing frequency deviation. Stimulus onset at 0 ms. (b) The dependence of the mean difference-wave peak amplitude (composed of MMN and of the enhancement of the N1 component peaking at about 100 ms) on the magnitude of frequency deviation. (c) The dependence of the MMN peak latency on the magnitude of frequency deviation. (Data from Tiitinen et al. 1994).

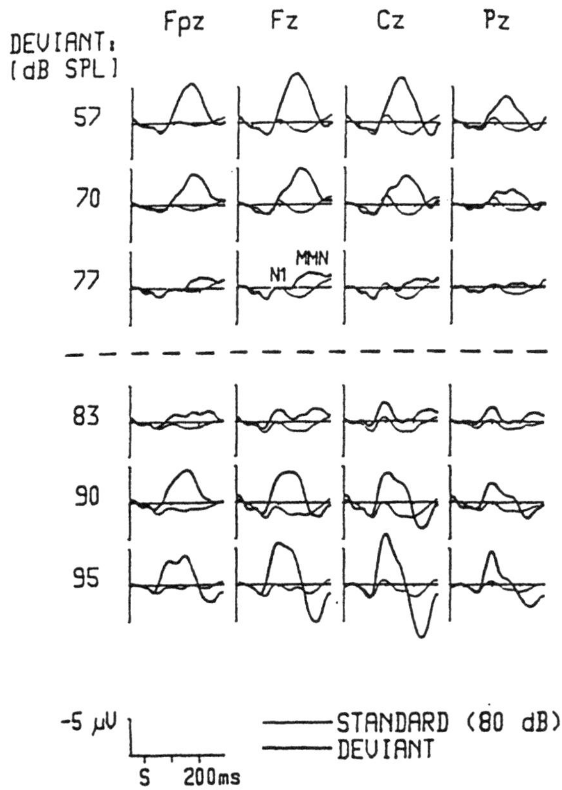

FIG. 12.14. Grand-average frontal-pole (Fpz), frontal (Fz), vertex (Cz), and parietal (Pz) ERPs to standard stimuli of 80 dB (thin line) and to deviant stimuli of different intensity (thick line) as indicated on the left side of the figure. (From Näätänen, Paavilainen, Alho, Reinikainen, & Sams, 1989. Copyright © 1989 by Elsevier Science Publishers, Ireland. Reprinted with permission, and from Näätänen, Paavilainen, Lavikainen, Alho, Reinikainen, Teder, Sams, Strelets, & Rosenfeld, unpublished data).

further decreased, the MMN component became larger and occurred earlier, making it impossible to measure the N1 and the MMN separately. The MMN, in general, is large in amplitude in this study because of the short ISI of 460 ms.

Consequently, quite paradoxically, it may be concluded that the weaker the stimulus intensity, the larger was the response elicited. This suggests that the MMN-generator mechanism in fact responded to the difference between the deviants and standards, not to the stimulus per se. Consistent with this, when presented without the intervening, loud standard stimuli, the soft 57-dB stimuli elicited no MMN but rather a large N1 (Fig. 12.15). Therefore, it is unlikely that any intensity-specific neurons (Brugge & Reale,

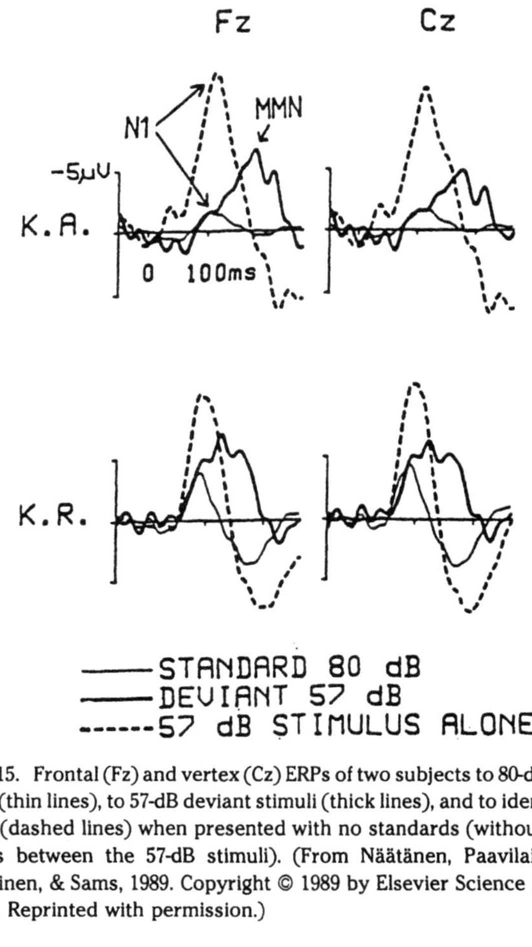

FIG. 12.15. Frontal (Fz) and vertex (Cz) ERPs of two subjects to 80-dB standard stimuli (thin lines), to 57-dB deviant stimuli (thick lines), and to identical 57-dB stimuli (dashed lines) when presented with no standards (without changing the ISIs between the 57-dB stimuli). (From Näätänen, Paavilainen, Alho, Reinikainen, & Sams, 1989. Copyright © 1989 by Elsevier Science Publishers, Ireland. Reprinted with permission.)

1985; Pantev, Hoke, Lenertz, & Lütkenhöner, 1989) could account for the MMN for the intensity decrements.

When deviant stimuli were intensity increments rather than decrements, the MMN was again elicited, and its amplitude was increased with the increasing intensity difference. This time, however, also the N1 component was enhanced in response to the deviants, and this enhancement was proportional to the intensity increment (Fig. 12.14), which accords with the known intensity dependence of the N1 amplitude (Davis, Bowers, & Hirsh, 1968; Picton et al., 1970).

Intensity-change effects can be better understood by looking down the Fpz column in Fig. 12.16 showing the deviant-standard difference waves. The N1 to the deviant stimulus (peaking at about 100 ms) became larger than that to the standard stimulus as the deviant stimulus became more intense than the standard stimulus and, further, this N1 enhancement in-

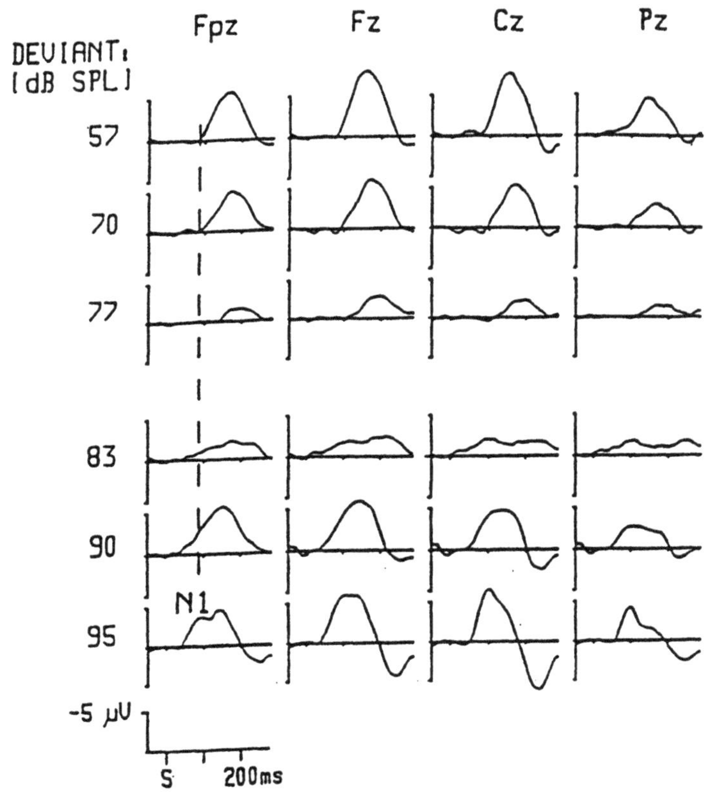

FIG. 12.16. Difference waves for the data presented in Fig. 12.14 obtained by subtracting ERPs to standards from those to the corresponding deviants. (From Näätänen, Paavilainen, Lavikainen, Alho, Reinikainen, Teder, Sams, Strelets, & Rosenfeld, unpublished data).

creased with increasing intensity. By contrast, the MMN, with a peak latency between 150 to 200 ms, gradually decreased in amplitude and increased in latency as the deviant stimulus became more intense (and therefore became closer in intensity to the 80-dB standard stimulus). Then, after the standard-stimulus intensity was passed, the MMN became gradually larger in amplitude and shorter in latency again, as the deviant stimulus became yet more intense (and therefore became further away in intensity from the 80-dB standard). In other words, the N1 amplitude was a linear function of intensity, whereas the MMN amplitude was a curvilinear function of intensity, with the zero point matching the standard-stimulus intensity.

Thus, the MMN generator responded to intensity deviation irrespective of whether this intensity deviation was an intensity decrement or increment. The N1 generator, in contrast, responded to stimulus intensity directly, that is, regardless of the relation of this intensity to that of the standard stimulus: The N1 amplitude was largest for intensity-increment deviants, and larger for standards than for intensity-decrement deviants. Consequently, whereas stimulus deviation was necessary for MMN elicitation, the N1 was also elicited by standards, that is, by stimulus repetitions. The insensitivity of the N1 to the relation between the stimuli in the block was also evidenced by the N1 latency, which in contrast to the MMN latency did not vary as a function of stimulus deviation. So, the N1 is a response to individual stimuli, whereas the MMN responds to the relation (difference) between consecutive stimuli, thus exemplifying a second-order response, one representing a difference signal generated in a comparison between two consecutive stimuli.

These data therefore strongly suggest that the brain process generating the MMN was based on a neural representation of the previous, standard stimuli, that is, on Sokolov's neuronal model and, further, that the very process generating the MMN greatly resembled the neuronal-mismatch process postulated by Sokolov. Importantly, what seemed to matter was only the deviation, not whether it was an intensity increment or decrement. In contrast, the P3a was considerably larger for intensity increments that were much more attention catching than intensity decrements. It appears that this generator mechanism was sensitive both to stimulus change (apparently receiving an input from the MMN generator) and transient energy increase, the two factors causing OR-types of responses in Sokolov's OR theory, as already mentioned.

Besides frequency or intensity changes in simple tones, an MMN can be elicited by other kinds of changes, too, such as change in the spatial locus of origin of a sound (Paavilainen, Karlsson, Reinikainen, & Näätänen, 1989; Schröger & Wolff, 1996; Winkler, Tervaniemi, Schröger, Wolff, & Näätänen, 1998), rise time (Lyytinen et al., 1992), duration (both by duration increments and decrements; Näätänen, Paavilainen, Reinikainen, et al., 1989; see also Kaukoranta et al., 1989), and by ISI decrements (Ford & Hillyard, 1981; Näätänen, Jiang, Lavikainen, Reinikainen, & Paavilanen, 1993; Nordby, Roth, & Pfefferbaum, 1988; for analogous MEG data, see Hari, Joutsiniemi, Hämäläinen, & Vilkman, 1989). In addition, an MMN is also elicited by changes in complex stimuli such as in the phonetic structure of a sound (Aaltonen, Niemi, Nyrke, & Tuhkanen, 1987; Aaltonen, Tuomainen, Laine, & Niemi, 1993; Kraus, McGee, Sharma, Carrell, & Nicol, 1992, 1995; Maiste, Wiens, Hunt, Scherg, & Picton, 1995; Sams, Aulanko, Aaltonen, & Näätänen, 1990; Sharma, Kraus, McGee, Carrell, & Nicol, 1993; for corroborating MEG data, see Aulanko, Hari, Lounasmaa, Näätänen, & Sams, 1993) or in a complex spectrotemporal stimulus pattern (Schröger, Näätänen, & Paavilainen, 1992; Schröger, Paavilainen, & Näätänen, 1994; Näätänen, Schröger, Karakas, Tervaniemi, & Paavilainen, et al., 1993; for analogous magnetic data, see Alho, Kujala, Paavilainen, Summala, Näätänen, 1993; Alho, Tervaniemi, et al., 1996). Also, changes in rhythmic stimulus patterns elicit an MMN (Imada, Hari, Loveless, & McEvoy, 1993). In fact, it appears that an MMN can be elicited by any discriminable change in an auditory stimulus (Kraus, McGee, Micco, Sharma, Carrell, & Nicol, 1993; Kraus, McGee, Carrell, et al., 1995; Lang, Nyrke, Ek, Aaltonen, Raimo, & Näätänen, 1990).

MMN: Evidence for the Involvement of a Memory Trace. In order to entertain the relation of the MMN to the OR theory, it is of course necessary to provide compelling evidence against the possibility that the response to stimulus change is due just to this infrequent stimulus activating fresh afferent elements, those not activated by the frequent, standard stimulus. This evidence may be summarized as follows:

1. The MMN is only elicited by stimulus (or event) change. Thus, single stimuli presented at long ISIs corresponding to those between the deviants in the MMN paradigm do not activate the neural populations generating an MMN (see Fig. 12.15; Kraus, McGee, Micco, Sharma, Carrell, & Nicol, 1993; Näätänen, Paavilainen, Alho, Reinikainen, & Sams, 1989). This conclusion is supported by MEG data indicating that the auditory-cortex locus generating an MMN is not activated by deviants when standards are omitted (Sams, Hämäläinen, Antervo, Kaukoranta, Reinikainen, & Hari, 1985);
2. An MMN is elicited by intensity decrements at such a large amplitude and duration (Näätänen, Paavilainen, Alho, Reinikainen, & Sams, 1989) that it is very hard to attribute these responses to specific soft-intensity tuned neurons. The same applies to the MMN elicited by duration decrements (Kaukoranta, Sams, Hari, Hämäläinen, & Näätänen, 1989; Näätänen, Paavilainen, & Reinikainen, 1989);
3. An MMN is elicited by stimuli presented after occasional shorter-duration ISIs in stimulus blocks with otherwise constant ISIs (Ford & Hillyard, 1981; Näätänen, Jiang, et al., 1993; Nordby et al., 1988);
4. An MMN is also elicited by stimulus omission when very short ISIs are used (Yabe, Tervaniemi, Reinikainen, & Näätänen, 1997; Yabe, Tervaniemi, Sinkkonen, Huotilainen, Ilmoniemi, & Näätänen, 1998) and by a partial stimulus omission of one element of a compound stimulus (Nordby, Hammerborg, Roth, & Hugdahl, 1994; Winkler & Näätänen, 1993).

On the basis of the evidence presented, the fresh afferent elements hypothesis of MMN generation can be regarded as being definitely ruled out. Rather than being generated by mere activation of fresh afferent elements, the MMN is caused by a process that registers the stimulus difference or change, that is, by a process that represents the neural code of this change.

This of course implicates an involvement of a neural representation (neuronal model) of the standard stimulus in the process generating the MMN.

However, the ISI in a stimulus block must not be very long; otherwise no MMN can be elicited even by deviants that deviate widely from the standards. The largest MMNs are usually obtained when the ISI is shorter than 0.5 s (cf. Näätänen, Paavilainen, Alho, Reinikainen, & Sams, 1987); when the ISI is prolonged to 5 or 10 s, then the MMN is only small in amplitude (see Böttcher-Gandor & Ullsperger, 1992; Czigler, Csibra, & Csontos, 1992; Mäntysalo & Näätänen, 1987; Sams, Hari, Rif, & Knuutila, 1993), apparently disappearing with the further prolongation of the ISI (cf. Sams et al., 1993). These data consequently suggest limited durations of the memory traces underlying MMN generation. Therefore, this mechanism cannot account for the OR to stimulus change when ISIs between stimuli are long such as 20 to 30 s, used in classical OR studies.

Some recent studies, however, suggest that the traces involved in MMN generation might in fact exceed in duration the ISIs with which an MMN can still be elicited. Such results were obtained by Cowan, Winkler, Teder, and Näätänen (1993; for corroborating results, see Winkler, Cowan, Csépe, Czigler, & Näätänen, 1996). Their data suggest that the trace has two phases (a) an active phase, during which an MMN is elicited if a deviant stimulus occurs; (b) a passive, "dormant" phase when a deviant stimulus cannot elicit an MMN but can elicit it when one "reminder" of the standard stimulus is presented to activate the trace shortly before the deviant stimulus occurs. The existence of the dormant trace was demonstrated by the result that in the beginning of a stimulus block, an MMN could not be elicited by a deviant stimulus after one standard when this standard differed from the standard of the previous block but could be elicited when the standard was the same as that in the previous block.

Converging evidence was provided by Näätänen, Schröger, Karakas, Tervaniemi, and Paavilainen (1993), who used novel complex spectrotemporal stimulus patterns as their standards and deviants. These authors found cumulative training effects suggesting a gradual development and informational refinement of the neural representation of that standard stimulus whose dormant phase therefore must have lasted throughout the whole session (Fig. 12.17). Consequently, it might be possible to use the sensory-memory trace reflected by MMN data in explaining the OR even when it occurs in the long-ISI paradigm. The mechanism cannot be the same in the two cases, however. With short ISIs, that is, when an MMN is elicited, the deviant stimulus automatically causes an attention switch (see below), whereas with a very long ISI, the MMN mechanism can no more be activated by stimulus change. However, when ISIs are very long, then each stimulus triggers, as judged from the strong N1 response to stimulus onset, a conscious evaluation of this stimulus with reference to the dormant sen-

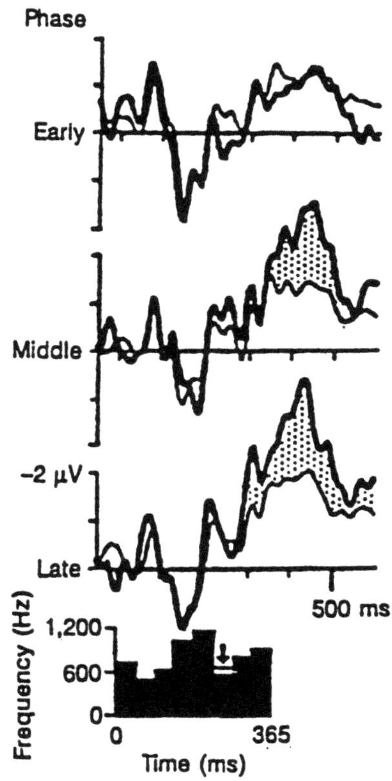

FIG. 12.17. Grand-average ERPs (seven subjects) at Cz to standard serial sound patterns (thin lines) and to deviant patterns (thick lines) occurring among standard patterns with a probability of 0.1. The standard and deviant sound patterns, illustrated at the bottom, consisted of eight consecutive tones of different frequencies. In the deviant patterns, the frequency of the sixth tone (indicated by the arrow) was higher than in the standard patterns. ERPs were recorded during the early, middle, and late phases of a session in which sound patterns (1,200 in each phase) were presented to subjects concentrating on a reading task. The performance of the subjects belonging to this group improved during the session in a sound pattern discrimination test applied after each phase of the session. In these subjects, the MMN (shaded area) emerged first and then increased in amplitude during the session. Adapted from Näätänen, Schröger, Karakas, Tervaniemi, & Paavilainen, 1993).

sory-memory trace of the standard stimulus accessible to attention (see Näätänen, 1986a).

MMN: Is a Constant Standard Stimulus Necessary? Recent MMN research also outlined the range of the different types of sensory information that can be encoded in the neuronal models. One of the questions is whether the standard stimulus must be constant for an MMN to emerge. In natural conditions, the input to the auditory system varies continuously, for example, with head movements and with moving sound sources, even when the sound itself remains constant. This would render an MMN-generator mechanism that depends on the constancy of the standard-stimulus input quite useless.

This question was addressed by Winkler, Paavilainen, Alho, Reinikainen, Sams, and Näätänen (1990), who demonstrated that an MMN is elicited even when the standard stimulus is not constant but rather varies continuously in intensity (however within a rather narrow range). This MMN was elicited by a frequency change and also by an intensity change that was considerably larger than the extreme intensity deviation of the standard stimulus from the mean. The MMN amplitude both for the frequency and intensity change was smaller when the standard-stimulus variation in a block was larger, however (Fig. 12.18).

Corroborating MEG results were provided by Huotilainen et al. (1993), who obtained an magnetic equivalent (MMNm) of the electric MMN to frequency change even though several features of the standard stimulus varied in parallel. This MMNm was, however, smaller than when the standard stimulus was constant. In contrast, Gomes, Ritter, and Vaughan (1995) recently found that the MMN elicited by change in one stimulus feature is not attenuated when another standard-stimulus feature is varied even with a very large range. In addition, Aulanko et al. (1993) obtained an MMNm to a change of a CV-syllable even though the standard syllable varied through 10 different levels of the fundamental frequency.

Thus, it is clear that an MMN can be elicited even when the standard stimulus undergoes considerable variation. These data can be interpreted as suggesting that each feature of a stimulus is encoded in at least partially separate feature-specific neuronal populations of the central auditory system. This is supported by results indicating additivity of the MMN (or MMNm) amplitude when a deviant stimulus deviates in two features rather than just in one (Levänen, Hari, McEvoy, & Sams, 1993; Schröger, 1994). Gomes et al. (1995), using an ingenious experimental design, showed, however, that in addition to the individual features of a stimulus, also the feature conjunction constituting this particular stimulus is represented by the trace.

MMN as Evidence for Primitive Sensory Intelligence. Saarinen, Paavilainen, Schröger, Tervaniemi, and Näätänen (1992) demonstrated that traces involved in MMN process are able to encode even generalizations, or rules, abstracted from a set of extensively varying sensory information. In one of their conditions, standard stimuli were ascending tone pairs, the second member of the pair being about 10% higher in frequency than the first member of the pair, but the tone pairs of the block randomly occurred at very different frequency levels. Thus, the only invariant, unifying feature of the standards was that the pair was an ascending one. Correspondingly, the deviants were descending pairs, again randomly occurring at very different frequency levels.

Notwithstanding this continuous frequency variation of both standards and deviants, an MMN was elicited by these direction deviants (Fig. 12.19). The authors interpreted this result in terms of primitive sensory intelligence. They proposed that sensory-memory neurons are able to extract invariant features behind continuous sensory variation, that is, to form simple concepts, in this case of an ascending pair or a descending pair. It is remarkable that this concept formation could be accomplished at a rela-

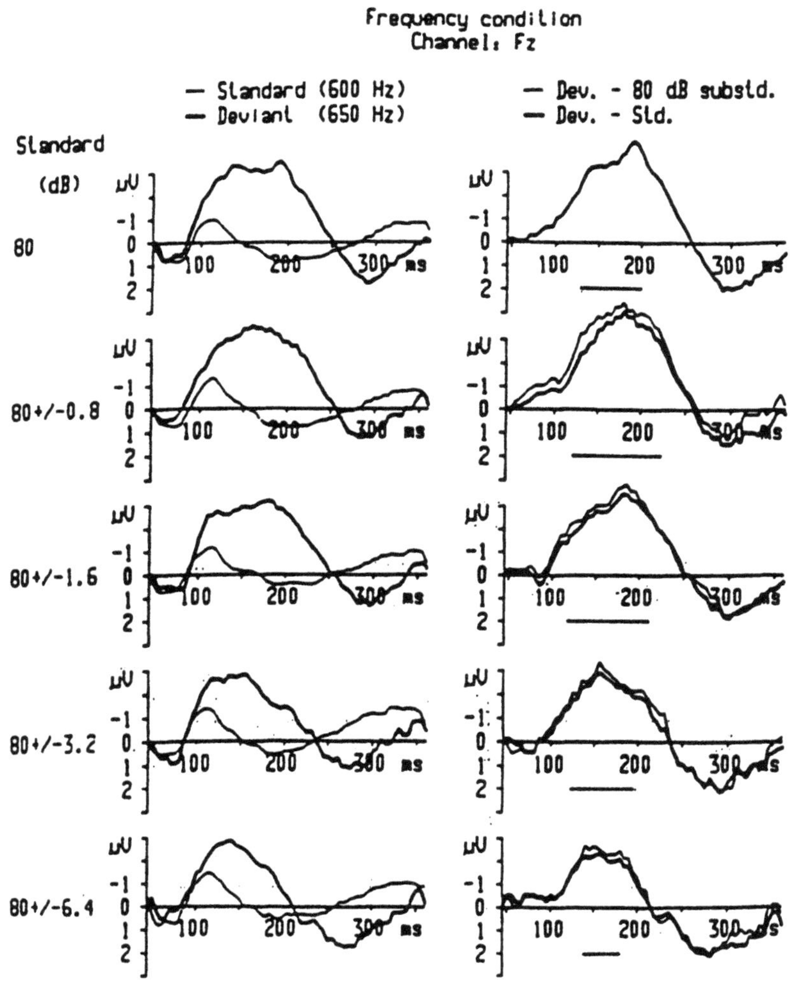

FIG. 12.18. LEFT: Grand-average frontal (Fz) ERPs to standard stimuli of 600 Hz (80 dB), averaged across the different substandards slightly varying in intensity around 80 dB, thin line; and to deviant stimuli of 650 Hz (thick line) for the different ranges of the standard-stimulus intensity variability as indicated on the left. RIGHT: The corresponding difference waves (thick line—deviant-stimulus ERP minus standard-stimulus ERP averaged across the different substandards; thin line—deviant-stimulus ERP minus ERP to 80-dB substandards). Intervals with significant ($p < .01$ in point-to-point *t*-tests) differences between ERPs to deviants and standards are underlined. (From Winkler, Paavilainen, Alho, Reinikainen, Sams, & Näätänen, 1990. Copyright © 1990 by the Society for Psychophysiological Research. Reprinted with permission).

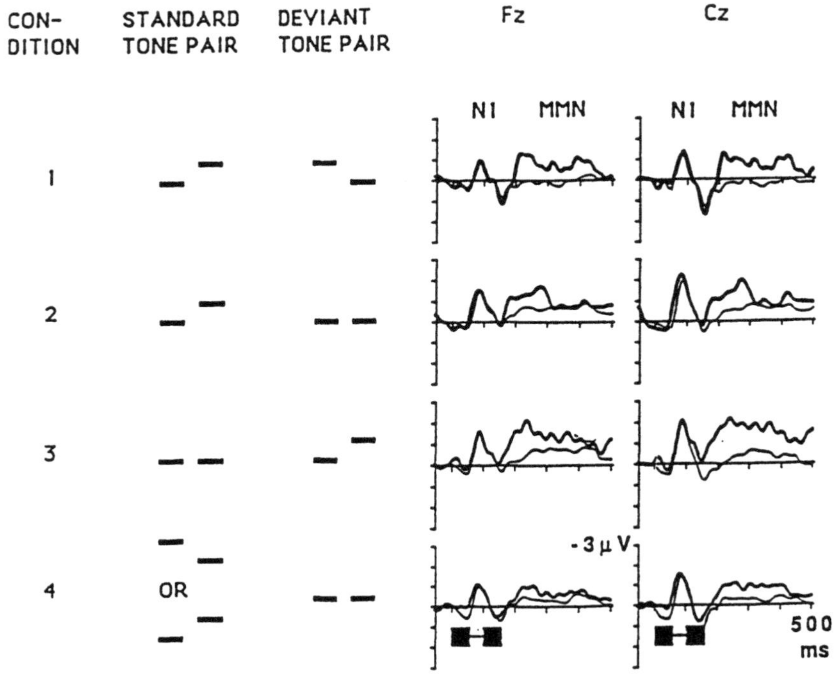

FIG. 12.19. Grand-average frontal (Fz) and central (Cz) ERPs to the standard and deviant tone pairs in the four experimental conditions illustrated schematically on the left. Standard and deviant tone pairs differed in the direction of the within-pair frequency change, but not in the (mean) absolute frequency that was randomly varied across 5 different frequency levels; thus there was no acoustically constant standard stimulus pair. The temporal course of a stimulus pair is shown below. Thin lines represent responses to the standard tone pairs and thick lines represent responses to the deviant pairs. The N1 wave was very similar to the standard and deviant tone pairs, whereas only the deviant tone pairs elicited MMN. (From Saarinen, Paavilainen, Schröger, Tervaniemi, & Näätänen, 1992. Copyright © 1992 by Rapid Communications of Oxford Ltd. Reprinted with permission).

tively low, still sensory level of stimulus processing and, apparently, in the absence of attention.

This automaticity was supported by the results of Paavilainen, Saarinen, Tervaniemi, and Näätänen (1995). They were able to replicate the finding in a rapid-rate, dichotic, selective-listening paradigm for the ignored stimulus stream, however only when the stimuli were presented to the *right* ear. Maybe this primitive concept formation is a left-hemisphere ability.

An analogous MEG result was obtained by Pardo and Sams (1993). Their standards were frequency glides starting at very different frequency levels, deviants being equivalent frequency glides but ones presented backwards.

The recent results of Paavilainen, Jaramillo, and Näätänen (1998) further extended these findings by showing, among other things, that the inputs to the two ears can also converge into a single interaural abstract-feature trace. This was done by presenting the two tones forming an ascending pair to different ears, with the first tone of a pair being always presented to the left ear and the second tone always to the right ear. In another condition, a still more complicated setup was used where even the order of ear stimulation was randomized. Nevertheless, an MMN was elicited by the deviant, descending pairs in both conditions. The behavioral discrimination tests performed after the ERP sessions suggested a dissociation between the neural mechanisms generating the abstract-feature MMN and those underlying the behavioral (conscious) responses, subjects usually not being able consciously to discriminate deviant stimuli. For a very recent review on MMN studies suggesting the existence of primitive intelligence at the level of auditory cortex, see Näätänen, Tervaniemi, Sussman, Paavilainen, and Winkler (2001).

Representations of Stimulus Events as Neural Models. The results discussed previously imply that stimulus representations encode stimulus *events* rather than mere static stimulus features (see also Port, 1991). This is clear also from studies using complex spectrotemporal stimulus patterns as standards. In one of these studies, Schröger et al. (1994) found that occasionally reversing the order of two frequency segments in an eight-segment pattern elicited a distinct MMN. Thus, the complex pattern was stored with its temporal relationships (the order of the segments) rather than just all the different frequencies present in the pattern.

The importance of time in sensory information encoded in the neural representations is also demonstrated by the MMN elicited by shortening the constant ISI between the stimuli of a block (Ford & Hillyard, 1981; Näätänen, Jiang, et al., 1993; Nordby et al., 1988). In addition, the assumption of an event rather than a stimulus being encoded by the traces is also supported by the somewhat paradoxical result that an MMN can also be elicited by stimulus similarity (repetition) rather than difference, if viewed from the perspective of individual stimuli. Nordby et al. (1988) showed that an occasional stimulus repetition in a regularly alternating sequence of two tones elicits an MMN. This result clearly indicates that what was encoded in the trace was the (alternating) stimulus sequence, not any individual stimulus.

Neural Models as Predictions of Future Stimulus Events. If time is precisely encoded in these representations of the past events, then this information about the temporal regularities of the events of the immediate past might be automatically used to *extrapolate* (the timing of) these events in the immediate future. Näätänen (1992) proposed that the sensory systems involved in storing sensory information from the past events might in fact use this information to form (automatic) predictions of future events, that is, they might actually be of extrapolatory nature. According to this hypothesis, these neurons encode the repeating spatio-temporal response pattern of the afferent neurons and project it to the immediate future. Thus, for example, if a tone is repeated at constant ISIs of 1 s, then this rhythm is soon adopted by a population of extrapolatory neurons representing this tone so that they start to undergo oscillatory changes replicating this rhythm. Then, these oscillatory changes become synchronized moment-by-moment, with no temporal lag, to the phase of the ongoing sequence of the sensory events.

Therefore, one could characterize this code not only as a memory trace of past auditory events but also as a primitive "prediction" of the immediate sensory future, as a future-oriented or anticipatory sensory code. If sensory events correspond to this prediction (in this case, the stimulus occurs at its regular moment), then these extrapolatory processes are reinforced and become stronger and more accurate. In contrast, if the prediction is violated by sensory events, the stimulus occurring too early or being different, then an MMN is generated and the extrapolatory processes representing the prediction are weakened or terminated. At any moment of time, only a certain stimulus, or stimulus absence, would correspond to the (momentary) state of the neuronal population, that is, to the specific anticipation represented, with events deviating from the anticipated event at any instant triggering an MMN. The extrapolated events could, apparently, be also much more complex than just repetitions of the same stimulus with regular ISIs. For example, an alternation of two different stimuli at regular ISIs might also be encoded by the extrapolatory mechanism (cf. Nordby et al., 1988).

Consequently, the sensory neurons involved could be divided into three basic categories: (a) afferent neurons analyzing the present sensory input (feature detectors); (b) sensory-memory neurons; (c) extrapolatory neurons forming predictions of future sensory events on the basis of repetitive spatio-temporal activation patterns of the afferent neurons encoded by sensory-memory neurons. In this case, it would be this automatically generated prediction of sensory events rather than just a memory of past events that is continuously compared with the current sensory input if sensory events display some temporal regularities (Näätänen, 1992; Winkler et al., 1996). It is remarkable that all these cognitive processes are of automatic nature.

This hypothesis involving extrapolatory sensory-level neurons seems to have been verified by Tervaniemi, Maury, and Näätänen (1994). Their standards were composed of a continuously descending sequence of tones with equal steps, and their deviants were either tone repetitions or tones ascending to the preceding frequency. The MMN was elicited by these deviant events, which was interpreted by the authors as evidence for automatic extrapolatory sensory activity. This is because this MMN was elicited by a deviation not from an actually presented stimulus but rather from the next one in the stimulus sequence had it continued regularly, that is, from one that appeared to be automatically predicted on the basis of the regular stepwise frequency decrements in the preceding sequence of standard stimuli.

MMN: Its Intracranial Origins. Several studies have tried to locate the cerebral generators of the MMN and its magnetic equivalent MMNm. The involvement of the auditory cortex in MMN generation was initially suggested by Näätänen et al. (1978) on the basis of the relatively large MMN amplitudes recorded over the temporal cortices (sites T3 and T4). The first conclusive evidence, however, was provided by the MEG recordings of Hari, Hämäläinen, Ilmoniemi, Kaukoranta, Reinikainen, Salminen, Alho, Näätänen, and Sams (1984). These authors found an MMNm to a slight change in the frequency of a simple tone, with an equivalent current dipole (ECD) located in supratemporal auditory cortex (see also Sams, Hämäläinen, et al., 1985). Further evidence was obtained by Kaukoranta et al. (1989) who obtained an MMNm to decrement in tone duration, and by Lounasmaa, Hari, Joutsiniemi, and Hämäläinen (1989) who found an MMNm to intensity reduction. In keeping with these results, Sams, Kaukoranta, Hämäläinen, and Näätänen (1991) were able to locate equivalent current dipoles for MMNm to frequency, intensity, and duration changes in the supratemporal plane but could not determine whether these MMNms originated from the same locus or from different loci. This study also suggested that the MMNm is generated somewhat anteriorly to the N1m, an observation corroborated by a number of subsequent studies (e.g., Csépe, Pantev, Hoke, Hampson, & Ross, 1992; Hari, Rif, Tiihonen, & Sams, 1992). Also the source of an MMNm elicited by an infrequent shortening of the ISI of a block was located on the supratemporal plane (Hari et al., 1989; Levänen et al., 1993).

In addition, subsequent studies demonstrated a supratemporal auditory-cortex MMNm also for reversal in the direction of a short-duration frequency glide (Pardo & Sams, 1993; Sams & Näätänen, 1991), for the frequency change of a continuous tone (Lavikainen, Huotilainen, Ilmoniemi, Simola, & Näätänen, 1995), of one segment of a complex spectrotemporal stimulus pattern (Alho et al., 1993), and of one subtone of a musical chord (Alho et al., 1996). Furthermore, a generator of the MMNm to a change of a vowel of the subject's mother tongue was located to the supratemporal cortex of the left hemisphere by Näätänen et al. (1997) and Rinne et al. (1999).

Using Scherg's dipole-modelling method, Scherg, Vajsar, and Picton (1989) demonstrated that the scalp distribution of the electric MMN elicited by a frequency change may be modelled with generators (dipoles) located in the left and right auditory cortices. Scherg et al. (1989) actually observed that when the frequency change was small, the negativity elicited could be modelled with one dipole source in the supratemporal auditory cortex of each hemisphere, whereas two dipoles in each hemisphere were needed to explain the negativity elicited by a large frequency change. One of these two dipoles was regarded as the "true" MMN generator, one that was also activated by the small frequency change. The other generator, one activated somewhat earlier, was posterior to this generator, in keeping with the MEG data reviewed previously, and appeared to account for the enhanced supratemporal N1 component (see also Lang et al., 1990). A sound markedly differing in frequency from the preceding sound usually elicits an enhanced supratemporal N1 component for it activates new nonrefractory, frequency-specific neurons (Butler, 1968).

Separate MMN generators in each supratemporal auditory cortex were also suggested by Giard, Perrin, Pernier, and Bouchet's (1990) scalp-current density (SCD) maps. These authors recorded MMNs to changes of the frequency of unattended tones presented to a given ear while the subject was attending to the opposite-ear tones. The SCD analysis indicated that the supratemporal auditory cortex in the hemisphere contralateral to the stimulated ear contributes more strongly to the MMN than does the ipsilateral auditory cortex.

MMNm data also suggest hemispheric asymmetries. Consistent with electric MMN recordings (Giard et al., 1990; Giard et al., 1995; Paavilainen, Alho, Reinikainen, Sams, & Näätänen, 1991; Scherg et al., 1989), Levänen, Ahonen, Hari, McEvoy, and Sams (1996) found that the MMNm was larger and slightly earlier over the right than left hemisphere irrespective of the ear of stimulus delivery (when simple auditory stimuli are used).

These electric and magnetic findings suggest a predominant role of the right hemisphere in sensory memory for the physical features of (nonverbal) auditory stimuli and/or in the processing of changes in these features. Moreover, although Levänen et al. (1996) found a single supratemporal ECD as providing a sufficient account for the MMNm generated in the left hemisphere, they needed two adjacent supratemporal ECDs, with temporally overlapping activity, to satisfactorily explain the MMNm generated in the right hemisphere.

Kropotov, Näätänen, Sevostianov, Alho, Reinikainen, and Kropotova (1995) recorded MMNs directly from the temporal cortex in two patients with intracranial electrodes implanted for diagnosis and therapy. These temporal MMNs, peaking at around 200 ms from stimulus onset, were elicited by deviant tones (1100 Hz) occurring in a sequence of standard tones (1000 Hz) both when the patients ignored the tones (reading a book) and when they attended to the tones in order to press a button to occasional frequency changes (Fig. 12.20). No MMN to the deviant tones of the ignored auditory input was found in recordings from electrodes inserted in the hip-

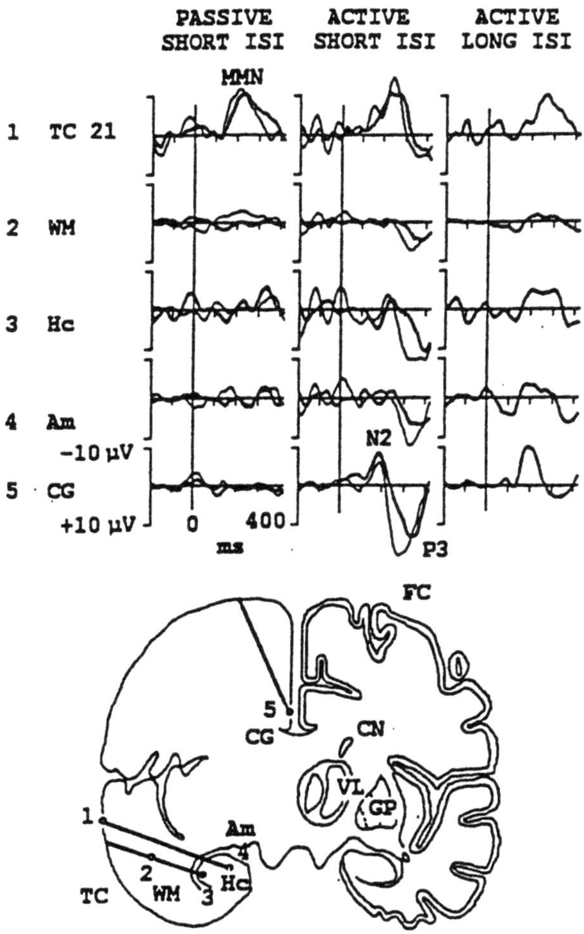

FIG. 12.20. *Top:* Difference waves derived by subtracting the ERP to standard tones (1000 Hz) from that to deviant tones (1100 Hz) for the passive short-ISI condition and for the active short-ISI and long-ISI conditions in different brain locations as indicated on the left. For the short-ISI conditions, ERPs were recorded twice (thick and thin lines) with an interval of several days. Data are from a single patient. *Bottom:* A schematic illustration of the electrode locations and lateral trajectories of insertion of the electrode bundles on the frontal cross-section of the brain of this patient. In reality, the bundles of electrodes were not located in the same cross-section and are shown on the same plane only for illustrative purposes. The numbers represent electrode locations from which ERPs (top) were recorded. (AM = amygdala; CG = cingulate gyrus; CN = caudate nucleus; FC = frontal cortex; GP = globus pallidus; HC = hippocampus; MMN = mismatch negativity; TC = temporal cortex: Brodmann 21; VL = ventrolateral nucleus of the thalamus; WM = the white matter between the temporal cortex and the hippocampus). (From Kropotov, Näätänen, Sevostianov, Alho, Reinikainen, & Kropotova (1995). Copyright © 1995 by Society for Psychophysiological Research. Reprinted with permission).

pocampus, the amygdala, the basal ganglia, and the ventrolateral nucleus of the thalamus. In these structures, a P3 positivity, sometimes preceded by an N2 negativity, was observed in response to deviant tones when they were target stimuli to be responded to (cf. Halgren, Squires, Wilson, Rohrbaugh, Babb, & Crandall, 1980; Kropotov & Ponomarev, 1991). An MMN directly from the auditory cortex (posterior supratemporal plane) was recorded also by Halgren et al. (1995a, 1995b).

The first evidence for separate generator mechanisms for changes in different auditory features was reported by Paavilainen et al. (1991); see also Näätänen (1990). These authors found that the MMN polarity reversal was relatively strongest for duration changes, and stronger for frequency than intensity changes. These effects were obtained for both hemispheres (but they were stronger for the right hemisphere) and for both contra- and ipsilateral stimuli.

These findings were corroborated and extended by Giard et al. (1995), who compared ERP scalp topographies of these three MMNs with one another. It was found that the MMN scalp topography varied according to the type of stimulus change. The dipoles fitting the scalp distributions of the three MMNs were all located in the supratemporal auditory cortex but they differed in orientation and/or location. This suggests that at least partially different supratemporal neuronal populations generated these MMNs. Thus, provided that a sensory-memory trace for the physical feature of a sound is located where the MMN is generated (Näätänen, 1992), these results indicate that at least partially different neuronal populations underlie sensory-memory representations for sound frequency, intensity, and duration and, further, that by using the MMN, one might even be able to roughly localize these representations.

Converging evidence was provided by Aaltonen et al. (1993). In their two aphasic patients with posterior left-hemisphere lesions, a prominent MMN was elicited by frequency change of a simple tone, whereas no MMN was elicited by vowel change. (In contrast, in patients with anterior left-hemisphere lesions, both MMNs could be observed). This suggests that the auditory cortex of the patients with posterior lesions could perform simple frequency discrimination but was incapable of phonetic discrimination, at least between the two vowels used (the Finnish /i/ vs. /y). Further converging evidence for separate generator mechanisms for the different MMNs was obtained by Schröger (1995), who showed that MMNs for frequency and location changes are additive, that is, a deviant stimulus deviating in both features elicits an MMN with an amplitude equalling the sum of the separate MMNs for the corresponding frequency and location changes.

In addition, Levänen et al. (1996) recently found that MMNms to changes in tone frequency, duration, and ISI are generated in different parts of the auditory cortex, suggesting that at least partially different supratemporal neuronal populations are involved in representing these features. Converging evidence was provided by Levänen et al. (1993), who found MMN additivity when a frequency-deviant stimulus was presented too early in a block with a constant ISI. Consistent with Schröger's (1995) results mentioned earlier, the MMNm elicited by this stimulus deviating from the standard stimulus in two features equalled the sum of the separate MMNms for these two features.

Furthermore, Alho et al.'s (1996) MEG study suggested that simple and complex sounds are represented in auditory cortex in at least partially different loci. It was found that the ECD for a frequency change of a simple tone was lateral to that for the same frequency change when it occurred in one element of a chord or of a sequential pattern of five tones. The two latter ECDs were very similarly located (Fig. 12.21).

Moreover, Tiitinen, Alho, Huotilainen, Ilmoniemi, Simola, and Näätänen's (1993) MEG data suggest a tonotopic organization of the neurophysiological basis of frequency representation in sensory memory. These authors reported that the orientation of the supratemporal ECD for the MMNm depends on tone frequency. They delivered, in separate blocks, standard tones of either 250, 1000, or 4000 Hz, which were occasionally replaced by a deviant tone with a 10% higher frequency than the standard tone of the same block. The ECD for the MMNm was less vertically oriented on the sagittal plane for higher frequencies, this clockwise rotation of the ECD with increasing frequency (in the right auditory cortex) suggesting that the MMNm might be generated, at least in part, in a tonotopically organized area of the curved supratemporal auditory cortex.

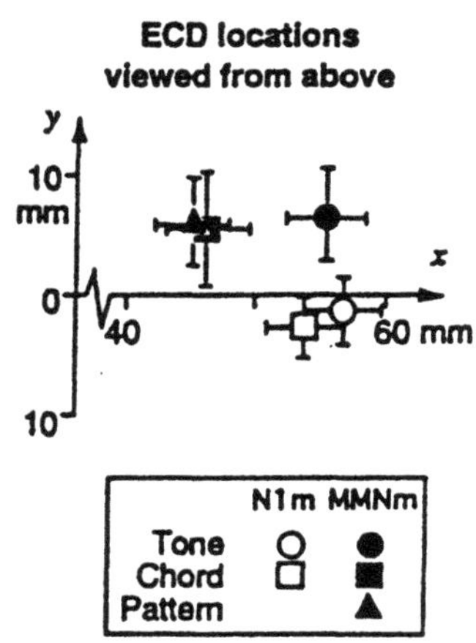

FIG. 12.21. Average locations of equivalent current dipoles (ECDs) in the auditory cortex of the right hemisphere (viewed from above) for the N1m to the standard tone and the standard chord and for the MMNm to the deviant tone, deviant chord, and deviant pattern. The vertical and horizontal bars indicate the standard errors of the mean ECD coordinates. The x axis is defined by the line connecting the left and right preauricular points. The y axis points toward the nasion. (From Alho, Tervaniemi, Huotilainen, Lavikainen, Tiitinen, Ilmoniemi, Knuutila, & Näätänen, 1996. Copyright © 1996 by Society for Psychophysiological Research. Reprinted with permission).

Also, the ECD for the N1m to standard tones changed in orientation clockwise with higher standard-tone frequencies, this finding according with the previous results that indicate that the N1m generator is located in the tonotopic auditory cortex (Elberling, Bak, Kofoed, Lebech, & Saermark, 1982; Pantev, Hoke, Lehnertz, Lütkenhöner, Anogianakis, & Wittkowski, 1988). Interestingly, different tonotopic regions of auditory cortex (see Merzenich & Brugge, 1973; Morel, Garraghty, & Kaas, 1993) might contribute to the N1m and MMNm, as the MMNm dipoles were located, in agreement with the studies already reviewed, anteriorly to the N1m dipoles. However, as already mentioned, both the MMN and MMNm appear to have several generator sources at least in the right auditory cortex (Levänen et al., 1996; Paavilainen et al., 1991). It is possible that these responses are in part generated in the tonotopic primary auditory cortex and in part in some anterior (tonotopic or nontonotopic) region of the auditory cortex.

There is also evidence for the generation of an MMN subcomponent on the lateral surface of the temporal lobe. Paavilainen et al.'s (1991) MMNs for frequency, intensity, and duration changes appeared to consist of two subcomponents of which the one peaking at 150 to 200 ms inverted in polarity at the electrode sites below the auditory cortex, whereas the other, peaking at 200 to 300 ms, did not. The polarity inversion of the earlier subcomponent was consistent with supratemporal origin, while the latter, noninverting subcomponent was probably generated by a radially oriented dipole on the lateral aspect of the temporal lobe. Also data in cats suggested an MMN generator in secondary auditory cortex (Csépe, Karmos, & Molnár, 1987).

Evidence exists for a frontal MMN generator. Näätänen and Michie (1979) proposed that the MMN has two components, a sensory-specific one generated by an automatic, preperceptual change-detection process, and a frontal one, generated by a frontal process associated with attention switch (orienting response) to stimulus change. However, it was only Giard et al. (1990) who, in their study, provided convincing evidence for this suggestion. In addition to the bilateral sensory-specific MMN subcomponent in supratemporal auditory cortex, their SCD maps suggested a further subcomponent, one originating from the frontal lobe. The estimated frontal generator was located predominantly in the right hemisphere, which might explain the right-hemisphere preponderance of the MMN scalp distribution observed in several studies (e.g., Paavilainen et al., 1991). Because the right frontal cortex in particular appears to play an important role in the control of attention (for reviews, see Fuster, 1989; Knight, 1991; Roland, 1993), the frontal MMN subcomponent might be associated with involuntary switching of attention to a change in the acoustic environment (Giard et al., 1990; Näätänen, 1992; Näätänen & Michie, 1979).

Some converging evidence for the frontal subcomponent of the MMN was obtained by Alho, Woods, Algazi, Knight, and Näätänen (1994). These authors found attenuated MMNs in patients with lesions in dorsolateral prefrontal cortex. In addition, the MEG recordings of Levänen et al. (1996) also provided some support for the frontal subcomponent of the MMN.

So, it is clear that the MMN has several intracerebral sources. The principal source seems to be the supratemporal auditory cortex where the MMN is generated from different feature-specific regions, depending on the feature in which the deviant stimulus violates the representation of the standard stimulus. In addition, there seem to be, at least in the right hemisphere, one or two further auditory-cortex generators, and probably also a frontal-cortex, predominantly right-hemispheric generator. However, it is also possible that there are subcortical generators for the MMN. In the cat and guinea pig, these structures possibly involve the medial geniculate body (Csépe, Karmos, & Molnár, 1989) and some nonspecific regions of the thalamus (Kraus, McGee, Carrell, King, Littman, & Nicol, 1994), but it is unclear to what extent these results can be generalized to humans. Finally, also some thalamo-cortical loop in MMN generation might exist in humans (Mäkelä et al., 1998).

A very recent PET study (Näätänen et al., unpublished data) corroborates and extends the present view on the intracranial MMN generators provided by electric and magnetic studies. A frequency change in a binaural tone caused considerable activation in both left and right auditory cortices, accompanied by an activation focus in the right frontal cortex. In addition, there was a bilateral parietal activation focus that could not be predicted on the basis of previous electric and magnetic studies. When deviant stimuli were presented alone, the same right-frontal focus was found, but there was no noticeable extra activation in the auditory cortices compared with a condition in which standards alone were presented. This is consistent with the results of electric and magnetic studies in that no MMN (or MMNm) is elicited by infrequent sounds presented with no standard sounds.

MMN and Attention Switch. Näätänen (1979) and Näätänen and Michie (1979) proposed that stimulus change is preconsciously detected in the auditory cortex, the code for stimulus change being formed there, which subsequently triggers frontal activation associated with the OR. Subsequently, Näätänen (1985, 1990; see also Giard et al., 1990) qualified the proposal involving the functional significance of the frontal activation by associating it with attention switch, regarded by him as the core event of the nonsignal OR (Näätänen, 1986a), more specifically, with a call from the preattentive mechanisms to focal attention (Öhman, 1979; see also Öhman, 1992). Öhman's interpretation is supported by data (Lyytinen et al., 1992) demonstrating that an MMN can be elicited even with no SCR or HR response (Figure 12.22), as well as by evidence (e.g., Alho & Sinervo, 1997; Näätänen & Gaillard, 1983) for MMN occurrence even in response to nondetected devi-

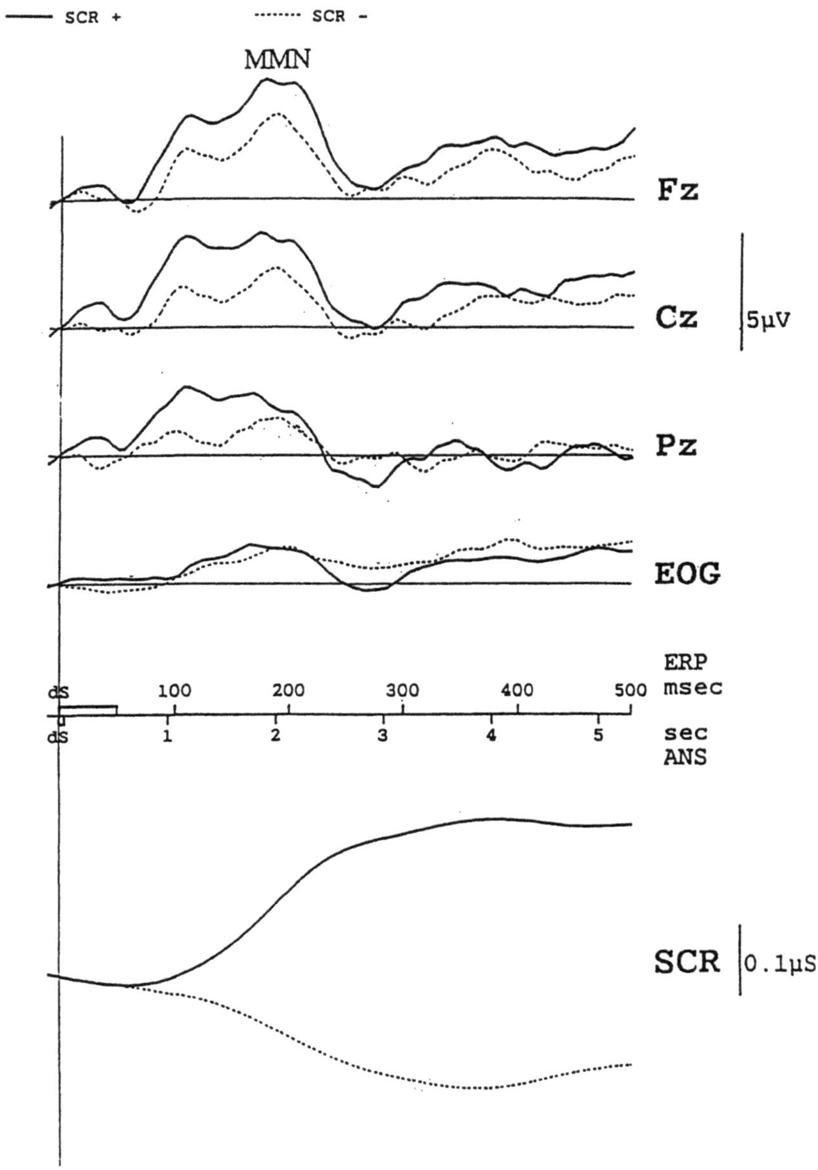

FIG. 12.22. Across-subject averaged ERPs, EOG, and SCR curves for pitch-deviant tones for trials classified according to whether or not an SCR occurred on a trial (SCR+, thick line: SCR−, dashed line). (From Lyytinen, Blomberg, & Näätänen, 1992. Copyright © 1992 by Society for Psychophysiological Research. Reprinted with permission).

ants when the subject is instructed to try to detect these deviants (Figure 12.23).

So, the occurrence of the MMN does not guarantee that the deviant stimulus has succeeded in causing an involuntary attention switch to this stimulus change. The call may not always be answered (Öhman, 1979). Instead, it appears that if the P3a follows the MMN, then attention switch has taken place (Näätänen 1985, 1990). According to several authors (e.g., Näätänen, 1990; Squires et al., 1975; Snyder & Hillyard, 1976), the P3a is a sign of the activation of an attention-switching mechanism. This is supported by data showing that when the primary task is very demanding (e.g., search for and circling words related to a specified theme in a matrix of letters), then the MMN to deviants in the to-be-ignored input sequence is not followed by a P3a (Duncan & Kaye, 1987), but that when the primary task is more relaxed (reading), then the MMN is accompanied by the P3a (Sams, Paavilainen, et al., 1985). In addition, Lyytinen and Näätänen (1987) and Lyytinen, Blomberg, and Näätänen (1992) found that the P3a following an MMN to slight frequency deviations tended to correlate with ANS responses, possible indicators of the occurrence of an attention switch. Convincing evidence for a relation between the P3a and the SCR was obtained by Halgren and Marinkovic (1995) in response to occasional novel, irrelevant sounds presented in an auditory discrimination task (Figure 12.24).

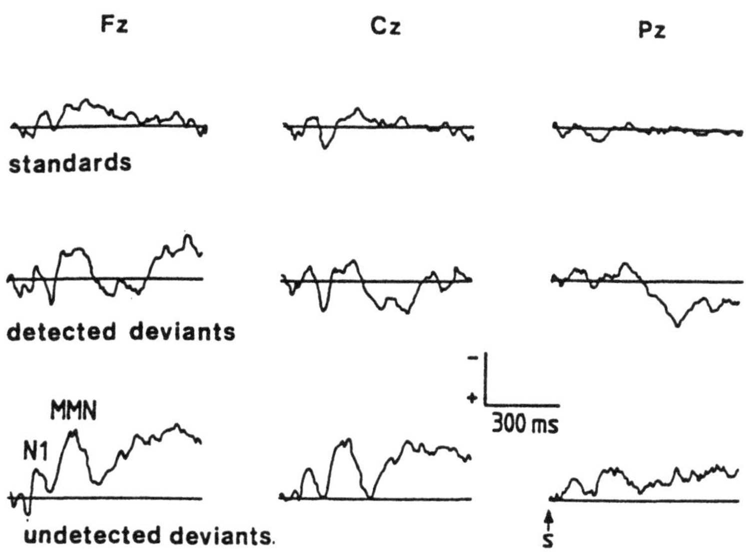

FIG. 12.23. Frontal (Fz), vertex (Cz), and parietal (Pz) ERPs of one subject to standard stimuli of 1000 Hz as well as to detected and undetected deviant stimuli of 1010 Hz. Notice also the slow positivity only to detected deviants. (Unpublished data of Loveless, Simpson, & Näätänen, 1979).

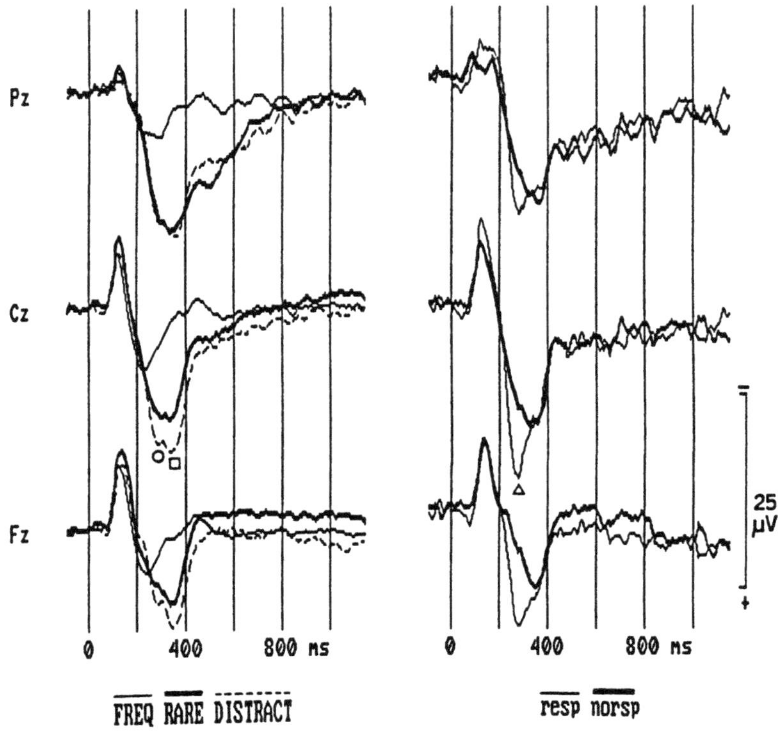

FIG. 12.24. (Left) Brain potentials recorded from the human scalp during an auditory discrimination task. Interspersed among frequent tones (thin lines), are rare target tones to which the subject pressed a key (thick lines), and occasional unique, strange, distracting sounds to which the subject made no response (dashed lines). Both targets and distractors evoked a large P3 component, with peaks at 285 ms (circle; termed P3a) and 330 ms (square; termed P3b). Depth recordings identify distinct generating systems for the P3a (including cingulate and rectal gyrus) and the P3b (including hippocampal formation and lateral orbital cortex). (Right) Correlation of the P3a with the autonomic orienting complex. The brain potentials evoked by rare distractor sounds were divided into two groups, according to whether the sounds did (thin line) or did not (thick line) also evoke an electrodermal response. Trials with autonomic responses also evoke a large P3a, especially at frontal (Fz) and central (Cz) electrode sites (triangle). (From Halgren & Marinkovic, 1995. Reprinted with permission).

Lyytinen, Blomberg, and Näätänen (1992) also found that the P3a occurred at a larger amplitude at an early phase than later in the session. Similar results were obtained by May, Tiitinen, Sinkkonen, and Näätänen (1994), who found a P3a to deviants only during the first quarter of a long session, whereas the MMN was elicited approximately at the same amplitude throughout this extended session (Figure 12.25). It appears that when the same de-

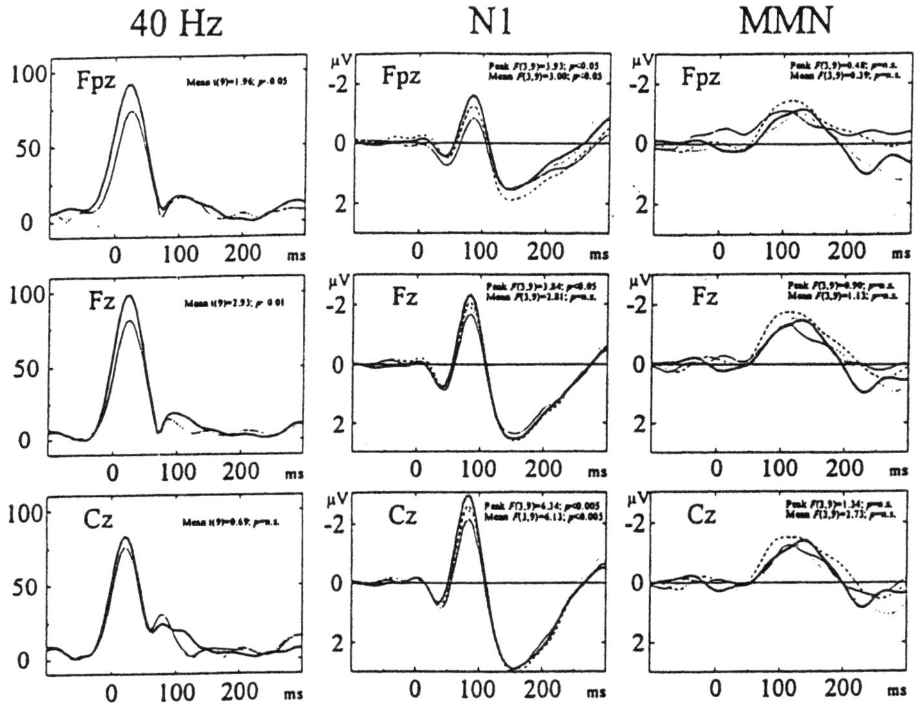

FIG. 12.25. The 40-Hz (left column), N1 (middle column), and MMN (right column) responses from electrodes Fpz, Fz, and Cz. The thick and thin lines represent the responses from the first and last subsession, dashed and dotted lines from the second and third subsession, respectively. The results of the statistical analyses of the attenuating effect of time-on-session on the response amplitudes are shown in the upper right corners. The 40-Hz and N1 responses attenuated during the experiment but the MMN response did not. Notice that a distinct P3a was elicited only during the first quarter of the session. (From May, Tiitinen, Sinkkonen, & Näätänen, 1994. Copyright © 1994 by Rapid Communications of Oxford Ltd. Reprinted with permission).

viant stimulus occurs repeatedly, it gradually loses its attention-catching ability; that is, the involuntary attention-switch response habituates.

Several studies (Alho et al., 1990; Knight et al., 1989) suggested that the P3a amplitude of an individual might provide an index of his/her distractability by irrelevant sounds and sound changes. Alho et al. (1990) found a large P3a to sound changes in prematurely born infants at the age of 6 months, which did not occur in full-term infants of the same conceptual age, suggesting enhanced distractability in preterm infants (Figure 12.26).

Further converging evidence for the relationship of the P3a to attention switch is provided by the results showing that intensity increments and decrements of a comparable magnitude elicited very similar MMNs, whereas the P3a was considerably larger in amplitude for intensity increments than dec-

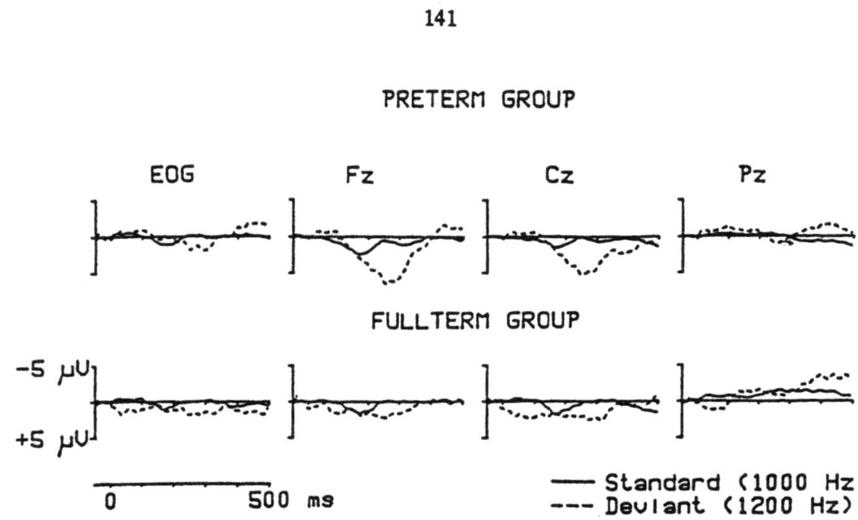

FIG. 12.26. Grand-average ERPs to deviant (dashed lines) and standard tones (continuous lines) for the preterm and full-term groups at Fz, Cz, and Pz, and at the EOG electrode above the right eye. Stimulus onset at 0 ms. (From Alho, Sajaniemi, Niittyvuopio, Sainio, & Näätänen, 1990. Copyright © 1990 by Tilburg University Press. Reprinted with permission).

rements (see Näätänen, 1992). Intensity increments are much more attention-catching, obtrusive, than intensity decrements behaviorally. Similarly, when Knight et al.'s (1989) deviants were occasional novel sounds, such as dog barking, engine starting, or telephone ringing, these certainly attention-catching sounds elicited a very large P3a irrespective of whether they occurred in the to-be-attended or ignored input in selective dichotic listening (see also Halgren & Marinkovic, 1995). The large amplitude of this P3a response might be in part explained by a strong MMN process elicited by such a novel sound. (In general, the P3a amplitude is larger for larger magnitudes of stimulus deviation; see Näätänen, 1992.) However, some novelty evaluation following transitory attention switch to the novel sound not presented previously in the session might have further increased the P3a amplitude.

In sum, in unattended stimulus sequences, the P3a to stimulus change appears to reflect the occurrence of an attention switch. This is suggested by the fact that the P3a accompanies the MMN in most cases and, further, that it is usually larger in amplitude when attention switch occurred more probably such as when the magnitude of stimulus deviation was larger (Näätänen, 1992), when the probability of stimulus deviation was lower (Näätänen et al., 1983), when deviants occurred early rather than late in the session (May et al., 1994), or when the primary task was more (Duncan & Kaye, 1987) than less (Sams, Paavilainen, et al., 1985) demanding.

Consequently, it appears that in the cerebral OR initiation, the P3a generator process forms a necessary early link in the chain of brain processes from the MMN generation in auditory cortex to those possibly reticular ones forming the final pathway to the OR (see Lynn, 1966). However, the full OR is not necessarily elicited when the P3a is elicited. It is possible that the occurrence of the attention switch (indicated by the P3a) is the earliest, and most sensitive, lowest-threshold process of all the different kinds of OR types of processes. These processes might consequently be seen as forming a continuum with regard to their threshold of activation with slight stimulus changes. Hence, when no P3a follows the MMN, then the occurrence of stimulus change would not intrude into the subject's conscious awareness. However, when a (small) P3a is elicited, then the stimulus change would be consciously perceived, that is, a transitory attention switch would occur and would probably be accompanied by the most sensitive of the further OR types of changes such as the SCR. Further, when the magnitude of stimulus deviation is increased, then a larger-amplitude P3a is elicited, one presumably accompanied by higher-threshold OR types of responses. The ANS responses can, apparently, be arranged according to their triggering thresholds, so that with a gradual increase of the magnitude of stimulus deviation, a certain ANS response emerges first, followed by other ANS responses one-by-one as the magnitude of stimulus deviation is further increased. Several studies have shown that the rank order of the sensitivity of the different ANS measures varies between different individuals but is relatively constant within an individual (see Sternbach, 1966).

Under some circumstances, however, the P3a is preceded by an N2b even in passive conditions, most typically when novel sounds are used as deviants (Halgren & Marinkovic, 1995; Knight et al., 1989), or when the magnitude of frequency deviation of a tone pip is wide (Näätänen et al., 1982), that is, when sound deviation is highly obtrusive. It may be assumed that when the N2b–P3a occurs in passive conditions, then a full-scale OR is elicited (see Näätänen & Gaillard, 1983).

An N2b in passive conditions was obtained with early blinded young adults by Kujala et al. (1995; see also Alho et al., 1993). These authors found that small frequency deviations elicited a larger-amplitude MMN in these than in control subjects. This large MMN in the blind was followed by a relatively early N2b that was absent in the control subjects (Fig. 12.27). It appears that in the course of their lifelong strong dependence on auditory information, the attention-catching function of the brain mechanisms tuned to sound changes had been considerably sensitized in these early blinded subjects.

The hypothesis of the MMN generator as an involuntary attention trigger is strongly supported by Schröger's (1996) results from a selective dichotic-listening experiment. He found that the RT to an infrequent softer-intensity

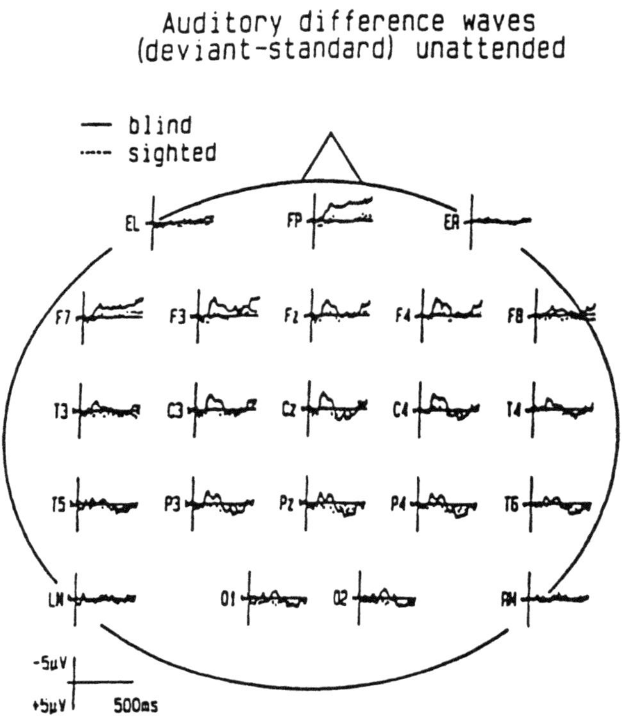

FIG. 12.27. Grand-mean difference waves at 22 scalp sites obtained by subtracting ERPs to standard tones from those to deviant tones during attention to somatosensory stimuli (LM, left mastoid, RM, right mastoid). (From Kujala, Alho, Kekoni, Hämäläinen, Reinikainen, Salonen, Standertskjöld-Nordenstam, & Näätänen, 1995. Copyright ©1995 by Springer-Verlag. Reprinted with permission).

stimulus in the right ear increased and the hit rate decreased when this target stimulus was preceded, with a 200-ms lead time, by a frequency deviant instead of a standard, in the left ear. Furthermore, these effects were proportional to the magnitude of the frequency change: When the frequency deviation was 50 Hz (standard 700 Hz), then the RT increased by 12 ms, and when the deviation was 200 Hz, then the RT prolongation was 26 ms. In addition, both frequency deviations elicited an MMN, whereas the wider frequency deviation also elicited N2–P3a waves. According to Schröger (1996), this performance decrement was probably due to attentional capture by the deviants of the to-be-ignored channel. He further proposed that the data pattern obtained supports the hypothesis that "the neural processes generating the MMN may be involved in a mechanism of passive attention switch" (pp. 88–89).

Schröger's (1996) conclusions were supported by Alho et al. (1997) and Escera et al. (1998). These studies found that task-irrelevant MMN- and P3a-eliciting deviant tones and novel sounds prolonged the RT and decreased the number of correct responses to successive visual stimuli that were to be discriminated in a forced-choice RT task. In these studies, the subject's task was to press one button when the visual stimulus was a digit and another button when it was a number (Alho et al., 1997), or one button to an odd digit and another button to an even digit (Escera et al., 1998). Each visual target stimulus was preceded by a sound with a duration of 200 ms, which commenced 300 ms before the visual stimulus and was either a standard tone (600 Hz), a deviant tone (700 Hz or 660 Hz in Alho et al., 1997, and Escera et al., 1998, respectively) or a novel sound (in Escera et al., 1988) like those used by Knight et al. (1989). To keep attention more efficiently away from the sounds, Alho et al. (1997) presented together with the sound a visual warning stimulus that informed the subject of whether a visual target stimulus will follow (a Go trial) or not (a No-Go trial).

Despite this attentional manipulation, the RT was increased and the hit rate decreased for visual targets preceded by a deviant tone (700 Hz) in comparison to the targets preceded by a standard tone (600 Hz). Moreover, Alho et al. (1997) observed an N1 attenuation in the ERP to visual stimuli preceded by deviant tones, which further indicated that attention was indeed involuntarily drawn away from the visual task by a preceding deviant tone eliciting an MMN and a P3a. Interestingly, Jääskeläinen, Alho, Escera, Winkler, et al. (1996), using the same paradigm as that employed by Escera et al. (1998), demonstrated that the detrimental effects of deviant and novel sounds on the RT and the accuracy in the visual forced-choice discrimination task were abolished by a small dose of ethanol, indicating that even small amounts of alcohol dramatically reduce involuntary attention to changes in the auditory environment. This might be one source of increased risk associated with drunken driving (Näätänen & Summala, 1976).

In conclusion, it was proposed before that when a deviant sound occurs, the first *specific* response to stimulus change is the difference signal indexed by the sensory-specific subcomponents of the MMN preconsciously generated in auditory cortex, which then activates some predominantly right-hemispheric, frontal structures associated with the control of the direction of attention. However, this frontal activation does not necessarily lead, as it further appears, to transitory attention switch to the eliciting sound change; this frontal activation could therefore be associated with Öhman's (1979, 1992) call for focal attention by preattentive, automatic processes. Further, if the call is answered, that is, a transitory attention switch occurs, the subject consciously perceiving the sound change, then the P3a generator is also activated and can therefore provide an index for the occurrence of an attention switch. It is possible, however, that, as already mentioned, the P3a amplitude is determined by, besides the strength of the MMN process (depending on the magnitude of stimulus change and on the recency of a similar stimulus change; Ritter, Deacon, Gomes, Javitt, & Vaughan, 1995; Sams, Alho, & Näätänen, 1983), also by a higher-level recognition of the deviant as the same as, or as different from, the previous deviants, or as familiar/unfamiliar in general. It was further proposed that the different ANS–OR indicators are triggered when the strength of the P3a-generator activation reaches certain preset individual levels needed for their release and, further, that novelty evaluation occurring as a consequence of the transitory attention switch might cause the occurrence of ANS responses even at very low levels of P3a activation. Finally, if the N2b process is also triggered, then a well-defined OR with its typical ANS indices can probably be observed.

At this point, it is important to make a distinction between novelty evaluation and significance evaluation following attention switch to a deviant stimulus. Novelty evaluation means the processing that determines how new or unfamiliar the present input is relative to the previous stimuli. There are two dimensions in novelty associated with stimulus change: the nature/magnitude of the change and the recency/frequency of similar changes in the past. Thus, the outcome of the novelty evaluation is affected, besides the type and magnitude of the change, also by when in the past, and how often, the present deviant stimulus occurred. It was proposed previously that novelty evaluation in these kinds of paradigms is based on automatic change detection performed by the MMN-generating brain process that causes transitory attention switch to the deviant stimulus, permitting this stimulus to enter higher memory systems (Näätänen, 1992). Significance evaluation in turn involves, according to the present hypothesis, semantic activation caused by the contact, as a result of attention switch, of the input with the semantic memory.

ATTENDED SOUNDS PRESENTED WITH SHORT ISIS

Figure 12.28 schematically illustrates the ERP components occurring when the subject is presented with auditory stimuli at short ISIs while being instructed to detect and to respond to occasional deviant stimuli (a typical signal case of OR studies but with short ISIs). The N1 and P2 amplitudes are then rather similar as, or somewhat larger than, in the passive condition (Näätänen, 1992). The MMN amplitude is usually unaffected by attention.

In contrast, the N2b (Renault & Lesévre, 1978, 1979; for a review, see Näätänen & Gaillard, 1983), a sharp negativity peaking at about 200 ms with a broad midline distribution (Näätänen et al., 1982; Sams et al., 1990), is usually elicited only in attend conditions. The N2b is, however, elicited, as already mentioned, also in passive conditions when widely deviant (Näätänen

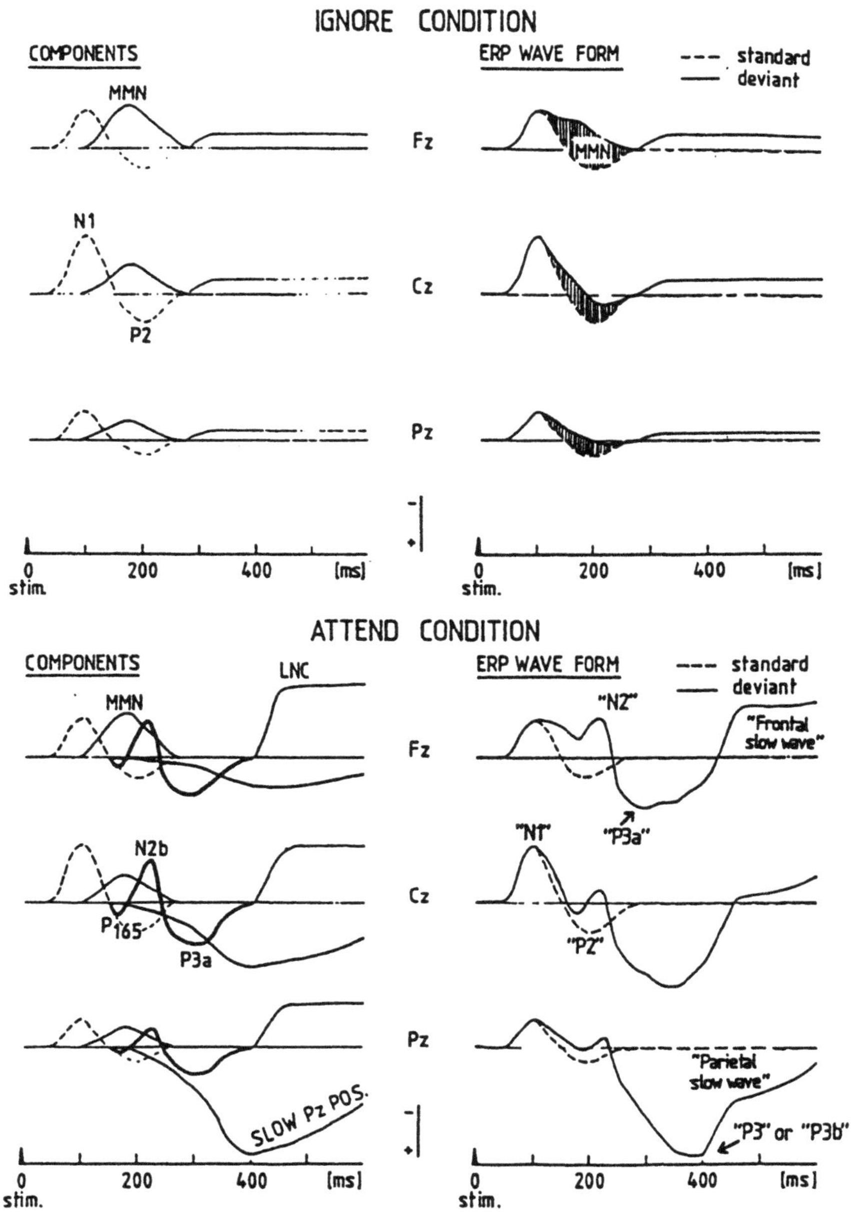

FIG. 12.28. A simplified schematic illustration of the frontal (Fz), vertex (Cz), and parietal (Pz) ERPs (right side) to standard (dashed line) and deviant (solid line) stimuli and the corresponding ERP components (left side) in the oddball paradigm. They are derived separately for the ignore (top) and attend (bottom) conditions. (Adapted from Näätänen, Sams, & Alho, 1986. Copyright © 1986 by Elsevier Science Publishers BV [Biomedical Division]. Reprinted with permission).

et al., 1982) or otherwise obtrusive stimuli (Lyytinen et al., 1992) are used. It has been proposed that the N2b reflects brain events associated with a transient arousal response and the OR (Loveless, 1983, 1986; Näätänen et al., 1982; Näätänen & Gaillard, 1983).

The N2b is almost always followed by the P3a. The N2b–P3a association is indeed very strong (Courchesne, Hillyard, & Galambos, 1975; Loveless, 1983, 1986; Näätänen et al., 1982; Renault & Lesévre, 1978, 1979; Snyder & Hillyard, 1976; Squires, Donchin, Herning, & McCarthy, 1977; Squires, Squires, & Hillyard, 1975); therefore, the two have often been referred to as the N2–P3a or N2b–P3a wave complex. The N2b can, however, occur also without the P3a (Knight, 1990; Ritter, Paavilainen, Lavikainen, Reinikainen, & Näätänen, 1992). The P3a, in turn, is usually seen without a preceding N2b in response to deviant stimuli in *Ignore* conditions (Sams, Paavilainen, et al., 1985a; for a review, see Näätänen, 1992).

Figure 12.29 shows ERPs to slightly deviant stimuli in Sams, Paavilainen, et al. (1985) discrimination condition. (The corresponding reading-condition data were illustrated in Fig. 12.13). The large negative peak after the N1 in response to the deviant stimuli in this figure is composed mainly of the N2b component. The N2b is better seen in Fig. 12.30 displaying the difference waves obtained by subtracting standard-stimulus ERPs from those to detected deviants. The remaining sharp negativity provides quite a good estimate for the sum of the N2b and MMN components, for the P2 component is cancelled in this subtraction. The early portion of the negativity is mainly due to the MMN component, the late portion principally to the N2b component.

In Fig. 12.31, ERPs to deviants in the *Ignore* condition were subtracted from those to detected deviants of the discrimination condition. Because the MMN component is totally, or almost totally, cancelled in this subtraction, the remaining sharp negative peak gives quite a reliable estimate of the N2b component. It is seen that the N2b latency becomes systematically shorter as the stimulus difference is increased. The same is true with regard to the subsequent, posteriorly largest, late positivity.

The most conspicuous aspect of the deviant-stimulus ERP under the *Attend* condition is the late parietal positivity, as shown in Figs. 12.29, 12.30, and 12.31, which also peaks earlier when the magnitude of deviation is increased. This slow parietal process constitutes a major component of the P3 wave, the most intensely studied aspect of the ERP (Sutton, Braren, Zubin, & John, 1965; for reviews, see Donchin & Coles, 1988; Johnson, 1988; Pritchard, 1981; Roth, 1983; Ruchkin & Sutton, 1983; Verleger, 1988). In the present context, the slow parietal positive component probably is the first ERP component that reflects not only the detection of stimulus deviation but also the recognition of the stimulus as a target, that is, stimulus significance. This is suggested by the results of oddball studies with two different

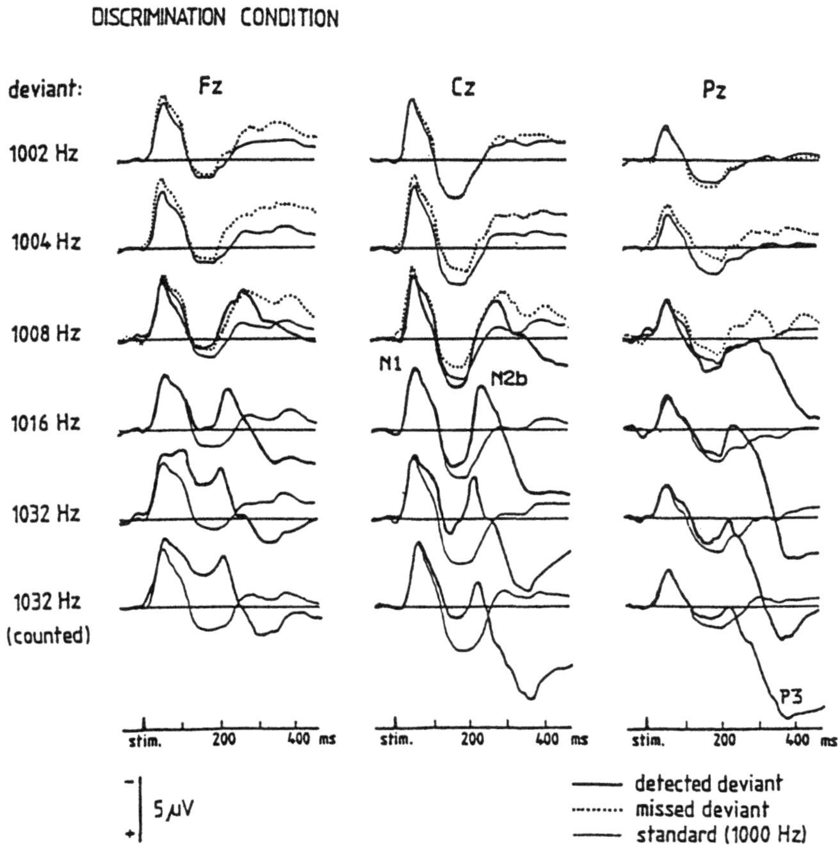

FIG. 12.29. Frontal (Fz), vertex (Cz), and parietal (Pz) grand-average ERPs to detected deviants (thick line), missed deviants (dotted line), and correctly rejected standards (thin line) in a discrimination condition when the standard stimulus was 1000 Hz and the deviant stimulus, in separate blocks, 1002 to 1032 Hz. The subject was instructed to press a button on discovering a deviant stimulus, except when the deviant stimuli were to be counted (bottom row). (From Sams, Paavilainen, Alho, & Näätänen, 1985. Copyright © 1985 by Elsevier Science Publishers, Ireland. Reprinted with permission).

deviant stimuli, one designated as a target and the other as a nontarget, a paradigm proposed by Näätänen (1975). In one of these studies, Courchesne, Courchesne, and Hillyard (1978), using visual stimuli, found a larger late positivity to the target than to an equally rare and equally widely deviant nontarget deviant. Corroborating results were provided by Courchesne, Hillyard, and Courchesne's (1977) visual study and Roth, Ford, and Kopell's (1978) auditory study. In contrast, Näätänen et al. (1982), presenting their equivalent target and nontarget deviants at a considerably smaller probability (2% each), found no significant difference in the slow parietal posi-

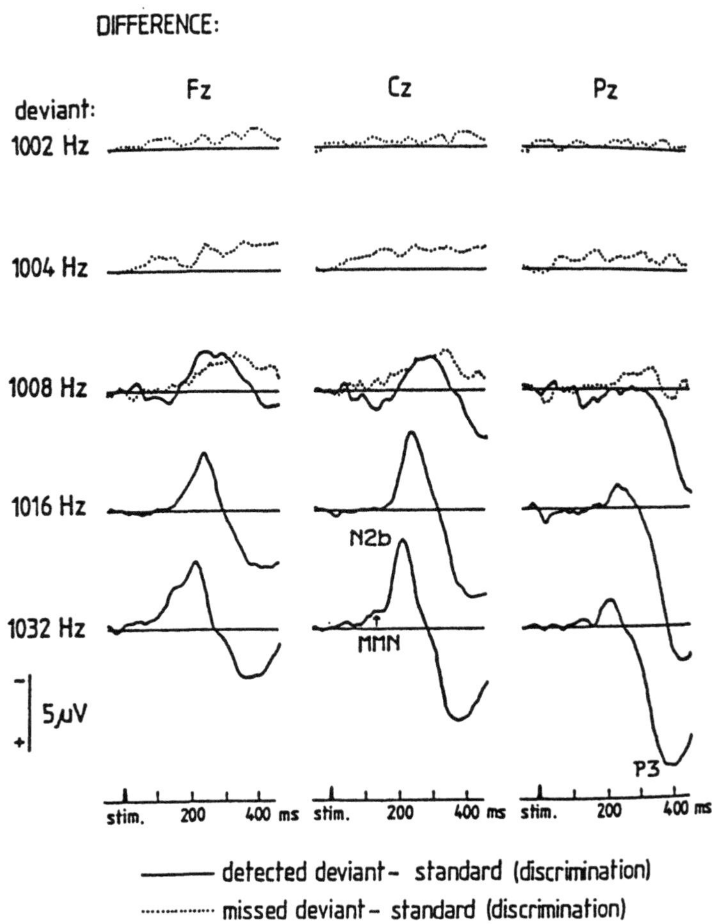

FIG. 12.30. Frontal (Fz), vertex (Cz), and parietal (Pz) grand-average difference waves obtained by subtracting ERPs to the correctly rejected standards from those to detected deviants (continuous line) and missed deviants (dotted line) in the discrimination condition when the standard stimulus was 1000 Hz and the deviant stimulus, in separate blocks, 1002 to 1032 Hz. The subject was instructed to press a button on discovery of a deviant stimulus. (The same data as those presented in Fig. 12.29). (From Sams, Paavilainen, Alho, & Näätänen, 1985. Copyright © 1985 by Elsevier Science Publishers, Ireland. Reprinted with permission).

tivity elicited by the two deviants. The authors suggested that the very low probabilities used "may have resulted in all deviants eliciting 'significance responses' usually elicited only by targets, leaving no room for any specific target effect beyond the effect of stimulus deviance." This is tantamount to saying that highly infrequent environmental changes are biologically significant (Näätänen et al., 1982, p. 84; Sutton, 1979).

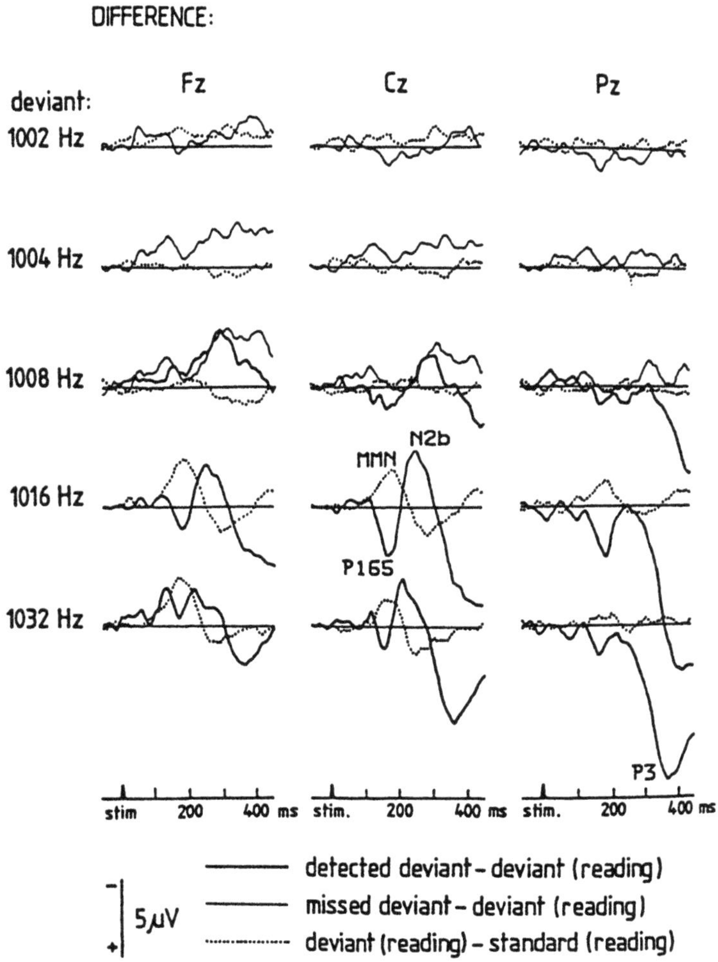

FIG. 12.31. Frontal (Fz), vertex (Cz), and parietal (Pz) grand-average difference waves obtained by subtracting (1) ERPs to reading-condition deviants from those to detected deviants in the discrimination condition (thick line), (2) ERPs to reading-condition deviants from those to missed deviants in the discrimination condition (thin line), and (3) ERPs to standards from those to deviants (dotted line) in the reading condition. The standard stimulus was 1000 Hz and the deviant stimuli, in separate blocks, 1002 to 1032 Hz. The subject was instructed to press a button on discovery of a deviant stimulus. The same data as in Figs. 12.29 and 12.30. (Unpublished figure from Sams, Paavilainen, Alho, & Näätänen, 1985).

Sams, Paavilainen, et al. (1985) averaged ERPs elicited by deviant stimuli at the discrimination threshold (deviants at 1008 Hz) separately for the trials at which the deviant stimulus was and was not discriminated. Figures 12.29, 12.30, and 12.31 show that (a) the large, late parietal positivity was elicited by the discriminated 1008-Hz deviants only, the trace for the nondiscriminated targets remaining negative throughout the averaging epoch, and, further, that (b) the process generating this (statistically significant) negativity, possibly the N2b, is initiated at the same time by the discriminated and nondiscriminated deviants, but it lasts considerably longer for the nondiscriminated deviants, the process apparently failing to reach the threshold for conscious discrimination (see also Loveless, 1986). A similar, though nonsignificant, long-duration shift is also seen for the clearly subliminal, 1004-Hz deviants.

Thus, it appears that if the process generating the possible N2b negativity succeeded in triggering the slow parietal positivity, then a conscious discrimination of stimulus deviation probably occurred on this trial, whereas if no positivity ensued, then the preconscious discrimination process failed to result in conscious discrimination. Whether the N2b process is vigorous enough might in turn be determined by (a) the strength of the MMN-generating process preceding it, and (b) the strength of the temporary facilitatory coupling between the MMN and N2b generators. With increasing facilitation, the MMN generator succeeds, presumably, more easily in triggering the N2b process. This temporary facilitatory connection might constitute the central element in the neurophysiological basis of an attentive set to discriminate physical stimulus changes in the oddball task (Näätänen, 1992).

Näätänen (1992) provided a summary of the behavior of these ERP components in the oddball situation as follows:

> The MMN and P3a are related to physical stimulus deviation but not to stimulus significance, for instance, whether the stimulus is a target or not. For the MMN (but probably not for the P3a; Ritter et al., 1992), this stimulus deviation can also be a repetition of the previous stimulus in a regularly alternating pattern, that is, a repetition that forms a deviation against the temporal patterning of stimulation (Nordby et al., 1988; Tervaniemi et al., 1994). Further, the MMN is usually elicited independently of attention, whereas the P3a elicitation often requires at least a minimal amount of attention.
>
> The N2b is usually elicited by a physical stimulus deviation but may also be elicited by infrequent stimulus repetition in an attended stimulus sequence (Näätänen, 1986b; Ritter et al., 1992; see also the data of Duncan-Johnson & Donchin, 1982). (In unattended input sequences, only wide deviations may elicit an N2b; Näätänen et al., 1982). The N2b is not related to stimulus significance, however. This was shown by the result that, given an attentive set, the N2b is elicited by both target and nontarget deviants in oddball situations

(Alho, Lavikainen, Reinikainen, Sams, & Näätänen, 1990; Näätänen et al., 1982; Nordby et al., 1988).

The slow parietal positive component is specifically related to stimulus significance, for it responds differentially to target and nontarget deviants, at least when they are not very infrequent (Näätänen, Simpson, & Loveless, 1982). Furthermore, this positivity is elicited by the target irrespective of whether it is a stimulus deviation or repetition (Ritter et al., 1992; Sams et al., 1983, 1984). In addition, this component probably cannot be elicited in the absence of attention.

The slow frontal negative component seems to be related to both stimulus change and significance (McCallum, Barrett, & Pocock, 1989; Näätänen et al., 1982; Sams et al., 1983, 1984).

It appears that the complex sequence of endogenous components, starting with the N2b and the early phase of the slow parietal positivity (Näätänen, 1975; Sams, Paavilainen, et al., 1985), is triggered by the cerebral process generating the MMN. Consistent with this, Novak, Ritter, Vaughan, and Wiznitzer (1990) found that this late sequence of endogenous components, as well as the release of the motor response in an RT task, were time-locked to the MMN generator process. For more recent corroborating results, see Tiitinen et al. (1994). Previously, Renault and Lesévre (1979) found that the duration of their ramp-like negativity (N2a), elicited by stimulus omission in a sequence of regularly spaced visual stimuli, determined the latencies of the subsequent components. This N2a cannot, however, be regarded as a strict equivalent for the auditory MMN (see Czigler & Csibra, 1990; Näätänen & Gaillard, 1983).

Further converging evidence for the MMN generator process initiating the sequence of brain processes leading to the conscious discrimination of stimulus deviation was provided by Lang et al. (1990), who found that behavioral pitch discrimination between two sequentially presented tones correlated with the sensitivity of the mechanism generating MMN to frequency change in passive oddball conditions.

In conclusion, the MMN generator process seems to form the first, preconscious step in discriminating stimulus deviation also in *Attend* conditions. This process initiates the chain of further cerebral processes generating the post-MMN endogenous ERP components that lead to conscious discrimination of stimulus deviation. The N2b process has, apparently, to exceed some threshold; otherwise, the endogenous sequence is prematurely terminated and no conscious discrimination occurs (Näätänen, 1992).

Consequently, as already suggested, voluntary attention in an oddball task might be characterized as "internal monitoring" of the possible occurrence of the MMN process, that is, as a temporary functional link between the automatic preconscious change-detection mechanism and the limited-capacity system (Näätänen et al., 1982). The presence of this coupling would be reflected by the attention-induced facilitation of the functional connection between the MMN mechanism and further cerebral discriminatory processes, so that even a very weak MMN process would be sufficient to trigger these further processes. This temporary facilitatory link is also reflected by the result mentioned above that those later processes, as well as the motor response, seem to be time-locked to the MMN generator process (Novak et al., 1990; Tiitinen et al., 1994). The earliest of the further discriminatory processes triggered by the MMN generator probably mediate, according to Näätänen (1992), between the preconscious discrimination of stimulus deviation by the MMN mechanism and the conscious discrimination of this deviation by the limited-capacity system. The critical borderline between the preconscious and conscious processes in discriminating stimulus deviation under the attentive set might lie in the temporarily facilitated connection between the N2b generator process and the generators of the subsequent positivities (cf. Sams, Paavilainen, et al., 1985).

It is well-established that targets of an attended stimulus sequence cause intense OR types of changes. In this case, the closest ERP correlates of the OR might be the N2b–P3a and the slow parietal positivity, perhaps also the slow frontal negativity. It appears that the N2b–P3a is primarily related to stimulus deviation, whereas the slower waves reflect stimulus significance also. To determine the relation of these ERP measures to the ANS indices of the OR, it is important to study their covariation in a paradigm that enables one to determine whether the responses are primarily related to stimulus deviation or significance. This could be accomplished by using two equivalent deviants, designating one deviant as a target and the other deviant as a nontarget, as already mentioned. If the response in question is similarly elicited by both deviants, then it is related to stimulus deviation under these circumstances, whereas if this response is clearly larger to the target than to the nontarget deviant, then significance evaluation affects the response.

This paradigm was employed by Lyytinen (unpublished data) who used two different deviant stimuli in the same sequence of tones presented at constant 750-ms ISIs. The standard tone was 1000 Hz, and one of the deviants was 1030 Hz and served as the target. The other deviant, always a nontarget one, was a rise-time deviant, one rising to full intensity (74 dB) in 2 ms, whereas the rise time of the standard and the target was 24 ms.

It was found that the SCR and the HR responses were almost exclusively confined to the target deviants (see Fig. 12.32). In contrast, the N2b–P3a to nontarget (rise-time) deviants was much larger than that to target (frequency) deviants, thus suggesting a dissociation between this ERP wave complex and the OR, as indexed by ANS measures. However, a later positivity, one peaking at about 400 ms (Fig. 12.32), was visible only in response to target deviants, thus suggesting a relationship with the OR. Further support for this relationship is provided in Fig. 12.33 where ERPs to targets are

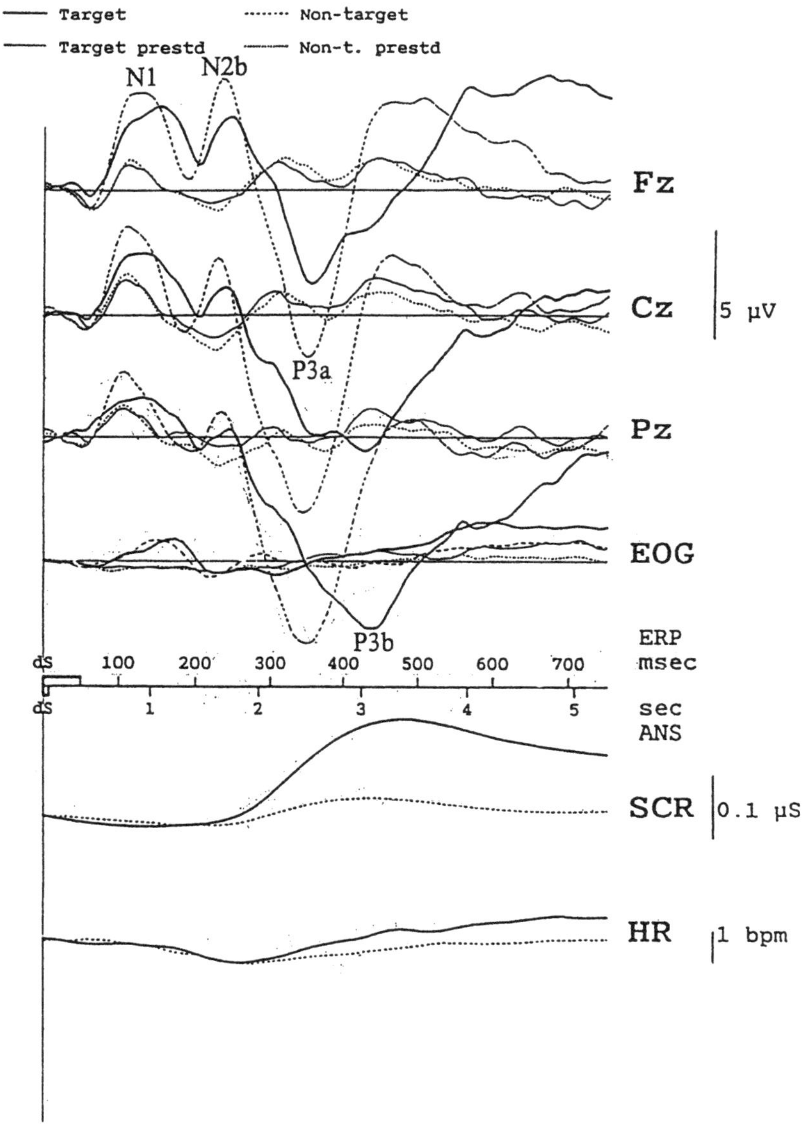

FIG. 12.32. *Top:* ERPs at Fz, Cz, and Pz and the EOG to targets, the standards preceding the targets (target prestd), to the nontarget deviants (non-target, shorter rise-time), and to the standards preceding the nontarget deviants (nont. prestd). *Bottom:* SCR and HR responses to targets and nontarget deviants. (Lyytinen, unpublished data).

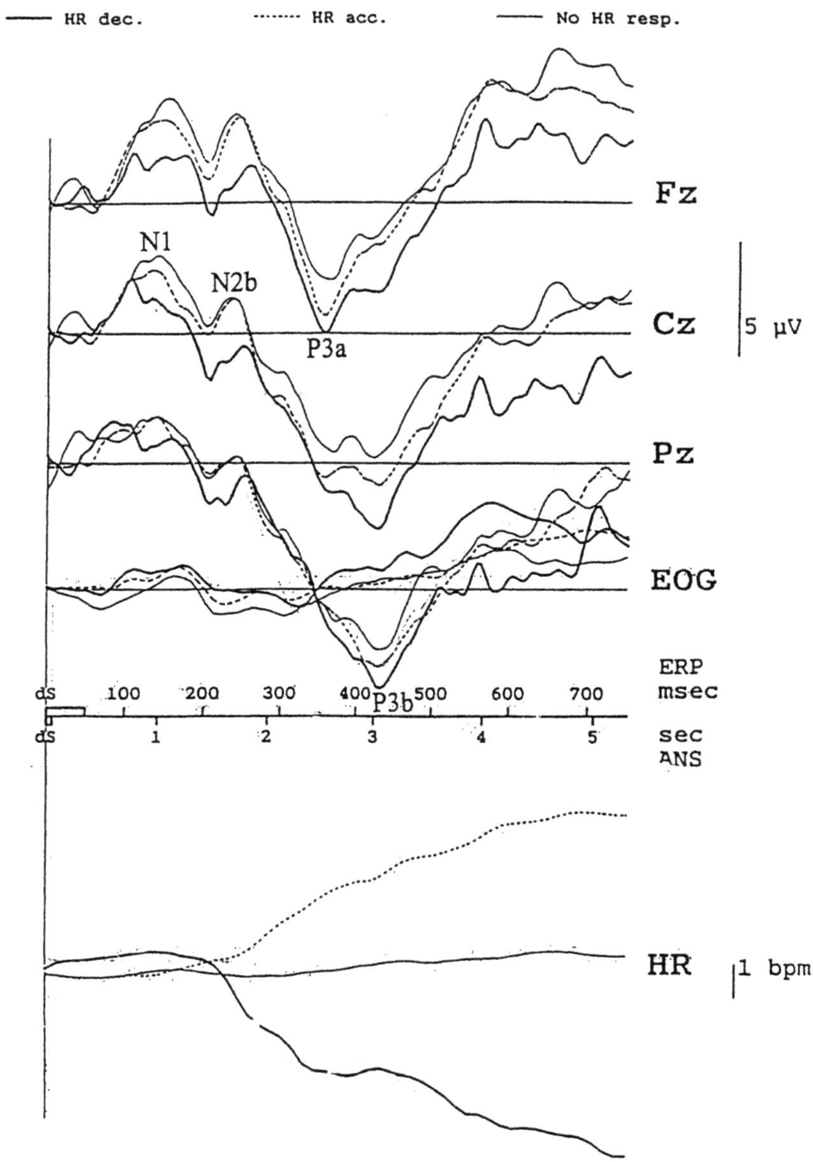

FIG. 12.33. ERPs at Fz, Cz, and Pz and the EOG to targets classified according to whether targets elicited HR acceleration (HR acc.), HR deceleration (HR dec.), or no HR response (no HR resp.) (bottom). (Lyytinen, unpublished data).

presented separately for HR deceleration, HR acceleration, and no-HR response trials. It can be seen that when the target caused HR deceleration (a well-established OR index), the late positivity (P3b) was larger than when the target caused either HR acceleration or no HR response. Similarly, when the target caused a SCR, then the slow positivity seen in Fig. 12.34 was considerably larger than when no SCR was elicited. This positivity, however, was more of the P3a than P3b type, judging from its somewhat shorter peak latency and more widespread midline distribution than those of the late positivity to targets (Fig. 12.32). In fact, a separate P3b can be observed in the Cz and Pz leads in Fig. 12.34.

Additional evidence dissociating the N2b–P3a from the ANS–OR was provided by ERP responses to nontarget deviants classified according to the occurrence and direction of the HR response (Fig. 12.35). It can be seen that the N2b–P3 was quite similar for the HR deceleration, HR acceleration, and no-HR response trials (though the P3 amplitude was somewhat smaller for no-HR response than for HR-response trials).

Further still, ERPs to nontarget deviants classified according to whether an SCR occurred at the trial or not disclosed only a small difference, with the N2b–P3 for the SCR trials being only slightly larger than that for the no-SCR trials (Fig. 12.36). In the same vein, although both the N2b–P3 and the ANS responses attenuated in amplitude from the first half of the session to the second half, this effect was proportionally much more dramatic for the ANS measures that were practically extinguished during the second half of the session in which an N2b–P3 of considerable size was still elicited (Fig. 12.37). In contrast, for the ANS responses to the target, habituation was much slower and proportionally comparable to the attenuation of the P3a type of positivity to these targets (Fig. 12.38).

In a subsequent study of Lyytinen (unpublished data), the rise-time of the standards was 20 ms. There were two deviants in the block, one with a fast rise-time (2 ms) and the other with a slow rise-time (40 ms). Otherwise, all three stimuli, with a duration of 400 ms, were identical. In different blocks, the subject was instructed to count either the fast or slow rise-time deviants.

When the deviant stimulus was a nontarget, it elicited ANS responses only when it was the fast rise-time deviant (Fig. 12.39). This deviant also elicited a large N2b–P3a complex, one much larger and earlier than that for the slow rise-time deviant (but no slow, late positivity, cf. Fig. 12.39). In order for the slow rise-time deviant to elicit well-defined ANS responses, it had to be made as the target (Fig. 12.40). Then, the ERP was also affected, the most conspicuous change being the emergence of the large, late positivity with a parietal maximum. This late positivity was much larger in amplitude at trials at which an SCR was elicited than when it was not elicited (Fig. 12.41).

Making the fast rise-time deviant as the target (Fig. 12.42) enhanced the ANS responses also to this stimulus but to a considerably smaller extent

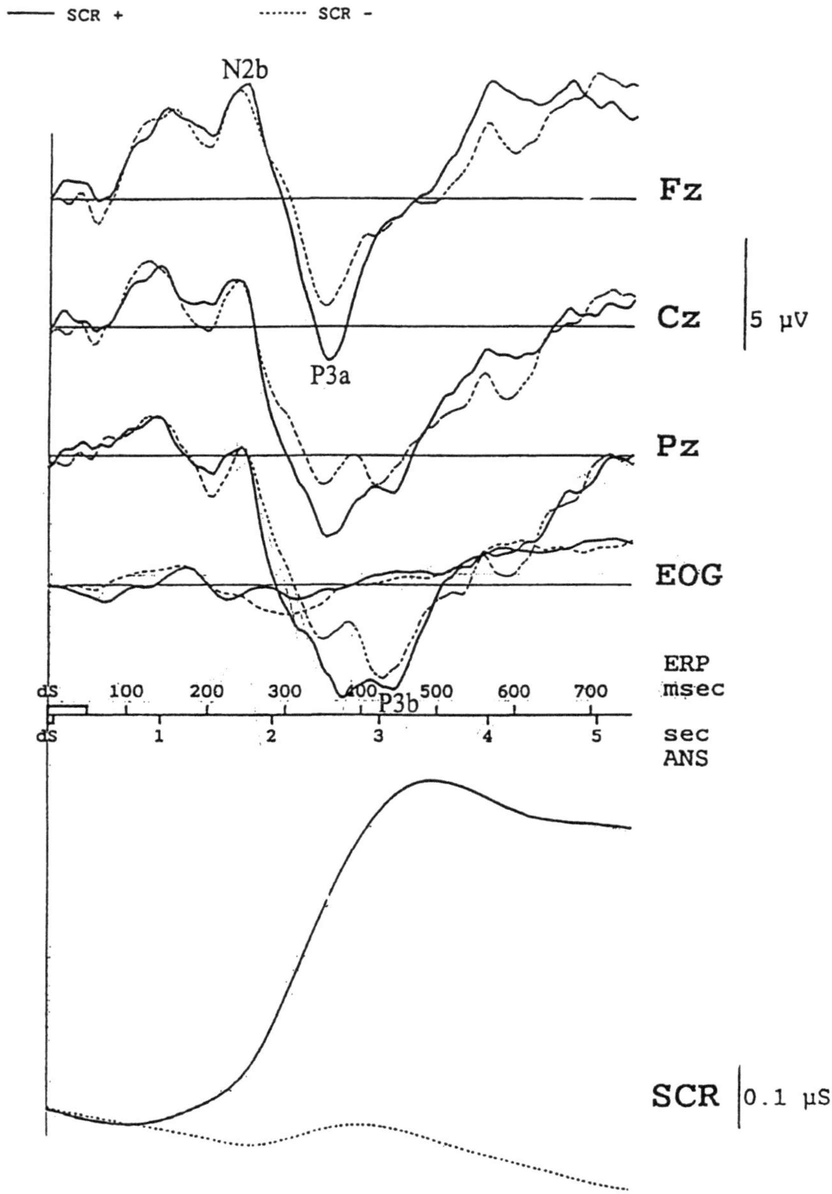

FIG. 12.34. ERPs at Fz, Cz, and Pz and the EOG to targets classified according to whether or not targets elicited a SCR (SCR+ and SCR−, respectively) (bottom). (Lyytinen, unpublished data).

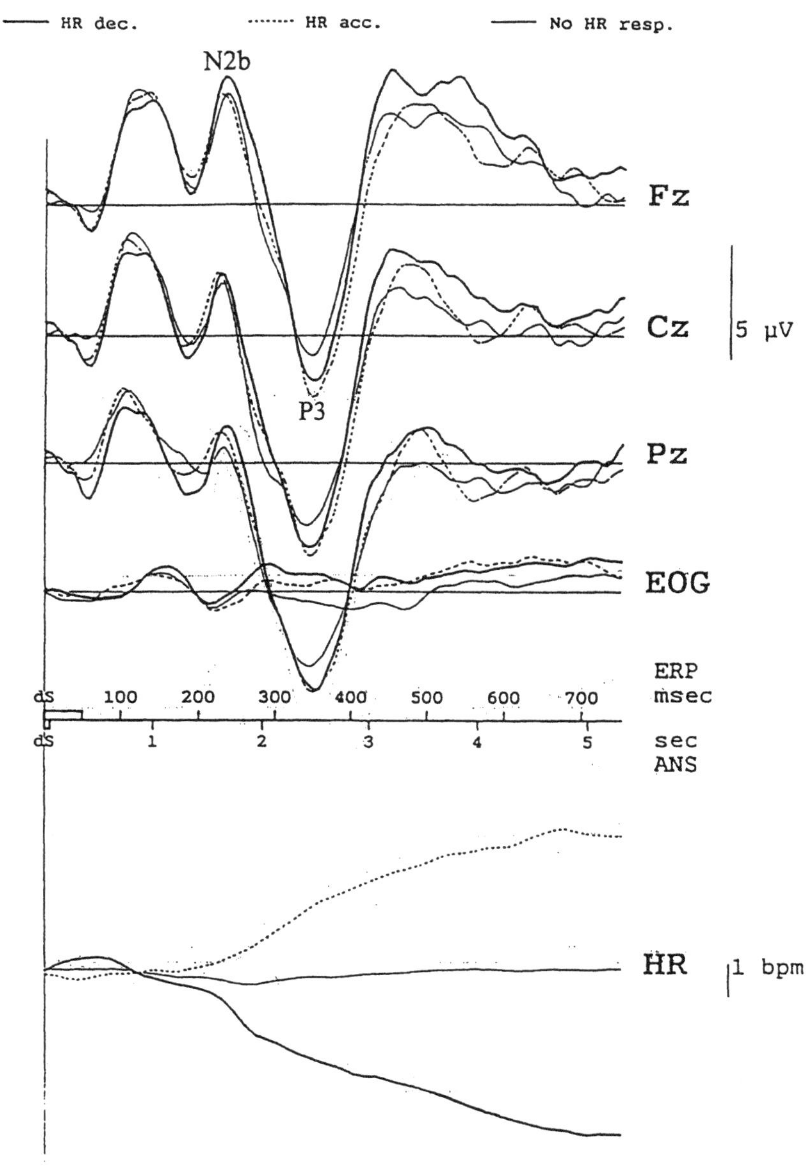

FIG. 12.35. ERPs at Fz, Cz, and Pz and the EOG to nontarget deviants classified according to whether these stimuli elicited HR acceleration (HR acc.), HR deceleration (HR dec.), or no HR response (no HR resp.) (bottom). (Lyytinen, unpublished data).

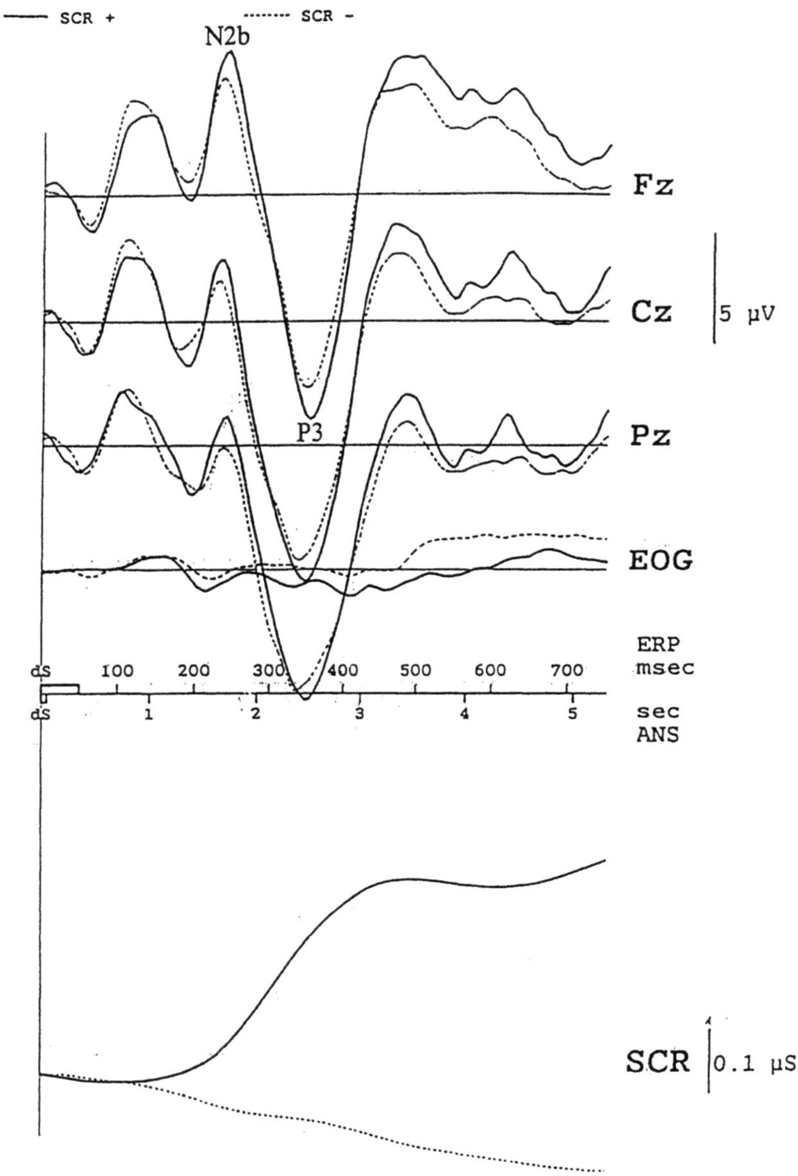

FIG. 12.36. ERPs at Fz, Cz, and Pz, and the EOG to nontarget deviants classified according to whether or not they elicited a SCR (SCR+ and SCR–, respectively) (bottom). (Lyytinen, unpublished data).

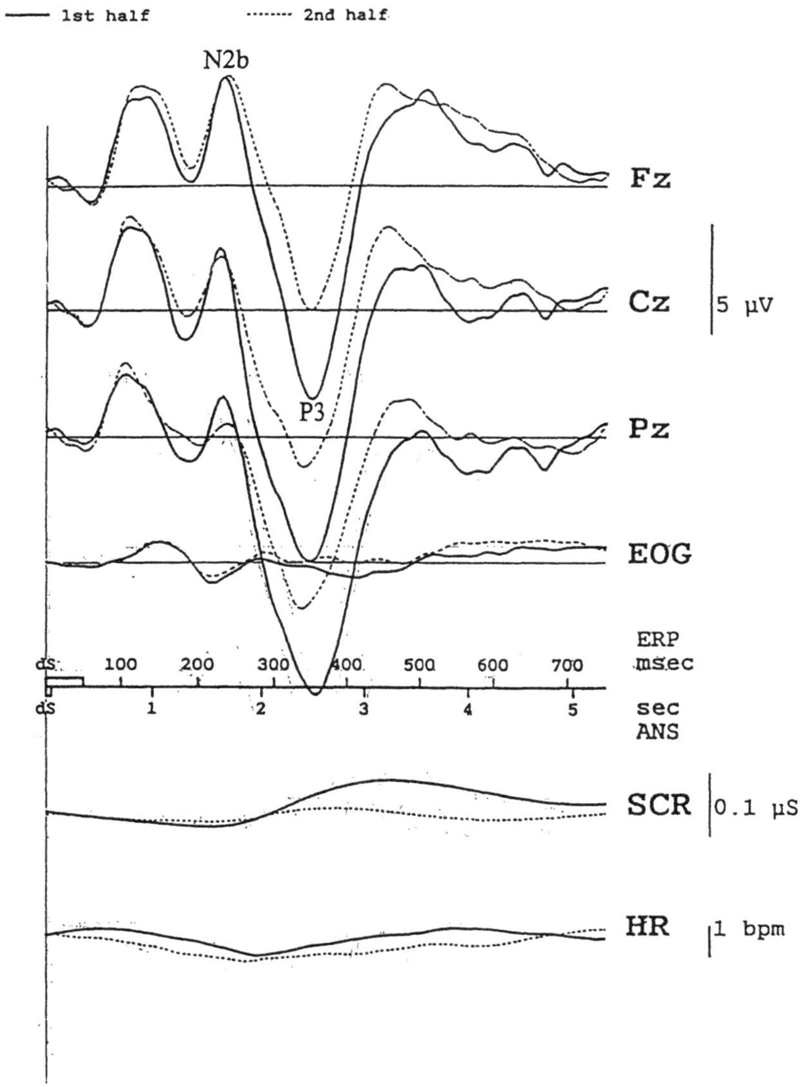

FIG. 12.37. ERPs at Fz, Cz, and Pz, and the EOG, SCR, and HR responses to *nontarget* deviants separately for the first and the second half of the session (Lyytinen, unpublished data).

than it enhanced these responses to the slow rise-time deviant (Fig. 12.40). Also the P3 amplitude was enhanced when the fast rise-time deviant was the target, this effect being strongest at the parietal electrode. This positivity was followed by a relatively sharp frontal negativity with a duration of about 200 ms. Also, this ERP wave was quite remarkably enhanced in amplitude by designating the fast rise-time deviant as the target.

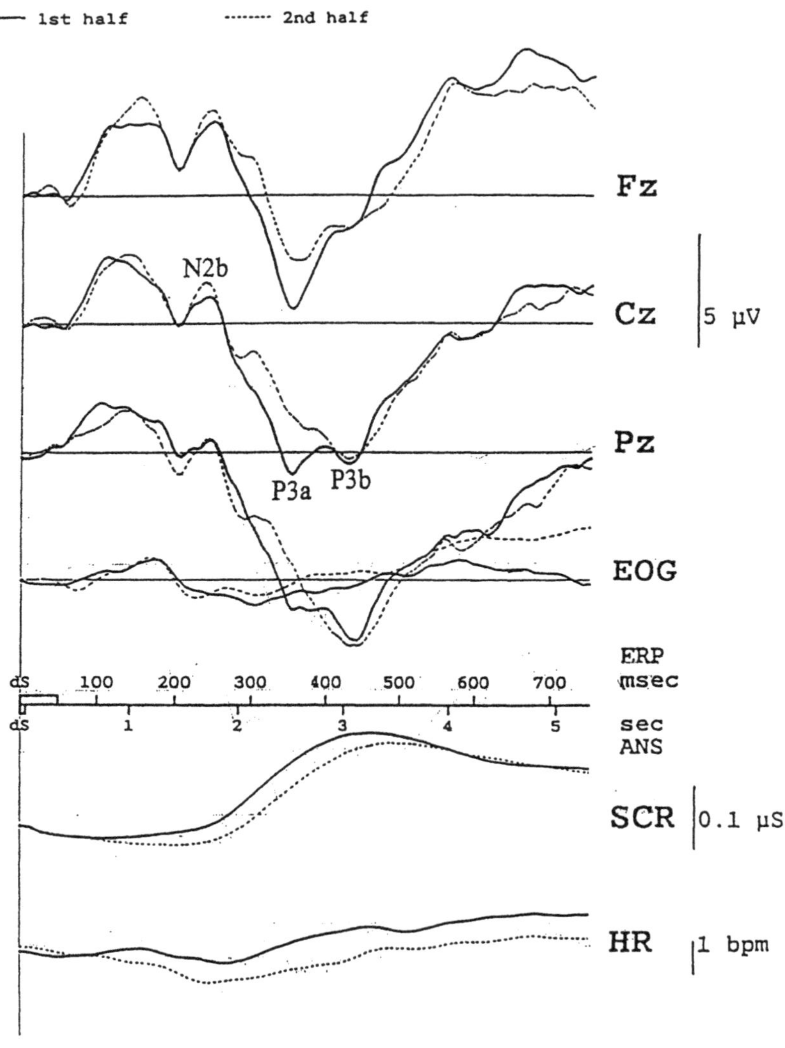

FIG. 12.38. ERPs at Fz, Cz, and Pz, and the EOG, SCR, and HR responses to *targets* separately for the first and the second half of the session (Lyytinen, unpublished data).

Figure 12.43 compares the responses to the two deviants when they were targets. A clear dissociation between the ANS and ERP responses can be seen in that whereas the ANS responses are quite similar to the two deviants, the ERPs are very different. For the fast rise-time deviant, the N2b–P3 is much larger in amplitude and earlier in latency than that for the slow rise-time deviant. These data thus provide a clear dissociation between the N2b–P3 and

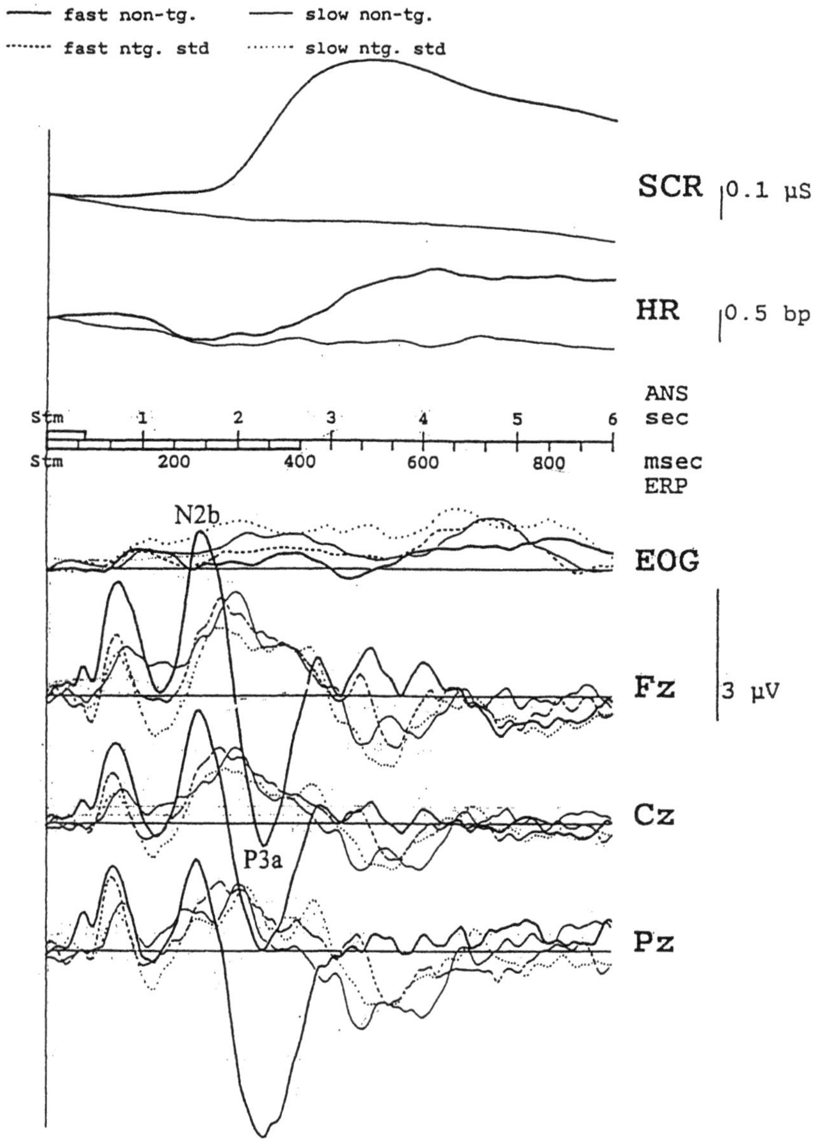

FIG. 12.39. SCR, HR response, EOG, and ERPs at Fz, Cz, and Pz for the fast rise-time nontarget deviant ("fast nontg."), for the preceding standard (fast ntg. std), for the slow rise-time nontarget deviant (slow nontg.), and for the preceding standard (slow ntg. std). (Lyytinen, unpublished data).

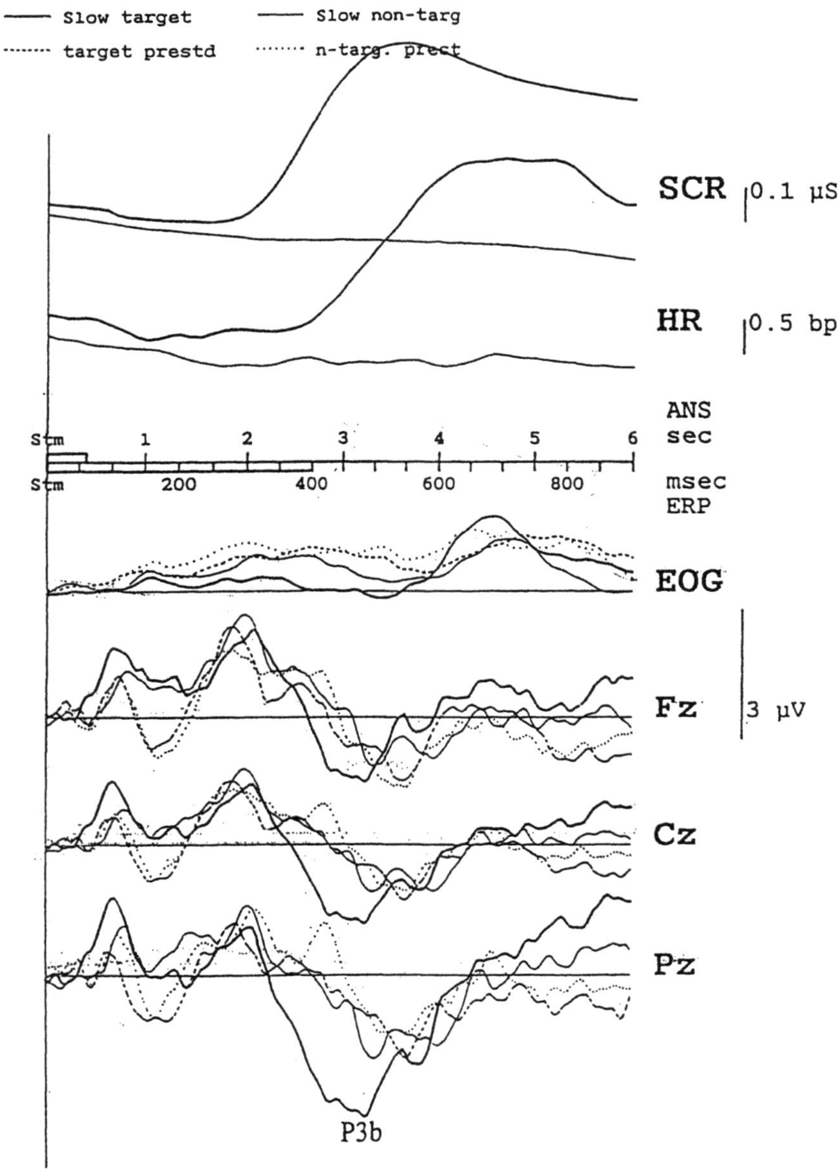

FIG. 12.40. SCR, HR response, EOG, and ERPs at Fz, Cz, and Pz for the slow rise-time target (slow target), for the preceding standard (target prestd), for the slow rise-time nontarget deviant ("slow nontarg"), and for the preceding standard (n-targ prest.). (Lyytinen, unpublished data).

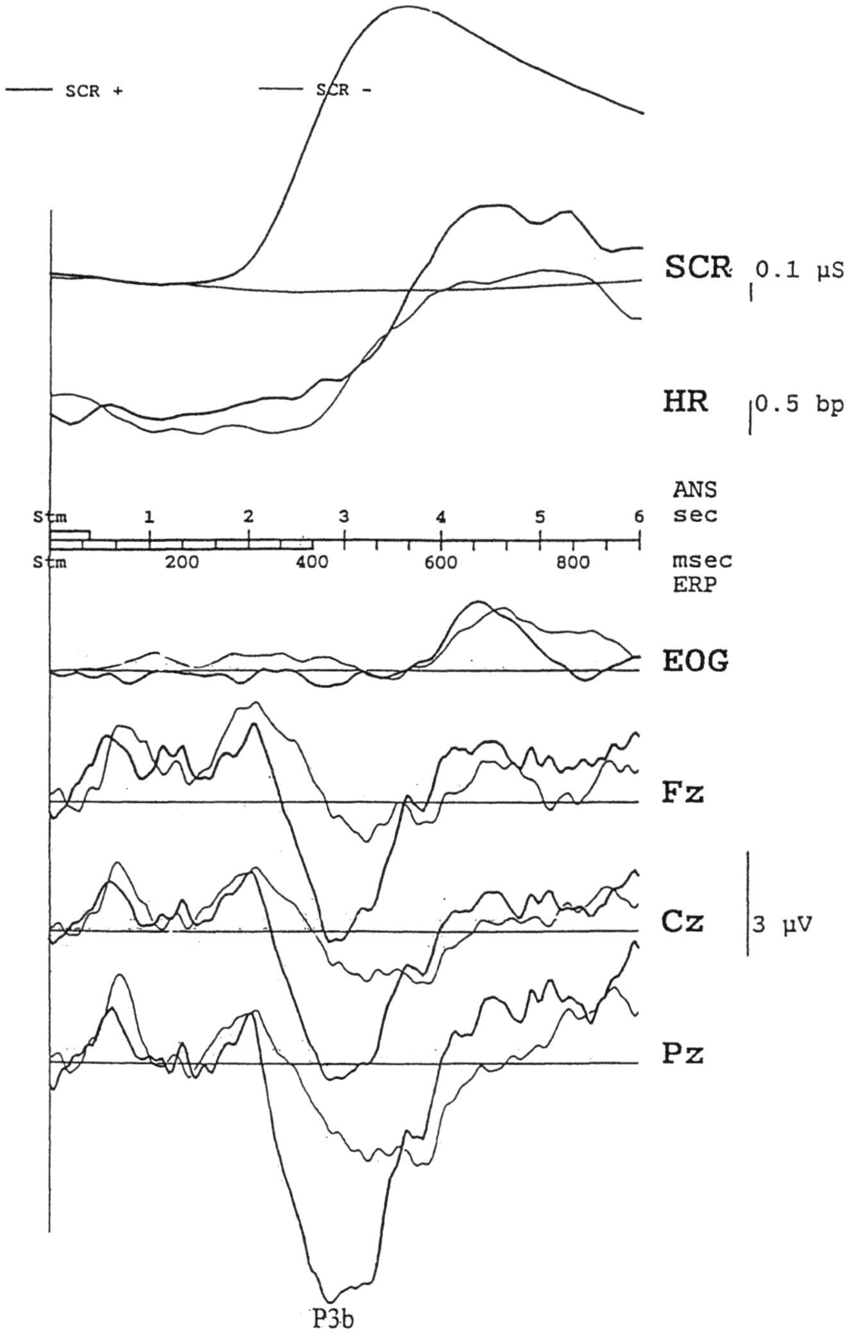

FIG. 12.41. SCR, HR response, EOG, and ERP at Fz, Cz, and Pz to the slow rise-time targets classified according to whether these targets elicited an SCR or not (SCR+ and SCR−, repectively). (Lyytinen, unpublished data).

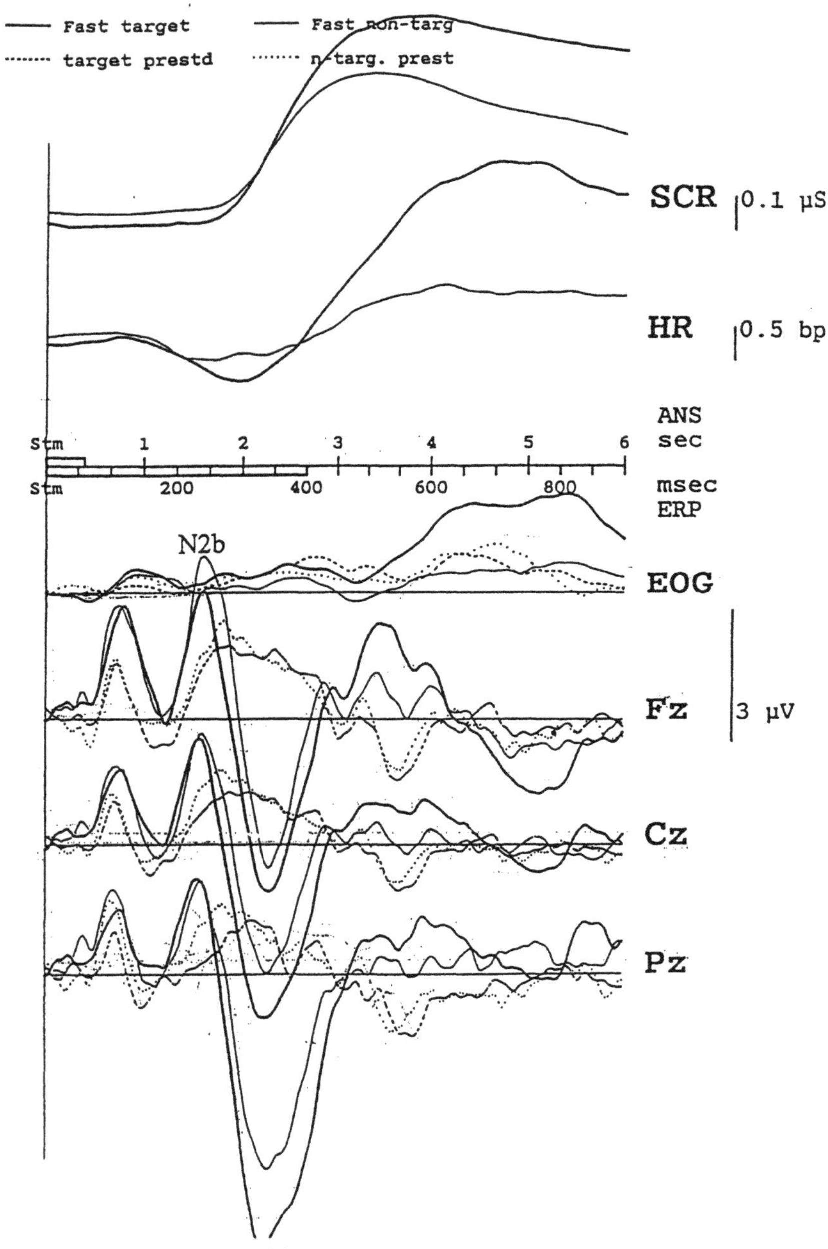

FIG. 12.42. SCR, HR response, EOG, and ERP at Fz, Cz, and Pz to the fast rise-time targets (fast target), to the preceding standards (target prestd), fast non-target deviants (fast non-targ), and to the preceding standards (n-targ. prest). (Lyytinen, unpublished data).

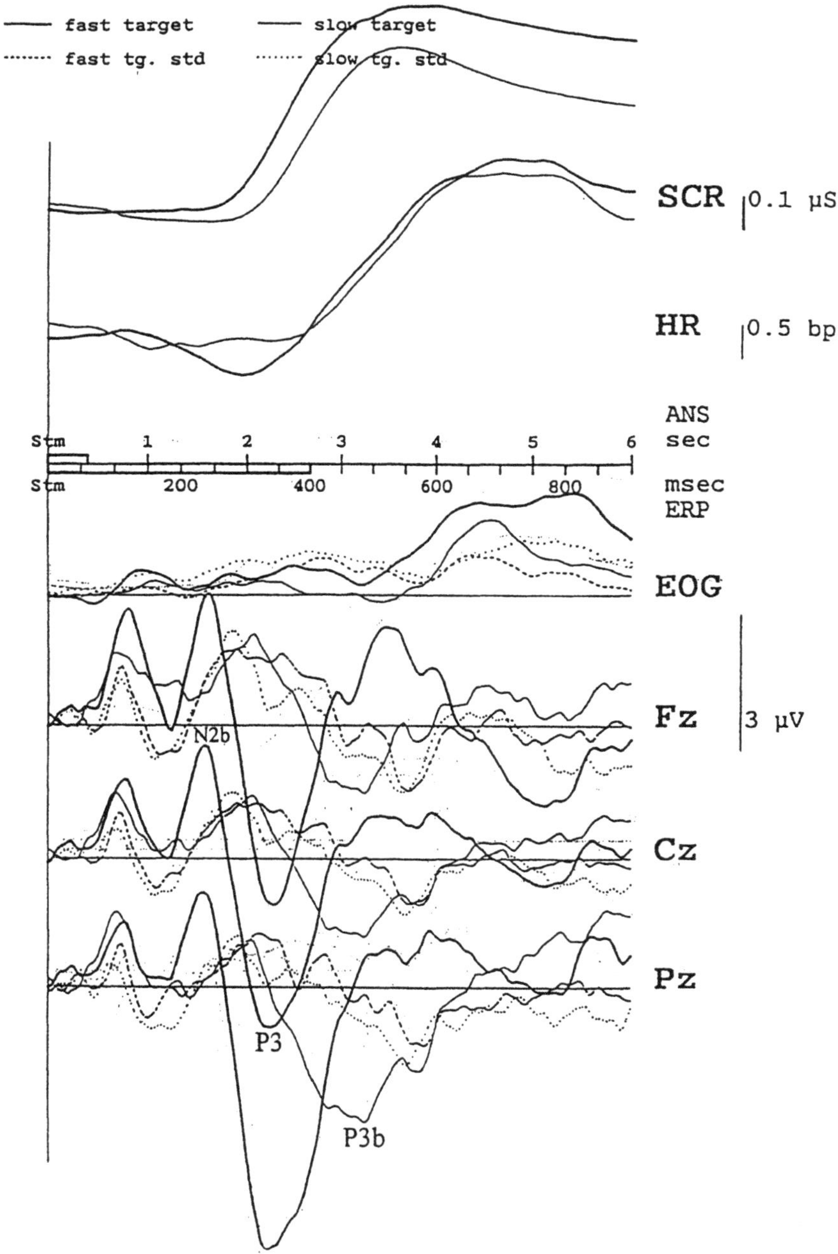

FIG. 12.43. SCR, HR response, EOG, and ERP at Fz, Cz, and Pz to fast rise-time targets (fast target), to the preceding standards (fast tg. std), to slow rise-time targets (slow target), and to the preceding standards (slow tg. std). (Lyytinen, unpublished data).

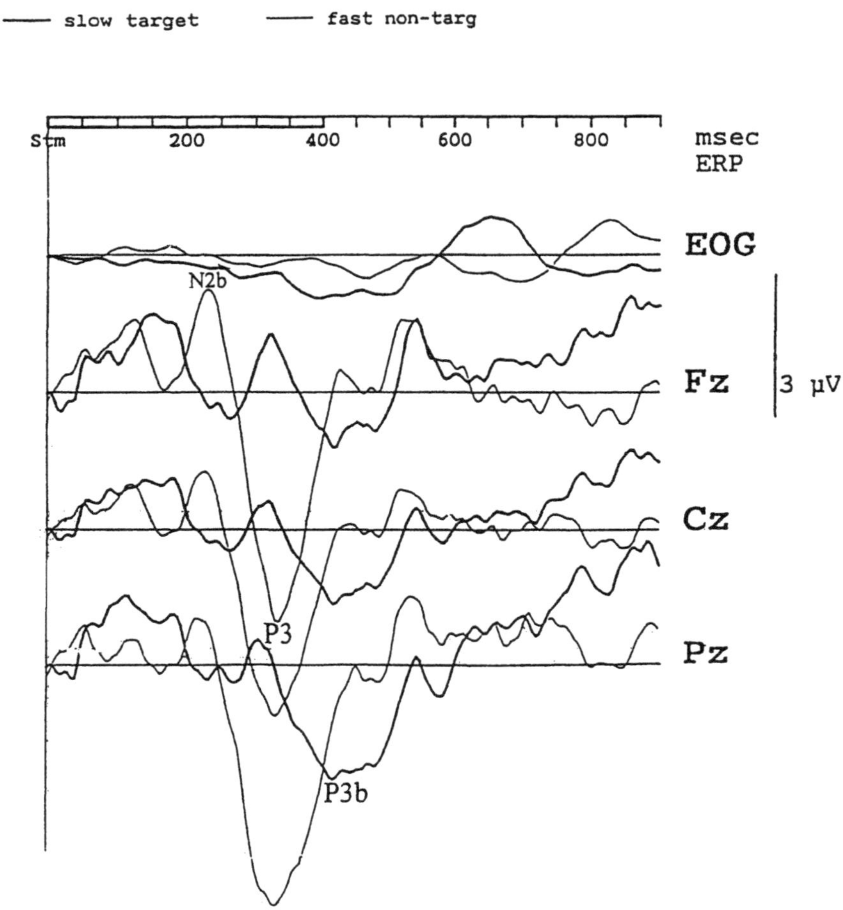

FIG. 12.44. Deviant-standard difference waves for the EOG, Fz, Cz, and Pz electrodes separately for slow rise-time targets (slow target) and fast rise-time nontarget deviants (fast nontarg.). (Lyytinen, unpublished data).

ANS responses, indicating that the cerebral processes involved in the generation of this wave complex do not, at least not to any major degree, determine the strength of the ANS responses. So, for these ERP amplitudes, the physical stimulus features (the eliciting stimulus and its difference from the previous ones) play a crucial role, whereas stimulus significance (target vs. nontarget) is the most important determinant of the ANS responses.

These conclusions are further illustrated in Fig. 12.44 showing deviant-standard difference waves when the slow rise-time deviant was the target and the fast rise-time deviant was the nontarget deviant. It can be seen that the N2b–P3 amplitude is much larger and earlier for the nontarget than target deviant, highlighting physical stimulus deviation as its main determinant. Interestingly, the target-deviant ERP shows a late, very slow negativity with a broad midline distribution, which cannot be seen in the ERP elicited by the nontarget deviant.

In summary, when the subject is instructed to attend to a sound sequence presented with short ISIs typical to ERP studies, target deviants requiring some response (button press, counting, etc.) elicit in a large proportion of trials ANS responses commonly regarded as indices of an OR such as a SCR or a HR response. These responses seem to be primarily related to stimulus significance rather than deviation per se as they are considerably larger or more frequent in *Attend* (Lyytinen, unpublished data) than in *Ignore* conditions (Lyytinen et al., 1992). Further converging evidence was provided by the result (Lyytinen, unpublished data) that the one of the two deviants designated as the target in these attention conditions elicited considerably larger/more frequent ANS responses than did the nontarget. In fact, in this study, the more obtrusive, nontarget deviant elicited almost no ANS responses (see Fig. 12.32). In a further experiment, Lyytinen (unpublished data) found, however, that also nontarget deviants elicited ANS responses but that these were much smaller than those to the same deviant when it was the target and, further, that these ANS responses occurred only when the nontarget deviant was the fast rise-time deviant but did not occur when the nontarget deviant was a slow rise-time deviant (see Figs. 12.39–12.44). The dependence of ANS responses on dynamogenic stimulus factors in their elicitation by a nontarget deviant supports Sokolov's view of OR elicitation including both memory (mismatch with a neuronal model) and dynamogenic factors. (However, as mentioned before, this ANS-response dependence on dynamogenic factors cannot always be found (Lyytinen, unpublished data). As far as ERPs are concerned, the MMN was, presumably, elicited by target and nontarget deviants alike (although in the data presented, the MMN could not be measured because of component overlap). Deviants also elicited the N2b–P3 complex that was clearly earlier and larger for more widely deviating deviants (Figs. 12.39, 12.43, & 12.44). This indicates the important role of physical stimulus deviation in the elicitation of this response. (Consistent with this, an N2b–P3a was elicited by fast rise-time deviants also in *Ignore* conditions; Lyytinen et al., 1992.) The P3–it was not possible to distinguish a separate P3a–was larger in amplitude, whereas the N2b was not affected, when the deviant was the target than when it was the nontarget (Figs. 12.41 & 12.42). This demonstrates the role of stimulus significance in the elicitation of the present P3. The effect of significance on this positivity was more robust for the slow (Fig. 12.41) than for the fast rise-time deviant (Fig. 12.42). For slow rise-time deviants, this target effect seemed to emerge in the form of a P3b (Figs. 12.43 & 12.44).

As is now clear, the ERP and ANS measures in response to deviants show some remarkable covariation but also dissociation. ERP components, in general, showed a relatively stronger dependence on physical stimulus factors, whereas the ANS responses depended more on stimulus significance. Halgren and Marinkovic (1995) distinguished between the afferent and efferent limbs of OR types of processes. The present results lend credibility to this distinction by suggesting that the ERP responses belong mainly to the afferent limb and the ANS responses to the efferent limb of the OR, in this way contributing to the solution of the significance conroversy.

THE CONTRIBUTION OF AUDITORY ERPS FOR UNDERSTANDING THE OR IN THE CLASSICAL OR PARADIGM

The classical OR paradigm was of course the long-ISI paradigm. This paradigm yielded the ANS responses that gave impetus to Sokolov's influential OR theory. The first stimulus elicited a large OR that attenuated and extinguished with stimulus repetition. When ERPs are recorded using this paradigm, a very large N1 or N1–P2 is typically observed in response to the first stimulus, which may be attenuated with stimulus repetition but only to a quite modest extent. The ANS responses, in contrast, are considerably attenuated in amplitude and eventually vanish with stimulus repetition. The modest amount of the N1-amplitude decrement, observed both in Attend and Ignore conditions, may be related to the long ISI in this paradigm approaching or exceeding the time needed for the full recovery of the different brain processes contributing to the scalp-recorded N1 wave. Of these processes, those generating the nonspecific component of the N1 wave need the longest time, perhaps 30 s until full recovery (see Hari et al., 1982; Näätänen & Picton, 1987). Näätänen (1986a) proposed that each clearly audible sound presented after a long interval causes (a) an attention switch, by activating certain N1 generators, to this stimulus (for a model, see Näätänen 1990, 1992), and thus (b) its conscious fast recognition as the same as, or different from, the previous stimuli of the situation, or context, as well as (c) its semantic interpretation. Näätänen (1986a) further proposed that if there is some attenuation in the N1 amplitude, this occurs, at least in part, because of gradual state changes toward diminished cortical excitability as a function of time-on-session. These state factors mainly affect the generator of the nonspecific N1 (Näätänen & Picton, 1987).

It is therefore likely that the relatively much smaller N1-amplitude reduction with stimulus repetition than that of the SCR might in part be accounted for by the multicomponent nature to the N1 wave. More specifically, possibly the nonspecific component, being very sensitive to, besides stimulus repetition, decreased vigilance, in fact attenuated in a manner resembling SCR habituation, whereas the supratemporal and other N1 subcomponents remained relatively constant throughout this stimulus block, accounting for the quite sizable N1 wave observed even in response to the last stimuli of the long-ISI block.

The first stimulus may sometimes elicit also some N2 and P3 kind of activity that is not present in response to the second stimulus. The fast disappearance of these responses might indicate their relation to the OR. If so, then the recognition of the second stimulus as the same as the first stimulus in the evaluation process initiated by the stimulus-onset triggered attention switch intervenes and inhibits the stimulus-initiated process from activating the OR centers of the brain. With regard to the behavior of the so-called 0-wave, the slow frontal negativity, as a function of stimulus repetition, the situation is somewhat unclear.

When a deviant stimulus occurs in this long-ISI sequence, ANS responses are often re-elicited, whereas the ERP is usually not affected (the ISI being too long for the deviant stimulus being able to elicit an MMN), indicating its inability to reflect change detection, or its experienced significance, that caused ANS responses to reappear. The ANS responses may also show some dishabituation, whereas ERPs to the first standard after the deviant were shown to have no, or only a very modest, recovery (for an illustration, see the small P2-amplitude enhancement in signal conditions in Fig. 12.4). Such a recovery might be associated with the improved functional state of the organism as a consequence of the subject having noticed a target or a deviant stimulus at the preceding trial (see Näätänen, 1975) rather than with any genuine dishabituation, which in essence is a release from response inhibition maintained by some neural representation (neuronal model) of the standard stimulus.

So, it appears clear that in the classical OR paradigm, that involving long ISIs such as 30 s, ERPs are much less informative than in the typical short-ISI paradigms. This is evident when one examines ERP effects emerging as a function of stimulus repetition and change, ERP differences between *Attend* and *Ignore* conditions, or those between targets and nontargets. These are manipulations that are so effective with regard to a host of ANS variables, and also have strong effects on ERPs in short-ISI paradigms. In contrast, when long ISIs are used, these manipulations exert only a relatively modest influence on the ERPs. For instance, when the initial stimulus is repeated, the ERP change is far from being dramatic. Under such circumstances, ERPs seem in general to reflect the immediate physical stimulus features, and the state of the organism, more closely than the context, physical or psychological, in which the stimulus is presented (cf. Roth et al., 1982).

Consequently, ERPs in these longer ISI paradigms do not, in general, reflect the OR. They are not useless for this OR research, however, as they suggest the route along which each input presented with long ISIs may reach the level of significance evaluation (resulting in ANS responses) by revealing the powerful attention-switching mechanisms (reflected in the N1) activated by each stimulus when presented with long ISIs. Moreover, some further ERP data (Cowan et al., 1993; Näätänen, Schröger, et al., 1993) suggest the existence of long-term sensory traces that are available to attention switching and might therefore provide sensory information for these evaluative processes.

THE CONTRIBUTION OF ERPS FOR UNDERSTANDING THE OR IN SHORT-ISI PARADIGMS

When short ISIs are used, the import of the ERPs for the understanding of the OR is considerable. On the basis of ERP data, the cerebral processes in the initiation of the OR to stimulus change can be reconstructed in a quite detailed manner. Most importantly, these studies have revealed the MMN, an index of preperceptual change detection in the brain. The MMN data provide strong evidence for a neuronal-mismatch type of process as an automatic detector of change in the acoustic environment. This neuronal-mismatch process may initiate the chain of further brain processes leading to the OR to the stimulus change. In essence, it has been well established that the MMN is generated by a local signal representing no individual stimulus but rather stimulus change. This is a case of Sokolov's (1975) *disconcordance response*. As for further criteria, this response should, according to Sokolov, be elicited even in the absence of attention, should be stronger and faster for wider stimulus deviations, and should be elicited even with no perceived significance of the stimulus change. All these conditions are met by MMN data (for a review, see Näätänen, 1992). Furthermore, consistent with the OR theory, the MMN data implicate a gradual development of a precise neural representation (the neuronal model) for the repeating stimulus, which is involved in the change-detection (neuronal mismatch) process.

There are, however, also some important differences between the change detection as reflected by the MMN and the brain events postulated by Sokolov to initiate the OR:

- The occurrence of change detection as indexed by the MMN does not necessarily result in the OR, at least with stimulus changes of a small magnitude in *Ignore* conditions (Lyytinen et al., 1992), whereas the OR theory suggests that the neuronal-mismatch process invariably results in an OR. It appears, however, that wide stimulus changes cause frequent ANS responses even in *Ignore* conditions. Within the framework of the OR theory, it would be natural to assume that the neuronal-mismatch process has to exceed a certain threshold in order to cause the OR centers of the brain to trigger an OR. Consistent with this, the OR is known to be stronger for wider stimulus deviations (Sokolov, 1975). However, if stimulus changes of even quite a considerable magnitude do not elicit an OR in a person ignoring that stimulus sequence, then it appears to be the MMN (and perhaps the involuntary attention switch) rather than the fully developed OR that behaves according to the OR theory. The MMN occurrence is not necessarily accompanied by ANS responses, whereas a transitory attention switch to stimulus change is likely to be intimately linked with the MMN (cf. Schröger, 1996). Thus the neuronal-mismatch process would cause attention switch resulting in stimulus evaluation whose outcome in turn would determine whether ANS responses will be triggered. One might well regard attention switch as the core event of the OR on the grounds that in a sudden encounter with a novel stimulus, it is of utmost importance first in a very short time to be able to roughly determine what is going on, which cannot take place without attention being switched to the essential aspects of the new situation (Näätänen, 1986a, 1992).

- The OR theory postulated neuronal models with a very long duration such as half a minute or even longer, which by a great margin exceed the longest ISIs with which an MMN can still be elicited, and thus the estimated durations of the neuronal models underlying MMN generation. This does not, however, dissociate the two trace systems from one another. Recent studies (Cowan et al., 1993, Näätänen, Schröger, et al., 1993; Winkler et al., 1996) showed that the traces involved in MMN generation can be either in an active or passive state and, further, that the passive state lasts much longer than the active state. In the active state, MMN elicitation is possible by a deviant stimulus, whereas when the trace is in a passive state, the sensory information contained is accessible via attention switch caused by each stimulus onset with long ISIs.

Quite parsimoniously, then, it could be that with short ISIs, the change-detection process is automatic because of the automatic neuronal-mismatch process made possible by the presence of an active trace, causing an attention switch to the deviant stimulus and therefore possibly resulting in OR elicitation. With long ISIs, in contrast, the strong N1 processes elicited by each stimulus trigger an automatic attention switch. Thus, with short ISIs, stimulus change would be automatically detected, attention switch being triggered only by deviant stimuli, whereas with long ISIs, each stimulus triggers attention switch and thus a conscious evaluation process in which stimulus change is then detected and significance evaluated. According to this hypothesis, both routes to change detection use the same memory representations, but with long ISIs attention is needed to "read" the sensory information contained by the trace to higher systems because of the passive state of the trace preventing the deviant stimulus from automatically activating the change-detection mechanism.

- According to the OR theory, the cerebral initiation of the OR is basically the same for the first stimulus of a sequence and for stimulus change in that sequence. In both cases, the activation of cortical feature detectors has, the theory postulates, an unblocked entry to the hippocampal novelty neurons. This is because in the case of the first-stimulus OR, there is, of course, no synaptic inhibition in the route from the feature detectors to the hippocampal novelty neurons, whereas for the deviant stimulus, a different set of cortical feature detectors is activated, those connected to the novelty neurons of the hippocampus via uninhibited synapses.

  In contrast, the MMN is elicited by stimulus change only, the first stimulus not being sufficient. This was first demonstrated by the magnetic recordings of Sams, Hämäläinen, et al. (1985). These authors found that stimuli presented at very long ISIs did not activate the auditory-cortex locus that was activated by deviant stimuli in the normal short-ISI paradigm. Corroborating results were obtained by Lounasmaa et al. (1989) and, with electrical recordings, by Näätänen, Paavilainen, Alho, Reinikainen, and Sams (1989) and Kraus et al. (1993, 1995). These data clearly indicate that in MMN elicitation, sensory input violating some existing neuronal representation is essential, not simply the sensory input having, presumably, an unblocked access to the hippocampus. Anticipating such results in their review, Näätänen and Gaillard (1983) proposed a distinction of the OR into an initial OR and a change OR, here following a previous similar suggestion of O'Gorman (1979). Näätänen and Gaillard further proposed that the MMN process elicited by stimulus change initiates a sequence of further brain processes which may lead to OR release to stimulus change, whereas the nonspecific component of the N1 is associated with the initial OR (and with the OR to stimuli presented with very long ISIs, of course).

- A further difference between the OR and the cerebral mechanisms of the MMN involves the assumed locus of the neuronal model. On the OR theory, the neuronal model resides, as a stimulus-specific inhibition pattern, in the matrix of the synaptic connections from the feature detectors to the hippocampal novelty neurons. The MMN data, in contrast, suggest that the auditory cortex is the principal locus of MMN generation, implicating that also the underlying neural stimulus representation, the neuronal model resides there, as far as the auditory modality is concerned. According to some further MMN data, also some neuronal populations of auditory cortex possess the degree of plasticity required for representing sensory information for quite long periods of time, in particular in view of the evidence for passive, dormant neural stimulus representations (Cowan et al., 1993; Näätänen, Schröger, et al., 1993; see also Näätänen et al., 1997).

However, the contrast to the hippocampal locus of the neuronal models by the OR theory is alleviated by the more recent data pointing to the existence of other MMN generators also outside the auditory cortex. In particular important here are the cat recordings of Csépe et al. (1989) suggesting a possible hippocampal MMN source. However, it is clear, of course, that a reliable demonstration of a hippocampal MMN generator in the cat brain does not implicate the existence of a hippocampal MMN source also in the human brain.

CHAPTER

13

Addendum: Underlying Principles of Information Processing

The Man–Neuron–Model strategy of psychophysiological research suggests an integration of different levels of analysis to reach a deeper understanding of psychological phenomena. Such an explanation bridges the neuronal level of information processing with cognitive functions in the framework of a model built up from neuron-like elements. A model like this must fulfill two functions. Overall, the model has to simulate the respective cognitive phenomenon. At the same time, each neuron-like element participating in a particular model (or an element of a model) of a cognitive process has to correspond to a response of a real neuron recorded under psychophysical experimental conditions. To link the results of single unit recordings often obtained in animal experiments with the psychophysical data of cognitive research studies in man, it is particularly useful to examine event-related potentials (ERPs). The configuration of an ERP results from contributions of neuronal populations involved in information processing. The comparison of ERPs and spikes in animal experiments can reveal the neuronal basis of cognitive functions in humans when psychophysical procedures are accompanied by the recording of ERPs.

There are different types of neurons participating in the handling of information within neuronal networks. Parallel and sequential stages of information processing can be distinguished. The input stimuli are initially coded by receptors, but even at this level, parallel networks may be found. Several types of receptors may constitute an ensemble. The excitations of the receptors within the ensemble can be regarded as components of an excitation vector. From this perspective, parallel information processing is closely associated with vector coding. The input stimuli are represented in neuronal nets by means of excitation vectors.

The ensemble of receptors is connected with an ensemble of predetectors in such a way that at the predetector level a new excitation vector is generated—a predetector excitation vector. The role of the predetectors is to normalize the excitation vectors. This is a procedure making receptor excitation vectors at the level of the predetectors of a constant length. The transfer of information from receptors to predetectors is achieved by parallel neurocomputing—multiplication of presynaptic transmitter outputs by their respective postsynaptic weights. The constant length of the predetector excitation vector suggests that different stimuli evoking such excitation vectors can be represented on the surface of a sphere in the Euclidean space of the dimensionality determined by the number of the predetectors constituting a respective neuronal ensemble.

The predetector excitation vector acts in parallel on a map of feature detectors that are characterized by sets of synaptic contacts. Each set of synaptic contacts is specific with respect to particular detectors. Such a set of synaptic contacts can be regarded as a link vector. The detector sums the products obtained by multiplication of presynaptic transmitter output and postsynaptic weight. This sum is an inner product of an input predetector excitation vector and a link vector specific to a given detector. The predetector excitation vector acting on the detector map is of a constant magnitude due to the process of normalization at the predetector level. The link vectors of the detectors are also of a constant length. Insofar as the excitation and link vectors are of constant length, their inner product characterizing the response of the detector depends only on the angle between a predetector excitation vector and a link vector. If the angle between these vectors is zero, then the response of the detector will be maximal. If the angles are orthogonal to each other, then no response in the detector will be generated. The detectors constituting a map are characterized by link vectors of specific orientation. The predetector excitation vector evoked by a stimulus generates on the detector map a relief of excitations with an excitation maximum on the detector having a link vector collinear to the predetector excitation vector. Thus, the input stimulus is coded by specific location of the excitation maximum on the detector map. The sequential transfer of information from the receptor level via predetectors up to the feature detector level is performed by parallel processing.

A remarkable property of link vectors at the detector level is their stability. The weights of synapses on feature detectors are not modified by the repeated presentation of a stimulus, the responses of the detectors then remain unchanged. The detector map composed from detectors with link vectors of constant length constitutes a sphere. This means that all detectors of a given map are located on a spherical surface in the space of a dimensionality specified by the number of synapses connecting a given detector with its respective predetector. It is evident that the number of predetectors equals the number of respective synapses on the detector, suggesting that predetector space and feature detector space are of the same dimensionality. Each detector with a specific link vector is selectively tuned to a particular predetector vector and to the stimulus generating such an excitation vector.

The main conclusion extracted from an analysis of vector coding of stimuli is that the vector code does not contradict the topical representation of stimuli in the brain known as somatotopic, retinotopic, and tonotopic mapping. Furthermore, the vector code makes mapping representation a universal principle that can be applied to any stimuli that do not move against the receptor surface. It is sufficient to change the combination of excitation of receptors constituting an ensemble on a local area of receptive surface.

What is the mechanism by which the detector map with a relief of excitation on it controls different behavioral acts? To answer this, the concept of a command neuron has to be added. A command neuron extends its axons to a set of premotor neurons. Such a set of premotor neurons connected to a specific command neuron can be regarded as a neuronal ensemble. The combination of excitations evoked in premotor neurons due to spiking of the command neuron constitutes a premotor neuron excitation vector. This excitation vector acts in parallel on a population of motor neurons. A motor neuron is characterized by a specific set of synapses, thus selectively tuning this motor neuron to a particular premotor neuron excitation vector and hence also selectively tuning it to activation of the command neuron that generates such an excitation vector. In terms of external space, each area of the extrapersonal space is represented by a specific command neuron, the total space being represented by a map of common neurons. To move from one point of the space to a neighboring one, it is necessary to excite the neighboring command neuron that represents it. To organize a behavioral act such as reaching an external object, with respect to a particular area of the external space using command neurons as a code, one has to specify a trajectory of motion on the map of command neurons representing the external space. The trajectory of such reaching behavior is given by a sequence of excitations of command neurons on the map of command neurons. Each command neuron is linked with such a set of premotor neurons and selectively tuned motor neurons that translocate a working organ into the predetermined area. By shifting the excitations from one command neuron to another, the working organ is moved along a specific trajectory being translocated step-by-step in space.

How is the trajectory of motion in space projected onto the map of command neurons? To answer this question, consider again the detector map. A simple version of the detector map is the retinotopic projection. Such a detector map is projected, in a parallel manner, on every command neuron coding different areas of the external space. All detectors of the detector map converging on the command neuron are represented by specific synapses on the dendrites of the command neuron. In this way, the map of detectors is transformed on each command neuron into a map of synaptic contacts where each synapse corresponds to a particular detector. Two types of synapses on the command neuron can be differentiated. The nonplastic synapses connect detectors of a local area of the detector map with a command neuron that translocates the working organ into the area of external space that is represented by given locus on the retinotopic map. All other detectors of the detector map are linked with command neurons through plastic synapses. One may say that for each position of the stimulus on the detector map, there is a stable link to a corresponding command neuron. At the same time, each detector of the detector map is connected to each command neuron via plastic synapses. During associative learning, the plastic synapses are enhanced due to reinforcement. Nonreinforcement results in a weakening of plastic synapses that results in the process of inhibition. If the stimulus moves across the retina, local detectors stimulate respective command neurons via nonplastic synapses. The sequential excitation of command neurons from the command neuron map specifies the trajectory of working organ movement in space.

It has to be emphasized that, although all local detectors are projected onto each command neuron, only one local detector can trigger the response of that command neuron. The other detectors can effectively stimulate that command neuron only after the elaboration of a conditioned reflex when a local detector increases its plastic contact with the command neuron due to reinforcement. When one regards the command neuron as a unit on which a detector map is projected, then the concept of a synaptic map arises. In this synaptic map, each detector of the detector map is represented by a single synapse. Of particular interest are the plastic synapses modified by learning. Negative learning or habituation (presentation of a stimulus without subsequent reinforcement) results in a formation on the synaptic map of a command neuron: a relief of decreased synaptic weights reproducing the shape of the applied stimulus.

Associative learning (classical or instrumental conditioning characterized by application of subsequent reinforcement) results in a formation of a configuration of increased synaptic weights simulating the input stimulus. In both cases, the configuration of modified synapses keeps information about the shape of the stimulus. Accordingly, this configuration is a kind of stimulus model. Because this model is constructed from neuronal elements, it can be called *neuronal model* of a stimulus. The command neuron with a positive neuronal model characterized by a relief of increased (prepotentiated) synapses will be selectively tuned to the stimulus that was used in the conditioning procedure. Negative learning will make this command neuron selectively depressed with respect to the nonreinforced stimulus. The probability of conditioned response elicitation is greater the more exact is the correspondence between the stimulus and the positive neuronal model established on the synaptic map of the command neurons. As has been emphasized, the detector map is projected onto all command neurons in parallel.

Negative learning occurs also in parallel, decreasing the efficiency of the stimulus in triggering any reaction. Associative learning is selective however, with respect to the conditioned stimulus and with respect to the command neuron being reinforced. This means that among synapses between a given detector and all command neurons, only those that constitute a synaptic map of this command neuron will be potentiated. In this way, a specific stimulus is switched via specific detectors with a command neuron of specific behavior. The mechanism of such selective switching is based on Hebbian (1949) Law that states: The weights of synapses being excited by reinforcement increase; the excited synapses not followed by reinforcement decrease their weights.

A detector map is a mechanism for representation of a continuously changing environment. The plastic synaptic map on command neurons underlying elaboration and extinction of conditioned reflexes is however changeable, but in higher vertebrates, there exists an additional specific neuronal mechanism of long-term permanent memory. The neurons of permanent memory collect information from different detector maps and become selectively tuned for a stimulus pattern. Such pattern-selective gnostic units incorporate complex experiences into brain structures. The memory cells represent events without any reference to specific behaviors. It does not mean, however, that they cannot contribute to particular behavioral acts. The memory cell can establish synaptic contact with command neurons in a similar way that feature detectors do. The difference is that memory cells represent more complex events and also that they are created under the influence of external stimulation. Being connected to a command neuron, memory units trigger specific behaviors consequent to complex stimuli for which they are selectively tuned. Another difference between feature detectors and memory units may be that feature detectors are stimulated under natural conditions via respective receptors. Memory units excite each other, creating internal representations of scenes subjectively experienced as *recollection*.

Even more important is that corresponding excitations of several memory units constitute a new complex that can be registered in an additional memory unit. This implies that the experiences obtained directly via sensory organs can be extended by their combination recorded in memory. Some of such combinations can be realized in practice, thus constituting the basis for productive or original thinking. The memory units can be linked with some other memory units encoding verbal stimuli that become symbolic representations of events encoded in event-related memory units. Understanding of a word is related to the excitation of a population of event-related memory cells. Through the links between verbal-related and event-related memory cells, two cognitive operations are performed: categorization of an event when an event excites event-related memory cells linked with verbal-related ones and understanding of the meaning of a word when a word excites a population of event-related memory units via a verbal-related memory cell.

Thus, when an event occurring that requires no specific action is analyzed by feature detectors, there is representation on a collection of detector maps by selective loci, which is recorded as a complex by an event-related memory cell and categorized by a verbal-related memory cell. If an event is reinforced, the respective feature detectors and event-related memory cell potentiate their synapses with an appropriate command neuron. A specific response can then be triggered via feature detectors or event-related memory cells. During learning, not all long-term memory units operate but only that limited subset that recruits neurons for operating or working memory. The neurons involved in working memory are tuned selectively to different events compared with their prototypes in long-term memory. There are also different variations of each event-selective unit of working memory. They respond in different time-intervals after the presentation of a stimulus, and they constitute one memory cell from a long-term memory map categorized by selected verbal-related memory cells.

Glossary

ADAPTATION. *Adaptation* indicates adjustment to a particular surrounding. Sensory *adaptation* is a modification of the thresholds under the influence of background stimulation–an increase of thresholds under a high level of background stimulation and a decrease otherwise.

CHANNEL. The *channel* is a term used to identify a pathway at different levels. At the macrolevel, the term *channel* is applied to the cells selectively tuned to a particular stimulus. In this case, the *channel* might refer to a *neuronal ensemble*. The term *channel* can be used in place of *detector* and *command neuron* emphasizing the common features referred to by the *labelled line principle*.

At the microlevel, the term *channel* refers to ionic channels of the neuronal membrane having selective characteristics for passing different ions.

COMMAND NEURON. The *command neuron* is characterized by a specific behavioral response evoked by its direct intracellular stimulation. The command neuron is responsible for a specific behavioral act or its fragment. The complex composition of the response evoked by a *command neuron* is due to a set of linked motor neurons.

The input signals reaching the command neuron are from detectors, gnostic units, and memory cells. The *command neurons* are supported by specific *modulatory neurons* that change the efficiency of the command neuron operations.

CONSTANT DETECTORS. The *constant detectors* are detectors with modifiable weights of synapses controlled by another set of detectors. They differ from nonconstant detectors that have unmodifiable synapses. The *constant detectors* represent the next stage of information processing following the stage of aconstant detectors. Thus, the receptive field of a parietal cortex neuron is "attached" to a specific locus of extrapersonal space. This is achieved by modification of the links from local retinotopically organized detectors of area 17 by signals coming from the eye muscles and corollary discharge of eye movement command neurons.

DECLARATIVE MEMORY. *Declarative memory* is a general term for semantic and episodic memory that are contextually linked cognitive forms of memory. *Declarative memory* is characterized by an indirect relation to behavior. The content of *declarative memory* can be analyzed and handled without immediate overt behavior so that final behavior influenced by this memory can be postponed with regard to the time of remembering.

DETECTOR. The *detector* is a neuron that is selectively tuned to a particular stimulus. The response of the detector equals a sum of pairwise products of incoming excitations and synaptic weights. In terms of linear algebra, the response of the detector is given by the scalar product of the *excitation vector* and its *link vector.*

f_g—single synaptic excitation; the synapse g
c_{gq}—single synaptic weight for synapse g of the detector q
d_q—response in the detector q

$$d_q = \sum_{g=1}^{s} f_g c_{gq} = (F, C_q) = |F| \times |C| \cos Fl$$

where Fl is the angle between excitation vector F and link vector C_q of a given detector q, assuming that lengths of excitation vector F and link vector C_q are of constant lengths: the $|F|$ = const, $|C|$ = const. The selective tuning of each detector depends on the orientation of link vector C_q.

DETECTOR EXCITATION VECTOR. *Detector excitation vector* is a set of excitations evoked by a particular stimulus in an array of *detectors*. The *detector excitation vector* generated by a stimulus S_l is produced by *predetector excitation vector* via a fan of *link vectors* specific for each detector. The detector excitation vector evoked by stimulus S_l is given by a matrix equation:

$\|C_{gq}\|$—matrix of weights of synapses in an array of detectors
$\|f_{gl}\|$—column vector F_l of predetector excitations evoked by stimulus S_l

$\|d_{ql}\|^T$—transposed detector excitation vector D_l evoked by stimulus S_l

$\|d_{ql}\|^T = \|c_{gq}\| \times \|f_{gl}\|$

DETECTOR MAP. The *detector map* is a set of detector neurons involved in the projection of a given stimulus on a specific locus of an internal quasi-receptive surface composed from the detectors. The *detector map* is a topological map in the sense that coordinates on the map are given by *link vectors* characterizing each detector. Because of the constant lengths of *link vectors*, the *detector map* is a hypersphere in n-dimensional space where n equals the number of predetectors and, respectively, the number of synaptic contacts of the link vector. The stimulus is represented by the position of the excitation maximum on the *detector map*.

DISHABITUATION. *Dishabituation* refers to the recovery of the response to the stimulus, the responses to which were previously habituated. This results from the presentation of a novel stimulus.

ELABORATION. The *elaboration* (of a conditioned reflex, conditioned inhibition) is a term used to emphasize the process of formation of a specific reflex. When termination of *elaboration* is to be emphasized, the term *establishment* is used which refers to the idea that a particular behavior has already been formed.

ESTABLISHMENT. The *establishment* (of a conditioned reflex, conditioned inhibition) means the termination of the process of formation of a given behavioral act. The actual process of its formation is given by the term *elaboration.*

EXCITATION VECTOR. *Excitation vector* is a general term used for the quantitative characterization of excitations evoked by a given stimulus in a set of cells taking part in coding of that stimulus. Depending on the type of cells, *receptor excitation vector, predetector excitation vector, detector excitation vector* may be distiguished. In a general form, the excitation vector is

$$X = (x_1, x_2, \ldots x_i, \ldots x_n)$$

where x_i is the excitation of a cell *i* and $i = 1, 2, \ldots n$ is an index of a respective cell. The excitation vector is used to define the excitations in an ensemble of cells involved in coding of a particular subset of signals.

EXTRAPOLATORY REFLEXES. The *extrapolatory reflexes* constitute a complex unconditioned reflex with an incorporated mechanism of target extrapolation. The characteristic feature of *extrapolatory reflexes* is such a behavioral act that is directed not to the observed target position but to the position where the target will appear according to its unobserved motion. The strong genetic contribution suggests that the extrapolatory mechanism is prewired in the process of natural selection as an important neuronal mechanism linked with the frontal lobes.

EXTRAPOLATING NEURONS. *Extrapolating neurons* are neurons elaborating conditional reflexes to time in combination with specific stimulus features and generating spikes in accordance with a stimulating schedule.

FOVEATION. *Foveation* is a process of translocation of the stimulus on the fovea of the retina. *Foveation* can be achieved by saccadic eye and head movements. *Foveation* also refers to the process of keeping the target on the fovea using compensatory and following eye movements interacting with following head movements. *Foveation* is at the heart of the *targeting reflex* that is in turn a motor subsystem of the *orienting reflex.*

GNOSTIC UNIT. The *gnostic unit* is a neuron which is selectively tuned to a particular complex stimulus. The *gnostic units* can be genetically prewired or formed as a *long-term memory unit* in the process of learning. When formed, such a *long-term memory unit* operates as a stable detector of complex events. *Gnostic units* take part in identification of faces, shapes, and phonemes. The brain lesions containing *gnostic units* result in a specific type of discrimination of complex signals.

HABITUATABLE SYNAPSE. Habituatable synapse is a plastic synapse demonstrating prolonged decrease of its strength under repeated activation of respective presynaptic fibers.

HABITUATION. The habituation is a gradual decrement of both complex behavioral acts and single isolated responses. The term *habituation* is used for the description of processes differing from *adaptation* and is characterized by an increase of the threshold of response evocation. The habituation is stimulus selective and occurs without threshold elaboration. Fatigue is characterized by the absence of recovery of efficiency after additional stimulation. *Habituation* is characterized by *dishabituation*—the recovery of response after its initiation from a novel stimuluus.

HEBBIAN SYNAPSE. The *Hebbian synapse* is a plastic synapse with postsynaptic modification of synaptic weight due to association of activation of a particular synapse with spiking of postsynaptic neuron.

INFORMATION REGULATOR. The information regulator is a mechanism that adjusts the arousal level in accordance with the information flow. The input signals in such a control device are measured by entropy with respect to the probabilities of internal hypotheses. Each hypothesis is characterized by an a priori probability that changes after the arrival of a stimulus and becomes a posteriori probability. This a posteriori probability is a priori with respect to the next step of information handling. The input signals prove and disprove some of the hypotheses so that the entropy of the total set of hypotheses is modified. The entropy of a priori hypotheses determines the level of arousal. The greater the entropy, the higher the arousal level. If a new stimulus, characterized by a low a priori probability, appears, its a posteriori probability rises. In turn, the high probability stimuli become lower. Thus the probabilities of the hypotheses become more equal. This results in an increase of entropy that parallels the increase of arousal. The switching on of that arousal mechanism is characterized by the entropy threshold–such an increase in entropy that only evokes the arousal. The reduction of entropy is characterized by an increase in the a posteriori probability of one of the hypotheses. The particular magnitude of probability constitutes the threshold of response evocation. The decrease of entropy of a set of hypotheses due to an input signal defines the amount of information obtained in the framework of a given hypothesis.

LABELED LINE. The *labeled line* is a term emphasizing that response and stimulus coding are related to specific neurons activated selectively by the execution of a behavioral act and stimulus coding, respectively. The *labeled line* principle in sensory coding is expressed in selectively tuned *detectors*, in response generation–in activation of command neurons. The *labeled line* principle suggests that each sensory event is represented by a specific neuron, and each behavioral act is initiated in a specific neuron.

LATENT LEARNING. *Latent learning* is characterized by processes that are not expressed at the behavioral level, but occur within the neuronal net. The behavioral act is determined by a spike discharge in a command neuron. But before a spike discharge is generated, the process of learning can occur at the synaptic level and is expressed only in modifications of postsynaptic potentials. Repeated stimulus presentation without its reinforcement results in a decrement of the excitatory postsynaptic potential, producing negative latent learning.

The systematic reinforcement of a stimulus can augment the amplitude of excitatory postsynaptic potential in the range when it does not reach the threshold of firing. Such a process would characterize *latent learning* because it can influence the effect in subsequent sessions when the firing threshold might suddenly be reached.

LATERAL INHIBITION. The term *lateral inhibition* describes the inhibitory links between parallel channels that are used to sharpen the response characteristic of the unit. Lateral inhibition is evoked with a fixed delay after the excitations evoked by a stimulus reach a plateau level and follow a particular time after the termination of excitation. A simultaneous sharpening of response characteristics of units affected by lateral inhibitory links is a mechanism of simultaneous contrast increasing differences between responses. The resultant inhibition is related to the opposite reaction being produced following the offset of stimulus.

LINK VECTOR. The *link vector* is a vector of synaptic weights of a given cell connecting it with several input cells. The link vectors differ depending on the level of connected cells. The *link vectors* between the receptors and predetectors that participate in orthogonalization of the *receptor excitation vector* depend on the composition of receptor excitations. The *link vectors* between the second stage of *predetectors* and a given *detector* are characterized by constant length. Thus the *link vector* of the *detector*, d_q is given by:

$$C_q = (c_{q1}, c_{q2}, \ldots c_{qg}, \ldots c_{qm})$$

where $g = 1, \ldots$ m—index of synaptic contact; $q = 1, \ldots$ 2—index of a detector. The length of the line vector is of a constant value:

$$|C_q| = \text{constant}$$

LONG-TERM MEMORY UNIT. The *long-term memory unit* is a specific neuron selectively tuned to a particular complex stimulus in the process of learning. When formed, *long-term memory units* operate as *gnostic units* to extract information from the environment as related to the content of memory. A map of *long-term memory units* constitutes the mechanism of *declarative memory*. It differs from *procedural memory* that is related to change of plastic synapses within the reflex arc, mainly between *detectors* and *command neurons*. The *long-term memory units* differ also from short-term memory units that function as operating memory units or working memory units. It is assumed that the *long-term memory unit* can be copied for operating in the process of matching signals against a stimulus trace.

MATCH SIGNAL. The *match signal* is a spike discharge evoked by a coincidence of input signal and a memory trace of a specific stimulus extracted from long-term memory and copied in operating memory. Via *detectors*, the input stimuli reach the *operating memory unit* and result in a maximal spike discharge when the appropriate synaptic contacts are activated. The *match signal* is fed to the *command neuron* to perform behavior dependent on *declarative memory*. That is represented by *long-term memory* units used as a container of experience for operative control in operating memory units. In the ERPs, the match signal is expressed in *processing negativity*.

MEMORY UNIT. A *memory unit* refers to a neuron becoming selectively tuned to a particular stimulus or a combination of stimuli in the process of learning. *Long-term memory units* are located in the anterior ventral temporal cortex and encode highly abstract properties.

MISMATCH NEGATIVITY. Mismatch negativity is a negative event-related potential in the range of 100 ms latency, triggered by a deviant stimulus presented with a low probability among a standard stimulus given with a high probability. Occurring in specific projection areas, *mismatch negativity* is generated by plastic short-term memory units characterized by decasecond trace life time. The generation of *mismatch negativity* is a preattentive stage of information processing influencing the triggering of the *orienting reflex*.

MISMATCH SIGNAL. A *mismatch signal* is generated by the lack of coincidence between the neuronal model of the stimulus and the input signal. Two types of *mismatch signals* can be differentiated, the short-term traces (iconic and echoic memories) and the medium-term trace. The units responsible for the short-term mismatch signal are located in projection brain areas. Such a mismatch signal is expressed in the *mismatch negativity*. The medium-term trace, related to the novelty neurons of the hippocampus, generate mismatch parallel to the *orienting-reflex* evocation. It is expressed in the nonspecific NI component that habituates in parallel with the *orienting reflex* components. The signal generated in hippocampal novelty detectors is sent to the brain stem activating system for triggering NI and arousal.

MODULATORY NEURON. The *modulatory neuron* is an interneuron characterized by action on the synaptic connection between other neurons and between neurons and peripheral cells. The *modulatory neuron* acts via an increase–decrease of calcium flow in the calcium *channels* of the synaptic terminals. Producing no observable effect, the modulatory neuron significantly modifies the synaptic efficiency as evidenced by the application of a following test-stimulus on the neuronal net influenced by the modulatory neuron.

NEURONAL ENSEMBLE. The *neuronal ensemble* is a collection of nerve cells involved in the process of stimulus coding. The excitations of cells constituting a *neuronal ensemble* can be quantitatively characterized by an *excitation vector*. The excitations of cells related to the *neuronal ensemble* correspond to the components of the *excitation vector*. The *neuronal ensem-*

ble as a coding mechanism does not contradict the detector-selective tuning. Thus the *neuronal ensemble* of *predetectors* constitutes a basic generation of a *predector excitation vector* that evokes an excitation maximum on the *detector map* in a detector selectively tuned to a particular stimulus.

NEURONAL MODEL. The *neuronal model* of a stimulus is related to the selective habituation of *the orienting reflex*. It is suggested that in the process of repeated presentations of a standard stimulus, plastic synapses of *detectors* on *novelty neurons* are selectively depressed in accordance with stimulus features. The pattern of the modified synapses on the matrix composed of all feature detectors is a model of stimulus. Once the *neuronal model* of stimulus is established, it operates as a selective filter, rejecting the standard stimulus. The mismatch signal generated as a result of a match of input signal against *the neuronal model* triggers the *orienting reflex*.

NOVELTY NEURONS. *Novelty neurons* are the pyramidal neurons of the hippocampus having plastic synapses that are selectively habituated by stimulus repetition and are responsive to any deviant stimulus.

OPERATING MEMORY UNIT. *Operating memory unit* refers to a neuron that is selectively active after presentation of a cue stimulus during delay of the response. These neurons are located in the prefrontal cortex.

ORIENTING REFLEX. The *orienting reflex* is an *unconditioned reflex* evoked by stimulus novelty and significance. Significant stimuli are announced as continously novel. The nonsignal, not significant stimuli are characterized by stimulus-selective habituation. The signal stimuli or significant stimuli evoke the orienting response as if they are novel. Significance is created by unconditioned stimuli used as reinforcement in the process of learning. In humans, stimulus significance can be produced by verbal instruction announcing a specific stimulus as a goal of action. The *orienting reflex* can be evoked by sensory stimuli and verbal stimuli due to perceptual and/or semantic difference. It is assumed that the *orienting reflex* can also be triggered by a new combination of memory traces taking part in the creative thinking process.

PARALLEL INFORMATION PROCESSING. *Parallel information processing* is a general term to characterize the simultaneous handling of information in a set of units. In computer science, parallel information processing refers to a set of parallel processors. In the nervous system, parallel information processing refers to a number of parallel fibers represented by a receptive surface. Different features within local patches of the receptive surface are coded in parallel. This is achieved by two levels of neurons, the *predetectors* and *detectors*. The *predetectors* as an ensemble of cells generate an *excitation vector.* Such *predetector excitation vectors* are generated in parallel in different patches of the receptive surface. Within each *predetector* ensemble, the *predetector excitation vector* acts, again in parallel, on a set of *detectors*, generating simultaneously a detector excitation vector. The process results in the evocation of an excitation maximum in particular levels of the detector map on a detector selectively tuned to a given stimulus. The detector excitation vector acts in parallel on a set of command neurons. The selection of a unique behavior pattern depends on two factors: learning (to what degree the *plastic link vector* connecting detectors with a given command neuron is close to the detector excitation vector evoked by the stimulus) and emotional state (activation of specific modulatory neuron that increases the excitation level of a given command neuron). After the command neuron is activated, the subsequent process is effected by the parallel involvement of motor neurons that determine the behavioral response pattern.

PLASTIC LINK VECTOR. The *plastic link vector* is composed of plastic synaptic weights modified in the process of learning. The *plastic link vector* is modified by its summation with the *detector excitation vector* multiplied by a scalar product of the initial *plastic link vector* and *the detector excitation vector.* The normalization of the components of a new *plastic link vector* keeps the length of the *plastic link vector* constant. In the process of iterative summations of detector excitation vector and *plastic link vector,* the latter approaches the *detector excitation vector*—both becoming collinear.

PLASTIC SYNAPSE. *Plastic synapse* refers to a synapse characterized by modification of its strength in the process of stimulation of presynaptic fibers.

PREDETECTOR. A *predetector* is a neuron which takes part in the coding of signals as a member of a *neuronal ensemble.* The excitations of the *predetector* constituting a *neuronal ensemble* are characterized by a *predetector excitation vector.* The role of predetectors located between receptors and *detectors* is to adjust the excitations of receptors for efficient handling at the *detector* level. One such function is orthogonalization, which represents the excitations of *predectors* as coordinates of stimuli in Euclidian space. The other function is the normalization of the *predector excitation vectors,* so that the stimulus code is given as its specific position on the surface of the hypersphere.

PREDETECTOR EXCITATION VECTOR. The *predetector excitation vector* is a set of excitations evoked by a particular stimulus in neurons preceding the detector level of information processing. Two types of *predetector excitation vector* can be differentiated. The first type is characterized by an orthogonal coordinate system with the length of the vector depending on stimulus intensity.

$$|x| = (x_1^2 + x_2^2 + \dots x_i^2 \dots + x_n^2)^{1/2}$$
$$|x| = f(I)$$

The second type of predetector vector is characterized by normalization of the orthogonal components, so that the length of the vector is constant for all stimuli in the set:

$$|x| = \text{constant}$$

Thus, a normalized excitation vector represents stimuli on the surface of a hypersphere in n-dimensional space, where n equals the number of predetectors involved in stimulus coding.

PREDICTIVE CONTROL. *Predictive control* refers to an adjustment of a system in accordance with an expected value of an input signal. Thus, predictive control is based on an extrapolation of the signal time course in the future. In a neuronal network, *predictive control* is realized by *time-coding neurons* that are selectively tuned to specific time intervals and *extrapolating neurons*, which generate bursts of spikes with specific intervals corresponding to the time intervals of the stimulus presentation. The mechanism of interval-selective spike generation can be explained by an intensification of synapses converging on *extrapolating neurons* from such *time-coding* neurons that are selectively tuned to the reinforced time-interval.

PROCEDURAL MEMORY. *Procedural memory* refers to skill and simple conditioning. The operations of procedural memory are expressed in behavioral acts independent of cognitive representational storage. The main mechanism of procedural memory is related to plastic synapses connecting *detectors* and *gnostic units* with *command neurons* responsible for different behavioral acts.

PROCESSING NEGATIVITY. *Processing negativity* refers to the negative wave overlapping brain evoked potentials triggered by an attended stimulus.

RECEPTOR EXCITATION VECTOR. The *receptor excitation vector* is a set of excitations evoked in receptors by the action of a particular stimulus. At the receptor level, the components of the excitation vector are given not in an orthogonal coordinate system, but in an affine one. An example of the *receptor excitation vector* is a combination of excitations of three types of cones contributing to color coding. In a general form, receptor excitation vector is given by:

$$(r = r_1, r_2, \ldots r_i, \ldots r_n)$$

where r_i is the excitation of a particular receptor; $i = 1, 2, \ldots n$ is the index of the receptor.

REFLEX. The *reflex* is a term used for indication of specific behavioral acts. The innate reflexes are labelled as unconditioned reflexes as opposed to learning-dependent conditioned reflexes. The conditioned reflexes are classified as classical and operant (or instrumental) conditioned reflexes. The difference between classical and operant conditioned reflexes refers to the self-generated activity as an additional cue used in the *elaboration* of operant conditioned reflexes.

RESPONSE. *Response* is a broad term applied to any evoked activity of an organism—behavioral or cellular. The term *response* may be used to indicate separate components of unconditioned and conditioned *reflexes*. The application of this term to complex biological acts is misleading. Thus, there is *orienting reflex*, *defensive reflex*, *adaptive reflex*, but there is also *skin galvanic response*.

SAMENESS NEURONS. The *sameness neurons* generate spikes when the stimulus becomes familiar to the subject after a number of presentations; otherwise, they are inhibited. The output signals from *sameness neurons* are transmitted to the synchronizing (moderating) brain system that takes part in the induction of sleep. Thus, repeated stimulus presentations can switch on the synchronizing EEG pattern leading to sleep.

SELF-ADJUSTABLE FILTER. The *self-adjustable filter* is a device that changes its response characteristic in the presence of a stimulus without tutor assistance. In the nervous system, such a self-adjustable filter is *elaborated* during *habituation*. This filter rejects the signal close to the applied standard in the process of *habituation* and the posing of other signals deviating from the standard. At the neuronal level, such a filter results from the depression of synaptic efficiency of the *detectors* on novelty neurons. The enhancement of the *detector* synapsing on *sameness neurons* results in passing a repeated standard and rejecting a stimulus that deviates from the standard. Thus, the self-adjustable filters produced by complex stimuli can by characterized as areas in a multidimensional space rejecting or passing complex stimuli.

SIMILARITY. *Similarity* is a term characterizing the closeness of stimuli under observation. The subjective estimation of similarity is given in numbers from 0 (minimal similarity) up to 9 (maximal similarity). The similarity between stimuli S_i and S_j can be measured by means of response probability vectors evoked by a set of test stimuli under two different conditions of learning, when stimulus S_i and stimulus S_j were reinforced respectively.

$$S_i \text{ and } S_j \text{ similarity} = \cos FI_{ij} = \frac{(P_i, P_j)}{|P_i|\,|P_j|},$$

where FI is the angle between response probability vector P_i and P_j obtained with test stimuli under reinforcement of stimulus S_i and S_j, respectively.

TARGETING REFLEX. The *targeting reflex* indicates a composition of motor responses that results in a relocation of the stimulus to the most sensitive area of the receptive surface. The most well known are eye movements, resulting in a *foveation* of the stimulus where it can be investigated in detail.

TIME-CODING NEURONS. The *time-coding neurons* are neurons which are selectively tuned to particular time intervals, so that each one responds only to stimuli of a specific duration. The change of the stimulus results in a shift of excitation along an array of selective *time-detectors*. The organization of time analysis is based on general principles of the neuronal coding of events. The input neurons for time-*detectors* are time-*prededectors*—neurons that gradually respond to a stimulus duration. One type of time-*predetectors* increases the firing rate as the stimulus duration increases, the other type decreases spiking with increase of stimulus duration. The participation of *time-coding neurons* is evident so far only for the coding of short time intervals.

VECTOR CODING. The *vector coding* is a representation of an input signal by a combination of excitations in a *neuronal ensemble*. These excitations constitute an *excitation vector*. The stimulus coded by an *excitation vector* is projected on a *detector map*. The next stage of *the vector coding* is represented by the levels of excitation maximum on the *detector map*. This projection of the stimulus on the *detector map* is achieved by a *link vector*. The distribution of excitations on the *detector map* constitutes a detector excitation vector.

The generation of a behavioral act is performed by connecting the *detector excitation vector* with the *command neuron* via a *plastic link vector* that is transformed in accordance with following reinforcement. Positive and negative reinforcements make the *plastic link vector* either collinear or orthogonal respectively, with the *detector excitation vector*. In this way, the *command neurons* become selectively tuned (collinear relation) or selectively inhibited (orthogonal relation) toward the stimulus under the learning conditions.

With respect to the behavioral response, *vector coding* means that the *command neuron* excitation initiates motor neuron activity by means of a fan of synaptic links that generate an output *excitation vector* characterizing the behavioral response pattern.

References

Aaltonen, O., Niemi, P., Nyrke, T., & Tuhkanen, J. M. (1987). Event-related brain potentials and the perception of a phonetic continuum. *Biological Psychology, 24,* 197–207.

Aaltonen, O., Tuomainen, J., Laine, M., & Niemi, P. (1993). Cortical differences in tonal frequency versus vowel processing as revealed by an ERP component called the mismatch negativity (MMN). *Brain and Language, 44,* 139–152.

Alcaini, M., Giard, M. H., Thevenet, M., & Pernier, J. (1994). Two separate frontal components in the N1 wave of the human auditory evoked response. *Psychophysiology, 31,* 611–615.

Alexandrov, Y., & Järvilehto, T. (1993). Activity versus reactivity in psychology and neuropsychology. *Ecological Psychology, 5,* 85–103.

Alho, K., Escera, C., Diaz, R., Yago, E., & Serra, J. M. (1997). Effects of involuntary auditory attention on visual task performance and brain activity. *Neuroreport, 8,* 3233–3237.

Alho, K., Huotilainen, M., Tiitinen, H., Ilmoniemi, R. J., Knuutila, J., & Näätänen, R. (1993). Memory-related processing of complex sound patterns in human auditory cortex: A MEG study. *NeuroReport, 4,* 391–394.

Alho, K., Kujala, T., Paavilainen, P., Summala, H., & Näätänen, R. (1993). Auditory processing in visual brain areas of the early blind: Evidence from event-related potentials. *Electroencephalography and Clinical Neurophysiology, 86,* 418–427.

Alho, K., Lavikainen, J., Reinikainen, K., Sams, M., & Näätänen, R. (1990). Event-related potentials in selective listening to frequent and rare stimuli. *Psychophysiology, 27,* 73–86.

Alho, K., Sainio, K., Sajaniemi, N., Reinikainen, K., & Näätänen, R. (1990). Event-related brain potential of human newborns to pitch change of an acoustic stimulus. *Electroencephalography and Clinical Neurophysiology, 77,* 151–155.

Alho, K., & Sinervo, N. (1997). Preattentive processing of complex sounds in the human brain. *Neuroscience Letters, 233,* 33–36.

Alho, K., Tervaniemi, M., Huotilainen, M., Lavikainen, J., Tiitinen, H., Ilmoniemi, R. J., Knuutila, J., & Näätänen, R. (1996). Processing of complex sounds in the human auditory cortex as revealed by magnetic brain responses. *Psychophysiology, 33,* 369–375.

Alho, K., Woods, D. L., Algazi, A., Knight, R. T., & Näätänen, R. (1994). Lesions of frontal cortex diminish the auditory mismatch negativity. *Electroencephalography and Clinical Neurophysiology, 91,* 353-362.

Anokhin, P. K. (1974). *Biology and neurophysiology of the conditioned reflex and its role in adaptive behavior*. Oxford: Pergamon.

Aulanko R., Hari, R., Lounasmaa, O. V., Näätänen, R., & Sams, M. (1993). Phonetic invariance in the human auditory cortex. *NeuroReport, 4*, 1356–1358.

Balaban, P. M., Zakharov, I. S., & Chistyakova, M. V. (1988). Role of serotonergic cells in aversive learning in Helix. In J. Salanki & K. S. Rozsa (Eds.), *Neurobiology of invertebrates: Transmitters, modulators and receptors* (pp. 519–531). Budapest: Akademia Kiado.

Batuev, A. S. (1981). *Vysshiye integrativnye sistemy mozga (Higher integrating brain systems)*. Leningrad: Nauka.

Becker, D. E., & Shapiro, D. (1980). Directing attention toward stimuli affects the P300 but not the orienting response. *Psychophysiology, 17*, 385–389.

Berger, H. (1929). Uber das Electroenkephalogramm des Menschen. *Archiev fur Psychiatrie, 87*, 527–570.

Bernstein, A. S. (1969). To what does the orienting response respond? *Psychophysiology, 6*, 338–350.

Bernstein, A. S. (1979). The orienting response as novelty and significance detector: Reply to O'Gorman. *Psychophysiology, 16*, 263–273.

Bernstein, A. S. (1981). The orienting response and stimulus significance: Further comments. *Biological Psychology, 12*, 171–185.

Blowers, G. H., Spinks, J. A., & Shek, D. T. L. (1986). P300 and the anticipation of information within an orienting response paradigm. *Acta Psychologica, 61*, 91–103.

Böttscher-Gandor, C., & Ullsperger, P. (1992). Mismatch negativity in event-related potentials to auditory stimuli as a function of varying interstimulus interval. *Psychophysiology, 29*, 546–550.

Brugge, J. F., & Reale, R. A. (1985). Auditory cortex. In A. Peters & E. G. Jones (Eds.), *Cerebral cortex, Vol. 4. Association and auditory cortices* (pp. 229–271). New York: Plenum.

Brusentsov, N. P. (Ed.). (1982). *Basisnyi Fortran (Basic Fortran)*. Izdatelstvo Moscovskogo Universiteta, Moscow.

Butler, R. A. (1968). Effect of changes in stimulus frequency and intensity on habituation of the human vertex potential. *Journal of the Acoustical Society of America, 44*, 945–950.

Butler, R. A. (1972). The auditory evoked response to stimuli producing periodicity pitch. *Psychophysiology, 9*, 233–237.

Butter, R. A., & Harlow, H. F. (1954). Persistence of visual exploration in monkeys. *Journal of Comparative & Physiological Psychology, 47*, 258–263.

Caspers, H. (1961). Changes of cortical D.C. potentials in the sleep-wakefulness cycle. In G. E. W. Wolstenholme & M. O'Conner (Eds.), *The nature of sleep* (pp. 237–253). London: Churchill.

Cheour-Luhtanen, M., Alho, K., Kujala, T., Sainio, K., Reinikainen, M., Renlund, M., Aaltonen, O., Eerola, O., & Näätänen, R. (1995). Mismatch negativity indicates vowel discrimination in newborns. *Hearing Research, 82*, 53–58.

Cheour-Luhtanen, M., Alho, K., Sainio, K., Reinikainen, K., Renlund, M., Aaltonen, O., Eerola, O., & Näätänen, R. (1997). The mismatch negativity to speech sounds at the age of three months. *Developmental Neuropsychology, 13*, 167–174.

Cheour-Luhtanen, M., Alho, K., Sainio, K., Rinne, T., Reinikainen, K., Pohjavuori, M., Renlund, M., Aaltonen, O., Eerola, O., & Näätänen, R. (1996). The ontogenetically earliest discriminative response of the human brain. *Psychophysiology, Special Report, 33*, 478–481.

Courchesne, E., Courchesne, R. Y., & Hillyard, S. A. (1978). The effect of stimulus deviation on P3 waves to easily recognized stimuli. *Neuropsychologia, 16*, 189–199.

Courchesne, E., Hillyard, S. A., & Courchesne, R. Y. (1977). P3 waves to the discrimination of targets in homogeneous and heterogeneous sequences. *Psychophysiology, 14*, 590–597.

Courchesne, E., Hillyard, S. A., & Galambos, R. (1975). Stimulus novelty, task relevance and the visual evoked potential in man. *Electroencephalography and Clinical Neurophysiology, 39*, 131–143.

Cowan, N., Winkler, I., Teder, W., & Näätänen, R. (1993). Memory prerequisites of the mismatch negativity in the auditory event-related potential. *Journal of Experimental Psychology: Human Perception and Performance, 19*, 909–921.

Csépe, V., Karmos, G., & Molnár, M. (1987). Evoked potential correlates of stimulus deviance during wakefulness and sleep in cat: Animal model of mismatch negativity. *Electroencephalography and Clinical Neurophysiology, 66*, 571–578.

Csépe, V., Karmos, G., & Molnár, M. (1989). Subcortical evoked potential correlates of early information processing: Mismatch negativity in cats. In E. Basar & T. H. Bullock (Eds.), *Springer series in brain dynamics 2* (pp. 279–289). Berlin: Springer-Verlag.

Csépe, V., Pantev, C., Hoke, M., Hampson, S., & Ross, B. (1992). Evoked magnetic responses to minor pitch changes: Localization of the mismatch field. *Electroencephalography and Clinical Neurophysiology, 84*, 538–548.

Czigler, I., & Csibra, G. (1990). Event-related potentials in a visual discrimination task: Negative waves related to detection and attention. *Psychophysiology, 32*, 153–190.

Czigler, I., Csibra, G., & Csontos, A. (1992). Age and inter-stimulus interval effect on event-related potentials to frequent and infrequent auditory stimuli. *Biological Psychology, 33*, 195–206.

Davis, H., Bowers, C., & Hirsh, S. K. (1968). Relations of the human vertex potential to acoustic input: Loudness and masking. *Journal of the Acoustical Society of America, 43*, 431–438.

Davis, H., Osterhammel, P. A., Wier, C. C., & Gjerdingen, D. B. (1972). Slow vertex potentials; Interactions among auditory, tactile, electric and visual stimuli. *Electroencephalography and Clinical Neurophysiology, 33*, 537–545.

Donchin, E. (1981). Surprise! . . . Surprise? *Psychophysiology, 18*, 493–513.

Donchin, E., & Coles, M. G. H. (1988). Is the P300 component a manifestation of context updating? *Behavioral and Brain Sciences, 11*, 357–374.

Donchin, E., Heffley, E., Hillyard, S. A., Loveless, N., Maltzman, I., Öhman, A., Rösler, F., Ruchkin, D., & Siddle, D. (1984). Cognition and Event-Related Potentials; II. The Orienting Reflex and P300. In R. Karrer, J. Cohen, & P. Tueting (Eds.), *Brain and information: Event-related potentials* (pp. 39–57). New York: Annals of the New York Academy of Sciences.

Duncan, C. C., & Kaye, W. H. (1987). Effects of clonidine on event-related potential measures of information processing. In R. Johnson, Jr., J. W. Rohrbaugh, & R. Parasuraman (Eds.), Current Trends in Event-Related Potential Research (pp. 527–531). *Electroencephalography and Clinical Neurophysiology, Suppl. 40.* Amsterdam: Elsevier.

Duncan-Johnson, C. C., & Donchin, E. (1982). The P300 component of the event-related brain potential as an index of information processing. *Biological Psychology, 14*, 1–52.

Elberling, C., Bak, C., Kofoed, B., Lebech, J., & Saermark, K. (1982). Auditory magnetic fields. Source location and "tonotopic organization" in the right hemisphere of the human brain. *Scandinavian Audiology, 11*, 61–65.

Escera, C., Alho, K., Winkler, I., & Näätänen, R. (1998). Neural mechanisms of involuntary attention to acoustic novelty and change. *Journal of Cognitive Neuroscience, 10*, 590–604.

Fedorovskaya, E. A. (1992a). Perceptual color space is isomorphic with semantic color space. *Man, Neuron, Model: Email Communications in Psychophysiology, 1.* Retrieved March 26, 2001 from World Wide Web: http://www.hku.hk/psycho/vol1.html

Fedorovskaya, E. A. (1992b). Memory color space is isomorphic with semantic color space. *Man, Neuron, Model: Email Communications in Psychophysiology, 1.* Retrieved March 26, 2001 from World Wide Web: http://www.hku.hk/psycho/vol1.html

Feigenberg, I. M. (1969). Probabilistic prognosis and its signifigance in normal and pathological subjects. In M. Cole & I. Maltzman (Eds.), *A handbook of contemporary Soviet psychology* (pp. 354–369). New York: Basic Books.

Ford, J. M., & Hillyard, S. A. (1981). Event-related potentials (ERPs) to interruptions of a steady rhythm. *Psychophysiology, 18*, 322–330.

Ford, J. M., Roth, W. T., Dirks, S. J., & Kopell, B. S. (1973). Evoked potential correlates of signal recognition between and within modalities. *Science, 181*, 465–466.

Ford, J. M., Roth, W. T., & Kopell, B. S. (1976a). Auditory evoked potentials to unpredictable shifts in pitch. *Psychophysiology, 13*, 32–39.

Ford, J. M., Roth, W. T., & Kopell, B. S. (1976b). Attention effects on auditory evoked potentials to infrequent events. *Biological Psychology, 4*, 65–77.

Frey, M. von, & Golgman, A. (1914). Der zeitliiche Verlauf der Einslellung bei der Druckempfindungen. *Zeitschrift fur Biologie, 65*, 183–191.

Fruhstorfer, H. (1971). Habituation and dishabituation of the human vertex response. *Electroencephalography and Clinical Neurophysiology, 30*, 306–312.

Fruhstorfer, H., Järvilehto, T., Soveri, P., Lumio, J., & Partanen, J. (1970). *Spinal excitability changes during an auditory vertex response in man.* Unpublished manuscript.

Fruhstorfer, H., Soveri, P., & Järvilehto, T. (1970). Short-term habituation of the auditory evoked response in man. *Electroencephalography and Clinical Neurophysiology, 28*, 153–161.

Fuster, J. M. (1989). *The prefrontal cortex: Anatomy, physiology, and neuropsychology of the frontal lobe* (2nd ed.). New York: Raven.

Gaillard, A. W. K. (1976). Effects of warning-signal modality on the contingent negative variation (CNV). *Biological Psychology, 4*, 139–154.

Germana, J. (1969). Central efferent processes and autonomic behavioral integration. *Psychophysiology, 6*(1), 70–78.

Giard, M. H., Lavikainen, J., Reinikainen, K., Perrin, F., Bertrand, O., Pernier, J., & Näätänen, R. (1995). Separate representation of stimulus frequency, intensity, and duration in auditory sensory memory: An event-related potential and dipole-model analysis. *Journal of Cognitive Neuroscience, 7*, 133–143.

Giard, M. H., Perrin, F., Echallier, J. F., Thevenet, M., Froment, J. C., & Pernier, J. (1994). Dissociation of temporal and frontal components in the human auditory N1 wave: A scalp current density and dipole model analysis. *Electroencephalography and Clinical Neurophysiology, 92*, 238–252.

Giard, M. H., Perrin, F., Pernier, J., & Bouchet, P. (1990). Brain generators implicated in the processing of auditory stimulus deviance: A topographic ERP study. *Psychophysiology, 27*, 627–640.

Gjerdingen, D. E., & Tomsic, R. (1970). Recovery functions of human cortical potentials evoked by tones, shocks, vibrations and flashes. *Psychonomic Science, 19*, 228–229.

Gomes, S. H., Ritter, W., & Vaughan, H. G., Jr. (1995). The nature of pre-attentive storage in the auditory system. *Journal of Cognitive Neuroscience, 7*, 81–94.

Graham, F. K. (1973). Habituation and dishabituation of responses innervated by the autonomic nervous system. In H. V. S. Peeke & M. J. Hertz (Eds.), *Habituation: Vol. I. Behavioral studies* (pp. 163–218). London: Academic Press.

Graham, F. K. (1979). Distinguishing among orienting, defense and startle. In H. D. Kimmel, E. H. van Olst, & J. F. Orlebeke (Eds.), *The orienting reflex in humans* (pp. 137–167). Hillsdale, NJ: Lawrence Erlbaum Associates.

Graham, F. K. (1989). SPR Award, 1988. For distinguished contributions to psychophysiology: Evgeny Nikolaevich Sokolov. *Psychophysiology, 26*, 385–391.

Graham, F. K. (1992). Attention: The heartbeat, the blink, and the brain. In B. A. Campbell, H. Hayne, & R. Richardson (Eds.), *Attention and information processing in infants and animals: Perspectives from human and animal research* (pp. 3–29). Hillsdale, NJ: Lawrence Erlbaum Associates.

Granit, R. (1955). Brain control of the sense systems. *Acta Psychologica, 11*, 117–118.

Grechenko, T. N., & Sokolov, E. N. (1987). (Neurophysiology of learning and memory). In P. G. Kostyuk (Ed.), *Handbook of physiology: Mechanisms of memory* (pp. 132–172) (in Russian). Leningrad: Nauka.

Halgren, E., Baudena, P., Clarke, J. M., Heit, G., Liégeois, C., Chauvel, P., & Musolino, A. (1995a). Intracerebral potentials to rare target and distractor auditory and visual stimuli. I. Superior temporal plane and parietal lobe. *Electroencephalography and Clinical Neurophysiology, 94*, 191–220.

Halgren, E., Baudena, P., Clarke, J. M., Heit, G., Marinkovic, K., Devaux, B., Vignal, J. P., & Biraben, A. (1995b). Intracerebral potentials to rare target and distractor auditory and visual stimuli. II. Medial, lateral, and posterior temporal lobe. *Electroencephalography and Clinical Neurophysiology, 94*, 229–250.

Halgren, E., & Marinkovic, K. (1995). Neurophysiological networks integrating human emotions. In M. S. Gazzaniga (Ed.), *The cognitive neurosciences* (pp. 1137–1151). Cambridge, MA: MIT Press.

Halgren, E., Squires, N. K., Wilson, C. L., Rohrbaugh, J. W., Babb, T. L., & Crandall, P. H. (1980). Endogenous potentials generated in hippocampal formation and amygdala by infrequent events. *Science, 210*, 703–705.

Hari, R., Hämäläinen, M., Ilmoniemi, R., Kaukoranta, E., Reinikainen, K., Salminen, J., Alho, K., Näätänen, R., & Sams, M. (1984). Responses of the primary auditory cortex to pitch changes in a sequence of tone pips: Neuromagnetic recordings in man. *Neuroscience Letters, 50*, 127–132.

Hari, R., Joutsiniemi, S.-L., Hämäläinen, M., & Vilkman, V. (1989). Responses of human auditory cortex to change in temporal stimulation patterns. *Neuroscience Letters, 99*, 164–168.

Hari, R., Kaila, K., Katila, T., Tuomisto, T., & Varpula, T. (1982). Interstimulus interval dependence of the auditory vertex response and its magnetic counterpart: Implications for their neural generation. *Electroencephalography and Clinical Neurophysiology, 54*, 561–569.

Hari, R., Rif, J., Tiihonen, J., & Sams, M. (1992). Neuromagnetic mismatch fields to single and paired tones. *Electroencephalography and Clinical Neurophysiology, 82*, 152–154.

Hartline, H. K. (1949). Inhibition of activity of visual receptors by illuminating nearby retinal areas in the Limulus eye. *Federation Proceedings, 8*, 69–75.

Hay, I. S., & Davis, H. (1971). Slow cortical evoked potentials: Interactions of auditory, vibrotactile and shock stimuli. *Audiology, 10*, 9–17.

Hebb, D. O. (1949). *The organization of behavior: A neuropsychological theory*. New York: Wiley.

Huotilainen, M., Ilmoniemi, R. J., Lavikainen, J., Tiitinen, H., Alho, K., Sinkkonen, J., Knuutila, J., & Näätänen, R. (1993). Interaction between representations of different features of auditory sensory memory. *NeuroReport, 4*, 1279–1281.

Imada, T., Fukuda, K., Kawakatsu, M., Masjiko, T., Odaka, K., Hayashi, M., Aihara, K., & Kotani, M. (1993, August). Mismatch fields evoked by a rhythm passage. In L. Deecke, C. Baumgartner, G. Stroink, & S. J. Williamson (Eds.), *Advances in biomagnetism* (pp. 118–119). Ninth International Conference on Biomagnetism, Vienna.

Imada, T., Hari, R., Loveless, N., McEvoy, L., & Sams, M. (1993). Determinants of the auditory mismatch response. *Electroencephalography and Clinical Neurophysiology, 87*, 144–153.

Ivanov-Smolenski, A. G. (1927). Ob issledovatelskom ili orientirovochnom uslovnom reflekse. (Concerning investigatory or orienting conditioned reflex). *Russkii fisiologicheskii zhurnal, 10*, 321–342.

Izmailov, Ch. A., & Sokolov, E. N. (1991). Spherical model of color and brightness discrimination. *Psychological Science, 2*(4), 249–259.

Izmailov, Ch. A., & Sokolov, E. N. (1992). A semantic space of color names. *Psychological Science, 3*(2), 105–110.

Izmailov, Ch. A., Sokolov, E. N., & Chernorizov, A. M. (1989). *Psikhofiziologiya tsvetovogo zrenia (Psychophysiology of color vision)*. Moscow: Izdatelstvo Moskovskopgo Universiteta.

Jääskeläinen, I. P., Alho, K., Escera, C., Winkler, I., Sillanaukee, P., & Näätänen, R. (1996). Effects of ethanol and auditory distraction on forced choice reaction time. *Alcohol, 13*, 153–156.

Jasper, H. H. (1958). The ten-twenty electrode system of the international federation. *Electroencephalography and Clinical Neurophysiology, 10*, 371–375.

Johnson, R., Jr. (1988). The amplitude of the P300 component of the event-related potential: Review and synthesis. *Advances in Psychophysiology, 3*, 69–137.

Kahneman, D. (1973). *Attention and effort*. Englewood Cliffs, NJ: Prentice-Hall.

Kaukoranta, E., Sams, M., Hari, R., Hämäläinen, M., & Näätänen, R. (1989). Reactions of human auditory cortex to a change in tone duration. *Hearing Research, 41*, 15–22.
Kevanishvili, Z. S., Pantev, C., & Khachidze, O. A. (1979). Intramodal and interaural interactions of the human slow auditory evoked potential. *Archives of Otorhinolarynlogy, 222*, 211–219.
Khananashvili, M. M. (1978). *Informatsionnye nevrozy (Informational neuroses)*. Leningrad: Nauka.
Kimmel, H. D., Olst, F. H. van, & Orlebeke, J. F. (Eds.). (1979). *The orienting reflex in humans*. Hillsdale, NJ: Lawrence Erlbaum Associates.
Klinke, R., Fruhstorfer, H., & Finkenzeller, P. (1968). Evoked responses as a function of external and stored information. *Electroencephalography and Clinical Neurophysiology, 25*, 119–122.
Knight, R. T. (1990). Neural mechanisms of event related potentials: Evidence from human lesion studies. In J. W. Rohrbaugh, R. Parasuraman, & R. Johnson, Jr. (Eds.), *Event-related brain potentials: Basic issues and applications* (pp. 3–18). New York: Oxford University Press.
Knight, R. T. (1991). Evoked potential studies of attention capacity in human frontal lobe lesions. In H. S. Levin, H. M. Eisenberg, & A. L. Benton (Eds.), *Frontal lobe function and dysfunction* (pp. 139–153). New York: Oxford University Press.
Knight, R. T., Scabini, D., Woods, D. L., & Clayworth, (1989). Contributions of temporal-parietal junction to the human auditory P3. *Brain Research, 502*, 109–116.
Kohonen, T. (1990). The self-organizing map. *Proceedings of the IEEE, 18*, 1464–1480.
Konorski, J. M. (1948). *Conditioned reflexes and neuron organization*. London: Cambridge University Press.
Kraus, N., McGee, T., Carrell, T. D., King, C., Littman, T., & Nicol, T. (1994). Discrimination of speech-like signals in the auditory thalamus and cortex. *Journal of the Acoustical Society of Audiology, 3*, 39–51.
Kraus, N., McGee, T., Carrell, T. D., Sharma, A., Koch, D., Kinf, C., Tremblay, K., & Nicol, T. (1995). Neurophysiologic bases of speech discrimination. *Ear and Hearing, 16*, 19–37.
Kraus, N., McGee, T., Micco, A., Sharma, A., Carrell, T. D., & Nicol, T. (1993). Mismatch negativity in school-age children to speech stimuli that are just perceptibly different. *Electroencephalography and Clinical Neurophysiology, 88*, 123–130.
Kraus, N., McGee, T., Sharma, A., Carrell, T. D., & Nicol, T. (1992). Mismatch negativity event-related potential elicited by speech stimuli. *Ear and Hearing, 13*, 158–164.
Kravkov, S. V. (1948). *Vzaimodeistviye organov chuvstv. (Interaction of sensory organs)*. Leningrad: Academy of Sciences of USSR.
Kropotov, J., & Ponomarev, V. A. (1991). Subcortical neuronal correlates of component P300 in man. *Electroencephalography and Clinical Neurophysiology, 72*, 1270–1277.
Kropotov, J. D., Näätänen, R., Sevostianov, A. C., Alho, K., Reinikainen, K., & Kropotova, O. V. (1995). Mismatch negativity to auditory stimulus change recorded directly from the human temporal cortex. *Psychophysiology, 32*, 418–422.
Krupa, D. J., & Thompson, R. F. (1997). Reversible inactivation of the cerebellar interpositus nucleus completely prevents acquisition of the classically conditioned eye-blink response. *Learning and Memory, 3*, 545–556.
Kujala, T., Alho, K., Kekoni, J., Hämäläinen, H., Reinikainen, K., Salonen, O., Standertskjöld-Nordenstam, C.-G., & Näätänen, R. (1995). Auditory and somatosensory event-related brain potentials in early blind humans. *Experimental Brain Research, 104*, 519–526.
Kumatsu, H., Ideura, Y., Kaji, S., & Yamane, S. (1992). Color selectivity of neurons in the inferior temporal cortex of the awake macaque monkey. *Journal of Neuroscience, 12*, 408–424.
Lacey, J. I. (1967). Somatic response patterning and stress: Some revisions of activation theory. In M. Appley & R. Trumbull (Eds.), *Psychological stress: Issues in research* (pp. 14–37). New York: Appleton-Century-Crofts.
Lang, H., Nyrke, T., Ek, M., Aaltonen, O., Raimo, I., & Näätänen, R. (1990). Pitch discrimination performance and auditory event-related potentials. In C. H. M. Brunia, A. W. K. Gaillard, A. Kok, G. Mulder, & M. N. Verbaten (Eds.), *Psychophysiological brain research* (Vol. 1; pp. 294–298). Tilburg: Tilburg University Press.

Larsson, L. E. (1956). The relation between the startle reaction and the nonspecific EEG response to sudden stimuli with a discussion on the mechanism of arousal. *Electroencephalography and Clinical Neurophysiology, 8*, 631–644.

Larsson, L. E. (1960a). Sensitization of the startle blink and nonspecific electroencephalographic response. *Electroencephalography and Clinical Neurophysiology, 12*, 727–733.

Larsson, L. E. (1960b). Correlation between the psychological significance of stimuli and the magnitudes of the startle blink and evoked EEG potentials in man. *Acta Physiologica Scandinavica, 48*, 276–294.

Lavikainen, J., Huotilainen, M., Ilmoniemi, R. J., Simola, J. T., & Näätänen, R. (1995). Pitch change of a continuous tone activates two distinct processes in human auditory cortex: A study with whole-head magnetometer. *Electroencephalography and Clinical Neurophysiology, 96*, 93–96.

Leppänen, P., Eklund, K., & Lyytinen, H. (1997). Event-related brain potentials to change in rapidly presented acoustic stimuli in newborns. *Developmental Neuropsychology, 13*(2), 175–204.

Levänen, S., Ahonen, A., Hari, R., McEvoy, L., & Sams, M. (1996). Deviant auditory stimuli activate human left and right auditory cortex differently. *Cerebral Cortex, 6*, 288–296.

Levänen, S., Hari, R., McEvoy, L., & Sams, M. (1993). Responses of the human auditory cortex to changes in one versus two stimulus features. *Experimental Brain Research, 97*, 177–183.

Lindsley, D. B. (1960). Attention, consciousness, sleep and wakefulness. In J. Field, H. W. Magoun, & V. E. Hall (Eds.), *Handbook of physiology, Section I, Vol. III*, 1553–1593. Washington, DC: American Physiological Society.

Livingston, R. B. (1958). Central control of afferent activity. In *Henry Ford Hospital—International Symposium: Reticular formation of the brain*. Boston: Little, Brown.

London, I. D. (1954). Research on sensory interaction in the Soviet Union. *Psychological Bulletin, 51*, 531–568.

Lounasmaa, O. V., Hari, R., Joutsiniemi, S.-L., & Hämäläinen, M. (1989). Multi-SQUID recordings of human cerebral magnetic fields may give information about memory processes. *Europhysics Letters, 9*, 603–608.

Loveless, N. E. (1979). Event-related slow potentials of the brain as expressions of orienting function. In H. D. Kimmel, E. H. van Olst, & J. F. Orlebeke (Eds.), *The orienting reflex in humans* (pp. 77–100). Hillsdale, NJ: Lawrence Erlbaum Associates.

Loveless, N. E. (1983). The orienting response and evoked potentials in man. In D. Siddle (Ed.), *Orienting and habituation: Perspectives in human research* (pp. 71–108). New York: Wiley.

Loveless, N. E. (1986). Potentials evoked by temporal deviance. *Biological Psychology, 22*, 149–167.

Loveless, N. E., & Sanford, A. J. (1974a). Effects of age on the contingent negative variation and preparatory set in a reaction-time task. *Journal of Gerontology, 29*, 52–63.

Loveless, N. E., & Sanford, A. J. (1974b). Slow potential correlates of preparatory set. *Biological Psychology, 1*, 303–314.

Lu, J.-L., Williams, S. J., & Kaufman, L. (1992). Behavioral lifetime of human auditory sensory memory predicted by physiological measures. *Science, 258*, 1668–1670.

Luria, A. R. (1973). *Osnovy neuropsikhologii (Foundations of neuropsychology)*. Moscow: Izdatelstvo Moscovskogo Universiteta.

Luria, A. R., & Homskaya, E. D. (1970). Frontal lobes and regulation of arousal process. In D. I. Mostofsky (Ed.), *Attention: Contemporary theory and analysis* (pp. 301–330). New York: McGraw-Hill.

Lynn, R. (1966). *Attention, arousal, and the orientation reaction*. Oxford: Pergamon.

Lyytinen, H. (1983). A component analysis of multi-channel arousal patterns. In R. Sinz & M. R. Rosenzweig (Eds.), *Psychophysiology: Memory, motivation and event-related potentials in mental operations, 1980* (pp. 413–420). Amsterdam: Elsevier/North-Holland Biomedical Press.

Lyytinen, H. (1984). The psychophysiology of anticipation and arousal. *Jyväskylä Studies in Education, Psychology and Social Research, 52*.

Lyytinen, H. (1985). Preparation, execution and experience: A multivariate evaluation of ANS–SNS patterns. In F. Klix, R. Näätänen, & K. Zimmer (Eds.), *Psychophysiology foundations and applications* (pp. 291–311). Amsterdam: Elsevier/North-Holland Biomedical Press.

Lyytinen, H. (1989). When do ANS- and ERP-measures covary? *Psychophysiology, 26,* 4A, S42.

Lyytinen, H., Aro, M., & Leppäsaari, T. (1992). Automatic auditory attention and arousal. *International Journal of Psychology, 27*(3–4), 394–395.

Lyytinen, H., Blomberg, A. P., & Näätänen, R. (1992). Event-related potentials and autonomic responses to a change in unattended auditory stimuli. *Psychophysiology, 29,* 523–534.

Lyytinen, H., & Näätänen, R. (1987). Autonomic and ERP responses to deviant stimuli: Analysis of covariation. In R. Johnson, Jr., R. Parasuraman, & J. W. Rohrbaugh (Eds.), Current Trends in Event-related potential research (pp. 108–117). *Electroencephalography and Clinical Neurophysiology. Suppl. 40.* Amsterdam: Elsevier.

MacAdam, D. L. (1963). Nonlinear relations of psychometric scale values to chromaticity differences. *Journal of Optical Society of America, 27,* 294–306.

MacLean, V., Öhman, A., & Lader, M. (1975). Effects of attention, activation, and stimulus regularity on short-term "habituation" of the averaged evoked response. *Biological Psychology, 3,* 57–69.

MacMillan, N. A. (1973). Detection and recognition of intensity changes in tone and noise: The detection–recognition disparity. *Perception and Psychophysics, 13,* 65–75.

Maiste, A. C., Wiens, A. S., Hunt, M. J., Scherg, M., & Picton, T. W. (1995). Event-related potentials and the categorical perception of speech sounds. *Ear and Hearing, 16,* 67–89.

Mäkelä, J. P., Hari, R., & Leinonen, L. (1988). Magnetic responses of the human auditory cortex to noise/square wave transitions. *Electroencephalography and Clinical Neurophysiology, 69,* 423–430.

Mäkelä, J. P., Salmelin, R., Kotila, M., Salonen, O., Laaksonen, R., Hokkanen, L., & Hari, R. (1994). Modification of neuromagnetic cortical signals by thalamic infarctions. *Electroencephalography and Clinical Neurophysiology, 106,* 433–443.

Maltzman, I. (1979). Orienting reflexes and significance: A reply to O'Gorman. *Psychophysiology, 16,* 274–282.

Mäntysalo, S., & Näätänen, R. (1987). The duration of a neuronal trace of an auditory stimulus as indicated by event-related potentials. *Biological Psychology, 24,* 183–195.

Marcel, A. J. (1983). Conscious and unconscious perception—Experiments on visual masking and word recognition. *Cognitive Psychology, 15,* 197–237.

May, P., Tiitinen, H., Sinkkonen, J., & Näätänen, R. (1994). Long-term stimulation attenuates the transient 40-Hz response. *NeuroReport, 5,* 1918–1920.

McCallum, W. C., Barrett, K., & Pocock, P. V. (1989). Late components & auditory event-related potentials to eight equiprobable stimuli in a target detection task. *Psychophysiology, 26,* 683–694.

Megela, A. L., & Teyler, T. J. (1979). Habituation of the human evoked potential. *Journal of Comparative and Physiological Psychology, 6,* 1154–1170.

Merzenich, M. M., & Brugge, J. F. (1973). Representation of the cochlear partition of the superior temporal plane of the macaque monkey. *Brain Research, 50,* 275–296.

Miyashita, Y. (1988). Neuronal correlate of visual associative long-term memory in the primate temporal cortex. *Nature, 335,* 817.

Morel, A., Garraghty, P. E., & Kaas, J. H. (1993). Tonotopic organization, architectonic fields, and connection of auditory cortex in macaque monkeys. *Journal of Comparative Neurology, 335,* 437–459.

Näätänen, R. (1975). Selective attention and evoked potentials in humans—A critical review. *Biological Psychology, 2,* 237–307.

Näätänen, R. (1979). Orienting and evoked potentials. In H. D. Kimmel, E. H. van Olst, & J. F. Orlebeke (Eds.), *The orienting reflex in humans* (pp. 61–75). Hillsdale, NJ: Lawrence Erlbaum Associates.

Näätänen, R. (1982). Processing negativity: An evoked-potential reflection of selective attention. *Psychological Bulletin, 92*, 605–640.

Näätänen, R. (1985). Selective attention and stimulus processing: Reflections in event-related potentials, magnetoencephalogram and regional cerebral blood flow. In M. I. Posner & O. S. M. Marin (Eds.), *Attention and performance XI* (pp. 355–373). Hillsdale, NJ: Lawrence Erlbaum Associates.

Näätänen, R. (1986a). The orienting response theory: An integration of informational and energetical aspects of brain function. In R. G. J. Hockey, A. W. K. Gaillard, & M. Coles (Eds.), *Adaptation to stress and task demands: Energetical aspects of human information processing* (pp. 91–111). Dordrecht: Martinus Nijhoff.

Näätänen, R. (1986b). N2 and automatic versus controlled processes: A classification of N2 kinds of ERP components. In W. C. McCallum, R. Zappoli, & F. Denoth (Eds.), *Cerebral psychophysiology: Studies in event-related potentials* (pp. 169–172). Electroencephalography and Clinical Neurophysiology. Suppl. 38. Amsterdam: Elsevier.

Näätänen, R. (1988). Implications of ERP data for psychological theories of attention. *Biological Psychology, 26*, 117–163.

Näätänen, R. (1990). The role of attention in auditory information processing as revealed by event-related potentials and other brain measures of cognitive function. *Behavioral and Brain Sciences, 13*, 201–288.

Näätänen, R. (1992). *Attention and brain function.* Hillsdale, NJ: Lawrence Erlbaum Associates.

Näätänen, R., & Gaillard, A. W. K. (1983). The N2 deflection of ERP and the orienting reflex. In A. W. K. Gaillard & W. Ritter (Eds.), *EEG correlates of information processing: Theoretical issues* (pp. 119–141). Amsterdam: North-Holland.

Näätänen, R., Gaillard, A. W. K., & Mäntysalo, S. (1978). Early selective-attention effect on evoked potential reinterpreted. *Acta Psychologica, 42*, 313–329.

Näätänen, R., Gaillard, A. W. K., & Mäntysalo, S. (1980). Brain potential correlates of voluntary and involuntary attention. In H. H. Kornhuber & L. Deecke (Eds.), Motivation, motor and sensory processes of the brain: Electrical potentials, behaviour and clinical use. *Progress in Brain Research, 54* (pp. 343–348). Amsterdam: Elsevier.

Näätänen, R., Jiang, D., Lavikainen, J., Reinikainen, K., & Paavilainen, P. (1993). Event-related potentials reveal a memory trace for temporal features. *NeuroReport, 5*, 310–312.

Näätänen, R., Lehtokoski, A., Lennes, M., Cheour, M., Huotilainen, M., Iivonen, A., Vainio, M., Alku, P., Ilmoniemi, R. J., Luuk, A., Allik, J., Sinkkonen, J., & Alho, K. (1997). Language-specific phoneme representations revealed by electric and magnetic brain responses. *Nature, 385*, 432–434.

Näätänen, R., & Lyytinen, H. (1989). Event-related potentials and the orienting response to nonsignal stimuli at fast stimulus rates. In N. Bond & D. Siddle (Eds.), *Psychobiology: Issues and applications* (pp. 185–195). Amsterdam: Elsevier.

Näätänen, R., Medvedev, S. V., Pakhomov, S. V., Roudas, M. S., Zeffiro, T., Tervaniemi, M., Reinikainen, K., & Alho, K. (Unpublished data). *Brain mechanisms of attention switch to infrequent sounds.*

Näätänen, R., Medvedev, S. V., Pakhamov, S. V., Roudas, M. S., Zeffiro, T., Tervaniemi, M., van Zuijen, T. L., Reinikainen, K., & Alho, K. (unpublished manuscript). *Preattentive processing of sound changes in multiple brain areas: A PET study.*

Näätänen, R., & Michie, P. T. (1979). Early selective attention effects on the evoked potential. A critical review and reinterpretation. *Biological Psychology, 8*, 81–136.

Näätänen, R., Paavilainen, P., Alho, K., Reinikainen, K., & Sams, M. (1987). Inter-stimulus interval and the mismatch negativity. In C. Barber & T. Blum (Eds.), *Evoked potentials III* (pp. 392–397). London: Butterworths.

Näätänen, R., Paavilainen, P., Alho, K., Reinikainen, K., & Sams, M. (1989). Do event-related potentials reveal the mechanism of auditory sensory memory in the human brain? *Neuroscience Letters, 98*, 217–221.

Näätänen, R., Paavilainen, P., Lavikainen, J., Alho, K., Reinikainen, K., Teder, W., Sams, M., Strelets, V., & Rosenfeld, J. (unpublished data).

Näätänen, R., Paavilainen, P., & Reinikainen, K. (1989). Do event-related potentials to infrequent decrements in duration of auditory stimuli demonstrate a memory trace in man? *Neuroscience Letters, 107*, 347–352.

Näätänen, R., & Picton, T. W. (1987). The N1 wave of the human electric and magnetic response to sound: A review and an analysis of the component structure. *Psychophysiology, 24*, 375–425.

Näätänen, R., Sams, M., & Alho, K. (1986). The mismatch negativity: The ERP sign of a cerebral mismatch process. In C. W. McCallum, R. Zappoli, & F. Denoth (Eds.), *Cerebral Psychophysiology. Electroencephalography and Clinical Neurophysiology, 38*, 172–178.

Näätänen, R., Sams, M., Alho, K., Paavilainen, P., Reinikainen, K., & Sokolov, E. N. (1988). Frequency and location specificity of the human vertex N1 wave. *Electroencephalography and Clinical Neurophysiology, 69*, 523–531.

Näätänen, R., Sams, M., Järvilehto, T., & Soininen, K. (1983). Probability of deviant stimulus and event-related brain potentials. In R. Sinz & M. Rosenzweig (Eds.), *Psychophysiology: Memory, motivation and event-related potentials in mental operations* (pp. 397–405). VEB Gustav Fischer Verlag, Jena.

Näätänen, R., Schröger, E., Karakas, S., Tervaniemi, M., & Paavilainen, P. (1993). Development of a memory trace for complex sound patterns in the human brain. *NeuroReport, 4*, 503–506.

Näätänen, R., Simpson, M., & Loveless, N. E. (1982). Stimulus deviance and evoked potentials. *Biological Psychology, 14*, 53–98.

Näätänen, R., & Summala, H. (1976). *Road-user behavior and traffic accidents*. New York: Elsevier.

Näätänen, R., Tervaniemi, M., Sussman, E., Paavilainen, P., & Winkler, I. (2001). "Primitive intelligence" in the auditory cortex. *Trends in Neurosciences, 24*, 283–288.

Niemi, P., & Näätänen, R. (1981). Foreperiod and simple reaction time. *Psychological Bulletin, 89*, 133–162.

Nordby, H., Hammerborg, D., Roth, W. T., & Hugdahl, K. (1994). ERPs for infrequent omissions and inclusions of stimulus elements. *Psychophysiology, 31*, 544–552.

Nordby, H., Roth, W. T., & Pfefferbaum, A. (1988). Event-related potentials to time-deviant and pitch-deviant tones. *Psychophysiology, 25*, 249–261.

Novak, G., Ritter, W., Vaughan, H. G., Jr., & Wiznitzer, M. L. (1990). Differentiation of negative event-related potentials in an auditory discrimination task. *Electroencephalography and Clinical Neurophysiology, 75*, 255–275.

O'Gorman, J. G. (1979). The orienting reflex: Novelty or significance detector? *Psychophysiology, 16*, 253–262.

Öhman, A. (1979). The orienting response, attention and learning: An information-processing perspective. In H. D. Kimmel, E. H. van Olst, & J. F. Orlebeke (Eds.), *The orienting reflex in humans* (pp. 443–471). Hillsdale, NJ: Lawrence Erlbaum Associates.

Öhman, A. (1992). Orienting and attention: Preferred preattentive processing of potentially phobic stimuli. In. B. A. Campbell, H. Hayne, & R. Richardson (Eds.), *Attention and information processing in infants and adults. Perspectives from human and animal research* (pp. 263–295). Hillsdale, NJ: Lawrence Erlbaum Associates.

Öhman, A., & Lader, M. (1972). Selective attention and "habituation" of the auditory averaged evoked response in humans. *Physiology and Behavior, 8*, 79–85.

Paavilainen, P., Alho, K., Reinikainen, K., Sams, M., & Näätänen, R. (1991). Right-hemisphere dominance of different mismatch negativities. *Electroencephalography and Clinical Neurophysiology, 78*, 466–479.

Paavilainen, P., Jaramillo, M., & Näätänen, R. (1998). Binaural information can converge in abstract memory traces. *Psychophysiology, 35*, 483–487.

Paavilainen, P., Karlsson, M.-L., Reinikainen, K., & Näätänen, R. (1989). Mismatch negativity to change in spatial location of an auditory stimulus. *Electroencephalography and Clinical Neurophysiology, 73*, 129–141.

Paavilainen, P., Saarinen, J., Tervaniemi, M., & Näätänen, R. (1995). Mismatch negativity to changes in abstract sound features during dichotic listening. *Psychophysiology, 9*, 243–249.

Palikhova, T. A. (1991). Multiple site of spike generation in snail neurones. In D. A. Sakharov & W. Winlow (Eds.), *Simpler nervous systems* (pp. 775–786). Manchester: Manchester University Press.

Palikhova, T. A., & Arakelov, G. G. (1990). Monosynaptic connections in the central nervous system of the snail: Receptive fields of the presynaptic neurones. *Zhurnal Visshey Nervnoi Deyatelnosty, 40*(6), 1186–1189.

Pantev, C., Hoke, M., Lehnertz, K., & Lütkenhöner, B. (1989). Neuromagnetic evidence of an amplitopic organization of the human auditory cortex. *Electroencephalography and Clinical Neurophysiology, 72*, 225–231.

Pantev, C., Hoke, M., Lehnertz, K., Lütkenhöner, B., Anogianakis, G., & Wittkowski, U. (1988). Tonotopic organization of human auditory cortex revealed by transient auditory evoked magnetic fields. *Electroencephalography and Clinical Neurophysiology, 69*, 160–170.

Pardo, P. J., & Sams, M. (1993). Human auditory cortex responses to rising versus falling glides. *Neuroscience Letters, 159*, 43–45.

Pavlov, I. P. (1927). *Conditioned reflexes*. Oxford: Clarendon Press.

Picton, T. W., Goodman, W. S., & Bryce, D. P. (1970). Amplitude of evoked responses to tones of high intensity. *Acta Otolaryngology, 70*, 77–82.

Picton, T. W., Woods, D. L., & Proulx, G. B. (1978). Human auditory sustained potentials. 2. Stimulus relationships. *Electroencephalography and Clinical Neurophysiology, 45*, 198–210.

Port, R. F. (1991). Can complex temporal patterns be automatized? *Behavioral and Brain Sciences, 14*, 762–764.

Posner, M. I., & Raichle, M. E. (1995). Images of mind. *Behavioral and Brain Sciences, 18*(2), 327–383.

Pribram, K. H., & McGuinness, D. (1975). Arousal, activation, and effort in the control of attention. *Psychological Review, 82*(2), 116–149.

Pritchard, W. S. (1981). Psychophysiology of P300. *Psychological Bulletin, 89*, 506–540.

Razran, G. (1971). *Mind in evolution. An east–west synthesis of learned behavior and cognition*. Boston: Houghton Mifflin.

Renault, B., & Lesévre, N. (1978). Topographical study of the emitted potential obtained after the omission of an expected visual stimulus. In D. Otto (Ed.), *Multidisciplinary perspectives in event-related brain potential research*, EPA 600/9-77-043 (pp. 202–208). Washington, DC: U.S. Government Printing Office.

Renault, B., & Lesévre, N. (1979). A trial-by-trial study of the visual omission response in reaction time situations. In D. Lehmann & E. Callaway (Eds.), *Attention and performance XI* (pp. 147–167). Hillsdale, NJ: Lawrence Erlbaum Associates.

Rinne, T., Alho, K., Alku, P., Holi, M., Sinkkonen, J., Virtanen, J., Bertrand, O., & Näätänen, R. (1999). Analysis of speech sounds is left-hemisphere predominant at 100–150 ms after sound onset. *Neuroreport, 10*, 1113–1117.

Ritter, W., Deacon, D., Gomes, H., Javitt, D. C., & Vaughan, H. G., Jr. (1995). The mismatch negativity of event-related potentials as a probe of transient auditory memory: A review. *Ear and Hearing, 16*, 51–66.

Ritter, W., Paavilainen, P., Lavikainen, J., Reinikainen, K., & Näätänen, R. (1992). Event-related potentials to repetition and change of auditory stimuli. *Electroencephalography and Clinical Neurophysiology, 83*, 306–321.

Ritter, W., Simson, R., & Vaughan, H. G., Jr. (1972). Association cortex potentials and reaction time in auditory discrimination. *Electroencephalography and Clinical Neurophysiology, 33*, 547–555.

Ritter, W., Simson, R., Vaughan, H. G., Jr., & Friedman, D. (1979). A brain event related to the making of a sensory discrimination. *Science, 203*, 1358–1361.

Ritter, W., Vaughan, Jr., H. G., & Costa, L. D. (1968). Orienting and habituation to auditory stimuli: A study of short term changes in average evoked responses. *Electroencephalography and Clinical Neurophysiology, 25*, 550–556.

Rohrbaugh, J. W. (1984). The orienting reflex: Performance and central nervous system manifestations. In R. Parasuraman & D. R. Davies (Eds.), *Varieties of attention* (pp. 323–373). New York: Academic Press.

Rohrbaugh, J. W., & Gaillard, A. W. K. (1983). Sensory and motor aspects of the contingent negative variation. In A. W. K. Gaillard & W. Ritter (Eds.), *Tutorials in ERP research: Endogenous components* (pp. 269–310). Amsterdam: North-Holland.

Rohrbaugh, J. W., Syndulko, K., & Lindsley, D. B. (1976). Brain wave components of the contingent negative variation in humans. *Science, 191*, 1055–1057.

Rohrbaugh, J. W., Syndulko, K., & Lindsley, D. B. (1978). Cortical slow negative waves following non-paired stimuli: Effects of task factors. *Electroencephalography and Clinical Neurophysiology, 45*, 551–567.

Rohrbaugh, J. W., Syndulko, K., & Lindsley, D. B. (1979). Cortical slow negative waves following non-paired stimuli: Effects of modality, intensity, and rate of stimulation. *Electroencephalography and Clinical Neurophysiology, 46*, 416–427.

Roland, P. E. (1993). *Brain activation*. New York: Wiley.

Rolls, E. (1989). The representation and storage of information in neuronal networks in the primate cerebrale cortex and hippocampus. In R. Durbin, Ch. Miall, & G. Nitchison (Eds.), *The computing neuron* (pp. 125–159). Wokingham: Addison-Wesley.

Roth, W. T. (1973). Auditory evoked responses to unpredictable stimuli. *Psychophysiology, 10*, 125–137.

Roth, W. T. (1983). A comparison of P300 and skin conductance response. In A. W. K. Gaillard & W. Ritter (Eds.), *Tutorials in event-related potential research: Endogenous components* (pp. 177–199). Amsterdam: North-Holland.

Roth, W. T., Blowers, G. H., Doyle, C. M., & Kopell, B. S. (1982). Auditory stimulus intensity effects on components of the late positive complex. *Electroencephalography and Clinical Neurophysiology, 54*, 132–146.

Roth, W. T., Dorato, K. H., & Kopell, B. S. (1984). Intensity and task effects on evoked physiological responses to noise bursts. *Psychophysiology, 21*, 466–481.

Roth, W. T., Ford, J. T., & Kopell, B. S. (1978). Long-latency evoked potentials and reaction time. *Psychophysiology, 15*, 17–23.

Roth, W. T., & Kopell, B. S. (1969). The auditory evoked response to repeated stimuli during a vigilance task. *Psychophysiology, 6*, 301–309.

Rothman, H. H., Davis, H., & Hay, I. S. (1970). Slow evoked cortical potentials and temporal features of stimulation. *Electroencephalography and Clinical Neurophysiology, 29*, 225–232.

Ruchkin, D. S., & Sutton, S. (1983). Positive slow wave and P300: Association and disassociation. In A. W. K. Gaillard & W. Ritter (Eds.), *Tutorials in event-related potential research: Endogenous components* (pp. 233–250). Amsterdam: North–Holland.

Rust, J. (1977). Habituation and the orienting response in the auditory cortical evoked potential. *Psychophysiology, 14*, 123–126.

Ruusuvirta, T., Korhonen, T., Penttonen, M., Arikoski, J., & Kivirikko, K. (1995a). Hippocampal event-related potentials to pitch deviances in an auditory oddball situation in the cat: Experiment I. *International Journal of Psychophysiology, 20*, 33–39.

Ruusuvirta, T., Korhonen, T., Penttonen, M., Arikoski, J., & Kivirikko, K. (1995b). Behavioral and hippocampal evoked responses in an auditory oddball situation when an unconditioned stimulus is paire with deviant tones in the cat: Experiment II. *International Journal of Psychophysiology, 20*, 41–47.

Saarinen, J., Paavilainen, P., Schröger, E., Tervaniemi, M., & Näätänen, R. (1992). Representation of abstract attributes of auditory stimuli in the human brain. *NeuroReport, 3*, 1149–1151.

Sallinen, M., & Lyytinen, H. (1997). Mismatch negativity during objective and subjective sleepiness. *Psychophysiology, 34*(6), 694–702.

Sallinen, M., Kaartinen, J., & Lyytinen, H. (1994). Is the appearance of mismatch negativity during stage 2 sleep related to the elicitation of K-complex? *Electroencephalography and Clinical Neurophysiology, 91*, 140–148.

Sallinen, M., Kaartinen, J., & Lyytinen, H. (1996). Processing of auditory stimuli during tonic and phasic periods of REM sleep as revealed by event-related brain potentials. *Journal of Sleep Research, 5*, 220–228.

Sallinen, M., Kaartinen, J., & Lyytinen, H. (1997). Precursors of the evoked K-complex in event-related brain potentials in stage 2 sleep. *Electroencephalography and Clinical Neurophysiology, 102*, 363–373.

Sams, M., Alho, K., & Näätänen, R. (1983). Sequential effects on the ERP in discriminating two stimuli. *Biological Psychology, 17*, 41–48.

Sams, M., Alho, K., & Näätänen, R. (1984). Short-term habituation and dishabituation of the mismatch negativity of the ERP. *Psychophysiology, 21*, 434–441.

Sams, M., Aulanko, R., Aaltonen, O., & Näätänen, R. (1990). Event-related potentials to infrequent changes in synthesized phonetic stimuli. *Journal of Cognitive Neuroscience, 2*, 344–357.

Sams, M., Hämäläinen, M., Antervo, A., Kaukoranta, E., Reinikainen, K., & Hari, R. (1985). Cerebral neuromagnetic responses evoked by short auditory stimuli. *Electroencephalography and Clinical Neurophysiology, 61*, 254–266.

Sams, M., Hari, R., Rif, J., & Knuutila, J. (1993). The human auditory sensory memory trace persists about 10 s: Neuromagnetic evidence. *Journal of Cognitive Neuroscience, 5*, 363–370.

Sams, M., Kaukoranta, E., Hämäläinen, M., & Näätänen, R. (1991). Cortical activity elicited by changes in auditory stimuli: Different sources for the magnetic N100m and mismatch responses. *Psychophysiology, 28*, 21–29.

Sams, M., & Näätänen, R. (1991). Neuromagnetic responses of the human auditory cortex to short frequency glides. *Neuroscience Letters, 121*, 43–46.

Sams, M., Paavilainen, P., Alho, K., & Näätänen, R. (1985). Auditory frequency discrimination and event-related potentials. *Electroencephalography and Clinical Neurophysiology, 62*, 437–448.

Scherg, M., Vajsar, J., & Picton, T. W. (1989). A source analysis of the late human auditory evoked potentials. *Journal of Cognitive Neuroscience, 1*, 336–355.

Schröger, E. (1994). An event-related potential study of sensory representations of unfamiliar tonal patterns. *Psychophysiology, 31*, 175–181.

Schröger, E. (1995). Processing of auditory deviants with changes in one versus two stimulus dimensions. *Psychophysiology, 32*, 55–65.

Schröger, E. (1996). A neural mechanism for involuntary attention shifts to changes in auditory stimulation. *Journal of Cognitive Neuroscience, 8*, 527–539.

Schröger, E., & Wolff, C. (1996). Mismatch response of the human brain to changes in sound location. *NeuroReport, 7*, 3005–3008.

Schröger, E., Näätänen, R., & Paavilainen, P. (1992). Event-related potentials reveal how non-attended complex sound patterns are represented by the human brain. *Neuroscience Letters, 146*, 183–186.

Schröger, E., Paavilainen, P., & Näätänen, R. (1994). Mismatch negativity to changes in a continuous tone with regularly varying frequencies. *Electroencephalography and Clinical Neurophysiology, 92*, 140–147.

Sharma, A., Kraus, N., McGee, T., Carrell, T., & Nicol, T. (1993). Acoustic versus phonetic representation of speech as reflected by the mismatch negativity event-related potential. *Electroencephalography and Clinical Neurophysiology, 88*, 64–71.

Shek, D. T. L., & Spinks, J. A. (1985). The effect of the orienting response on sensory discriminability. *Perceptual and Motor Skills, 61*, 987–1003.

Shek, D. T. L., & Spinks, J. A. (1986). A study of the attentional changes accompanying orienting to different types of change stimuli. *Acta Psychologica, 61*, 153–166.

Siddle, D. A. T. (1979). The orienting response and stimulus significance: Some comments. *Biological Psychology, 8*, 303–309.

Siddle, D. (Ed.). (1983). *Orienting and habituation: Perspectives in human research*. Chichester: Wiley.

Siddle, D. A. T., & Spinks, J. A. (1992). Orienting, habituation, and the allocation of processing resources. In B. A. Campbell, H. Hayne, & R. Richardson (Eds.), *Attention and information processing in infants and adults: Perspectives from human and animal research* (pp. 227–262). Hillsdale, NJ: Lawrence Erlbaum Associates.

Simons, R. F., Rockstroh, B., Elbert, T., Fiorito, E., Lutzenberger, W., & Birbaumer, N. (1987). Evocation and habituation of autonomic and event-related potential responses in a non signal environment. *Journal of Psychophysiology, 1*, 45–59.

Simson, R., Vaughan, H. G., Jr., & Ritter, W. (1976). The scalp topography of potentials associated with missing visual or auditory stimuli. *Electroencephalography and Clinical Neurophysiology, 40*, 33–42.

Simson, R., Vaughan, H. G., Jr., & Ritter, W. (1977). The scalp topography of potentials in auditory and visual discrimination tasks. *Electroencephalography and Clinical Neurophysiology, 42*, 528–535.

Singer, W. (1990). Search for coherence: A basic principle of cortical self-organization. *Concepts in Neuroscience, 1*, 1–26.

Snyder, E., & Hillyard, S. A. (1976). Long-latency evoked potentials to irrelevant deviant stimuli. *Behavioral Biology, 16*, 319–331.

Sokolov, E. N. (1960). Neuronal models and orienting reflex. In M. A. B. Brazier (Ed.), *The central nervous system and behavior* (pp. 187–276). Madison, NJ: Madison Printing.

Sokolov, E. N. (1963). *Perception and the conditioned reflex*. Oxford: Pergamon Press.

Sokolov, E. N. (1966). Orienting reflex as information regulator. In A. Leontev, A. Luria, & S. Smirnov (Eds.), *Psychological research in the USSR* (pp. 334–360). Moscow: Progress.

Sokolov, E. N. (1969a). *Mekhanizmy pamyati (Mechanisms of memory)*. Moscow: Izdatelstvo Moscovskogo Universiteta.

Sokolov, E. N. (1969b). The modeling properties of the nervous system. In M. Cole & I. Maltzman (Eds.), *A handbook of contemporary Soviet psychology* (pp. 671–704). New York: Basic Books.

Sokolov, E. N. (1975). The neuronal mechanisms of the orienting reflex. In E. N. Sokolov & O. S. Vinogradova (Eds.), *The neuronal mechanisms of the orienting reflex* (pp. 217–235). Hillsdale, NJ: Lawrence Erlbaum Associates.

Sokolov, E. N., & Vinogradova, O. S. (1957). Sootnosheniye orientirovochnykh i oboronitelnykh refleksov pri deistvii zvukovykj razdrazhitelei. Sbornik Ostatochyi slukh u tugoukhikj i glukhonyemykh detei. [The relationship of orienting and defensive reflexes evoked by sound stimuli. In *Collection of papers: Residual hearing in partially deaf and deafmute children*]. Moscow: Academy of Pedagogical Sciences.

Sokolov, E. N., & Vinogradova, O. S. (Eds.). (1975). *The neuronal mechanisms of the orienting reflex*. Hillsdale, NJ: Lawrence Erlbaum Associates.

Somjen, G. (1972). *Sensory coding in the mammalian nervous system*. New York: Meredith Corporation.

Spinks, J. A. (1984). The effects of different types of distractors on visual search performance: The role of the orienting response. *Psychophysiology, 21*, 599–600.

Spinks, J. A. (1989). The orienting response and anticipation of information processing demands. In N. W. Bond & D. A. T. Siddle (Eds.), *Psychobiology: Issues and applications* (pp. 149–161). Amsterdam: North-Holland.

Spinks, J. A., Blowers, G. H., & Shek, D. T. L. (1985). The role of the orienting response in the anticipation of information: A skin conductance response study. *Psychophysiology, 22*, 385–394.

Spinks, J. A., & Kramer, A. (1991a). Capacity views of information processing: Autonomic nervous system measures. In J. R. Jennings & M. G. H. Coles (Eds.), *Handbook of cognitive psychology: Central and autonomic nervous system approaches* (pp. 208–229). Chichester, UK: Wiley.

Spinks, J. A., & Kramer, A. (1991b). Capacity views of information processing: Integration. In J. R. Jennings & M. G. H. Coles (Eds.), *Handbook of cognitive psychology: Central and autonomic nervous system approaches* (pp. 229–249). Chichester, UK: Wiley.

Spinks, J. A., & Shek, D. T. L. (1982). The effect of orienting activity following a warning stimulus on subsequent information processing. *Psychophysiology, 19,* 589.

Spinks, J. A., & Siddle, D. A. T. (1976). Effects of stimulus information and stimulus duration on amplitude and habituation of the electrodermal orienting response. *Biological Psychology, 4,* 29–39.

Spinks, J. A., & Siddle, D. (1983). The functional significance of the orienting response. In D. Siddle (Ed.), *Orienting and habituation: Perspectives in human research* (pp. 237–314). Chichester, UK: Wiley.

Spinks, J. A., & Siddle, D. A. T. (1985). The effects of anticipated information on skin conductance and cardiac activity. *Biological Psychology, 20,* 39–50.

Squires, K. C., Donchin, E., Herning, R. I., & McCarthy, G. (1977). On the influence of task relevance and stimulus probability on event-related potential components. *Electroencephalography and Clinical Neurophysiology, 42,* 1–14.

Squires, N. K., Squires, K. C., & Hillyard, S. A. (1975). Two varieties of long-latency positive waves evoked by unpredictable auditory stimuli in man. *Electroencephalography and Clinical Neurophysiology, 38,* 387–401.

Sternbach, R. A. (1966). *Principles of psychophysiology.* New York: Academic Press.

Suga, N. (1965). Functional properties of auditory neurons in the cortex of echolocating bats. *Journal of Physiology, 181,* 671–700.

Surwillo, W. W. (1975). Reaction-time variability, periodicities in reaction-time distributions, and the EEG gating-signal hypothesis. *Biological Psychology, 3,* 247–261.

Sutton, S. (1979). P300—Thirteen years later. In H. Begleiter (Ed.), *Evoked brain potentials and behavior* (pp. 107–126). New York: Plenum.

Sutton, S., Braren, M., Zubin, J., & John, E. R. (1965). Evoked potential correlates of stimulus uncertainty. *Science, 150,* 1187–1188.

Tanner, W. P., & Swets, J. A. (1954). A decision-making theory of visual detection. *Psychological Review, 61,* 401–409.

Tervaniemi, M., Mayry, S., & Näätänen, R. (1994). Neural representations of abstract stimulus features in the human brain as reflected by the mismatch negativity. *NeuroReport, 5,* 844–846.

Thompson, R. F. (1980). *Introduction to physiological psychology.* New York: Harper & Row.

Thompson, R. F., & Spencer, W. A. (1966). Habituation: A model phenomenon for the study of neuronal substrates of behavior. *Psychological Review, 73,* 16–43.

Thorpe, W. (1956). *Learning and instincts in animals.* Cambridge, England: Cambridge University Press.

Tiitinen, H., Alho, K., Huotilainen, M., Ilmoniemi, R. J., Simola, J., & Näätänen, R. (1993). Tonotopic auditory cortex and the magnetoencephalographic (MEG) equivalent of the mismatch negativity. *Psychophysiology, 30,* 537–540.

Tiitinen, H., May, P., Reinikainen, K., & Näätänen, R. (1994). Attentive novelty detection in humans is governed by pre-attentive sensory memory. *Nature, 372,* 90–92.

Tolman, E. C. (1955). Performance vectors and the unconscious. *Acta Psychogica, 1,* 31–40.

Tomita, T. (1965). Electrophysiological study of the mechanisms subserving color coding in the fish retina. *Cold Spring Harbor Symposium on Quantitative Biology, 30,* 559–566.

Tomita, T., Kaneko, A., Murakami, M., & Pautler, E. L. (1967). Spectral response curves of single cones in the carp. *Vision Research, 7,* 519–533.

Torgerson, W. S. (1958). *Theory and methods of scaling.* New York: Wiley.

Turpin, G. (1983). Effects of stimulus intensity on cardiovascular activity. *Psychophysiology, 20,* 611–624.

Turpin, G., & Siddle, D. A. T. (1978). Cardiac and forearm, plethysmographic responses to high-intensity auditory stimulation. *Biological Psychology, 6,* 267–281.

Verbaten, M. N., Poclofs, J. W., Sjouw, W., & Slangen, J. L. (1986). Different effects of uncertainty and complexity on single trial visual ERPs and the SCR-OR in non-signal conditions. *Psychophysiology, 23*, 254–262.

Verleger, R. (1988). A critique of the context updating hypothesis and an alternative interpretation of P3. *Behavioral and Brain Sciences, 11*, 343–427.

Vinogradova, O. S. (1975). The hippocampus and the orienting reflex. In E. N. Sokolov & O. S. Vinogradova (Eds.), *The neuronal mechanisms of orienting reflex* (pp. 128–154). Hillsdale, NJ: Lawrence Erlbaum Associates.

Vinogradova, O. S. (1976). *Hippokamp i pamyat (The hippocampus and memory)*. Moscow: Nauka.

Vinogradova, O. S., & Sokolov, E. N. (1957). Sootnosheniye reaktsii sosudov ruki i golovy i nekotorykh bezuslovnykh refleksakh u chelovyeka (The relationship of vascular responses of the hand and the head of some unconditioned reflexes in humans). *Fiziologicheskii zhurnal SSSR, 43*, 24–31.

Voittonis, N. Yu. (1949). *Predystoria intellecta (Prehistory of intelligence)*. Moscow: Isdatelstvo Academii Nauk.

Von Bekesy, G. (1967). *Sensory inhibition*. Princeton, NJ: Princeton University Press.

Wastell, D. G. (1980). Temporal uncertainty and the recovery function of the auditory EP. In C. Barber (Ed.), *Evoked potentials* (pp. 491–495). Lancaster: MTP Press.

Winkler, I., Cowan, N., Csépe, V., Czigler, I., & Näätänen, R. (1996). Interactions between transient and long-term auditory memory as reflected by the mismatch negativity. *Journal of Cognitive Neuroscience, 8*, 403–415.

Winkler, I., & Näätänen, R. (1993). Event-related brain potentials to infrequent partial omissions in series of auditory stimuli. In H.-J. Heinze, G. R. Mangun, & T. F. Münte (Eds.), *New developments in event-related potentials* (pp. 219–216). Boston: Birkhäuser.

Winkler, I, Paavilainen, P., Alho, K., Reinikainen, K., Sams, M., & Näätänen, R. (1990). The effect of small variation of the frequent auditory stimulus on the event-related brain potential to the infrequent stimulus. *Psychophysiology, 27*, 228–235.

Winkler, I., Tervaniemi, M., Schröger, E., Wolff, C., & Näätänen, R. (1998). Preattentive processing of auditory spatial information in humans. *Neuroscience Letters, 242*, 49–52.

Woods, D. L. (1990). The physiological basis of selective attention: Implications of event-related potential studies. In J. W. Rohrbaugh, R. Parasuraman, & R. Johnson, Jr. (Eds.), *Event-related brain potentials: Basic issues and applications* (pp. 178–209). New York: Oxford University Press.

Woods, D. L., & Elmasian, R. (1986). The habituation of event-related potentials to speech sounds and tones. *Electroencephalography and Clinical Neurophysiology, 65*, 447–459.

Woods, D. L., & Knight, R. T. (1986). Electrophysiologic evidence of increased distractibility after dorsolateral prefrontal lesions. *Neurology, 36*, 212–216.

Yabe, H., Tervaniemi, M., Reinikainen, K., & Näätänen, R. (1997). Temporal window of integration revealed by MMN to sound omission. *NeuroReport, 8*, 1971–1974.

Yabe, H., Tervaniemi, M., Sinkkonen, J., Huotilainen, M., Ilmoniemi, R., & Näätänen, R. (1998). The temporal window of integration of auditory information in the human brain. *Psychophysiology, 35*, 615–619.

Yaeger, D. (1967). Behavioral measures and theoretical analysis of spectral sensibility and spectral saturation of the goldfish (*Carasus auatus*). *Vision Research, 7*, 707–727.

Yarbus, A. L. (1965). *Rol dvizhenii glaz v processe vospriyatiz izobrazhenii (The role of eye movements in the process of image perception)*. Moscow: Nauka.

Young, G., & Housholder, A. S. (1938). Discussion of a set of points in terms of their mutual distances. *Psychometrica, 3*, 19–21.

Zeki, S. (1990). Colour vision and functional specification in the visual cortex. *Discussion in Neuroscience, 1*(2), 1–64.

Zimachev, M. M., Shekhter, E. D., Sokolov, E. N., Izmailov, Ch. A., Näätänen, R., & Nyman, G. (1991). Razlichenie tsvetovykh signalov setchatkoi lyagushki (Differentiation of color signals by the retina of the frog). *Zhurnal Vysshei Nervnoi Deyatelnost, 41*, 518–527.

Author Index

U-V

W

Y

Z

Subject Index

For Product Safety Concerns and Information please contact our EU
representative GPSR@taylorandfrancis.com
Taylor & Francis Verlag GmbH, Kaufingerstraße 24, 80331 München, Germany

www.ingramcontent.com/pod-product-compliance
Ingram Content Group UK Ltd.
Pitfield, Milton Keynes, MK11 3LW, UK
UKHW022115190926
475702UK00013B/1448

* 9 7 8 0 4 1 5 6 5 2 5 3 7 *